T0134532

Communications
in Computer and Information Science   **841**

Commenced Publication in 2007
Founding and Former Series Editors:
Alfredo Cuzzocrea, Xiaoyong Du, Orhun Kara, Ting Liu, Dominik Ślęzak,
and Xiaokang Yang

More information about this series at http://www.springer.com/series/7899

Renu Rameshan · Chetan Arora
Sumantra Dutta Roy (Eds.)

Computer Vision, Pattern Recognition, Image Processing, and Graphics

6th National Conference, NCVPRIPG 2017
Mandi, India, December 16–19, 2017
Revised Selected Papers

 Springer

Editors
Renu Rameshan
Indian Institute of Technology Mandi
Mandi, Himachal Pradesh
India

Sumantra Dutta Roy
Indian Institute of Technology
New Delhi
India

Chetan Arora
Indraprastha Institute of Information
  Technology
New Delhi
India

ISSN 1865-0929   ISSN 1865-0937   (electronic)
Communications in Computer and Information Science
ISBN 978-981-13-0019-6   ISBN 978-981-13-0020-2   (eBook)
https://doi.org/10.1007/978-981-13-0020-2

Library of Congress Control Number: 2018941552

Printed on acid-free paper

This Springer imprint is published by the registered company Springer Nature Singapore Pte Ltd.
part of Springer Nature
The registered company address is: 152 Beach Road, #21-01/04 Gateway East, Singapore 189721,
Singapore

Preface

The 6th National Conference on Computer Vision, Pattern Recognition, Image Processing and Graphics (NCVPRIPG 2017) was held at Mandi, Himachal Pradesh, during December 16–19, 2017. NCVPRIPG 2017 was organized by the Indian Institute of Technology Mandi in association with the Indian Unit for Pattern Recognition and Artificial Intelligence (IUPRAI). The NCVPRIPG series of conferences aims to bring together researchers and practitioners from the allied areas of computer vision, graphics, image processing, and pattern recognition, in order to promote community-wide discussions of ideas that will influence and foster continued research in the field. Over the years the conference has grown into a vibrant national conference with participations from many students and researchers in the field.

These proceedings contain the papers accepted and presented at the conference (including those presented in the oral as well as poster sessions). The papers showcased original contemporary research spanning various broad themes such as video processing, image and signal processing, segmentation, retrieval, captioning, and various pattern recognition applications. Out of a total of 147 papers submitted to the conference, 48 were accepted and presented, following an elaborate double-blind review process. After the review process, the final decision process was carried out by the Program Chairs based on the review comments. The conference involved eight oral sessions with a total of 25 papers presented, and two poster sessions containing a total of 23 papers. The papers in the proceedings are the revised versions which were submitted after incorporating the review comments.

The conference hosted plenary talks by Dr. Guna Seetharaman (Naval Reseach Lab, United States), Dr. Nikhil Rasiwasia (Amazon), and Dr Siddhartha Chaudhuri (Adobe Research and IIT Bombay) Prof A. N. Rajagopalan from IIT Madras was the general chair. There were also sessions by industry and special sessions covering topics on virtual reality and rolling shutter cameras. Two research challenges were also held in connection with NCVPRIPG 2017: to automatically detect auto-rickshaws in an image, and the second to automatically detect birds in an image. The conference was sponsored by Mathworks, Kovid Labs, Vehant Technologies, Punjab National Bank, and IIT Mandi.

March 2018

Renu Rameshan
Chetan Arora
Sumantra Dutta Roy

NCVPRIPG 2017 Organization

General Chair

A. N. Rajagopalan   IIT Madras, India

Program Co-chairs

Renu Rameshan   IIT Mandi, India
Sumantra Dutta Roy   IIT Delhi, India
Chetan Arora   IIIT Delhi, India

Organizing Co-chairs

Anil Sao   IIT Mandi, India
A. D. Dileep   IIT Mandi, India
Padmanabhan Rajan   IIT Mandi, India
Arnav Bhavsar   IIT Mandi, India
Veena Thenkanidiyoor   NIT Goa, India

Publication Co-chairs

Aditya Nigam   IIT Mandi, India
Gaurav Sharma   IIT Kanpur, India

Tutorials Chair

Rajib Jha   IIT Patna, India

Program Committee

A. N. Rajagopalan   Indian Institute of Technology Madras, India
Aditya Nigam   Indian Institute of Technology Mandi, India
Aditya Tatu   Dhirubhai Ambani Institute of Information
                             and Communication Technology, Gandhinagar, India
Amlan Chakrabarti   University of Calcutta, India
Angshuman Paul   Indian Statistical Institute Kolkata, India
Anil K. Tiwari   Indian Institute of Technology Jodhpur, India
Anil Kumar Sao   Indian Institute of Technology Mandi, India
Anoop Namboodiri   International Institute of Information Technology,
                             Hyderabad, India
Anubha Gupta   Indraprastha Institute of Information Technology,
                             Delhi, India

Arijit Sur	Indian Institute of Technology Guwahati, India
Arnav Bhavsar	Indian Institute of Technology Mandi, India
Arun Pujari	University of Hyderabad, India
Ashish Anand	Indian Institute of Technology Guwahati, India
Asif Ekbal	Indian Institute of Technology Patna, India
Balaraman Ravindran	Indian Institute of Technology Madras, India
Bhabotosh Chanda	Indian Statistical Institute Kolkata, India
Bidyut Kumar Patra	National Institute of Technology Rourkela, India
Brejesh Lal	Indian Institute of Technology Delhi, India
C. Chandra Shekhar	Indian Institute of Technology Madras, India
C. V. Jawahar	International Institute of Information Technology, Hyderabad, India
Chetan Arora	Indraprastha Institute of Information Technology, Delhi, India
Chiranjoy Chattopadhyay	Indian Institute of Technology Jodhpur, India
Debdoot Sheet	Indian Institute of Technology Kharagpur, India
Deepti Bathula	Indian Institute of Technology Ropar, India
Dileep A. D.	Indian Institute of Technology Mandi, India
Dipti Patra	National Institute of Technology Rourkela, India
D. Guru	Mysore University, India
Gaurav Harit	Indian Institute of Technology Jodhpur, India
Gaurav Sharma	Indian Institute of Technology Kanpur, India
Gorthi Subramanyam	Indian Institute of Space Science and Technology, Thiruvananthapuram, India
Indu Sreedevi	Delhi Technological University, India
Jayanta Mukhopadhyay	Indian Institute of Technology Kharagpur, India
Jiji C. V.	University of Kerala, India
Jorg Peters	University of Florida, USA
Jyotindra Sahambi	Indian Institute of Technology Ropar, India
Karunesh Gupta	Birla Institute of Technology and Science Pilani, India
Kaushik Mitra	Indian Institute of Technology Madras, India
Laxmidhar Behera	Indian Institute of Technology Kanpur, India
Maheshkumar H. Kolekar	Indian Institute of Technology Patna, India
Manish Khare	Dhirubhai Ambani Institute of Information and Communication Technology, Gandhinagar, India
Manisha Verma	Indian Institute of Technology Gandhinagar, India
Md Mansoor Roomi	Thiagarajar College of Engineering, India
Mehul Raval	Ahmedabad University, India
Mohan Kankanhalli	National University of Singapore, Singapore
Niloy Mitra	University College London, UK
Nitin Raje	Dhirubhai Ambani Institute of Information and Communication Technology, Gandhinagar, India
Pabitra Mitra	Indian Institute of Technology Kharagpur, India
Padmanabhan Rajan	Indian Institute of Technology Mandi, India

Paramanand Chandramouli	University of Siegen, Germany
Partha Bhowmick	Indian Institute of Technology Kharagpur, India
Partha Das	Indian Institute of Technology Kharagpur, India
Partha Mohanta	Indian Statistical Institute Kolkata, India
Partha Pratim Roy	Indian Institute of Technology Roorkee, India
Pratik Chattopadhyay	Indian Institute of Technology BHU, India
Preeti Rege	College of Engineering Pune, India
Prem Kalra	Indian Institute of Technology Delhi, India
Prithwijit Guha	Indian Institute of Technology Guwahati, India
Puneet Goyal	Indian Institute of Technology Ropar, India
Rajbabu Velmurugan	Indian Institute of Technology Bombay, India
Rajesh Kumar	GIFS, Aurangabad, India
Rajib Jha	Indian Institute of Technology Patna, India
Rajlaxmi Chouhan	Indian Institute of Technology Jodhpur, India
Rakesh Jadon	Madhav Institute of Technology and Science, Gwalior, India
Ram Pachori	Indian Institute of Technology Indore, India
Raman Balasubramanian	Indian Institute of Technology Roorkee, India
Renu M. Rameshan	Indian Institute of Technology Mandi, India
Shanmuganathan Raman	Indian Institute of Technology Gandhinagar, India
Sharat Chandran	Indian Institute of Technology Bombay, India
Snehasis Mukherjee	Indian Institute of Information Technology Sri City, Chittoor, India
Soumitra Samanta	Indian Statistical Institute Kolkata, India
Srimanta Mandal	Indian Institute of Technology Madras, India
Sriparna Saha	Indian Institute of Technology Patna, India
Suman Mitra	Dhirubhai Ambani Institute of Information and Communication Technology, Gandhinagar, India
Sumantra Dutta Roy	Indian Institute of Technology Delhi, India
Sumeet Agarwal	Indian Institute of Technology Delhi, India
Surya Prakash	Indian Institute of Technology Indore, India
Suyash Awate	Indian Institute of Technology Bombay, India
Swapan Parul	Indian Statistical Institute Kolkata, India
Swapna Agarwal	Indian Statistical Institute Kolkata, India
Tapabrata Chakraborti	Otago University, Auckland, New Zealand
Ujjwal Maulik	Jadavpur University, Kolkata, India
Umapada Pal	Indian Statistical Institute Kolkata, India
V. Vijaya Saradhi	Indian Institute of Technology Guwahati, India
Veena Thenkanidiyoor	National Institute of Technology Goa, India
Venkatesh Kamat	University of Goa, India
Venkatesh Babu R.	Indian Institute of Science, Bangalore, India
Vinay Namboodiri	Indian Institute of Technology Kanpur, India
Vivek Kanhangad	Indian Institute of Technology Indore, India
Yash Vasavada	Dhirubhai Ambani Institute of Information and Communication Technology, Gandhinagar, India

Contents

Image and Signal Processing

Segmentation, Retrieval, Captioning

Pattern Recognition Applications

Video Processing

Visual Odometry Based Omni-directional Hyperlapse

Prachi Rani[1(✉)], Arpit Jangid[1], Vinay P. Namboodiri[2], and K. S. Venkatesh[1]

[1] Department of Elecrical Engineering, Indian Institute of Technology Kanpur,
Kanpur, India
prachi.rani03@gmail.com, arpitjangid999@gmail.com, venkats@iitk.ac.in
[2] Computer Science and Engineering Department,
Indian Institute of Technology Kanpur, Kanpur, India
vinaypn@iitk.ac.in

Abstract. The prohibitive amounts of time required to review the large
amounts of data captured by surveillance and other cameras has brought
into question the very utility of large scale video logging. Yet, one recognizes that such logging and analysis are indispensable to security applications. The only way out of this paradox is to devise expedited browsing,
by the creation of hyperlapse. We address the hyperlapse problem for
the very challenging category of intensive egomotion which makes the
hyperlapse highly jerky. We propose an economical approach for trajectory estimation based on Visual Odometry and implement cost functions
to penalize pose and path deviations. Also, this is implemented on data
taken by omni-directional camera, so that the viewer can opt to observe
any direction while browsing. This requires many innovations, including
handling the massive radial distortions and implementing scene stabilization that need to be operated upon the least distorted region of the
omni view.

1 Introduction

With time, high quality video cameras becoming cheaper and the growth of social
media platforms that give the opportunity to share videos have resulted in people
making videos more often. Recently the popularity of 360° view cameras like
Ricoh Theta has attracted people to shoot the videos of their fun activities like
bike riding, running, mountain climbing etc. Cheap storage devices have made
storage of long videos easy but it is quite time consuming to watch and navigate
through such large videos. One simple way to watch these videos in a short time is
to speed them up in order to create timelapse videos. This results in a watchable
short video in case of stationary cameras. But with camera motion, which is
actually the case most of the time with hand held or head mounted cameras,
this will heighten the apparent motion resulting in a nauseating jumble. Some
adaptive fast forward approaches [14] try to adjust the speeds in different parts
of the video so that stationary scenes are sampled sparsely while dynamic scenes

© Springer Nature Singapore Pte Ltd. 2018
R. Rameshan et al. (Eds.): NCVPRIPG 2017, CCIS 841, pp. 3–13, 2018.
https://doi.org/10.1007/978-981-13-0020-2_1

are sampled densely. Some timelapse and hyperlapse approaches combined with video stabilization have also been suggested for conventional cameras.

Storyboard summarization based on keyframes selection is proposed in [17,18]. Video stabilization techniques can directly be combined with timelapse (before or after). In [4,12] the camera path is generated by estimating pose using feature mapping and this path is used to create a new smooth path for the camera for stabilization. In [10,11], based on structure-from-motion (SfM) they render the scene for a novel smooth camera path. Hyperlapse app from Instagram uses the approach of stabilization after uniform frame skipping [6] and for stabilization they use hardware stabilization approach of Karpenko *et al.* [7]. Hardware based stabilization approaches involve dampening of camera motion using mechanical means like inertial sensors (gyroscopes and accelerometers) with gimbals. As instagram's approach uses inertial sensor data, it cannot be applied to existing videos.

Non-uniform timelapse with varying skipping rate across the video as a function of scene content is proposed in [3]. The most sophisticated approach for hyperlapse creation is from Kopf *et al.* [8] which is based on SfM so computationally very expensive. Joshi *et al.* [5] came up with real time hyperlapse creation approach based on optimal selection of frames using frame matching and poses hyperlapse as a frame sampling problem by optimizing an energy function. Very recently a saliency based hyperlapse approach for 360° videos have been proposed [9]. They generate hyperlapse by optimizing over saliency and motion smoothness followed by saliency aware frame selection.

Our work is based on smart sampling of the input frames depending on a cost function which works upon the camera path obtained by visual odometry [16]. We include the following costs in the cost function: (a) pose change cost between frames, (b) smooth path deviation cost by fitting a smooth approximate path to the VO camera path, (c) velocity and acceleration costs. The idea is to sample more frames when pose change of camera is significant. This method can be used for normal cameras as well as for omni-cameras, but creating omni-summaries is different from normal in terms of handling massive radial distortion and applying stabilization on the basis of the least distorted spatial regions of input video.

2   Framework

The proposed algorithm can be divided in two main parts: Visual Odometry (VO) and selection of frames based on VO.

2.1   Visual Odometry for Omnidirectional Camera

Preparing images in 'Ready for VO' form: As VO is a feature matching based process, all the video frames must be undistorted. The Ricoh Theta S camera consists of two fish-eye lenses each giving a view of more than $\frac{4\varPi}{2}$ steradian. In recorded video, frames are depicted as two discs side by side, with each showing one hemispherical view captured by one lens. Since the view is captured as a spherical image, it is very much distorted at the edges of each of the discs, and is hence difficult to restore. Observing that the central part is least distorted, we crop the central part from either of the discs and undistort this part only. This cropped part is undistorted using Scaramuzza's OCamCalib toolbox for MATLAB [15]. We observed that central 400×400 part proved to be good enough in case of 1920×1080 resolution. In case of 1280×720 resolution this size reduces to 300×300. This is not a very strict restriction but optimal in the sense that the above stated size frames can be undistorted well and in the final cropped version enough number of robust feature points can be found for VO. If we crop a bigger portion, there will remain some distortion and if we crop smaller portion there may not be enough features in the final cropped frame for VO.

The manufacturing company of Ricoh Theta S provides an app RICOH THETA [2] which converts the image in the 2 disc form of into equi-rectangular form. This equi-rectangular form video can be used to look into any specific direction using the same app. This feature of the app makes available hyper-lapse data in equirectangular form, which is very convenient.

Finding VO: Visual odometry (VO) is the process of estimating the egomotion of an agent observing the changes in images of the attached camera due to induced motion. Two consecutive camera frames at different camera positions are related by rigid body transformation $\mathbf{T}_{k,k-1} \in \mathbb{R}^{4 \times 4}$ given as:

$$\mathbf{T}_{k,k-1} = \begin{bmatrix} \mathbf{R}_{k,k-1} & \mathbf{t}_{k,k-1} \\ 0 & 1 \end{bmatrix} \tag{1}$$

where $\mathbf{R}_{k,k-1} \in \mathbb{R}^{3 \times 3}$ is the rotation matrix and $\mathbf{t}_{k,k-1} \in \mathbb{R}^{3 \times 1}$ is the translational vector. Our main task is to compute the relative transformations $\mathbf{T}_{k,k-1}$ and then to get the full trajectory of the camera by concatenating the transformations. Main components of the VO system are shown in Fig. 1(f). Our algorithm does not include last step of VO which is bundle adjustment. Rotation and translation are extracted from the essential matrix $\mathbf{E}$ by 2-D to 2-D motion estimation and $\mathbf{E}$ can be computed from 2-D to 2-D feature correspondences. Nister's five-point algorithm has been used for motion estimation [13]. After extracting $\mathbf{R}$ and $\mathbf{t}$, $\mathbf{T}_{k,k-1}$ is obtained and camera pose can be found incrementally as shown in Fig. 1(g):

$$\mathbf{C}_k = \mathbf{C}_{k-1}\mathbf{T}_{k,k-1} \tag{2}$$

2.2   VO Based Hyperlapse Algorithm

We propose a cost function based on VO and choose frames which follow the target speed-up rate, yet keep their pose close to the smooth path and the pose change between consecutive frames is also minimal. The following costs are included:

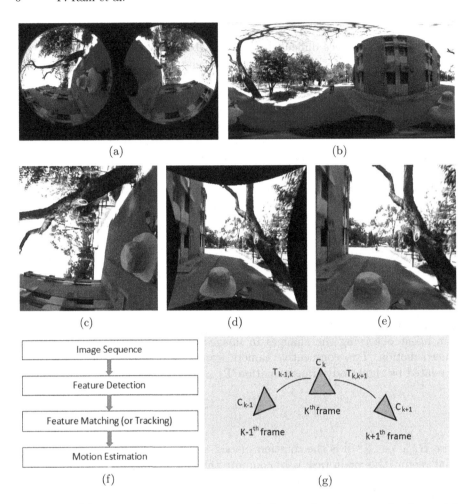

Fig. 1. (a), (b) are one omni-frames in two circle form and equi-rectangular frame. (c), (d) are 400×400 central cropped part and its undistorted version and (e) is 300×300 part used for VO. (f) is block diagram of VO system used in our algorithm [16], (g) is illustration of VO process.

Pose Change Cost: One observation is that even minor camera pose change causes significant content change in consecutive frames (rotation causes more change than translation) assuming the environment is sufficiently diverse. So, in pose change cost, more weight is given to orientation change. Camera poses are obtained as 7D vectors (x, y, z and 4D quaternions) and 6D vectors (x, y, z and 3D Euler's angles (pitch, roll and yaw)). Pose change cost is computed as:

$$C_n(i,j) = \|P_{xyz}(j) - P_{xyz}(i)\|$$
$$+ Q_p * \|P_{pitch}(j) - P_{pitch}(i)\| + Q_y * \|P_{yaw}(j) - P_{yaw}(i)\|$$
$$+ Q_r * \|P_{roll}(j) - P_{roll}(i)\|$$
$$(3)$$

Here $P_{xyz}(j)$ is 3D translation coordinates, $P_{pitch}(j), P_{yaw}(j)$ and $P_{roll}(j)$ are the rotation coordinates of the jth camera frame and Q_p, Q_r, Q_y are weights given to pitch, roll and yaw change respectively.

Smoothness Deviation Cost: For the resultant hyperlapse to look good in terms of frame-to-frame transitions, frames should be sampled such that they lie near to a smooth camera path. For the obtained camera path P as a sequence of 7D pose vectors, a smooth camera path S is obtained by fitting a cubic spline on the camera path obtained from VO as shown in Fig. 2 and the cost for j^{th} frame is defined as:

$$C_d(j) = \|P_{xyz}(j) - S_{xyz}(j)\| + w * \|P_{quat}(j) - S_{quat}(j)\| \qquad (4)$$

Here $P_{xyz}(j)$ and $S_{xyz}(j)$ are 3D translation coordinates for actual and smooth camera path respectively, $P_{quat}(j)$ and $S_{quat}(j)$ are 4D quaternions vectors for actual and smooth camera path respectively for j^{th} camera frame.

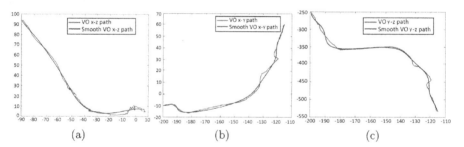

(a)   (b)   (c)

Fig. 2. VO path and smooth path obtained by spline fitting.

Velocity and Acceleration Costs: As in [5], to ensure that our result achieves the desired speedup we use a velocity cost when the frame skip deviates from the target speedup v.

$$C_s(i,j,v) = min(\|(j-i) - v\|_2^2, \tau_s) \qquad (5)$$

Here i,j are consecutive frames to be selected in hyperlapse, v is target speed up. Previous costs lead to selecting frames such that it balances between following a smooth camera path versus violating target speed-up. There can be cases where violating speed-up rate may lead to frames following a smooth path but it might cause a perceptual jump due to sudden change in speed-up rate. To avoid these sudden jumps in speed-up rate causing perceptual jumps, we use an acceleration cost:

$$C_a(h,i,j) = min(\|(j-i)-(i-h)\|_2^2, \tau_a) \qquad (6)$$

Here h, i, j are consecutive frames to be selected in hyperlapse video, τ_s and τ_a are the upper bounds so that not a large number of frames are skipped.

Adaptive Target Speed Up: Parts of the input video where there is sudden camera movement, at the same global speed-up result might be jerky at those places as we are not using frame-to-frame matching. Taking inspiration from equal motion hyperlapse of [5] we define adaptive speed-up depending upon the change in camera pose:

$$Q_d(i) = P_{quat}(i+1) - P_{quat}(i) \qquad (7)$$
$$Q_{ds}(i) = f_{sigm}(\|Q_d(i)\|) \qquad (8)$$
$$f_{sigm}(x) = \frac{1}{1+e^{-a(x-c)}} \qquad (9)$$
$$v_{ad}(i) = \frac{median(Q_{ds})}{Q_{ds}(i)} \qquad (10)$$

Here $P_{quat}(i+1)$, $P_{quat}(i)$ are quaternions vectors for actual camera path for $(i+1)^{th}$ and i^{th} frames respectively, a, c are sigmoid parameters and $v_{ad}(i)$ is target speed up for i^{th} frame.

Finding Optimal Path: Using all the costs, the total cost with different weights for different components is defined as:

$$C(h,i,j,v) = l_sC_s(i,j,v) + l_aC_a(h,i,j) + l_nC_n(i,j)$$
$$+ l_d(C_d(i) + C_d(j)) \qquad (11)$$

For obtaining optimal path P, define the cost of a path p for a given target speed-up v as:

$$\Phi(p,v) = \sum_{t=1}^{T-1} C(p(t-1),p(t),p(t+1),v) \qquad (12)$$
$$P = \underset{p}{arg\ min}\ \Phi(p,v) \qquad (13)$$

Optimum path calculation is done using Algorithm 1, inspired from [5], which consists of two passes. The first pass builds a dynamic cost matrix D_v (function of target speed-up v). For i^{th} frame, the next frame is to be chosen from among the window of w successive frames.

Algorithm 1. Frame selection

Input: v
Initialization:
for $i = 1$ to g do
    for $j = i+1$ to $i + w$ do
        $D_v(i,j) = l_d(C_d(i) + C_d(j)) + l_n C_n(i,j) + l_s C_s(i,j,v_{ad}(i))$
    end for
end for
First Pass: populate D_v
for $i = g$ to T do
    for $j = i+1$ to $i + w$ do
        $c = l_d(C_d(i) + C_d(j)) + l_n C_n(i,j) + l_s C_s(i,j,v_{ad}(i))$
        $D_v(i,j) = c + min_{k=1}^{w}[D_v(i-k,i) + l_a C_a(i-k,i,j)]$
        $T_v(i,j) = c + arg\ min_{k=1}^{w}[D_v(i-k,i) + l_a C_a(i-k,i,j)]$
    end for
end for
Second Pass: track back min cost path
$(s,d) = arg\ min_{i=T-g,j=i+1}^{T,i+w} D_v(i,j)$
$\mathbf{p} = <d>$
while $s > g$ do
    $\mathbf{p} = prepend\ (\mathbf{p},s)$
    $b = T_v(s,d)$
    $d = s, s = b$
end while
Return: p

The algorithm populates D_v by iterating over its entries, where each element $D_v(i,j)$ represents the running minimal cost path with last two frames as i and j. At each step of constructing D_v, cost functions C_d, C_n, and C_s are evaluated at i and j, and the preceding frame h with the lowest cost is searched for, which depends on the previous costs and C_a. h is stored in a traceback matrix T_v for the second pass of the algorithm. After fully populating D_v, the second pass finds an optimal path by finding the minimal cost in the rows and columns of D_v.

3   Observations and Results

Since this is VO based process which is a feature matching based process, we can not use very low resolution cameras (either conventional or omni cameras like Ricoh Theta S) as low resolution frames increase the possibility of wrong feature matching which might ruin the accuracy of VO. For conventional cameras (GoPro Hero 4), we need not do any extra-preprocessing like cropping before undistortion as the inherent distortion is not too severe so the bigger full size frames can be used for VO. Using cropped frames for VO (relatively fewer features for matching) in case of the Ricoh camera does not change the VO quality much. We compare the odometry obtained from both cameras by matching different numbers of features after making a video capture with both cameras fixed rigidly to one another (so that their motions are identical, barring a small constant displacement), and choose that number for which the shape of VOs match the most. One more key observation here is that only the shape of VO matters, not their absolute values. On comparing the VO from both spheres, we observe that the shape is related irrespective of which disc we use for VO Fig. 3(b), thus confirming that the VO from any Ricoh sphere can undoubtedly be used for hyperlapse. The displacement in curves is observed because of the opposite direction of VO process accumulation error.

VO of raw video captured by head mounted camera can directly be used for hyperlapse, no unnecessary jerks are observed in hyperlapse but raw input videos captured by hand held camera are shaky due to induced vibrations in hand because of vehicle as in Fig. 3(a) so VO is not smooth. So VO of raw videos captured by hand held Ricoh Theta S can not be used directly for hyperlapse as unnecessary jerks can be observed in hyperlapse. In this case, a prior stage of stabilization is applied before the VO as shown in Fig. 3(a).

We compare our method against Instagram's method (timelapse followed by stabilization) for conventional cameras by creating VO based hyperlapse with centrally cropped and undistorted frames. The measures used for comparison are the number of frames selected at sharp camera path points, mean and standard deviation of consecutively selected frames at these sharp camera path points. We also introduce a standard deviation based measure which is defined as follows:

$$measure = \frac{No.\ of\ non\ zero\ pixels\ in\ std.\ dev.\ image}{Total\ pixels\ in\ std.\ dev.\ image} \qquad (14)$$

Better method:

1. selects more number of frames.
2. gives lesser ghostly mean and standard deviation.
3. gives lesser standard deviation based measure.

In Table 1 and Fig. 4, we see that for our method, as compared to instagram's, more frames are selected at sharp turns and standard deviation based measure is also lesser. In Fig. 3(c), we see that mean and standard deviation for our method are less ghostly.

The poststabilization of omnidirectional hyperlapse is an issue in dual sphere format. Dual fisheye sphere format video is not accepted by RICOH THETA app for converting into equirectangular form (which is of main interest) after any modification. This app accepts only raw videos captured by Ricoh Theta S. So an alternative approach is to apply hyperlapse on equirectangular video which can be stabilized by facebook stabilization app for equirectangular videos [1] (to be launched in near future) and then we can use this stabilized hyperlapse to see into any specific direction using RICOH THETA app. Prestabilization for VO is done by combining all 'Ready for VO' frames into a video and stabilizing that sequence. This is equivalent to stabilizing all full frames, converting them to 'Ready for VO' form and then finding VO.

Table 1. Standard deviations based measure of 5 consecutive frames in case of 3× speed up and of 3 consecutive frames in case of 6× speed up is listed in table. This measure is defined as per Eq. 14. Also, number of chosen frames for different video slots at different speed ups have been shown in table.

	Standard deviation based measure		No. of frames chosen	
	Timelapse + stabilization	Our method	Timelapse + stabilization	Our method
Slot1 at 3×	0.9870	0.9531	26	40
Slot1 at 6×	0.9934	0.9490	13	20
Slot2 at 3×	0.9527	0.9220	33	46
Slot2 at 6×	0.9749	0.9456	18	30
Slot3 at 3×	0.9997	0.9985	29	46
Slot3 at 6×	0.9986	0.9951	15	25

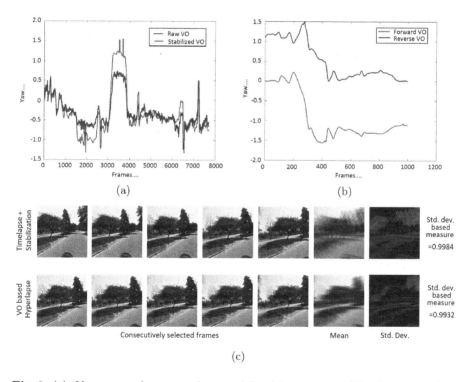

Fig. 3. (a): Yaw curves for raw and pre-stabilized input video. (b): Yaw curves from different spheres. (c): Consecutive selected frames and their mean and standard deviation. In case of VO based hyperlapse mean and standard deviation are less ghosted. We are comparing at a speedup of 3× with 'timelapse followed by stabilization' which is equivalent to instagram's hyperlapse technique. Numerical value of standard deviation based measure has been calculated as per Eq. 14.

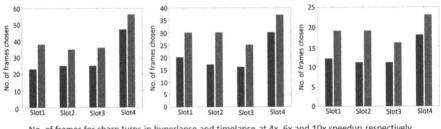

No. of frames for sharp turns in hyperlapse and timelapse at 4x, 6x and 10x speedup respectively.

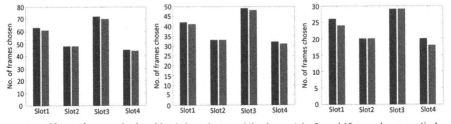

No. of frames for normal going video in hyperlapse and timelapse at 4x, 6x and 10x speedup respectively.

■ Hyperlapse   ■ Timelapse

Fig. 4. Comparision of number of frames chosen in ours and Instagram's hyperlapse technique for different video slots at different speed ups. In case of normal going video number of frames selected in both are same which ensures that dense sampling takes place at sharp camera motion points only.

4   Conclusion

Our work of creating hyperlapse for egocentric videos is a novel approach based on Visual Odometry. Moreover, we implement our approach on omni-directional camera so that there is no question of losing information in any direction and user is also allowed to select post capture viewing direction. To handle the issue of egomotion we use cost function based approach and introduce various costs which helps the hyperlapse to become smooth. To handle omni-directional camera (excessive distortion) we introduce some pre-processing steps like cropping and undistortion. We also state the problems faced while trying to stabilize the omni-directional video.

Acknowledgment. This project is a part of postgraduate dissertation research work at Indian Institute of Technology Kanpur, India, financially supported by the Indian government organization *Defence Research and Development Organisation.*

References

1. 360 video stabilization: a new algorithm for smoother 360 video viewing. https://code.facebook.com/posts/697469023742261/360-video-stabilization-a-new-algorithm-for-smoother-360-video-viewing/
2. Ricoh theta app. https://theta360.com/en/support/download/

3. Bennett, E.P., McMillan, L.: Computational time-lapse video. ACM Trans. Graph. **26**(3), 102 (2007)
4. Grundmann, M., Kwatra, V., Essa, I.: Auto-directed video stabilization with robust L1 optimal camera paths. In: Proceedings of the 2011 IEEE Conference on Computer Vision and Pattern Recognition, CVPR 2011, pp. 225–232 (2011)
5. Joshi, N., Kienzle, W., Toelle, M., Uyttendaele, M., Cohen, M.F.: Real-time hyperlapse creation via optimal frame selection. ACM Trans. Graph. **34**(4), 63:1–63:9 (2015)
6. Karpenko, A.: The technology behind hyperlapse from instagram. http://instagram-engineering.tumblr.com/post/95922900787/hyperlapse
7. Karpenko, A., Jacobs, D., Baek, J., Levoy, M., Virji, S.: Digital video stabilization and rolling shutter correction using gyroscopes (2011)
8. Kopf, J., Cohen, M.F., Szeliski, R.: First-person hyper-lapse videos. ACM Trans. Graph. **33**(4), 78:1–78:10 (2014)
9. Lai, W., Huang, Y., Joshi, N., Buehler, C., Yang, M., Kang, S.B.: Semantic-driven generation of hyperlapse from 360° video. CoRR abs/1703.10798 (2017)
10. Liu, F., Gleicher, M., Jin, H., Agarwala, A.: Content-preserving warps for 3D video stabilization. ACM Trans. Graph. **28**(3), 44:1–44:9 (2009)
11. Liu, F., Gleicher, M., Wang, J., Jin, H., Agarwala, A.: Subspace video stabilization. ACM Trans. Graph. **30**(1), 4:1–4:10 (2011)
12. Matsushita, Y., Ofek, E., Ge, W., Tang, X., Shum, H.Y.: Full-frame video stabilization with motion inpainting. IEEE Trans. Pattern Anal. Mach. Intell. **28**(7), 1150–1163 (2006)
13. Nistér, D.: An efficient solution to the five-point relative pose problem. IEEE Trans. Pattern Anal. Mach. Intell. **26**(6), 756–777 (2004)
14. Petrovic, N., Jojic, N., Huang, T.S.: Adaptive video fast forward. Multimed. Tools Appl. **26**(3), 327–344 (2005)
15. Scaramuzza, D.: OcamCalib: omnidirectional camera calibration toolbox for matlab. https://sites.google.com/site/scarabotix/ocamcalib-toolbox
16. Scaramuzza, D., Fraundorfer, F.: Visual odometry [tutorial]. IEEE Robot. Autom. Mag. **18**(4), 80–92 (2011)
17. Xiong, B., Grauman, K.: Detecting snap points in egocentric video with a web photo prior. In: Fleet, D., Pajdla, T., Schiele, B., Tuytelaars, T. (eds.) ECCV 2014. LNCS, vol. 8693, pp. 282–298. Springer, Cham (2014). https://doi.org/10.1007/978-3-319-10602-1_19
18. Lee, Y.J., Ghosh, J., Grauman, K.: Discovering important people and objects for egocentric video summarization. In: CVPR, vol. 2, no. 6, pp. 1346–1353 (2012)

Classification of Human Actions Using 3-D Convolutional Neural Networks: A Hierarchical Approach

Shaival Thakkar[(✉)] and M. V. Joshi

Dhirubhai Ambani Institute of Information and Communication Technology,
Gandhinagar 382007, Gujarat, India
shaivalthakkar@gmail.com, mv_joshi@daiict.ac.in

Abstract. In this paper, we present a hierarchical approach for human action classification using 3-D Convolutional neural networks (3-D CNN). In general, human actions refer to positioning and movement of hands and legs and hence can be classified based on those performed by hands or by legs or, in some cases, both. This acts as the intuition for our work on hierarchical classification. In this work, we consider the actions as tasks performed by hand or leg movements. Therefore, instead of using a single 3-D CNN for classification of given actions, we use multiple networks to perform the classification hierarchically, that is, we first perform binary classification to separate the hand and leg actions and then use two separate networks for hand and leg actions to perform classification among target action categories. For example, in case of KTH dataset, we train three networks to classify six different actions, comprising of three actions each for hands and legs. The novelty of our approach lies in performing the separation of hand and leg actions first, thus making the subsequent classifiers to accept the features corresponding to either hands or legs only. This leads to better classification accuracy. Also, the use of 3-D CNN enables automatic extraction of features in spatial as well as temporal domain, avoiding the need for hand crafted features. This makes it one of the better approaches when it comes to video classification. We use the KTH, Weizmann and UCF-sports datasets to evaluate our method and comparison with the state of the art methods shows that our approach outperforms most of them.

1 Introduction

Automatic action recognition has gained more importance in the recent years. This is due to its wide areas of applications which include intelligent surveillance systems, automated video retrieval systems and modern gaming systems which use action recognition. The task of automatic action recognition is a nontrivial one due to challenges such as occlusions, different lighting conditions and other problems. However, deep structures such as 3-D CNN [1] have proved to be

© Springer Nature Singapore Pte Ltd. 2018
R. Rameshan et al. (Eds.): NCVPRIPG 2017, CCIS 841, pp. 14–23, 2018.
https://doi.org/10.1007/978-981-13-0020-2_2

robust enough to overcome such challenges. Most of the work in the field of action recognition comprises of two stages: Calculation of hand crafted features [2–5] which act as descriptors of the input videos and classification of actions using these descriptors with the help of classifiers such as Support Vector Machine (SVM) [6,7] and others. Such methods require mathematical models to calculate the hand crafted features. However, such mathematical models may fail to adapt to real world data and to capture the change in every individual's way of performing an action.

Deep structures such as Convolutional neural networks (CNNs) [8] have proven to perform better in case of image data but even such networks cannot be used efficiently for action recognition. This is because, CNNs perform the convolution operation in the spatial domain only. However, in case of action recognition, important information is contained in the temporal domain which requires convolution in temporal domain. Convolution in temporal domain can extract features which are representative of the information contained in this domain. This extension of the convolution operation in temporal domain is known as 3-D convolution which is the central idea of 3-D CNN.

1.1   3-D Convolution

In CNNs, we learn filters and generate feature maps at each convolutional layer by convolving these filters with the input images. In case of traditional CNNs or 2-D CNNs, 2-D filters are learnt, the inputs to which are single-channel or multi-channel still images. These filters use single image as input whereas in case of 3-D CNNs, 3-D filters are learnt which require a collection of frames of a video as input and that number of frames determines the temporal dimension of the filter. For *eg* if a filter with a temporal dimension of 3 is learnt, the first three frames from the input video are used to generate a feature map at all spatial locations for the next layer and then frame numbers 2, 3 and 4 and so on. Figures 1 and 2 show the difference between 2-D convolution and 3-D convolution and the working of 3-D convolution can be observed in Fig. 2.

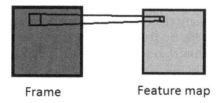

Frame   Feature map

Fig. 1. 2-D convolution operation on a single channel input frame

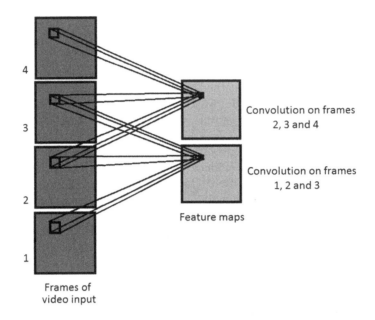

Fig. 2. 3-D convolution operation

2   Hierarchical Classification

Human actions are performed by hands or by legs or in some cases, both. Generally, an action can be categorized as that performed by hands (clapping, waving, *etc.*) or by legs (walking, running, *etc.*). This intuition is used in our approach to obtain the classification hierarchically, that is, first perform binary classification and then use two separate networks for target action classification. For the purpose of explaining the approach, let us consider the classification of actions of the KTH dataset, which has 6 actions. These are boxing, hand clapping, hand waving which are hand actions and walking, jogging, running correspond to the leg actions. Instead of performing classification directly into the 6 target action categories, we classify these actions into those performed by hands or by legs, initially, and then classify the actions into their target categories. We use three 3-D CNNs to perform the classification hierarchically. The block diagram representation of our approach is shown in Fig. 3.

The first of the three networks (3-D CNN 1 in Fig. 3) performs binary classification among hand and leg actions. Since the hand and leg actions are well separated, this network can classify them accurately (with 100% accuracy), which makes it possible to perform classification hierarchically. Our algorithm checks the output of 3-D CNN 1 and if the input video is classified as hand action, the same input video is automatically given to 3-D CNN 2 which performs the classification among the target action classes of boxing, hand clapping and hand waving which are hand actions. Similarly, if the input video is classified as leg

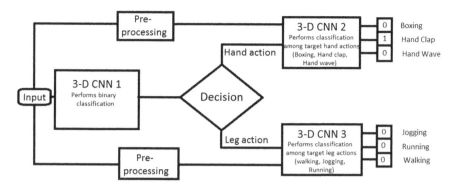

Fig. 3. Block diagram representation of our approach

action by 3-D CNN 1, then the same input video is automatically given to 3-D CNN 3 for classification among leg actions *viz.* walking, jogging and running. Figure 3 shows the classification of an input video as being of the hand clapping action class. The architecture, training, testing, inputs to the 3-D CNNs and the pre-processing blocks are explained in the next section.

3   3-D Convolutional Neural Networks

The basic architecture of all the three networks, shown in Fig. 3, is the same except for the output layer. The output layer of 3-D CNN 1 has just one output unit since it performs binary classification. The output layer of the other two networks have 3 units each, as indicated in Fig. 3 and they perform classification among the three target action classes.

3.1   Network Architecture

The basic architecture of the 3-D CNNs used in our work is shown in Fig. 4. The architecture and filter sizes have been decided heuristically after extensive experimentations and checking the results for various architectures and filter sizes. The network has an input layer of dimension $80 \times 60 \times 25$ which means that each input video patch consists of 25 frames with a spatial resolution of 80×60 pixels. Then, we have two 3-D convolutional layers with 14 and 6 filters respectively, each of size $5 \times 5 \times 5$, followed by a max pooling layer with mask size of 3×3. We then have one more 3-D convolutional layer with 4 filters of size $3 \times 3 \times 5$ followed by a 3×3 max pooling layer. Finally, we have a fully connected layer which converts the output of the max pooling layer into a 128-D vector. At the end, we have an output layer with one unit (binary classification) in case of 3-D CNN 1 and three units (three class classification) in case of 3-D CNNs 2 and 3.

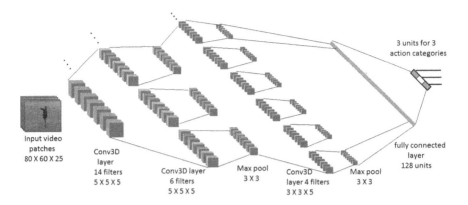

Fig. 4. Example of a figure caption.

3.2   Pre-processing/Inputs to the Network

The input video to the first network corresponds to alternate gray-scale images (i.e. frame numbers 1, 3, 5, 7 and so on) with no pre-processing. Here, use of alternate frames allows us to cover a longer duration of video, so that the actions are well defined. This also controls the complexity of the network due to reduced number of input frames. However, inputs to the other two networks undergo pre-processing before being fed to the network. In the case of 3-D CNN 2, used for classifying hand actions, we use alternate frame subtractions (i.e. 1–3, 3–5, 5–7 and so on) as pre-processing. By doing so, one can consider only those portions that change temporally. Few of the pre-processed frames of hand waving action class are shown in Fig. 5.

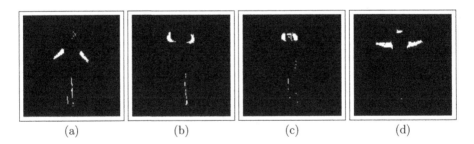

Fig. 5. Pre-processed frames of hand waving action class (image values boosted to improve visibility in the paper)

For the 3-D CNN used to classify leg actions (3-D CNN 3), alternate frame subtractions cannot be used. This is due to the fact that, in actions such as walking or jogging, the position of a human may not change significantly across the frames and hence, the subtraction may cause loss of information. Hence, in this case we use background subtraction as pre-processing. Here, we find a background frame from the input which corresponds to a frame that has minimum or no foreground. This is done by finding a frame which has the least number of interest points or no interest points. To do this, we make use of Space time interest points (STIPs) [2]. By doing so, we can keep the entire human body intact in the frames. Some of the pre-processed frames of running action class are shown in Fig. 6. Thus, with 50 frames as input, 3-D CNN 1 uses 25 alternate frames. Alternate frame subtractions generate 25 frames as input to 3-D CNN 2 from the available frames and the 25 alternate frames with the background subtraction are input to 3-D CNN 3. The use of subtraction of images instead of the actual images allows the networks to focus, only on the areas which change across the frames, ignoring the redundant information.

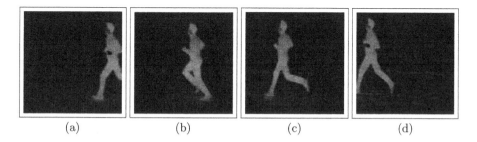

| (a) | (b) | (c) | (d) |

Fig. 6. Pre-processed frames of running action class

3.3 Training and Testing

We train the first network using the entire training data by considering boxing, hand clapping and hand waving belonging to one class and the rest of the actions belonging to the other class. Similarly, 3-D CNN 2 and 3-D CNN 3 are trained using training data of hand and leg actions, respectively, with the input pre-processing steps as explained in Sect. 3.2. We use the back-propagation algorithm [9] for training. After training the three networks, testing is performed as shown in Fig. 3. An unknown test sample is given as input to the first network, say of the hand waving class. The first network classifies it as hand action after which, the further classification is done by 3-D CNN 2. Therefore, the same test input is automatically applied as input to 3-D CNN 2 (after the pre-processing steps) which in turn classifies it as hand waving action.

4 Experiments

We use KTH and Weizmann datasets for evaluation and compare our results with few of the state of the art methods. The approach that we propose in this paper is more focussed on action recognition in applications such as surveillance and not for other applications such as video retrieval and KTH and Weizmann datasets are more suitable for surveillance applications. In addition, we perform experiments on UCF-sports data set to demonstrate the efficacy of our approach on more complex actions.

Most of the experiments have been carried out on a system with Intel fourth Gen I5 processor and NVIDIA Ge-force 920 m gpu with 4 GB of RAM, running windows 10 (except for some parameter tuning on NVIDIA Ge-force GTX Titan X gpu). We use python 3.5 (Anaconda3) and Keras deep learning library with Theano back-end on the software front.

4.1 Experiment on KTH Dataset

As explained earlier, KTH dataset [10] has 6 actions *viz.* boxing, hand clapping, hand waving, walking, jogging, and running. 25 persons perform these 6 actions repeatedly in 4 different scenarios *viz.* outdoor, outdoor with scale variation, outdoor with different clothes and indoor. Therefore, we have $25 \times 4 \times 6 = 600$ videos in the dataset. Each video is divided in 4 sub-sequences. As of now 2391 sub-sequences are available. On an average, each sub-sequence has a duration of 2–4 s. All the videos are shot using a static camera with frame rate of 25 fps. We use data of 16 persons for training and that of 9 persons for testing. The data is divided into train and test set according to the split suggested in [10]. Table 1 shows category-wise and average performance comparison with some of the state of the art methods. One can observe a significant performance boost from using a single 3D-CNN (refer [1] for confusion matrix with only 1 3D-CNN). The results also show that our approach outperforms most of the state of the art methods in 3 out of the 6 categories and also has the best average performance among the methods listed in Table 1.

Table 1. Category-wise and overall comparison with state of the art methods for KTH dataset

Method	Box	Clap	Wave	Jog	Run	Walk	Avg
Schuldt *et al.* [10]	97.9	59.7	73.6	60.4	54.9	83.8	71.7%
Dollar *et al.* [11]	93	77	85	57	85	90	81.2%
Niebles *et al.* [12]	98	86	93	53	88	82	83.3%
Jhuang *et al.* [13]	92	**98**	92	85	87	96	91.7%
Ji *et al.* [1]	90	94	**97**	84	79	97	90.2%
Laptev *et al.* [14]	97	95	91	89	80	**99**	91.8%
Wang *et al.* [15]	-	-	-	-	-	-	94.2%
Hao *et al.* [16]	-	-	-	-	-	-	94%
Our approach	**100**	95.2	93.1	**90**	**94.5**	97.3	**95.02%**

4.2   Experiment on Weizmann Dataset

Weizmann dataset [17] is a comparatively smaller dataset consisting of 90 videos but has more number of actions compared to KTH dataset. It has 10 actions *viz.* walking, running, jumping forward, galloping sideways, bending, one hand wave, two hand wave, jumping in place, jumping jack and skipping forward. These 10 actions are performed by 9 persons. In this case, we consider walking, running, galloping sideways, jumping forward and skipping forward as leg actions and the rest of the actions as hand actions and perform an experiment similar to what was done in the case of KTH dataset. We use the data of 8 randomly selected persons for training and that of a single person for testing and report 5-fold cross validation accuracy. The results and comparison with few of the state of the art methods are shown in Table 2 which shows that our approach achieves the best result in case of Weizmann dataset as well.

Table 2. Results on Weizmann dataset

Method	Recognition accuracy
Gorelick *et al.* [17]	97.83%
Brahman and Nanni [18]	97.8%
Fathi and Mori [19]	100%
Our approach	**100%**

4.3   Experiment on UCF-sports Dataset

UCF-sports dataset [20] contains 10 actions as well. They are Diving, Golf Swing, Kicking, lifting, horse riding, running, skating, bench swing, side swing and walking. Here, we consider walking, running, skating, horse riding, and kicking as leg actions and the rest as hand actions. We use 5-fold cross validation in this case as well. The recognition accuracy obtained and comparison with different approaches is as shown in the table below. One can see that our approach performs better on this data set as well (Table 3).

Table 3. Results on UCF-sports dataset

Method	Recognition accuracy
Wand *et al.* [21]	85.6%
Kovashka and Grauman [22]	87.2%
Weinzaepfel *et al.* [23]	90.5%
Ravanbaksh *et al.* [4]	97.8%%
Our approach	**98%**

5   Conclusion

This paper focused on a raw pixel based method for action recognition. We proposed a hierarchical way of classifying human actions by classifying them into hand and leg actions before classifying them into their target action categories. From the experiments conducted by us, we can conclude that performing classification hierarchically, gives better performance, since it reduces the confusion between the classes and allows learning of better and focussed features. Also, using subtraction of images rather than the actual images makes it better. This is because, only the area which changes in the frames can be concentrated upon, ignoring the redundant information. We compare the results achieved by our approach with few of the state of the art methods and we can see that our approach outperforms most of the state of the art methods.

We would like to thank NVIDIA Corporation for provision of the Titan X gpu, which enabled us to do network selection and parameter tuning very quickly.

References

1. Ji, S., Xu, W., Yang, M., Yu, K.: 3D convolutional neural networks for human action recognition. IEEE Trans. Pattern Anal. Mach. Intell. **35**(1), 221–231 (2013)
2. Laptev, I., Lindeberg, T.: Space-time interest points. In: 2003 Proceedings of the Ninth IEEE International Conference on Computer Vision, vol. 1, pp. 432–439, October 2003
3. Scovanner, P., Ali, S., Shah, M.: A 3-dimensional sift descriptor and its application to action recognition. In: Proceedings of the 15th ACM International Conference on Multimedia, Series MM 2007, pp. 357–360. ACM, New York (2007). http://doi.acm.org/10.1145/1291233.1291311
4. Ravanbakhsh, M., Mousavi, H., Rastegari, M., Murino, V., Davis, L.S.: Action recognition with image based CNN features, CoRR, vol. abs/1512.03980 (2015). http://arxiv.org/abs/1512.03980
5. Baumann, F.: Action recognition with HOG-OF features. In: Weickert, J., Hein, M., Schiele, B. (eds.) GCPR 2013. LNCS, vol. 8142, pp. 243–248. Springer, Heidelberg (2013). https://doi.org/10.1007/978-3-642-40602-7_26
6. Cortes, C., Vapnik, V.: Support-vector networks. Mach. Learn. **20**(3), 273–297 (1995). https://doi.org/10.1023/A:1022627411411
7. Boser, B.E., Guyon, I.M., Vapnik, V.N.: A training algorithm for optimal margin classifiers. In: Proceedings of the Fifth Annual Workshop on Computational Learning Theory, Series COLT 1992, pp. 144–152. ACM, New York (1992). http://doi.acm.org/10.1145/130385.130401
8. Krizhevsky, A., Sutskever, I., Hinton, G.E.: Imagenet classification with deep convolutional neural networks. In: Proceedings of the 25th International Conference on Neural Information Processing Systems, Series NIPS 2012, pp. 1097–1105. Curran Associates Inc., USA (2012). http://dl.acm.org/citation.cfm?id=2999134.2999257
9. Mitchell, T.M.: Machine Learning, 1st edn. McGraw-Hill Inc., New York (1997)
10. Schuldt, C., Laptev, I., Caputo, B.: Recognizing human actions: a local SVM approach. In: 2004 Proceedings of the 17th International Conference on Pattern Recognition, ICPR 2004, vol. 3, pp. 32–36, August 2004

11. Dollar, P., Rabaud, V., Cottrell, G., Belongie, S.: Behavior recognition via sparse spatio-temporal features. In: Proceedings of the 14th International Conference on Computer Communications and Networks, Series ICCCN 2005, Washington, DC, USA, pp. 65–72. IEEE Computer Society (2005). http://dl.acm.org/citation.cfm? id=1259587.1259830

12. Niebles, J.C., Wang, H., Fei-Fei, L.: Unsupervised learning of human action categories using spatial-temporal words. Int. J. Comput. Vis. **79**(3), 299–318 (2008). https://doi.org/10.1007/s11263-007-0122-4

13. Jhuang, H., Serre, T., Wolf, L., Poggio, T.: A biologically inspired system for action recognition. In: 2007 IEEE 11th International Conference on Computer Vision, pp. 1–8, October 2007

14. Laptev, I., Marszalek, M., Schmid, C., Rozenfeld, B.: Learning realistic human actions from movies. In: 2008 IEEE Conference on Computer Vision and Pattern Recognition, pp. 1–8, June 2008

15. Wang, H., Kläser, A., Schmid, C., Liu, C.L.: Action recognition by dense trajectories. In: CVPR 2011, pp. 3169–3176, June 2011

16. Hao, Z., Lu, L., Zhang, Q., Wu, J., Izquierdo, E., Yang, J., Zhao, J.: Action recognition based on subdivision-fusion model. In: Proceedings of the British Machine Vision Conference (BMVC), pp. 50.1–50.12. BMVA Press, September 2015. https://doi.org/10.5244/C.29.50

17. Gorelick, L., Blank, M., Shechtman, E., Irani, M., Basri, R.: Actions as space-time shapes. Trans. Pattern Anal. Mach. Intell. **29**(12), 2247–2253 (2007)

18. Brahnam, S., Nanni, L.: High performance set of features for human action classification (2009)

19. Fathi, A., Mori, G.: Action recognition by learning mid-level motion features. In: 2008 IEEE Conference on Computer Vision and Pattern Recognition, pp. 1–8, June 2008

20. Soomro, K., Zamir, A.R.: Action recognition in realistic sports videos. In: Moeslund, T.B., Thomas, G., Hilton, A. (eds.) Computer Vision in Sports. ACVPR, pp. 181–208. Springer, Cham (2014). https://doi.org/10.1007/978-3-319-09396-3_9

21. Wang, H., Ullah, M.M., Klaser, A., Laptev, I., Schmid, C.: Evaluation of local spatio-temporal features for action recognition. In: Cavallaro, A., Prince, S., Alexander, D. (eds.) British Machine Vision Conference, BMVC 2009, London, United Kingdom, pp. 124.1–124.11. BMVA Press, September 2009. https://hal.inria.fr/inria-00439769

22. Kovashka, A., Grauman, K.: Learning a hierarchy of discriminative space-time neighborhood features for human action recognition. In: 2010 IEEE Computer Society Conference on Computer Vision and Pattern Recognition, pp. 2046–2053, June 2010

23. Weinzaepfel, P., Harchaoui, Z., Schmid, C.: Learning to track for spatio-temporal action localization, CoRR, vol. abs/1506.01929 (2015). http://arxiv.org/abs/1506.01929

SmartTennisTV: Automatic Indexing of Tennis Videos

Anurag Ghosh$^{(\boxtimes)}$ and C. V. Jawahar

CVIT, KCIS, IIIT, Hyderabad, India
anurag.ghosh@research.iiit.ac.in, jawahar@iiit.ac.in

Abstract. In this paper, we demonstrate a score based indexing approach for tennis videos. Given a broadcast tennis video (BTV), we index all the video segments with their scores to create a navigable and searchable match. Our approach temporally segments the rallies in the video and then recognizes the scores from each of the segments, before refining the scores using the knowledge of the tennis scoring system. We finally build an interface to effortlessly retrieve and view the relevant video segments by also automatically tagging the segmented rallies with human accessible tags such as 'fault' and 'deuce'. The efficiency of our approach is demonstrated on BTV's from two major tennis tournaments.

1 Introduction

Sports streaming websites are very popular with many services like TennisTV and WatchESPN offering full game replays on demand. Millions of users use these services for entertainment, education and other purposes. However, tennis matches are usually very long, often running into hours. It's very hard to infer playing styles and patterns of players without investing hundreds of hours of viewing time. Thus, it's cumbersome to find "useful" parts. Streaming websites provide the video as-is, i.e. it's only possible to access the video stream sequentially. However, in case of sports and other event-rich video streams, an useful extension is to provide random access (like accessing an array) grounded in events along with sequential access, so that extensions like skipping to next event, filtering events etc. can be provided.

In this paper, we focus on constructing a point wise index of a tennis match and thus providing random access to the match. We propose a method to segment out the match into a set of rallies, then automatically extract the scorecard and the scores. Using tennis domain knowledge, we construct a novel algorithm to refine our extracted scores. We then demonstrate the utility of the automatically constructed index by building an interface to quickly and effortlessly retrieve and view the relevant point, game and set segments along with providing human accessible tags.

There are multiple challenges in this scenario. The tennis match videos are recorded from multiple camera angles and edited to have different kind of shots, to capture various emotions and drama along with the game play. With respect

© Springer Nature Singapore Pte Ltd. 2018
R. Rameshan et al. (Eds.): NCVPRIPG 2017, CCIS 841, pp. 24–33, 2018.
https://doi.org/10.1007/978-981-13-0020-2_3

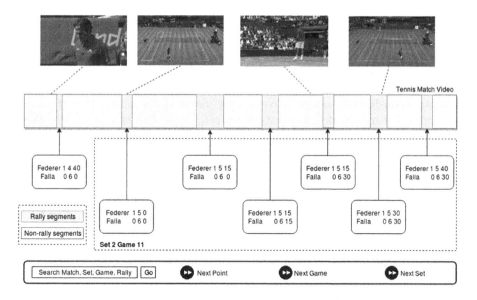

Fig. 1. We aim to provide random access to tennis match videos and construct a point wise index of a tennis match so that a user can access, jump and skip "points", "games" and "sets".

to extracting scores, the score board is never at a fixed position or in a specific format and the score digits are not constrained by font, size, and color (Fig. 1).

The major contributions of this paper are,

1. An effective score recognition algorithm using domain knowledge which can be adapted for different games. Here, we do our experiments on tennis videos by using the tennis domain knowledge.
2. We propose a score based indexing system, to navigate and retrieve segments from large volumes of video data with considerable ease.
3. Our method also enables many applications of indexing, we demonstrate one such application, human accessible event tagging.

Section 2 discusses advances and related work in literature. Section 3 forms the core of the paper, describing our core approach. Lastly, Sect. 4 provides a brief background of tennis and a high level description of our dataset(s), describes the implementation details and the experiments we performed along with obtained results.

2   Related Work

Sports Understanding: Using domain specific cues, several researchers have previously worked on improving sports understanding (specially tennis), with strides made in video summarization and automatically generating highlights [1–3], generating descriptions [10] and automatically segmenting coarse temporal scenes [5], annotating players [4,14] and tracking the ball [13,15].

Sports Video Indexing and Applications: Xu et al. [12] and Miyamori et al. [9] focus on semantic annotations exploiting tennis domain knowledge to build retrieval systems based on positions and actions. Sukhwani et al. [11] proposed a dictionary learning method for frame level fine grained annotations for a given video clip, but their annotations are also computed at the level of actions, useful in the context of computing player statistics. Kolekar et al. [6] use audio features to detect events in soccer scenes and generate highlights. Liu et al. [7] perform mutlimodal analysis to generate tennis video highlights while Connaghan et al. [8] attempt to segment out game into point, game and set, however, perform no score keeping and use multiple cameras to perform the task. However, these methods do not attempt to robustly index point level information to enable retrieval from the point of view of a viewer. Our work differs from all of these as we attempt to annotate point level information for a match.

Scorecard and Score Extraction: Liao et al. [16] focus only on detecting the scorecard while Miao et al. [17] focuses on both detection and extraction of scores, however the algorithm is specific for Basketball. Tesseract [18] is the commonly used OCR pipeline to detect text from images and documents which have a plain background. Convolutional Recurrent Neural Network (CRNN) [20] is applicable for performing end-to-end scene text recognition while Textspot [19] introduces a Fully Convolutional Regression Network (FCRN) which performs end-to-end scene text detection and for recognition, uses the intermediary stage of the pipeline based on the lexicon-encoding CNN from Jaderberg et al. [21].

3   Approach

Our goal is to automatically create an index for tennis videos. We begin by describing a method to automatically segment rallies. Then we detect and

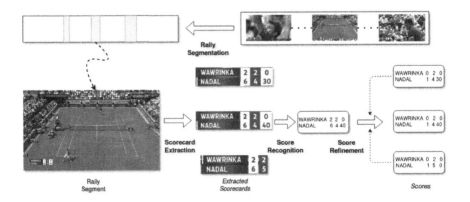

Fig. 2. Our approach is illustrated in this figure. We start by temporally segmenting out the rallies, extracting the scoreboard and then recognizing the scores where we use contextual and domain knowledge to refine the recognized scores.

localize the scorecard in each of these rallies and recognize the text to abstract out the game score state to annotate the video with the accessible tags. An overview of our pipeline can be seen in Fig. 2.

3.1   Rally Segmentation

Our method of segmenting out rallies stems from the observation that in BTV's, the camera is only overhead when the rally is in play and nowhere else. The background is mostly static after the serve begins, and remains the same till a player wins a point. HOG features are appropriate in such a scenario, so we extract frames from the Segment Dataset, downscale them, and extract HOG features. We then learn a χ-squared kernel SVM to label a frame either as a rally frame or a non-rally frame. Then, we use this learned classifier to label each frame of the BTV as part of a rally or otherwise and smoothen this sequence using Kalman filter to remove any false positives/negatives to obtain the segmented rallies.

3.2   Scorecard Extraction

We utilize the observation that the scorecard position is stationary in a rally, while the camera pans and moves around to cover the game. However, the score-card may disappear and is not necessarily of the same size across the game as opposed to the assumptions in [17]. So, to overcome these issues, we extract the scorecard independently from each rally segment instead of assuming a single scorecard template.

We adapt the method described in [16]. We start by finding the gradient for each frame (say $I_x(i, j, t)$) using the sobel filter, and then calculate the normalized temporal sum for each frame using, $I_{norm}(i, j, n) = \frac{1}{n} \sum_{t=1}^{n} I_x(i, j, t)$. Then, we subtract I_x and I_{norm} to obtain the temporally correlated regions I_g. Further, we binarize the image using the following equation,

$$I_r(i, j, t) = (1 - \frac{I_x(i, j, t)}{max_{t,i,j}(I_x)}) I_{norm}(i, j, t) \qquad (1)$$

Empirically, the scorecard is found in one of the corners of the frame, we identify the four regions of size $(h/5, w/2)$ in the corners as the regions to search for the scorecard. Note, w and h are the width and height of the frame respectively. We identify the coarse scorecard region by selecting the region with the maximum number of white pixels in the specified regions in $I_r(i, j, t)$ summed over time. Further, after we have identified the coarse region, we apply morphological operators to remove small aberrations present and fit a rectangle which encloses the scorecard area. Our qualitative results can be seen in Fig. 3(a).

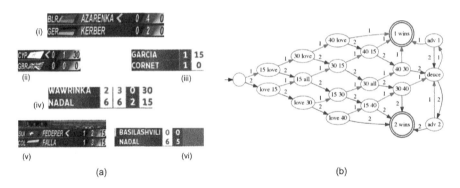

Fig. 3. (a) Depicts some of the extracted scorecards from different matches from our dataset. As one can see, the scorecards detected are of different sizes and formats, and differences across tournaments is noticeable. We have also included some of our failure cases, (v) and (vi) have extra regions that have been detected. (b) Depicts the tennis point automaton that can be constructed from the tennis scoring system which is used to refine our extracted scores.

3.3   Score Recognition

Traditional OCR based methods like Tesseract [18] can recognize text printed on a clear background however need the image to be preprocessed if the background is textured and shaded, and the contrast in the text fragments varies widely. However, with the advent of deep learning based OCR and scene text detection methods, a more general approach can be formulated.

To recognize scores, we experiment with three different methods, Tesseract, CRNN and Textspot. Textspot combines FCRN [19] which is an end to end text detection network, which constructs a field of predictors where each predictor is responsible for detecting a word if the word centre falls within the corresponding cell, akin to the YOLO network architecture. The recognition is performed by the intermediary stage of the pipeline based on the lexicon-encoding CNN from Jaderberg et al. [21]. CRNN [20] is a scene text recognition network which treats the image as a sequence of strips. It proceeds by treating a CNN as a feature extractor to extract feature maps and construct a sequence of feature vectors. The sequence is fed into a bi-directional LSTM to obtain label sequence probabilities and CTC loss is employed to obtain labels. We adapt and perform a comparison of the various score recognition baselines in Sect. 4.

3.4   Score Refinement

To further refine our recognized scores, we use the knowledge of the tennis scoring system. As any structured game, score keeping in tennis is governed by a set of rules and thus, can be modeled as a finite automaton. Tennis in specific can be modeled as 3 automatons, one each for tracking the point, game and set score (see Fig. 3(b)). Also, the vocabularies for point, game and set are restricted, so, we find errors by checking if the value belongs to the vocabulary or not. For instance, the vocabulary for a point score is restricted to $\{0, 15, 30, 40, AD\}$.

Let $J = (game_1, set_1, point_1, game_2, set_2, point_2)$ be the score state where game, set and point have the same meanings as in tennis. Firstly, we exploit the fact that the game and set scores are usually remain constant in a window, and thus replace errors with the mode of the value in the temporal window (with exceptions for score change within the window).

Consider the tennis scoring automaton T which is composed of score states and the transition function is constructed using the tennis scoring rules. Then we define a function $nextStates(s)$ which returns all possible states for the next game state. Likewise, $previousStates(s)$ provides the set of originating states for the current state s. For instance, from Fig. 3(b), if we assume that we are at state $s = (0, 0, 30, 0, 0, 30)$ (referred to as 30 all in the figure), the function $previousStates(s)$ will return $\{(0, 0, 30, 0, 0, 15), (0, 0, 15, 0, 0, 30)\}$ and $nextStates(s)$ would return $\{(0, 0, 40, 0, 0, 30), (0, 0, 30, 0, 0, 40)\}$.

Assuming that the set of scores is $S = \{s_1, s_2...s_n\}$, and that s_i is erroneous (using vocabulary constraints), we compute the set $P = nextStates(s_{i-1}) \cap previousStates(s_{i+1})$, then we find the corrected score using,

$$s_i' = \underset{p \in P}{\arg\max} \frac{1}{|J|} \sum_{j \in J} \delta(s_i(j), p_i(j)) \tag{2}$$

where J is the set of game score states and δ is the Kronecker delta function. This equation is only needed if there are more than one possible score. It is to be noted that this method is extensible to any game which follows a structured scoring system like tennis.

4 Experiments and Results

4.1 Dataset

A tennis match is divided into sets, each set is divided into games and each game has certain number of points or rallies. We restrict ourselves to "singles" matches and work with broadcast tennis video (BTV) recordings at 720p for 10 matches. 5 matches are taken from the French Open 2017 and remaining matches are from London Olympics 2012 for all our experiments. For performing rally segmentation, we created a "Rally Dataset" by manually annotating 2 matches into rally and non rally segments. The training and test set images are derived by dividing all the images in a 50–50 split. For evaluating score extraction, we further annotated 4 matches with score of each segment using the automated segmented rallies from our described algorithm. All together, we have annotated 1011 rallies to create the "Match Scores Dataset".

4.2 Rally Segmentation

For learning the rally segmentation classifier, we extracted every 10th frame from Rally Dataset and cross validated using a 0.8 split to find the optimal values of

Fig. 4. The developed interface supports the indexing and retrieval of a match as a point, game and set.

the hyper-parameters C and the period of the χ-squared kernel. The optimal value of C is 0.05 and the period of the χ-squared kernel SVM is found to be 3.

The mean $F1$ score on the test set for the task was found to be 97.46%, the precision for the non-rally segments was 98.94% and the rally segments was 95.41%.

4.3 Score Recognition

For employing Tesseract, we carefully preprocess the scorecard image and threshold the image manually. For each tournament such a preprocessing step needs to be manually defined. To train the CRNN, which is constrained to recognize words as sequences, we divided the scorecard to two parts horizontally. For employing Textspot, we don't train the network and use the model trained on "Synth-Text in the Wild" dataset as [19] note state-of-the-art performance on standard benchmarks. However, we post-process the text detection boxes and sort them to extract the scores. We used edit distance instead of the usual text recognition metrics because the "spaces" between scores (in the recognized string) are relevant in our case. For instance, CRNN removes repetitions of numbers, which causes the decrease in accuracy. Table 1 here presents our experimental results

Table 1. Averaged edit distance for score recognition (lower is better)

Match	Textspot	CRNN	Tesseract-P
Match 1 (186 rallies)	0.2070	0.4272	0.2612
Match 2 (218 rallies)	0.2178	0.4476	0.3780

on a subset of the matches and as we can see, Textspot performed the best and thus, for the next set of experiments we use that as our baseline.

4.4 Score Refinement

It is important to reiterate that our aim is not to recognize the text in the scorecard, but rather capture the game score state. To evaluate our results, we formulate a new metric, which inputs computed game state C_i and the actual game state G_i, and computes the following (for a set of rallies say R),

$$AC(R) = \sum_{i \in R} \frac{1}{|J|} \sum_{j \in J} \delta(C_i(j), G_i(j)) \tag{3}$$

where J and δ as defined earlier.

Table 2. Averaged score accuracy AC(R) for our method and the defined baseline, FCRN (higher is better)

Match	Textspot	Ours
Match 1 (186 rallies)	79.30%	91.66%
Match 2 (218 rallies)	77.90%	80.58%
Match 3 (201 rallies)	92.45%	95.19%
Match 4 (194 rallies)	85.22%	92.18%

As can be seen from Table 2, our refinement algorithm shows a consistent improvement in the averaged score accuracy across matches over the best performing baseline method, Textspot [19]. However, as it is apparent, the performance of our method is dependent on the performance of the baseline score recognition and that is possibly the reason in the relatively meager improvements in score accuracy in the second match.

4.5 Event Tagging

Further, we automatically tagged common tennis events of importance to viewers such as "fault", "deuce" and "advantage" using simple rules which define these tennis terms and our extracted scores. We compare our accuracy with and without score refinement and can observe that there is an improvement corresponding to improvement in the score accuracy. Accuracy for each tag per match (the matches are same as Table 2) can be seen in Table 3.

Table 3. Averaged accuracy score of automatic event tagging (in percentage)

	Match 1		Match 2		Match 3		Match 4	
	Textspot	Ours	Textspot	Ours	Textspot	Ours	Textspot	Ours
Fault	66.66	70.83	52.24	56.71	87.87	90.90	84.44	84.44
Deuce	100.0	100.0	73.68	78.94	100.0	100.0	94.73	94.73
Advantage	100.0	100.0	77.77	77.77	100.0	100.0	95.65	95.65
Overall	75.00	79.41	60.58	64.43	92.45	94.33	89.65	89.65

5   Conclusion

We have presented an approach to create a tennis match index based on recognizing rallies and scores, supporting random access of "points" (Fig. 4) tagged with common tennis events. Further extensions to this work are numerous, such as providing point based semantic search and performing tennis player analytics using videos instead of expensive sensor-based technologies.

References

1. Huang, Y.P., Chiou, C.L., Sandnes, F.E.: An intelligent strategy for the automatic detection of highlights in tennis video recordings. Expert Syst. Appl. **36**(6), 9907–9918 (2009)
2. Ghanem, B., Kreidieh, M., Farra, M., Zhang, T.: Context-aware learning for automatic sports highlight recognition. In: 21st International Conference on Pattern Recognition (ICPR), pp. 1977–1980. IEEE (2012)
3. Hanjalic, A.: Generic approach to highlights extraction from a sport video. In: International Conference on Image Processing (ICIP), vol. 1, pp. I–1. IEEE (2003)
4. Mentzelopoulos, M., Psarrou, A., Angelopoulou, A., García-Rodríaguez, J.: Active foreground region extraction and tracking for sports video annotation. Neural Process. Lett. **37**(1), 33–46 (2013)
5. Zhang, Y., Zhang, X., Xu, C., Lu, H.: Personalized retrieval of sports video. In: Proceedings of the International Workshop on Workshop on Multimedia Information Retrieval, pp. 313–322 (2007)
6. Kolekar, M.H., Sengupta, S.: Bayesian network-based customized highlight generation for broadcast soccer videos. IEEE Trans. Broadcast. **61**(2), 195–209 (2015)
7. Liu, C., Huang, Q., Jiang, S., Xing, L., Ye, Q., Gao, W.: A framework for flexible summarization of racquet sports video using multiple modalities. Comput. Vis. Image Underst. **113**(3), 415–424 (2009)
8. Connaghan, D., Kelly, P., O'Connor, N.E.: Game, shot and match: event-based indexing of tennis. In: 2011 9th International Workshop on Content-Based Multimedia Indexing (CBMI), pp. 97–102. IEEE (2011)
9. Miyamori, H., Iisaku, S.-I.: Video annotation for content based retrieval using human behavior analysis and domain knowledge. In: Fourth IEEE International Conference on Automatic Face and Gesture Recognition Proceedings, pp. 320–325. IEEE (2000)

10. Sukhwani, M., Jawahar, C.: TennisVid2Text: fine-grained descriptions for domain specific videos. In: Proceedings of the British Machine Vision Conference (BMVC), pp. 117.1-117.12. BMVA Press, September 2015
11. Sukhwani, M., Jawahar, C.: Frame level annotations for tennis videos. In: International Conference on Pattern Recognition (2016)
12. Xu, C., Wang, J., Lu, H., Zhang, Y.: A novel framework for semantic annotation and personalized retrieval of sports video. IEEE Trans. Multimed. **10**(3), 421–436 (2008)
13. Yan, F., Christmas, W., Kittler, J.: All pairs shortest path formulation for multiple object tracking with application to tennis video analysis. In: British Machine Vision Conference (2007)
14. Yan, F., Kittler, J., Windridge, D., Christmas, W., Mikolajczyk, K., Cox, S., Huang, Q.: Automatic annotation of tennis games: an integration of audio, vision, and learning. Image Vis. Comput. **32**(11), 896–903 (2014)
15. Zhou, X., Xie, L., Huang, Q., Cox, S.J., Zhang, Y.: Tennis ball tracking using a two-layered data association approach. IEEE Trans. Multimed. **17**(2), 145–156 (2015)
16. Liao, S., Wang, Y., Xin, Y.: Research on scoreboard detection and localization in basketball video. Int. J. Multimed. Ubiquit. Eng. **10**(11), 57–68 (2015)
17. Miao, G., Zhu, G., Jiang, S., Huang, Q., Xu, C., Gao, W.: A real-time score detection and recognition approach for broadcast basketball video. In: IEEE International Conference on Multimedia and Expo, pp. 1691–1694 (2007)
18. Smith, R.: An overview of the Tesseract OCR engine. In: Ninth International Conference on Document Analysis and Recognition, vol. 2, pp. 629–633 (2007)
19. Gupta, A., Vedaldi, A., Zisserman, A.: Synthetic data for text localisation in natural images. In: Proceedings of the IEEE Conference on Computer Vision and Pattern Recognition, pp. 2315–2324 (2016)
20. Shi, B., Bai, X., Yao, C.: An end-to-end trainable neural network for image-based sequence recognition and its application to scene text recognition. IEEE Trans. Pattern Anal. Mach. Intell. **39**, 2298–2304 (2016)
21. Jaderberg, M., Simonyan, K., Vedaldi, A., Zisserman, A.: Synthetic data and artificial neural networks for natural scene text recognition. arXiv preprint arXiv:1406.2227 (2014)

Flow-Free Video Object Segmentation

Aditya Vora[(✉)] and Shanmuganathan Raman

Electrical Engineering, Indian Institute of Technology Gandhinagar,
Gandhinagar 382355, Gujarat, India
{aditya.vora,shanmuga}@iitgn.ac.in

Abstract. Segmenting foreground object from a video is a challenging
task because of large deformations of objects, occlusions, and background
clutter. In this paper, we propose a frame-by-frame but computationally
efficient approach for video object segmentation by clustering visually
similar generic object segments throughout the video. Our algorithm
segments object instances appearing in the video and then performs clustering in order to group visually similar segments into one cluster. Since
the object that needs to be segmented appears in most part of the video,
we can retrieve the foreground segments from the cluster having maximum number of segments. We then apply a track and fill approach in
order to localize the object in the frames where the object segmentation
framework fails to segment any object. Our algorithm performs comparably to the recent automatic methods for video object segmentation
when benchmarked on DAVIS dataset while being computationally much
faster.

1 Introduction

Video object segmentation is the task of separating a foreground object from the
background in a video. Previous algorithms for video object segmentation make
use of optical flow in order to localize foreground object in each frame of the
video [1–5]. However, computing optical flow in each frame is a computationally
expensive task especially when the spatial resolution of the video frame is large.
Also, because of the inaccuracies of the optical flow estimation at the boundaries
of the object, it becomes a challenging task to model the temporal consistency
of the object segmentation and this leads to error propagation over time. As a
result, it becomes practically infeasible to scale these algorithms to longer video
sequences with a larger spatial resolution. Thus, instead of computing dynamic
cues of object proposals from the optical flow in each frame in order to localize
the object, we perform a non-parametric clustering of object proposals, which
will enable us to localize the foreground object segments in each frame of the
video. Because of the fact that the object that needs to be segmented appears
throughout the frames consistently irrespective of deformations and occlusions,
we can obtain the foreground segments by selecting the cluster that has the
most number of object proposals. Moreover, when we consider the clustering
process in our algorithm, the features are computed using a convolutional neural

© Springer Nature Singapore Pte Ltd. 2018
R. Rameshan et al. (Eds.): NCVPRIPG 2017, CCIS 841, pp. 34–44, 2018.
https://doi.org/10.1007/978-981-13-0020-2_4

network (CNN) [6] which helps us to restrict the spatial resolution of the segment to the network architecture (i.e., 224 × 224). Because of this, the clustering process takes almost constant time irrespective of the spatial resolution of the original video. Due to this advantage, our algorithm can scale up to longer video sequences with larger spatial resolutions. In order to localize the object properly in the frames, where either the detection framework might have failed to detect the segment or the presence of noise in the clustering process, we employ a track and fill approach in order to estimate the segments in those frames. First, we track the object in the frames where the segmentation is not available in order to get a loosely bounded window around the object. Then, we compute the average mask of the segments that are already detected in the nearest set of frames. We utilize this average mask to initialize the GrabCut algorithm [7], using an approach similar to that described by Kuettel and Ferrari [8].

In this work, the following major contributions are made:

– Given a video sequence, our algorithm discovers, segments as well as clusters generic objects, where the category of the objects appearing in the video is assumed to be unknown.
– We propose a flow-free algorithm for video object segmentation that instead makes use of the cluster information in order to obtain localized segments throughout the frames of the video.
– We extend the segmentation transfer on images [8] to videos in order to obtain temporally consistent segments.

2   Related Work

Fully Automatic Approaches: Fully automatic methods for video object segmentation are grouped into several categories. First, we have the algorithms which oversegment the frames of the video into space-time superpixels with similar appearance and motion [9,10]. We focus on generating an accurate spatio-temporal tube of binary masks which are well aligned around the boundaries of the foreground object. Other category of algorithms exploits long term motion cues in the form of dense trajectories which are derived using dense optical flow in order to get the final object level segmentation [1,2]. However, because of the assumption that the object moves with only a single type of translation, these technique sometimes fail to give proper results with non-rigid objects. Only recently, methods based on finding region proposals were proposed [4,5]. All these methods generate thousands of object-like space-time segments and try to rank them based on some static or dynamic cues and after selecting some best ranked segments they try to associate these segments across the space and time of the video. In [11], the authors tries to expand the concept of saliency object detection to videos. Although it is a unsupervised approach it is based on the assumption that the object motion is dissimilar from the surroundings. In [3], a fast algorithm for video object segmentation was proposed which tries to localize the object in the video based on the motion boundaries computed from optical flow.

Supervised Approaches: Supervised approaches for video object segmentation requires the user to manually annotate some of the frames in the video and the algorithms then propagates the information to the rest of the frames [12,13]. Other than this, some algorithms require user to annotate the first frame of the video with the corresponding segmentation and then track the object in the rest of the video [14,15]. Maerki *et al.* recently proposed a semi-automatic algorithm to video object segmentation that operates in the bilateral space achieving good accuracy [16]. These algorithms use motion in order to primarily propagate information to the other frames of the video. Caelles *et al.* proposed an approach that uses annotation of the first frame and then using the generic semantic information of the fully convolutional neural network transfers the foreground segment information to the rest of the frames [17].

3   Proposed Approach

Given a video, we need to discover and segment the foreground object appearing in the video. The overview of our approach is shown in Fig. 1.

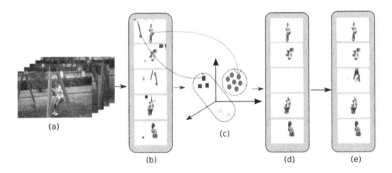

Fig. 1. Strategy for video object segmentation. (a) Input video with spatial resolution 854×480 from the DAVIS dataset [18]. (b) Top-5 region proposals of each frame are unioned. (c) Mean Shift Clustering on the features extracted from the FC6 layer of VGG-16 CNN model [6]. Cluster with most segments is shown in red which represents the foreground segment, while non-object segments are shown in blue and green. (d) Result after clustering. (e) Final segmentation after track and fill. (Color figure online)

3.1   Extracting Object Like Candidates

Several previous video segmentation algorithms [4,5] compute category independent bag of regions in each frame and rank them such that the top ranked region contains the segments of different objects. The most popular technique for generating these regions was proposed by Endres and Hoiem [19]. This technique however has the following drawbacks. (i) It generates thousands of regions for each frame of the video. As a result, it becomes extremely challenging to associate thousands of these regions from different objects while maintaining temporal connections for each of them across all the sequences. (ii) It is computationally too expensive. It takes about few minutes/frame in order to generate candidate regions in each frame. (iii) Top most proposals are always not aligned around the object. As shown in the Fig. 2(a), (c) which is the union of top-5 regions generated using the technique in [19], it almost covers the entire image with its top most regions which requires further processing in order to improve the spatial accuracy of the segment.

(a)   (b)   (c)   (d)

Fig. 2. $(a), (c)$: Union of top-5 proposals generated from [19]. $(b), (d)$: Union of top-5 proposals generated from [20].

Deepmask is a discriminative CNN which is trained to perform object instance segmentation over the image given as input [21]. Sharpmask on the other end is another object instance segmentation model which is built over deepmask to generate refined object segments [20]. It first generates a coarse mask with a bottom-up approach using deepmask and then fuses appearance information from the fine layers of the network using a refinement module in order to obtain spatially accurate segments of the object instances in each test image. This bottom-up/top-down architecture for segmentation has high recall capability using fewer masks which can be seen in Fig. 2(b), (d). It gives reasonably good localization of the object by selecting very few region proposals. We use the publicly available pre-trained model of sharpmask [20,21]. As compared to the technique in [19], the segmentation mask that is generated is properly aligned to the object. We select top-k region proposals from this model so that we can obtain the preliminary mask of that particular frame. Selecting appropriate value of k is necessary as it will affect the results in the following ways: (1) Selecting lower value of k will not be able to localize the object properly and thus will not lead to spatially accurate segments. (2) Selecting higher value of k will lead to more non-object like proposals in each frame and thus will affect the clustering accuracy. As a result, we select $k = 5$, which we keep unchanged throughout our experiments.

Given a video $\mathcal{V}$ with a set of N frames, for each frame $\mathcal{V}_i \in \mathcal{V}$, we process them using the pre-trained model of sharpmask [20]. This model is applied to the entire set of frames and is able to generate a set of region proposals $\mathcal{B}_i = \{b_{i,1}, b_{i,2}, \ldots, b_{i,k}\}$ for each frame. Here we had selected $k = 5$ and the masks are binarized with a threshold of 0.2. Then in order to obtain a preliminary mask $\mathcal{S}_i$ for each frame i, we take the union of all the k region proposals

$S_i = b_{i,1} \cup b_{i,2} \ldots \cup b_{i,k}$ corresponding to that frame which are generated by the segmentation framework. As a result, we now obtain N preliminary masks $S = \{S_1, S_2, \ldots, S_N\}$ corresponding to each frame of the video.

3.2   Clustering of Visually Similar Generic Objects

Preliminary segmentation mask obtained by taking the union of top-5 region proposals generated from the sharpmask consists of region proposals covering the foreground object as well as some noisy region proposals that do not represent any object. This can be seen in Fig. 1(b). In order to filter out these non-object like segments and to localize the foreground segment well throughout all frames we take the clustering approach. We extract a 4096 dimensional descriptor from the FC6 layer of VGG-Net [6] for each region proposal in the frame. We use the publicly available pre-trained VGG-16 model for feature extraction [6]. This gives us a general feature level representation of each proposal appearing in each frame of the video. We then normalize each feature vector using the L_2 norm. After computing these features for each region proposal, we do a mean shift clustering on these computed features. The main reason for using mean shift clustering is the fact that it does not make any assumption about the predefined shape of the data clusters and it can automatically decide over the optimal number of clusters based on the window size. Since the feature similarity among the foreground segments is high across all the frames of the video there is a high probability that these foreground segments will be accommodated into one cluster, whereas the rest of the noisy segments that do not represent any object will be scattered across different clusters based on the feature differences across the segments. In order to select the foreground segments we select the cluster that has maximum number of segments. This will automatically filter out the noisy proposals that are scattered into different clusters.

3.3   Tracking and Filling

Sometimes there is a chance that the object that needs to be segmented remains undetected in few frames of the video as it gets missed by the segmentation detection framework. It might also be possible that some object segments of few frames are lost due to the inefficiency of the clustering process. Some techniques use segmentation tracking strategies in order to fill out these regions. We propose a technique in order to properly localize objects in undetected frames which is based on segmentation transfer approach. Segmentation transfer techniques are used to estimate the segmentation on a new test image from the set of images for which the segmentation masks are already known. Our idea of track and fill is based on the segmentation transfer technique proposed by [8]. The entire pipeline of tracking and filling step is explained in Fig. 3.

   We first discover the frame X where the segment is undetected. We then find the nearest set of p frames N_p from the generated object cluster. These selected set of frames are then used to compute the soft segmentation mask M. In order to do so, we first localize the region where we need to transfer the average

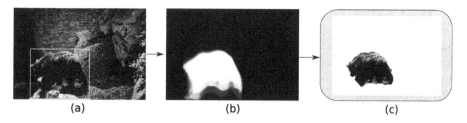

(a)   (b)   (c)

Fig. 3. Approach to track and fill. (a) We detect window for segmentation transfer by tracking the object to the frame X where the segment is undetected. (b) Soft segmentation mask M of p nearest frames are obtained by taking pixel wise mean across all the frames. Here p = 10. (c) Final mask is predicted using GrabCut by initializing it using the average mask.

segmentation mask. For this, we track the region from the nearest frame where the segment is present to the frame X. We use compressive tracking algorithm for this purpose [22]. After getting this bounding box window on the test image X, we resize all the p windows of N_p containing their respective segments to the size of the bounding box region on the test image. These resized windows are denoted as W_p. Then these windows are pixel-wise averaged in order to obtain the soft segmentation mask M. We use this soft-segmentation mask M in order to initialize the GrabCut algorithm.

We formulate the problem as an energy minimization problem which can be solved using graph-cut. Given a test image X, neighbouring windows W_p of all neighbouring frames N_p and soft segmentation mask M, we would like to label each pixel $x_i \in X$ as foreground ($c_i = 1$) or background ($c_i = 0$) which will result into labelling C of the entire frame X. The energy function that needs to be minimized is given by $E(C) = \sum_i \phi_i(r_i) + \sum_{ij \in \epsilon} \psi_{ij}(c_i, c_j)$. It has two terms, first is the unary potential ϕ_i and second is the pairwise potential ψ_{ij}. Unary potential ϕ_i is the data term which is obtained from the soft segmentation mask M and is given as $\phi_i(c_i) = -\log P(x_i|c_i) - \log Q_i(c_i)$, where i is the index of the pixel in the test image X. The two terms in the unary potential are $P(x_i|c_i)$ which is the appearance based model and $Q_i(c_i)$ is the location based model. Appearance based model uses Gaussian mixture model (GMM) on the RGB color space to model the foreground and the background. We fit two GMMs, P_1 for foreground and P_0 for background. Location based model Q defines in what location of the image is likely to contain foreground/background. For foreground, it is given as $Q_i(c_i = 1) = M(i)$ and for background, it is given as $Q_i(c_i = 0) = 1 - M(i)$. The pairwise potential ψ_{ij} is the standard penalty term used in many standard graph cut algorithms which is given by $\psi_{ij}(c_i, c_j) = \gamma d^{-1}(i, j)[c_i \neq c_j]e^{-\beta|x_i - x_j|^2}$. Here the neighbourhood is selected using ϵ. Generally 8-neighbourhood is considered. It is designed to penalize neighbouring pixels to take different label values. Optimum labelling C^* is obtained by minimizing the energy function $E(C)$ which can be obtained by max-flow technique described in [23]. Solving this using GrabCut will result into segmentation in frame X.

4   Evaluation

Dataset: We evaluate our algorithm on the recently released DAVIS 2016 Dataset which is the most challenging dataset for the benchmarking of video object segmentation algorithms [18]. It consists of 50 high quality video sequences with resolution of 480p and 1080p. There is also a recently released DAVIS 2017 dataset [24] which has around 150 high quality videos with multiple object instances. In order to have a consistency in comparison with previous algorithms, we benchmark our algorithm on DAVIS 2016 dataset. We evaluate our algorithm on 480p video sequences as all other baseline algorithms which are compared with are evaluated on the same set of videos. The dataset on which we benchmark our algorithm contains only one object per video sequence. However, we can still extend the algorithm for segmenting multiple objects in the video. Instead of selecting the cluster with maximum segments we can put a threshold in cluster selection i.e. those clusters that have a larger number of segments then the given threshold will be selected thus filtering out the noisy segments. Moreover because of the feature similarity of the object of the same class the clustering algorithm will effectively separate out the segments of different objects into different clusters.

Metric: In order to measure the region similarity between the estimated segmentation masks and the ground truth, we make use of Jaccard index $\mathcal{J}$ which is measured as intersection-over-union between the estimated mask and the ground truth. Given the estimated mask M_{est} and corresponding ground truth mask M_{gt}, the Jaccard index $\mathcal{J}$ is computed as $\mathcal{J} = \frac{|M_{est} \cap M_{gt}|}{|M_{est} \cup M_{gt}|}$. We average out the Jaccard similarity score across all the frames of videos in the dataset in order to obtain the average intersection over union score which is represented as $\mathcal{J}$ Mean ($\mathcal{M}$) in Table 1. The higher the value of $\mathcal{M}$ the better the algorithm is. We also compute the $\mathcal{J}$ Decay ($\mathcal{D}$) which quantifies the error propagation over time because of the inaccuracies in segmentation tracking and $\mathcal{J}$ Recall ($\mathcal{O}$) which measures the fraction of sequences scoring higher than a threshold. Recall should be higher and decay should be lower for a better performing algorithm.

Baselines: We compare our technique with several other fully automatic state-of-the-art techniques for video object segmentation which are FST [3], SAL [24], KEY [5], MSG [1], TRC [25], CVOS [26] and NLC [11]. Our algorithm has $\mathcal{J}$ Mean ($\mathcal{M}$) of **0.598**, Recall ($\mathcal{O}$) of **0.731**, and Decay ($\mathcal{D}$) of **0.018**. As it can be seen from Table 1, our algorithm has comparable accuracy to NLC [11], whereas it performs better than all remaining automatic algorithms. This is because of the following reasons: (1) Foreground estimation in our algorithm is done using sharpmask [20] which uses structural information from various layers using a refinement module in order to estimate spatially accurate foreground segments. (2) Clustering of segments is done with VGG features [6] which are discriminative in nature and thus able to filter out the noisy segments from the frames in an efficient manner. (3) Track and fill takes care of the temporal consistency of the segments throughout the frames of the video. Because of these reasons, our algorithm is able to perform well in terms of $\mathcal{J}$ Mean ($\mathcal{M}$) than other algorithms. Moreover, our algorithm has a lower $\mathcal{J}$ Decay ($\mathcal{D}$) than all other algorithms which shows that our method has least error propagation over time thus giving consistent segmentation results. This is because our algorithm computes segments frame-by-frame through the segmentation model because of which each frame is treated independently and thus leading to less error propagation through time. This is not the case with algorithms that make use of optical flow because of error in estimation of optical flow at the boundaries of the object which gets accumulated over time, resulting into a much larger decay in segmentation quality over time.

Table 1. Evaluation of our algorithm on DAVIS dataset [18].

Evaluation on DAVIS dataset			
Method	$\mathcal{J}$ Mean ($\mathcal{M}$)	$\mathcal{J}$ Recall ($\mathcal{O}$)	$\mathcal{J}$ Decay ($\mathcal{D}$)
FST [3]	0.575	0.652	0.044
SAL [24]	0.426	0.386	0.084
KEY [5]	0.569	0.671	0.075
MSG [1]	0.543	0.636	0.028
TRC [25]	0.501	0.560	0.050
CVOS [26]	0.514	0.581	0.127
NLC [11]	**0.641**	0.731	0.086
Ours	0.598	**0.731**	**0.018**

Despite comparable accuracy, our algorithm is much more computationally efficient compared to the other fully automatic techniques. We perform the experiments in MATLAB environment on PC with Intel core i7 processor with NVIDIA Quadro K2200 GPU. Our algorithm takes 2 s/frame for object instance segmentation, 0.1 s/frame for feature extraction of all proposals in each frame and 3 s/frame for track and fill stage. The segmentation and feature extraction stage are fixed timing of our algorithm that are required for all the frames of the video. However, track and fill stage is the variable timing of our algorithm as actual computation time required by this stage depends on the number of frames in which the segment is undetected. We shall do a worst case analysis of our algorithm. If we assume that the track and fill stage is executed for all the frames of the video (i.e. segmentation framework fails to detect object in all the frames) then the average time required by our algorithm would be 5.1 s/frame. Compared to NLC technique which takes 12 s/frame as reported in the paper [11], our technique is around 2.5× faster in the worst case. Moreover, they have reported the timings on the SegTrack dataset which have lower resolution videos compared to DAVIS dataset. FST technique, however computes segmentation within 0.5 s/frame [3]. However, they assume that the optical flow and the superpixels are already available and thus are not included in the computation time calculation. As a result, if we add all these computational overheads,

42 A. Vora and S. Raman

the overall computation time surely will increase significantly as computing optical flow for a video with 480p resolution is a computationally expensive task. Figure 4 shows results of our algorithm on the DAVIS dataset. It can be seen that our algorithm gives good segmentation results throughout the video in challenging scenarios such as occlusions, fast movements, scale changes and cluttered backgrounds.

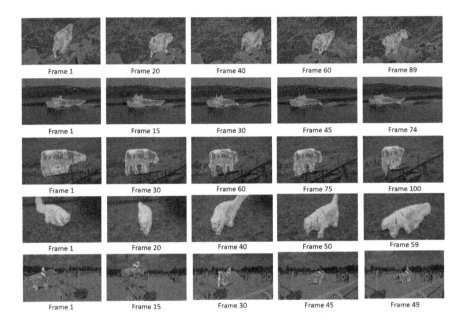

Fig. 4. Example results on DAVIS dataset [18].

5 Conclusion

We have presented a new approach for segmenting generic objects in the video, that instead of using optical flow to localize the object instances in the video, makes use of the cluster information to do so. Results show comparable accuracy with respect to the state-of-the-art techniques. Our method performs better than most of the fully automatic techniques while being much faster than these algorithms. As our algorithm treats each frame of the video independently, it gives rise to spatially accurate and temporally consistent segments unlike algorithms which make use of optical flow. In future, we plan to explore extensions of this algorithm by intelligently including optical flow for localizing the foreground object in the initial frames of the video and then search for a similar object instance in the remaining frames of the video.

References

1. Ochs, P., Brox, T.: Object segmentation in video: a hierarchical variational approach for turning point trajectories into dense regions. In: 2011 IEEE International Conference on Computer Vision (ICCV), pp. 1583–1590. IEEE (2011)
2. Brox, T., Malik, J.: Object segmentation by long term analysis of point trajectories. In: Daniilidis, K., Maragos, P., Paragios, N. (eds.) ECCV 2010. LNCS, vol. 6315, pp. 282–295. Springer, Heidelberg (2010). https://doi.org/10.1007/978-3-642-15555-0_21
3. Papazoglou, A., Ferrari, V.: Fast object segmentation in unconstrained video. In: Proceedings of the IEEE International Conference on Computer Vision, pp. 1777–1784 (2013)
4. Zhang, D., Javed, O., Shah, M.: Video object segmentation through spatially accurate and temporally dense extraction of primary object regions. In: Proceedings of the IEEE Conference on Computer Vision and Pattern Recognition, pp. 628–635 (2013)
5. Lee, Y.J., Kim, J., Grauman, K.: Key-segments for video object segmentation. In: 2011 IEEE International Conference on Computer Vision (ICCV), pp. 1995–2002. IEEE (2011)
6. Simonyan, K., Zisserman, A.: Very deep convolutional networks for large-scale image recognition. arXiv preprint arXiv:1409.1556 (2014)
7. Rother, C., Kolmogorov, V., Blake, A.: Grabcut: interactive foreground extraction using iterated graph cuts. In: ACM Transactions on Graphics (TOG), vol. 23, no. 3, pp. 309–314. ACM (2004)
8. Kuettel, D., Ferrari, V.: Figure-ground segmentation by transferring window masks. In: 2012 IEEE Conference on Computer Vision and Pattern Recognition (CVPR), pp. 558–565. IEEE (2012)
9. Grundmann, M., Kwatra, V., Han, M., Essa, I.: Efficient hierarchical graph-based video segmentation. In: 2010 IEEE Conference on Computer Vision and Pattern Recognition (CVPR), pp. 2141–2148. IEEE (2010)
10. Xu, C., Corso, J.J.: Evaluation of super-voxel methods for early video processing. In: 2012 IEEE Conference on Computer Vision and Pattern Recognition (CVPR), pp. 1202–1209. IEEE (2012)
11. Faktor, A., Irani, M.: Video segmentation by non-local consensus voting. In: BMVC, vol. 2, no. 7, p. 8 (2014)
12. Bai, X., Wang, J., Simons, D., Sapiro, G.: Video snapcut: robust video object cutout using localized classifiers. In: ACM Transactions on Graphics (ToG), vol. 28, no. 3, p. 70. ACM (2009)
13. Wang, T., Collomosse, J.: Probabilistic motion diffusion of labeling priors for coherent video segmentation. IEEE Trans. Multimed. **14**(2), 389–400 (2012)
14. Chockalingam, P., Pradeep, N., Birchfield, S.: Adaptive fragments-based tracking of non-rigid objects using level sets. In: 2009 IEEE 12th International Conference on Computer Vision, pp. 1530–1537. IEEE (2009)
15. Tsai, D., Flagg, M., Rehg, J.M.: Motion coherent tracking with multi-label MRF optimization. BMVC (2010)
16. Maerki, N., Perazzi, F., Wang, O., Sorkine-Hornung, A.: Bilateral space video segmentation. In: The IEEE Conference on Computer Vision and Pattern Recognition (CVPR) (2016)
17. Caelles, S., Maninis, K.-K., Pont-Tuset, J., Leal-Taixé, L., Cremers, D., Van Gool, L.: One-shot video object segmentation. In: Computer Vision and Pattern Recognition (CVPR) (2017)

18. Perazzi, F., Pont-Tuset, J., McWilliams, B., Van Gool, L., Gross, M., Sorkine-Hornung, A.: A benchmark dataset and evaluation methodology for video object segmentation. In: Proceedings of the IEEE Conference on Computer Vision and Pattern Recognition, pp. 724–732 (2016)
19. Endres, I., Hoiem, D.: Category independent object proposals. In: Daniilidis, K., Maragos, P., Paragios, N. (eds.) ECCV 2010. LNCS, vol. 6315, pp. 575–588. Springer, Heidelberg (2010). https://doi.org/10.1007/978-3-642-15555-0_42
20. Pinheiro, P.O., Lin, T.-Y., Collobert, R., Dollár, P.: Learning to refine object segments. In: Leibe, B., Matas, J., Sebe, N., Welling, M. (eds.) ECCV 2016. LNCS, vol. 9905, pp. 75–91. Springer, Cham (2016). https://doi.org/10.1007/978-3-319-46448-0_5
21. Pinheiro, P.O., Collobert, R., Dollar, P.: Learning to segment object candidates. In: Advances in Neural Information Processing Systems, pp. 1990–1998 (2015)
22. Zhang, K., Zhang, L., Yang, M.-H.: Real-time compressive tracking. In: Fitzgibbon, A., Lazebnik, S., Perona, P., Sato, Y., Schmid, C. (eds.) ECCV 2012. LNCS, vol. 7574, pp. 864–877. Springer, Heidelberg (2012). https://doi.org/10.1007/978-3-642-33712-3_62
23. Boykov, Y., Kolmogorov, V.: An experimental comparison of min-cut/max-flow algorithms for energy minimization in vision. IEEE Trans. Pattern Anal. Mach. Intell. **26**(9), 1124–1137 (2004)
24. Wang, W., Shen, J., Porikli, F.: Saliency-aware geodesic video object segmentation. In: Proceedings of the IEEE Conference on Computer Vision and Pattern Recognition, pp. 3395–3402 (2015)
25. Fragkiadaki, K., Zhang, G., Shi, J.: Video segmentation by tracing discontinuities in a trajectory embedding. In: 2012 IEEE Conference on Computer Vision and Pattern Recognition (CVPR), pp. 1846–1853. IEEE (2012)
26. Taylor, B., Karasev, V., Soatto, S.: Causal video object segmentation from persistence of occlusions. In: Proceedings of the IEEE Conference on Computer Vision and Pattern Recognition, pp. 4268–4276 (2015)

SSIM-Based Joint Bit-Allocation Using Frame Model Parameters for 3D Video Coding

Y. Harshalatha$^{(\boxtimes)}$ and Prabir Kumar Biswas

Indian Institute of Technology Kharagpur, Kharagpur, India
{harshalatha.y,pkb}@ece.iitkgp.ernet.in

Abstract. Optimum bit-allocation between texture video and depth map in 3D video results in better virtual view quality. To incorporate this, rate distortion optimization (RDO) property is used. The RDO in 3D video implies minimization of synthesis distortion at available rate. Several bit-allocation methods proposed in literature have not considered perceptual quality improvement. In this paper, we propose bit-allocation criteria that results in better visual quality of synthesized view. To achieve this, visual quality metrics are to be incorporated and structural similarity (SSIM) index is one of the metric that measures perceived quality. As SSIM gives similarity measure, we used dSSIM as distortion metric in mode decision and motion estimation instead of traditional metrics like mean square error (MSE) or sum of squared error (SSE). Synthesis distortion is modeled using dSSIM and joint bit-allocation is formulated as optimization problem that is solved using Lagrange multiplier method. Model parameters are determined at frame level for more accurate calculation of quantization parameters. BD-Rate evaluation shows a reduction in bit rate with improved SSIM.

1 Introduction

3D video is finding vast application areas by replacing the conventional 2D video. With multiple 2D videos at the input, 3D video processing complexity increases. Multiview video plus depth (MVD) format reduces the number of views to be transmitted, thus reducing the encoding complexity. Depth-image-based rendering (DIBR) [1] algorithm is used at the decoder side to synthesize intermediate views. Factors like compression distortion, depth inaccuracy and so on worsen the quality of generated views. Bit-allocation is one of the solution to enhance the quality of the synthesized view.

Optimized bit-allocation is a challenging task and researchers reported different methods in [2–7]. In all these methods, mean square error (MSE) is used to measure synthesis distortion. We replace MSE with structural similarity (SSIM) index that takes care of human visual characteristics and thus improves perceptual quality.

© Springer Nature Singapore Pte Ltd. 2018
R. Rameshan et al. (Eds.): NCVPRIPG 2017, CCIS 841, pp. 45–53, 2018.
https://doi.org/10.1007/978-981-13-0020-2_5

In this paper, initially, we used dSSIM as distortion metric for mode decision and motion estimation rate distortion optimization (RDO). For joint bit-allocation, we experimentally derived dSSIM-based synthesis distortion model. dSSIM model is converted to MSE-based model and Rate-Quantization (R-Q) and Distortion-Quantization (D-Q) models are used to solve bit-allocation problem. Bit-allocation algorithm is implemented using H.264 based 3DV-ATM encoder.

The contribution of the paper is explained in Sect. 2. RDO for 3D video is briefly discussed in Sect. 3 followed by SSIM-based RDO in Sect. 3.1. Joint Bit-allocation is described in Sect. 4. Section 5 discusses experimental results and paper is concluded in Sect. 6.

2   Contribution of the Paper

Perceptual quality improvement of synthesized views in 3D video is not much addressed in literature. Inspired by traditional 2D video schemes [8–14] to improve perceptual quality, we extended the idea of SSIM-based RDO to 3D video. Further, we derived view synthesis distortion model in terms of dSSIM and solved bit-allocation problem using Lagange multiplier method. Frame model parameters are used in computing quantization step. Proposed bit-allocation method efficiently allocates optimal bits between texture and depth maps along with improvement in visual quality.

3   RDO in 3D Video

MVD data consisting of texture videos and depth map sequences are input to the 3DV-ATM. Encoding these sequences follow a specific pattern. For example, if we consider the case of 2-view input, encoder will have two texture videos and corresponding depth views as input. Here, coding order can be T0T1D0D1 or T0D0T1D1 and so on where T0, T1 are texture views and D0, D1 are depth views. At an instance, one frame of either texture video or depth map is encoded. 3DV-ATM encoder uses complex procedure of variable-block mode decision and motion estimation to improve the encoding efficiency. Each macroblock of either texture video or depth map is partitioned into different block size for both intra and inter prediction. Initially, motion estimation RDO (Eq. 1a) is carried out which is followed by mode decision RDO (Eq. 1b). In mode decision RDO, RD cost is computed for each mode and the mode with minimum cost is selected.

$$J_{ME} = D_{ME} + \lambda_{ME} R_{ME} \tag{1a}$$

$$J_{MD} = D_{MD} + \lambda_{MD} R_{MD} \tag{1b}$$

where D_{ME} is prediction error, R_{ME} is the number of bits associated with motion vectors, D_{MD} is distortion between original and reconstructed blocks, R_{MD} is the number of bits associated with mode and quantization parameter.

λ_{ME} and λ_{MD} are the Lagrange multipliers used in motion estimation and mode decision RDO respectively. In both motion estimation and mode decision RDO, Lagrange optimization is used. Lagrange multiplier is the slope of the RD curve.

3.1   SSIM-Based RDO for 3D Video

In motion estimation and mode decision RDO, metrics used to measure distortion are sum of squared error (SSE) or sum of absolute differences (SAD). In order to improve perceptual quality, SSIM (Eq. 2) [15] is used. As SSIM is a measure of similarity, dSSIM is used as distortion metric as in Eq. 3.

$$SSIM(x, y) = \frac{(2\mu_x\mu_y + C_1)(2\sigma_{xy} + C_2)}{(\mu_x^2 + \mu_y^2 + C_1)(\sigma_x^2 + \sigma_y^2 + C_2)} \tag{2}$$

where, μ_x and σ_x are mean and standard deviation of block x respectively, μ_y and σ_y are mean and standard deviation of block y respectively, and σ_{xy} is cross-correlation between image blocks. C_1 and C_2 are used to limit the range of SSIM values when mean and variance are close to zero.

$$dSSIM = \frac{1}{SSIM} \tag{3}$$

$$\lambda_i = \frac{2\sigma_{x_i}^2 + C_2}{\exp(\frac{1}{M} \sum\limits_{j=1}^{M} \log(2\sigma_{x_j}^2 + C_2))} \lambda_{SSE} \tag{4}$$

where σ_{x_i} is the local variance of ith macroblock, M is total number of macroblocks in a frame. Instead of using dSSIM to measure distortion in RDO, Yeo et al. [13] related it to SSE and derived expression for modified Lagrange multiplier as in Eq. 4. We incorporated the same Lagrange multiplier in 3DV-ATM and found that value of λ_i lies at point A as shown in Fig. 1. Scaling of Lagrange multiplier is the simple way of fixing optimum point on RD curve (Point B in Fig. 1).

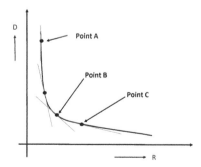

Fig. 1. Lagrange multiplier on RD curve

Thus, we modified Lagrange multiplier as in Eq. 5 with an empirical scaling factor S_f [16].

$$\lambda_{new} = \frac{2\sigma_{x_i}^2 + C_2}{S_f \left(\exp(\frac{1}{M} \sum\limits_{j=1}^{M} \log(2\sigma_{x_j}^2 + C_2)) \right)} \lambda_{SSE} \tag{5}$$

4   Joint Bit-Allocation

Texture video and depth map equally contribute to the quality of synthesized views and thus optimal bit-allocation plays a significant role. Bit-allocation problem is formulated as in Eq. 6, where view synthesis distortion is minimized at a given rate constraint.

$$\min_{(R_t, R_d)} D_v$$
$$s.t. \quad R_t + R_d \le R_c \tag{6}$$

R_t and R_d are the bitrates of texture video and depth map respectively and D_v is synthesis distortion. In literature, synthesis distortion D_v is modeled as linear combination of texture distortion D_t and depth distortion D_d as in Eq. 7.

$$D_v = AD_t + BD_d + C \tag{7}$$

A, B, and C are the parameters that depend on factors causing distortion like compression, depth inaccuracy and so on. Both D_t and D_d are measured using MSE.

Our aim is to improve perceptual quality of synthesized views and thus bit-allocation problem is reformulated as in Eq. 8. In order to improve visual quality, dSSIM of synthesized view is to be minimized.

$$\min_{(R_t, R_d)} dSSIM_v$$
$$s.t. \quad R_t + R_d \le R_c \tag{8}$$

where, $dSSIM_v$ is synthesis distortion measured using dSSIM as distortion metric. In order to relate synthesis distortion with texture and depth distortion in terms of dSSIM, we performed encoding followed by view synthesis. dSSIM is computed between original and reconstructed texture video ($dSSIM_t$) as well as original and reconstructed depth map ($dSSIM_d$). For synthesis distortion ($dSSIM_v$), dSSIM is calculated between original synthesized view (using original texture video and depth map) and synthesized view at the decoder. Relation between $dSSIM_t$, $dSSIM_d$ and $dSSIM_v$ is obtained through curve fitting to get the expression as in Eq. 9 (Fig. 2).

$$dSSIM_v = y_t \cdot dSSIM_t + y_d \cdot dSSIM_d + z \tag{9}$$

where y_t, y_d, and z are model parameters. For efficient bit-allocation, we need to obtain optimal values of quantization parameter for texture video and depth

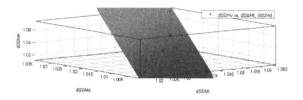

Fig. 2. Relationship between dSSIM of virtual view, texture video and depth map

map. As SSIM cannot be related to quantization parameter [17], we used SSIM-MSE relation [13] and converted Eq. 9 as given in Eq. 10.

$$dSSIM_v = \frac{y_t}{2\sigma^2_{x_t} + C_2}D_t + \frac{y_d}{2\sigma^2_{x_d} + C_2}D_d + z \tag{10}$$

$$dSSIM_v = p_1 D_t + p_2 D_d + c \tag{11}$$

where $p_1 = \frac{y_t}{2\sigma^2_{x_t}+C_2}$ and $p_2 = \frac{y_d}{2\sigma^2_{x_d}+C_2}$.

Texture and depth maps were pre-encoded to derive D-Q models which are linear. R-Q models are also assumed to be linear.

$$D_t = \alpha_t Q_t + \beta_t \tag{12a}$$

$$D_d = \alpha_d Q_d + \beta_d \tag{12b}$$

$$R_t = a_t Q_t^{-1} + b_t \tag{12c}$$

$$R_d = a_d Q_d^{-1} + b_d \tag{12d}$$

where Q_t and Q_d are quantization steps of texture video and depth map respectively. a_t, a_d, b_t, b_d, α_t, α_d, β_t, β_d are the parameters calculated from pre-encoding the texture video and the depth sequences. To determine model parameters original sequences are encoded with different quantization steps. Using frame rate and distortion the model parameters are determined for each frame separately.

The bit-allocation problem is framed (Eq. 13) and minimized to get optimum values of Q_t and Q_d as in Eqs. 14a and 14b respectively.

$$\min \quad (p_1 D_t + p_2 D_d)$$
$$s.t. \quad (a_t Q_t^{-1} + b_t + a_d Q_d^{-1} + b_d) \leq R_c \tag{13}$$

$$Q_t = \frac{a_t + \sqrt{\frac{K_1 a_t a_d}{K2}}}{R_c - b_t - b_d} \tag{14a}$$

$$Q_d = \sqrt{\frac{K_2 a_d}{K_1 a_t}}Q_t \tag{14b}$$

where $K_1 = p_1 \alpha_t$ and $K_2 = p_2 \alpha_d$.

5   Results

SSIM-based joint bit-allocation is proposed and implemented using 3DV-ATM encoder [18]. We used 3D-AVC mode of 3DV-ATM which is an extension of H.264/AVC. Virtual view synthesis is performed using view synthesis reference software VSRS 3.0 [19]. Balloons and Breakdancer [20,21] sequences are used in the experiments.

Performance of SSIM-based RDO is investigated by encoding the sequences with different quantization parameters ranging from 20 to 44 and compared with original 3DV-ATM RDO. In both cases, synthesized views were generated using (i) original texture and depth maps (original synthesized view) and (ii) reconstructed texture and depth maps (reconstructed synthesized view). SSIM is measured between original and reconstructed virtual views at different bit rates and graph is plotted by considering rate along horizontal axis and SSIM along vertical axis. RD curves for Kendo, Balloons and Breakdancer are shown in Figs. 3 and 4. Table 1 gives the BD-Rate [22] figures which shows improvement in SSIM at reduced rate.

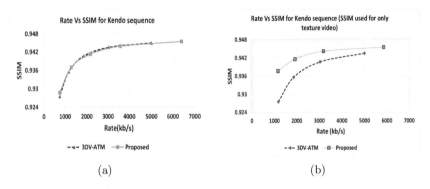

Fig. 3. SSIM Vs Rate for Kendo sequence when view 2 synthesized from views 1 and 3, when SSIM is used as distortion metric

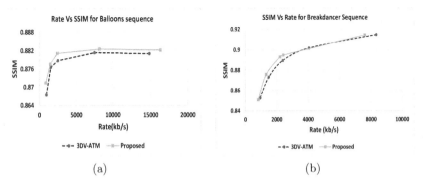

Fig. 4. SSIM Vs Rate for (a) balloons sequence and (b) breakdancer sequence. In both cases view 2 is synthesized from views 1 and 3 with SSIM as distortion metric

Table 1. Performance of SSIM-based RDO compared with SSE-based RDO

Sequence	ΔSSIM	ΔRate
Kendo	0.0015	-6.2971
Balloons	0.0017	-7.0832
Breakdancer	0.0048	-15.4161

5.1   Bit-Allocation Results

For bit-allocation, Q_t and Q_d of Eqs. 14a and 14b are to be computed. This requires model parameters a_t, a_d, b_t, b_d, α_t, α_d, β_t, β_d to be determined which is done through pre-encoding. These parameters will remain same for whole sequence. However, each frame in a sequence will have different details and model parameters vary for each frame. Thus, we determined model parameters for each frame which resulted in more accurate calculation of quantization step for each frame. We compared SSIM-based joint bit-allocation with model based joint bit-allocation. In both cases we measured SSIM of virtual views and plotted RD curve as shown in Fig. 5. BD-Rate measurement shown in Table 2 also shows an improvement in SSIM and reduction in rate.

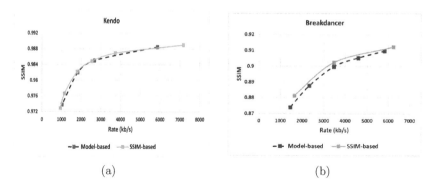

(a)   (b)

Fig. 5. RD curve for bit allocation

Table 2. BD-rate comparison

Sequence	ΔSSIM	ΔRate
Kendo	0.0003	-6.6795
Breakdancer	0.0004	-7.2763

We compared the performance of proposed algorithm with SSIM-based bit allocation algorithm [23] that uses sequence parameters for computing quantization step. As frame parameters compute quantization step for each frame, performance of bit allocation algorithm is improved. The RD curves are as shown in Fig. 6.

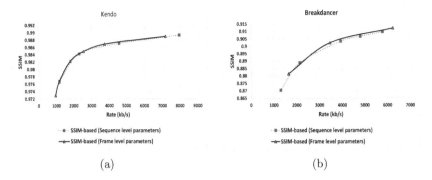

Fig. 6. Comparison of SSIM-based bit allocation algorithm with sequence and frame parameters

6 Conclusions

Perceptual quality-based joint bit-allocation is proposed in this paper. As a first step, SSIM-based RDO is implemented using modified Lagrange multiplier. For joint bit-allocation, synthesis distortion model is experimentally derived in terms of dSSIM. Model is converted to MSE-based model in order to relate with quantization step. We derived optimum quantization step for both texture video and depth map. Model parameters are computed for each frame in a sequence and thus quantization parameter was calculated for every frame. Objective evaluation is done by measuring BD-Rate which shows improved performance of proposed algorithm. In the proposed algorithm, we considered the linear model for synthesis distortion. However, the relationship of depth distortion with synthesis distortion is nonlinear. This factor can be considered for further improvement of the algorithm.

References

1. Fehn, C.: A 3D-TV approach using depth-image-based rendering (DIBR). In: Proceedings of VIIP, vol. 3 (2003)
2. Fehn, C.: Depth-image-based rendering (DIBR), compression, and transmission for a new approach on 3D-TV. In: Electronic Imaging 2004, pp. 93–104. International Society for Optics and Photonics (2004)
3. Yuan, H., Chang, Y., Li, M., Yang, F.: Model based bit allocation between texture images and depth maps. In: International Conference On Computer and Communication Technologies in Agriculture Engineering (CCTAE), vol. 3, pp. 380–383. IEEE (2010)
4. Yuan, H.H., Chang, Y., Huo, J., Yang, F., Lu, Z.: Model-based joint bit allocation between texture videos and depth maps for 3-D video coding. IEEE Trans. Circ. Syst. Video Technol. **21**(4), 485–497 (2011)
5. Zhu, G., Jiang, G., Yu, M., Li, F., Shao, F., Peng, Z.: Joint video/depth bit allocation for 3D video coding based on distortion of synthesized view. In: IEEE International Symposium on Broadband Multimedia Systems and Broadcasting (BMSB), pp. 1–6. IEEE (2012)

6. Shao, F., Jiang, G., Lin, W., Yu, M., Dai, Q.: Joint bit allocation and rate control for coding multi-view video plus depth based 3D video. IEEE Trans. Multimedia **15**(8), 1843–1854 (2013)
7. Yang, C., An, P., Shen, L.: Adaptive bit allocation for 3D video coding. Circ. Syst. Sig. Process. **36**, 1–23 (2016)
8. Mai, Z.-Y., Yang, C.-L., Po, L.-M., Xie, S.-L.: A new rate-distortion optimization using structural information in H.264 I-frame encoder. In: Blanc-Talon, J., Philips, W., Popescu, D., Scheunders, P. (eds.) ACIVS 2005. LNCS, vol. 3708, pp. 435–441. Springer, Heidelberg (2005). https://doi.org/10.1007/11558484_55
9. Huang, Y.-H., Ou, T.-S., Chen, H.H.: Perceptual-based coding mode decision. In: Proceedings of IEEE International Symposium on Circuits and Systems (ISCAS), pp. 393–396 (2010)
10. Chen, Z., Lin, W., Ngan, K.N.: Perceptual video coding: challenges and approaches. In: Proceedings of IEEE International Conference on Multimedia and Expo (ICME), pp. 784–789 (2010)
11. Huang, Y.-H., Ou, T.-S., Su, P.-Y., Chen, H.H.: Perceptual rate-distortion optimization using structural similarity index as quality metric. IEEE Trans. Circ. Syst. Video Technol. **20**(11), 1614–1624 (2010)
12. Cui, Z., Gan, Z., Zhu, X.: Structural similarity optimal MB layer rate control for H. 264. In: Proceedings of IEEE International Conference on Wireless Communications and Signal Processing (WCSP), pp. 1–5 (2011)
13. Yeo, C., Tan, H.L., Tan, Y.H.: On rate distortion optimization using SSIM. IEEE Trans. Circ. Syst. Video Technol. **23**(7), 1170–1181 (2013)
14. Zhao, T., Wang, J., Wang, Z., Chen, C.W.: SSIM-based coarse-grain scalable video coding. IEEE Trans. Broadcast. **61**(2), 210–221 (2015)
15. Wang, Z., Bovik, A.C., Sheikh, H.R., Simoncelli, E.P.: Image quality assessment: from error visibility to structural similarity. IEEE Trans. Image Process. **13**(4), 600–612 (2004)
16. Harshalatha, Y., Biswas, P.K.: Rate distortion optimization using SSIM for 3D video coding. In: 23rd International Conference on Pattern Recognition (ICPR), pp. 1261–1266. IEEE (2016)
17. Chen, H.H., Huang, Y.-H., Su, P.-Y., Ou, T.-S.: Improving video coding quality by perceptual rate-distortion optimization. In: IEEE International Conference on Multimedia and Expo (ICME), pp. 1287–1292 (2010)
18. 3DV-ATM Reference Software 3DV-ATMv5.lr2. http://mpeg3dv.nokiaresearch.com/svn/mpeg3dv/tags/3DV-ATMv5.1r2/. Accessed 06 Jan 2017
19. View Synthesis Reference Software VSRS3.5. ftp://ftp.merl.com/pub/avetro/3dv-cfp/software/. Accessed 06 Jan 2017
20. Fujii Laborotory, Nagoya University. http://www.fujii.nuee.nagoya-u.ac.jp/multi view-data/. Accessed 06 Jan 2017
21. Zitnick, C.L., Kang, S.B., Uyttendaele, M., Winder, S., Szeliski, R.: High-quality video view interpolation using a layered representation. In: ACM Transactions on Graphics (TOG), vol. 23, no. 3, pp. 600–608. ACM (2004)
22. Bjontegaard, G.: Calculation of Average PSNR Differences Between RD - curves. ITU-TQ.6/SG16 VCEG 13th Meeting. http://wftp3.itu.int/av-arch/video-site/0104_Aus/
23. Harshalatha, Y., Biswas, P.K.: SSIM-based joint-bit allocation for 3D video coding. Multimedia Tools Appl. (2017, in Press). https://doi.org/10.1007/s11042-017-5327-0

Trajectory Based Integrated Features for Action Classification from Depth Data

Parul Shukla[1(✉)], Noopur Arora[2], and Kanad K. Biswas[3]

[1] Indian Institute of Technology, Delhi, India
parulpandey.iitd@gmail.com
[2] Works Application, Singapore, Singapore
[3] Bennett University, Greater Noida, Uttar Pradesh, India

Abstract. We present an approach for Human Action Recognition based on amalgamation of features from depth maps and body-joint data. This *Integrated* feature set consists of depth features based on gradient orientation and motion energy, in addition to features from 3D- skeleton data capturing its statistical details. Feature selection is carried out to extract a relevant set of features for action recognition. The resultant set of features are evaluated using SVM classifier. We validate our proposed method on various benchmark datasets for Action Recognition such as MSR-Daily Activity and UT-Kinect dataset.

1 Introduction

Human Action Recognition has been one of the most important areas of research and innovation in computer vision for over a decade. With the advent of new high quality cameras and their extensive use, the task of human action recognition has become important for applications such as content based video retrieval, surveillance, human-computer interaction.

Action recognition from color frames has seen tremendous improvements over the year. Wang et al. [1] extract feature trajectories by tracking Harris 3D interest point with KLT tracker. HOG, HOF and other trajectory aligned features are calculated to form the final feature vector. Nowadays, the amount of RGB videos available has increased, resulting in a paradigm shift. Now, deep learning based methods, provide more scalable and accurate recognition solutions. It may, however, be noted that 'deep' models require huge amount of data to achieve better generalization, and in case of smaller datasets their application is limited due to increased chances of overfitting.

Rapid development of image sensing technologies, in particular cost-effective depth sensors, has added a 'new' dimension to the task of action recognition. Depth maps, available using these sensors, provide several advantages over the conventional color images. They are indicative of the shape and geometry of the objects/person in the scene. For action recognition, this is more beneficial as compared to the color or texture details from RGB. In addition to it, the depth images are insensitive to the illumination changes in the scene, hence, effective in

R. Rameshan et al. (Eds.): NCVPRIPG 2017, CCIS 841, pp. 54–65, 2018.
https://doi.org/10.1007/978-981-13-0020-2_6

scenarios where the region of interest is a person. The availability of 3D skeleton model further aids extraction of joints' based pose and motion features.

Among the existing depth maps based methods, representative images such as Motion History Images and other motion maps provide an efficient and simpler solution for extracting motion and shape features for action recognition. Yang et al. [2] compute the difference of two consecutive frames and add them throughout the video to form Depth Motion Maps from which HOG features are calculated. In [3], the authors divide the video into overlapping blocks along the time domain, Motion History Template (MHT) and Binary Shape Template (BST) are calculated for each block and gradient analysis is performed to get the motion and shape information respectively. It may be noted that depth map-based methods often suffer from the limitations of sensors such as undefined depth points (black regions in depth maps). Additionally, scene clutter often limits the applicability of these features.

3D-skeleton based methods, on the other hand, provide an efficient and faster method for extracting 'person-centric' pose and motion features. Yang and Tian [4] calculate motion, posture and offset features from skeleton data followed by PCA to get 'Eigenjoints'. Kruthiventi and Babu [5] use a combination of 3D edge vectors that connect important joint positions in the skeleton and 3D trajectory vectors that connects joints positions from previous and current frames. Recently, Liu et al. [6] have proposed Long Short Term Memory [7] based approach with trust gates for action recognition from 3D skeleton data. However, it is important to note that 3D-skeleton based methods rely on accurate estimation and tracking of body-joints in every frame. It, therefore, seems imperative to use features from different modalities such as depth maps, skeleton data to mitigate the drawbacks of single-sourced data.

Amongst fusion-based methods, Wang et al. [8] use data mining to obtain important joints and calculate Local Occupancy Patterns around these joint positions. Zhu et al. [9] perform fusion by computing spatio-temporal RGB features around detected interest points and frame-wise, pair-wise distance of skeleton joint positions. Chaaraoui et al. [10] combine joint features from normalized skeleton data and shape features from silhouette data by concatenating the two feature vectors. In [11], relative and temporal joint distance is augmented with gradient features from ROI consisting of person.

In this paper, we present trajectory-based *integrated* features from both 3D body-joints' data as well as depth maps. Our approach involves estimating local gradient orientations in the local neighborhood of each joint from 3D stack of depth data. The obtained features are augmented with features describing statistical properties of the 3D body-joint trajectory and motion map descriptor. The final set of features is further processed to remove irrelevant features using ReliefF [12] method. This fusion-based approach differs from [8,10], in that, it does not use expensive operations such as *apriori* mining or multiple kernel learning and instead of a mere concatenation, it uses *feature selection* to reduce the number of irrelevant features. Figure 1 illustrates the pipeline of the proposed approach. It is an improvement over [11] since it involves gradient computation around a joint instead of the whole 3D ROI involving person. The proposed approach can be readily implemented and used in case of smaller datasets. It is evaluated on well-known datasets UT-Kinect Action and MSR-DailyActivity datasets.

The remainder of the paper is organized as follows: Sects. 2, 3 and 4 present our proposed features. Section 5 presents experiments and results. Finally, Sect. 6 concludes the paper.

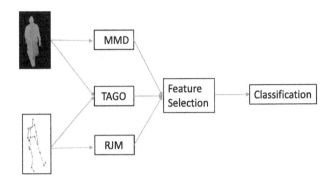

Fig. 1. Pipeline of proposed approach. Motion Map Descriptor (MMD), Trajectory Aligned Gradient Orientation (TAGO) and Range of Joint Motion (RJM) are the constituent features used in the proposed approach.

2   Trajectory Aligned Gradient Orientation

In this section, we describe the features obtained using *both* depth maps and 3D skeleton data provided by Kinect. Depth maps are intensity images where the depth is encoded in terms of image intensity and are suitable for representing shape of an object. A popular way of representing shape in images involves using intensity gradients wherein local object appearance and shape can be described by the distribution of intensity gradients [13]. Gradients have been used earlier in the literature for action recognition from RGB data [1, 14–16]. These approaches differ in the orientation binning process and the region used for constructing histograms. In [1], points from RGB frames are sampled densely and tracked using dense optical flow field. Descriptors such as HOG, HOF, MBH are computed along the trajectories. This method considers the shape and motion information along trajectory of sampled points. Inspired by this, we extract gradient-based descriptors along joint trajectory. With Kinect, the skeleton data and trajectory of joint is readily available and the need for explicit sampling and tracking of points is eliminated. We use *both*, the 3D skeleton data and depth map sequence to define *Trajectory Aligned Gradient Orientation (TAGO)* feature describing the local information along the joint trajectory.

Since human action involves movement of joints, the location of a joint and the area around the joint provide vital cues about the action being performed.

We exploit this by considering a small neighbourhood around the joint to extract local appearance and shape information. To accomplish this, firstly a fixed number of frames (N) are sampled from the complete sequence of frames in order to take into account the variation in the speed of actions. The 3D location of each joint is converted into corresponding image (depth map) coordinate using the camera parameters. Subsequently, a 3D cell is considered around each joint with the given location of joint as the center of the cell. Gradient-based descriptor are computed within each cell. The use of trajectory for describing local shape information has certain advantages over that of [11], in that, only the neighbourhood around a joint is considered for computing the gradient, resulting in reduction in redundant features.

Formally, let $(P_1, P_2, ..., P_N)$ be the trajectory of a joint j where $P_i = (x_i, y_i)$ is the spatial position of joint j in the *sampled* frame i. It is to be noted that P_i is the location obtained after projecting the 3D joint location onto the depth image plane. A 3D spatio-temporal cell of size $\Delta_x * \Delta_y * \Delta_t$ is defined around a trajectory point P_i with P_i as the center of the cell. Figure 2 illustrates the process of creating trajectory-aligned cells.

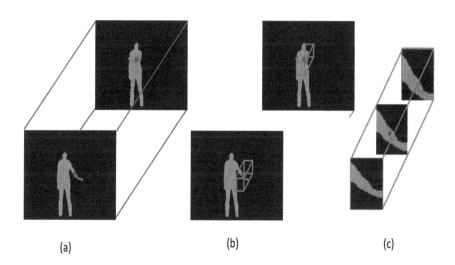

(a)   (b)   (c)

Fig. 2. Trajectory Aligned Gradient features. (a) Skeleton position of 'elbow' joint indicated with a red circle. (b) Cells along joint trajectory with 'joint' at the center of the cell. (c) Cell consisting of $\Delta t = 3$. (Depth image from [18])

To describe the local appearance and shape of a cell, we compute intensity gradients. Let $H(i, j, k)$ be the depth value at pixel location (i, j) and sampled frame k, then gradients are computed as:

$$D_x = H(i, j + 1, k) - H(i, j - 1, k) \tag{1}$$

$$D_y = H(i + 1, j, k) - H(i - 1, j, k) \tag{2}$$

$$D_t = H(i, j, k+1) - H(i, j, k-1) \tag{3}$$

Using these, gradient magnitude (M) and orientations (θ, ϕ) can be obtained as:

$$M = \sqrt{D_x^2 + D_y^2 + D_t^2} \, , \; M \geq 0 \tag{4}$$

$$\phi = \arccos(D_t/M) \, , \; 0 \leq \phi \leq \pi \tag{5}$$

$$\theta = \arctan(D_y/D_x) \, , \; 0 \leq \theta \leq 2\pi \tag{6}$$

The resultant gradient magnitude (M) and orientations (θ, ϕ) are used to compute TAGO descriptors by considering n_θ and n_ϕ bins. Every pixel within the 3D cell votes towards the corresponding orientations weighted by gradient magnitude, similar to HOG computation. This results in two histograms, h_θ and h_ϕ of dimensions n_θ and n_ϕ respectively, for each cell. Subsequently, each histogram is normalized. Concatenation of θ-histogram and ϕ-histogram results in a $n_\theta + n_\phi$ dimensional gradient-based descriptor for each cell. Such descriptors are concatenated along every cell to give final TAGO feature descriptor corresponding to a joint. A total of $N * n_j * (n_\theta + n_\phi)$ TAGO features are obtained for n_j number of joints. Typical choice of parameters used is $\Delta_x = \Delta_y = 10$, $\Delta_t = 3$ (indicating a cell with spatial extent of 10 pixels in both directions and temporal extent of 3 frames), $n_\theta = 12 \; n_\phi = 6$.

3   Range of Joint Motion

In this section, we describe the features extracted using *only* skeleton data. Pose-based and motion features have been a popular choice of feature description, where features such as pair-wise joint difference per frame, joint difference across frames have often been used to describe pose and motion of a joint locally [4,5]. We, on the other hand, extract features describing the *Range of Joint Motion* (*RJM*). The RJM captures the global statistics of the movement of a joint. In particular, this feature describes the maximum displacement of a joint from the mean of the joint trajectory for a sample. Statistically this is similar to measuring the dispersion of a joint's trajectory.

Given a video and a joint j, let μ_x^j be the mean of joint positions along the x axis. Likewise, let μ_y^j and μ_z^j be the mean along y and z axes respectively. We define *Maximum* Displacement from Mean (MDM_x, MDM_y, MDM_z) as follows:

$$MDM_x^j = \max_f (|x_f^j - \mu_x^j|) \tag{7}$$

where (x_f^j, y_f^j, z_f^j) is the position of joint j in frame f. It may be noted that, here the joint position refers to the 3D coordinate of joint. For n_j number of joints , we have $n_j * 3$ such features per video. The choice of RJM as a feature descriptor is based on the fact that statistical dispersion helps in capturing the variability of distribution. In the context of action recognition, RJM can be used to distinguish between actions such as 'walk' and 'punch' since the maximum

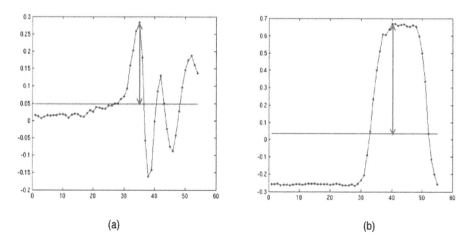

(a)   (b)

Fig. 3. Range of joint motion. Horizontal axis represents frame number. Vertical axis represents the location (x-coordinate or y-coordinate) of joint. (a) Location (x-coordinate) of 'hand' joint for 'High Arm Wave Action'. $MDMx_x^j$ is indicated in green. (b) Location (y-coordinate) of 'hand' joint for 'High Arm Wave Action'. MDM_y^j is indicated in green. (Color figure online)

displacement from mean trajectory will be negligible in case of 'punch' vis-à-vis 'walk' for joints corresponding to legs. Another advantage of RJM is that it results in reduced number of features in comparison to RJD and TJD features of [11] at the same time capturing the global characteristics of action.

4   Motion Map Descriptor

In this section, we describe the features obtained using *only* depth maps. We use the sequence of depth maps to obtain three binary masks corresponding to the three principal planes. These masks can be obtained by projecting a depth map onto the principal planes. In case, the scene consists of other objects, a mask corresponding to person can be easily extracted by projecting the 3D skeleton joints onto the depth map and extracting region around the skeletal model. This is followed by summation of difference of consecutive masks as follows:

$$MM^i = \sum_{t=2}^{N} |S_t^i - S_{t-1}^i| \tag{8}$$

where $i \in \{1,2,3\}$ for the three planes and S_t is the binary mask at time frame t. Repeating this for each principal plane results in three representative motion maps. Motion maps are non-binary images, where every pixel-value in the motion map is indicative of the motion at that pixel. Motion Map Descriptors (MMD) are obtained by computing HOG descriptors for each map MM^i, which can be easily obtained using MATLAB's in-built function. The number of features, in this case, depend on the choice of different HOG parameters such as number of orientation bins, cell size, block size etc. For example, with 9 orientation bins, block size as 4 and number of blocks as 10, a total of $9 * 4 * 10 = 360$ MMD features are obtained corresponding to a single principal plane.

5   Experiments

The final feature descriptors consist of TAGO, RJM and MMD concatenated together. This concatenated feature vector is termed as *Trajectory based Integrated Features* or **TIF**. It is possible that a few features might be irrelevant. For example, in case of MMD, HOG descriptors extracted from 'non-person' region of the motion map are not relevant for classification. Feature selection methods can be used to remove such features. We have used RELIEFF [12,17] method in our experiments. This results in a ranking of the features by taking into account how similar is the value of that feature for k nearest neighbors (samples) of the same class (nearest hits) and how distinct are the values of that feature for k nearest neighbors for each of the other classes (nearest misses). Prior probability of each class is taken into account while estimating the quality factor for an attribute. Let the length of the final feature vector (concatenated TAGO, RJM, MMD) be γ. RELIEFF yields a ranking of features. We select $\hat{\gamma}$ top-ranked features. $\hat{\gamma}$ is chosen by measuring the performance of selected top-ranked features on validation set. The accuracy on validation set is noted by varying the number of selected features. $\hat{\gamma}$ is the number of top-ranked features that yield highest accuracy on the validation set. Classification is performed on these $\hat{\gamma}$ features using SVM with RBF kernel. Feature selection (FS) has advantage over other dimension reduction techniques such as PCA, in that, the features obtained with PCA do not have the same meaning as before. Whereas, FS results in a selection of features from the original pool of features while retaining their original meaning. The proposed approach is evaluated on MS-Daily Activity 3D [19] and UTKinect [20] datasets.

5.1   MSR-Daily Activity

The MSR-Daily Activity dataset [19] consist of a set of 16 actions such as "drink", "eat", "read book" etc. Each action is performed by 10 actors in two different poses "sitting" and "standing" resulting in 320 samples. This is a more challenging dataset as this covers activities that involve human-object interaction and other human activities performed in daily life. Evaluation is performed using 'cross subject' scenario as in [19], where, half of the subjects are used for training and the remaining for testing. The performance of entire feature set has been compared with that of reduced feature set obtained using RELIEFF algorithm in Table 1 . From a total of 6024 features, 3400 top ranking features were selected using ReliefF. Figure 4(a) illustrates the proportion of features in the final set. Figure 4(b) illustrates the accuracy obtained with different features. It may be noted that the combined or TIF features yield higher accuracy than individual features. Further, feature selection results in higher classification accuracy.

Table 1. Comparative results on MSR daily activity 3D dataset

Method		Accuracy
DMM-HOG [2]		43.13%
Joint positions feature [8]		68.00%
Cuboid descriptor [23]		73.60%
Moving pose [24]		73.80%
HOG [25]		79.10%
HON4D [26]		80.00%
HDMM [27]		81.88%
Integrated features [11]		85.62%
Actionlet ensemble [8]		85.75%
SNV [28]		86.25%
DSTIP [29]		88.2%
Ours	**TIF** (Without FS)	85.44%
	TIF (With FS)	**89.20%**

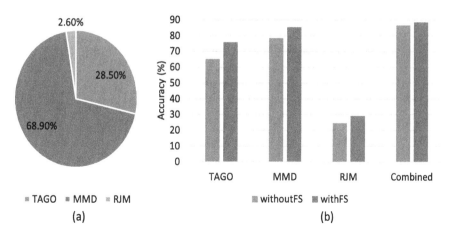

Fig. 4. Result analysis on MSR-Daily activity dataset. (a) Proportion of features in final 'selected' feature-set. (b) Classification accuracy using different features. 'Combined' refers to the TIF features.

5.2   UT-Kinect

The UT-Kinect Dataset [20] consist of 10 actions namely "walk", "sit down", "stand up' etc. There are 10 subjects and each subject performs each action twice resulting in 200 samples. Evaluation is done using Leave-One-Out-Cross-Validation (LOOCV) scenario [20], wherein, all-but-one sample is used for training and the remaining for testing. This step is repeated until each sample is tested once and the overall average accuracy is reported. Table 2 reports the results obtained. From a total of 6024 features, 800 top ranked features were selected based on ranking obtained through ReliefF. In comparison to MSR Daily Activity dataset, higher accuracy is obtained on UT-Kinect dataset. This can be attributed to the fact that the RJM features are more discriminative in case of UTK than MSR dataset as UTK dataset consists of actions with more inter-class variations. This can be further observed from Figs. 4(b) and 5(b). This further illustrates that if the actions differ significantly from each other, then with stable joint estimation, even simple feature such as RJM alone can be useful for classification.

Figure 5 illustrates the result analysis on UT-Kinect dataset. As with MSR-Daily Activity dataset, the proportion of MMD features in the selected

Table 2. Comparative results on UT-Kinect dataset

Method		Accuracy
DSTIP [29]		85.8%
Integrated features [11]		87.44%
SNV [28]		88.89%
MHT + BST [3]		90.00%
HDMM [27]		90.91%
HOJ3D [20]		90.92%
Fusion [22]		91.90%
View-time invariant [30]		95.00%
Skeleton data [21]		95.10%
Ours	**TIF** (Without FS)	88.38%
	TIF (With FS)	**95.96**%

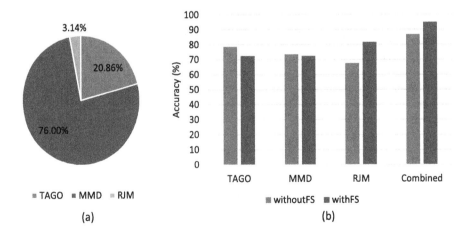

(a)   (b)

Fig. 5. Result analysis on UT-Kinect dataset. (a) Proportion of features in final 'selected' feature-set. (b) Classification accuracy using different features. 'Combined' refers to the TIF features.

feature-set is more than other features, followed by TAGO, with RJM being least in number. Also, the combined or TIF features yield higher accuracy than individual features and feature selection results in higher classification accuracy in case of TIF features.

6 Conclusion

In this paper we have presented a new approach for action recognition, Trajectory-based Integrated Features or TIF set, by integrating features such as Trajectory Aligned Gradient Orientation (TAGO), Range of Joint Motion (RJM) and Motion Map Descriptor (MMD) from depth maps and 3D skeleton data. TAGO improves upon the traditional depth-based HOG, by considering a neighborhood around body-joints for constructing descriptors, as most of the motion-centric detail can be obtained from 3D joint and its surrounding area. RJM, on the other hand, captures the global statistics of joint motion such as the displacement of the joint positions from the mean trajectory. In order to reduce the number of irrelevant features, we use the ReliefF method. The selected top-ranked features are used to train a SVM classifier. Experimental results reveal that there is performance improvement *with feature selection*. The improvement in classification accuracy with TIF indicates the discriminative power of the proposed method. A possible extension of the proposed approach would be to construct class-specific models for classification, wherein, feature selection could be used to select features relevant for representing a particular class.

References

1. Wang, H., Klaser, A., Schmid, C., Liu, C.-L.: Dense trajectories and motion boundary descriptors for action recognition. Int. J. Comput. Vis. **103**, 60–79 (2013)
2. Yang, X., Zhang, C., Tian, Y.: Recognizing actions using depth motion maps-based histograms of oriented gradients. In: Proceedings of the 20th ACM International Conference on Multimedia, MM 12, pp. 1057–1060 (2012)
3. Jetley, S., Cuzzolin, F.: 3D activity recognition using motion history and binary shape templates. In: Jawahar, C.V., Shan, S. (eds.) ACCV 2014. LNCS, vol. 9008, pp. 129–144. Springer, Cham (2015). https://doi.org/10.1007/978-3-319-16628-5_10
4. Yang, X., Tian, Y.: EigenJoints based action recognition using naive Bayes nearest neighbor. In: CVPR Workshop (2012)
5. Kruthiventi, S., Babu, R.: 3D action recognition by learning sequence of poses. In: ICVGIP (2014)
6. Liu, J., Shahroudy, A., Xu, D., Wang, G.: Spatio-temporal LSTM with trust gates for 3D human action recognition. In: Leibe, B., Matas, J., Sebe, N., Welling, M. (eds.) ECCV 2016. LNCS, vol. 9907, pp. 816–833. Springer, Cham (2016). https://doi.org/10.1007/978-3-319-46487-9_50
7. Hochreiter, S., Schmidhuber, J.: Long short-term memory. Neural Comput. **9**(8), 1735–1780 (1997)

8. Wang, J., Liu, Z., Wu, Y., Yuan, J.: Mining actionlet ensemble for action recognition with depth cameras. In: Proceedings of the 2012 IEEE Conference on CVPR, pp. 1290–1297 (2012)
9. Zhu, Y., Chen, W., Guo, G.: Fusing spatiotemporal features and joints for 3D action recognition. In: CVPRW (2013)
10. Chaaraoui, A.A., Padilla-Lopez, J.R., Florez-Revuelta, F.: Fusion of skeletal and silhouette based features for human action recognition with RGBD sensors. In: ICCV Workshops (2013)
11. Arora, N., Shukla, P., Biswas, K.K.: Integrating depth-HOG and spatio-temporal joints data for action recognition. In: International Conference on Computer Graphics, Visualization and Computer Vision (WSCG) (2016)
12. Kononenko, I., Simec, E., Sikonja, M.R.: Overcoming the myopia of inductive learning algorithms with RELIEFF. Appl. Intell. **7**, 39–55 (1997)
13. Dalal, N., Triggs, B.: Histograms of oriented gradients for human detection. In: CVPR (2005)
14. Scovanner, P., Ali, S., Shah, M.: A 3-dimensional SIFT descriptor and its application to action recognition. In: 15th International Conference on Multimedia, pp. 357–360 (2007)
15. Klaser, A., Marszaek, M., Schmid, C.: A spatio-temporal descriptor based on 3D gradients. In: British Machine Vision Conference, pp. 995–1004 (2008)
16. Perez, E.A., Mota, V.F., Maciel, L.M., Sad, D., Vieira, M.B.: Combining gradient histograms using orientation tensors for human action recognition. In: ICPR, pp. 3460–3463 (2012)
17. Robnik-Sikonja, M., Kononenko, I.: Theoretical and empirical analysis of ReliefF and RReliefF. Mach. Learn. **53**, 23–69 (2003)
18. Li, W., Zhang, Z., Liu, Z.: Action recognition based on a bag of 3D points. In: CVPR (2010)
19. Wang, J., Liu, Z., Wu, Y., Yuan, J.: Mining actionlet ensemble for action recognition with depth cameras. In: CVPR, pp. 1290–1297 (2012)
20. Xia, L., Chen, C., Aggarwal, J.: View invariant human action recognition using histograms of 3D joints. In: CVPR Workshop (2012)
21. Cippitelli, E., Gasparrini, S., Gambi, E., Spinsante, S.: A human activity recognition system using skeleton data using RGBD sensors. J. Comput. Intell. Neurosci. **2016**, 21 (2016)
22. Zhu, Y., Chen, W., Guo, G.: Fusing spatio-temporal features and joints for 3D action recognition. In: Computer Vision and Pattern Recognition Workshops (2013)
23. Dollar, P., Rabaund, V., Cottrell, G., Belongie, S.: Behaviour recognition via sparse spatio temporal features. In: PETS (2005)
24. Zanfir, M., Leordeanu, M. and Sminchisescu, C.: The moving pose: an efficient 3D kinematics descriptor for low-latency action recognition and detection, In: ICCV (2013)
25. Laptev, I., Marszalek, M., Schmid, C., Rozenfeld, B.: Learning realistic human actions from movies. In: CVPR (2008)
26. Oreifej, O., Liu, Z.: Histogram of oriented 4D normals for activity recognition from depth sequences. In: CVPR (2013)
27. Wang, P., Li, W., Gao, Z., Zhang, J., Tang, C., Ogunbona, P.: deep convolutional neural networks for action recognition using depth map sequences. In: CVPR (2015)
28. Yang, X., Tian, Y.: Super normal vector for activity recognition using depth sequences. In: CVPR (2014)

29. Xia, L., Aggarwal, J.K.: Spatio-temporal depth cuboid similarity feature for activity recognition using depth camera. In: CVPR (2013)

30. Liu, Z., Feng, X., Tian, Y.: An effective view and time-invariant action recognition methods based on depth videos. In: Visual Communications and Image Processing (2015)

Anomaly from Motion: Unsupervised Extraction of Visual Irregularity via Motion Prediction

Avishek Majumder$^{(\boxtimes)}$, R. Venkatesh Babu$^{(\boxtimes)}$, and Anirban Chakraborty$^{(\boxtimes)}$

Indian Institute of Science, Bangalore 560012, Karnataka, India
{avishekm,venky,anirban}@iisc.ac.in

Abstract. The problem of automatically extracting anomalous events from any given video is a problem that has been researched from the early days of computer vision. It has still not been fully solved, showing that it is indeed not a trivial problem. The various challenges involved are lack of proper definition, varying scene structure and objects of interest in the scene, just a few to name.

In this paper we propose a novel method to extract outliers from motion alone. We employ a stacked LSTM encoder-decoder structure to model the regular motion patterns of the given video sequence. The discrepancy between the motion predicted using the model and the actual observed motion in the scene is analyzed to detect anomalous activities. We perform extensive experimentation on the benchmark datasets of crowd anomaly analysis. We report State of the Art results across all the datasets.

Keywords: RNN · Anomaly · Crowded scenes · LSTMs
Video surveillance · Machine learning · Computer vision

1 Introduction

With ever-increasing population in this world, the need for intelligent surveillance systems are increasing everyday. Accurate, reliable and scalable systems which can be deployed across scenes with little hassle are the demands of the current era. Almost all existing methods employ a human in the loop, who has the sole responsibility to react to a situation based on visual cues, often simultaneously coming from multiple sources. A human operator is unreliable due to various reasons, for example, their mood, and fatigue. Fatigue can have severe consequences in certain situations, where attention to certain subtle details in a scene is necessary.

Prompt recognition of suspicious events is a topic of great importance in video surveillance. An abnormal event/anomaly is often defined as an outlier, i.e., either different from its spatio-temporally neighboring events or is rarely observed throughout the video. Due to the lack of proper definition for anomaly, the video anomaly detection task becomes particularly challenging. In certain

© Springer Nature Singapore Pte Ltd. 2018
R. Rameshan et al. (Eds.): NCVPRIPG 2017, CCIS 841, pp. 66–77, 2018.
https://doi.org/10.1007/978-981-13-0020-2_7

scenes, anomaly might be a function of time, in another, it might be uniform. Considering a traffic crossing at any junction, based on the traffic signal, only certain motions in the scene might be applicable. In another scenario, a static scene of a public place might not have such strict restrictions on the motion. In that situation, detecting anomalous activity becomes even more difficult.

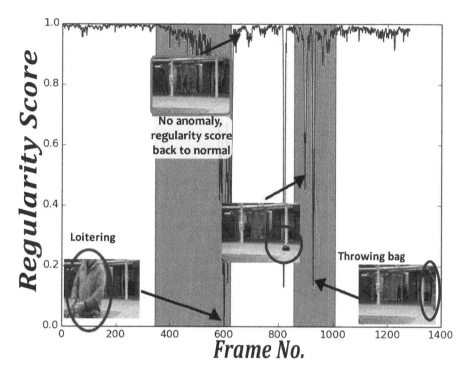

Fig. 1. Temporal regularity score is used to detect anomalous events. The red area are the marked ground truth. The regularity scores go down to local minimas in case of anomalous events occurring. In the first minima, loitering person is detected. In the second one, a person throwing bag is detected. (Color figure online)

Besides these challenges, certain physical restrictions are automatically embedded into the task of automated anomaly detection. Anomaly, by nature, is sparse and spurious in any scene. Because of this nature, we don't have access to annotated anomalies. This forces the models to learn using unsupervised methods.

The recent advancement of Convolutional Neural Networks for tackling computer vision task has gained huge popularity, simply due to the fact that these models can efficiently extract higher level information from raw data. For the task of anomalous event detection, Convolution Neural Networks have been used as well [3,8,9,19,21].

In this work, we present a novel recurrent neural network based anomaly detection method. Even though the idea of using RNNs for anomaly detection is not a novel one [4,14], we present a very shallow two layer LSTM network, working on a much sparser signal than the appearance domain. Specifically, we use a stacked LSTM encoder-decoder framework to model the *normal* motion patterns in a provided video sequence. Our model takes in the spatial distribution of estimated motion in a sequence of frames, and predicts the motion in the subsequent frame in the sequence. The difference between predicted motion and the actual observed motion is analyzed to detect and localize abnormal activities in the test video sequence (Fig. 1).

2   Related Work

Starting from the early days of computer vision, researchers have been trying various ways to detect and extract novel, interesting or anomalous events from huge sequence of videos, both online [2,12,20] and offline [8,19]. Both of the methods have great applications in forensics, surveillance and security. While the online method is good for making real time decisions, it also is much more challenging since the computation pipeline has to be very fast. The offline method, on the other hand, is a great way to extract information from an existing video segment and further analyze it.

The methods such as Mixture of probabilistic principle component analysis (MPPCA) [10], Social Force (SF) [15], Chaotic Invariants [18], SF + MPPCA [13] have used carefully extracted features by hand-crafted filters, and then fitted them to any statistics to determine if an event is regular or irregular. MPPCA method models the local regular events using Markov Random Fields. Methods such as Chaotic Invariants and Social Force utilize the particle trajectories of the objects in the scenes. The Social Force method computes a bag of Forces, from the interaction of the particle vectors among each other. The SF + MPPCA method divides the scene into small non overlapping patches, and then computes local patch statistics for the particular locations, thus modelling the normal statistics.

Besides these there has been spectacular amount of work using CNNs. AMDN [19] splits the image into patches of various sizes, re-scales them and trains a stacked auto-encoder system. They then use a one class SVM on top of the learnt features to determine if anomaly occurs. They do this to 3 modalities, appearance or raw frames, motion vectors and appearance and motion vectors combined. The work by Hasan et al. [8] uses an end-to-end fully convolutional network to reconstruct a volume of 10 frames. During testing if the reconstruction does not match the frame being tested for, it is considered anomalous. Spatial Temporal CNN [21] uses both training as well as testing data to classify frames into anomalous and non anomalous frames.

Most of the methods which yield good results using deep learning techniques either process the full frame and reconstruct it back, or break it into patches for reconstructing each patch separately. Most of these methods use more than one modality associated with the data, such as appearance, motion or both. In our method, we predict the motion in a *future* frame using RNN from existing data instead of reconstructing it. We use the motion modality of the data as it is sparse and easier to regress, yet not losing any motion information associated with the scene. Our assumption for training this model is that the video sequences are coming from surveillance cameras, where the video does not suffer from camera motion. Besides, even if there exists motion in background which is considered 'normal', then there should be enough examples in the training set such that our model can learn the statistics of the motion in the background. Also, if at all our method fails to model some minor portion of the background motion, it would only increase the number of false detections, which are considered less malicious than missing to flag true anomalies.

3   Methodology

For the current task, we use a stacked LSTM architecture. Our model consists of two stacked LSTMs. The LSTMs were intended to be used as encoder decoder. The first one contains just 128 units to enforce encoding only the most important features in the sequence. The second one contains 512 units for reconstruction or prediction of optical flow. Figure 2 shows the architecture of our model. The following sections describe the method in detail.

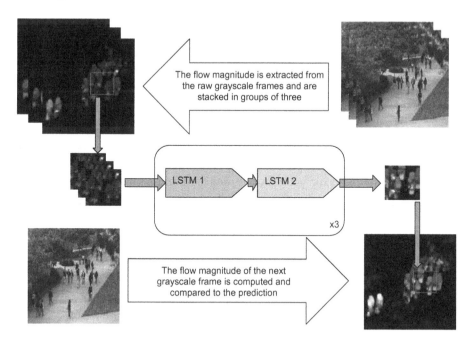

Fig. 2. Flow RNN architecture. As shown in the figure, we first extract the dense optical flow magnitude from the gray scale frames. We stack them together to form the sequence, and split them into patches of size 32×32. We then train the LSTMs to predict the future flow.

3.1   RNN : LSTM

Before going into the details of our method, this section will briefly discuss the RNN unit used by our method and how it is used.

Traditionally, neural networks are acyclic directed graphs. RNNs or recurrent neural network units are composed of neurons in a network which have connections from their output to input, thus creating a loop or cycle. These kinds of units are important when dealing with sequential data. It is typically observed in a scene that the estimated motion is highly correlated in time. The motion vectors from frame 1 change slightly both in direction and magnitude to produce the next one. Thus we chose RNNs to model the temporal evolution of the data.

LSTMs [7] are a special class of RNN units, which have four gates associated with each cell. The four gates are input gate (i_t), forget gate (f_t), cell state (c_t) and hidden state (h_t). LSTMs were chosen for their particular success with recurrent tasks. They are capable of learning and remembering sequential data. The following are the equations for the 4 gates respectively:

$$i_t = \sigma_i(x_t W_{xi} + h_{t-1} W_{hi} + w_{ci} \odot c_{t-1} + b_i) \tag{1}$$

$$f_t = \sigma_f(x_t W_{xf} + h_{t-1} W_{hf} + w_{cf} \odot c_{t-1} + b_f) \tag{2}$$

$$c_t = f_t \odot c_{t-1} + i_t \odot \sigma_c(x_t W_{xc} + h_{t-1} W_{hc} + b_c) \tag{3}$$

$$o_t = \sigma_o(x_t W_{xo} + h_{t-1} W_{ho} + w_{co} \odot c_t + b_o) \tag{4}$$

$$h_t = (1 - u_t) \odot h_{t-1} + u_t \odot c_t \tag{5}$$

Where σ denotes *tanh* non-linearity. The LSTM unit contains 3 gates, input (i_t), forget (f_t) and output (o_t) respectively. It also maintains two internal states, a cell state (c_t) and a hidden state (h_t). The weights control the parts of the features which are to be passed and which are to be forgotten. From the above Eq. (3), we see that the cell state combines the current input with the previous hidden state, to update its current cell state, which is again used in Eq. 5, to update the current hidden state. Due to the gating mechanism of LSTMs, they can selectively keep certain pieces of information for long periods of time, and use them to find sequential patterns. The objective function for our task is to minimize the squared error between the predicted and actual motion vectors.

$$L(Y_t, \hat{Y}_t) = \sum_n \|\mathbf{y_t^n} - \mathbf{\hat{y}_t^n}\|_2^2 \tag{6}$$

In Eq. (6), Y_t is the actual optical flow of the frame at time t and $\hat{Y}_t$ is the corresponding prediction of the optical flow of the frame. This is split into n patches of size 32×32, and stretched into vectors $\mathbf{y_t^n}$ and $\mathbf{\hat{y}_t^n}$ respectively. The euclidean distance between these vectors are computed and added for all the n patches to get the frame-wise error scores. These scores are normalized with respect to the full video to get the final regularity scores.

3.2   Anomaly from Optical Flow

As the concept of detecting anomaly is not well defined, we describe anomaly as objects which do not follow the usual motion patterns of the given scene.

Specifically, we intend to catch abrupt motions, or motions which are faster/slower or even in a direction that is not typically observed in the scene. According to the definitions of anomaly in the datasets under study, the usual behaviour is context dependant and is typically understood from the past history.

We start by taking the individual scenes, and extract their dense optical flow magnitudes by Farneback algorithm [6]. We do not consider the direction since while feeding to the LSTM, we send a temporal sequence of optical flow magnitudes. Such a sequence can automatically encode the motion direction in the scene when the temporal evolution of the flow magnitude is modelled.

3.3   Training Procedure

We train three separate LSTM encoder decoder networks of different scales, at resolutions of 224×224, 64×64 and 32×32 and extract the dense opticals flows. The optical flows are then stacked into groups of 3 to form sequences of shape $3 \times 224 \times 224$, $3 \times 64 \times 64$, $3 \times 32 \times 32$ respectively. We then split the flow sequence into patches of 32×32. This yields 49, 4 and 1 patches from each sequence of the scene respectively. The idea behind using three scales is to have three expert networks with different context information. We feed the sequences to the stacked RNNs. The stacked RNNs predicts what would be the next flow in the sequence shown. Keeping the learning rate fairly low $(1e{-}6)$, we let the network overfit on the training data. Since the network has limited capacity, it only learns what the "normal" statistics might be. So even if some anomalous events creep into the training data, it would be overridden by the massive amount of normal data statistics.

During testing we find the outliers by their error signatures. That is, when the network predicts the next flow of the sequence, we compute the prediction error between the actual observed optical flow magnitude of the predicted frame and the prediction. Naturally the network would produce large prediction errors when outliers or anomalies occur in the scene. We min-pool the error maps of the three scales, to only keep the most significant errors where all three networks are in consensus.

4   Experiments and Results

We use the min pooled prediction error to compute the regularity score of the scene. We scale the errors between 0 to 1 for each scene, and then invert it such that an error of 1 gives a regularity score of 0. For detecting anomaly, we need to isolate the dominant minima of the error sequence. For this we use persistence1D [11] algorithm to extract the minimas of the error. We then use a sliding window to accumulate all the minimas occuring in the part of window as the same anomalous event. We consider an anomaly as correctly detected if the prediction and the ground truth has atleast 50% temporal (frame) overlap.

Table 1. Comparison of anomaly detection across datasets with different ablations. We compare the different scales of the training, along with the fusion strategy. We found min-pooling to be the best way to fuse the scores of the three scales.

Dataset		Anomaly detection					
Name	# Anomalies	True positive/false alarm					
		224×224	64×64	32×32	Mean pool	Max pool	Min pool
CUHK avenue	47	43/13	43/16	43/17	43/19	43/19	43/13
UCSD Ped 1	40	39/2	39/3	39/4	39/1	39/3	39/1
UCSD Ped 2	12	12/1	12/1	12/1	12/1	12/1	12/1
Subway entry	66	62/11	63/8	61/15	61/11	60/11	64/11
Subway exit	19	17/4	17/3	10/12	17/2	17/3	18/4

We use various pooling techniques, as well as check the results and outcomes of the individual scales. The following Table 1 summarizes our findings. From the comparison, we conclude that min pooling has the maximum recall rate, even though precision is slightly off. And in cases of Anomaly detection, it is always better to compromise on precision, as false positives are not considered as malicious as false negatives.

4.1 Datasets

In this section, we briefly describe each dataset and the associated normal and abnormal behaviours. Some of the behaviours are simply fast moving objects, while some are more conceptual like loitering and jumping turnstiles. All the scenes are fixed surveillance camera feeds, so the usual challenges like unavailability of sound, low resolution video and compression artifacts are there.

UCSD Pedestrian Dataset [13]. This dataset is the most widely used dataset for pedestrian crowd analysis containing two different scenes. The Pedestrian 1 dataset is a scene of a pedestrian walkway going through the scene vertically. This scene suffers from occlusion due to foliage as well as huge crowd. The scene also suffers from slight change in scale between the entry and exit points of the pedestrians. Due to the scale change the anomalous objects in the scene exhibit different motion magnitude depending on their location. Objects in the front of the scene, being closer to the camera, produces large motion, while the same objects farther away in the scene produce smaller motion vectors.

The Pedestrian 2 dataset is slightly simpler, as the scene has a horizontal pedestrian walkway, so the change in scale and motion is not there. Nevertheless, the occlusion of anomalous objects behind the regular objects poses serious challenge, as well as the type of the anomalous objects are greatly varying. Both scene contains small vehicles, cyclists, skateboarders, wheelchairs as anomalous objects.

CUHK Avenue Dataset [12]. This dataset is yet another most widely used benchmark for anomaly detection. The scene consists of a stationary camera, and normal motion consists of people walking by. The anomalies in this scene are not just running or cycling, but are also conceptual anomalies such as loitering, throwing things, etc.

Table 2. Comparison of anomaly detection across datasets. *Uses older dataset. DNR: Did not report.

Dataset		Anomaly detection				
Name	# Anomalies	True positive/false alarm				
		Ours	Hasan [8]	Lu [12]	Medel [14]	Chong [5]
CUHK avenue	47	43/13	**45/4**	12/1*	40/2	44/6
UCSD Ped 1	40	39/1	38/6	DNR	**40/7**	DNR
UCSD Ped 2	12	**12/1**	**12/1**	DNR	**12/1**	DNR
Subway entry	66	**64/11**	61/15	57/4	62/14	61/9
Subway exit	19	18/4	17/5	**19/2**	19/37	18/10

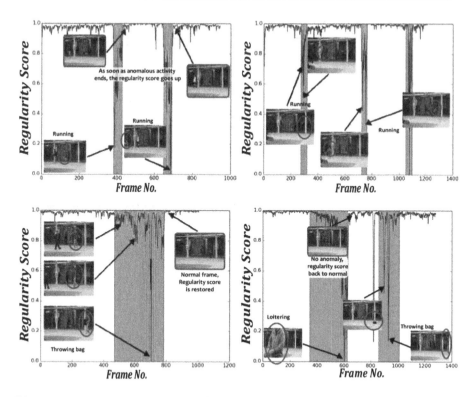

Fig. 3. Regularity score for CUHK Avenue. The red areas are the marked anomalous region, where we see local minima is achieved by our method, to signify irregular activity. Best viewed on digital display zoomed. (Color figure online)

Subway Entry and Exit Dataset [1]. This dataset contains a scene of an entry to and exit from a subway station. Like CUHK Avenue, this dataset contains anomalies which are difficult to detect using only low level motion cues. Some example cases of anomaly in this dataset are people walking in opposite direction, people jumping turnstiles, etc.

UMN Abnormal Crowd Dataset [15]. This dataset contains some events which might cause a commotion or stampede in a crowded scene. This dataset has also been used to benchmark anomaly detection algorithms.

4.2   Results

Table 2 summarizes our findings on various datasets. Some of the regularity scores are shown in Figs. 3, 4, 5 and 6. The regularity score goes down significantly during all anomalous events, suggesting irregular motion patterns in those scenes.

We also test our method on the UMN abnormal crowd behaviour detection, and show that it performs better or on-par with all the existing algorithms.

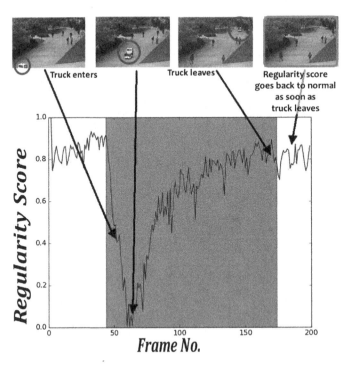

Fig. 4. Regularity score for UCSD Ped 1. The red area is the ground truth anomalous region. During the occurrence of anomalous activities, we observe that the regularity score goes down to a local minimum. (Color figure online)

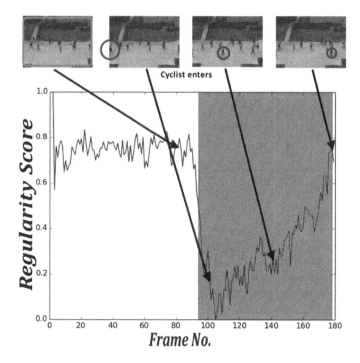

Fig. 5. Regularity score for UCSD Ped 2. The red area is the actual anomalous region, and the score goes down to local minima suggesting the presence of an anomalous object. In this particular case, we see how the regularity scores drop as soon as the cyclist enters the scene. (Color figure online)

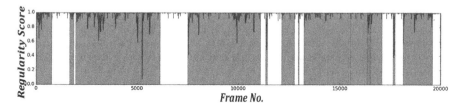

Fig. 6. Regularity score for Subway Entry. The ground truth is annotated as the red region in the graph, and we see significant drop in regularity scores in those areas. (Color figure online)

Table 3 summarizes the results on UMN dataset. We choose AUC to measure our performance for this dataset, since in this dataset, we encounter a global anomalous behaviour, where all the participants in the scene behave in abnormal way. In these scenarios, it is not enough to just identify the anomalous event but to localize the event temporally.

From the results, we see that our model's performance is better or on-par with the state of the art methods in most of the cases.

Table 3. AUC comparison of UMN dataset.

Method	AUC
Optical flow	84%
SFM [15]	96%
Chaotic Invariants [18]	**99%**
Commotion [16]	98%
TCP [17]	98%
Ours	**99%**

5   Conclusion

In this work we use a very sparse representation of motion to predict regularity in motion. We use three small networks, at different scales, due to the unavailability of large training data. Our experiments show how multiscale model helps in improving the results of the anomalous event detection. Since the data is sparse we could afford to regress the future prediction instead of reconstructing. In case of dense data, most regression models usually fail and converge to an average of the input data.

Acknowledgment. This work is supported by Science and Engineering Research Board (SERB), Department of Science and Technology (DST), Government of India (Proj No. SB/S3/EECE/0127/2015).

References

1. Adam, A., Rivlin, E., Shimshoni, I., Reinitz, D.: Robust real-time unusual event detection using multiple fixed-location monitors. IEEE Trans. Pattern Anal. Mach. Intell. **30**(3), 555–560 (2008)
2. Chaker, R., Al Aghbari, Z., Junejo, I.N.: Social network model for crowd anomaly detection and localization. Pattern Recognit. **61**, 266–281 (2017)
3. Chen, B., Marlin, B., de Freitas, N., et al.: Deep learning of invariant spatio-temporal features from video. In: Deep Learning and Unsupervised Feature Learning Workshop, NIPS 2010 (2010)
4. Chong, Y.S., Tay, Y.H.: Modeling representation of videos for anomaly detection using deep learning: a review. arXiv preprint arXiv:1505.00523 (2015)
5. Chong, Y.S., Tay, Y.H.: Abnormal event detection in videos using spatiotemporal autoencoder. In: Cong, F., Leung, A., Wei, Q. (eds.) ISNN 2017. LNCS, vol. 10262, pp. 189–196. Springer, Cham (2017). https://doi.org/10.1007/978-3-319-59081-3_23
6. Farnebäck, G.: Two-frame motion estimation based on polynomial expansion. In: Bigun, J., Gustavsson, T. (eds.) SCIA 2003. LNCS, vol. 2749, pp. 363–370. Springer, Heidelberg (2003). https://doi.org/10.1007/3-540-45103-X_50
7. Gers, F.A., Schmidhuber, J., Cummins, F.: Learning to forget: continual prediction with LSTM (1999)

8. Hasan, M., Choi, J., Neumann, J., Roy-Chowdhury, A.K., Davis, L.S.: Learning temporal regularity in video sequences. In: Proceedings of the IEEE Conference on Computer Vision and Pattern Recognition, pp. 733–742 (2016)
9. Hu, X., Hu, S., Huang, Y., Zhang, H., Wu, H.: Video anomaly detection using deep incremental slow feature analysis network. IET Comput. Vis. **10**(4), 258–265 (2016)
10. Kim, J., Grauman, K.: Observe locally, infer globally: a space-time MRF for detecting abnormal activities with incremental updates. In: IEEE Conference on Computer Vision and Pattern Recognition, CVPR 2009, pp. 2921–2928. IEEE (2009)
11. Kozlov, Y., Weinkauf, T.: Persistence1D: extracting and filtering minima and maxima of 1D functions (2015). http://people.mpi-inf.mpg.de/weinkauf/notes/persistence1d.html. Accessed 11 Jan 2015
12. Lu, C., Shi, J., Jia, J.: Abnormal event detection at 150 FPS in MATLAB. In: Proceedings of the IEEE International Conference on Computer Vision, pp. 2720–2727 (2013)
13. Mahadevan, V., Li, W., Bhalodia, V., Vasconcelos, N.: Anomaly detection in crowded scenes. In: 2010 IEEE Conference on Computer Vision and Pattern Recognition, CVPR, pp. 1975–1981. IEEE (2010)
14. Medel, J.R., Savakis, A.: Anomaly detection in video using predictive convolutional long short-term memory networks. arXiv preprint arXiv:1612.00390 (2016)
15. Mehran, R., Oyama, A., Shah, M.: Abnormal crowd behavior detection using social force model. In: IEEE Conference on Computer Vision and Pattern Recognition, CVPR 2009, pp. 935–942. IEEE (2009)
16. Mousavi, H., Nabi, M., Kiani, H., Perina, A., Murino, V.: Crowd motion monitoring using tracklet-based commotion measure. In: 2015 IEEE International Conference on Image Processing, ICIP, pp. 2354–2358. IEEE (2015)
17. Ravanbakhsh, M., Nabi, M., Mousavi, H., Sangineto, E., Sebe, N.: Plug-and-play CNN for crowd motion analysis: an application in abnormal event detection. arXiv preprint arXiv:1610.00307 (2016)
18. Wu, S., Moore, B.E., Shah, M.: Chaotic invariants of Lagrangian particle trajectories for anomaly detection in crowded scenes. In: 2010 IEEE Conference on Computer Vision and Pattern Recognition, CVPR, pp. 2054–2060. IEEE (2010)
19. Xu, D., Song, J., Yan, Y., Ricci, E., Sebe, N., et al.: Learning deep representations of appearance and motion for anomalous event detection. In: BMVC. BMVA Press (2015)
20. Yuan, Y., Fang, J., Wang, Q.: Online anomaly detection in crowd scenes via structure analysis. IEEE Trans. Cybern. **45**(3), 548–561 (2015)
21. Zhou, S., Shen, W., Zeng, D., Fang, M., Wei, Y., Zhang, Z.: Spatial-temporal convolutional neural networks for anomaly detection and localization in crowded scenes. Signal Process. Image Commun. **47**, 358–368 (2016)

Recognizing Human Activities in Videos Using Improved Dense Trajectories over LSTM

Krit Karan Singh and Snehasis Mukherjee[(⊠)]

Indian Institute of Information Technology SriCity, Sri City, India
snehasis.mukherjee@iiits.in

Abstract. We propose a deep learning based technique to classify actions based on Long Short Term Memory (LSTM) networks. The proposed scheme first learns spatial temporal features from the video, using an extension of the Convolutional Neural Networks (CNN) to 3D. A Recurrent Neural Network (RNN) is then trained to classify each sequence considering the temporal evolution of the learned features for each time step. Experimental results on the CMU MoCap, UCF 101, Hollywood 2 dataset show the efficacy of the proposed approach. We extend the proposed framework with an efficient motion feature, to enable handling significant camera motion. The proposed approach outperforms the existing deep models for each dataset.

Keywords: Dense trajectories · LSTM · CNN · RNN
Human activities

1 Introduction and Related Works

Machine recognition of human activity have been an active research area during the last few years because of its potential impact on several application areas including surveillance, robotics and healthcare. With the recent advancements in the big data analysis techniques, a handful of different sophisticated techniques are available to explore in recognizing several complex human activities in run-time. This paper proposes a technique for classifying human activities into a sufficiently large number of classes in run-time.

Several efforts have been made for recognizing human activities in video [1]. The general approach for activity recognition consists of the two major steps: extracting motion related features [2–4] from the videos and classifying the features into different action classes [5]. Laptev et al. proposed Space Time Interest Points (STIP) detector, based on the extension of Harris corner detector in temporal space [2]. Efforts have been made for recognizing human activities using some other spatio-temporal features like Motion- Scale Invariant Feature Transform (MoSIFT) [3] and sparse features [4]. However, such spatio-temporal features are unable to handle challenges like camera shake and background clutter.

© Springer Nature Singapore Pte Ltd. 2018
R. Rameshan et al. (Eds.): NCVPRIPG 2017, CCIS 841, pp. 78–88, 2018.
https://doi.org/10.1007/978-981-13-0020-2_8

Another line of approach relies on optical flow based features to get the advantage of motion information [6–9,11]. In [6,7], Mukherjee et al. minimized the effect of camera shaking by introducing Gradient-Weighted Optical Flow (GWOF) feature, where the optical flow of each frame is point-wise multiplied with the gradient. Wang et al. introduced Warped Optical Flow (WOF) by measuring the gradient on the Optical flow matrix of each frame [8]. In [9], effect of background clutter is minimized by multiplying WOF with the image gradient. Efforts have been made by analyzing the motion trajectories across frames during activity [10]. All these approaches have the limitation of dealing with unnecessary motion information at the background. Buddubariki et al. introduced Gradient Flow- Space Time Interest Point (GF-STIP) features to extract motion information only at the spatio temporal interest points, and find the motion trajectories based on GF-STIP [11]. Extracting motion features only at the interest points, helps in reducing the effect of motion of background pixels during action. Another good effort was made by Mukherjee and Singh in [22], where GWOF features were calculated only at the 3D joint points of the person during action. However, for a big dataset like UCF101 [12], some Deep Learning framework is necessary.

Recently, Deep Learning techniques are gaining interest of researchers for classifying human activities in big datasets [13–17]. Taylor et al. proposed a multi-stage architecture combining convolutional fully connected layers, where a convolutional Restricted Boltzman Machine (ConvRBM) extracts motion related features from each pair of successive frames at the lowest layer [13]. Ji et al. proposed 3D ConvNet approach for action recognition, where spatio-temporal features are extracted by a Convolutional Neural Network (CNN) [14]. Tran et al. extended the concept of 3D ConvNet by applying Fisher vector encoding on the learned feature [15]. Karpathy et al. applied their video classification approach for action recognition, by proposing an architecture for two types of spatio-temporal resolutions: high and low resolutions, then combining them to train the CNN [16]. Wang et al. extracted the motion trajectories and fed them into the 3D ConvNet [17]. However, the problem of camera shake and cluttered background, are not addressed so far.

Singh et al. extended the concept of Trajectory Pooled 3D ConvNet Descriptor (TDD) described in [17], to apply for egocentric action recognition, where the extreme camera shake was handled by stabilizing the video using trajectory [5]. Inspired by [5], the proposed approach feeds an improved version of trajectory feature into a Deep network. The improved version of the trajectory is obtained by using GF-STIP features, instead of optical flow [11]. Hence, we get the trajectories of only selected points, reducing the ambiguities in motion information, extracted from the background. The second contribution of the proposed approach lies in the use of LSTM network for classifying the action following [18]. An overview of the proposed approach is shown in Fig. 1.

2   Extracting Motion Trajectories

We extract motion trajectories in two steps: extracting GF-STIP feature [11] and finding the trajectories.

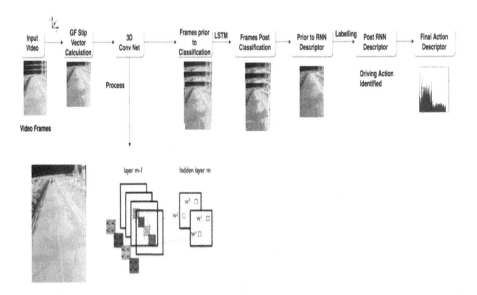

Fig. 1. The proposed framework for action recognition.

2.1   Extracting GF-STIP Features

We extract the GF-STIP features from each frame for analyzing the motion of objects (human) present in the video, following [11]. We minimize the effect of camera motion by extracting motion features only at spatio-temporal interest points, rather than analyzing the motion of the whole frame (including background). We extract STIP points from each frame using [2]. We obtain the Gradient Weighted Optical Flow (GWOF) at the STIP points following [7], by pixel-wise multiplying optical flow with image gradient, for each frame. Since the image gradient is almost zero at the background pixels, the result vector gets very less value at the background pixel, after multiplying optical flow with gradient. The result vector gets a high value at the object silhouette, when the edge pixels have high gradient value. Hence, GWOF feature can reduce the effect of background motion during action [7]. However, for cluttered background, this GWOF feature is not effective, due to high gradient value at the background pixels as well. For this reason, we extract GF-STIP feature where GWOF features are extracted only at those pixels which are spatio-temporally important. The cluttered background pixels are not selected as STIP points and hence, the result feature minimizes the effects of both camera shake and cluttered background. Figure 2 shows examples of some frames taken from the benchmark datasets,

Fig. 2. Sample frames from benchmark datasets, and the GF-STIP feature plotted on it. CMU (a) Walking, (b) Running, (c) Basketball; UCF (d) Situp, (e) Running, (f) Kicking; Holleywood 2 (g) Kissing, (h) Sit down, (i) Driving; Egocentric (j) Driving, (k) Cricket and (l) Badminton actions.

where the GF-STIP features are plotted on the frames. We can observe that, even for cluttered background frames like UCF101 dataset, the GF-STIP feature points are mostly concentrated at the human silhouette. Next we find the motion trajectories from the GF-STIP features.

2.2   Finding Motion Trajectories

We track the point P_t of the tth frame of the video, using median filtering on a dense optical flow field as follows,

$$P_{t+1} = P_t + K . D, \tag{1}$$

where K is the kernel of the median filter and D is the dense optical flow at point P_t. Points of subsequent frames are concatenated to find the trajectory [10]. The shape S of an L length trajectory is defined by a sequence of normalized displacement vectors $\Delta P_t = (P_{t+1} - P_t)$,

$$S = \frac{\Delta P_t, \dots, \Delta P_{t+L-1}}{\sum_{j=t}^{t+L-1} \|P_j\|}, \tag{2}$$

where $\|P_j\|$ is the magnitude of the vector P_j.

From each frame, HOG and HOF features are extracted. We obtain Motion Boundary Histogram (MBH) feature from WOF following [10]. We concatenate the three histograms obtained from HOG, HOF and MBH, along with the trajectory (obtained from (2)), using L1-norm to find the initial trajectories. Note that, we follow the same procedure as [10] to find the trajectories, except that, the HOF and MBH are extracted from the GF-STIP feature, instead of optical flow feature, to reduce the effect of motion of the background pixels during action.

The trajectories are modified by estimating the homography across frames. The homography is estimated using SURF features [21]. The SURF features are matched across consecutive frames, based on the nearest neighbor rule using RANSAC algorithm [23], and tracked using dense optical flow. Next we train a deep network with the modified trajectories.

3   Deep Architecture

We use 3D ConvNet for the proposed action recognition scheme, as 3D version of the CNN architecture takes care of the spatio temporal information of the video. Instead of feeding the raw video data, we feed the GF-STIP features extracted from each frame of the video, to the 3D-CNN model.

3.1   Space-Time Features with 3D-CNN

The 3D-CNN architecture used in this study, comprises of 10 layers. There are two rotating convolutional, amendment and sub-examining layers C1, R1, S1 and

C2, R2, S2 followed by a third convolution layer C3 and two neuron layers N1 and N2. The extent of the 3D input layer is $34 \times 54 \times 9$, comparing to 9 progressive casings of 34×54 pixels each. Layer C1 is made of 7 highlight maps of size $28 \times 48 \times 5$ pixels. Every unit in each element is associated with a 3D $7 \times 7 \times 5$ neighborhood into the information retina. Layer R1 is made of 7 highlight maps, each associated with one feature outline C1, and essentially applies supreme esteem to its information. Layer S1 is made of 7 highlight maps of size $14 \times 24 \times 5$, each associated with one component feature map in R1. S1 performs sub-testing at a figure of 2 spatial space, intending to fabricate strength to little spatial contortions. The interface particle plot between S1 and C2 follows the same standard portrayed in [18] hence, C2 layer has 35 highlight maps performing $5 \times 5 \times 3$ convolutions. Layers R2 and S2 follow a similar guideline portrayed for R1 and S1. Layer C3 comprises of 5 highlight maps completely associated to S2 and performs $3 \times 3 \times 3$ convolutions. Each C3 include delineate $3 \times 8 \times 1$ qualities, and the information is encoded in a vector. This vector is the descriptor of the spatial information associated with the video. Layers N1 and N2 contain an established multilayer perception with one neuron for each activity in the yield layer. This design compares to a sum of 17,169 trainable parameters. To prepare this architecture, we utilize the calculation proposed in [18]. Next we describe how the learned features are used to feed a recurrent neural network (RNN) classifier, which is trained to recognize the actions based on the temporal evolution of features.

3.2 Evolution of RNN Features

We use the LSTM architecture for recognition of actions through RNN features, as described in [18]. This system utilize an exceptional hub called Steady Error Carousel (SEC), that considers consistent blunder flag engendering through time. The second entry to LSTM is the utilization of multiplicative entryways to control the entrance to the CEC. With a specific end goal to characterize the activity sequences, we propose to utilize a Repetitive Neural Organize design with one concealed layer of LSTM cells. The information layer of this RNN comprises in 120 C3 yield values for each time step. LSTM cells are completely associated with these data sources and have likewise repetitive associations with all the LSTM cells.

The yield layer of the proposed neural network model comprises of neurons associated with LSTM, for yields at every time step. We have tried a few system setup, varying the quantity of covered up LSTM in the proposed module. A setup of 50 LSTM was observed to be a decent trade off for this classification task. This architecture corresponds to about 2,000 trainable parameters. The network was trained with online back propagation through time. Figure 3 shows sample action descriptors learned by the proposed model. We can observe that, the descriptors are similar for the same actions but different across actions.

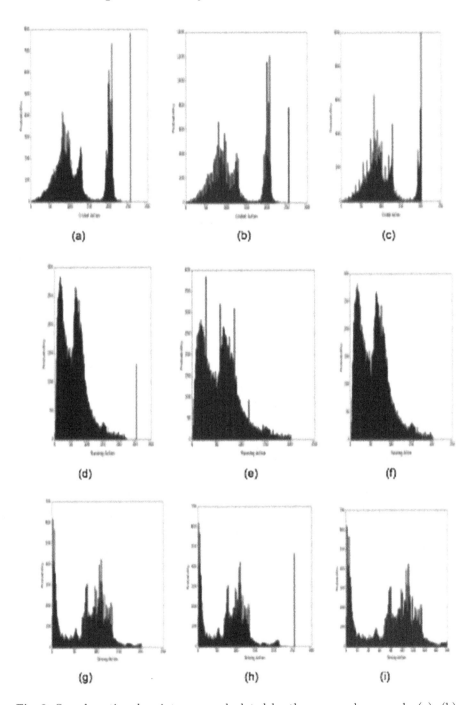

Fig. 3. Sample action descriptors, as calculated by the proposed approach. (a), (b), (c) kissing action descriptors, (d), (e), (f) running action descriptors and (g), (h), (i) driving action descriptors from Holleywood 2 dataset.

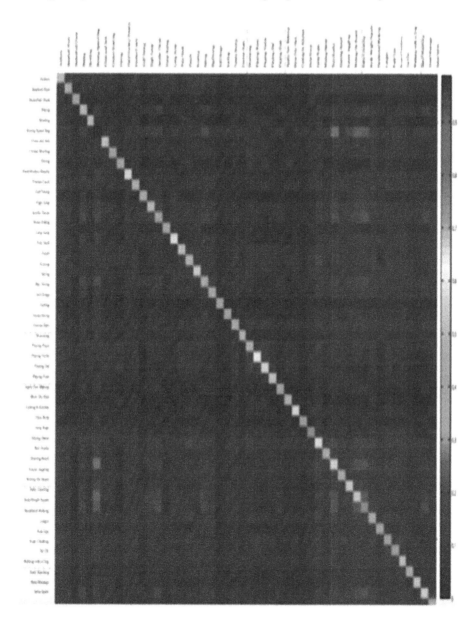

Fig. 4. Confusion matrix for UCF 101 dataset

4   Experiments and Results

We experimented with three benchmark datasets: CMU [19], UCF 101 [12] and Hollywood 2 [20] datasets. CMU Mocap dataset consists of 6 actions (Running, Walking, Kicking, Skating, Basketball and Boxing) and Holleywood 2 dataset contains 6 actions (Eat, Kiss, Run, Drive, Situp and Sit Down). The UCF 101 is a big dataset consisting of 101 action classes. All the datasets contain background clutter, dynamic illumination changes and camera movements. Large variation between the classes introduced by changes in camera viewpoint, shapes and sizes of different actors, different dressing styles, changes in execution rate of activity, individual styles of actors increase the level of difficulty.

Table 1. Confusion matrix for CMU Mocap dataset [19]

Actions	Ru	Wa	Ki	Sk	Ba	Bo
Running (Ru)	24	3	0	0	0	0
Walking (Wa)	0	30	0	0	2	0
Kicking (Ki)	0	0	20	0	0	0
Skating (Sk)	0	0	0	9	0	0
Basketball (Ba)	1	0	0	0	39	0
Boxing (Bo)	0	0	4	0	0	24

Table 2. Confusion matrix for Hollywood 2 dataset [20]

Actions	Ea	Ki	Rn	Dr	Su	Sd
Eat (Ea)	29	1	0	0	0	0
Kiss (Ki)	0	41	0	0	0	1
Run (Rn)	0	0	9	0	0	0
Drive (Dr)	0	0	0	19	0	0
Sit up (Su)	0	0	0	0	39	0
Sit down (Sd)	0	0	0	0	0	15

Tables 1 and 2 show the confusion matrices for the proposed approach applied to CMU and Holleywood 2 datasets respectively. Figure 4 shows the confusion matrix for UCF 101. Table 3 shows the accuracy of applying the proposed method on benchmark datasets compared to the state-of-the-art.

For the UCF 101 and the Hollywood 2 datasets, the proposed approach outperforms the state-of-the-art due to its ability to reduce the effect of background pixel motion during action, using the GF-STIP feature. Especially, the proposed deep architecture based on LSTM, can easily work on huge datasets like UCF 101. However, the proposed method does not performed well compared to the competing methods on CMU MoCap dataset. This may be due to the lack of sufficient number of training videos available in the dataset, to train a deep network model. Moreover, the videos in CMU MoCap dataset does not have the challenges like camera shaking, which causes background pixel motion during action. As a result, the competing methods work better on the dataset.

Table 3. Results of applying the proposed approach on the benchmark datasets compared to the competing approaches.

Methods	UCF101	CMU	Hollywood 2
Donahue et al. [18]	91.1	92.1	93.4
Singh et al. [5]	91.8	95.4	95.6
Proposed method	93.9	92.3	96.6

5 Conclusion

We have proposed a combination of 3D CNN and RNN architectures for action recognition, where an improved version of trajectories are fed into the Deep architecture for classification. The proposed method demonstrates better results on benchmark datasets compared to the state-of-the-art. This study shows that trajectories extracted from the videos can be better classified by Deep architectures, compared to raw input video. The GF-STIP based Deep network can be experimented on Egocentric datasets, which is a future research direction.

Acknowledgements. The authors wish to acknowledge the generous financial support provided by the Science and Engineering Research Board (SERB) of the Department of Science and Technology (DST), the Government of India, for conducting this research work. The financial support was provided through the project numbered ECR/2016/000652.

References

1. Ziaeefar, M., Bergevin, R.: Semantic human activity recognition: a literature review. Pattern Recognit. **48**(8), 2329–2345 (2015)
2. Laptev, I., Marszalek, M., Schmid, C., Rozenfeld, B.: Learning realistic human actions from movies. In: CVPR, pp. 1–8 (2008)
3. Chen, M.Y., Hauptmann, A.: MoSIFT: recognizing human actions in surveillance videos. Technical report CMU-CS-09-161. Carnegie Mellon University (2009)
4. Dollar, P., Rabaud, V., Cottrell, G., Belongie, S.: Behavior recognition via sparse spatio-temporal features. In: Joint IEEE International Workshop on Visual Surveillance and Performance Evaluation of Tracking and Surveillance, pp. 65–72 (2005)
5. Singh, S., Arora, C., Jawahar, C.V.: First person action recognition using deep learned descriptors. In: CVPR 2016 (2016)
6. Mukherjee, S., Biswas, S.K., Mukherjee, D.P.: Recognizing human action at a distance in video by key poses. IEEE Trans. Circ. Syst. Video Technol. **21**(9), 1228–1241 (2011)
7. Mukherjee, S., Biswas, S.K., Mukherjee, D.P.: Recognizing interactions between human performers by 'Dominating Pose Doublet'. Mach. Vis. Appl. **25**(4), 1033–1052 (2014)
8. Wang, H., Klaser, A., Schmid, C., Liu, C.-L.: Dense trajectories and motion boundary descriptors for action recognition. Int. J. Comput. Vis. **103**(1), 60–79 (2013)

9. Mukherjee, S.: Human action recognition using dominant pose duplet. In: Nalpantidis, L., Krüger, V., Eklundh, J.-O., Gasteratos, A. (eds.) ICVS 2015. LNCS, vol. 9163, pp. 488–497. Springer, Cham (2015). https://doi.org/10.1007/978-3-319-20904-3_44

10. Wang, H., Schmid, C.: Action recognition with improved trajectories. In: ICCV, pp. 3551–3558 (2013)

11. Buddubariki, V., Tulluri, S.G., Mukherjee, S.: Event recognition in egocentric videos using a novel trajectory based feature. In: ICVGIP, pp. 76:1–76:8. ACM (2016)

12. Soomro, K., Zamir, A.R., Shah, M.: UCF101: a dataset of 101 human action classes from videos in the wild. In: CRCV-TR-12-01, November 2012

13. Taylor, G.W., Fergus, R., LeCun, Y., Bregler, C.: Convolutional learning of spatio-temporal features. In: Daniilidis, K., Maragos, P., Paragios, N. (eds.) ECCV 2010. LNCS, vol. 6316, pp. 140–153. Springer, Heidelberg (2010). https://doi.org/10.1007/978-3-642-15567-3_11

14. Ji, S., Xu, W., Yang, M., Yu, K.: 3D convolutional neural networks for human action recognition. IEEE T-PAMI $35(1)$, 221–231 (2013)

15. Tran, D., Bourdev, L., Fergus, R., Torresani, L., Paluri, M.: Learning spatiotemporal features with 3D convolutional networks. In: ICCV (2015)

16. Karpathy, A., Toderici, G., Shetty, S., Leung, T., Sukthankar, R., Fei-Fei, L.: Large-scale video classification with convolutional neural networks. In: CVPR (2014)

17. Wang, L., Qiao, Y., Tang, X.: Action recognition with trajectory-pooled deep convolutional descriptors. In: CVPR (2015)

18. Donahue, J., Hendricks, L., Guadarrama, S., Rohrbach, M., Venugopalan, S., Saenko, K., Darrell, T.: Long-term recurrent convolutional networks for visual recognition and description. In: CVPR (2015)

19. CMU MoCap dataset. http://mocap.cs.cmu.edu/. Accessed Dec 2016

20. Marszalek, M., Laptev, I., Schmid, C.: Actions in context. In: CVPR (2009)

21. Bay, H., Tuytelaars, T., Van Gool, L.: SURF: speeded up robust features. In: Leonardis, A., Bischof, H., Pinz, A. (eds.) ECCV 2006. LNCS, vol. 3951, pp. 404–417. Springer, Heidelberg (2006). https://doi.org/10.1007/11744023_32

22. Mukherjee, S., Singh, K.K.: Human action and event recognition using a novel descriptor based on improved dense trajectories. Multimed. Tools Appl. (2017). https://doi.org/10.1007/s11042-017-4980-7

23. Fischler, M.A., Bolles, R.C.: Random sample consensus: a paradigm for model fitting with applications to image analysis and automated cartography. Commun. ACM $24(6)$, 381–395 (1981)

Saliency Driven Video Motion Magnification

Manisha Verma[1](✉) ⓘ, Ramyani Ghosh[2], and Shanmuganathan Raman[1]

[1] Electrical Engineering, IIT Gandhinagar, Gandhinagar, Gujarat, India
manisha.verma89@gmail.com, shanmuga@iitgn.ac.in
[2] Computer Science Engineering, PES University, Bengaluru, Karnataka, India
ramyani.ghosh@gmail.com

Abstract. The main goal of the proposed work is to detect certain spatial and temporal changes in videos that are not visible to the human eye and magnify them in order to make them perceptible while making sure that the background noise is not amplified. We apply Eulerian motion magnification on only the salient area of each frame of the video. The salient object is processed independent of the rest of the image using alpha matting aided by scribbles. We demonstrate the need to isolate the salient object from background motions and propose a simple and efficient way to do so. The proposed algorithm is tested on videos with imperceptible motion along with background motion to illustrate the significance of the proposed method. We compare the proposed method with linear and phase based Eulerian motion magnification techniques.

1 Introduction

Our environment constantly undergoes changes in color and motion. A lot of these changes are so subtle that they are imperceptible to the human eye. Needless to say, revealing these invisible changes via video processing can find numerous applications and provide interesting study in many research problems. The analysis of these changes gives significantly valuable information that is not visible naturally. Important phenomena such as human pulse from the wrist can be studied through these methods of video magnification. Efficiency, accuracy, and computational simplicity are necessary in order to use these concepts and obtain easily functional results.

Previously, Lagrangian and Eulerian magnification methods have been applied in order to make these changes visible in videos [1,2]. Lagrangian method works on the optical flow of each pixel in the video and magnifies the motion. On the other hand, Eulerian motion magnification evaluates temporal changes in two consecutive frames and magnifies accordingly. Most of the existing video magnification techniques, such as Eulerian Video Magnification (EVM), involve magnification of all the motions in the video uniformly. This process tends to unnecessarily magnify large motions in the background and may lead to noise. The unwanted magnification of all motions in the video disrupts the study of the phenomenon of amplification of imperceptible motion.

R. Rameshan et al. (Eds.): NCVPRIPG 2017, CCIS 841, pp. 89–100, 2018.
https://doi.org/10.1007/978-981-13-0020-2_9

In this paper, we discuss the use of saliency detection in order to isolate the salient region in the video [3]. Our approach is to detect the region of interest (ROI) so that video magnification can be selectively applied while leaving other motions or variations unchanged. In doing so, we have used saliency detection to get a primary idea of ROI and then apply image matting in order to get a near perfect ROI with fuzzy boundary. For motion magnification, we use Eulerian motion magnification technique which includes both linear and phase based methods. Eulerian approach is faster than Lagrangian as it uses temporal change of full frame at a time and not the optical flow of each pixel. We analyze the results of both linear and phase based Eulerian methods on the ROI.

The main contributions of the proposed work are as follows:

- We propose a fully automatic motion magnification method in order to magnify only the ROI using saliency and EVM.
- While magnifying only the ROI, the proposed approach is able to reduce noise because of the presence of the background motion.

The rest of the paper is organized as follows. Section 2 presents a brief literature review related to the problem. Saliency, image matting, and motion magnification are briefly illustrated in Sect. 3. Section 3.4 presents the proposed framework. Section 4 shows the experiments and results. Finally, the paper has been concluded in Sect. 5.

2   Related Work

Magnification of motion in videos is a field that has been explored by researchers for many years now. Numerous approaches have been made and there are multiple techniques for efficient video magnification. A Lagrangian approach was introduced by Liu *et al.* where pixel trajectories were magnified in order to magnify the motion [1]. Wang *et al.* proposed "cartoon animation filter", where an input signal was modified to make it look more animated [4]. Wu *et al.* proposed a motion magnification technique for subtle changes in the video by the method of EVM [2]. It uses Laplacian pyramids for spatial decomposition and temporal filters to calculate the temporal difference and magnification is performed on the temporal difference using an amplification factor. Further, it was improved by using complex steerable pyramids. Wadhwa *et al.* utilized the concept of phase in optical flow to develop the phase based video motion magnification [5] which was further improvised using Riesz pyramid in order to perform real-time phase based motion amplification [6]. In the Riesz pyramid, the image features are phase shifted only along their dominant directions as opposed to complex steerable pyramids where it is done for every orientation.

These methods have found numerous applications over the years. Balakrishnan *et al.* tracked subtle head motions by performing principal component analysis (PCA) and used it to extract heart rate and beat lengths from videos [7]. Eulerian magnification and empirical mode decomposition (EM-EMD) have been used to differentiate between emotional and physical stress on performing frequency division processing [8]. Face spoofing detection and facial expression recognition has been performed using Eulerian motion magnification [9,10]. Detection of pulse transit time and finger vein liveliness detection have been performed using the Eulerian color amplification [11,12].

Elgharib *et al.* used a layer based magnification that enables the magnification of small motions within large ones [13]. They used manually marked scribbles and image matting to single out the ROI and magnify subtle motions in that region. Kooji *et al.* selectively magnified motion based on the depth of layers using bilateral filters that require additional depth map information along with input video [14]. Zhang *et al.* proposed motion magnification using acceleration [15]. Instead of magnifying linear changes, they chose to magnify acceleration to avoid magnification of large motions. The proposed approach also aims to magnify the subtle motions and avoid large background motions. It does not require any additional information to locate the object of interest as it does in [13,14].

3 Saliency Driven Motion Magnification

3.1 Saliency Detection

Visual saliency is the property that makes a region or a group of regions in an image distinctively stand out from its surroundings. In the proposed work, we have used saliency detection using structure matrix decomposition (SMD) [3]. It calculates the saliency of any part of an image by calculating its color and pattern distances from its immediate surroundings. It is performed by segmenting the image into super pixels and comparing the color distances between adjacent super pixels. Simple Linear Iterative Clustering (SLIC) is used to divide the image into superpixels which makes comparison and detection easier. Superpixels simplify the extraction of features (color, edge, and texture) and help to form a feature matrix. Model based on structure matrix decomposition to detect salient object is as follows.

$$\min_{\mathrm{B,F}} \Psi(\mathrm{B}) + a\Omega(\mathrm{F}) + b\Theta(\mathrm{B,F}) \quad \mathrm{s.t.} \quad \mathrm{M} = \mathrm{B} + \mathrm{F}, \tag{1}$$

where M, B, and F are the feature matrix, background, and salient foreground respectively. $\Psi(.)$ is a low-rank constraint, $\Omega(.)$ is a structured sparsity regularization, $\Theta(.,.)$ is an interactive regularization term to enlarge the distance between the subspaces drawn from B and F, and a, b are positive parameters.

Distance between feature subspaces of salient objects (F) and background (B) is calculated using following distance measure.

$$d(\mathrm{B, F}) = ||\mathrm{BB}^T - \mathrm{FF}^T||_M^2 \tag{2}$$

SMD works by generating an index tree. Index tree is constructed from a high-level prior map obtained from location, color, and background priors. This guides the matrix decomposition, enabling better detection. On incorporating the feature matrix and the high-level prior map, it defines the low rank part and the structured sparse part. Saliency map example for three video frames are shown in Fig. 1.

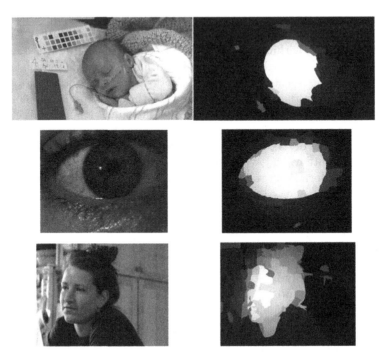

Fig. 1. Saliency examples. First and second columns represent first frames of videos and their saliency maps respectively.

3.2   Image Matting

In order to find the ROI with accuracy, image matting is performed. To do image matting, all the color and the pattern variations of the foreground need to be detected and isolated from the background while making sure that the boundary of the foreground is maintained. This is done with the help of scribbles. In order to draw appropriate scribbles, we have used super pixel segmentation and Bezier curves [16]. Initially, the salient map of the first frame is obtained using SMD based saliency detection as described in Sect. 3.1. A gray scale saliency map is converted into black and white image as an approximation of background and foreground regions using a threshold parameter. To get the region in which scribbles are to be drawn, we must make sure that no scribbles are drawn on the boundary of the object as this may cause ambiguity in the detection of the edges of the ROI in image matting. To avoid that, we invert the black and white regions and erode the boundaries, thus, effectively shrinking our detected region away from its borders. Once the above steps are done, we draw scribbles in the foreground and background regions followed by the process of alpha matting.

Scribbles: Scribbles are randomly generated using Bezier curves that are drawn on the image to distinguish between regions [16]. The scribbles are generated such that their shape and curvature ensure that the maximum variations in color and pattern of the ROI are covered and thus included in the final matte. First, the superpixels are computed to divide the foreground and background regions. The Bezier curves are generated by first selecting a random pixel within the superpixel. The next pixel is obtained by finding the mirror image of the first pixel with respect to the centroid of the current superpixel. The remaining points are placed within the superpixel by rotating and translating the same point by a random angle. The curve is then drawn by connecting six points inside the superpixel. Thus, random scribbles are generated in each superpixel.

Matting: Matting is a technique to find a gray scale approximation of foreground and background image regions with a fuzzy boundary. Matting is performed using a trimap (a pre-segmented image with absolute background, absolute foreground and unknown region) or scribbled image. An image intensity can be written as the combination of background and foreground as follows.

$$I(x,y) = \alpha(x,y)F(x,y) + (1 - \alpha(x,y))B(x,y) \tag{3}$$

where $I(x,y), F(x,y), B(x,y)$, and $\alpha(x,y)$ are pixel intensity, foreground intensity, background intensity, and foreground opacity at the position (x,y) respectively. We have utilized closed form image matting method using a scribbled image. It assumes smoothness in foreground and background in the local region of the neighborhood of each pixel and minimizes a cost function in α in order to calculate the matte.

3.3   Motion Magnification

Motion magnification methods magnify the motion in order to make it more visual. Motion magnification for subtle changes makes it possible to convert imperceptible into perceptible motion. In the proposed work, we have analysed linear and phase based Eulerian motion magnification techniques in order to magnify salient region in the video. Brief descriptions of both the methods are given below.

Linear Eulerian Video Magnification: Linear EVM decomposes the video frames into a Laplacian pyramid [2]. Temporal filters are applied on spatial bands to detect the variations in specific frequencies. Temporal processing is uniformly performed within each band of every two consecutive frames and their temporal differences are obtained. The extracted temporal differences are multiplied by the magnification factor. The magnified temporal differences are reconstructed and added back to the original frame in order to produce desired results.

A simple translational motion is considered to connect temporal processing and motion magnification [2]. If the linear displacement function is $d(t)$, image intensity as a function of the linear motion is given by:

$$A(x,t) = f(x + d(t)) \tag{4}$$

The magnified intensity can then be given by the expression:

$$\bar{A}(x,t) = f(x + (1 + \beta)d(t)) \tag{5}$$

where β is the magnification factor. This is a simple method with very low computational cost involved, however it works for small magnification factors and magnifies background noise with an increment in the magnification factor.

Phase-Based Motion Magnification: Phase based motion magnification uses the concept of the phase and applies magnification to phase differences in order to magnify the motion [5]. This method of video magnification uses complex steerable pyramids. The motion is amplified in selected frequency bands by performing temporal processing. Small motions are amplified by modifying the local phase variations in a complex steerable pyramid for every orientation and scale. Once magnification is applied, the original video is reconstructed from the pyramid.

3.4   Framework

We have used both linear and phase based methods to magnify the video for salient region. Since the motion of desired object is very less, scribbles are drawn only on the first frame of the video and it is assumed that the scribbles will be on the right place throughout the video as the object has no large motion. The method has two phases, the first is to obtain foreground object and the second is to apply magnification to the foreground object only.

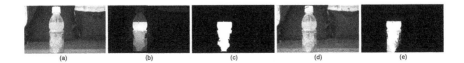

Fig. 2. (a) Video frame, (b) Saliency map, (c) Threshold, (d) Scribbles and (e) Alpha matte.

Pipeline of the proposed work with linear and phase based methods is as follows.

3.5   Phase 1

Initially, the video is uploaded and saliency map of the first frame is calculated using structured matrix decomposition (SMD) saliency detection [3] as shown in Fig. 2(b). The saliency map has gray scale intensities where light to dark represents higher saliency to lower saliency of object. To determine the foreground object, gray scale saliency map is thresholded and a black & white image is obtained for a possible foreground and background approximation (Fig. 2(b)). The foreground and background object boundaries are eroded before drawing scribbles in order to maintain the scribbles only inside the object and not on the boundaries. After erosion, the foreground and the background images are divided into super pixels and at the centroid of each super pixel, Bezier curves are drawn [16,17] (Fig. 2(d)). Image matting is performed with the help of closed form alpha matting as shown in Fig. 2(e).

3.6   Phase 2

In phase two, we have used both linear and phase based methods to magnify the salient region. Work flows of both the methods are as follows.

Linear: Input video frames are decomposed into sub-band images using the Laplacian pyramid. Every pixel of each sub-band image is passed through a temporal filter and temporal difference of two consecutive frames is obtained. Temporal difference is magnified using a magnification factor and multiplied with the alpha matte (calculated in Phase 1) in order to remove the magnification of the background. The magnified temporal difference of foreground region is reconstructed using the Laplacian pyramid and added back to the original frame. The process is applied to all the video frames in order to obtain the resultant video.

Phase Based: Alpha matte is multiplied with all the video frames and complex steerable pyramids are calculated for each frame. Phase difference is calculated between the frames and magnified in order to magnify motion. After magnification, pyramid is reconstructed in the original form and summed up with the background of each frame (inversion of alpha matte), and hence the motion magnified video is produced.

4   Experiments and Results

Experiments have been performed on various videos which were previously used in [2,5] for motion magnification and new videos with large background motions. The proposed method uses both the linear and the phase based motion magnification. Hence, experiments have been performed to test both the techniques and results have been compared with both the previous methods [2,5]. Threshold parameter which is used to convert saliency map to approximate background and foreground (black and white), is kept empirical (approximately .45 and can be adjusted as required) as motion magnification of the foreground is significant and it should not be missed and small intervention of background as false foreground is acceptable. Moreover, this parameter can be set automatically according to intensities of saliency map. Motion magnification parameters depend on the frequency which needs to be magnified. A few experimental results are presented here to show the absence of noise in the proposed method as compared to the previous methods. Space-time graphs for a particular pixel range are plotted in order to measure the difference in motion from the original video and the motion magnified video.

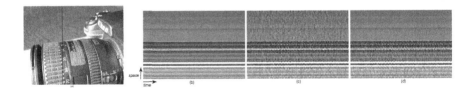

Fig. 3. (a) First frame of camera sequence with highlighted black line, (b) space-time plot of original video of highlighted black line, (c) motion magnified plot using [2], and (d) motion magnified plot using the proposed method.

In all the experiment figures, first original frame of video is shown with some highlighted pixels with black line, which are shown in space-time intensity plot. In Fig. 3, variations of camera video sequence are shown. Figure 3(a) is first image of camera video sequence and horizontal black line is shown for original video, linear Eulerian motion magnification and saliency driven linear motion magnification in Fig. 3(b), (c) and (d). Camera motion is nearly invisible to human eyes as shown very straight in Fig. 3(b). Motion magnified video using [2] is shown to be producing noise along with motion magnification for camera.

In Fig. 4, variations of eye video sequence are shown. Figure 4(a) is first image of eye video sequence and vertical black line is shown for original video, linear Eulerian motion magnification and saliency driven linear motion magnification in Fig. 4(b), (c), and (d). Eye ball movement is nearly invisible as it is seen to be straight in Fig. 4(b). Motion magnified video using [2] is shown to be producing noise due to magnification surrounding motions.

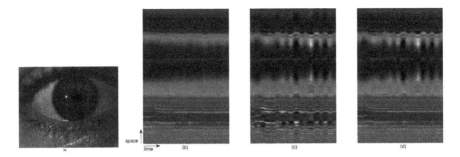

Fig. 4. (a) First frame of eye sequence with highlighted black line, (b) space-time plot of original video of highlighted black line, (c) motion magnified plot using [2], and (d) motion magnified plot using the proposed method.

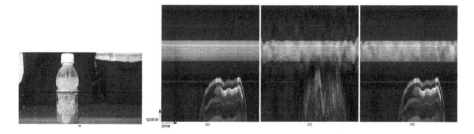

Fig. 5. (a) First frame of bottle sequence with highlighted black line, (b) space-time plot of original video of highlighted black line, (c) motion magnified plot using [5], and (d) motion magnified plot using the proposed method. (Color figure online)

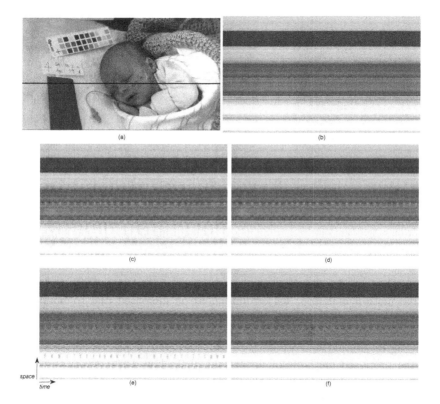

Fig. 6. (a) First frame of baby video, (b) space-time plot of original video, (c) motion magnified plot using [2], (d) motion magnified plot using the proposed method with linear motion magnification, (e) motion magnification using [5], and (f) motion magnified plot using the proposed method with phase based motion magnification.

In Fig. 5, the results of the phase based method are shown on a video sequence of a juice bottle, where a bottle of juice is still and the background has large motions over different times. As shown in Fig. 5(a), the bottle is still all over the period (yellow stripe) and after a few frames there is motion in the video. In the

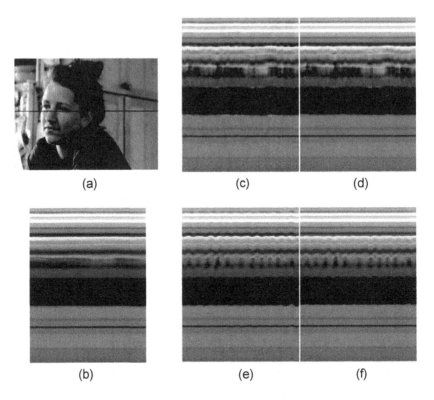

Fig. 7. (a) First frame of woman video, (b) space-time plot of original video, (c) motion magnified plot using [2], (d) motion magnified plot using the proposed method with linear motion magnification, (e) motion magnification using [5], and (f) motion magnified plot using the proposed method with phase based motion magnification.

magnified video using [5], the large motion is magnified along with the bottle's invisible motion and also, background noise is increased due to unnecessary magnification. On the contrary, the proposed method detected the salient object (bottle) and magnified the desired motion.

In Fig. 6, comparisons of both the linear and the phased based methods with the proposed methods of linear and phase based framework are shown. In Fig. 6(a), the first frame of the baby sequence is shown with highlighted black line to show the variation over time. In Fig. 6(b), the space-time plot of the original frame is shown that represents almost no change over time. In Figs. 6(c) and 6(d), plots of motion magnified videos are shown of [2] and the proposed framework with linear motion magnification. It is clearly visible that the proposed method has overcome the noise and magnifies only the breath of the baby. On the other hand, phase based method produces more significant amplification and the proposed phase based method removes the other outliers except the breath as shown in Figs. 6(e) and (f).

Again in Fig. 7, space-time plot of for both linear and phase-based motion magnification are shown. Similarly as Fig. 6, in this example also first frame of woman video is shown with a black line (Fig. 7(a)). In Fig. 7(b), variation of spatial intensities are shown over time, where movement is negligible. In Fig. 7(c–f), motion magnified space-time plots are illustrated. Linear motion magnification using [2] and the proposed saliency method are shown in Figs. 7(c) and 7(d) respectively. As compare to [2], the proposed method avoid unnecessary motion magnification in background of woman. Similarly, motion magnification using [5] and the proposed method (using phase based) are shown in Figs. 7(e) and 7(f). Phase-based method produce less noise as compare to linear motion magnification. However, the proposed saliency method helps in removing noise because of outliers.

5   Conclusion

In this paper, we have proposed an efficient method to automatically detect the ROI and apply magnification selectively. We combine object detection techniques with EVM and presented a model that effectively amplifies only the motions of the salient object, thus eliminating background noise and making the result more significant to video magnification applications. We would like to improve this work by processing foregrounds such as transparent objects for which matting is not directly applicable.

Acknowledgement. The authors would like to thank SERB-DST for support through Young Scientists Startup Research Grant.

References

1. Liu, C., Torralba, A., Freeman, W.T., Durand, F., Adelson, E.H.: Motion magnification. ACM Trans. Graph. **24**(3), 519–526 (2005)
2. Wu, H.Y., Rubinstein, M., Shih, E., Guttag, J., Durand, F., Freeman, W.: Eulerian video magnification for revealing subtle changes in the world. ACM Trans. Graph. **31**(4), 1–8 (2012)
3. Peng, H., Li, B., Ling, H., Hu, W., Xiong, W., Maybank, S.J.: Salient object detection via structured matrix decomposition. IEEE Trans. Pattern Anal. Mach. Intell. **39**(4), 818–832 (2017)
4. Wang, J., Drucker, S.M., Agrawala, M., Cohen, M.F.: The cartoon animation filter. ACM Trans. Graph. **25**(3), 1169–1173 (2006)
5. Wadhwa, N., Rubinstein, M., Durand, F., Freeman, W.T.: Phase-based video motion processing. ACM Trans. Graph. **32**(4), 80 (2013)
6. Wadhwa, N., Rubinstein, M., Durand, F., Freeman, W.T.: Riesz pyramids for fast phase-based video magnification. In: Proceedings of IEEE International Conference on Computational Photography, pp. 1–10 (2014)
7. Balakrishnan, G., Durand, F., Guttag, J.: Detecting pulse from head motions in video. In: Proceedings of the IEEE Conference on Computer Vision and Pattern Recognition, pp. 3430–3437 (2013)
8. Hong, K.: Classification of emotional stress and physical stress using facial imaging features. J. Opt. Technol. **83**(8), 508–512 (2016)

9. Bharadwaj, S., Dhamecha, T.I., Vatsa, M., Singh, R.: Computationally efficient face spoofing detection with motion magnification. In: Proceedings of the IEEE Conference on Computer Vision and Pattern Recognition Workshops, 105–110 (2013)
10. Park, S.Y., Lee, S.H., Ro, Y.M.: Subtle facial expression recognition using adaptive magnification of discriminative facial motion. In: Proceedings of the 23rd ACM International Conference on Multimedia, pp. 911–914. ACM (2015)
11. He, X., Goubran, R.A., Liu, X.P.: Using Eulerian video magnification framework to measure pulse transit time. In: 2014 IEEE International Symposium on Medical Measurements and Applications (MeMeA), pp. 1–4. IEEE (2014)
12. Raghavendra, R., Avinash, M., Marcel, S., Busch, C.: Finger vein liveness detection using motion magnification. In: 2015 IEEE 7th International Conference on Biometrics Theory, Applications and Systems (BTAS), pp. 1–7. IEEE (2015)
13. Elgharib, M., Hefeeda, M., Durand, F., Freeman, W.T.: Video magnification in presence of large motions. In: Proceedings of the IEEE Conference on Computer Vision and Pattern Recognition, pp. 4119–4127 (2015)
14. Kooij, J.F.P., van Gemert, J.C.: Depth-aware motion magnification. In: Leibe, B., Matas, J., Sebe, N., Welling, M. (eds.) ECCV 2016. LNCS, vol. 9912, pp. 467–482. Springer, Cham (2016). https://doi.org/10.1007/978-3-319-46484-8_28
15. Zhang, Y., Pintea, S.L., van Gemert, J.C.: Video acceleration magnification. arXiv preprint arXiv:1704.04186 (2017)
16. Sonane, B., Ramakrishnan, S., Raman, S.: Automatic video matting through scribble propagation. In: Proceedings of the Tenth Indian Conference on Computer Vision, Graphics and Image Processing, vol. 87, no. (1–87), p. 8 (2016)
17. Achanta, R., Shaji, A., Smith, K., Lucchi, A., Fua, P., Süsstrunk, S.: SLIC superpixels. Technical report (2010)

Detecting Missed and Anomalous Action Segments Using Approximate String Matching Algorithm

Hiteshi Jain$^{(\boxtimes)}$ and Gaurav Harit

Indian Institute of Technology Jodhpur, Jodhpur, India
{jain.4,gharit}@iitj.ac.in

Abstract. We forget action steps and perform some unwanted action movements as amateur performers during our daily exercise routine, dance performances, etc. To improve our proficiency, it is important that we get a feedback on our performances in terms of where we went wrong. In this paper, we propose a framework for analyzing and issuing reports of action segments that were missed or anomalously performed. This involves comparing the performed sequence with the standard action sequence and notifying when misalignments occur. We propose an exemplar based Approximate String Matching (ASM) technique for detecting such anomalous and missing segments in action sequences. We compare the results with those obtained from the conventional Dynamic Time Warping (DTW) algorithm for sequence alignment. It is seen that the alignment of the action sequences under conventional DTW fails in the presence of missed action segments and anomalous segments due to its boundary condition constraints. The performance of the two techniques has been tested on a complex aperiodic human action dataset with Warm up exercise sequences that we developed from correct and incorrect executions by multiple people. The proposed ASM technique shows promising alignment and missed/anomalous notification results over this dataset.

Keywords: Missed action · Anomalous action
Dynamic Time Warping · Approximate String Matching

1 Introduction

Assisting the users while performing their daily exercise routine, dance practice, etc. helps them improve their proficiency. This assistance has long been into existence from human experts like therapists, dance experts, etc. However, the increased expenses of dance classes, therapy sessions and activities that require trainers, discourage people to include these in their daily routine. To overcome this, computer vision community has recently been persuaded to make automatic training systems that provide visual hints to the performers and motivate them to perform better by giving them appropriate feedbacks.

© Springer Nature Singapore Pte Ltd. 2018
R. Rameshan et al. (Eds.): NCVPRIPG 2017, CCIS 841, pp. 101–111, 2018.
https://doi.org/10.1007/978-981-13-0020-2_10

Researchers have recently made attempts to develop automatic assessment and feedback systems for many use cases - sports [1], health care [2], entertainment [3], physical exercises [4], etc. Long-term human actions like warm-up exercise, dance performances consists of time-sequential postures. While performing such actions, the amateur performers tend to miss or wrongly perform a few segments of these long term action sequences. To the best of our knowledge, automated technique to report missed and anomalous human action segments have not been developed in the past. As a part of this work, we compare the performance of people to the gold performance instances and provide a feedback to performers on where they miss a posture subsequence or perform an anomalous pose sequence in between using a string matching technique. The proposed framework has been tested on 24 warm up exercise sequences. Results are compared with those obtained using the Dynamic Time Warping (DTW) algorithm [12], a time-series similarity measurement which minimizes the effects of shifting and distortion in time to detect similar performances.

2   Related Work

Action quality assessment is a less explored area in computer vision. Past works include a few promising attempts towards action specific assessment that tell how well people perform basketball activity, coordinated human activity etc. discussed in [6–8]. However, these works are action specific assessments and do not generalize.

Generalized assessment is broadly classified into two category of works - first where a generalized model is developed from training videos, and the test videos are compared against the model to find the scores. The second category includes exemplar based works where a test sequence is compared with a single gold standard action performance and the scores are evaluated. Among the learning based methods, Pirsiavah et al. [1] have proposed a generic framework to evaluate human actions based on postures and provide feedback on how they can improve their actions. They trained a regression model from spatio-temporal pose features to scores obtained from expert judges. Following this, Venkataraman et al. [9] introduced the approximate entropy-based feature over poses and used them with SVM regressors to achieve the state-of-the-art performance in action quality assessment [1]. Exemplar based methods include works [2,3] where dance and rehabilitation performances are assessed against the performance by a dance teacher and medical expert. These works use standard rule based methods, dynamic time warping alignments to assess the performances.

Both of these approaches work towards overall score evaluation of the performers and do not attempt towards reporting of details like missed action segments or anomalous action segments. As a part of this work we develop an exemplar based string matching technique that can help notify performers for where they missed an action or have performed an anomalous action.

3   Proposed Approach

As a part of this section, we first define how we represent action sequences in terms of pose sequences and then propose our method to find missed and anomalous segments in the video using Approximate String Matching technique.

3.1   Pose Estimation

We use the stacked hourglass network [5] for human pose estimation. This deep pose model gives state-of-the-art pose estimates over two benchmark datasets, FLIC and MPII Human pose dataset. For each frame the network estimates a pose with 16 joint locations (right ankle, right knee, right hip, left hip, left knee, left ankle, pelvis, neck, thorax, head, right wrist, right elbow, right shoulder, left shoulder, left elbow, left wrist). The joint locations of a pose are normalized relative to the head position thus making them translation invariant [1].

Let $p_x^{(j)}(t)$ be the x component of the jth joint in the tth frame then the normalized joint has its x coordinate given as $s_x^{(j)}(t) = p_x^{(j)}(t) - p_x^h(t)$, where $p_x^h(t)$ is the x coordinate of the head location of the human. Further, the normalized joint points are represented using 8 vectors (Fig. 1) of the form: $(rK \rightarrow rA)$, $(rH \rightarrow rK)$, $(lK \rightarrow lA)$, $(lH \rightarrow lK)$, $(rE \rightarrow rW)$, $(rS \rightarrow rE)$, $(lE \rightarrow lW)$, $(lS \rightarrow lE)$, where K, A, H, E, W, S denote knee, ankle, hip, elbow, wrist and shoulder respectively and prefix l, r indicate left or right. As an example, vector v_1, that connects *right knee* and *right ankle*, is given by $v_1 = [v_x \ v_y] = [(s_x^{rK} - s_x^{rA}) \ (s_y^{rK} - s_y^{rA})]$.

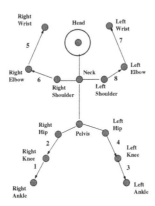

Fig. 1. Pose-vector representation

3.2   Approximate String Matching Algorithm

Approximate String Matching (ASM) has been originally used to solve string matching problem. Given the test video Q composed of pose symbols $q_1, q_2, q_3,$ $\ldots, q_M$ and the standard template video A with pose symbols $a_1, a_2, a_3, \ldots, a_N$,

ASM finds the smallest number of edit operations that can transform Q into A i.e. ASM finds how test pattern Q is generated from the standard sequence A by calculating the minimum edit distance between Q and A. Let $d_e(i,j)$ denote the minimum edit distance to transform the first j symbols of Q into the first i symbols of A. At each symbol q_j, the editing operations are as follows:

1. *Substitution:* The pose symbol a_i is approximately matched with pose symbol q_j or is substituted by pose symbol q_j with an additional cost $\delta(a_i, q_j)$.
2. *Insertion:* There is an extra pose symbol a_i in A which needs to be inserted into Q with an insertion cost $\delta(\epsilon, a_i)$.
3. *Deletion:* There is an extra pose symbol q_j in Q which needs to be deleted from Q with a deletion cost $\delta(q_j, \epsilon)$.

ASM can be solved using dynamic programming and the edit distance at grid (i,j) is defined as:

$$
d_e(i,j) = \begin{cases} d_e(i-1,j-1), & \text{if } cost(a_i, q_j) \le th \\ \min \begin{pmatrix} d_e(i-1,j-1) + \delta(a_i, q_j) \\ d_e(i,j-1) + \delta(\epsilon, a_i) \\ d_e(i-1,j) + \delta(q_j, \epsilon) \end{pmatrix}, & \text{otherwise} \end{cases}
$$

i.e. the edit distance at grid (i,j) remains unaltered if the difference between the two poses a_i and q_j is less than a threshold th which is set to 0.5 for our experiments. This difference between the poses $cost(a_i, q_j)$ is the sum of cosine distances for all the 8 pose vectors. For k^{th} pose vector for frames i and j of sequences Q and V, the cosine distance is computed as

$$
dist_{v_k}^{ij} = (v_k^i \ldots v_k^j)/(\|v_k^i\| \, \|v_k^j\|)
$$

The three operation costs - insert, delete and substitution costs are all set to 1.

Once all the operations needed to transform the test sequence Q to the standard sequence A are determined, the next step is to interpret these operations. A burst of insert operations implies that there is action segment which is missing in the test sequence Q at location s, the starting point of the burst of insertions. Similarly, a burst of delete operations implies that there is action segment which is anomalously performed in the test sequence Q at location s, where the burst of deletions start. This segment does not exist in the standard sequence A and is thus anomalous. Substitution operations occur when the poses in the two sequences are not significantly different i.e. a little adjustment of the pose of the performer is sufficient. Figure 2 illustrates the different operations and their interpretations regarding missed actions and anomalous actions on our standard sequence and one of the test sequences from the dataset.

DTW has been used to align similar movements [10,11] to formulate action similarity scores that measure the difference between two time series with different durations. In the next section we examine how conventional DTW algorithm can be used to find missing and anomalous action segments and discuss the problems encountered by this technique. The notification accuracies from the ASM technique is then compared with the baseline DTW algorithm in Sect. 5.

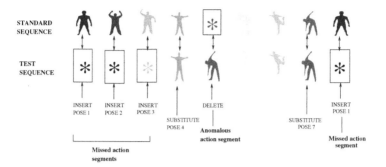

Fig. 2. Approximate String Matching illustration

4   Conventional Dynamic Time Warping

Given a test action pose sequence Q and a compared action video A, our system aims to find: (1) all video segments in the standard action sequence A that are missed by the performer during his performance Q. (2) all video segments in the performer's action sequence Q that do not occur in the standard sequence A and are anomalous. This requires aligning the two sequences and reporting whenever there are misalignments.

Dynamic Time Warping is a widely used exemplar based sequence matching approach. It is a nonlinear time warping scheme that aims to find the best warping function between any two input signals which gives the minimal total distance. It is tolerant to some degree of time variation between the sequences. The technique uses some constraints to reduce the search space which are -

- **monotonicity constraint** - that prevents the warping path from going back in time axis
- **boundary conditions** - that limits the warping path to start from the first time instance and end at the last time instance for both the test and the standard sequences.

Given a test sequence Q composed of poses $\{q_1, q_2, q_3, \ldots, q_M\}$ and a compared action video sequence A containing poses $\{a_1, a_2, a_3, \ldots, a_N\}$, a DTW table of size $M \times N$ is created and the boundaries are set as infinity. For $1 \leq i \leq M$ and $1 \leq j \leq N$, each grid (i, j) is filled with a minimum warping distance defined by

$$d_w(i, j) = min \begin{pmatrix} d_w(i - 1, j - 1) \\ d_w(i, j - 1) \\ d_w(i - 1, j) \end{pmatrix} + cost(i, j)$$

The DTW method backtracks from the end grid (M, N) to the start grid (1, 1) and construct the entire alignment path which is invariant to temporal transformation.

The existence of missing action segments is marked by the existence of a single frame of the performer's sequence Q aligned to multiple frames from the standard sequence A with count $> th$. Likewise the existence of a single frame of the standard sequence A aligned to multiple frames with count $> th$ from the performer's sequence Q marks the beginning of anomalous action segments as can be seen in Fig. 3.

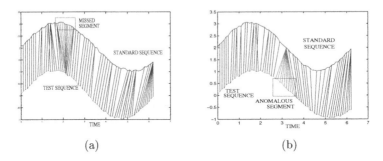

(a)   (b)

Fig. 3. DTW alignment: (a) with missed actions (b) anomalous actions

However, the alignment of two sequences by the conventional DTW in the presence of such segments is not appropriate. The boundary conditions force the initial and end frames of both the sequences to match to each other leading to misalignment in the rest of the sequence. The misalignment due to boundary conditions can be seen in Fig. 4 where in (a) alignment between two sequences: standard sequence $\{1\,2\,3\,4\,5\,6\,7\,1\}$ and test sequence: $\{3\,4\,5\,6\,7\}$ is illustrated. The boundary condition of DTW forces both the sequences to align from the first frame and finish aligning at the last frames of both the sequences. This leads to misaligned action segments 1 and 4 in the beginning and action segments 7 and 1 at the end and result into action segments that are incorrectly classified as an anomaly or a missed action (false alarms and missed alarms). Figure 4(b) illustrates alignment of example sequence with an anomalous segment and clearly shows misalignments both at the end and the middle of the sequence.

This however is not the case in the ASM technique which is not constrained to begin matching at the initial frame or match the last frames of the two sequences. If there are some action segments missed by a performer at the beginning of the execution, a sequence of insert frame operations are performed until a correctly matching segment is seen. This insert frame operations signify a missed action segment. Similar is the case for anomalous actions, where the delete frame operations are performed until the frames of query sequence and standard gold sequence are matched.

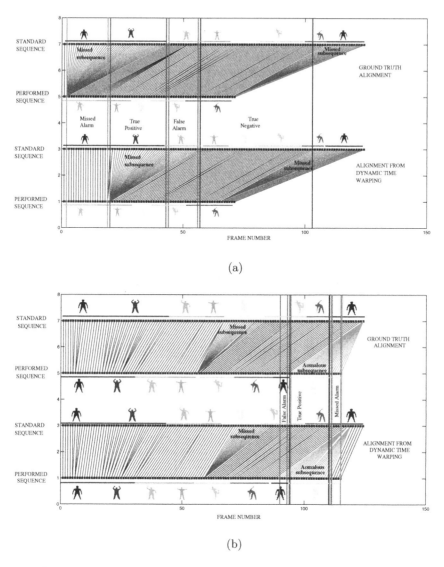

Fig. 4. Alignment from Conventional DTW: (a) *alignment with red lines* - missed frames alignment (b) *alignment with green lines* - anomalous frames alignment (c) *alignment with blue lines* - alignment of performed sub-actions (Color figure online)

5   Experiments and Results

Dataset: We developed a *Warm up exercises* dataset with 25 videos of which 1 was a correct action execution while 24 were incorrect executions. The complete sequence consists of 7 sub-actions with the first sub-action repeated at the end as shown in Fig. 5. By incorrect sequences we mean that some of the poses were missed or some anomalous sub-action was performed. The videos were shot for 3 subjects who were asked to perform the sequence while missing some sub-actions and performing anomalous actions. Some of the sample frames from the dataset are shown in Fig. 6. The trimmed sequences of 25 performances are as shown in Fig. 7, where sequence 1 is the correct sequence while the rest are incorrect.

Evaluation: We evaluate the proposed system as a notification module. The accuracy of our notification system can be measured in terms of precision/recall metric. The correctness of a notification is measured in a δ neighborhood of

Fig. 5. Warm up exercise sequence

Fig. 6. Dataset frames

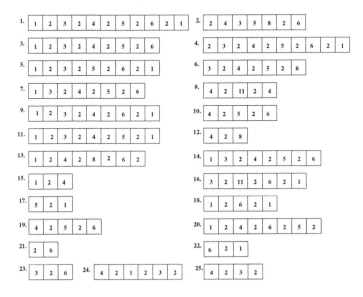

Fig. 7. Action sequences

Table 1. Performance accuracy for missed action notification (under tolerance of 25 frames)

Technique	Precision	Recall
ASM	1	1
DTW	0.836	0.874

Table 2. Performance accuracy for anomalous action notification (under tolerance of 25 frames)

Technique	Precision	Recall
ASM	1	1
DTW	0.758	0.91

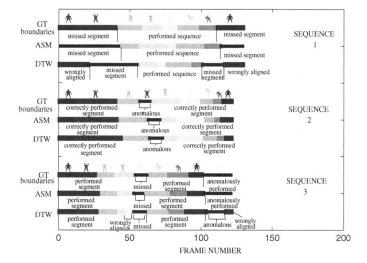

Fig. 8. Qualitative results of notification and segmentation modules: Ground truth (GT) illustrates the correct notification and segmentation boundaries and compared to ASM and DTW based boundaries

boundaries of groundtruth missed or groundtruth anomalous sub-actions. This means that if a notification of missed segment or anomalously performed action is given in the δ neighborhood of the groundtruth time, it is counted as correct. In our experiments, δ is set as 25 frames, i.e. roughly within 1 second of when it was missed based on the frame rate of 25 fps. Tables 1 and 2 list the accuracies of notification module towards missed action and anomalous action detection. It can be seen that the Approximate String Matching technique can correctly notify for all anomalous action and missed action steps while the conventional Dynamic Time Warping technique fails to report the same. The lower precision recall in case of DTW is mostly attributed to the misalignment caused due to boundary conditions.

Further, segmentation accuracies of the two algorithms is measured. The sub-action boundaries are identified after aligning the test sequence with the standard template. Segmentation accuracies were found to be 86.54% and 67.15% for ASM and DTW respectively. Thus it is seen that ASM outperforms the baseline DTW both as notification and alignment module. Figure 8 shows the qualitative results of segmentation and notification modules for three test sequences. It can be seen that DTW technique results in misaligned segments that are false alarms and missed alarms. ASM in contrast, shows no misaligned segments leading to a precision/recall of 1. However, discrepancies in sub-action boundary alignments leads to a reduced segmentation accuracy.

6 Conclusion

Action quality assessment is an important research area that has recently attracted many computer vision researchers. Works in past have evaluated performer's scores against gold standard performances. As a part of this work we attempt to make a notification module that can report for missed and anomalous action segments in the performance. We demonstrate how the string matching techniques can be extended to pose sequence matching and detect missed and anomalous action segments in the performances and compare its performance with the baseline Dynamic Time Warping technique for alignment. It is seen that the ASM technique successfully notifies all missed and anomalous actions in the videos while the Dynamic time warping technique fails to align properly and gives incorrect notifications due to its boundary conditions.

Acknowledgment. We thank Divya Srivastava, Arnav Chopra, Aayush Sarda, Kushagra Surana and Rohil Surana for contributing towards creating dataset of Warm Up Exercise videos and their constant support throughout the work.

References

1. Pirsiavash, H., Vondrick, C., Torralba, A.: Assessing the quality of actions. In: Fleet, D., Pajdla, T., Schiele, B., Tuytelaars, T. (eds.) ECCV 2014. LNCS, vol. 8694, pp. 556–571. Springer, Cham (2014). https://doi.org/10.1007/978-3-319-10599-4_36
2. Su, C.-J.: Personal rehabilitation exercise assistant with kinect and dynamic time warping. Int. J. Inf. Educ. Technol. **3**(4), 448 (2013)
3. Alexiadis, D.S., Daras, P.: Quaternionic signal processing techniques for automatic evaluation of dance performances from MoCap data. IEEE Trans. Multimed. **16**(5), 1391–1406 (2014)
4. Jain, H., Harit, G.: A framework to assess sun salutation videos. In: Proceedings of the Tenth Indian Conference on Computer Vision, Graphics and Image Processing, p. 29. ACM (2016)
5. Newell, A., Yang, K., Deng, J.: Stacked hourglass networks for human pose estimation. In: Leibe, B., Matas, J., Sebe, N., Welling, M. (eds.) ECCV 2016. LNCS, vol. 9912, pp. 483–499. Springer, Cham (2016). https://doi.org/10.1007/978-3-319-46484-8_29
6. Perše, M., Kristan, M., Perš, J., Kovačič, S.: Automatic Evaluation of Organized Basketball Activity using Bayesian Networks. Citeseer, Princeton (2007)
7. Jug, M., Perš, J., Dežman, B., Kovačič, S.: Trajectory based assessment of coordinated human activity. In: Crowley, J.L., Piater, J.H., Vincze, M., Paletta, L. (eds.) ICVS 2003. LNCS, vol. 2626, pp. 534–543. Springer, Heidelberg (2003). https://doi.org/10.1007/3-540-36592-3_51

8. Gordon, A.S.: Automated video assessment of human performance. In: Proceedings of AI-ED, pp. 16–19 (1995)
9. Venkataraman, V., Vlachos, I., Turaga, P.: Dynamical regularity for action analysis. In: BMVC, p. 67-1 (2015)
10. Su, C.-J., Chiang, C.-Y., Huang, J.-Y.: Kinect-enabled home-based rehabilitation system using dynamic time warping and fuzzy logic. Appl. Soft Comput. **22**, 652–666 (2014)
11. Hu, M.-C., Chen, C.-W., Cheng, W.-H., Chang, C.-H., Lai, J.-H., Wu, J.-L.: Real-time human movement retrieval and assessment with kinect sensor. IEEE Trans. Cybern. **45**(4), 742–753 (2015)
12. Sakoe, H., Chiba, S.: Dynamic programming algorithm optimization for spoken word recognition. IEEE Trans. Acoust. Speech Sign. Process. **26**(1), 43–49 (1978)

Parametric Reshaping of Humans in Videos Incorporating Motion Retargeting

Suresh Prakash[(✉)] and Prem Kalra

IIT Delhi, Delhi, India
sureshiitdcs@gmail.com, pkalra@cse.iitd.ac.in

Abstract. We propose a system capable of changing the shape of humans in monocular video sequences. Initially, a 3D model is fit over each frame of the video sequence in a spatio-temporally coherent manner, using the feature points provided by the user in a semi-automatic interface and the silhouette correspondences obtained from background subtraction. The 3D morphable model learned from laser scans of different human subjects is used to generate a model having the shape parameters like height, weight, leg length, etc. specified by the user. The deformed model is then retargeted to transfer the semantics of the motion, like step size of the person. This retargeted model is used to perform a body-aware warping of the foreground of each frame. Finally, the warped foreground is composited over the inpainted background. Spatio-temporal consistency is achieved through the combination of automatic pose fitting and body-aware frame warping. Motion retargeting makes the system produce visually pleasing and natural results like the motion of a taller human is higher than that of the human before warping. We have demonstrated the results of shape changes on different subjects with a variety of actions.

Keywords: Video retouching · Video editing · Reshaping humans
Application of motion retargeting

1 Introduction

Image editing tools like Adobe Photoshop, GIMP, etc., allow body retouching operations to local regions. Thus, in order to achieve globally consistent shape change (height increase/decrease, weight increase/decrease, etc.) of humans in single images, it requires a collection of large number of local modifications. Moreover, this change is neither applicable to different subjects nor to the same subject in different poses. [14] proposed a system for reshaping human subjects in images. Background artifacts are produced by this method and these artifacts are eliminated by a method proposed by [8]. Applying this method to each

Electronic supplementary material The online version of this chapter (https://doi.org/10.1007/978-981-13-0020-2_11) contains supplementary material, which is available to authorized users.

frame of the video requires fitting pose in every single frame. Fitting the pose manually in every frame is not only a tedious process but also lacks consistency across frames and therefore creates sliding effects in motion. Therefore, we need a method to consistently track human pose for the whole video sequence.

[6] proposed a combined pose and shape tracking approach followed by MLS warping for achieving shape change of humans in videos. However, the major drawback of their method is that it does not maintain the motion semantics like step size when the shape of the human is changed. For this purpose, motion retargeting becomes important. The major difference of our method as compared to [6] is that we apply motion retargeting after pose tracking, which transfers the motion to the reshaped model in a semantically correct way. This difference could be clearly observed in our results.

[11] proposed a system for reshaping human videos captured using special acquisition devices like Kinect. However, our system works well with the videos captured using normal acquisition devices and does not need any special devices for the video acquisition. [13] tries to produce 3D models in the desired shape and pose by adjusting the semantic parameters. However, we try to address a different problem of reshaping human subjects in video footages. After retargeting, we apply the body-aware reshaping method proposed by [8] to each frame rather than applying MLS as suggested by [6]. Reshaping method by [8] does not require precise tracking, thereby reducing human intervention. The proposed system has immediate applications in movie post-production to change the semantic attributes of actors like height, weight, etc.

2   Previous Work

2.1   Image Warping and Reshaping

Image warping methods like Moving Least Squares [15] allow users to manipulate an image through a set of control handles specified on it and propagate changes from the control handle to the rest of the image. However, these methods are not context based and therefore the warping result is highly dependent on the fitting quality. [14] proposed a warping approach for the parametric reshaping of humans in images to adhere the human shape to the specified semantic attributes by resizing the human body along and orthogonal to the skeletal bones in order to achieve global consistency. The artifacts produced by this method, especially in the background, are removed by warping only the foreground, as presented by [8]. However, applying [8] to each frame in the video requires the subject pose to be defined in each of the frames in a spatio-temporally consistent manner. Moreover, doing so does not produce natural results without motion retargeting.

2.2   Video Reshaping

[6] applied the parametric reshaping of humans to videos in a spatio-temporally consistent way using Moving Least Squares warping method. However, their method produces visible artifacts when there are drastic variations in the semantic attributes. Their method also requires very accurate tracking (of both pose

and shape) due to the MLS warping approach. Moreover, they do not perform background inpainting, limiting the amount of decrease in the semantic attributes. The approach also requires pose ambiguities to be corrected manually, when the shape parameters are modified over the normal range. The approach does not produce natural motion, especially when the shape edits create changes in skeletal dimensions, due to the lack of motion retargeting. For example, the results produced by their method creates unnatural effects like a dwarf taking longer steps, when the height of the actor is decreased.

3   Proposed Approach

The whole process of video reshaping consists of the following steps:

– The human body, to be reshaped, is extracted by background subtraction
– The hard segmentation, thus obtained, is used to produce soft mask through matting
– The hole generated in the background is filled by a video-based inpainting algorithm [10]
– Pose of the 3D model is tracked with the help of feature correspondences and silhouette correspondences
– Motion retargeting is performed to transfer motion from one model to the other
– Body-aware image warping method is used to warp the foreground each frame in a spatio-temporally consistent manner
– The warped foreground is composited over the inpainted background

(a)   (b)   (c)   (d)   (e)   (f)

(g)   (h)

Fig. 1. Proposed reshaping pipeline. (a) Original frame; (b) Binary mask; (c) Soft mask; (d) Inpainted background; (e) Feature points; (f) Model fit; (g) Silhouette correspondences (Blue dots are projected model vertices and the red dots are silhouette pixels); (h) Reshaped and retargeted result (Weight decreased) (Color figure online)

3.1 Preprocessing

Binary Segmentation: We use "SnapCut" (a video segmentation tool)[1] proposed by [1] for background subtraction. We obtain the binary mask for each video frame through this method.

Image Matting: The mask obtained from binary segmentation may not capture fine details like hair and may be fuzzy in regions containing thin foreground boundaries like fingers. Therefore, we perform image matting (soft segmentation) technique proposed and implemented by [9]. In place of user interaction, we provide the binary mask obtained from binary segmentation as input for matting, called the scribble.

Background Inpainting: Though methods like Exemplar-based technique [3] works sufficient enough for images, it is not suitable for inpainting videos since there is no inter-frame information transfer. Therefore, we use the video based inpainting technique implemented by [10].

Finding Pixel-Vertex Correspondences: Since motion tracking in monocular video sequences is an ill-posed problem, we need additional user-input in form of feature points. The feature points, once specified on a frame, are tracked for the rest of the frames using a KLT tracker, as done in [6]. The trajectories, which are broken due to subject self-occlusion are linked manually through a user-interface. Once the feature points are specified, feature correspondences are found by assigning an unoccluded vertex in the 3D model, whose projection is nearest to the pixel under consideration. For the purpose of identifying silhouette correspondences, we use proximity and normal based approach as provided in [7]. These feature correspondences and silhouette correspondences are used in Pose Tracking (Sect. 3.3).

3.2 3D Morphable Model

The warping algorithm requires a regression function to generate new 3D models for the specified semantic attributes. For this purpose, the 3D morphable model database and the regression coefficients (PCA data) by [5] are used. Each 3D model M in this database has 6449 vertices and 12894 faces. Let us indicate the ith vertex of model M as v_i.

Skeleton: The skeletal hierarchy used in the system has 18 joints. Let the set of bones of the skeleton be represented as $B = \{(i, j) \mid i \text{ and } j \text{ are connected}\}$ It should be noted that each element of B is an ordered pair (i, j) such that i represents the index of the parent joint and j represents the index of the child

---

[1] SnapCut is implemented as RotoBrush tool in Adobe After Effects.

joint. Each 3D model is associated with three skeletons namely, the template skeleton, the posed skeleton and the final skeleton. Let us use the superscripts t, p and f for the template skeleton, posed skeleton and final skeleton of the original 3D model and T, P and F for the deformed 3D model, respectively. Let the ith joint position of the original template skeleton (template skeleton of the original 3D model) be represented as J_i^t, where $J_i^t \in \mathbb{R}^3$. Let the individual components of J_i^t be represented as $J_i^t(x)$, $J_i^t(y)$ and $J_i^t(z)$. The bone vector from joint i to joint j of the original template skeleton can be denoted as $\overrightarrow{b_{ij}^t} = J_j^t - J_i^t$ and let $\widehat{b_{ij}^t}$ be the normalized bone vector.

Shape Parameters: Shape parameters define the semantic attributes of the human body like height, weight, leg length, etc. Let $\Lambda = (\lambda_1, \lambda_2, \cdots, \lambda_{13})$ denote the shape parameters of the original 3D model, which is fit over the original foreground image to be warped. Let $\Lambda' = (\lambda_1', \lambda_2', \cdots, \lambda_{13}')$ denote the shape parameters of the deformed 3D model, according to which the frame needs to be warped. It should be noted that for any reshaping process, $\lambda_i' = \lambda_i$ except for the i corresponding to the parameter(s) being changed. Let M_Λ and $M_{\Lambda'}$ be the 3D models with the shape parameters Λ and Λ' respectively. The shape parameters (Λ and Λ'), once fixed, will remain the same for reshaping all the frames. Changing one shape parameter might affect some other parameter(s) since the semantic attributes of the models are directly correlated to each other.

Pose Parameters: Let s be the global uniform-scaling factor, t_x and t_y be the global-translations along x and y axes respectively and τ denote the global-rotation twist-vector, whose direction represents axis of rotation and magnitude represents the angle of rotation along that axis. The pose parameters contain the joint positions of the posed skeleton $(J_1^p, J_2^p, \cdots, J_{18}^p)$ and the global transformation parameters $(s, \tau, t_x$ and $t_y)$. Let us represent these parameters collectively as $\Phi = (\phi_1, \phi_2, \cdots)$. In the reshaping process, the pose parameters will vary from frame to frame. Let us assume that our video contains Q frames, numbered from 1 to Q and let us denote the pose parameters of frame q as Φ^q.

Linear Blend Skinning: For skinning transformation, we require skinning weights, which are the weights assigned for each vertex with respect to each of the bones. Let us call the weight of vertex v_i and bone (j, k) pair as $\alpha(i, (j, k))$. Let the original 3D model in the template pose be represented as M_Λ. The skinning weights are obtained directly from the Pinocchio library [2]. Given the template mesh M_Λ and the template skeleton, the Pinocchio library gives us the skinning weights α, provided the template skeleton can be embedded onto the mesh. The α values are normalized such that $\sum \alpha(i, (j, k)) = 1$ $\forall i$. Since the skinning weights can only be non-negative, this also implies that $0 \leq \alpha(i, (j, k)) \leq 1$ $\forall i$, $(j, k) \in B$. Let the Linear Blend Skinning transformation function be represented as

$\eta(\Phi, v_i)$ and the global transformation function (incorporating global scaling, translation and rotation) be represented as $\rho(\Phi, v_i)^2$.

Mesh Segmentation: Each vertex in the 3D model is associated with a particular body part based on the skinning weights α. Since each body part is distinctly identified using a bone, each vertex v_i corresponds to a bone (j, k) such that $(j, k) = \underset{(l, m)}{\text{argmax }} \alpha(i, (l, m))$. The segmented mesh is shown in Fig. 1(f) with each body part in a different color.

Correspondences: Let $M_\Lambda(\Phi)$ be the 3D model after applying the skinning transformations and global transformations for the pose parameters Φ. For the pose parameters Φ^q of frame q, the vertices of $M_\Lambda(\Phi^q)$ are denoted as $\rho(\Phi^q, v_i)$. Let V_b represent the set of boundary vertex indices of $M_\Lambda(\Phi^q)$. Let the ith feature point, specified by the user, be represented as f_i. Let s_i indicate the ith silhouette pixel. Let μ be the correspondence function such that $\mu(f_i) = j$ represents the ith feature point has a corresponding model vertex index j and $\mu(s_i) = k$ denotes the model vertex with index k corresponds to the ith silhouette pixel in frame q such that $k \in V_b$.

Let the feature points f_i and silhouette points s_i be collectively represented as p_i and the correspondence function $\mu(p_i)$ be shortly denoted as μ_i. Though the feature points and silhouette pixels will differ between different frames, they are simply denoted as f_i and s_i implicitly indicating that they are the feature points and silhouette pixels for the frame under consideration.

3.3 Pose Tracking

Pose tracking helps to reduce the amount of user input required in fitting the model to match the image contour. It also avoids the foot-skate artifacts produced while reshaping humans in the video. The goal of tracking is to find out Φ^2 to Φ^Q given the pose for frame 1, Φ^1. For this purpose, the correspondence function μ is used. The basis of pose tracking and minimizing the error using Taylor approximation is provided by [6]. However, certain regularization terms and constraints are introduced to keep the tracking smooth (Sect. 3.3). Due to the introduction of these constraints, the need for particle filter mentioned in [6] has been eliminated, thereby improving the performance of tracking. Figure 1(f) shows the pose fit for the frame shown in Fig. 1(a).

Error Term: Let E_f be the feature point error term and E_s be the silhouette error term. The total error term to be minimized is given as

$$E(\Phi) = E_f(\Phi) + E_s(\Phi) \tag{1}$$

---

[2] $\eta(\Phi, v_i)$ and $\rho(\Phi, v_i)$ are also written as $\eta_i(\Phi)$ and $\rho_i(\Phi)$ respectively for notational convenience.

$$E_f(\Phi) = \sum_{i \in U} \left\| f_i - \rho(\Phi, v_{\mu(f_i)}) \right\|_2^2 \tag{2}$$

$$E_s(\Phi) = \sum_j \left\| s_j - \rho(\Phi, v_{\mu(s_j)}) \right\|_2^2 \tag{3}$$

where $\| \bullet \|_2$ represents the 2D Euclidean norm and U denotes the set of valid feature point indices since a feature points might not be valid in all the frames.

The first component E_f measures the sum of distances between feature points f_i of the person tracked over time and the projected 3D vertex locations $\rho(\Phi, v_{\mu(f_i)})$ of the model $M_\Lambda(\Phi^q)$ that corresponds to the respective feature point. The second component E_s measures the misalignment of the silhouette boundary $\rho(\Phi, v_{\mu(s_j)})$ of the projected model $M_\Lambda(\Phi^q)$ with the foreground boundary pixel s_j. The goal of tracking is to assign $\Phi^q = \underset{\Phi}{\mathrm{argmin}}\ E(\Phi)$. However, finding the global minimum is difficult because, the function ρ is non-linear due to the presence of rotations. Therefore, (1) is linearized using Taylor approximation with Φ^{q-1} as the initial pose.

Linearization Using Taylor Approximation: Taylor approximation is an iterative process, based on partial derivatives. Let us consider $\Phi(k)$ as the pose parameters found after the kth iteration in tracking and hence $\Phi(0)$ denotes the initial guess. Since we pick the pose parameters of the previous frame as the initial guess, $\Phi(0) = \Phi^{q-1}$. The system of equations, which is solved iteratively, is of the form, $\mathbf{JX} = \mathbf{M}$, where $\mathbf{J}$ is the Jacobian matrix, $\mathbf{X}$ is the parameter shift vector, containing the pose parameter shifts $\Delta\phi_1, \Delta\phi_2, \cdots$ and $\mathbf{M}$ is the misfit vector, which stores the norms as mentioned in (2) and (3). During k^{th} iteration $(k \geq 1)$, i^{th} row, j^{th} column of $\mathbf{J}$ is given by

$$\mathbf{J}(i,\ j) = \left. \frac{\partial \rho(\Phi, v_{\mu_i})}{\partial \phi_j} \right|_{\Phi = \Phi(k-1)} \tag{4}$$

i^{th} row of $\mathbf{M}$ is given by $\mathbf{M}(i) = p_i - \rho(\Phi(k-1), v_{\mu_i})$

Since we obtain only the parameter shift vector $\mathbf{X}$, it is important to update the pose parameters for next iteration as $\Phi(i) = \Phi(i-1) + \mathbf{X}$, where we assume $\Phi(i)$ is represented as column vector. As the skinning transformation function ρ is not known in advance, the partial derivatives are computed numerically with $\delta = 10^{-5}$. The termination condition used in the system is $E(\Phi(n-1)) \leq E(\Phi(n))$, which also means that $\Phi^q = \Phi(n-1)$. In other words, if there are $n-1$ iterations for tracking, $E(\Phi(0)) > E(\Phi(1)) > \cdots > E(\Phi(n-1))$.

Regularization Terms and Constraints: During tracking, we solve for the posed skeletal joint positions $(J_1^p, J_2^p, \cdots, J_{18}^p)$ and the global transformation parameters $(s,\ \tau,\ t_x\ and\ t_y)$. Therefore, it becomes necessary to induce some constraints and regularization terms on the joint positions for successful tracking. A function is associated with each regularization term and constraint. The function is then, partially differentiated with respect to each parameter of that function at $\Phi(k-1)$ during k^{th} iteration and the numerical value obtained is stored in a new row of $\mathbf{J}$ along the column corresponding to the parameter with which the function is partially differentiated. Also, the misfit of that function at $\Phi(k-1)$ is added as the same row in $\mathbf{M}$.

Joint Position Regularization Term: To avoid huge deviations from its original position, each joint requires a position regularization term. A positive weight $w_p(j)$ is assigned for each joint j, whose magnitude represents the amount we penalize for deviation of that joint. Let consider the root joint index to be 1. A constant weight of 1 is assigned for each joint, except for the root joint, whose weight is specified to be 10^4. That is, $w_p(1) = 10^4$ *and* $w_p(j) = 1 \; \forall j \geq 2$. Such a high weight for the root joint is necessary because we want the root joint position of the template skeleton and the posed skeleton to be same, $J_1^t = J_1^p$. By penalising the root translation heavily, we force the root joint translation also to accumulate in the global translation parameters t_x and t_y.

Bone Length Regularization Term: While tracking, the bone lengths should be fixed, because only then the transformations will be rigid. Since we are tracking based on positions rather than rotations, it is crucial to have bone length regularization term. $\forall (i, j) \in B$, we want $\|\overrightarrow{b_{ij}^p}\|$ to be equal to $\|\overrightarrow{b_{ij}^t}\|$. However, through this regularization term, we can only provide a soft constraint, but not a hard constraint on the bone lengths. This is because of the fact that penalizing bone length variations heavily restricts the free translation of the joints. Therefore, we specify a soft constraint on the bone length and correct the length after every iteration. A constant weight of $w_l = 1$ is used for all the bones.

Bone Vector Regularization Term: This regularization term smooths out the sudden jerks appearing to the bones along the frames. This term specifies that the direction of a bone vector $\overrightarrow{b_{ij}^p}$ of pose Φ^q should not deviate much from that of the pose Φ^{q-1} for $(i, j) \in B$, which in turn, implies that $\overrightarrow{b_{ij}^p}$ of pose $\Phi(k)$ should not deviate much from $\overrightarrow{b_{ij}^p}$ of pose $\Phi(k-1)$. We can consider vector dot product of the bone vectors, before and after k^{th} iteration, to achieve this goal. A constant weight of $w_v = 1$ is used for all the bones to penalize deviations in the vector direction.

Bone Orientation Constraint: This constraint is important for maintaining the configuration of the skeleton during tracking. This constraint specifies that the deviation of template bone vector $\overrightarrow{b_{ij}^t}$ and the posed bone vector $\overrightarrow{b_{ij}^p}$ should be minimized $\forall (i, j) \in B$. However, it becomes necessary to choose the weights carefully, otherwise, it is possible for the bones to become "stiff". For the bones forming the torso of the skeleton, the weight $w_o(i, j) = 1$ is used and for the remaining bones (that form the limbs and head), a weight of $w_o(i, j) = 0.01$ is used. By specifying this constraint, we have forced all whole body rotations to the global rotation parameter, τ.

3.4   Motion Retargeting

When we reshape by changing semantic attributes like height, the respective skeletal structure also differs. Therefore, applying the same motion to the deformed skeleton may make the motion quite unnatural. For example, when the height of a subject is decreased, the movement and the step-size should be in accordance with the deformed (shorter) skeleton. This problem is addressed by motion retargeting. Retargeting makes the resulting video look more natural in a spatio-temporally coherent manner.

For the purpose of motion retargeting, the tracked pose parameters applied for the original template skeleton is taken as the source animation and the deformed template skeleton (skeleton located through the deformed mesh) is taken to be the target skeleton. Therefore, the inputs for motion retargeting are the original template joint positions J^t, the original posed, global transformed joint positions J^f for frames 1 to Q and the deformed template joint positions J^T. The original posed joint positions are obtained as

$$J_i^f = T_{(t_x, t_y, 0)} R_\tau \cdot J_i^p \tag{5}$$

where T_X represents the translation matrix for translation by X, R_X represents the rotation matrix for rotation by twist vector X.

Retargeting[3] gives new transformed joint positions for the deformed skeleton J^{F_r}, whose positions were J^F before retargeting. In order to cater for small mismatches between the original skeletal configuration and the retargeted deformed skeletal configuration, retargeting is performed in two stages. In the first stage, the original skeleton itself is retargeted to get joint positions J^{f_r} and in the second stage, this output is pipelined as the source for retargeting the deformed skeleton. After retargeting, warping is carried out with the retargeted skeletal joints J^{f_r} and J^{F_r} in place of the joints J^f and J^F respectively.

3.5   Transferring Pose to Deformed Model

Matching Deformed Template Skeleton: The original template skeleton J^t and the deformed template skeleton J^T needs to be in the same configuration for transferring pose parameters from the original skeleton to the deformed skeleton. Let $(1, 2)$ denote the root bone that spans from root joint 1 to joint 2. Initially, the root joint position J_1 of the template skeletons are matched by translating the deformed template skeleton by the offset between the root joints, $J_1^t - J_1^T$. Then, starting from the root bone, the following transformation is applied $\forall (i, j) \in B$ in BFS order of the skeletal hierarchy (though DFS would also work equivalently).

$$J_j^T = \begin{cases} J_i^T + R\left(\theta\left(\widehat{b_{ij}^T}, \widehat{b_{ij}^t}\right), \overrightarrow{b_{ij}^T}\right) & \text{if } (i, j) = (1, 2) \\ J_i^T + R\left(\theta\left(\widehat{b_{kl}^t}, \widehat{b_{ij}^t}\right), \overrightarrow{b_{kl}^T}\right) * \|\overrightarrow{b_{ij}^T}\| & \text{if } (i, j) \neq (1, 2) \end{cases} \tag{6}$$

where bone (k, l) is the parent of bone (i, j), $\theta(X, Y)$ denotes twist between vectors X and Y and $R(W, Z)$ indicates rotation of vector Z by twist W.

---

[3] Retargeting is performed using Maya Human IK interface.

Transferring Posed Skeleton Angles: After we obtain the pose parameters Φ^q for the original mesh $M_\Lambda(\Phi^q)$ by tracking (or through manual user input in case of frame 1), the same pose parameters have to be applied for the deformed mesh $M_{\Lambda'}$, in order to have both meshes in the same pose. For this purpose, initially, the root joint position J_1^P of the original posed skeleton is copied to that of the deformed posed skeleton, $J_1^P = J_1^p$. After this, in BFS order of the skeletal hierarchy $\forall (i, j) \in B$, the following transformation is applied.

$$J_j^P = J_i^P + R\left(\theta\left(\widehat{b_{ij}^t},\ \widehat{b_{ij}^p}\right),\ \overrightarrow{b_{ij}^T}\right) \tag{7}$$

where $\theta(X,\ Y)$ denotes twist between vectors X and Y and $R(W,\ Z)$ indicates rotation of vector Z by twist W. After this step, the skinning transformations and global transformations are applied to the mesh vertices of $M_{\Lambda'}$ with the same global transformation parameters, t_x, t_y, s and τ to obtain $M_{\Lambda'}(\Phi^q)$.

Vertical Translation to Match Source Position: Since the pose transformation to the deformed mesh is carried out by anchoring the root joint, the meshes $M_\Lambda(\Phi^q)$ and $M_{\Lambda'}(\Phi^q)$ will be at located at different heights (from the ground). To fix this, apart from the global translation t_y, an additional translation along y axis $t_{y'}$ is required by the model $M_{\Lambda'}(\Phi^q)$, which would match the joint with the lowest y-valued vertex (assuming the y axis is positive upwards) in the posed, global-transformed original skeleton.

$$t_{y'} = J_i^f(y) - J_i^F(y) \ \bigg|\ i = \underset{j}{\operatorname{argmin}}\ J_j^f(y) \tag{8}$$

3.6 Body-Aware Frame Warping

The basic reshaping model for images has been proposed by [14]. The background artifacts produced by this method are eliminated by a method proposed by [8]. After tracking the pose in each frame (Sect. 3.3), we apply [8] method using the retargeted skeleton to obtain the corresponding reshaped frame. Thanks to the body-aware warping technique and separation of foreground before warping, we do not need a very accurate pose tracking in order to obtain decent results.

Therefore, our method requires matching a 3D morphable model by manually adjusting its pose and shape parameters, to match the human body in the first frame of the video. Also, the user specifies feature points broken due to occlusion, in addition to providing a set of feature point positions in the first frame. Then, the user specifies the desired offsets of the semantic attributes. The 3D model is morphed to meet the semantic attributes specified by the user. The changes in the fitted model with respect to its retargeted 3D skeleton are then used to guide warping a single frame. The body-aware warping coherently resizes the body parts along the direction and perpendicular to the bone axes of the 3D-skeleton, to incorporate the length changes in corresponding directions. With the help of feature points and silhouette information obtained from the binary mask, the pose for the 3D model is estimated in every frame and each frame is warped in the same manner.

4   Results

We demonstrate the results on video sequences with various actions by different actors in the supplementary material[4]. In all these examples, the user inputs required are in form of segmentation and feature point specification. Apart from this, no user correction of pose was necessary due to the body-aware warping technique. This implies that tracking is sufficient enough for warping even in case of presence of moderately loose clothing as shown in the examples. Therefore, once the segmentation and feature points are available, the whole of the process is automatic. Figure 3 shows that our system is capable of reshaping with consistency even in case of severe occlusion and rapid motion like jumping. Figure 4 shows reshaping two subjects in a single video sequence. Reshaping with retargeting, in this case, is done in two passes, one for each subject. The results in Fig. 2 depicts how our system works even with non-orthogonal camera angles

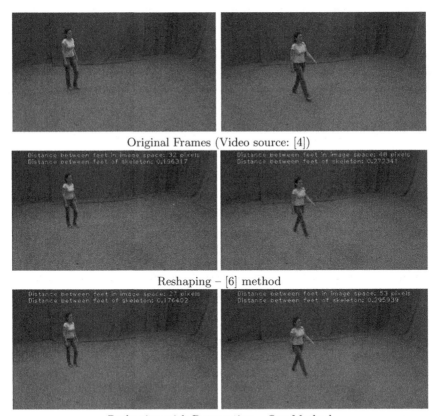

Original Frames (Video source: [4])

Reshaping – [6] method

Reshaping with Retargeting – Our Method

Fig. 2. Height and leg length of the subject are increased

---

[4] reshaping_with_retargeting.mp4.

Original Frames

Retargeted and Reshaped frames

Fig. 3. Weight of the subject is decreased

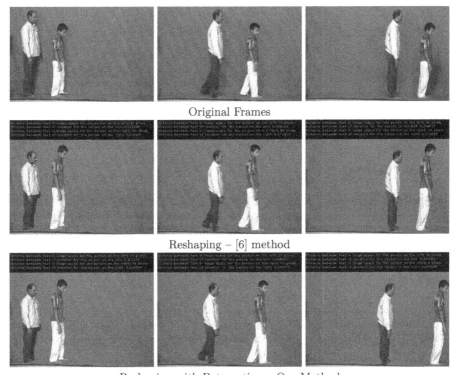

Original Frames

Reshaping – [6] method

Reshaping with Retargeting – Our Method

Fig. 4. Height of the subject on the left hand side is reduced and the height of the subject on the right hand side is increased (It can be clearly noticed that retargeting produces natural results)

Original Frames

Retargeted and Reshaped Frames

Fig. 5. Weight of the subject is increased

having two shape parameters changed (height and leg length) simultaneously. The results in Figs. 2 and 4 show that retargeting produces natural motion by comparing them with [6]. Figure 5 shows the result of increasing the weight of the subject, who is jogging in the video sequence, again proving the tracking performance even in case of rapid motion of the subjects.

5   Conclusions

The system we propose allows easy reshaping of humans in videos to produce natural and visually pleasing results. Our method is based on tracking pose of a 3D model to fit the human actor to be reshaped, followed by motion retargeting to the reshaped 3D model and finally applying a body-aware warping method. We show the results on video sequences with various types of actors with different actions.

Acknowledgements. We would like to thank University of Surrey (Gkalelis et al. [4]) for permitting us to use their video footages. We thank Hasler et al. [5] and Starck and Hilton [12] for making their datasets available. We also thank Newson et al. [10] for making their source code publicly available. We extend our gratitude to Ganesh and Aswinn for being the test subjects.

References

1. Bai, X., Wang, J., Simons, D., Sapiro, G.: Video SnapCut: robust video cutout using localized classifiers. ACM Trans. Graph. (TOG) **28**(3) (2009)
2. Baran, I., Popovic, J.: Automatic rigging and animation of 3D characters. ACM Trans. Graph. (TOG) **29**(3) (2007)

3. Criminisi, A., Perez, P., Toyama, K.: A region filling and object removal by exemplar-based image inpainting. IEEE Trans. Image Process. **13**(9), 1200–1212 (2004)
4. Gkalelis, N., Kim, H., Hilton, A., Nikolaidis, N., Pitas, I.: The i3DPost multi-view and 3D human action/interaction. In: CVMP (2009)
5. Hasler, N., Stoll, C., Sunkel, M., Rosenhahn, B., Seidel, H.-P.: A statistical model of human pose and body shape. In: Computer Graphics Forum (Proceedings of the Eurographics 2008), vol. 2 (2009)
6. Jain, A., Thormahlen, T., Seidel, H.-P., Theobalt, C.: MovieReshape: tracking and reshaping of humans in videos. Trans. Graph. **29**(6), 148:1–148:10 (2010)
7. Kraevoy, V., Sheffer, A., Van De Panne, M.: Modelling from contour drawings. In: SBIM (2009)
8. Kumar, H., Arora, N., Dhaliwal, J.S., Kalra, P., Chaudhuri, P.: Improved interactive reshaping of humans in images. In: 21st International Conference on Computer Graphics, Visualization and Computer Vision (2013)
9. Levin, A., Lischinski, D., Weiss, Y.: A closed-form solution to natural image matting. IEEE Trans. Pattern Anal. Mach. Intell. **30**(2), 228–242 (2008)
10. Newson, A., Almansa, A., Fradet, M., Gousseau, Y., Perez, P.: Video inpainting of complex scenes. SIAM J. Imaging Sci. **17**(4), 1993–2019 (2014)
11. Richter, M., Varanasi, K., Hasler, N., Theobalt, C.: Real-time reshaping of humans. In: International Conference on 3D Imaging, Data Processing, Visualization and Transmission (3DIMPVT) (2012)
12. Starck, J., Hilton, A.: Surface capture for performance based animation. IEEE Comput. Graph. Appl. **27**, 21–31 (2007)
13. Yang, Y., Yu, Y., Zhou, Y., Du, S., Davis, J., Yang, R.: Semantic parametric reshaping of human body models. In: Second International Conference on 3D Vision (2014)
14. Zhou, S., Fu, H., Liu, L., Cohen-Or, D., Han, X.: Parametric reshaping of human bodies in images. ACM Trans. Graph. (Proc. ACM SIGGRAPH) **29**(3), 1–10 (2010). Article No. 126
15. Schaefer, S., McPhail, T., Warren, J.: Image deformation using moving least squares. ACM Trans. Graph. **25**(3), 533–540 (2006)

Enhanced Aggregated Channel Features Detector for Pedestrian Detection Using Parameter Optimisation and Deep Features

Blossom Treesa Bastian[(✉)] and C. V. Jiji

College of Engineering Trivandrum, Thiruvananthapuram, Kerala, India
{blossombastian,jijicv}@cet.ac.in

Abstract. Aggregated Channel Features (ACF) proposed by Dollar *et al.* provide strong framework for pedestrian detection. Many variants of ACF detector achieved state of the art result using deep features along with aggregated channel features. In this paper we propose a hybrid method for pedestrian detection using a parameter optimized variant of ACF detector with decorrelated channels as region proposer followed by a deep CNN for feature extraction. Our proposed method effectively handles the issues of false positives and detection of small instances of pedestrians. The proposed detector gives the best result among the different variants of the ACF detectors in Caltech dataset with the best localization and is second to the best performing detector available till date.

Keywords: Pedestrian detection · ACF detector · Boosting algorithm

1 Introduction

Owing to the diverse applications in vision based systems, pedestrian detection from images is still an active area of research. There have been significant improvements in the detection performance on bench mark datasets over the last decade. Most of the prevailing techniques rely on either hand crafted features followed by a classifier or deep networks for detecting pedestrian instances of varying resolutions. As a matter of fact, the top performing techniques use a combination of hand crafted features and deep features for enhanced performance [2,18].

Aggregated Channel Features (ACF) detector proposed by Dollar *et al.* [4] which utilizes hand crafted features derived from LUV color channels and various HOG channels remains as one of the classic stand alone pedestrian detectors. Moreover, most of the state of the art methods using hand designed features are based on ACF detector. Hybrid approaches normally use stand alone detectors based on hand designed features as region proposers to generate all the possible locations of the object. This is followed by a deep CNN which extracts fixed

© Springer Nature Singapore Pte Ltd. 2018
R. Rameshan et al. (Eds.): NCVPRIPG 2017, CCIS 841, pp. 126–135, 2018.
https://doi.org/10.1007/978-981-13-0020-2_12

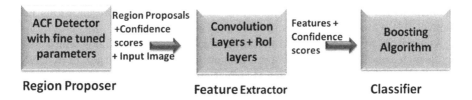

Fig. 1. Block diagram

length feature vector for each region proposal and finally a classifier predicts the scores for the regions. Many state of the art variants of ACF detector were widely used as region proposers [10].

Nevertheless, Zhang *et al.* [23] observed a failure of deep CNNs in providing additional gains when used with very strong region proposer (best performance as stand alone detectors) in pedestrian detection. This limited success of deep CNNs with strong region proposers are due to two reasons: (1) no effective mining for hard negatives, (2) non discriminative features obtained for small instances of pedestrians. However, Zhang *et al.* [22] came up with solutions to these issues by using a classifier with multiple bootstrapping stages and using deep features from convolutional layers with low stride value. In light of this observation, we propose a hybrid approach for pedestrian detection using the ACF detector with fine-tuned parameters and decorrelated channels as the region proposer. Later, these well-defined proposals are fed to a CNN for feature extraction and finally classification is achieved through a boosting algorithm which effectively bootstrap many times for hard negatives. Also deep features are extracted from higher resolution convolutional layers to avoid non discriminative features obtained for small instances of pedestrians. Figure 1 demonstrates the basic work flow of the proposed pedestrian detector. Eventually our proposed detector attained best results in Caltech dataset when compared with all other hybrid methods in pedestrian detection with much better localisation.

2   Related Work

Success of deep CNNs for image classification and object detection [9,11] motivated researchers to use deep networks for pedestrian detection. Hence, many methods used the well structured architecture of R-CNN [9], where a region proposer is used to find out the region of interest followed by a deep convolutional network for extracting features, classification and finally for getting the bounding box. Initially deep network based pedestrian detectors used HOG/linSVM [3] and DPM [7] as region proposers. Ever since the introduction of ICF [5], most popular pedestrian detector based on hand crafted features, ICF and its improved versions like ACF [4], LDCF [13], SCF [1] etc. were the most effective region proposers. Also the architecture of the deep network underwent rapid changes. Starting from custom made deep networks, more and more deeper networks which are capable of extracting more high level representations like AlexNet [11], GoogLeNet [16], and VGG [17] were employed.

Apart from above mentioned methods, there are other methods which used the deep features but have different frameworks other than that of R-CNN. Among which TA_CNN [19] achieved reduction in false positives by using more high level representations, obtained with a deep network trained on semantic task which includes both pedestrian attributes and scene attributes. DeepParts method [18] effectively handled occlusions by learning separate detectors for complementary parts of a pedestrian using deep network. Cai *et al.* [2] proposed a complexity aware cascading of features where complex channels extracted using deep networks are combined with existing ICF channels at higher stages of boosting algorithm. Scale aware-Fast RCNN [12] introduced by Li *et al.* used two separately learned sub network to detect pedestrian instances of different scales.

Our detector proposed in this work is a variant of ACF detector with fine-tuned parameters and appropriate channel filtering followed by an RCNN based deep network.

3   Proposed Method

3.1   Fine Tuned ACF Detector as Region Proposer

The ACF detector proposed by Dollar *et al.* for pedestrian detection used 10 lower resolution channels extracted from the input image as features. These are constituted of three LUV color channels, normalized gradient magnitude of the input image and the last six channels corresponding to the gradient histogram which are computed using HOG features for six different orientation bins. These channels are then vectorized and fed to a learned boosting algorithm to get detection output.

In order to reduce the local correlation among the above channels, we computed the eigen vectors corresponding to the covariance matrix of the 10 channels and the top four eigen vectors are used to filter the channels as proposed by Nam *et al.* [13]. These locally decorrelated channels further enhanced the performance of boosting algorithm.

Using the above filtered channels as features, we performed a detailed analysis by varying four significant parameters of the detector to optimize the performance in Caltech dataset. The four parameters we considered are described below.

1. **Sliding Window Size:** By increasing the sliding window size, the number of features available for learning will get increased and thereby the discriminative power of the detector get enhanced. Although, raising the window size beyond a limit, resulted in large number of features which increased computations and also resulted in missing out small instances. Hence an optimum window size of 120×60 was used as a trade-off between these two factors.

2. **Training Dataset Size:** More number of high and low resolution instances can be detected by increasing the training dataset size but increasing beyond a limit resulted in over fitting of the classifier. In Caltech dataset number of images available for training can be varied by changing the number of frames taken from the videos (six set of videos are available for training in the Caltech pedestrian dataset). The training dataset obtained by taking every third frame (42782 images) provided the best detector performance.

3. **Sliding Window Stride:** Sliding window stride value defines the number of pixels skipped in between adjacent sliding window scans. Even though increasing the stride value will reduce computations, the detector will also miss out small instances of pedestrians. So we reduced the stride value from four in the baseline detector to two in order to detect more small instances of pedestrians.

4. **Number of Bootstrapping Stages:** Each bootstrapping stage mines the training dataset for hard negatives. We increased the bootstrapping stages from four to five and thus reduced the number of false positives.

Table 1. Parameters values of the baseline detector and the proposed ACF variant

Parameter	Sliding window size	Training dataset size	Sliding window stride	Number of bootstrapping stages
Values of the baseline detector [6]	64×32	4250	4	4
Values of proposed ACF variant	120×60	42782	2	5

The optimized parameter set was tabulated in Table 1. A detailed experimental analysis for parameter optimisation of ACF detector done by the authors is available in [20]. The stand alone detector gave enhanced performance compared to other different versions of the ACF detector [1,13,24]. This motivated us to employ this configuration as a region proposer for the proposed hybrid detector. A typical region proposals for an input image is shown in Fig. 2.

Fig. 2. Input and output of region proposer.

3.2 Deep Features Extraction

Fast-RCNN architecture [8] which takes an entire image and a set of region proposals as input was used to extract fixed length deep features for the regions generated by ACF detector mentioned above. The network first processes the whole image with several convolutional and max pooling layers to produce a convolutional feature map. Then, for each region proposal, a region of interest (RoI) pooling layer extracts a fixed-length feature vector from this convolutional feature map. In Fast-RCNN, output of the final convolution layer is fed to the RoI layer to extract features. In final convolution layer the stride value will be higher and will produce flat features for region proposals of smaller size, which will eventually results in missing out smaller pedestrian instances. Instead of taking feature map from final convolutional layer we fed the RoI layer with output from more than one fine resolution convolution layers and output of RoI layer is simply concatenated and form the final deep feature vector (Fig. 3).

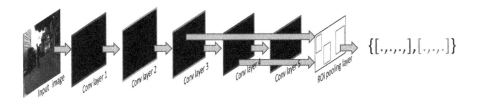

Fig. 3. Deep feature extraction.

3.3 Boosting Algorithm

In order to effectively bootstrap the training phase for multiple times, we used a boosting algorithm on the deep features obtained from the RoI layer of Fast-RCNN framework. Initially, the training set consists of feature vectors of positive regions (regions having higher overlapping threshold with ground truth) and the same number of feature vectors obtained from randomly sampled negative regions (regions having lower overlapping threshold with ground truth). In each bootstrapping stage, training set is further enriched with features of hard negative regions. We used the confidence score produced by the proposal generator to calculate the initial weights of training set features. Weights are calculated as follows:

$$w_i = \frac{1}{2}log\frac{s_i}{1-s_i} \tag{1}$$

where w_i is the weight of feature vector of ith region and s_i the confidence produced by the region proposer for i^{th} region.

4 Experiments and Results

We tested our region proposer and the proposed detector on the standard Caltech testing dataset. The testing dataset consists of 4024 images with 847 instances of pedestrians with reasonable height (>50 pixels). We used the ground truth annotations provided by [23] for comparing the result. Performance of the proposed detector and other state of the art pedestrian detectors were compared using the ROC curve plotted between miss rate and false positives per image (fppi) and log average miss rate in the range of $[10^{-2}, 10^0]$.

4.1 Region Proposer: ACF Detector with Fine Tuned Parameters and Decorrelated Channels

In Sect. 3.1 we mentioned the fine tuned parameter values used to achieve best result for ACF detector. Table 2 shows the step by step reduction in miss rate achieved by the ACF detector using these values. Table 3 provides the comparison between different variants of ACF detector and our proposed ACF detector with fine tuned parameters and decorrelated channels in terms of miss rate. We did the comparison for two values of overlapping threshold (OT) between the ground truth and the detected results. For both cases, our detector achieved best

Table 2. Step by step reduction in the miss rate of baseline ACF detector by changing each parameter

Specifications	Miss rate
Baseline ACF detector	27.72%
+Window size	22.96%
+Training dataset size	17.45%
+AdaBoost parameters	16.14%
+Stride	15.73%
+Filtering using [13]	12.72%

Table 3. Miss rate values of state of the art ACF variants and the proposed ACF variant

Detector	Miss rate for OT = 0.5	Miss rate for OT = 0.7
ACF	27.72%	38.30%
CCF [21]	23.7%	68.6%
Katamari [1]	22.2%	49.0%
LDCF	22.03%	58.11%
SpatialPooling [14]	21.6%	46.7%
RotatedFilters [23]	16.3%	41.3%
CheckerBoards [23]	13.47%	38.67%
Proposed ACF variant	12.72%	25.94%

result. For an overlapping threshold of 0.7, the proposed ACF variant produced superior performance over the other methods, since it has got better localisation of the detected result. Hence we used the proposed ACF variant as the region proposer.

4.2 Deep Features Extraction Using VGG Net

VGG19 ConvNet was used to get the convolutional feature map of the input image. This network was pre-trained on ImageNet dataset [15] and fine tuned on Caltech dataset. In VGG-net there are totally 19 convolutional layers and the final convolutional layer is $Conv5\_3$ (stride value $= 16$ pixels). As per the discussion in Sect. 3.2, RoI pooling layer was fed with feature map outputs from layers having less stride. Here we used the feature map output of $Conv4\_3$ (stride value $= 8$ pixels) layer and $Conv3\_3$ (stride value $= 4$ pixels) layer (as shown in Fig. 3). These two convolutional feature maps of the input image is fed to the RoI pooling layer along with the bounding box values generated from the region proposer. RoI pooling layer produces a fixed length vector of size $37,632$ for each bounding box created by the region proposer.

4.3 Boosting Algorithm: AdaBoost

AdaBoost algorithm was used for the classification of deep features. AdaBoost classifier is a cascade of weak classifiers and here the weak classifiers are decision trees. We employed seven stages of bootstrapping for learning the classifier (starting from a classifier with 64 decision trees and then 128, 256, 512, 1024, 1536 and in the final stage 2048 decision trees). Each bootstrapping stage adds 10,000 additional negatives to the training set. The confidence scores produced by the region proposer for each bounding box were fed as the initial weights of feature vector.

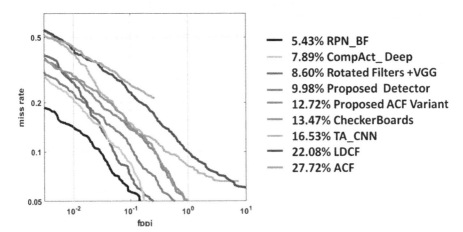

Fig. 4. ROC curves for state of the art pedestrian detectors along with our proposed detector for an overlapping threshold of 0.5

4.4   Results

Figures 4, 5 and 6 provide comparisons between state of the art pedestrian detection methods and the proposed detector for different values of overlapping threshold. RPN_BF [22] is a fully CNN based method, where as CompactAct-Deep [2], Rotated Filters+VGG [23] and TA_CNN are hybrid methods. When the overlapping threshold is 0.5, the proposed detector achieved comparable result with the above mentioned hybrid methods (Fig. 4). But for increased overlapping threshold our method have an upper hand over all the hybrid methods and became only second best to RPN_BF (best result in Caltech Dataset) as depicted in

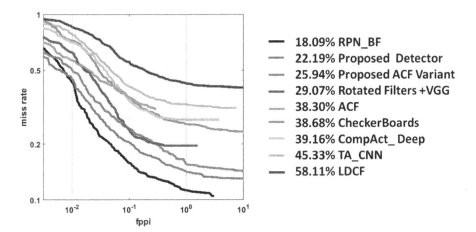

Fig. 5. ROC curves for state of the art pedestrian detectors along with our proposed detector for an overlapping threshold of 0.7

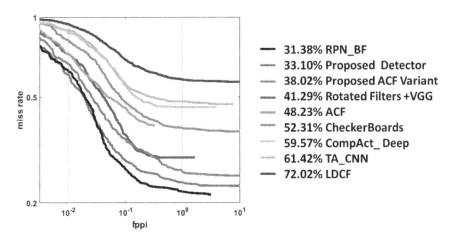

Fig. 6. ROC curves for state of the art pedestrian detectors along with our proposed detector for an overlapping threshold of 0.75

Figs. 5 and 6. As a matter of fact, the performance gap between the proposed detector and RPN_BF reduces to ∼2% for an overlapping threshold of 0.75 (Fig. 6). Performance comparisons show that our detector has better localized detection results in comparison to all other hybrid methods used for pedestrian detection.

5 Conclusion

In this paper we proposed a hybrid method for pedestrian detection using an improved variant of ACF detector as region proposer and the architecture of Fast-RCNN for deep feature extraction. Region proposal generated by proposed variant of ACF detector had better localisation with ground truth. Usage of AdaBoost as classifier reduced false positives and deep feature extraction from high resolution convolutional layers resulted in detection of more small instances of pedestrians. Proposed detector achieved much better performance than existing hybrid methods in Caltech dataset and is the best among the ACF variants in terms of localisation and miss rate. Our method achieved the second best result in comparison with all the currently available pedestrian detectors in Caltech dataset.

Acknowledgements. We gratefully acknowledge for the research fellowship (3501/ (NET-DEC.2014)) provided by the University Grants Commission (UGC) Govt. of India.

References

1. Benenson, R., Omran, M., Hosang, J., Schiele, B.: Ten years of pedestrian detection, what have we learned? In: Agapito, L., Bronstein, M.M., Rother, C. (eds.) ECCV 2014. LNCS, vol. 8926, pp. 613–627. Springer, Cham (2015). https://doi.org/10.1007/978-3-319-16181-5_47
2. Cai, Z., Saberian, M., Vasconcelos, N.: Learning complexity-aware cascades for deep pedestrian detection. In: Proceedings of the IEEE International Conference on Computer Vision, pp. 3361–3369 (2015)
3. Dalal, N., Triggs, B.: Histograms of oriented gradients for human detection. In: Proceedings of the IEEE Conference on Computer Vision and Pattern Recognition, vol. 1, pp. 886–893 (2005)
4. Dollár, P., Appel, R., Belongie, S., Perona, P.: Fast feature pyramids for object detection. IEEE Trans. Pattern Anal. Mach. Intell. **36**(8), 1532–1545 (2014)
5. Dollár, P., Tu, Z., Perona, P., Belongie, S.: Integral channel features (2009)
6. Dollar, P., Wojek, C., Schiele, B., Perona, P.: Pedestrian detection: an evaluation of the state of the art. IEEE Trans. Pattern Anal. Mach. Intell. **34**(4), 743–761 (2012)
7. Felzenszwalb, P.F., Girshick, R.B., McAllester, D., Ramanan, D.: Object detection with discriminatively trained part-based models. IEEE Trans. Pattern Anal. Mach. Intell. **32**(9), 1627–1645 (2010)
8. Girshick, R.: Fast R-CNN. In: Proceedings of the IEEE International Conference on Computer Vision, pp. 1440–1448 (2015)

9. Girshick, R., Donahue, J., Darrell, T., Malik, J.: Rich feature hierarchies for accurate object detection and semantic segmentation. In: Proceedings of the IEEE Conference on Computer Vision and Pattern Recognition (2014)
10. Hosang, J., Omran, M., Benenson, R., Schiele, B.: Taking a deeper look at pedestrians. In: Proceedings of the IEEE Conference on Computer Vision and Pattern Recognition, pp. 4073–4082 (2015)
11. Krizhevsky, A., Sutskever, I., Hinton, G.E.: Imagenet classification with deep convolutional neural networks. In: Pereira, F., Burges, C.J.C., Bottou, L., Weinberger, K.Q. (eds.) Advances in Neural Information Processing Systems 25, pp. 1097–1105. Curran Associates, Inc., New York (2012)
12. Li, J., Liang, X., Shen, S., Xu, T., Feng, J., Yan, S.: Scale-aware fast R-CNN for pedestrian detection. arXiv preprint arXiv:1510.08160 (2015)
13. Nam, W., Dollár, P., Han, J.H.: Local decorrelation for improved pedestrian detection. In: Advances in Neural Information Processing Systems, pp. 424–432 (2014)
14. Paisitkriangkrai, S., Shen, C., van den Hengel, A.: Strengthening the effectiveness of pedestrian detection with spatially pooled features. In: Fleet, D., Pajdla, T., Schiele, B., Tuytelaars, T. (eds.) ECCV 2014. LNCS, vol. 8692, pp. 546–561. Springer, Cham (2014). https://doi.org/10.1007/978-3-319-10593-2_36
15. Russakovsky, O., Deng, J., Su, H., Krause, J., Satheesh, S., Ma, S., Huang, Z., Karpathy, A., Khosla, A., Bernstein, M., Berg, A.C., Fei-Fei, L.: ImageNet large scale visual recognition challenge. Int. J. Comput. Vis. (IJCV) **115**(3), 211–252 (2015)
16. Simonyan, K., Zisserman, A.: Very deep convolutional networks for large-scale image recognition. arXiv preprint arXiv:1409.1556 (2014)
17. Szegedy, C., Liu, W., Jia, Y., Sermanet, P., Reed, S., Anguelov, D., Erhan, D., Vanhoucke, V., Rabinovich, A.: Going deeper with convolutions. In: Proceedings of the IEEE Conference on Computer Vision and Pattern Recognition, pp. 1–9 (2015)
18. Tian, Y., Luo, P., Wang, X., Tang, X.: Deep learning strong parts for pedestrian detection. In: Proceedings of the IEEE International Conference on Computer Vision, pp. 1904–1912 (2015)
19. Tian, Y., Luo, P., Wang, X., Tang, X.: Pedestrian detection aided by deep learning semantic tasks. In: Proceedings of the IEEE Conference on Computer Vision and Pattern Recognition, pp. 5079–5087 (2015)
20. Bastian, B.T., Jiji, C.V.: Aggregated channel features with optimum parameters for pedestrian detection. In: Shankar, B.U., Ghosh, K., Mandal, D.P., Ray, S.S., Zhang, D., Pal, S.K. (eds.) PReMI 2017. LNCS, vol. 10597, pp. 155–161. Springer, Cham (2017). https://doi.org/10.1007/978-3-319-69900-4_20
21. Yang, B., Yan, J., Lei, Z., Li, S.Z.: Convolutional channel features. In: Proceedings of the IEEE International Conference on Computer Vision, pp. 82–90 (2015)
22. Zhang, L., Lin, L., Liang, X., He, K.: Is faster R-CNN doing well for pedestrian detection? In: Leibe, B., Matas, J., Sebe, N., Welling, M. (eds.) ECCV 2016. LNCS, vol. 9906, pp. 443–457. Springer, Cham (2016). https://doi.org/10.1007/978-3-319-46475-6_28
23. Zhang, S., Benenson, R., Omran, M., Hosang, J., Schiele, B.: How far are we from solving pedestrian detection? In: Proceedings of the IEEE Conference on Computer Vision and Pattern Recognition, pp. 1259–1267 (2016)
24. Zhang, S., Benenson, R., Schiele, B.: Filtered channel features for pedestrian detection. In: Proceedings of the IEEE Conference on Computer Vision and Pattern Recognition, pp. 1751–1760 (2015)

Image and Signal Processing

Unsupervised Segmentation of Speech Signals Using Kernel-Gram Matrices

Saurabhchand Bhati$^{(\boxtimes)}$, Shekhar Nayak, and K. Sri Rama Murty

Department of Electrical Engineering, IIT Hyderabad, Hyderabad, India
{ee12b1044,ee13p1008,ksrm}@iith.ac.in

Abstract. The objective of this paper is to develop an unsupervised method for segmentation of speech signals into phoneme-like units. The proposed algorithm is based on the observation that the feature vectors from the same segment exhibit higher degree of similarity than the feature vectors across the segments. The kernel-Gram matrix of an utterance is formed by computing the similarity between every pair of feature vectors in the Gaussian kernel space. The kernel-Gram matrix consists of square patches, along with the principle diagonal, corresponding to different phoneme-like segments in the speech signal. It detects the number of segments, as well as their boundaries automatically. The proposed approach does not assume any information about input utterances like exact distribution of segment length or correct number of segments in an utterance. The proposed method out-performs the state-of-the-art blind segmentation algorithms on Zero Resource 2015 databases and TIMIT database.

Keywords: Blind segmentation · Gaussian kernel
Kernel-Gram matrix · Phonetic segmentation

1 Introduction

Speech signal can be considered as a sequence of basic phonemic units. Most of the automatic speech recognition (ASR) systems depend on accurate recognition of these basic units. Even, the speech synthesis systems rely on synthesizing acoustic waveforms for these basic units. Automatic segmentation of speech into phoneme-like units plays an important role in several speech applications including speech recognition, speech synthesis and audio search [1–3]. Segmentation of speech forms a crucial initial step in the acoustic segment modelling which finds applications in audio search [4] and unsupervised transfer learning [5]. Speech segmentation in an unsupervised manner is an important step in zero-resource speech processing [6]. Segmentation of speech into basic units involves detecting the time instants at which the vocal tract system transitioned from one state to another state. However, the transition is not abrupt, rather it happens in a continuum, making it difficult to unambiguously detect the time instant of transition. As a result, accurate identification of phoneme boundaries is difficult even

© Springer Nature Singapore Pte Ltd. 2018
R. Rameshan et al. (Eds.): NCVPRIPG 2017, CCIS 841, pp. 139–149, 2018.
https://doi.org/10.1007/978-981-13-0020-2_13

for human beings. There could be differences between the boundary locations marked by two different experts.

Automatic approaches to speech segmentation can be broadly categorized into supervised and unsupervised methods. Supervised methods are mainly model-based, and employ probabilistic models of the phonemes to classify the acoustic regions into phonemes. Hidden Markov models (HMM) are typically used to model the acoustic features extracted from the phonemes [7]. If sequence of phones is available for an utterance then the boundaries can be determined with forced alignment using Viterbi algorithm [8]. Though the supervised approaches deliver high performance, they require a large amount of manually transcribed data. Moreover, phoneme models are specific to the language on which they are trained, and cannot be readily used to segment speech data from other languages. Segmentation methods that fine-tune parameters on a validation set suffer from the same problem. These approaches can not be applied to a new target language without the required amount of manual supervision.

Unsupervised approaches to speech segmentation, on the other hand, do not require manually transcribed speech data. In fact, it has been argued that unsupervised segmentation is similar to the perception of speech by infants [9]. Unsupervised approaches are metric-based, and use the distance between the adjacent regions to detect the change points in the audio stream [10]. Support vector machines were employed to detect abrupt spectral changes which were marked as segment boundaries [11]. Maximum spectral transition was used for detecting boundaries [12] and a "jump function" was proposed for identifying changes in audio signal [13]. Segmentation has also been formulated as a clustering problem [14–16]. Boundary models were used for capturing the characteristics of the signal around a boundary [17,18]. Segmentation by recognition was proposed where a probabilistic model was used to determine whether a feature belongs to a segment or not [19]. An agglomerative algorithm was proposed for speech segmentation, which begins with as many numbers of segments as the number of frames in the speech signal, and successively combines the pair of most similar adjacent segments in each iteration, till the required number of segments is met [20]. Time-frequency speech spectrograms were used for speech segmentation and the intensity changes in spectrogram were hypothesized as potential change points [21]. Spectrogram and Mel cepstral coefficients were used for segmentation and the results were combined from both the features to give final segment end points [22]. Microcanonical Multiscale Formalism (MMF) was used for segmentation which analyzes the local dynamics of speech from a multiscale perspective [23]. A 2-D filter that moves along diagonal in correlation matrix obtained using FFT features was proposed for estimating the segment boundaries [24]. A non-parametric Bayesian approach was proposed for acoustic model discovery [25].

In this paper, a local similarity measure for unsupervised phonetic segmentation of speech signals is proposed which is motivated by the observation of distance matrix, shown in Fig. 1. This depicts the distance between every pair of feature vectors extracted from the speech signal. Features from the same segment exhibit higher degree of similarity (or lesser distance), than the features from two different segments. From the distance matrix, the sequence of features having a higher degree of similarity are separated and labeled as a segment. Since we process the features extracted from the signal in a sequential manner, it does not require the entire signal at the same time. Moreover, the number of segments can be automatically determined from speech signal.

The rest of the paper is organized as follows: Sect. 2 discusses the proposed similarity measure for unsupervised phonetic segmentation of speech. Section 3 presents experimental evaluation and effectiveness of the proposed method. Finally, paper is concluded in Sect. 4.

2   Segment Detection from Kernel-Gram Matrix

Let the sequence of states of the vocal-tract system during the production of a speech signal be represented by a sequence of feature vectors $\mathbf{X} = (x_1, x_2, \ldots, x_N)$, where x_i denotes the d-dimensional feature vector extracted from i^{th} frame of the speech signal, and N is the total number of frames. The objective of speech segmentation is to divide the sequence $\mathbf{X}$ into K non-overlapping contiguous segments $\mathbf{S} = (s_1, s_2, \ldots s_K)$, where s_j denotes j^{th} segment that begins at frame b_j and ends at frame e_j. The segmentation algorithm should ensure that feature vectors in each of the segment s_j are acoustically similar, and represent a phoneme-like unit. Hence the segmentation algorithm should determine the number of segments and detect their beginning and end points from the acoustic similarity of the feature vectors $\mathbf{X}$.

In the absence of any information about the source distribution, we propose to detect the segment boundaries from the Gram matrix obtained using Gaussian kernel [26]. We assume that two feature vectors from the same segment must have a higher degree of similarity than two feature vectors from different segments. This assumption is justified as the feature vectors from the same segment are drawn from the same source distribution, while the feature vectors from different segments are drawn from different source distributions.

In the proposed approach, the similarity between two feature vectors x_i and x_j is computed using Gaussian kernel as

$$G(i,j) = \exp\left(-\frac{||x_i - x_j||}{h}\right) \tag{1}$$

where $||.||$ denotes the Euclidean norm of a vector and h is a free parameter which can be used to adjust the width of the Gaussian kernel. Kernel-Gram matrix G can be obtained by computing the similarity between every pair of feature vectors in the sequence $\mathbf{X}$.

Gram matrix computed from 13-dimensional Mel-frequency cepstral coefficient (MFCC) features, extracted from a speech utterance is shown in Fig. 1(a). The intensity of a pixel at (i, j) indicates the similarity $G(i, j)$ between the feature vectors x_i and x_j. The region around the principal diagonal corresponds to temporally closer segments. The square patches of higher degree of similarity along the diagonal correspond to acoustically similar segment. Manually marked phoneme boundaries are also shown in the Fig. 1. It is observed that the manually marked boundaries, shown in red colour, coincide exactly with the square patches along the principal diagonal. In this work, the task of speech segmentation is equivalent to identifying the square patches along the main diagonal of the Gram matrix.

As segment boundaries occur in a small neighborhood around the diagonal, the search space can be restricted to a small region parallel to the diagonal. This is analogous to constraining the dynamic time warping path using Itakura parallelogram [27]. The length constraints are shown in Fig. 1(a) with dotted lines. As Gram matrix is symmetric, it is enough to compute the upper triangular portion of the Gram matrix. These two constraints lead to significant reduction in computational complexity. The similarity values are higher when the column index j is close to the row index i, i.e., around diagonal, indicating that the frames i and j belong to same segment. On the other hand, as the column index j moves away from the row index i, the similarity values decrease indicating that the frames i and j belong to different segments.

A density-based algorithm is used for identifying the segment boundaries from the kernel gram matrix. We share some concepts such as reachability and ϵ neighbourhood with DBSCAN [28] algorithm which are used in the calculation of segment boundaries.

A frame, x_j, is in ϵ neighbourhood of x_i if $1-G(i,j) < \epsilon$. Given an appropriate ϵ, all the features that are from the same segment as that of x_i will be in ϵ neighbourhood of x_i. Since segments are continuous only consecutive frames can be in a segment. For frame x_i, we check consecutive frames for the neighbourhood and maintain a run length (number of neighbours) l_i for each frame.

A frame x_{i+l_i} is temporally reachable from x_i, if all the frames in between x_i, x_{i+l_i} are in ϵ neighbourhood of frame x_i. The first temporally unreachable frame from x_i can be considered as the end of the segment containing the x_i frame. However, making a decision with just one single frame could be erroneous due to noise in data. Hence, we use K-step temporal unreachability, i.e., K successive frames being unreachable, to identify the boundary of the segment containing x_i. The chances of making an erroneous estimate decrease with increase in K. So for a frame x_i, the end point is estimated at $i + l_i$ if and only if x_{i+l_i} is temporally reachable by x_i and all the frames $x_{i+l_i+1}, \ldots, x_{i+l_i+K}$ are not in ϵ neighbourhood of x_i.

A frame in the beginning of the segment will have the highest number of neighbours and a frame, in the end, will have the lowest number of neighbours. For each frame, we construct the neighbourhood graph, which is basically the sum of all the similarities in the K-point reachability of that frame. Neighbourhood graph is given as

$$N_G(i) = \Sigma_{j=i}^{l_i} G(i,j) \tag{2}$$

where l_i is the run length of x_i frame. For a frame, in the beginning, the value of N_G will be highest since the maximum number of frames contribute to it. As we move towards the end of the segment the value of N_G will keep decreasing

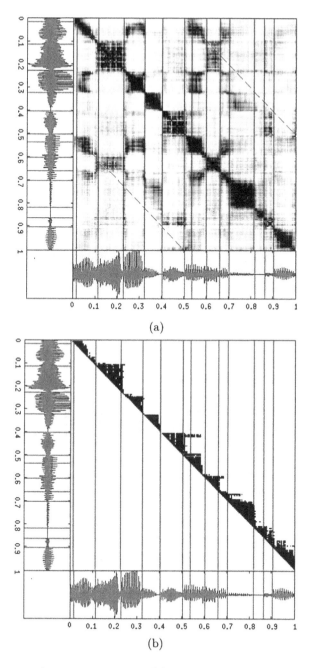

Fig. 1. Illustration of similarity matrices. (a) Kernel-Gram matrix between every pair of feature vectors extracted from the speech signal. (b) End point detected by each frame. Red lines indicate manually marked phoneme boundaries. (Color figure online)

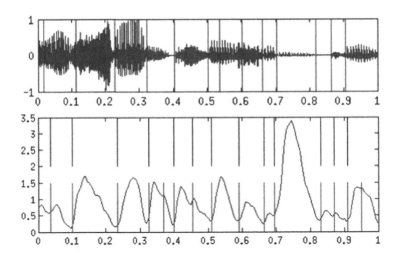

Fig. 2. Top - speech signal with manually marked boundaries. Bottom - segment profile with detected boundaries shown in Red lines. Black lines show manually marked boundaries. (Color figure online)

as shown in Fig. 2. At the end point, the N_G will be minimum, ideally zero. The location of minimas in N_G gives the location of end points of all the segments in the given utterance.

Given the reachability threshold ϵ and parameter K in K-step temporal unreachability, any utterance can be segmented into phoneme-like units. The segmentation performance critically depends on the choice of ϵ. Acoustic properties of the segments differ across segments. For example, a frame taken from voiced segment will be more similar to another frame taken from voiced segment as compared to a frame taken from an unvoiced segment. This makes finding a global ϵ very hard which is consistent across different segments. So, we use an ϵ value that adapts itself according to the acoustic properties of the segment.

To automatically determine the value of ϵ and to allow different segments to use separate ϵ threshold, we develop a simple algorithm. The algorithm is based on the observation that similarity between frames of the same segment is higher than the average similarity. New threshold for x_i frame is given as

$$\epsilon_i = \frac{\sum_{j=i}^{\tau} G(i,j)}{\tau} \tag{3}$$

where τ is the diagonal window constraint. For each frame, a different ϵ is computed automatically using the acoustic properties of the segment in consideration.

After getting segment boundaries, minimum length criteria is used for avoiding segments that are not possible. Minimum length is fixed to be 20 ms. K is chosen to be equal to the minimum length of the segment because if there is a segment boundary then at least minimum length number of frames will be temporally unreachable after the boundary. For longer segments, the number of unreachable points will exceed minimum length.

3 Experimental Evaluation

The speech segmentation algorithm proposed in the paper was evaluated on TIMIT [29] and Zero Resource 2015 databases: Tsonga and English [30]. The following sections explain the performance evaluation on both the benchmarks. The kernel width is simply kept 1 and the algorithm determines the value of ϵ automatically.

3.1 Experimental Evaluation on TIMIT

TIMIT dataset has been used for evaluation segmentation algorithms [12, 21–24]. All the sentences were manually transcribed and segmented at phone level using 61 phone labels. In this work, we have used MFCC features to represent the state of the vocal-tract system at a given instant of time. The segment boundaries are extracted from the kernel-Gram matrix, computed from the MFCC features, as discussed in Sect. 2. Let N_C be the number of correctly detected boundaries (within a given tolerance interval), N_T is the total number of detected boundaries and N_G is the total number manual boundaries. The performance of the proposed algorithm is evaluated, by comparing the detected boundaries with the manually marked boundaries, using the following intermediate metrics:

- Hit Rate (HR): It is the fraction of reference boundaries that are correctly detected (N_C/N_G). It is also called recall rate of the segmentation system.
- Over Segmentation (OS): It represents how many extra (less) boundaries are detected as compared to reference boundaries $((N_T - N_G)/N_G)$.
- False Alarm (FA): The fraction of incorrectly detected boundaries $((N_T - N_C)/N_T)$.

The overall quantification of segmentation algorithm is done with a global measure, F score, which combines all the intermediate scores.

$$F = \frac{2*(1 - FA)*HR}{1 - FA + HR} \qquad (4)$$

There is another global measure, R, which emphasizes more on over segmentation (OS). It argues that recall rate can be increased by inserting random boundaries without changing the algorithm.

$$r_1 = \sqrt{(1 - HR)^2 + (OS)^2}; \; r_2 = \frac{-OS + HR - 1}{\sqrt{2}} \qquad (5)$$

The final metric is defined as

$$R = 1 - \frac{|r_1| + |r_2|}{2} \qquad (6)$$

We use metrics R and F for evaluating the segmentation algorithm. The performance of the proposed algorithm is given in Table 1. For $h = 1$, approximately 73% of the detected boundaries fall within the 20 ms tolerance interval from the manually marked boundaries Table 2.

Table 1. Performance comparison of speech segmentation algorithms for 20 ms tolerance window. The * mark represents use of a validation set for parameter fine tuning.

Method	F	R
Kernel width (h = 1)	0.76	0.79
Dusan and Rabiner [12]	0.71	0.73
Khanagha et al. [23]	0.74	0.77
Stan et al. [22] *	0.76	0.80
Leow et al. [21] *	0.75	0.78
Rasanen et al. [24] *	0.76	0.78

Table 2. Results (in percentage) for STD task on Zerospeech 2015 databases: English and Xitsonga (in brackets). The best scores for each evaluation metric are highlighted in bold.

System	Boundary		
	Precision	Recall	F-score
Baseline [31]	44.1 (22.3)	4.7 (5.6)	8.6 (8.9)
Vseg [32]	**76.1** (26.2)	28.5 (26.3)	41.4 (26.3)
EnvMin [32]	75.7 (16.3)	27.4 (24.4)	40.3 (19.5)
Osc [32]	75.7 **(29.2)**	33.7 (39.4)	46.7 (33.5)
CC-PLP [33]	39.6 (19.4)	7.5 (11.2)	12.7 (14.2)
CC-FDPLS [33]	35.4 (18.8)	38.5 (64)	36.9 (29)
Proposed	41.2 (22.5)	**71.1 (74.8)**	**52.2 (34.6)**

The agglomerative algorithm proposed by Qiao et al., requires the number of expected segments as input [20]. This method uses manual transcriptions for calculating the exact number of segments for the input utterance. The neural network based segmentation method proposed by Vuuren et al. [34] used transcriptions for entire train data to learn the probability distribution of segment lengths. Both these approaches achieve very high performance but due to their strong prior requirements, recent works [22,23] have put them in the category of semi-supervised approaches and performance comparison is done only with zero or minimal fine tuning approaches. We follow the same practice. Stan et al. [22] used a small validation set for adjusting the minimum peak height in probability function. Also, the beginning and end silence regions were trimmed to

50 ms which contribute a high number of spectral discontinuities in input signal. Leow et al. [21] found the best performing system by evaluating the performance and then choosing the parameters of the best system. In the proposed method, the kernel width is simply kept 1. The proposed algorithm selects the optimal number of segments automatically.

3.2 Zero Resource 2015

We also evaluate the performance of the proposed segmentation method on the zero speech challenge 2015 datasets. This dataset consists of 10.5 h of casual conversations in American English, and 5 h of read speech in Xitsonga. The aim of the challenge (Track 2) was to discover recurring speech patterns in an unsupervised manner. Evaluation kit for measuring quality of discovered sub-words were provided as part of the challenge. Segments are clustered and combined to discover large segments but the boundaries are not altered during that step. In the present work, we only evaluate the segmentation performance. Recall measures the probability of finding a manual boundary within 30 ms of a discovered boundary. Precision measures the probability that a discovered boundary is within 30 ms of a manual boundary. The F-score is the harmonic mean of precision and recall. If the algorithm predicts boundaries only where manual boundaries are, then both precision and recall will be 1. The recall can be increased by predicting more boundaries but that would decrease the precision. Similarly, precision can be increased by predicting limited number of boundaries. The precision and recall can be traded off for each other. The F-score combines both of them and is used as a global measure for segmentation evaluation.

4   Summary and Conclusion

This study presents a new method for segmenting speech signals into phoneme like segments and a quantitative analysis between automatically detected boundaries and manually segmented boundaries on TIMIT database and Zero Resource 2015 database. The proposed algorithm achieves very high performance regardless of the language, recording environments or length of the utterances. In the proposed approach, all the frames estimate the end point of the segment they belong to. The individual decisions are then combined to give final end point decision. It reduces the deviation between predicted boundaries and manual boundaries. This is analogous to ensemble learning where several weak classifiers are combined to achieve performance on par with a single strong classifier. The proposed algorithm achieves the best performance among the blind segmentation algorithm on both databases.

Factors such as K point unreachability, adaptive threshold for each frame and combination of several end points improve the overall performance of the algorithm. We believe that performance can be improved by using more information rich features. The method presented in the paper can also be used in other sequence segmentation problems.

References

1. Rabiner, L.R.: A tutorial on hidden Markov models and selected applications in speech recognition. Proc. IEEE **77**(2), 257–286 (1989)
2. Moulines, E., Charpentier, F.: Pitch-synchronous waveform processing techniques for text-to-speech synthesis using diphones. Speech Commun. **9**(5–6), 453–467 (1990)
3. Furui, S.: Digital Speech Processing: Synthesis, and Recognition. CRC Press, Boca Raton (2000)
4. Wang, A., et al.: An industrial strength audio search algorithm. In: ISMIR, vol. 2003, pp. 7–13, Washington, D.C. (2003)
5. Pan, S.J., Yang, Q.: A survey on transfer learning. IEEE Trans. Knowl. Data Eng. **22**(10), 1345–1359 (2010)
6. Gales, M.J., Young, S.J.: Robust continuous speech recognition using parallel model combination. IEEE Trans. Speech Audio Process. **4**(5), 352–359 (1996)
7. Brugnara, F., Falavigna, D., Omologo, M.: Automatic segmentation and labeling of speech based on hidden Markov models. Speech Commun. **12**(4), 357–370 (1993)
8. Demuynck, K., Laureys, T.: A comparison of different approaches to automatic speech segmentation. In: Sojka, P., Kopeček, I., Pala, K. (eds.) TSD 2002. LNCS (LNAI), vol. 2448, pp. 277–284. Springer, Heidelberg (2002). https://doi.org/10.1007/3-540-46154-X_38
9. Scharenborg, O., Ernestus, M., Wan, V.: Segmentation of speech: child's play? (2007)
10. Rybach, D., Gollan, C., Schluter, R., Ney, H.: Audio segmentation for speech recognition using segment features. In: IEEE International Conference on Acoustics, Speech and Signal Processing, ICASSP 2009, pp. 4197–4200. IEEE (2009)
11. Davy, M., Godsill, S.: Detection of abrupt spectral changes using support vector machines an application to audio signal segmentation. In: 2002 IEEE International Conference on Acoustics, Speech, and Signal Processing (ICASSP), vol. 2, pp. 1313–1316. IEEE (2002)
12. Dusan, S., Rabiner, L.: On the relation between maximum spectral transition positions and phone boundaries. In: Ninth International Conference on Spoken Language Processing (2006)
13. Aversano, G., Esposito, A., Marinaro, M.: A new text-independent method for phoneme segmentation. In: Proceedings of the 44th IEEE 2001 Midwest Symposium on Circuits and Systems, MWSCAS 2001, vol. 2, pp. 516–519. IEEE (2001)
14. Goodwin, M.M., Laroche, J.: Audio segmentation by feature-space clustering using linear discriminant analysis and dynamic programming. In: IEEE Workshop on Applications of Signal Processing to Audio and Acoustics, pp. 131–134. IEEE (2003)
15. Estevan, Y.P., Wan, V., Scharenborg, O.: Finding maximum margin segments in speech. In: IEEE International Conference on Acoustics, Speech and Signal Processing, ICASSP 2007, vol. 4, pp. 937–940. IEEE (2007)
16. Park, A.S., Glass, J.R.: Unsupervised pattern discovery in speech. IEEE Trans. Audio Speech Lang. Process. **16**(1), 186–197 (2008)
17. Micallef, P., Chilton, T.: Automatic identification of phoneme boundaries using a mixed parameter model. In: Fifth European Conference on Speech Communication and Technology (1997)
18. van Santen, J.P., Sproat, R.: High-accuracy automatic segmentation. In: EUROSPEECH (1999)

19. Chang, J.W., Glass, J.R.: Segmentation and modeling in segment-based recognition. In: Fifth European Conference on Speech Communication and Technology (1997)
20. Qiao, Y., Shimomura, N., Minematsu, N.: Unsupervised optimal phoneme segmentation: objectives, algorithm and comparisons. In: IEEE International Conference on Acoustics, Speech and Signal Processing, ICASSP 2008, pp. 3989–3992. IEEE (2008)
21. Leow, S.J., Chng, E.S., Lee, C.-H.: Language-resource independent speech segmentation using cues from a spectrogram image. In: 2015 IEEE International Conference on Acoustics, Speech and Signal Processing (ICASSP), pp. 5813–5817. IEEE (2015)
22. Stan, A., Valentini-Botinhao, C., Orza, B., Giurgiu, M.: Blind speech segmentation using spectrogram image-based features and Mel cepstral coefficients. In: 2016 IEEE Spoken Language Technology Workshop (SLT), pp. 597–602. IEEE (2016)
23. Khanagha, V., Daoudi, K., Pont, O., Yahia, H.: Phonetic segmentation of speech signal using local singularity analysis. Digit. Signal Proc. **35**, 86–94 (2014)
24. Rasanen, O., Laine, U., Altosaar, T.: Blind segmentation of speech using non-linear filtering methods. In: Speech Technologies. InTech (2011)
25. Lee, C., Glass, J.: A nonparametric Bayesian approach to acoustic model discovery. In: Proceedings of the 50th Annual Meeting of the Association for Computational Linguistics: Long Papers, vol. 1, pp. 40–49. Association for Computational Linguistics (2012)
26. Vert, J.-P., Tsuda, K., Schölkopf, B.: A primer on kernel methods. In: Kernel Methods in Computational Biology, pp. 35–70 (2004)
27. Rabiner, L.R.: Multirate Digital Signal Processing. Prentice Hall PTR, Upper Saddle River (1996)
28. Ester, M., Kriegel, H.-P., Sander, J., Xu, X., et al.: A density-based algorithm for discovering clusters in large spatial databases with noise. In: KDD, vol. 96, no. 34, pp. 226–231 (1996)
29. Garofolo, J.S., Lamel, L.F., Fisher, W.M., Fiscus, J.G., Pallett, D.S.: DARPA TIMIT acoustic-phonetic continuous speech corpus CD-ROM. NIST speech disc 1-1.1. NASA STI/Recon Technical report N, vol. 93 (1993)
30. Versteegh, M., Thiolliere, R., Schatz, T., Cao, X.-N., Anguera, X., Jansen, A., Dupoux, E.: The zero resource speech challenge 2015. In: Interspeech, pp. 3169–3173 (2015)
31. Jansen, A., Van Durme, B.: Efficient spoken term discovery using randomized algorithms. In: IEEE Workshop on Automatic Speech Recognition and Understanding (ASRU), pp. 401–406. IEEE (2011)
32. Räsänen, O., Doyle, G., Frank, M.C.: Unsupervised word discovery from speech using automatic segmentation into syllable-like units. In: Sixteenth Annual Conference of the International Speech Communication Association (2015)
33. Lyzinski, V., Sell, G., Jansen, A.: An evaluation of graph clustering methods for unsupervised term discovery. In: Sixteenth Annual Conference of the International Speech Communication Association (2015)
34. Vuuren, V., Bosch, L., Niesler, T.: Unconstrained speech segmentation using deep neural networks. In: Proceedings of the International Conference on Pattern Recognition Applications and Methods, ICPRAM 2015, vol. 1, pp. 248–254 (2015)

Design of Biorthogonal Wavelet Filters of DTCWT Using Factorization of Halfband Polynomials

Shrishail S. Gajbhar[(⊠)] and Manjunath V. Joshi

DA-IICT, Gandhinagar, Gujarat, India
{shrishail_gajbhar,mv_joshi}@daiict.ac.in

Abstract. In this paper, we propose a new approach for designing the biorthogonal wavelet filters (BWFs) of Dual-Tree Complex Wavelet Transform (DTCWT). Proposed approach provides an effective way to handle the frequency response characteristics of these filters. This is done by optimizing the free variables obtained using factorization of generalized halfband polynomial (GHBP). The designed filters using proposed approach have better frequency response characteristics than those obtained by using binomial spectral factorization approach. Also, their associated wavelets show improved *analyticity* in terms of qualitative and quantitative measures. Transform-based image denoising using the proposed filters shows better visual as well as quantitative performance.

Keywords: Wavelet transform · Complex wavelet
Spectral factorization

1 Introduction

In recent years, Dual-Tree Complex Wavelet Transform (DTCWT) has gained popularity as one of the important transform-domain processing tools in wide range of multimedia applications such as image [1] and video denoising [2], fusion [3], watermarking [4] to name a few. Unlike discrete wavelet transform (DWT), it offers better directionality, near-shift invariance and phase information with limited redundancy. In practice, DTCWT is implemented using two branches of DWT referred to as primal (filter bank: h) and dual (filter bank: g) tree and outputs of these are considered as the real and imaginary parts of the complex coefficient representation of an input signal. With the use of orthogonal/biorthogonal finite impulse response (FIR) filters in these trees, the transform is approximately *analytic* with a redundancy factor of just 2^m for an input of m-dimensional (m-D) signal, while the directionality is $2^{(m-1)} \times (2^m - 1)$. The idea for constructing *dual-tree complex wavelet transform* (DTCWT) was first proposed by Nick Kingsbury [5,6] and subsequently developed by Selesnick in [7,8]. We refer to [9] as an excellent tutorial paper on various aspects of DTCWT.

Although, DTCWT output representation is complex valued, real-valued filter coefficients are used in the construction and no complex arithmetic is

© Springer Nature Singapore Pte Ltd. 2018
R. Rameshan et al. (Eds.): NCVPRIPG 2017, CCIS 841, pp. 150–162, 2018.
https://doi.org/10.1007/978-981-13-0020-2_14

required which is very much advantageous. However, design of such filters is quite challenging [10], since the filter coefficients need to satisfy various constraints. Selesnick [7] was the first researcher to arrive at certain conditions that must be satisfied by the DTCWT filters in order to have desired *analyticity* property. He showed that if the wavelet functions associated with the two trees of DTCWT are Hilbert transform pairs, the transform is completely analytic and shift-invariant. Since, obtaining perfect analyticity is difficult using compactly supported filters, approximate analyticity and near shift-invariance can be achieved using FIR orthogonal/biorthogonal wavelet filters [8]. In order to have these properties, filters must satisfy *perfect reconstruction* (PR), *vanishing moment* (VM) and *half-sample delay* (HSD) constraints as minimum requirements. HSD condition plays the role of coupling between two trees of DTCWT to have approximate Hilbert transform relationship. Intuitively, the HSD requirement given by Selesnick is equivalent to Kingsbury's [6] idea of doubling the sampling rate at each scale thus largely removing the aliasing caused by downsamplers and making the transform nearly shift-invariant [9]. The concept of *generalized* HSD is used in [11,12] to obtain M-band extensions of orthogonal and biorthogonal DTCWT, respectively. Theoretical details about the necessary and sufficient conditions in case of orthogonal and biorthogonal DTCWT filters can be found in [13,14], respectively.

Traditional wavelet filter design techniques cannot be used directly to design DTCWT filters since they only consider PR and VM conditions. Considering the much needed HSD requirement, various approaches are proposed in the literature to obtain orthogonal/biorthogonal DTCWT filters [9,10].

In this paper, we only consider the design of biorthogonal FIR filters by modifying the common factor approach [8]. The filters designed using common factor approach [8] have poor frequency response since it uses maximum number of vanishing moments i.e., zeros at $z = -1$ or $\omega = \pi$ resulting in zero degrees of freedom to shape the filter response characteristics. Hence, it is desired to have filters with good frequency response characteristics to minimize the *inherent* residual amplitude distortion present in the maximally decimated filter banks used in the two trees of DTCWT.

The paper is organized as follows. In Sect. 2, we give the background to understand the DTCWT basics and briefly describe the common factor technique. In Sect. 3, proposed approach is described while Sect. 4 details the design examples of the proposed approach along with their qualitative and quantitative measures. In Sect. 5, we discuss image denoising application using the designed filters. Section 6 concludes the paper.

2   Background Review

Figure 1 shows core structure of the DTCWT. It has two trees consisting of 2-channel filter banks that use 1-D biorthogonal wavelet filters.

In Tree-1, the filters $\tilde{h}_0(n)$ and $\tilde{h}_1(n)$ represent the analysis lowpass and highpass filters, respectively. Similarly, the $h_0(n)$ and $h_1(n)$ represent the same

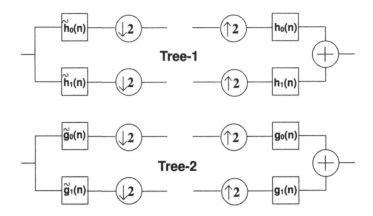

Fig. 1. Two trees of 2-channel filter banks used in DTCWT construction

on the synthesis side referred to as synthesis lowpass and highpass filters. They are related to each other as follows

$$\tilde{h}_1(n) = -(-1)^n h_0(n), \ \ 0 \leq n \leq N - 1$$
$$h_1(n) = (-1)^n \tilde{h}_0(n), \ \ 0 \leq n \leq \tilde{N} - 1. \tag{1}$$

Here, $\tilde{N}$ and N represent lengths of the filters $\tilde{h}_0(n)$ and $h_0(n)$, respectively. Similar relations hold good in the case of filters in Tree-2.

Let, $\phi_h(t)$ and $\phi_g(t)$ be the synthesis scaling functions of Tree-1 and Tree-2, respectively and $\psi_h(t)$ and $\psi_g(t)$ be their corresponding wavelet functions. Then the two-scale equations associated with these are given as

$$\phi_h(t) = \sqrt{2} \sum_n h_0(n) \phi_h(2t - n)$$
$$\psi_h(t) = \sqrt{2} \sum_n h_1(n) \phi_h(2t - n)$$
$$\phi_g(t) = \sqrt{2} \sum_n g_0(n) \phi_g(2t - n)$$
$$\psi_g(t) = \sqrt{2} \sum_n g_1(n) \phi_g(2t - n). \tag{2}$$

In a similar way one can define analysis wavelet functions $\tilde{\psi}_h(t)$ and $\tilde{\psi}_g(t)$. In order to have approximate analyticity of DTCWT, we require that $\psi_g(t) \approx \mathcal{H}\{\psi_h(t)\}$ and $\tilde{\psi}_g(t) \approx \mathcal{H}\{\tilde{\psi}_h(t)\}$ [7,8] representing Hilbert transform pairs criteria. This indicates that the synthesis and analysis wavelet functions of Tree-2 are *approximately* Hilbert transforms of Tree-1 wavelet functions. In Fourier domain, these relations are given as

$$\Psi_g(\omega) \approx \begin{cases} -j\Psi_h(\omega), & \omega > 0 \\ j\Psi_h(\omega), & \omega < 0. \end{cases} \tag{3}$$

Similar expressions exist for $\tilde{\Psi}_g(\omega)$. Here, $\Psi_h(\omega)$, $\Psi_g(\omega)$, $\tilde{\Psi}_h(\omega)$ and $\tilde{\Psi}_g(\omega)$ represent Fourier transforms of $\psi_h(t)$, $\psi_g(t)$, $\tilde{\psi}_h(t)$ and $\tilde{\psi}_g(t)$, respectively. Since, wavelet functions depend on the scaling functions which in turn depend on the lowpass filters associated with that scaling function, the problem of designing the Hilbert transform pairs of wavelet bases reduces to designing the lowpass filters that satisfy $g_0(n) \approx h_0(n-0.5)$ which is known as *half-sample delay* (HSD) constraint [9]. In Fourier domain, this can be expressed as

$$G_0(\omega) \approx e^{-j\frac{\omega}{2}} H_0(\omega) \tag{4}$$

where, $G_0(\omega)$ and $H_0(\omega)$ are Fourier transforms of $g_0(n)$ and $h_0(n)$, respectively. One can design these filters by approximating the magnitude and phase responses as

$$|G_0(\omega)| = |H_0(\omega)| \tag{5}$$

$$\angle G_0(\omega) = -\frac{\omega}{2} + \angle H_0(\omega). \tag{6}$$

Due to the nature of the Eq. (4), one of the two conditions given in Eqs. (5) and (6) is satisfied *exactly* or both are approximated. Common factor design method satisfies the magnitude condition exactly while phase condition is approximately met by using maximally flat all pass filters which is reviewed in the next subsection since proposed approach is based on the same.

2.1   Common Factor Technique

Common factor technique [8] proposed by Selesnick uses a two stage design process to approximate the relation given in Eq. (4) and finally obtains the required filters of DTCWT shown in Fig. 1. In the first stage, half-sample delay constraint is approximated using Thiran's maximally flat allpass filters [15]. Perfect reconstruction and vanishing moment constraints are imposed in the second stage by considering the use of *maxflat* halfband polynomial factorization approach. Both the stages are combined to obtain the final product filter $P(z)$ to design the biorthogonal wavelet filters. Here, we only need to design the product filter of one of the two trees i.e., either of the following two Eqs. (7) and (8) can be used.

$$P(z) = \tilde{H}_0(z)H_0(z) \tag{7}$$

$$= \tilde{G}_0(z)G_0(z). \tag{8}$$

Here, $\tilde{H}_0(z)$, $H_0(z)$, $\tilde{G}_0(z)$ and $G_0(z)$ are the $z-$transforms of $\tilde{h}_0(n)$, $h_0(n)$, $\tilde{g}_0(n)$ and $g_0(n)$, respectively. If the lengths of the filters $\tilde{h}_0(n)$ and $h_0(n)$ are $\tilde{N}$ and N, respectively, the filters of Tree-2 can be obtained using time-reversal relationship as

$$\tilde{g}_0(n) = \tilde{h}_0(\tilde{N}-1-n), \ \ 0 \leq n \leq \tilde{N}-1 \tag{9}$$

$$g_0(n) = h_0(N-1-n), \ \ 0 \leq n \leq N-1. \tag{10}$$

The filters $\tilde{h}_0(n)$ and $h_0(n)$ are obtained using polynomial factorization of the form $\tilde{H}_0(z) = \tilde{F}_0(z)D(z)$ and $H_0(z) = F_0(z)D(z^{-1})z^{-L}$, where $D(z)$ and $D(z^{-1})z^{-L}$ are chosen such that

$$A(z) = \frac{D(z^{-1})z^{-L}}{D(z)} = z^{-1/2}|_{z=1}. \tag{11}$$

which represents an all pass filter approximation of half-sample delay. Here, $D(z) \xrightarrow{z} d(n)$ represents a z-transform pair and L represents order of the filter $d(n)$ obtained using Eq. (12).

$$d(n+1) = d(n).\frac{(L-n)(L-n-0.5)}{(n+1)(n+1+0.5)}, \quad 0 \leq n \leq L-1 \tag{12}$$

where, $d(0) = 1$. Factors $\tilde{F}_0(z)$ and $F_0(z)$ are *maxflat* or *binomial* filters used in order to satisfy the *perfect reconstruction* and *vanishing moments* criteria and are of the form $\tilde{Q}(z)(1 + z^{-1})^{\tilde{K}}$ and $Q(z)(1 + z^{-1})^{K}$, respectively. The polynomials $\tilde{Q}(z)$ and $Q(z)$ are obtained by solving a set of linear equations by imposing halfband constraint on $P(z)$. Here, $\tilde{K}$ and K represent the number of VMs for $\tilde{h}_0(n)$ and $h_0(n)$, respectively. Since the filters are chosen to satisfy Eqs. (9) and (10), the magnitude condition given in Eq. (5) is exactly satisfied, whereas the phase condition given in Eq. (6) is approximated since the order L used is finite. Ideally L should be ∞ to satisfy the Eq. (11) exactly.

3   Proposed Approach

In the proposed approach, we use factorization of generalized halfband polynomial (GHBP) [16]. Here, we propose and design generalized halfband polynomial such that perfect reconstruction (PR) and vanishing moment (VM) and half-sample delay (HSD) constraints are satisfied for any values of the free variables. Given Eq. (7) or (8), we obtain the generalized halfband polynomial for $P(z)$ that satisfies PR, VM and HSD constraints in order to design the DTCWT filters of Tree-1 i.e., $\tilde{h}_0(n)$ and $h_0(n)$. There are three input parameters $\tilde{K}$, K and L. Here, $\tilde{K}$ and K represent number of vanishing moments for $\tilde{h}_0(n)$ and $h_0(n)$, respectively while L represents order of $d(n)$ i.e., denominator polynomial of an allpass filter used to approximate the HSD condition. Since, we wish to design $\tilde{h}_0(n)$ and $h_0(n)$ as real symmetric odd-length filters of arbitrary lengths, all the input parameters must be even. Let, n_f be the number of free variables used in the optimization to shape the frequency response characteristics. We then select the GHBP of order D given by

$$P^D(z) = a_0 + a_2 z^{-2} + \cdots + a_{(D/2)-1} z^{-(D/2)-1} + z^{-(D/2)}$$
$$+ a_{(D/2)-1} z^{-(D/2)+1} + \cdots + a_0 z^{-D}, \tag{13}$$

where the polynomial order D is chosen as $D = 2(M-1) + 4L + 8n_f$. Note that, order D is chosen such that it includes *desired* number of VMs, L^{th} order all-pass HSD approximation with n_f degrees of freedom available to shape the frequency responses of the filters. Here, $M = \tilde{K} + K$ represents total number of VMs required in the design. For $P^D(z)$ of order D, there exist maximum $(\frac{D}{2}+1)$ zeros at $z = -1$ and $\frac{(D+2)}{4}$ unknown variables i.e., a_i, $i = 0, 2, \ldots, (\frac{D}{2} - 1)$. By imposing M number of zeros at $z = -1$, the $P^D(z)$ can then be expressed as

$$P^D(z) = (1 + z^{-1})^M R(z) = (1 + z^{-1})^{\tilde{K}+K} R(z)$$
$$= \tilde{F}_0(z)F_0(z), \tag{14}$$

where, the term $(1 + z^{-1})$ represents the condition on vanishing moments i.e., zero at $z = -1$ or $\omega = \pi$ which decides smoothness or regularity of the wavelet functions and $R(z)$ is a remainder polynomial expressed in terms of free variables. Here, a double zero at $z = -1$ eliminates one degree of freedom from $P^D(z)$, thus $\frac{M}{2}$ unknown variables are expressed in terms of $n_f = \left(\frac{D+2}{4} - \frac{M}{2}\right)$ free variables in the remainder polynomial $R(z)$. With this, our modified product filter to design the lowpass filters of Tree-1 i.e., $\tilde{h}_0(n)$ and $h_0(n)$ can be chosen as

$$P(z) = P^D(z)D(z)D(z^{-1})z^{-L} \tag{15}$$
$$P(z) = P^D(z)D_L(z). \tag{16}$$

The polynomial factor $D_L(z) = D(z)D(z^{-1})z^{-L}$ used here represents *half-sample delay* constraint. Due to this, $P(z)$ is no longer a halfband polynomial and perfect reconstruction property of the designed filters is lost. Therefore, we impose halfband constraints on $P(z)$ to make it a halfband polynomial before the factorization step. Using Eq. (14), $P(z)$ can be then written as

$$P(z) = (1 + z^{-1})^{\tilde{K}+K} R(z)D_L(z) \tag{17}$$
$$P(z) = B(z)R(z). \tag{18}$$

Imposing Halfband Constraints: In Eq. (18), coefficients of the $B(z)$ polynomial are exactly known while $R(z)$ is a symmetric polynomial having unknown variables $a_i, i = 0, 2, \ldots, (D/2) - 1$ as coefficients. After collecting the terms of the product $B(z)R(z)$, we get $P(z)$ which has both odd and even powers of z i.e., it violates the halfband condition. Hence, coefficients of even powers of z are made 0 while the center term (or constant term) is chosen to be 1 in order to obtain the halfband polynomial $P(z)$. Remainder polynomial $R(z)$ in Eq. (18) is now expressed in terms of desired n_f number of free variables.

We use MATLAB optimization toolbox routine *fminunc* to obtain the filters $\tilde{H}_0(z)$ and $H_0(z)$ by minimizing the following objective function with respect to n_f number of free variables as

$$F_{obj} = \int_0^{\omega_p} \left|1 - \tilde{H}_0(\omega)\right|^2 d\omega + \int_{\omega_s}^{\pi} \left|\tilde{H}_0(\omega)\right|^2 d\omega$$

$$+ \int_0^{\omega_p} \left|1 - H_0(\omega)\right|^2 d\omega + \int_{\omega_s}^{\pi} \left|H_0(\omega)\right|^2 d\omega. \tag{19}$$

Here, ω_p and ω_s represent passband and stopband cut-off frequencies (in radian), respectively. Expressions for $\tilde{H}_0(\omega)$ and $H_0(\omega)$ are given as:

$$\tilde{H}_0(\omega) = (1 + z^{-1})^{\tilde{K}} R_1(z) D(z)|_{z=e^{j\omega}} \tag{20}$$

$$H_0(\omega) = (1 + z^{-1})^{K} R_2(z) D(z^{-1}) z^{-L}|_{z=e^{j\omega}}. \tag{21}$$

During the optimization, for given values of the free variables polynomial $R(z)$ is first evaluated and factorized into polynomials $R_1(z)$ and $R_2(z)$. Since, this factorization is not unique the objective function value is then computed for all possible combinations of real-valued symmetric polynomials $R_1(z)$ and $R_2(z)$. We choose them to be symmetric polynomials such that $\tilde{h}_0(n)$ and $h_0(n)$ obtained are real-valued biorthogonal filters having near-orthogonal frequency response characteristics. Due to *approximation* of the HSD condition using finite length polynomial, the designed filters have approximate linear-phase property.

4   Design Example

Input parameters chosen are $\tilde{K} = 2$, $K = 4$, $L = 2$ and $n_f = 1$. The lengths of the designed filters $\tilde{h}_0(n)$ and $h_0(n)$ is 11 and 13, respectively. Biorthogonal filters given in Table 3 of [8] also have the same lengths for the filters $\tilde{h}_0(n)$ and $h_0(n)$. These filters were obtained using *max-flat* factorization approach of Daubechies [17] with input parameters $\tilde{K} = K = 4$ and $L = 2$. We see from Table 1 that the filter coefficients obtained in our case are entirely different from [8]. Due to same lengths of the obtained filters and Selesnick's 11/13 filters [8], we compare the frequency response characteristics of both the filters. Figure 2 shows magnitude response comparison between proposed and Selesnick's 11/13 filters. It is clear that frequency response characteristics of the proposed filters are much better and closely mimic near-orthogonal filter response characteristics than those designed using maxflat approach. Wavelet plots for the proposed filters are shown in Fig. 3. Here, one can observe that apart from near-orthogonal frequency response characteristics of the designed filters, *analyticity* of their associated wavelets is also good. For $\omega < 0$, one see that the magnitude frequency plots of $|\tilde{\Psi}_h(\omega) + j\tilde{\Psi}_g(\omega)|$ and $|\Psi_h(\omega) + j\Psi_g(\omega)|$ have negligible frequency contents. Wavelets of the two trees are approximately Hilbert transform pairs of each other.

Table 1. Coefficients of the designed filters.

n	$\tilde{h}_0(n)$	$h_0(n)$
1	0.0015	0.0002
2	0.0007	−0.0001
3	0.0381	−0.0195
4	0.0080	0.0113
5	−0.3869	0.0772
6	−0.5781	−0.1724
7	−0.1584	−0.5473
8	0.0670	−0.3851
9	0.0055	0.0031
10	0.0025	0.0551
11	0.0003	−0.0149
12	-	−0.0088
13	-	0.0010

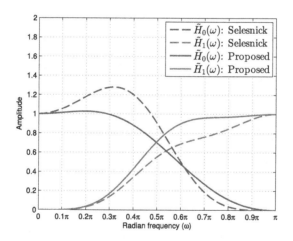

Fig. 2. Magnitude response comparison between Tree-1 analysis filters of the proposed 11/13 filters and Selesnick's 11/13 filters.

Apart from qualitative results, we also give quantitative evaluation of the designed filters using proposed approach to measure *analyticity* of their associated wavelets as well as *orthogonality* of their frequency response characteristics. The error measuring *analyticity* is quantified using two quantitative measures E_1 and E_2 given by Tay et al. in [18]. Ideally, E_1 and E_2 must be 0. For qualitative evaluation of the frequency response characteristics of the proposed

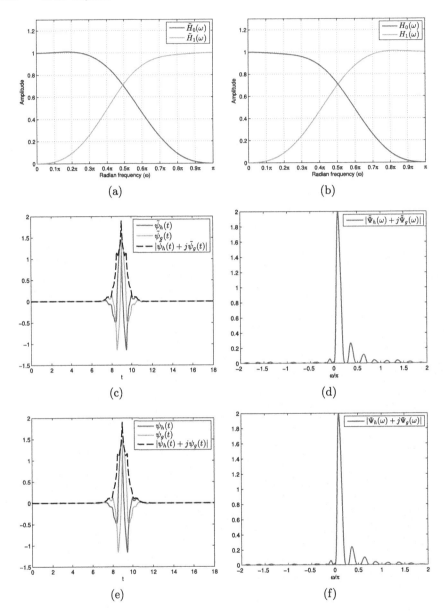

Fig. 3. Plots for the designed example (a) magnitude responses for analysis filters of Tree-1 i.e., $\tilde{H}_0(\omega)$ and $\tilde{H}_1(\omega)$ (b) magnitude responses for synthesis filters of Tree-1 i.e., $H_0(\omega)$ and $H_1(\omega)$. (c) Analysis wavelet functions $\tilde{\psi}_h(t)$, $\tilde{\psi}_g(t)$ and $|\tilde{\psi}_h(t) + j\tilde{\psi}_g(t)|$ (d) Magnitude frequency spectrum for $|\tilde{\Psi}_h(\omega) + j\tilde{\Psi}_g(\omega)|$ (e) Synthesis wavelet functions $\psi_h(t)$, $\psi_g(t)$ and $|\psi_h(t) + j\psi_g(t)|$ (f) Magnitude frequency spectrum for $|\Psi_h(\omega) + j\Psi_g(\omega)|$.

filters, we use two orthogonality measures given in [19,20]. They indicate how good the response characteristics match to the orthogonal filters which have ideal value of 0. Expression for the first measure used is $ON1 = \frac{1}{\pi} \int_0^\pi (2 - O(\omega))^2 d\omega$, where $O(\omega) = O(z)|_{z=e^{j\omega}}$ with $O(z) = H_0(z)H_0(z^{-1}) + H_1(z)H_1(z^{-1})$. Expression for the second measure is $ON2 = \left| |H_0\left(\frac{\pi}{2}\right)| - |H_1\left(\frac{\pi}{2}\right)| \right|$. Here, $H_0(z)$ and $H_1(z)$ denote analysis lowpass and highpass filters, respectively. Table 2 shows quantitative comparison of the filters designed using the proposed approach and common factor technique.

Table 2. Quantitative comparison of the filters.

	E_1 [18]	E_2 [18]	$ON1$ [19]	$ON2$ [20]
Proposed	0.0239	0.0008	0.0010	0.0145
Selesnick 11/13 [8]	0.0171	3.4E−04	0.0372	0.3510

5   Image Denoising Application

In this section, we show the performance of the proposed filter set for the image denoising application. We have used filters of the proposed set to obtain the 2-D DTCWT by using the construction given [9]. For comparing the image denoising performance, we have used the MATLAB software provided by Ivan W. Selesnick on his website [21]. We have compared our results with 2-D DTCWT obtained using Selesnick's 11/13 filters [8]. Additive white Gaussian noise (AWGN) of standard deviation σ is added to the original image in order to test the performance on noisy images. We have used *bivariate shrinkage* method [22] to obtain the denoised results. MATLAB implementation of the same can be found in the software mentioned above. Figure 4 shows image denoising results on widely used Lena image for AWGN of standard deviation $\sigma = 30$. It can be observed that image denoising performance of 2-D DTCWT obtained using proposed filter set outperforms Selesnick's 11/13 filters [8] in terms of Peak Signal-to-Noise Ratio (PSNR) value while considerable improvement is observed in case of recent image quality indicator values namely Structural Similarity Index Measure (SSIM) [23] and Feature Similarity Index Measure (FSIM) [24]. Both SSIM and FSIM have ideal value of 1. Denoising output shown in Fig. 4(d) for proposed filter set have better visual performance when compared to the output for Selesnick's filters shown in Fig. 4(c). Directional image features are better captured using the proposed filters due to better directional selectivity of their 2-D dual-tree directional wavelets. Also, due to near-orthogonality of the proposed filters, noise is better removed than that of Selesnick's filters.

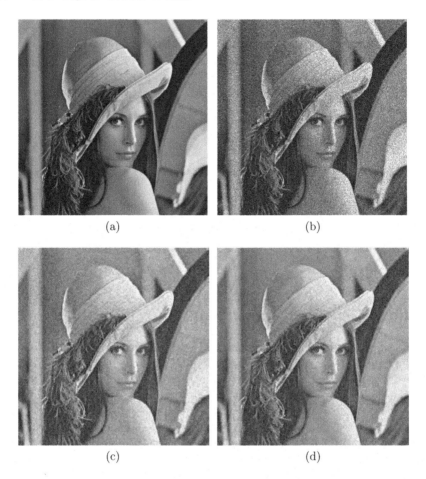

Fig. 4. Image denoising using 2-D DTCWT (a) original image (b) noisy image with $\sigma = 30$, PSNR $= 18.59$ dB. Denoising using (c) Selesnick's 11/13 filters [8], PSNR $= 28.73$ dB, SSIM [23] $= 0.73$ and FSIM [24] $= 0.90$. (d) proposed filters, PSNR $= 29.52$ dB, SSIM [23] $= 0.77$ and FSIM [24] $= 0.92$.

6   Conclusion

In this paper, we proposed a new approach to design the biorthogonal wavelet filters of DTCWT. The proposed approach is based on optimization of free variables obtained through factorization of generalized halfband polynomial. The designed filters using the proposed approach have better frequency response characteristics. Also, their associated wavelets show better analyticity in terms of qualitative as well as quantitative evaluation. Transform-based image denoising experiment using the proposed filters shows better performance in terms of qualitative and quantitative evaluation when compared to the filters designed using common factor approach.

References

1. Fierro, M., Ha, H.G., Ha, Y.H.: Noise reduction based on partial-reference, dual-tree complex wavelet transform Shrinkage. IEEE Trans. Image Process. **22**(5), 1859–1872 (2013)
2. Rabbani, H., Gazor, S.: Video denoising in three-dimensional complex wavelet domain using a doubly stochastic modelling. IET Image Process. **6**(9), 1262–1274 (2012)
3. Anantrasirichai, N., Achim, A., Kingsbury, N.G., Bull, D.R.: Atmospheric turbulence mitigation using complex wavelet-based fusion. IEEE Trans. Image Process. **22**(6), 2398–2408 (2013)
4. Asikuzzaman, M., Alam, M.J., Lambert, A.J., Pickering, M.R.: Robust DT-CWT based DIBR 3D video watermarking using chrominance embedding. IEEE Trans. Multimedia **18**(9), 1733–1748 (2016)
5. Kingsbury, N.: Image processing with complex wavelets. Philos. Trans. R. Soc. London A: Math. Phy. Eng. Sci. **357**(1760), 2543–2560 (1999)
6. Kingsbury, N.: Complex wavelets for shift invariant analysis and filtering of signals. Appl. Comput. Harmonic Anal. **10**(3), 234–253 (2001)
7. Selesnick, I.W.: Hilbert transform pairs of wavelet bases. IEEE Sig. Process. Lett. **8**(6), 170–173 (2001)
8. Selesnick, I.W.: The design of approximate Hilbert transform pairs of wavelet bases. IEEE Trans. Sig. Process. **50**(5), 1144–1152 (2002)
9. Selesnick, I.W., Baraniuk, R.G., Kingsbury, N.C.: The dual-tree complex wavelet transform. IEEE Sig. Process. Mag. **22**(6), 123–151 (2005)
10. Tay, D.B.H.: Designing Hilbert-pair of wavelets: recent progress and future trends. In: 6th International Conference on Information Communication & Signal Processing, pp. 1–5. IEEE (2007)
11. Chaux, C., Duval, L., Pesquet, J.C.: Image analysis using a dual-tree M-band wavelet transform. IEEE Trans. Image Process. **15**(8), 2397–2412 (2006)
12. Chaux, C., Pesquet, J.C., Duval, L.: 2D dual-tree complex biorthogonal M-band wavelet transform. In: 2007 IEEE International Conference on Acoustics, Speech and Signal Processing-ICASSP 2007, vol. 3, pp. III-845. IEEE (2007)
13. Yu, R., Ozkaramanli, H.: Hilbert transform pairs of orthogonal wavelet bases: necessary and sufficient conditions. IEEE Trans. Sig. Process. **53**(12), 4723–4725 (2005)
14. Yu, R., Ozkaramanli, H.: Hilbert transform pairs of biorthogonal wavelet bases. IEEE Trans. Sig. Process. **54**(6), 2119–2125 (2006)
15. Thiran, J.P.: Recursive digital filters with maximally flat group delay. IEEE Trans. Circ. Theory **18**(6), 659–664 (1971)
16. Patil, B.D., Patwardhan, P.G., Gadre, V.M.: On the design of FIR wavelet filter banks using factorization of a halfband polynomial. IEEE Sig. Process. Lett. **15**, 485–488 (2008)
17. Daubechies, I., et al.: Ten Lectures on Wavelets, vol. 61. SIAM, Philadelphia (1992)
18. Tay, D.B., Kingsbury, N.G., Palaniswami, M.: Orthonormal Hilbert-pair of wavelets with (almost) maximum vanishing moments. IEEE Sig. Process. Lett. **13**(9), 533–536 (2006)
19. Lightstone, M., Majani, E., Mitra, S.K.: Low bit-rate design considerations for wavelet-based image coding. Multidimension. Syst. Sig. Process. **8**(1–2), 111–128 (1997)

20. Rahulkar, A.D., Patil, B.D., Holambe, R.S.: A new approach to the design of biorthogonal triplet half-band filter banks using generalized half-band polynomials. Signal Image Video Process. **8**(8), 1451–1457 (2014)
21. Selesnick, I.W.: http://eeweb.poly.edu/iselesni/WaveletSoftware/. Accessed 04 Aug 2014
22. Sendur, L., Selesnick, I.W.: Bivariate shrinkage functions for wavelet-based denoising exploiting interscale dependency. IEEE Trans. Sig. Process. **50**(11), 2744–2756 (2002)
23. Wang, Z., Bovik, A.C., Sheikh, H.R., Simoncelli, E.P.: Image quality assessment: from error visibility to structural similarity. IEEE Trans. Image Process. **13**(4), 600–612 (2004)
24. Zhang, L., Zhang, L., Mou, X., Zhang, D.: FSIM: a feature similarity index for image quality assessment. IEEE Trans. Image Process. **20**(8), 2378–2386 (2011)

Single Noisy Image Super Resolution by Minimizing Nuclear Norm in Virtual Sparse Domain

Srimanta Mandal$^{(\boxtimes)}$ (iD) and A. N. Rajagopalan

Image Processing and Computer Vision Lab, Department of Electrical Engineering,
IIT Madras, Chennai 600036, India
in.srimanta.mandal@ieee.org, raju@ee.iitm.ac.in
http://www.ee.iitm.ac.in/ipcvlab/

Abstract. Super-resolving a noisy image is a challenging problem, and needs special care as compared to the conventional super resolution approaches, when the power of noise is unknown. In this scenario, we propose an approach to super-resolve single noisy image by minimizing nuclear norm in a virtual sparse domain that tunes with the power of noise via parameter learning. The approach minimizes nuclear norm to explore the inherent low-rank structure of visual data, and is further augmented with coarse-to-fine information by adaptively re-aligning the data along the principal components of a dictionary in *virtual sparse domain*. The experimental results demonstrate the robustness of our approach across different powers of noise.

Keywords: Super resolution · Noise · Nuclear norm
Virtual sparsity · Dictionary

1 Introduction

Super resolution (SR) techniques are quite useful in recovering high resolution (HR) image from low resolution (LR) image(s) by means of processing the image without any modification in hardware [1]. The LR image is believed to be formed by blurring followed by decimating the HR scene with some error, often termed as noise. Mathematically,

$$\mathbf{y} = \mathbf{LHx} + \mathbf{n}, \tag{1}$$

where $\mathbf{y} \in \mathbb{R}^N$ is the LR observation corresponding to the HR scene $\mathbf{x} \in \mathbb{R}^M$, $\mathbf{H} \in \mathbb{R}^{M \times M}$ is blur kernel, $\mathbf{L} \in \mathbb{R}^{N \times M}$ is responsible for decimation, and $\mathbf{n} \in \mathbb{R}^N$ is the noise $(M > N)$. SR techniques try to approximate $\mathbf{x}$ from $\mathbf{y}$, which is an ill-posed problem due to presence of $\mathbf{L}$, $\mathbf{H}$, and $\mathbf{n}$.

The ill-posed problem of SR is often addressed by complementary information from several LR images of the scene with sub-pixel shift precision or from some HR example images along with prior knowledge about the HR scene [2–6].

© Springer Nature Singapore Pte Ltd. 2018
R. Rameshan et al. (Eds.): NCVPRIPG 2017, CCIS 841, pp. 163–176, 2018.
https://doi.org/10.1007/978-981-13-0020-2_15

However, these classes of SR techniques may become inefficacious in absence of multiple sub-pixel shifted LR images or the example HR images. In such scenario exploring the redundancy present in target LR image across scales can be useful for SR [7–12]. However, presence of noise in the target image can degrade the SR performance. Only, few approaches have addressed the SR problem in noisy scenario [11,12]. The problem becomes more challenging, if the power of noise is not known a-priori [12].

In this paper, we propose to address the issue of SR from single image in presence of unknown power of noise. Here, we derive few parameters from the given LR image that reflect the power of noise with the help of algorithm developed by the approach of [12]. Unlike [12], we explore the intrinsic low-rank structure of visual data by minimizing the nuclear norm of the image in a virtual sparse domain. Here, we do not explicitly solve any sparse coding optimization. Instead, we select one dictionary from multiple choices, and re-align the data along the principal components of the dictionary with adaptive thresholding. Thus, the sense of sparsity comes in a virtual way, hence the word "virtual".

The rest of the paper is organized as follows: Sect. 2 briefs some of the related works. Section 3 describes the proposed SR work that consists of exploring low-rank structure of similar image patches and restoring HR image in virtual sparse domain. Experimental results are demonstrated in Sect. 4, and the paper is summarized in Sect. 5.

2 Related Works

Image SR approaches can be broadly classified into two categories based on the requirement of LR images of the scene: (i) Multi-frame SR, (ii) Single image SR. Classical multi-frame SR requires some LR sub-pixel shifted images of the scene such that the information from different views can be augmented to generate an HR image. Requirement of multiple LR images often becomes bottleneck for these kind of approaches. On the other hand, single image SR does not require multiple LR images. Nevertheless, it generally requires example HR images in order to import missing information of the target LR patch from similar patches from the database made up of the example images. However, absence of similar patches in the database may degrade the SR results.

This issue can be addressed by sparse representation framework, where a target patch is represented by a weighted combination of few patches. The patches from the database are represented as column vectors of an over-complete matrix, also known as *dictionary* [5,13–16]. Being a source of information, dictionary attracted lots of attention from the scientific community. As a result, it has several forms starting from simple analytical to advanced learning based multiple dictionaries [4,6,16–19]. In absence of example images, the patch similarity across scales can be investigated as is done by few approaches [7–11,20]. The working principle of these approaches is that similar image patches across scales can provide high frequency information for the target patch, as is the case of classical multi-frame SR. However, most of these approaches do not consider the presence of noise explicitly in the LR observation.

A few approaches have considered SR from a noisy LR observation [11,12]. The approach [11] addresses the problem as a combination of denoising and SR approaches. It derives two HR images by applying self-similarity based SR approach on the given LR image and the denoised version of the noisy LR image (achieved by a denoising algorithm). Further, the HR images are combined effectively by considering their orientations and frequency selective bands to produce the final HR image. On the other hand, the approach [12] undertakes the issue as SR problem with implicit blind denoising. The approach derives some parameters from the given LR image that reflect the power of noise, which are used in further processing of the LR image by restoring detail/non-local mean component of patch. The parameter estimation strategy of [12] becomes the basis of the proposed approach of SR in noisy case. As opposed to the approach [12], we explore the inherent low-rank structure of the image patches by minimizing the nuclear norm in virtual sparse domain. Further, we re-align group of similar patches along the principal components of the dictionary that is selected from multiple choices of dictionaries.

3   Proposed Approach

The proposed approach consists of mainly two stages: (a) Exploring low-rank structure of similar image patches, and (b) Restoration of image via virtual sparsity. Here, we discuss the stages in the following sub-sections.

3.1   Exploring Low-Rank Structure of Similar Image Patches

It has been explored that the low-rank assumption of matrix, composed of non-local similar patches of natural image is a good prior for image restoration tasks such as image denoising, image completion, and so on [21–24]. However, this prior has not received much attention in case of super resolution imaging. Here, we employ this prior information to super-resolve a noisy image.

First of all, the LR image $\mathbf{y}$ is interpolated onto an HR grid to produce an initial approximation. Overlapping patches are extracted from the initial approximation as $\mathbf{x}_i = \mathbf{P}_i(\mathbf{y}) \uparrow_l$, where $\mathbf{x}_i$ is the ith patch and $\mathbf{P}_i$ is the patch extraction matrix. In order to make low-rank assumption valid for the clean HR patches, we need to find a matrix of non-local similar patches for the clean HR image. Thus, we process the noisy image to find non-local similar patches to the ith patch by $||\mathbf{x}_i - \mathbf{x}_j||_2^2 \leq \epsilon, \forall j \neq i$. Finding similar patches in the entire image is time consuming process, hence we restrict ourselves to specific region surrounding the ith patch of the image[1]. The indices of patches within the region are denoted by the set $\boldsymbol{\zeta}_i$. All $\mathbf{x}_j$ that are similar to $\mathbf{x}_i$ are concatenated to form a matrix $\mathbf{X}_{i,m}$. The produced $\mathbf{X}_{i,m}$ is used to compute the detail component as

$$\mathbf{D}_{\mathbf{x}i,m} = \mathbf{X}_{i,m} - \mathcal{REP}\left[\sum_{j \in \zeta_i}\left\{\frac{1}{z}\exp\left(-\frac{||\mathbf{x}_i - \mathbf{x}_j||_2^2}{h}\right)\right\}\mathbf{x}_j\right]. \qquad (2)$$

---

[1] If we increase the area of the region to find similarity, a better result is expected in the cost of increased computational burden.

Here, $\mathcal{REP}[\cdot]$ repeats the vector "$\cdot$" to form a matrix of the same size as that of $\mathbf{X}_{i,m}$, z is the normalizing constant, and h controls the decay of the exponential function. Subtrahend of Eq. (2) is the weighted average of the non-local similar patches, which is also known as non-local mean ($\overline{\mathbf{X}_i}$) of the target patch. By assuming $\mathcal{D}_{\mathbf{x},i,m}$ to be the matrix for HR clean image, corresponding to $\mathbf{D}_{\mathbf{x}i,m}$, we can explore the low rank structure of $\mathcal{D}_{\mathbf{x},i,m}$ as

$$\hat{\mathcal{D}}_{\mathbf{x},i,m} = \arg\min_{\mathcal{D}_{\mathbf{x},i,m}} \left\{ ||\mathbf{D}_{\mathbf{x}i,m} - \mathcal{D}_{\mathbf{x},i,m}||_F^2 + \lambda\, \mathcal{R}\left(\mathcal{D}_{\mathbf{x},i,m}\right) \right\}. \tag{3}$$

Here, $\mathcal{R}\left(\mathcal{D}_{\mathbf{x},i,m}\right)$ is the rank of $\mathcal{D}_{\mathbf{x},i,m}$, and can be defined as the number of non-zero singular values σ_k of $\mathcal{D}_{\mathbf{x},i,m}$ i.e., $\mathcal{R}\left(\mathcal{D}_{\mathbf{x},i,m}\right) = \sum_k ||\sigma_k\left(\mathcal{D}_{\mathbf{x},i,m}\right)||_0$, where $||\cdot||_0$ is l_0 norm that counts the number of non-zero elements. However, minimization of $\mathcal{R}\left(\mathcal{D}_{\mathbf{x},i,m}\right)$ in this form is not convenient as it is non-convex as well as NP hard. Thus, the rank is replaced by its convex representation $\sum_k ||\sigma_k\left(\mathcal{D}_{\mathbf{x},i,m}\right)||_1$, which is also known as nuclear norm [22], and is generally represented as $||\mathcal{D}_{\mathbf{x},i,m}||_*$. So the Eq. (3) is modified as

$$\hat{\mathcal{D}}_{\mathbf{x},i,m} = \arg\min_{\mathcal{D}_{\mathbf{x},i,m}} \left\{ ||\mathbf{D}_{\mathbf{x}i,m} - \mathcal{D}_{\mathbf{x},i,m}||_F^2 + \lambda\, ||\mathcal{D}_{\mathbf{x},i,m}||_* \right\}. \tag{4}$$

The Eq. (4) can be solved by singular value decomposition of the matrix $\mathbf{D}_{\mathbf{x}i,m} = \mathbf{U}\mathbf{S}\mathbf{V}^T$, where the columns of $\mathbf{U}$ and $\mathbf{V}$ contain the left singular vectors and right singular vectors of $\mathbf{D}_{\mathbf{x}i,m}$, respectively. $\mathbf{S}$ is a diagonal matrix that contains the singular values of $\mathbf{D}_{\mathbf{x}i,m}$. It has been proved that by thresholding the singular value in conjunction with the unitary matrices $\mathbf{U}$ and $\mathbf{V}$, we can get a closed form solution to the Eq. (4) [25] as follows

$$\hat{\mathcal{D}}_{\mathbf{x},i,m} = \mathbf{U}\Gamma(\mathbf{S})_\lambda \mathbf{V}^T. \tag{5}$$

Here, $\Gamma(\cdot)_\lambda$ is a soft thresholding operator that operates on $\mathbf{S}$ to provide a *shrinked* $\mathbf{S}$.

$$\Gamma(\mathbf{S}_{k,k})_\lambda = \max\left(\mathbf{S}_{k,k} - \lambda, 0\right), \tag{6}$$

where, if elements of $\mathbf{S}$ are greater than λ, the operator shrinks those elements by a λ amount, otherwise it makes them zero. The parameter λ is derived from the noisy LR image by computing the ratio of first two singular values of the gradient components, as is done in the approach [12]. Depending on the power of noise, the parameter λ varies, and thus it adapts with the noise condition. Once, the low-rank approximation $\hat{\mathcal{D}}_{\mathbf{x},i,m}$ for clean HR image patch is achieved, we further process it to complement with coarse-to-fine information with the help of dictionaries in virtual sparse domain.

3.2   Restoring Image via Virtual Sparsity

Coarse-to-fine information plays an important role in super-resolving an image. In order to capture such information, we learn dictionaries from the patches, extracted from intra/inter-scale versions of the LR image [12]. The extracted patches are clustered based on their detail information using K-means clustering approach. Corresponding centroids $\mathbf{r}_k$ are the representative of each of these clusters. Finally, eigenvectors are computed from each cluster, and are kept column-wise in a matrix with descending order of corresponding eigenvalues. Each of these matrices is a dictionary $(\mathbf{A}_k)$, which contains similar patch information from different scales of the image. Thus, dictionary can provide coarse-to-fine information.

The learned $\mathbf{A}_k$s are used to add coarse-to-fine information with the low-rank approximation $\hat{\mathcal{D}}_{\mathbf{x},i,m}$ by projecting it on the dictionary. Thus, we select one of the dictionaries $\mathbf{A}_k$, based on the minimum distance between their corresponding centroids $\mathbf{r}_k$ and $\hat{\mathcal{D}}_{\mathbf{x},i,m}$. The selected dictionary is then used to complement $\hat{\mathcal{D}}_{\mathbf{x},i,m}$ as

$$\hat{\hat{\mathcal{D}}}_{\mathbf{x},i,m} = \mathbf{A}_k \Gamma(\mathbf{A}_k^T \hat{\mathcal{D}}_{\mathbf{x},i,m})_\lambda. \tag{7}$$

Here, $\hat{\mathcal{D}}_{\mathbf{x},i,m}$ is re-aligned along the principal components through projection onto the dictionary matrix $\mathbf{A}_k$. The projected elements are further shrinked by soft-thresholding operation, as has done in the earlier stage. This, operation also helps to reduce the effect of noise. The thresholded elements are then multiplied back with the dictionary to get back refined detail information corresponding to $\hat{\mathcal{D}}_{\mathbf{x},i,m}$.

It has to be noted that the described method does not involve solving any sparse coding optimization. Instead, the process selects one dictionary from many options and re-aligns the data along the principal components. Selection of one dictionary from multiples creates a sense of sparsity in the virtual coefficient vector, as can be observed in Fig. 1. Multiplying the virtual coefficient vector with the group of dictionaries will lead to the selected dictionary, which basically represents the test patches. In "actual sparsity", the coefficient vector is computed, and is used for data representation. On the contrary, we do not compute or use the coefficient vector explicitly. Hence, we have used the terminology "virtual sparsity".

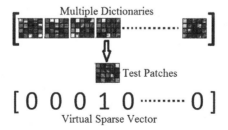

Fig. 1. Demonstration of virtual sparsity: selection of a dictionary from the multiple dictionaries for the test patches is forcing the corresponding coefficient of the "vector" to be 1 and rest of the coefficients are zero.

Once, the refined $\hat{\boldsymbol{\mathcal{D}}}_{\mathbf{x},i,m}$ is achieved, it can be compensated with the non-local mean to get back the grey-scale patches as

$$\hat{\mathbf{X}}_{i,m} = \hat{\boldsymbol{\mathcal{D}}}_{\mathbf{x},i,m} + \mathcal{REP}\left[\sum_{j \in \zeta_i}\left\{\frac{1}{z}\exp\left(-\frac{||\mathbf{x}_i - \mathbf{x}_j||_2^2}{h}\right)\right\}\mathbf{x}_j\right]. \tag{8}$$

The columns of $\hat{\mathbf{X}}_{i,m}$ contain the restored $\hat{\mathbf{x}}_i$s. After recovering all $\hat{\mathbf{x}}_i$s, they are used to recover the entire HR image, which has to be consistent with the LR image, if down-sampled in a similar way. Thus, we solve the following equation

$$\hat{\mathbf{x}} = \arg\min_{\hat{\mathbf{x}}}\left\{\sum_i ||\mathbf{P}_i\hat{\mathbf{x}} - \hat{\mathbf{x}}_i||_2^2 + \beta\,||\mathbf{y} - \mathbf{LH}\hat{\mathbf{x}}||_2^2\right\}, \tag{9}$$

where the first term is responsible for recovering the entire HR image from the patches and the second term is the data fidelity term. The Eq. (9) can be solved to derive a closed form solution, which is

$$\hat{\mathbf{x}} = \left(\sum_i \mathbf{P}_i^T\mathbf{P}_i + \beta\,\mathbf{H}^T\mathbf{L}^T\mathbf{LH}\right)^{-1}\left(\sum_i \mathbf{P}_i^T\hat{\mathbf{x}}_i + \beta\,\mathbf{H}^T\mathbf{L}^T\mathbf{y}\right). \tag{10}$$

The estimated $\hat{\mathbf{x}}$ is the restored clean HR image, which is examined qualitatively as well as quantitatively in the next section.

4   Experimental Results

In order to validate our approach, we performed experiments on standard images. The ground truth images are first blurred by a Gaussian kernel of size 7×7 with standard deviation 1.6. The blurred image is then decimated by factor 3 to generate the LR images. According to the process of LR image formation, we have added additive white Gaussian noise (AWGN) of standard deviations (σ_n) 5, 10 and 15, separately to test our approach. Bi-cubic interpolation technique is used on the LR image to achieve an initial approximation of the unknown HR scene. 6×6 dimensional patches are considered in our approach.

We have compared our results with some existing approaches including RP [15], SISU [13], ASDS [4], and NASR [12], quantitatively as well as qualitatively. For quantitative comparison, we have used peak signal-to-noise ratio (PSNR) and structural similarity index (SSIM) [26]. In case of color images, the images are first converted to YCbCr color space, and then the perceptually significant Y component is considered for SR and rest of the Cb and Cr components are interpolated and added back to the super-resolved Y component to get back the HR color image.

First of all, we show and compare the results qualitatively for noisy *Hat* ($\sigma_n = 5$), *Parrots* ($\sigma_n = 10$) and *Butterfly* ($\sigma_n = 15$) images in Figs. 2, 3 and 4, respectively. One can observe that across all the figures, our proposed

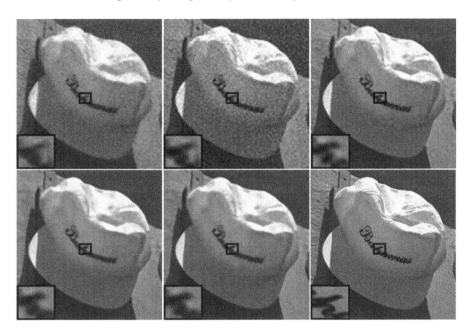

Fig. 2. Comparison of SR approaches for noisy *Hat* image (AWGN, $\sigma_n = 5$); Top left is the result of RP [5], top middle is the SR result of SISU [13], top right is the SR results of ASDS [4]. Bottom left represents the SR results of NASR [12], middle one is the result of the proposed approach and right bottom is the original image.

Table 1. Results of SR ($\uparrow 3$) for AWGN ($\sigma_n = 5$)

Images	Bi-cubic	RP [15]	SISU [13]	ASDS [4]	NASR [12]	Proposed
Barbara	22.68	23.76	**23.99**	23.29	23.71	23.73
	0.5739	0.6196	0.6082	0.5886	0.6462	**0.6485**
Bike	20.75	22.43	23.23	23.64	**23.88**	**23.88**
	0.5667	0.6442	0.6677	0.7279	0.7384	**0.7389**
Butterfly	20.74	23.04	24.84	25.68	26.49	**26.50**
	0.7036	0.7573	0.7566	0.8461	**0.8803**	0.8801
Girl	29.60	29.32	28.80	31.69	**31.70**	31.69
	0.7101	0.6713	0.6211	0.7529	**0.7531**	0.7528
Hat	27.00	27.91	27.81	29.52	29.59	**29.73**
	0.7479	0.7150	0.6439	0.7914	0.8191	**0.8226**
Lena	23.68	25.58	26.69	26.45	27.49	**27.52**
	0.6809	0.7274	0.7024	0.6968	0.7979	**0.7997**
Parrot	25.44	26.46	26.95	28.89	28.89	**28.90**
	0.7978	0.7491	0.6884	0.8451	0.8745	**0.8753**
Plants	27.62	28.70	28.60	31.04	**31.19**	**31.19**
	0.7607	0.7395	0.6840	0.8249	0.8416	**0.8422**

170   S. Mandal and A. N. Rajagopalan

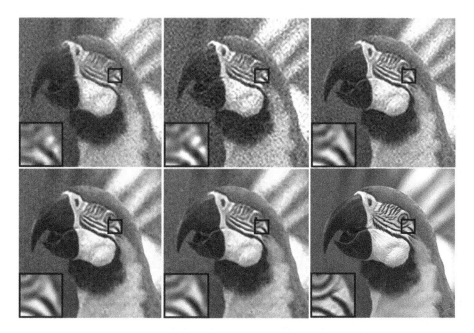

Fig. 3. Comparison of SR approaches for noisy *Parrots* image (AWGN, $\sigma_n = 10$); Top left is the result of RP [5], top middle is the SR result of SISU [13], top right is the SR results of ASDS [4]. Bottom left represents the SR results of NASR [12], middle one is the result of the proposed approach and right bottom is the original image.

Table 2. Results of SR ($\uparrow 3$) for AWGN ($\sigma_n = 10$)

Images	Bi-cubic	RP [15]	SISU [13]	ASDS [4]	NASR [12]	Proposed
Barbara	22.08	22.69	21.94	20.25	22.96	**22.98**
	0.4916	0.5061	0.4471	0.3564	0.5714	**0.5743**
Bike	20.62	21.47	21.40	22.55	23.09	**23.10**
	0.5430	0.5460	0.5310	0.6309	0.6846	**0.6857**
Butterfly	20.62	22.00	22.48	24.01	25.73	**25.74**
	0.6690	0.6447	0.6073	0.7148	**0.8573**	0.8573
Girl	28.76	26.37	24.19	27.95	**30.78**	30.77
	0.6584	0.5059	0.3922	0.5874	**0.7273**	0.7273
Hat	26.49	25.52	24.60	26.61	**28.63**	28.27
	0.6776	0.5236	0.4629	0.5717	**0.7940**	0.7885
Lena	22.97	24.00	23.39	21.49	25.54	**25.57**
	0.5749	0.5806	0.5074	0.4161	0.6879	**0.6909**
Parrot	25.07	24.65	23.77	26.25	28.07	**28.10**
	0.7300	0.5645	0.5001	0.6255	0.8073	**0.8094**
Plants	27.04	25.95	24.70	27.36	30.07	**30.09**
	0.6972	0.5525	0.4818	0.6212	0.8078	**0.8099**

Fig. 4. Comparison of SR approaches for noisy *Butterfly* image (AWGN, $\sigma_n = 15$); Top left is the result of RP [5], top middle is the SR result of SISU [13], top right is the SR results of ASDS [4]. Bottom left represents the SR results of NASR [12], middle one is the result of the proposed approach and right bottom is the original image.

approach is able to produce better results in terms of suppressing the effect of noise and in retaining subtle details as compared to the approaches of RP, SISU, and ASDS [4,13,15]. However, the proposed approach produces very close results with the approach NASR [12]. Note that the approach NASR solves the sparse coding optimization and uses edge preserving constraint [17]. On the other hand, our approach relies on the intrinsic low-rank structure of non-local similar patches, and its re-alignment along the principal components. However, differences among the results can be found in Tables 1, 2 and 3 in terms of PSNR (top) and SSIM values (bottom) presented in each row of the results. The bold fonts represent the best value in the corresponding row. It can be noticed that at higher power of noise few existing approaches [4,13,15] perform egregiously as compared to the simple bi-cubic interpolation approach. However, the proposed approach is robust enough to cope up with different powers of noise, and is able to out-perform most of the approaches by its simple yet effective low-rank structure assumption.

Table 3. Results of SR ($\uparrow$ 3) for AWGN ($\sigma_n = 15$)

Images	Bi-cubic	RP [15]	SISU [13]	ASDS [4]	NASR [12]	Proposed
Barbara	21.24	21.37	19.77	17.12	22.57	**22.60**
	0.4093	0.4068	0.3306	0.2197	0.5678	**0.5693**
Bike	20.42	20.34	19.42	20.92	**22.50**	22.50
	0.5117	0.4558	0.4207	0.5178	**0.6448**	0.6445
Butterfly	20.42	20.72	20.11	21.76	24.95	**24.96**
	0.6256	0.5468	0.5000	0.5822	0.8141	**0.8143**
Girl	27.68	23.82	20.96	24.32	29.56	**29.64**
	0.5946	0.3726	0.2513	0.4103	0.6916	**0.6929**
Hat	25.75	23.28	20.78	23.33	27.23	**27.29**
	0.5952	0.3847	0.2739	0.3849	0.7697	**0.7712**
Lena	21.99	**22.27**	20.59	17.64	19.92	19.92
	0.5749	**0.4596**	0.3730	0.2623	0.3607	0.3608
Parrot	24.52	22.74	20.64	23.18	**25.85**	25.85
	0.6481	0.4242	0.3106	0.4302	0.6346	0.6343
Plants	26.23	23.53	20.92	23.66	28.46	**28.65**
	0.6199	0.4070	0.3003	0.4258	0.7694	**0.7728**

4.1 Analysis and Discussion

Here, we discuss different aspects of our approach such as the robustness of our approach for other types of additive noises, the impact of only nuclear norm minimization technique against the proposed combination of nuclear norm and virtual sparsity. Further, the behavior of the proposed approach is analyzed for noiseless situation. Please note that the required computational time of our approach is dominated by the computation of singular value decomposition and principal component analysis of patches. Hence, the computational time is relied on the size of patch and number of patches to process.

Performance in Comparison to Non-Gaussian Noises. Here, we have shown the performance of the proposed approach for non-Gaussian additive noise such as Rayleigh and uniform noise. In order to maintain similar power of noise with the σ_n 10 of Gaussian case, the variances of Rayleigh and uniform noises are chosen to be 50 and 12, respectively. These noises are then used to form the noisy LR images to evaluate our approach. The performance of the proposed approach is shown in Fig. 5 in terms of average PSNR values that is obtained by averaging the PSNR values for 8 images.

It can be observed that the bars, colored by blue, green and red have almost similar heights under the condition of similar power of noise. This clearly demonstrates the robustness of our approach for different kinds of additive noises.

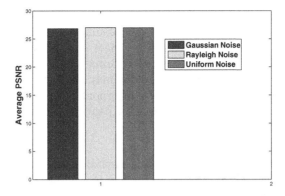

Fig. 5. The performance of the proposed approach – Gaussian noise vs. non-Gaussian noises: Average PSNR values of 8 images are shown for Gaussian noise (Blue) (variance = 100), Rayleigh noise (Green) (variance = 50) and Uniform noise (Red) (variance = 12). (Color figure online)

Impact of Nuclear Norm Minimization. In order to catch the impact of nuclear norm alone, we have released the augmentation of coarse-to-fine information in virtual sparse domain to obtain results on the same set of images. These results can be observed and compared in terms of PSNR and SSIM values against the combined approach in Fig. 6 for AWGN $\sigma_n = 10$. The blue colored bars represent the results of minimizing nuclear norm only, whereas the red colored bars represent the results of nuclear norm minimization along with augmentation of coarse-to-fine information in virtual sparse domain.

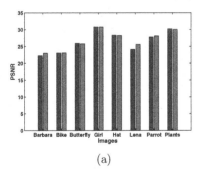
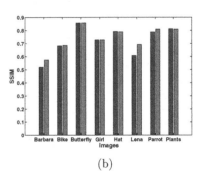

(a)   (b)

Fig. 6. Impact of minimizing nuclear norm alone (blue colored bars) vs the combination effect (the red colored bars) for AWGN ($\sigma_n = 10$): (a) PSNR comparison and (b) SSIM comparison. (Color figure online)

One can observe that the combined results are either better or almost similar to the results of using nuclear norm only. The reason being that natural image patches tend to recur within the image. Thus, the matrix, consisting of such patches should have low rank because of patch similarity. However, presence of noise leads to violation of such low-rank assumption. Hence, by minimizing the nuclear norm helps in suppressing the effect of noise. However, the noise-suppressed image may lack subtle detail information because of the low-rank assumption. Hence, rank minimization alone may not suffice to achieve an HR image. The detail information has been incorporated by re-aligning the data along the principal components of cluster of patches, containing coarse-to-fine information.

Behavior Towards Clean Images. It is inevitable for natural images to have some kind of noises. Hence, in this paper our focus has been to super-resolve noisy image. However, analysis of performance of the approach for clean images can be an addition to its arsenal of robustness. Thus we observe the behavior of the proposed approach in noise-free situation in Fig. 7 in terms of PSNR and SSIM values.

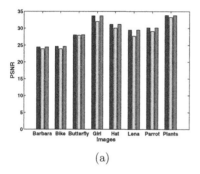 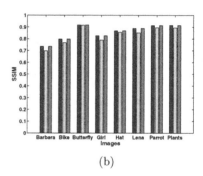

(a)   (b)

Fig. 7. Behavior towards clean (noise-free) images: (a) PSNR comparison and (b) SSIM comparison; Blue colored bar represents the result of NASR approach [12]; The results of minimizing nuclear norm only is depicted by green colored bar; The red colored bar represents the result of the proposed approach that combines the effectiveness of nuclear norm minimization as well as inclusion of coarse-to-fine information. (Color figure online)

In comparison to the existing approach NASR [12] (the blue colored bar), the performance of nuclear norm minimization alone (the green colored bar) is slightly lagging behind. This is because the restored image of nuclear norm minimization is lacking the subtle details, as explained earlier. However, re-aligning the data along the principal components of cluster of patches, containing coarse-to-fine information incorporates subtle details into the result. Thus, the red colored bar (the results of the proposed approach) is able to attain almost similar height to the blue colored bar (existing approach). Thus, it can be forwarded that the proposed approach can not only suppress the effect of noise in super-resolving a noisy image but it can also super-resolve a noise-free image upto a reasonable quality.

5   Summary

In this paper, we have proposed to super-resolve noisy image with unknown amount of noise. The inherent low-rank structure of non-local similar patches of clean HR images has been explored to achieve an HR clean image, which is further boosted with the coarse-to-fine information, learned from the LR image at different scales. This has been done in a virtual sparse domain by re-aligning the initial HR image along the principal components of the dictionary that has been selected effectively from multiple choices. The experimental results demonstrate the efficacy of the proposed approach in terms of suppressing the effect of noise as well as smearing.

References

1. Park, S.C., Park, M.K., Kang, M.G.: Super-resolution image reconstruction: a technical overview. IEEE Sig. Process. Mag. **20**(3), 21–36 (2003)
2. Stark, H., Oskoui, P.: High-resolution image recovery from image-plane arrays, using convex projections. J. Opt. Soc. Am. A **6**(11), 1715–1726 (1989)
3. Freeman, W., Jones, T., Pasztor, E.: Example-based super-resolution. IEEE Comput. Graph. Appl. **22**(2), 56–65 (2002)
4. Dong, W., Zhang, L., Shi, G., Wu, X.: Image deblurring and super-resolution by adaptive sparse domain selection and adaptive regularization. IEEE Trans. Image Process. **20**(7), 1838–1857 (2011)
5. Yang, J., Wright, J., Huang, T., Ma, Y.: Image super-resolution as sparse representation of raw image patches. In: IEEE Conference on Computer Vision and Pattern Recognition, pp. 1–8, June 2008
6. Mandal, S., Sao, A.K.: Employing structural and statistical information to learn dictionary(s) for single image super-resolution in sparse domain. Sig. Process. Image Commun. **48**, 63–80 (2016)
7. Glasner, D., Bagon, S., Irani, M.: Super-resolution from a single image. In: IEEE International Conference on Computer Vision (ICCV), pp. 349–356, September 2009
8. Yang, C.-Y., Huang, J.-B., Yang, M.-H.: Exploiting self-similarities for single frame super-resolution. In: Kimmel, R., Klette, R., Sugimoto, A. (eds.) ACCV 2010. LNCS, vol. 6494, pp. 497–510. Springer, Heidelberg (2011). https://doi.org/10.1007/978-3-642-19318-7_39
9. Vishnukumar, S., Nair, M.S., Wilscy, M.: Edge preserving single image super-resolution with improved visual quality. Sig. Process. **105**, 283–297 (2014)
10. Mandal, S., Bhavsar, A., Sao, A.: Super-resolving a single intensity/range image via non-local means and sparse representation. In: Indian Conference on Computer Vision, Graphics and Image Processing (ICVGIP), pp. 1–8, December 2014
11. Singh, A., Porikli, F., Ahuja, N.: Super-resolving noisy images. In: IEEE Conference on Computer Vision and Pattern Recognition (CVPR), pp. 2846–2853, June 2014
12. Mandal, S., Bhavsar, A., Sao, A.K.: Noise adaptive super-resolution from single image via non-local mean and sparse representation. Sig. Process. **132**, 134–149 (2017)

13. Zeyde, R., Elad, M., Protter, M.: On single image scale-up using sparse-representations. In: Boissonnat, J.-D., Chenin, P., Cohen, A., Gout, C., Lyche, T., Mazure, M.-L., Schumaker, L. (eds.) Curves and Surfaces 2010. LNCS, vol. 6920, pp. 711–730. Springer, Heidelberg (2012). https://doi.org/10.1007/978-3-642-27413-8_47

14. Timofte, R., De Smet, V., Van Gool, L.: A+: adjusted anchored neighborhood regression for fast super-resolution. In: Cremers, D., Reid, I., Saito, H., Yang, M.-H. (eds.) ACCV 2014. LNCS, vol. 9006, pp. 111–126. Springer, Cham (2015). https://doi.org/10.1007/978-3-319-16817-3_8

15. Yang, J., Wright, J., Huang, T., Ma, Y.: Image super-resolution via sparse representation. IEEE Trans. Image Process. **19**(11), 2861–2873 (2010)

16. Mandal, S., Bhavsar, A., Sao, A.K.: Depth map restoration from undersampled data. IEEE Trans. Image Process. **26**(1), 119–134 (2017)

17. Mandal, S., Sao, A.: Edge preserving single image super resolution in sparse environment. In: 20th IEEE International Conference on Image Processing (ICIP), pp. 967–971, September 2013

18. Yang, S., Wang, M., Chen, Y., Sun, Y.: Single-image super-resolution reconstruction via learned geometric dictionaries and clustered sparse coding. IEEE Trans. Image Process. **21**(9), 4016–4028 (2012)

19. Zhang, K., Tao, D., Gao, X., Li, X., Xiong, Z.: Learning multiple linear mappings for efficient single image super-resolution. IEEE Trans. Image Process. **24**(3), 846–861 (2015)

20. Huang, J.B., Singh, A., Ahuja, N.: Single image super-resolution from transformed self-exemplars. In: IEEE Conference on Computer Vision and Pattern Recognition (CVPR), pp. 5197–5206, June 2015

21. Wang, S., Zhang, L., Liang, Y.: Nonlocal spectral prior model for low-level vision. In: Lee, K.M., Matsushita, Y., Rehg, J.M., Hu, Z. (eds.) ACCV 2012. LNCS, vol. 7726, pp. 231–244. Springer, Heidelberg (2013). https://doi.org/10.1007/978-3-642-37431-9_18

22. Gu, S., Xie, Q., Meng, D., Zuo, W., Feng, X., Zhang, L.: Weighted nuclear norm minimization and its applications to low level vision. Int. J. Comput. Vis. **121**(2), 183–208 (2017)

23. Dong, W., Shi, G., Li, X., Ma, Y., Huang, F.: Compressive sensing via nonlocal low-rank regularization. IEEE Trans. Image Process. **23**(8), 3618–3632 (2014)

24. Dong, W., Shi, G., Li, X.: Nonlocal image restoration with bilateral variance estimation: a low-rank approach. IEEE Trans. Image Process. **22**(2), 700–711 (2013)

25. Cai, J.F., Cands, E.J., Shen, Z.: A singular value thresholding algorithm for matrix completion. SIAM J. Optim. **20**(4), 1956–1982 (2010)

26. Wang, Z., Bovik, A., Sheikh, H., Simoncelli, E.: Image quality assessment: from error visibility to structural similarity. IEEE Trans. Image Process. **13**(4), 600–612 (2004)

Near Real-Time Correction of Specular Reflections in Flash Images Using No-Flash Image Prior

Saikat Kumar Das$^{(\boxtimes)}$ ⓘ, Kunal Swami, Gaurav Khandelwal,
and Prashanth Rao Thakkalapally

Samsung R&D Institute India, Bangalore, India
{saikat.das1,kunal.swami,gaurav.k7,prashanth.th}@samsung.com

Abstract. In insufficient indoor light conditions, when images of paintings, documents and objects with glossy surfaces are captured using flash light, bright annoying specularities appear in the image which not only degrade the aesthetic quality, but also lead to loss of useful information. In this paper, we address the problem of specular reflections in images of aforementioned scenes, captured using flash light. We propose a novel specular reflection detection algorithm which utilizes flash/no-flash image pair to accurately detect specular reflections in flash image, while ignoring the inherent bright regions. The detected specular reflections are seamlessly recovered using Poisson image editing technique. Quantitative as well as qualitative comparison of the proposed detection method on our flash/no-flash image dataset shows that it significantly outperforms other eminent methods in literature. We also implement our solution in an Android smartphone to demonstrate its effectiveness in real-life scenarios.

Keywords: Flash/no-flash images
Specular reflection detection and removal · Smartphone application

1 Introduction

With the advent of mobile cameras, the practice of capturing and sharing of images of documents, class boards, notices, posters, IDs, paintings has become very convenient and commonplace. This particular segment of images tend to loose utility owing to noise and blurry appearance when captured under insufficient ambient light conditions. Often, annoying reflections and shadows of the photographer occlude important parts in the image (see Fig. 1a). To avoid these problems, an alternative is to capture such scenes using flash light. Flash images are relatively sharp, less noisy and also do not contain unwanted ambient shadows and reflections (see Fig. 1b). However, flash images are prone to undesirable annoying artifacts, such as specular reflections, sharp shadows and uneven

---

S. K. Das and K. Swami—Equal contribution.

© Springer Nature Singapore Pte Ltd. 2018
R. Rameshan et al. (Eds.): NCVPRIPG 2017, CCIS 841, pp. 177–189, 2018.
https://doi.org/10.1007/978-981-13-0020-2_16

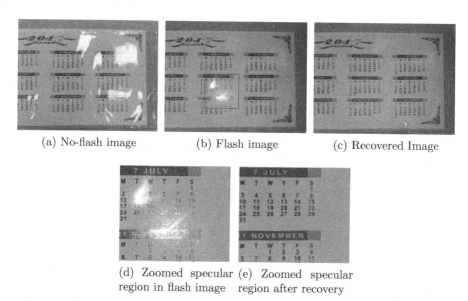

(a) No-flash image   (b) Flash image   (c) Recovered Image

(d) Zoomed specular (e) Zoomed specular
region in flash image   region after recovery

Fig. 1. Illustration of problems in flash and no-flash images and result of the proposed specular reflection correction algorithm in solving such problems. The two images in second row show in close up the area affected by flash image specularity (marked by the red box in Fig. 1b) and the result of the proposed specularity correction algorithm on the corresponding area, respectively. (Color figure online)

lighting. Specular reflections not only occlude important information, but they also degrade the overall aesthetic quality of an image. Moreover, many image enhancement and computer vision algorithms are designed with the assumption that all surfaces in a scene are purely Lambertian, i.e. all the reflections are diffused, but in practice their performance suffers due to violation of this assumption. Thus, if the specular reflections are corrected in a preprocessing step then the results of these subsequent algorithms can also be improved appreciably. In this paper, we try to address the problem of specular reflection detection and removal in images of aforementioned scenes, captured with flash light using flash/no-flash image pairs. Only a handful of prior works [1–4] take the problem of specular reflections in flash images into consideration, including an excellent work from Raskar *et al.* [1] and a recent work on document binarization by Kumar *et al.* [3] but while [1] suffers from poor performance due to only suppression of specularity affected image areas instead of completely replacing them, the method described in [3] lacks in generalizing the problem of specular reflection to color images as it specifically focuses on document binarization. We propose to use multi level detection masks for detecting specular reflections in a flash image using the no-flash prior to remove false detections and then use seamless cloning with Poisson image editing tools [5] to recover the detected image areas, again with information from the no-flash image. Also we target this algorithm as an user application on hand held mobile devices and as a preprocessing step to subsequent algorithms thus, making the proposed algorithm nearly real-time becomes an crucial parameter for its effectiveness.

1.1 Related Work

Flash/no-flash image pairs have been used in literature for solving widely varied problems like saliency detection [6], image segmentation [7], white-balance estimation [8–10], depth estimation [11], deblurring [12], denoising [2] and overall quality enhancement [13]. However, to the best of our knowledge, only Agrawal *et al.* [1] explicitly address the problem of specularities in flash image using flash/no-flash image pair. In their method [1], the specularity-free flash image is obtained by integrating the gradient field obtained by linearly weighting flash/no-flash image gradients using a saturation map. However, their method suffers from a problem which is inherent to usage of saturation mask—it only suppresses specularities to an extent rather completely removing them (see Fig. 4d), because the gradient values are mixed not replaced. Moreover, it also leads to unnecessary alteration of gradients even in the non-specular reflection regions; thus, effecting the appearance of entire flash image adversely (see Fig. 4d). Kumar *et al.* [3] specifically address the problem of specular flash hotspots in binarized document images by applying a window based two pass flash spot detection method. Although the second pass with lower threshold increases the accuracy of detection by extending the initial FSR region but fails to address the issue of false positives. Moreover, the recovery method used in [3] is only suitable for binarized images. Among other notable flash/no-flash works, [14] doesn't deal with the problem of specular reflections, while in [2] authors rely on user input to detect specularities.

Apart from flash/no-flash image based works, there are numerous other works in literature which deal with the problem of specular reflection removal [15]. Nayar *et al.* [16] proposed a method which uses a polarizer based on the observation that specular reflections are polarized compared to unpolarized diffused reflections. Feris *et al.* [4] and Yang *et al.* [17] proposed multiple image based solution to remove specular reflections based on the idea that specular reflections exhibit different characteristics under different lighting directions and viewing angles. Tan and Ikeuchi [18] removed highlights by iteratively shifting chromaticity of specular regions towards that of neighboring pixel having maximum diffused chromaticity; [19] applies similar approach in SUV color space, while Yang et al. [20, 21] improved this method by using bilateral filter. Kim *et al.* [22] proposed an optimization framework based on dark channel prior, while [23] presents a non-negative matrix factorization based method; both these methods are computationally expensive. Shen *et al.* [24] determine specular component of pixels with similar chromaticity by solving dichromatic equation under least squares criterion. In [25, 26] intensity ratio between maximum value and range value of diffuse pixels is used in order to separate diffuse and specular components. The polarization [16] and the multiple image based methods [4, 17] are not feasible for mobile devices, while the single image methods [18–27] deal with only small and weak specularities and don't have any information to recover specular regions. The flash image specularities are very strong, destroying the structural and color information in the image.

1.2 Our Contributions

In this paper, we propose a flash image specular reflection removal solution which does not have aforementioned drawbacks and is also suitable for mobile devices. Following are the major contributions of this work:

- A novel method of specular reflection detection in flash images which uses a pair of flash/no-flash images.
- Qualitative and quantitative evaluation of the proposed detection method which shows that it outperforms other eminent methods presented in [1,18, 24,25].
- A flash/no-flash image dataset for flash image specularity detection, along with ground-truth images.
- Implementation of the proposed solution in an Android smartphone device with real-time response to demonstrate its effectiveness in real-life scenarios.

2   Proposed Method

2.1   Detection Method

Overview and Motivation. Specularity detection methods based on simple thresholding [1,2] have following drawbacks. First, since only a single threshold is applied, these methods detect only the partial specular artifacts, i.e., mostly the central bright spots. Second, since the detection method is applied only on the flash image, some inherently bright non-specular regions are also falsely detected. The single image specularity detection methods [3,27,28] also suffer from these drawbacks. In proposed method, the first drawback is addressed by computing two detection masks from flash image, one with a higher threshold value, while other with moderate threshold value. The former mainly detects the central bright spots of specular artifacts, while the later additionally detects the surrounding specular regions of lesser intensity along with other moderate-intensity non-specular regions. A more accurate and complete detection of specular reflection regions is obtained by computing the common connected components between these two masks. In order to address the second drawback, we identify mutually exclusive bright regions between the flash and no-flash images. For this, we compute detection masks using no-flash image to determine inherent bright areas, which are then eliminated from the final detection mask.

The novelty of our approach is that, we compute multiple detection masks from flash/no-flash images and combine them to accurately detect specular reflection artifacts, while ignoring the inherent bright regions. The detection masks derived from the flash image act as **additive masks**, in the sense that they are used to detect *complete* specular regions. The detection masks derived from the no-flash image act as **subtractive masks**, in the sense that they are used to prevent false detection of inherent bright regions (Fig. 2).

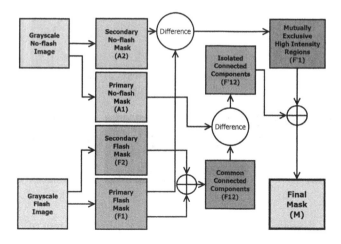

Fig. 2. Steps involved in our detection algorithm

Algorithm. First, we convert no-flash and flash images into grayscale. Next, we compute two masks from flash image (I_F), viz., ***primary flash mask (F_1)*** and ***secondary flash mask (F_2)***. Mask F_1 is computed with a high threshold T_1 so that only the regions which exhibit true specular characteristics, i.e., extremely high saturation are detected (see Fig. 3e).

$$F_1 = \{p \in I_F : |p| > T_1\} \tag{1}$$

p represents individual pixels of an image and $|p|$ denotes the intensity of that pixel. This mask mainly detects the central bright spots of specular regions, which in later stages, act as seed points to expand the detection of specular artifacts. Mask F_2 is computed using a relatively lower threshold value T_2, so that it additionally detects other moderately saturated areas—moderate-intensity specular regions surrounding the central bright specular hot-spots and other non-specular moderate-intensity regions (see Fig. 3f).

$$F_2 = \{p \in I_F : |p| > T_2\} \tag{2}$$

The non-specular moderate-intensity regions can be *isolated* from, lie in the *vicinity* of, or *overlap* with, the specular artifacts. The non-zero elements in F_2 are clustered and labeled with 8-connectivity rule [29], which gives us N number of individual clusters C_i, where i $= 1, 2, ...N$.

Using F_1 and labeled F_2 mask, we compute an ***intermediate mask (F_{12})*** which contains the common connected components between the two masks. Thus, mask F_{12} contains the central bright spots as well as their surrounding medium intensity specular regions (see Fig. 3g), while the *isolated* non-specular moderate intensity regions from mask F_2 are eliminated.

$$F_{12} = \{C_i \in F_2 : C_i \cap F_1 \neq \phi, \text{ for every i}\} \tag{3}$$

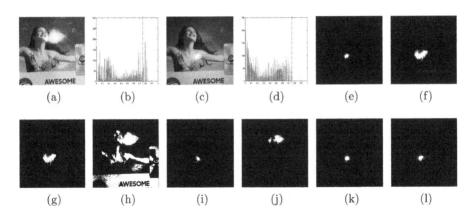

Fig. 3. Sample detection result: (a) No-flash image. (b) Histogram of (a). (c) Flash image. (d) Histogram of (c). (e) Mask F_1. (f) Mask F_2. (g) Mask F_{12}. (h) Mask A_1. (i) Mask F'_{12}. (j) Mask A_2. (k) Final mask. (l) Ground truth.

As mentioned above, mask F_{12} is prone to falsely detect moderately saturated non-specular areas as well if they have greater intensity than T_2. In order to prevent the detection of these inherent bright regions, we utilize no-flash image information. All the regions having intensity equal or higher than the threshold T_2 used for computing mask F_2 are candidates for false detection; hence, we compute a **primary no-flash mask** (A_1) using a threshold value T_3 which is slightly less than T_2. The threshold of mask A_1 is lowered in order to account for the absence of flash light intensity in no-flash image. All the regions that are detected in the mask A_1 (see Fig. 3h) are eliminated from the mask F_{12} to obtain a more accurate mask F'_{12} (see Fig. 3i).

$$F'_{12} = F_{12} - A_1 \text{ where, } A_1 = \{p \in I_A : |p| > T_3\} \tag{4}$$

However, when specular regions *overlap* with inherent bright regions, the previous step will eliminate the overlapping specular region from mask F'_{12} (see Fig. 3i). As a preventive measure, the over-saturated regions detected in F_1 should be added back to F'_{12}; however, if F_1 contains some inherent bright elements (already eliminated by A_1 from F_{12}), then simple addition of F_1 will result in their re-inclusion. To identify these false positives in F_1, we compute **secondary no-flash mask** (A_2) from no-flash image (see Fig. 3j) with a threshold T_4, similar to F_1.

$$A_2 = \{p \in I_A : |p| > T_4\} \tag{5}$$

$$M = F'_{12} + F'_1 \text{ where, } F'_1 = F_1 - A_2 \tag{6}$$

All the detected elements in A_2 are eliminated from F_1, generating a resultant mask F'_1, that contains only true positive elements from F_1, which can be safely added back to F'_{12} to create the **Final Mask** M (see Fig. 3k).

The optimal threshold values for various detection masks were empirically obtained as follows: $T_1 = 0.90$, this value is also used for detecting specularity in [1–3]. As already stated, $T_1 > T_2$ and as specular areas are always high in intensity so it is logical to narrow the candidate specular regions to the higher $1/4$ of the intensity range, thus $T_2 = 0.75$. This is also based on the fact that the number of specular pixels are generally very small compared to non-specular pixels and similarly very few pixels have intensities more than T_2 (see Fig. 3b and d). The other two thresholds, T_3 and T_4, decided in accordance to following relations established before: $T_1 \approx T_4$ and $T_2 \approx T_3$, are 0.70 (decreased to accommodate for absence of flash light) and 0.90 respectively. The effectiveness of these parameters is proven by the quantitative evaluation (see Table 1) on our diverse dataset.

2.2 Recovery Method

The detected specular regions in flash image are recovered from corresponding non-specular regions in no-flash image using Poisson image editing technique [5]. The gradient field for detected regions in flash image are replaced by corresponding no-flash image gradient field, calculated using a two point filter $[-1, 1]$. The pixel values in edited regions are recreated from gradient fields by solving following Laplace equation with boundary condition derived from the Poisson equation with Dirichlet boundary conditions (Eq. 4 in [5]):

$$\Delta \widetilde{f} = 0 \text{ over } \Omega, \widetilde{f}|_{\partial\Omega} = (f^* - g)|_{\partial\Omega} \tag{7}$$

The objective is to interpolate the unknown pixel values (scalar function f) inside the detected regions Ω using a membrane interpolant $\widetilde{f}$ of the mismatch between the known pixel values (scalar function f^*) of the boundary region $\partial\Omega$ of Ω and the no-flash image gradients (conservative vector g) i.e $(f^* - g)$ along $\partial\Omega$. Here $\widetilde{f}$ is the additive correction function to the conservative guidance vector g such that $f = g + \widetilde{f}$ and $\Delta. = [\frac{\partial^2.}{\partial x^2} + \frac{\partial^2.}{\partial y^2}]$. The known boundary pixels impose a unique solution constraint. This guided interpolation recovers the areas disfigured by the specular reflections. Poisson image editing generates specularity-free flash images without any noticeable artifacts. However, since the boundaries of specular regions in detection mask might not exactly coincide with the actual specular reflection boundaries, the boundary pixels in flash image belonging to specular regions might lead to reconstruction of the specular regions or cause blur artifacts. Therefore, the detection mask is dilated before recovery.

3   Experiment and Results

The proposed solution is implemented in an Android smartphone device to demonstrate its efficacy in real-life scenarios. The application is an extension of the Android application developed in [30]; with a single capture press, a pair of flash/no-flash images is captured which are just 70 ms apart on average,

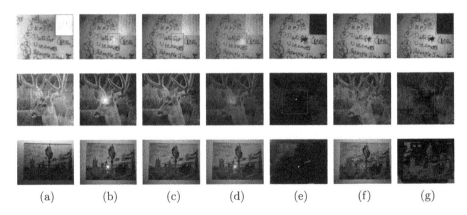

(a)   (b)   (c)   (d)   (e)   (f)   (g)

Fig. 4. (a) No-flash images, (b) flash images, (c) our result, (d) result of [1], (e) result of [18], (f) result of [24], (g) result of [25]. Qualitative comparison of the proposed algorithm. Pay attention to areas in red boxes, these areas signify that our method performs much better compared to other methods. (Color figure online)

thus, minimizing the relative motion between the two images. This allows us to use simpler motion models and fast feature detector-descriptors to register the images.

3.1   Dataset

As there is no flash/no-flash image dataset available for flash image specularity detection, we created our own dataset for evaluation and comparison purpose. Our dataset has 40 sets of flash/no-flash images. Ground truth images depicting the specular regions in of every flash image are manually created using various image editing softwares.

3.2   Image Registration

The nature of the proposed algorithm makes it crucial for the input images to have pixel level correspondence. The input image pair are captured rapidly one after the other. To reduce latency between the images, the flash image is captured before the no-flash image as pre-flash and 3 A statistics computation can be time consuming. The implementation of our system optimized camera application enables us to capture the two images with a minimum delay of 70 ms. However, even in case of images taken in such quick succession we still observed global motion between the two images due to shaking of the mobile device. Tripods and stands were not used in experiments to simulate real life conditions.

Fast image registration is employed by first identifying potential keypoints using FAST feature detector [31] and then finding the best matches using BRISK feature descriptor [32]. Both FAST detector and BRISK descriptors are widely used for their high-speed performance more than their accuracy. Although not entirely rotation and scale invariant but the detector-descriptor make up in speed what they lack in accuracy. This high-speed performance can be attributed to the binary nature of the feature description which can be compared efficiently using Hamming distance. As the motion between the images are not profound in most scenarios and does not generally include scale or rotation variance, aforementioned algorithms were deemed appropriate for our use. Moreover, binary feature descriptors such as BRISK have very low memory footprint. The outliers are excluded using RANSAC [33] and the no-flash image is warped using the estimated affine transformation between the matched points.

3.3   Results and Discussion

Figure 4 shows the qualitative results of the proposed solution compared to the methods in [1,18,24,25]. For comparison, we have used original source code provided by authors but as the code of the method described in [1] is not available publicly we evaluated the same using our implementation of the method in accordance to the literature. It is evident that our method generates superior quality flash images without specular artifacts. It can be seen in Fig. 4d, the saturation mask based approach adopted in [1] degrades overall image quality and also fails to completely remove the specular reflection artifacts. The single image methods in [18,24,25] fail to obtain accurate diffuse image component with correct structure and color information; moreover, the specular artifacts are also not recovered and appear completely black in the recovered image (see Fig. 4e–g). It can also be observed that in contrast to other methods, our method is able to differentiate between inherent bright regions and specular artifacts accurately. For e.g., [18,24,25] consider even moderately bright regions as specularity (see Fig. 4), in almost all the images in our database (Table 2).

Figure 5 shows the qualitative comparison of the specular components (detection mask in our case) obtained with different methods and it is evident that compared to other methods, the specularities are identified more accurately by our method. Table 1 shows the quantitative comparison of our detection method with [1,24]. Inspite of lower precision values compared to [1], the proposed method achieves significant higher recall rates and overall surpasses the existing arts by obtaining significantly better F-measure [34].

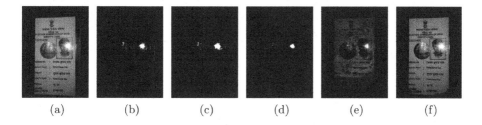

| (a) | (b) | (c) | (d) | (e) | (f) |

Fig. 5. Qualitative comparison of obtained specular components: (a) Flash image. (b) Ground truth. (c) Our result. (d) Result with [1]. (e) Result with [24]. (f) Result with [25].

Table 1. Quantitative result of our detection method

Method	Precision	Recall	F-measure
Proposed	0.80	**0.66**	**0.70**
Raskar et al. [1]	**0.94**	0.24	0.36
Shen et al. [24]	0.75	0.06	0.11

Table 2. Performance of proposed method on Samsung Galaxy C9 Pro device

Module	Detection	Recovery	Registration
Time	100 ms	150 ms	300 ms

3.4 Limitations

Although the proposed algorithm works as expected in most cases but under few environments, like severe low light condition, the quality of recovery gets limited

(a)   (b)   (c)   (d)   (e)

Fig. 6. (a) No-flash images, (b) flash images, (c) our result, (d) zoomed specular region in flash image, (e) zoomed corresponding specular region in after recovery. Images captured by users with the developed android application which embodies the proposed algorithm. Quality of the recovered images demonstrate how well the algorithm generalizes to wide variety of real-world scenes outside the lab environment.

by the amount of information in the no-flash image. It's crucial for the no-flash image to retain the gradient information (i.e. edges, corners and textures) of the original scene even if the color information is corrupted by noise and absence of light. Also if the no-flash image contains very strong ambient reflections which are not suppressed by the flash exposure or which coincide with the specularities then the recovered image tends to retain traces of those ambient reflections as well.

3.5 Performance

Proposed solution takes roughly 100 ms for detecting specular regions and 150 ms on average for recovery of the detected regions after moderate multi-threading and NEON optimization. We isolate and recover the smallest non-overlapping rectangles in parallel to speed up recovery. The performance data mentioned here is measured on a *Samsung Galaxy C9 Pro* device having ARM64-V8A based Qualcomm Snapdragon 653 octa-core processor (1.8 GHz) and 6 GB RAM with 0.5 MP (612×816) input images. Alignment of the input images introduces an additional delay of 300 ms.

4 Conclusion

An effective and real-time flash image specularity removal solution using flash/no-flash image pair is proposed here. The detection method is based on the idea of computing multiple detection masks from flash/no-flash images and combining them to accurately detect specularities in flash image. The quantitative and qualitative results obtained with the proposed solution show that it significantly outperforms prominent methods in literature. It is also shown that the existing methods fail to deal with the strong specularities of flash images. The proposed solution generates superior quality specularity-free flash images and is also realizable in mobile devices. The proposed algorithm also works sufficiently well in real world scenario as demonstrated by images taken by different users in Fig. 6. These images were captured by users without any guidance from the development team and also points to the practicality of the problem targeted.

References

1. Agrawal, A., Raskar, R., Nayar, S.K., Li, Y.: Removing photography artifacts using gradient projection and flash-exposure sampling. ACM Trans. Graph. **24**(3), 828–835 (2005)
2. Petschnigg, G., Szeliski, R., Agrawala, M., Cohen, M., Hoppe, H., Toyama, K.: Digital photography with flash and no-flash image pairs. ACM Trans. Graph. **23**(3), 664–672 (2004)
3. Kumar, J., Maltz, M., Bala, R.: Flash/no-flash fusion for mobile document image binarization. In: 2014 IEEE International Conference on Image Processing (ICIP), pp. 5871–5875, October 2014

4. Feris, R., Raskar, R., Tan, K.H., Turk, M.: Specular reflection reduction with multi-flash imaging. In: 17th Brazilian Symposium on Computer Graphics and Image Processing, Proceedings, pp. 316–321, October 2004
5. Pérez, P., Gangnet, M., Blake, A.: Poisson image editing. ACM Trans. Graph. **22**(3), 313–318 (2003)
6. He, S., Lau, R.W.H.: Saliency detection with flash and no-flash image pairs. In: Fleet, D., Pajdla, T., Schiele, B., Tuytelaars, T. (eds.) ECCV 2014. LNCS, vol. 8691, pp. 110–124. Springer, Cham (2014). https://doi.org/10.1007/978-3-319-10578-9_8
7. Sun, J., Sun, J., Kang, S.B., Xu, Z.B., Tang, X., Shum, H.Y.: Flash cut: foreground extraction with flash and no-flash image pairs. In: 2007 IEEE Conference on Computer Vision and Pattern Recognition, pp. 1–8, June 2007
8. DiCarlo, J.M., Xiao, F., Wandell, B.A.: Illuminating illumination. In: Color and Imaging Conference, vol. 9, pp. 27–34. Society for Imaging Science and Technology (2001)
9. Lu, C., Drew, M.S.: Practical scene illuminant estimation via flash/no-flash pairs. In: Color and Imaging Conference, vol. 14, pp. 84–89. Society for Imaging Science and Technology (2006)
10. Hui, Z., Sankaranarayanan, A.C., Sunkavalli, K., Hadap, S.: White balance under mixed illumination using flash photography. In: 2016 IEEE International Conference on Computational Photography (ICCP), pp. 1–10, May 2016
11. Raskar, R., Tan, K.H., Feris, R., Yu, J., Turk, M.: Non-photorealistic camera: depth edge detection and stylized rendering using multi-flash imaging. In: ACM SIGGRAPH 2004 Papers, SIGGRAPH 2004, pp. 679–688. ACM, New York (2004)
12. Zhuo, S., Guo, D., Sim, T.: Robust flash deblurring. In: 2010 IEEE Computer Society Conference on Computer Vision and Pattern Recognition, pp. 2440–2447, June 2010
13. Seo, H., Milanfar, P.: Computational photography using a pair of flash/no-flash images by iterative guided filtering. In: IEEE International Conference on Computer Vision (ICCV) (2011)
14. Eisemann, E., Durand, F.: Flash photography enhancement via intrinsic relighting. ACM Trans. Graph. **23**(3), 673–678 (2004)
15. Artusi, A., Banterle, F., Chetverikov, D.: A survey of specularity removal methods. Comput. Graph. Forum **30**(8), 2208–2230 (2011)
16. Nayar, S.K., Fang, X.S., Boult, T.: Separation of reflection components using color and polarization. Int. J. Comput. Vis. **21**(3), 163–186 (1997)
17. Yang, Q., Wang, S., Ahuja, N., Yang, R.: A uniform framework for estimating illumination chromaticity, correspondence, and specular reflection. IEEE Trans. Image Process. **20**(1), 53–63 (2011)
18. Tan, R.T., Ikeuchi, K.: Separating reflection components of textured surfaces using a single image. IEEE Trans. Pattern Anal. Mach. Intell. **27**(2), 178–193 (2005)
19. Mallick, S.P., Zickler, T., Belhumeur, P.N., Kriegman, D.J.: Specularity removal in images and videos: a PDE approach. In: Leonardis, A., Bischof, H., Pinz, A. (eds.) ECCV 2006. LNCS, vol. 3951, pp. 550–563. Springer, Heidelberg (2006). https://doi.org/10.1007/11744023_43
20. Yang, Q., Wang, S., Ahuja, N.: Real-time specular highlight removal using bilateral filtering. In: Daniilidis, K., Maragos, P., Paragios, N. (eds.) ECCV 2010. LNCS, vol. 6314, pp. 87–100. Springer, Heidelberg (2010). https://doi.org/10.1007/978-3-642-15561-1_7
21. Yang, Q., Tang, J., Ahuja, N.: Efficient and robust specular highlight removal. IEEE Trans. Pattern Anal. Mach. Intell. **37**(6), 1304–1311 (2015)

22. Kim, H., Jin, H., Hadap, S., Kweon, I.: Specular reflection separation using dark channel prior. In: 2013 IEEE Conference on Computer Vision and Pattern Recognition (CVPR), pp. 1460–1467, June 2013
23. Akashi, Y., Okatani, T.: Separation of reflection components by sparse non-negative matrix factorization. In: Cremers, D., Reid, I., Saito, H., Yang, M.-H. (eds.) ACCV 2014. LNCS, vol. 9007, pp. 611–625. Springer, Cham (2015). https://doi.org/10.1007/978-3-319-16814-2_40
24. Shen, H.L., Zhang, H.G., Shao, S.J., Xin, J.H.: Chromaticity-based separation of reflection components in a single image. Pattern Recogn. **41**(8), 2461–2469 (2008)
25. Shen, H.L., Zheng, Z.H.: Real-time highlight removal using intensity ratio. Appl. Opt. **52**(19), 4483–4493 (2013)
26. An, D., Suo, J., Ji, X., Wang, H., Dai, Q.: Fast and high quality highlight removal from a single image. CoRR abs/1512.00237 (2015)
27. Nguyen, T., Vo, Q., Kim, S., Yang, H., Lee, G.: A novel and effective method for specular detection and removal by tensor voting. In: 2014 IEEE International Conference on Image Processing (ICIP), pp. 1061–1065, October 2014
28. Park, J.B., Kak, A.C.: A truncated least squares approach to the detection of specular highlights in color images. In: IEEE International Conference on Robotics and Automation, Proceedings, ICRA 2003, vol. 1, pp. 1397–1403, September 2003
29. Rosenfeld, A.: Connectivity in digital pictures. J. ACM **17**(1), 146–160 (1970)
30. Swami, K., Das, S.K., Khandelwal, G., Vijayvargiya, A.: A robust flash image shadow detection method and seamless recovery of shadow regions. In: 2016 23rd International Conference on Pattern Recognition (ICPR), pp. 2836–2841, December 2016
31. Rosten, E., Drummond, T.: Machine learning for high-speed corner detection. In: Leonardis, A., Bischof, H., Pinz, A. (eds.) ECCV 2006. LNCS, vol. 3951, pp. 430–443. Springer, Heidelberg (2006). https://doi.org/10.1007/11744023_34
32. Leutenegger, S., Chli, M., Siegwart, R.Y.: BRISK: binary robust invariant scalable keypoints. In: 2011 International Conference on Computer Vision, pp. 2548–2555, November 2011
33. Fischler, M.A., Bolles, R.C.: A paradigm for model fitting with applications to image analysis and automated cartography. Commun. ACM **24**(6), 381–395 (1981). (reprinted in readings in computer vision, ed. ma fischler)
34. Goutte, C., Gaussier, E.: A probabilistic interpretation of precision, recall and F-score, with implication for evaluation. In: Losada, D.E., Fernández-Luna, J.M. (eds.) ECIR 2005. LNCS, vol. 3408, pp. 345–359. Springer, Heidelberg (2005). https://doi.org/10.1007/978-3-540-31865-1_25

A Method for Detecting JPEG Anti-forensics

Dinesh Bhardwaj[✉], Chothmal Kumawat, and Vinod Pankajakshan

Department of Electronics and Communication Engineering,
Indian Institute of Technology Roorkee, Roorkee, Uttarakhand, India
{dinesdec,cmeca.dec2015,vinodfec}@iitr.ac.in

Abstract. In this paper, a new approach is proposed for the detection of JPEG anti-forensic operations. It is based on the fact that when a JPEG anti-forensic operation is applied, the values of DCT coefficients are changed. This change decreases, especially in high frequency subbands, if we apply anti-forensic operation again. Hence, we propose to calculate a normalized difference between absolute values of DCT coefficients in 28 high frequency AC-subbands of the test image and its anti-forensically modified version. Based on this normalized feature, it is possible to differentiate between uncompressed and anti-forensically modified images. Experimental results show the effectiveness of the proposed method.

1 Introduction

The technological advancements have made digital cameras easily available and the increasing use of internet as a communication media made the digital images an easy way of conveying the visual information. But the digital images can be manipulated easily with the help of photo-editing softwares, even by non-professional users. These manipulations are known as image forgery in which a part of a realistic image is tampered. These forgeries have made the authenticity of digital images doubtful or we can say that the old saying "to see is to believe", might not be true in the case of digital images. In most of the cases, these forged images are not harmful, but if the same are used for malicious purposes such as evidences in the courtroom, or with the celebrities images, or as material for propaganda may defame an individual or organization. The doctored images/videos may create a negative environment or influence the public opinion. Many forensic techniques that can detect forgeries have been proposed in recent years. These forensic techniques detect the traces left by signal processing operations associated with forgery or fingerprints of acquisition devices [1].

Among the forensic techniques, JPEG forensics have received considerable research attention. This is due to the fact that the JPEG is the most widely used image compression standard. It introduces blocking artifacts across the boundaries of 8×8 sub-image blocks in spatial domain and DCT histogram artifacts in form of clustering of DCT coefficient around the integer multiple of quantization

© Springer Nature Singapore Pte Ltd. 2018
R. Rameshan et al. (Eds.): NCVPRIPG 2017, CCIS 841, pp. 190–197, 2018.
https://doi.org/10.1007/978-981-13-0020-2_17

step size in frequency domain. Furthermore, any forgery of a JPEG compressed image results in multiple compression artifacts in forged image. Based on these artifacts, various forensic techniques have been proposed in the literature to detect doctored images [2–4].

Most of the forensic techniques do not account for the possibility of anti-forensics. An adversary, who is familiar with the signal processing operations involved in the forgery, may develop an anti-forensic technique by removing the traces left by these operations. This results in an undetectable image forgery which can deceive forensic detectors. It is necessary for the forensic researchers to study any loophole in the forensic techniques, so that the undetectable image forgeries due to anti-forensic operation can be detected. In [5], Stamm *et al.* introduced the concept of JPEG anti-forensics to remove the JPEG histogram artifacts by adding an anti-forensic dither in the DCT-domain. In [6], the authors extended this work by removing blocking artifacts in addition to the dithering operation. Fan *et al.* [7] proposed another approach for concealing both the blocking and the DCT quantization artifacts with an improved trade-off between the forensic undetectability and perceptual quality of the anti-forensically modified image.

In response to these anti-forensics techniques, there are a few algorithms proposed which can detect the presence of anti-forensic operations. Valenzise *et al.* [8] observed that the addition of dithering noise in the DCT coefficients to remove histogram artifacts introduces grainy noise in the spatial domain. They proposed a technique to detect the presence of anti-forensic dither in a test image by computing the total variation (TV) in different recompressed versions (with different quality factors) of the test image. Lai and Böhme [9] proposed a calibrated feature which is based on the variance of DCT coefficients in high frequency subbands of test image and its calibrated version which is obtained by cropping the test image. Both these methods successfully detect the anti-forensic operation [5]. A machine learning based approach is proposed by Haodong Li *et al.* [10] for detecting various image operations as well as anti-forensic operations. Apart from the technique in [10], which is a computationally expensive machine learning based technique, there exists no technique which can detect the anti-forensic operations in [6,7]. This paper proposes a technique for differentiating uncompressed images from anti-forensically modified images. It is based on the change in the DCT coefficients due to anti-forensic operation.

The rest of this paper is organized as follows. Section 2 briefly discusses different anti-forensic methods. The proposed method is explained in Sect. 3. Section 4 presents the experimental results and performance analysis, and finally Sect. 5 concludes the paper.

2   JPEG Anti-forensic Methods

2.1   Stamm *et al.*'s Anti-forensic Method [6]

The DCT coefficients of an uncompressed image for a given AC subband follow the Laplacian distribution and JPEG compression converts this into discrete version [11]. In [6], for removing the JPEG histogram artifacts, a specially designed noise (anti-forensic dither) is added in the DCT subbands in such a way that the AC subbands follow the Laplacian distribution. The Laplacian parameter is estimated from the DCT coefficients of the compressed image for each AC subband by using maximum likelihood estimation (MLE). This dithering process adds grainy noise in the spatial domain which degrades the visual quality and disturbs the correlation of DCT coefficients. Further, JPEG blocking artifacts are removed by applying median filtering followed by the addition of zero mean Gaussian noise in spatial domain. The window size of the median filter and the variance of the noise can be adjusted according to quality factor of the JPEG image.

2.2   Fan *et al.*'s Anti-forensic Method [7]

The main disadvantage of Stamm's [6] anti-forensic method is that it degrades the quality of anti-forensically modified image. Fan *et al.*'s anti-forensic algorithm is a four step technique capable of fooling most of the forensic detectors based on JPEG compression artifacts. This approach achieves better visual quality as compared to [6]. In the first step, a deblocking is performed by using constrained TV-based minimization problem which is solved by projected subgradient method. It removes blocking artifacts and partially fills the gaps in the DCT histogram. In the second step, an adaptive local dithering signal model is used to fill the remaining gaps in DCT histogram. It is pointed out that in case of real data, the Laplacian model works well for the DCT coefficients quantized to zero whereas uniform model fits better for the other quantized DCT coefficients. As compared to [6], the Laplacian parameter for each quantization bin is estimated on the basis of weighted least-square fitting on the first round TV-based deblocked image. A second round TV based deblocking is performed to remove the small artifacts introduced during the histogram smoothing. Finally, decalibration is done to fool the calibrated feature based detector [9].

3   Proposed Detector

We propose a technique that can differentiate between uncompressed images and anti-forensically modified images. When an uncompressed image is JPEG compressed with a certain quality factor, the values of DCT coefficients will be clustered around the integer multiples of the corresponding quantization step size. As a result, gaps are introduced in the histogram of DCT coefficients in each subband. The application of anti-forensic operation on the JPEG compressed image tries to restore the DCT histogram similar to that of the uncompressed image. Figure 1(a) shows the histogram of DCT coefficients in a particular subband of an uncompressed image. Figure 1(b) shows the histogram of the DCT coefficients in the same subband after the JPEG compressed image is anti-forensically modified using the method proposed in [7]. Though the gaps in the DCT histogram are eliminated by the anti-forensic operation, there is a noticeable difference in the

DCT histograms of the uncompressed (Fig. 1(a)) and that of the anti-forensically modified image (Fig. 1(b)). If we compress the anti-forensically modified image and then apply the anti-forensic operation, there is difference between the histograms of the DCT coefficients of the resulting image, which has undergone the anti-forensic operation twice, and that of the image which has undergone anti-forensic operation once. Figure 1(c) shows the histogram of the DCT coefficients in the same subband for the image which had undergone anti-forensic operation twice. Figure 1(d) and (e) shows the absolute difference of the DCT histograms in Figs. 1(a), (b) and (b), (c) respectively. It can be observed form Figs. 1(d) and (e) that the change in the DCT histograms is more when the image is anti-forensically modified for the first time as compared to the change when an image is anti-forensically modified for the second time. It is also observed that this change in DCT histograms is more pronounced in the high frequency DCT subbands. Based on this observation, we propose a detector that can differentiate anti-forensically modified images from uncompressed images. The block diagram of the proposed detector is shown in Fig. 2. Let X be the given test image and X_d denotes its block-DCT transform. The test image is JPEG compressed with a quality factor Q_r and modified by the anti-forensic operation [7]. The resulting image is denoted by X_1 and its block-DCT transform is denoted by X_{1d}. For each of the 28 high frequency subbands (in zig-zag scan order), the

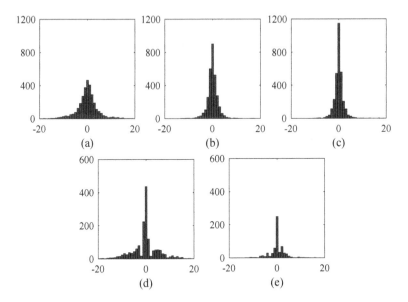

Fig. 1. DCT histograms of 51-th (in zig-zag scan order) AC subband for (a) uncompressed image. (b) image obtained by applying anti-forensic operation [7] on the compressed version of (a). (c) image obtained by applying anti-forensic operation [7] on the compressed version of (b). (d) the absolute difference of DCT histograms of (a) and (b). (e) the absolute difference of DCT histograms of (b) and (c).

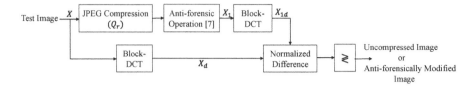

Fig. 2. Block diagram of proposed method

sum of absolute values of the DCT coefficients is computed for both X_d and X_{1d}, denoted by S_d^i and S_{1d}^i, respectively. Here, i is the subband index which varies from 37 to 64. Then the normalized difference (D) is calculated as

$$D = \sum_i \left| \frac{S_d^i - S_{1d}^i}{S_{1d}^i} \right|. \tag{1}$$

The given test image may be uncompressed or anti-forensically modified image. Hence, if the test image is uncompressed, the JPEG compression and anti-forensic operations are applied only once and the difference is calculated between DCT coefficients of uncompressed image and anti-forensically modified image. On the other hand, if the given test image had already undergone an anti-forensic operation, it is JPEG compressed and modified again by an anti-forensic operation. As a result, the difference is calculated between the given anti-forensically modified image and its anti-forensic version. Hence, the value of the proposed normalized difference (D) is small for anti-forensically modified image as compared to that of uncompressed image.

Now, the question arises, at what quality factor, the test image should be compressed and anti-forensically modified. If the test image is anti-forensically modified image, it had already been JPEG compressed by a certain quality factor (Q) and modified by an anti-forensic operation. It is observed that the normalized difference (D) will be less if we compress and anti-forensically modify the image at same quality factor i.e. $Q_r = Q$. But, the value of quality factor Q is not available to the forensic detector. Hence, we calculate a normalized feature (D) using a set of quality factors (Q_r) and the average normalized feature value $\overline{D}$ is used. In the experiments, we have used $Q_r = \{40, 50, ..., 80\}$. Finally, by applying a suitable threshold on $\overline{D}$, it is possible to differentiate between uncompressed and anti-forensically modified images.

4 Experimental Results

The performance of the proposed detector is evaluated on three standard datasets: UCID [12], Dresden [13] and Boss Base 1.01 [14]. There are total of 3691 images in which 1338 images are from UCID database, 353 images are from Dresden database and remaining 2000 images are taken from the Boss Base 1.01 database. Each image is converted into gray scale and are then JPEG compressed with 5 different quality factors: $Q = \{40, 50, ..., 80\}$. Each of these JPEG compressed images is anti-forensically modified by [7] which form a set of anti-forensic images. The average normalized difference $(\overline{D})$ feature is calculated for both uncompressed and anti-forensically modified images. Figure 3 shows the scatter plot of the average normalized difference for uncompressed images and anti-forensically modified images for quality factor $Q = 60$. It is observed that with a suitable threshold, we can effectively classify uncompressed images from anti-forensically modified images.

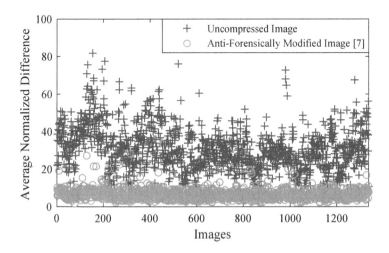

Fig. 3. Scatter plot of proposed feature at $Q = 60$ (UCID database)

The receiver operating characteristics (ROC) is used as the performance measure. The ROC curve gives the classification ability of the proposed feature: the closer the apex of the curve towards the top left corner, the higher is the classification ability i.e. high true-positive rate (TPR) and low false-positive rate (FPR). Figure 4 shows the ROC curves for the proposed detection method for different values of quality factor i.e. $Q = 40, 50, ..., 80$. We can observe that the performance degrades as the quality factor increases because higher the quality factor, lower is the quantization step size and lesser is the amount of noise added by the anti-forensic operation. We also tested proposed feature for the detection of anti-forensic operation [6]. We calculated the average normalized difference $(\overline{D})$ for uncompressed and anti-forensically modified images by [6] for three different quality factors i.e. $Q = 40, 60, 80$ and the corresponding ROC curves are shown in Fig. 5. The area under curve (AUC) for proposed detector at different quality factors are reported in Table 1. As expected, the AUC decreases with increase in the value of quality factor for both the anti-forensic techniques. These results show that the proposed detector can detect both the anti-forensic operations with a good accuracy.

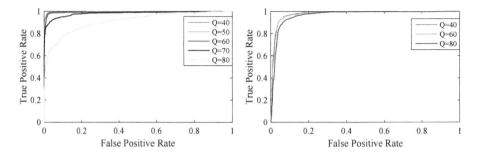

Fig. 4. Receiver operating character- **Fig. 5.** Receiver operating characteris-
istic (ROC) curve for detecting [7] tic (ROC) curve for detecting [6] (UCID
(UCID database) database)

Table 1. Performance of the proposed method in terms of AUC

Dataset	[7]			[6]		
	$Q = 40$	$Q = 60$	$Q = 80$	$Q = 40$	$Q = 60$	$Q = 80$
UCID [12]	0.99	0.99	0.91	0.98	0.98	0.97
Dresden [13]	0.98	0.96	0.93	0.99	0.99	0.99
Boss base 1.01 [14]	0.98	0.96	0.90	0.98	0.98	0.97

5   Conclusions

This paper proposed a technique for differentiating between uncompressed
images and anti-forensically modified JPEG images. The technique is based on
the change in values of DCT coefficients by an anti-forensic operation. A normalized difference feature is calculated for measuring these changes. Experimental
results show that the proposed method effectively classifies uncompressed images
from anti-forensically modified images. Future research includes the detection of
quality factor of the anti-forensically modified JPEG image.

References

1. Farid, H.: Image forgery detection. IEEE Sig. Process. Mag. **26**(2), 16–25 (2009)
2. Huang, F., Huang, J., Shi, Y.Q.: Detecting double JPEG compression with the
   same quantization matrix. IEEE Trans. Inf. Forensics Secur. **5**(4), 848–856 (2010)
3. Chen, Y.L., Hsu, C.T.: Detecting recompression of JPEG images via periodicity
   analysis of compression artifacts for tampering detection. IEEE Trans. Inf. Forensics Secur. **6**(2), 396–406 (2011)
4. Bianchi, T., Piva, A.: Image forgery localization via block-grained analysis of JPEG
   artifacts. IEEE Trans. Inf. Forensics Secur. **7**(3), 1003–1017 (2012)
5. Stamm, M.C., Tjoa, S.K., Lin, W.S., Liu, K.J.R.: Anti-forensics of JPEG compression. In: Proceedings of IEEE International Conference on Acoustics, Speech and
   Signal Processing, pp. 1694–1697, March 2010

6. Stamm, M.C., Liu, K.J.R.: Anti-forensics of digital image compression. IEEE Trans. Inf. Forensics Secur. **6**(3), 1050–1065 (2011)
7. Fan, W., Wang, K., Cayre, F., Xiong, Z.: JPEG anti-forensics with improved trade-off between forensic undetectability and image quality. IEEE Trans. Inf. Forensics Secur. **9**(8), 1211–1226 (2014)
8. Valenzise, G., Tagliasacchi, M., Tubaro, S.: Revealing the traces of JPEG compression anti-forensics. IEEE Trans. Inf. Forensics Secur. **8**(2), 335–349 (2013)
9. Lai, S., Böhme, R.: Countering counter-forensics: the case of JPEG compression. In: Proceedings of International Conference on Information Hiding, pp. 285–298 (2011)
10. Li, H., Luo, W., Qiu, X., Huang, J.: Identification of various image operations using residual-based features. IEEE Trans. Circ. Syst. Video Technol. **PP**(99), 1 (2016)
11. Lam, E.Y., Goodman, J.W.: A mathematical analysis of the DCT coefficient distributions for images. IEEE Trans. Image Process. **9**(10), 1661–1666 (2000)
12. Schaefer, G., Stich, M.: UCID - an uncompressed colour image database. In: Proceedings of SPIE, pp. 472–480, March 2004
13. Gloe, T., Bhme, R.: The 'Dresden Image Database' for benchmarking digital image forensics. In: Proceedings of the 25th Symposium on Applied Computing (ACM SAC 2010), vol. 2, pp. 1585–1591 (2010)
14. Bas, P., Filler, T., Pevný, T.: Break our steganographic system: the ins and outs of organizing boss. In: Proceedings of 13th International Conference on Information Hiding, pp. 59–70 (2011)

An End-to-End Deep Learning Framework for Super-Resolution Based Inpainting

Manoj Sharma[1,2(✉)], Rudrabha Mukhopadhyay[3], Santanu Chaudhury[1,2], and Brejesh Lall[2]

[1] Central Electronics Engineering Research Institute,
Pilani 333031, Rajasthan, India
mksnith@gmail.com, schaudhury@gmail.com
[2] Department of Electrical Engineering, IIT Delhi, New Delhi 110016, India
brejesh@ee.iitd.ac.in
[3] Heritage Institute of Technology, Kolkata 700107, India
rudrabha@gmail.com

Abstract. Image inpainting is an extremely challenging and open problem for the computer vision community. Motivated by the recent advancement in deep learning algorithms for computer vision applications, we propose a new end-to-end deep learning based framework for image inpainting. Firstly, the images are down-sampled as it reduces the targeted area of inpainting therefore enabling better filling of the target region. A down-sampled image is inpainted using a trained deep convolutional auto-encoder (CAE). A coupled deep convolutional auto-encoder (CDCA) is also trained for natural image super resolution. The pre-trained weights from both of these networks serve as initial weights to an end-to-end framework during the fine tuning phase. Hence, the network is jointly optimized for both the aforementioned tasks while maintaining the local structure/information. We tested this proposed framework with various existing image inpainting datasets and it outperforms existing natural image blind inpainting algorithms. Our proposed framework also works well to get noise resilient super-resolution after fine-tuning on noise-free super-resolution dataset. It provides more visually plausible and better resultant image in comparison of other conventional and state-of-the-art noise-resilient super-resolution algorithms.

Keywords: Convolutional auto-encoder (CAE)
Coupled deep convolutional auto-encoder (CDCA) · Deep learning
Blind and non-blind image inpainting · Super-resolution (SR)
Noise-resilient super-resolution

1 Introduction

Image inpainting aims to reconstruct missing regions and removal of unwanted parts of an image [1,2]. This area of research has earned a lot of significance over the course of time. Image inpainting can be classified as blind and non-blind

R. Rameshan et al. (Eds.): NCVPRIPG 2017, CCIS 841, pp. 198–208, 2018.
https://doi.org/10.1007/978-981-13-0020-2_18

based methods. Blind inpainting is a more complex problem to solve because there is no prior information provided to the network/algorithm about the exact position/location of the corrupted, missing or deteriorated regions of an image. Whereas, in non-blind inpainting the location of the regions to be filled are provided.

Recently, researchers have used deep learning algorithms for blind inpainting [3–6]. These algorithms work well for small region but filling of a big region is still an open challenge. To overcome this issue, we are proposing a new end-to-end deep learning framework for super-resolution based inpainting. Le Meur et al. [7] has shown importance of super-resolution based inpainting to fill larger regions. Aforementioned super-resolution based inpainting method was just a cascading of inpainting and super-resolution algorithm which was non-blind technique. It failed to preserve local structure/information but, our proposed framework jointly optimize both the tasks to get better results for blind inpainting.

Firstly, a convolutional auto-encoder (CAE) was trained for blind inpainting with down sampled version of images and a coupled deep convolutional auto-encoder (CDCA) [8] was trained for natural image super resolution (SR) separately. This results in learned CAE kernels/filters for blind inpainting and learned CDCA kernels for natural image SR. Then both of these networks were cascaded and the resulting network was initialized as a single integral network (CAE-CDCA) with pre-trained weights of the aforementioned networks. After that, the combined CAE-CDCA was fine-tuned on a data-set having down-sampled version of images with some missing region (corrupt LR images) as input and corresponding higher resolution (HR) ground truth images as a target. Here the parameters of CAE-CDCA is optimized by minimizing final SR loss. Filters/kernels were updated at each iteration and filters were learned for inpainting and super resolution simultaneously while preserving local texture information. The simple cascaded network fails to preserve local structure and high frequency information whereas our integrated CAE-CDCA is able to preserve the local structure by filling the missing region while optimizing inpainting and SR tasks jointly. A block diagram of the proposed framework is shown in Fig. 1.

We can adopt similar framework (CAE-CDCA) with few changes to get noise-free image SR. Sharma et al. [8] has given end to end deep learning framework to get noise-resilient SR. In contrast to stacked sparse auto-encoder (SSDA) used by [8] for image denoising, deep convolutional auto-encoder (CAE) is used in our framework. Since CAE provides a better resultant de-noised image in comparison to SSDA [9]. Firstly, CAE was trained for image de-noising and CDCA was trained for super-resolution separately. This results in learned CAE weights for de-noising and learned CDCA filters for super-resolution. Then both networks were cascaded (CAE-CDCA) and this cascaded network is finetuned as an integral network with pre-trained weights. After that, combined CAE-CDCA was fine-tuned on dataset having noisy-LR images as input and corresponding HR images as a target. Here the loss gradient was back-propagated till the first layer of CAE from the last layer of CDCA. Weights/filters were updated at each iteration and weights were learned to super-resolve and de-noising image simultaneously while preserving textural information.

The main reason behind using CDCA framework [8] of single image super-resolution (SISR) instead of other deep learning based SISR methods [9–16] is that CDCA architecture with 3 layers provides comparative results with other deep learning based SISR methods. Whereas, other architectures are very deep which require lots of computational complexity.

The rest of the paper is organized as follows. In Sect. 2 we mention related work. Section 3 covers proposed methodology for super-resolution based inpainting. Section 4 shows experimental result to show effectiveness of proposed framework and in last we conclude in Sect. 5.

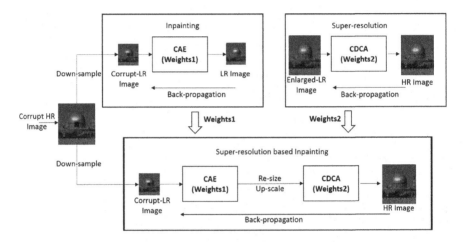

Fig. 1. Block diagram of deep learning framework for super-resolution based inpainting.

2   Related Work

In the first category of inpainting, researchers targeted to segment some specific regions from a given image and fill that region with similar patterns and textures present in the background [17]. This category covers only texture synthesis task at a particular location. Second category is of diffusion based techniques [18] which fills the targeted region by diffusing the information from known neighbouring regions. These diffusion based algorithms work well for small targeted regions but fail completely or give a blurring artifact for larger targeted regions. Exemplar based inpainting [15,17] and sparsity based inpainting [19,20] lie in the third category. These techniques work better to fill the missing region in comparison to diffusion based techniques but, there is a need to solve complex optimization problems during usage. Le Meur et al. [21] has presented new hybrid inpainting approach which uses both diffusion and exemplar based technique but with large computational complexity. Super-resolution based inpainting method [15] was able to fill larger regions but failed to preserve the local structure.

In the above mentioned methods, it is required to know the location of the missing region. Dong et al. [22] presented a wavelet based technique for blind inpainting and Liu et al. [23] have proposed tensor completion approach for prediction of missing regions. Recently, researchers have presented deep learning frameworks [3–6] for blind inpainting tasks, where deep learning frameworks learn end-to-end mapping between input with some missing region and targeted ground truth. After learning, we have to take the inference of the learned model to inpaint test images with missing region. These algorithms works better in filling smaller regions than earlier traditional approaches but not for larger missing regions. In recent years, generative adversarial network based inpainting approaches [24,25] have gained popularity for filling large missing regions, but these approaches fills the missing regions with arbitrary details which are quite different from the required context.

3 Methodology

3.1 Inpainting Using CAE

Let us consider that down-sampled natural image patches with some missing region (corrupt LR image patches) represented by y_i and corresponding down-sampled ground truth HR patches be represented by $x_i \ \forall i = 1, 2..n$, where n is the total number of patches in training dataset. We normalize both the input and target patches between [0 1] as a pre-processing step. We learn the blind inpainting function F_1 which converts y_i into x_i.

$$x_i = F_1(y_i, \theta_1) \tag{1}$$

Here, F_1 and θ_1 are blind inpainting function and parameters respectively. These parameters are same as used in the RED10 [3] architecture. The function F_1 is learned using similar convolution and de-convolution ten layer architecture. Size of patches used for training is $l \times h$. The function F_1 is learned by minimizing the following mean square error (MSE):

$$Loss_{Inpainting} = \frac{1}{n} \sum_{i=1}^{n} \frac{1}{2} \parallel x_i - F_1(y_i, \theta_1) \parallel_2^2 \tag{2}$$

3.2 Super-Resolution Using CDCA

Assuming up-sampled low-resolution natural image patches are represented as X_i and their corresponding ground truth HR patches represented as Z_i $\forall i = 1, 2..m$ where m is the total number of patches in SR training dataset. We normalize both the input and target patches between [0 1] as a pre-processing step. We learn the SR function F_2 which converts X_i into Z_i.

$$Z_i = F_2(X_i, \theta_2) \tag{3}$$

Here, F_2 and θ_2 are SR function and parameters respectively. The same parameters of CDCA [8] architecture is used. The function F_2 is learned by using same architecture and parameters as used in [8]. Size of patches used for training is $s.l \times s.h$. Where s is the desired super-resolution scaling. The function F_2 is learned by minimizing the following mean square error (MSE):

$$Loss_{SR} = \frac{1}{m} \sum_{i=1}^{m} \frac{1}{2} \parallel Z_i - F_2(X_i, \theta_2) \parallel_2^2 \tag{4}$$

3.3 SR Based Inpainting Using CAE-CDCA

The proposed framework for blind inpainting is shown in Fig. 1. and it comprises of the following steps:

1. Firstly, CAE architecture was learned for coarser version image inpainting. For this, we trained a CAE on a dataset having down-sampled natural image patches with some missing region (corrupt LR image patches) as an input and corresponding down-sampled HR ground truth patches as a target. Learning at coarser level reduces the area to inpaint which helps in preserving local structure information.
2. Then, the CDCA was learned for natural image SR on a dataset with natural LR image patches as input and the corresponding HR patches as target.
3. After having learned the CAE filters for blind inpainting and learned the CDCA filters/kernels for image super-resolution, we cascaded both these networks and termed it as CAE-CDCA. Then CAE-CDCA was treated as one integral network with pre-trained weights as shown in Fig. 1.
4. This CAE-CDCA was fine-tuned end-to-end on a dataset which consists of natural LR image patches with some missing region as an input and corresponding HR natural image patches as target. For end-to-end fine-tuning we use k number of patches in fine-tuning dataset.

After end-to-end fine-tuning, the combined network is jointly optimized for both the task (natural image inpainting at coarser level and SR) and preserves the local structure/information at the same time.

During fine-tuning, the final loss gradients were back-propagated from final layer of the CDCA to initial layer of the CAE. We want to learn the SR based inpainting function F such that $Z_i = F(y_i, \theta) \; \forall i = 1, 2..k$. Here, k is the total number of patches in fine-tuning dataset. The kernels/filters were learned to perform image inpainting at coarser level and SR, simultaneously by minimizing the final loss.

$$Loss_{final} = \frac{1}{k} \sum_{i=1}^{k} \frac{1}{2} \parallel Z_i - F(y_i, \theta) \parallel_2^2 \tag{5}$$

After learning the CAE-CDCA, we can inpaint any test image by down sampling that input image and by passing through the feed forward path of CAE-CDCA (taking inference of learned CAE-CDCA).

4 Experimental Results

4.1 Datasets

To train deep CAE for blind inpainting, we generated a large training database of 0.2 million corrupted and corresponding ground truth patches (size $= 64 \times 64$) using imagenet [26] and few images from ETH CIL database [27]. To create blind inpainting database, we corrupt the patches by using random masks at different locations. Our CDCA framework is trained on imagenet dataset for 2x SR dataset as given in [26]. Combined CAE-CDCA framework is fine-tuned on the dataset having down-sampled corrupted patches (64×64) as an input and corresponding ground truth patches (128×128) as a target. Fine-tuning is also done on imagenet dataset. We tested our framework on BSD300 dataset [28] and on remaining images from ETH CIL dataset. ImageNet dataset was used for fine-tuning our proposed deep learning framework to get noise-free super-resolution.

4.2 Experiments

To train CAE for blind inpainting, we take 10 layer architecture having 5 convolutional and 5 de-convolutional layers with ReLU as the activation function as given in RED10 [3]. At each convolutional and de-convolutional layer, the kernel size is 5×5, feature map is 64. we set batch size: 150 and learning rate: 10^{-4}.

To train CDCA for 2x SR of natural LR images, we use similar parameters as given in [8]. To learn convolutional feature maps, we take 9×9 filter size for first layer and 5×5 filter for the last two layers of the SR module. Feature maps used for first, second and third layers are 64, 32 and 1 respectively. We also set batch size: 150 and learning rate: 10^{-4}. Fine-tuning of CAE-CDCA was done on same parameters with a learning rate of 10^{-5} for the last layer and 10^{-4} for all other layers.

All these deep learning frameworks were trained and tested on a HP Z640 desktop workstation with 64 GB RAM, two Intel Xeon-E-5 processors and with GTX-1080 GPU support. All the experiments are performed on gray scale images. But the same framework can be extended to work on color images.

To generate noisy input, we add a different type of noises to the down-sampled ground-truth image patches using inbuilt functions in Matlab. Experiments have been conducted for noise resilient super-resolution. Proposed framework has been compared with conventional and state of art noise-free SR techniques.

4.3 Results

To verify effectiveness of proposed CAE-CDCA for blind inpainting, we have conducted several experiments as shown in Table 1. Proposed CAE-CDCA performs better in terms of PSNR and SSIM with comparison to state-of-the-art blind inpainting techniques. Mainly, we focus on larger missing region because state-of-the-art techniques like SSDA [5], BiCNN [4] and RED30 [3] performs

Table 1. Blind image inpainting results comparison on different images and dataset

Datasets	INPUT	INPUT	SSDA [5]	SSDA	BiCNN [4]	BiCNN	RED [3]	RED	Proposed	Proposed
Images	PSNR	SSIM	PSNR	SSIM	PSNR	SSIM	PSNR	SSIM	PSNR	SSIM
Image1	16.63	0.7823	20.16	0.7904	20.72	0.7984	25.2316	0.8075	28.36	0.8143
Image2	13.32	0.8104	24.04	0.8375	24.87	0.8654	25.03	0.9013	26.89	0.9704
Image3	18.41	0.8252	23.67	0.8276	24.89	0.8279	28.08	0.8311	29.71	0.8358
Set5+Set14	17.19	0.7129	20.28	0.7591	25.06	0.7878	26.23	0.8110	29.87	0.8765
BSD100	19.73	0.8359	22.60	0.8471	25.01	0.8901	27.39	0.9126	30.86	0.9416

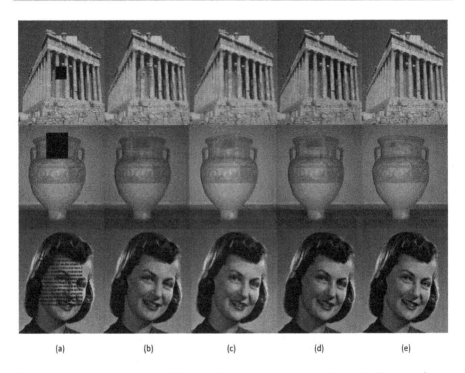

(a)   (b)   (c)   (d)   (e)

Fig. 2. Visual comparison of different blind inpainting algorithms for Image.1 (upper one), Image.2 (middle one) and Image.3 (lower one): (a) input, (b) BiCNN [4], (c) RED30 [3], (d) proposed, (e) ground truth.

exceptionally well for small region (missing line or region 1–10 pixel width) but for larger region, these algorithms fail to fill region with proper local texture/information. We get 3.12, 1.86, 1.64, 3.64 and 3.51 dB improvement for Image.1, Image.2, Image.3, Set5+Set14 [3] and BSD100 dataset [3] respectively from the RED30 [3]. To make fair comparison, we have also shown results of other state-of-the-art blind inpainting techniques (No comparison with non-blind inpainting techniques).

In Fig. 2, we have shown the visual comparison of different algorithms for blind inpainting. For Image.1, missing region is of size (32×32) at the mid of image. Here, the texture information in resultant image of proposed method is clearer than RED30 [3] and BiCNN [4] resultant image. In case of Image.2, missing region is of size (64×64) at random location. We can visualize that, proposed method is able to restore sharp edges of pot compared to other methods. We also show result on Image.3 with text as a mask. Here our result is visually comparable with RED30 [3] but gives much better results than BiCNN [4].

We are showing results with different mask at different locations to prove generalization and robustness of proposed framework. To make comparisons more generalized for all natural images, we compare all algorithms for BSD100 dataset images with random missing region (square of 32×32) at different locations. Our architecture performs inpainting at coarser version with 5 convolutional and 5 de-convolutional layers. Due to performing inpainting at down-sampled version, our framework have less computational complexity and reduced area to be inpainted (missing region). We use CDCA [8] to perform SR because it provides state-of-the-art results with less computational complexity (only 3 layer convolutional network). Thus, our combined CAE-CDCA provides better result with less complexity in comparison of RED30 [3] for blind inpainting.

We have also tested proposed framework (CAE+CDCA) for 3X and 4X SR on BSD100 dataset to fill more bigger region (missing region of size greater than 100×100). Our framework get $3.61\,dB$ and $3.87\,dB$ improvement in PSNR from RED30 [3] for inpainting missing region of size (120×120) using 3X and 4X SR, respectively. Our framework also works better than [8] for getting noise resilient SR. We get $0.87\,dB$, $1.19\,dB$ and $0.98\,dB$ improvement on BSD200 dataset for getting 2X, 3X and 4X noise (Gaussian noise with different variance) resilient super resolution, respectively.

Comparison of proposed framework with conventional and state of art 3x noise resilient image SR has been shown in Table 2. The table shows that results of proposed frameworks are better than state-of-art and traditional frameworks. Here, conventional method refers to best algorithm for image de-noising followed by best algorithm for image super-resolution (i.e, CAE+CDCA). Here, the + sign shows just cascading of methods. In Table 2, CAE+CDCA is just cascading of learned CAE for de-noising and learned CDCA for super-resolution (without fine-tuning). CAE-CDCA is proposed framework with fine-tuned weights of combined network. We have also compared the result of integrated architecture with cascaded network and the result shows that proposed framework performs better than a cascaded framework. In Table 2, results are shown on Set5, Set14 and BSD200 dataset with the gaussian noise of different variance (10, 20 and 30) for 3X super-resolution. To test the robustness of our architecture, we applied other noises as well. The improvement in PSNR, when compared to conventional method, was $2.2\,dB$ for blurring and $2.9\,dB$ for salt and pepper noise in case of 2x noise resilient SR. The test images for experiments were obtained from, set5, set14 and BSD200 dataset [28].

In Fig. 3, we can easily visualize that high-frequency information is far better than state of art and conventional approach. This figure clearly represents that conventional techniques are not able to recover high frequency and texture information.

Table 2. Comparison of different methods with gaussian noise for 3x noise resilient super-resolution

Algo./Datasets	Set5	Set14	BSD200	Set5	Set14	BSD200	Set5	Set14	BSD200
	$(\sigma = 10)$	$(\sigma = 10)$	$(\sigma = 10)$	$(\sigma = 20)$	$(\sigma = 20)$	$(\sigma = 20)$	$(\sigma = 30)$	$(\sigma = 30)$	$(\sigma = 30)$
	PSNR	PSNR	PSNR	PSNR	PSNR	PSNR	PSNR	PSNR	PSNR
SSDA+CDCA	29.11	26.47	24.65	28.59	26.28	25.06	28.17	25.96	23.08
CAE+CDCA	29.17	26.49	24.67	28.67	26.34	25.12	28.19	26.22	23.15
SSDA-CDCA	32.24	28.86	26.83	32.03	28.71	26.41	31.63	28.36	25.96
CAE-CDCA	32.53	28.99	27.06	32.49	28.99	26.94	31.72	28.48	26.33

Fig. 3. Noise resilient image SR (2x) comparison on lamma. (a) LR image with Gaussian noise ($\sigma = 30$). (b) Conventional. (c) Proposed CAE-CDCA. (d) Original.

5 Conclusion

We proposed a novel end-to-end deep learning based framework for blind inpainting which is more efficient in filling larger missing regions. Our framework performs inpainting at coarser level and super-resolution simultaneously preserving the local structure/information. We did exhaustive experiments with several state-of-the-art image inpainting techniques. Our framework can be easily adopted for getting noise-free super-resolution after fine-tunning on noise-free super resolution dataset. Experimental results show the effectiveness of our framework. End-to-end optimization is the main reason behind our better results. In future, we plan to experiment with color images for blind inpainting.

References

1. Bertalmio, M., Sapiro, G., Caselles, V., Ballester, C.: Image inpainting. In: Proceedings of the 27th Annual Conference on Computer Graphics and Interactive Techniques, SIGGRAPH (2000)
2. Guillemot, C., Le Meur, O.: Image inpainting: overview and recent advances. IEEE Signal Process. Mag. **31**(1), 127–144 (2014)
3. Mao, X.-J., Shen, C., Yang, Y.-B.: Image Denoising Using Very Deep Fully Convolutional Encoder-Decoder Networks with Symmetric Skip Connections. CoRR (2016)
4. Cai, N., Su, Z., Lin, Z., Wang, H., Yang, Z., Ling, B.W.K.: Blind inpainting using the fully convolutional neural network. Vis. Comput. **33**(2), 249–261 (2017)

5. Xie, J., Xu, L., Chen, E.: Image denoising and inpainting with deep neural networks. In: Advances in Neural Information Processing Systems, pp. 341–349 (2012)
6. Fawzi, A., Samulowitz, H., Turaga, D., Frossard, P.: Image inpainting through neural networks hallucinations. In: IEEE 12th Image, Video and Multidimensional Signal Processing Workshop, IVMSP (2016)
7. Le Meur, O., Ebdelli, M., Guillemot, C.: Hierarchical super-resolution-based inpainting. IEEE Trans. Image Process. **22**(10), 3779–3790 (2013)
8. Sharma, M., Chaudhury, S., Lall, B.: Deep learning based frameworks for image super-resolution and noise-resilient super-resolution. In: International Joint Conference on Neural Networks, IJCNN (2017)
9. Mao, X.-J., Shen, C., Yang, Y.-B.: Image Restoration Using Convolutional Auto-encoders with Symmetric Skip Connections. CoRR (2016)
10. Dong, C., Loy, C.C., He, K., Tang, X.: Learning a deep convolutional network for image super-resolution. In: Fleet, D., Pajdla, T., Schiele, B., Tuytelaars, T. (eds.) ECCV 2014. LNCS, vol. 8692, pp. 184–199. Springer, Cham (2014). https://doi.org/10.1007/978-3-319-10593-2_13
11. Kim, J., Kwon Lee, J., Mu Lee, K.: Accurate Image Super-Resolution Using Very Deep Convolutional Networks. CoRR (2015)
12. Wang, Z., Liu, D., Yang, J., Han, W., Huang, T.: Deep networks for image super-resolution with sparse prior. In: IEEE International Conference on Computer Vision, ICCV (2015)
13. Kim, J., Kwon Lee, J., Mu Lee, K.: Deeply-Recursive Convolutional Network for Image Super-Resolution. CoRR (2015)
14. Yang, W., Feng, J., Yang, J., Zhao, F., Liu, J., Guo, Z., Yan, S.: Deep Edge Guided Recurrent Residual Learning for Image Super-Resolution. CoRR (2016)
15. Ledig, C., Theis, L., Huszar, F., Caballero, J., Aitken, A.P., Tejani, A., Totz, J., Wang, Z., Shi, W.: Photo-Realistic Single Image Super-Resolution Using a Generative Adversarial. CoRR (2016)
16. Shi, W., Caballero, J., Huszar, F., Totz, J., Aitken, A.P., Bishop, R., Rueckert, D., Wang, Z.: Real-Time Single Image and Video Super-Resolution Using an Efficient Sub-Pixel Convolutional Neural Network. CoRR (2016)
17. Criminisi, A., Perez, P., Toyama, K.: Region filling and object removal by exemplar-based image inpainting. IEEE Trans. Image Process. **13**(9), 1200–1212 (2004)
18. Bertalmio, M., Bertozzi, A.L., Sapiro, G.: Navier-stokes, fluid dynamics, and image and video inpainting. In: Proceedings of the 2001 IEEE Computer Society Conference on Computer Vision and Pattern Recognition, CVPR (2001)
19. Ghorai, M., Mandal, S., Chanda, B.: Patch sparsity based image inpainting using local patch statistics and steering kernel descriptor. In: 23rd International Conference on Pattern Recognition, ICPR (2016)
20. Fadili, M.-J., Starck, J.-L., Murtagh, F.: Inpainting and zooming using sparse representations. Comput. J. **52**(1), 64–79 (2009)
21. Le Meur, O., Gautier, J., Guillemot, C.: Examplar-based inpainting based on local geometry. In: 18th IEEE International Conference on Image Processing, ICIP (2011)
22. Dong, B., Ji, H., Li, J., Shen, Z., Xu, Y.: Wavelet frame based blind image inpainting. Appl. Comput. Harmon. Anal. **32**(1), 268–279 (2012)
23. Liu, J., Musialski, P., Wonka, P., Ye, J.: Tensor completion for estimating missing values in visual data. IEEE Trans. Pattern Anal. Mach. Intell. TPAMI **35**(1), 208–220 (2013)

24. Pathak, D., Krähenbühl, P., Donahue, J., Darrell, T., Efros, A.A.: Context encoders: feature learning by inpainting. In: IEEE Conference on Computer Vision and Pattern Recognition, CVPR (2016)
25. Yeh, R., Chen, C., Lim, T.-Y., Hasegawa-Johnson, M., Do, M.N.: Semantic Image Inpainting with Perceptual and Contextual Losses. CoRR (2016)
26. Russakovsky, O., Deng, J., Su, H., Krause, J., Satheesh, S., Ma, S., Huang, Z., Karpathy, A., Khosla, A., Bernstein, M., Berg, A.C., Fei-Fei, L.: ImageNet large scale visual recognition challenge. Int. J. Comput. Vis. IJCV **115**(3), 211–252 (2015)
27. Image Inpainting Dataset of Computational Intelligence Lab - ETH Zürich, ETH-CIL Dataset (2012)
28. Martin, D., Fowlkes, C., Tal, D., Malik, J.: A database of human segmented natural images and its application to evaluating segmentation algorithms and measuring ecological statistics. In: 8th International Conference on Computer Vision, ICCV (2001)

Saliency Map Improvement Using Edge-Aware Filtering

Diptiben Patel[(✉)] and Shanmuganathan Raman

Electrical Engineering, Indian Institute of Technology Gandhinagar,
Gandhinagar 382355, Gujarat, India
{diptiben.patel,shanmuga}@iitgn.ac.in

Abstract. Content-aware applications in computational photography define the relative importance of objects or actions present in an image using a saliency map. Most saliency detection algorithms learn from the human visual system and try to find relatively important content as a salient region(s). This paper attempts to improve the saliency map defined by these algorithms using an iterative process. The saliency map of an image generated by an existing saliency detection algorithm is modified by filtering the image after segmenting into foreground and background. In order to enhance the saliency map values present in the salient region, the background is filtered using an edge-aware guided filter and the foreground is enhanced using a local Laplacian filter. The number of iterations required varies according to the image content. We show that the proposed framework enhances the saliency maps generated using the state-of-the-art saliency detection algorithms both qualitatively and quantitatively.

1 Introduction

The human visual system and the brain are remarkably fast in processing visual information in a fraction of time. The human visual system makes this process faster by focusing on a "distinctive and attentive" object or action and processing it first before the other regions. The human eye is fixated to a distinctive region with higher priority and spends much of the processing time on it as compared to the other non-distinctive regions. The distinctive region(s) is/are named as salient region(s) and the map describing its distinctiveness is called saliency map in computer vision. The goal of saliency detection algorithms is to estimate the fixation of a human eye according to the distinctiveness. The estimated saliency map is used in different applications to mimic the human visual system such that the modification of the scene induces as less visible artifacts as possible. The estimated saliency map is used in many computer vision applications such as image segmentation [1], object detection [2], image compression [3] and image enhancement [4], to name a few. The efficiency of these applications depends on the accuracy of the underlying saliency detection algorithm.

Rather than improving the existing saliency detection algorithms, can we improve the saliency maps generated by the state-of-the-art saliency detection

© Springer Nature Singapore Pte Ltd. 2018
R. Rameshan et al. (Eds.): NCVPRIPG 2017, CCIS 841, pp. 209–219, 2018.
https://doi.org/10.1007/978-981-13-0020-2_19

algorithms using some iterative process? In this work, the values in terms of the saliency map generated by a saliency detection algorithm are improved in the salient region of an image by modifying the original image in an iterative manner. Most of the saliency detection algorithms look for local contrast or edge details at first stage to estimate the saliency map of an image. Therefore, if the local contrast of an image is modified such that the edge details in the non-salient region are suppressed and those present in the salient region are enhanced, it can enable us to modify and improve the saliency map of an image. This motivation is behind the proposed framework to enhance the saliency map of an image generated using the existing saliency detection algorithms. The number of iterations required for the improvement in a given saliency map depends on the image content making it an adaptive algorithm.

The paper is organized as follows. Section 2 surveys various saliency detection algorithms and different criteria considered for defining saliency. The framework for improvement in the saliency map generated by existing saliency detection algorithms is proposed in Sect. 3. The results and the comparisons are discussed in Sect. 4. The paper is concluded with some pointers to future work in Sect. 5.

2 Related Work

Saliency detection algorithms use different features of an image to estimate the human eye fixations. In late 90's, Itti *et al.* have defined the saliency map using early visual features comprising of image intensity contrast, color contrast, and local orientation contrast computed at different Gaussian scales [5]. Harel *et al.* have proposed a graph-based visual saliency model in feature space using bottom-up approach [6]. The above-mentioned saliency detection algorithms do not take care of exact boundaries of salient regions. Achanta *et al.* have proposed frequency tuned saliency detection algorithm providing exact boundaries of salient regions imparting more frequency content across the boundaries using color and luminance features [7]. The saliency map of an image is estimated using local feature color contrast, sparse sampling, kernel density estimation and Bayesian theory model in [8]. Liu *et al.* have proposed learning based salient object detection algorithm which trains Conditional Random Field (CRF) algorithm using features: multi-scale contrast (local), center-surround histogram (regional), and color spatial distribution (global) [9]. While detecting eye fixations or salient regions, the context of the salient region is lost. Using local contrast, global features, visual organization rules, and some of the high-level features, the context of an image alongside salient region is preserved in [10]. Cheng *et al.* have proposed a saliency detection algorithm by combining histogram based contrast and region based contrast [11]. Murray *et al.* have proposed a saliency model based on low-level vision system at multi-scale decomposition using color and luminance channels [12]. Li *et al.* have proposed a learning based saliency detection algorithm which combines eye fixation and segmentation models in order to perform segmentation of the salient objects [13]. In [14], salient objects and distractors are separated by learning the distribution of projected features using principal component analysis. Borji *et al.* have proposed a patch based saliency detection algorithm which defines saliency of patches based on how they are different from surrounding patches and how often they occur in an RGB and Lab color space of an image [15]. Another patch based saliency detection algorithm defines the saliency of a patch using the distance from an average of all patches in the color space and the pattern space along the principal component directions [16]. The weighted dissimilarity between patches using multiple parameters is used to form a saliency map in [17].

Improving the saliency map generated by the saliency detection algorithms is a novel research area. Lei *et al.* have proposed a framework using Bayesian decision theory after finding rough saliency map from different saliency detection algorithms [18]. They enhanced the saliency map of an image using a conditional probability of pixels having similar color values with that of pixels with higher saliency value in rough saliency map. This framework will fail if the salient object contains different colors and is not captured in rough saliency map. Alternatively, we have proposed to improve the saliency map by modifying the image in order to enhance the saliency value present in the salient region in an iterative manner. From the saliency map generated using an existing saliency detection algorithm, foreground and background regions are found using image segmentation. The image is modified differently for foreground and background regions iteratively. This enables us to enhance the saliency values in the salient (foreground) region and to suppress the saliency values in the non-salient (background) region.

3   Proposed Approach

The purpose of saliency detection algorithm is to look for distinctive regions in an image where human eye fixates. The more the distinctiveness of a pixel, the more the saliency value assigned to a pixel. Most saliency detection algorithms fail to properly distinguish distinctive regions and sometimes assign the same value to a region in an image. Sometimes, they may not be able to assign consistent saliency value to the same object in an image. Our goal is to improve and make the saliency values concentrated in distinctive regions by enhancing the energy present in the distinctive regions iteratively. This can be achieved by smoothing out the non-distinctive region (background) and coarsening the distinctive region (foreground) while generating the saliency map in an iterative manner.

3.1   Methodology

The proposed framework for an improvement in a given saliency map S_0 of image I_0 is described below. Let the image I_0 be of size $M \times N$.

1. The saliency map of an image I_i generated using an existing saliency detection algorithm is S_i. The energy E_i of a saliency map S_i is defined as a squared sum of gray level co-occurrence matrices (GLCM [19]) C_{θ_j} in 4 directions $0°$, $45°$, $90°$, and $135°$ with the distance between given two pixels being 1 and is shown in Eq. (1).

$$E_i = \sum_{a=1}^{P} \sum_{b=1}^{P} \left(\sum_{j=1}^{4} C_{\theta_j}(a,b) \right)^2$$

$$C_{\theta_j}(a,b) = \sum_{x=1}^{M} \sum_{y=1}^{N} \begin{cases} 1, & S_i(x,y) = a \ \& \\ & S_i(x+x_{\theta_j}, y+y_{\theta_j}) = b \\ 0, & \text{Otherwise} \end{cases} \tag{1}$$

here, $i = 0, 1, \ldots, K$, $x = 1, 2, \ldots, M$, $y = 1, 2, \ldots, N$, $\theta \in \{0°, 45°, 90°, 135°\}$, $x_{\theta_j} \in \{-1, 0, 1\}$, $y_{\theta_j} \in \{-1, 0, 1\}$, K is the number of iterations, P is number of intensity levels in an image and E_i is the energy of the saliency map after the ith iteration.

2. The image I_i is segmented into foreground (FG_i) and background (BG_i) using kernel k-means algorithm described in [20]. The segmentation method proposed in [20] requires rectangular box R_i as a seed that includes foreground region (FG_i) which is a salient region in our case. We find this rectangular box R_i from binary map P_i using the saliency map S_i as shown in Eq. (2).

$$P_i(x,y) = \begin{cases} 1, & \text{if } S_i(x,y) \geq average(S_i) \\ 0, & \text{Otherwise.} \end{cases} \tag{2}$$

R_i of size $M \times N$ is a minimum area rectangle which contains all the 1's in P_i. The segmentation method outputs an image G_i with foreground region intact and background region with values 1. We generate the binary mask B_i (indicating foreground region) using G_i as shown in Eq. (3).

$$B_i(x,y) = \begin{cases} 1, & \text{if } G_i(x,y) \neq 1 \\ 0, & \text{Otherwise.} \end{cases} \tag{3}$$

3. As our goal is to propagate energy towards the salient region (foreground), we exaggerate the foreground region and apply smoothing on the background region of the image. We use local Laplacian filter T_l described in [21] to exaggerate the details in the foreground with $\sigma_r = 0.1$. The low pass filtering of the background region is performed using the guided filter T_g with filter size $w = 5$ and the guide image to be the same as the input image to be filtered. The modified image $I_{(i+1)}$ is generated by combining differently filtered foreground and background regions and it is as described in Eq. (4).

$$\begin{aligned} I_{(i+1)} &= FG_{(i+1)} + BG_{(i+1)} \\ &= (B_i \times T_l(I_i, \sigma_r)) + ((1 - B_i) \times T_g(I_i, I_i, w)) \end{aligned} \tag{4}$$

4. We repeat the steps 1–3 iteratively with the modified input image $I_{(i+1)}$. The summarized block diagram of iterative process is shown in Fig. 1. The number of iterations to be performed is dependent on the image content and is estimated as described in Sect. 3.2.

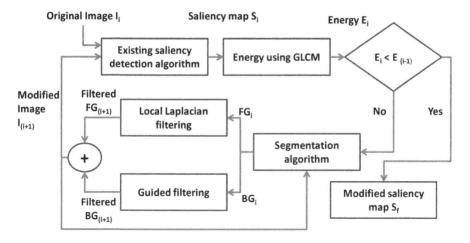

Fig. 1. The proposed saliency improvement framework.

3.2   Optimal Number of Iterations

The energy variation of a saliency map of modified images over the number of iterations is shown in Fig. 2. Observing the energy variations over the number of iterations, the energy E_i starts decreasing after some iteration. During initial iterations, as the smoothing of a background region tends to gain a constant intensity value, energy value E_i increases to achieve a value of 1. (Energy of a gray co-occurrence matrix of a constant intensity image is 1). After some iteration, exaggeration of foreground region starts dominating the effect of background region on energy and detail enhancement in foreground region reduces the energy value. As more enhancement of details in the foreground leads to saturation of intensity values, we stop the iterations when energy values start decreasing. The

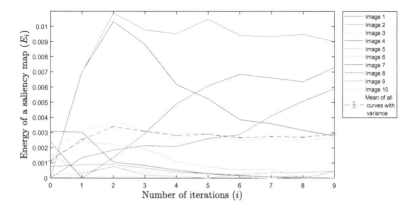

Fig. 2. Energy of the improved saliency map as a function of number of iterations. Each curve shows energy variation of a saliency map of modified images over the iterations.

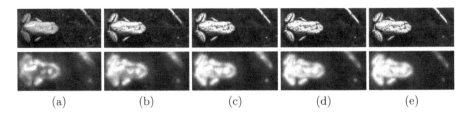

(a)   (b)   (c)   (d)   (e)

Fig. 3. Effect of iterative process on saliency map: Top row: modified images: (a) Original image, (b)–(e) modified images after $i = 1, 2, 3$ and 4 iterations, Bottom row: saliency maps of the corresponding modified images using existing saliency detection algorithm by [10].

same can be observed from Fig. 3. Figure 3 shows the modified images and their saliency maps after each iteration. From Fig. 3, it is observed that after a certain number of iterations, the intrusion of constant values in the background region and the saturation of exaggerated edges in the foreground region lead to decrease in the energy of a saliency map. Hence, the iterative process has to be stopped as soon as the energy value starts decreasing. The saliency map (S_f) of the modified image after the last iteration provides the improved version of the saliency map (S_0) of the original image. In this way, the number of iterations required for an improvement in the saliency map is adaptive depending on the given image.

4   Results and Discussions

We have tested the proposed framework on the MSRA salient object dataset [9] and compared the improvement in the saliency maps with their corresponding original saliency maps. The comparison is performed using several existing state-of-the-art saliency detection algorithms such as graph-based visual saliency (GBVS) approach [6], spatially weighted dissimilarity (SWD) based approach [17], non-parametric low level vision (NPL) based approach [12], context-aware saliency (CS) based approach [10], distinct patch (Patch) based approach [16], discriminative subspaces (DSRC) based approach [14], and kernel density estimation (KDE) based approach [8]. The maximum number of iterations is kept to 10 which is way higher than 4, the average number of iterations required to enhance the saliency map.

Visual comparison of the proposed approach for a number of images is shown in Fig. 4. Figure 4 shows the original images (Image), their ground truth binary saliency maps (GT), the saliency maps using the existing saliency detection algorithms (X), and their corresponding improved version (X_{SI}) obtained using the proposed framework. One can observe that the saliency map generated using an existing saliency detection algorithm is improved after the execution of the proposed approach for every state-of-the-art saliency detection algorithm.

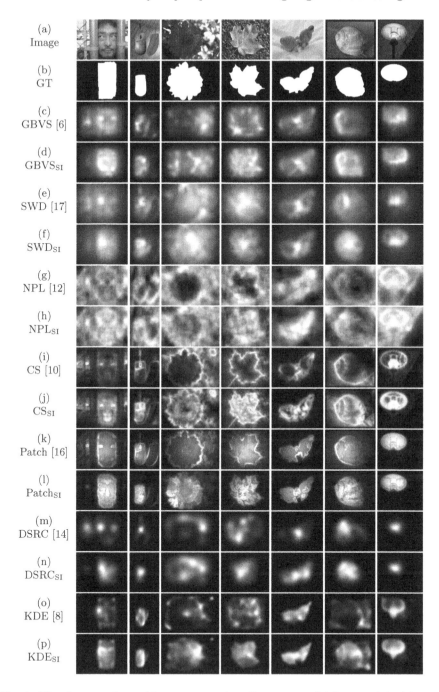

Fig. 4. Visual comparison of improvement in saliency map: (a) Input original images and (b) their ground truths, (c, e, g, i, k, m, o) Saliency maps using existing saliency detection algorithms and (d, f, h, j, l, n, p) modified saliency maps using proposed approach.

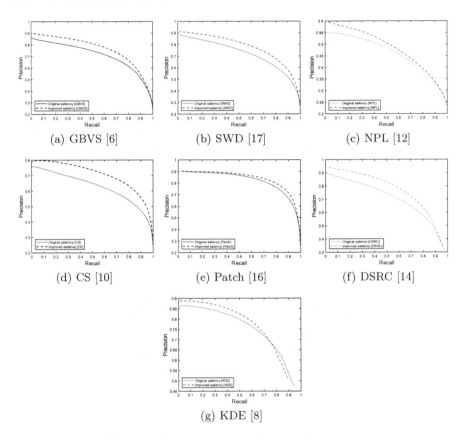

Fig. 5. Average precision - recall curves for saliency maps generated using existing saliency detection algorithms and modified saliency maps using proposed approach.

The objective evaluation of the results obtained using proposed framework is carried out using two measures: precision-recall measure and recently proposed structure measure [22]. Precision (Pr) and recall (Re) values with respect to a fixed threshold and the ground truth binary saliency map are calculated as shown in Eq. (5). S_T is thresholded binary saliency map and GT is ground truth map available with the dataset. For a fixed threshold value, better performance is identified by higher precision value and higher recall value. For each threshold, precision and recall values are averaged across the number of images. Figure 5 shows the graph of the average precision-recall values for different saliency detection algorithms considered in this study. It can be observed from Fig. 5 that the implementation of the proposed framework improves the saliency map generated using all the state-of-the-art saliency detection algorithms. We evaluate the quality of the proposed framework using F-measure F which is defined in Eq. (6).

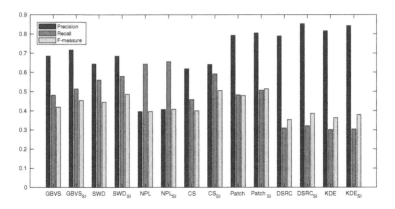

Fig. 6. Precision, recall and F-measure for saliency maps using existing saliency detection algorithms and their corresponding improvement using proposed approach.

$$Pr = \frac{\sum\limits_{x=1}^{M}\sum\limits_{y=1}^{N}(S_T \cap GT)}{\sum\limits_{x=1}^{M}\sum\limits_{y=1}^{N}S_T}, Re = \frac{\sum\limits_{x=1}^{M}\sum\limits_{y=1}^{N}(S_T \cap GT)}{\sum\limits_{x=1}^{M}\sum\limits_{y=1}^{N}GT} \tag{5}$$

$$F = 2\left(\frac{Pr \times Re}{Pr + Re}\right) \tag{6}$$

Using Eqs. (5) and (6), average Pr, Re and F values for the saliency maps obtained using different algorithms and their corresponding improved saliency maps obtained using the proposed framework are shown in Fig. 6. Higher precision and higher recall values indicate that the proposed framework improves the saliency map generated by all the saliency detection methods considered. We can observe that we tend towards salient object segmentation with a better suppression of non-salient regions using the proposed approach. Recently Fan *et al.* have proposed a structural similarity measure to evaluate region-aware and object-aware similarities between non-binary saliency map and ground truth (GT) [22]. Region-aware and object-aware structure similarities try to capture global structure and global distributions of foreground objects. The structure measure overcomes the pixel-wise comparison algorithms for better overall global structure comparison. Table 1 shows the structure measure values: the first row shows the

Table 1. Structure measure for saliency maps generated using existing saliency detection algorithms and their corresponding improvement using proposed approach.

	GBVS [6]	SWD [17]	NPL [12]	CS [10]	Patch [16]	DSRC [14]	KDE [8]
S_0	0.6677	0.6604	0.5032	0.6246	0.7096	0.5984	0.5900
S_f	0.6965	0.6989	0.5114	0.6934	0.7320	0.6170	0.5983

average values of structure measures of saliency maps generated using different existing saliency detection algorithms and the second row shows that of using proposed improvement framework. It is noted that S-values are increased by applying proposed improvement framework.

5   Conclusion

The proposed method introduces an iterative process to improve the saliency map obtained by an existing saliency detection algorithm. The saliency values are forced to be more concentrated in distinctive regions and suppressed in non-distinctive regions. This is achieved by smoothing non-distinctive or background regions and enhancing the details of distinctive or foreground regions using edge-preserving filters. The performance of the saliency improvement framework is shown to be effective using precision, recall, F-measure and recently proposed structure measure. The proposed saliency improvement technique can be used for various applications of computer vision which require salient object detection and segmentation. In future, we would like to extend the work for improving the salient object detection in videos.

References

1. Qin, C., Zhang, G., Zhou, Y., Tao, W., Cao, Z.: Integration of the saliency-based seed extraction and random walks for image segmentation. Neurocomputing **129**, 378–391 (2014)
2. Peng, H., Li, B., Ling, H., Hu, W., Xiong, W., Maybank, S.J.: Salient object detection via structured matrix decomposition. IEEE Trans. Pattern Anal. Mach. Intell. **39**(4), 818–832 (2017)
3. Ouerhani, N., Bracamonte, J., Hugli, H., Ansorge, M., Pellandini, F.: Adaptive color image compression based on visual attention. In: Proceedings of 11th International Conference on Image Analysis and Processing, pp. 416–421. IEEE (2001)
4. Zhao, J., Chen, Y., Feng, H., Xu, Z., Li, Q.: Infrared image enhancement through saliency feature analysis based on multi-scale decomposition. Infrared Phys. Technol. **62**, 86–93 (2014)
5. Itti, L., Koch, C., Niebur, E., et al.: A model of saliency-based visual attention for rapid scene analysis. IEEE Trans. Pattern Anal. Mach. Intell. **20**(11), 1254–1259 (1998)
6. Harel, J., Koch, C., Perona, P.: Graph-based visual saliency. In: Advances in Neural Information Processing Systems, pp. 545–552 (2006)
7. Achanta, R., Hemami, S., Estrada, F., Susstrunk, S.: Frequency-tuned salient region detection. In: IEEE Conference on Computer Vision and Pattern Recognition, CVPR 2009, pp. 1597–1604. IEEE (2009)
8. Rezazadegan Tavakoli, H., Rahtu, E., Heikkilä, J.: Fast and efficient saliency detection using sparse sampling and kernel density estimation. In: Heyden, A., Kahl, F. (eds.) SCIA 2011. LNCS, vol. 6688, pp. 666–675. Springer, Heidelberg (2011). https://doi.org/10.1007/978-3-642-21227-7_62
9. Liu, T., Yuan, Z., Sun, J., Wang, J., Zheng, N., Tang, X., Shum, H.-Y.: Learning to detect a salient object. IEEE Trans. Pattern Anal. Mach. Intell. **33**(2), 353–367 (2011)

10. Goferman, S., Zelnik-Manor, L., Tal, A.: Context-aware saliency detection. IEEE Trans. Pattern Anal. Mach. Intell. **34**(10), 1915–1926 (2012)
11. Cheng, M.-M., Mitra, N.J., Huang, X., Torr, P.H., Hu, S.-M.: Global contrast based salient region detection. IEEE Trans. Pattern Anal. Mach. Intell. **37**(3), 569–582 (2015)
12. Murray, N., Vanrell, M., Otazu, X., Parraga, C.A.: Saliency estimation using a non-parametric low-level vision model. In: IEEE Conference on Computer Vision and Pattern Recognition (CVPR), pp. 433–440. IEEE (2011)
13. Li, Y., Hou, X., Koch, C., Rehg, J.M., Yuille, A.L.: The secrets of salient object segmentation. In: Proceedings of the IEEE Conference on Computer Vision and Pattern Recognition, pp. 280–287 (2014)
14. Fang, S., Li, J., Tian, Y., Huang, T., Chen, X.: Learning discriminative subspaces on random contrasts for image saliency analysis. IEEE Trans. Neural Netw. Learn. Syst. **28**, 1095–1108 (2016)
15. Borji, A., Itti, L.: Exploiting local and global patch rarities for saliency detection. In: 2012 IEEE Conference on Computer Vision and Pattern Recognition (CVPR), pp. 478–485. IEEE (2012)
16. Margolin, R., Tal, A., Zelnik-Manor, L.: What makes a patch distinct? In: Proceedings of the IEEE Conference on Computer Vision and Pattern Recognition, pp. 1139–1146 (2013)
17. Duan, L., Wu, C., Miao, J., Qing, L., Fu, Y.: Visual saliency detection by spatially weighted dissimilarity. In: 2011 IEEE Conference on Computer Vision and Pattern Recognition (CVPR), pp. 473–480. IEEE (2011)
18. Lei, J., Wang, B., Fang, Y., Lin, W., Le Callet, P., Ling, N., Hou, C.: A universal framework for salient object detection. IEEE Trans. Multimed. **18**(9), 1783–1795 (2016)
19. Haralick, R.M., Shanmugam, K., et al.: Textural features for image classification. IEEE Trans. Syst. Man Cybern. **3**(6), 610–621 (1973)
20. Tang, M., Ben Ayed, I., Marin, D., Boykov, Y.: Secrets of GrabCut and kernel k-means. In: Proceedings of the IEEE International Conference on Computer Vision, pp. 1555–1563 (2015)
21. Paris, S., Hasinoff, S.W., Kautz, J.: Local Laplacian filters: edge-aware image processing with a Laplacian pyramid. ACM Trans. Graph. **30**(4), 68 (2011)
22. Fan, D.-P., Cheng, M.-M., Liu, Y., Li, T., Borji, A.: Structure-measure: a new way to evaluate foreground maps. arXiv preprint arXiv:1708.00786 (2017)

A Generative Adversarial Network for Tone Mapping HDR Images

Vaibhav Amit Patel[1(✉)], Purvik Shah[1], and Shanmuganathan Raman[2]

[1] Dhirubhai Ambani Institute of Information and Communication Technology Gandhinagar, Gandhinagar 382007, Gujarat, India
vaibhav290797@gmail.com, spurvik07@gmail.com
[2] Indian Institute of Technology Gandhinagar, Gandhinagar 382007, Gujarat, India
shanmuga@iitgn.ac.in

Abstract. A tone mapping operator converts High Dynamic Range (HDR) images to Low Dynamic Range (LDR) images, which can be seen on LDR displays. There has been a lot of research done in the direction of an optimal Tone Mapping Operator which maximizes Tone Mapping Quality Index (TMQI). However, since all the methods approximate Human Vision System in one or different way, none of them works for every type of images. We are proposing a novel generative adversarial network to learn a combination of these tone mapping operators. In order to get pixel level accuracy, we are using residual connections between same sized network layers. We compare this method with some of the existing tone mapping operators and observe that our method generates images with comparably high TMQI and indeed works on many different types of images. Because of the residual connections, the network can be scaled to very high dimensional images.

Keywords: High dynamic range imaging
Generative adversarial networks · Deep learning

1 Introduction

Human Visual System (HVS) can view a large dynamic range present in real world scenes. However, High Dynamic Range (HDR) images can only be seen on HDR displays. Conventional displays only support a low dynamic range (0–255) of intensity. Over time, there has been growing demand for more natural and realistic images. Nowadays, HDR images can be captured using common cameras through multi-exposure bracketing. To incorporate HDR images into an LDR display, one needs to map the higher range to a lower range. This approximation should happen in such a way that the structural similarity of the image and the naturalness are maintained. This approximation method is called tone mapping of an HDR image. Tone-mapping operators are used to achieve this process. Normally, they are classified into two categories depending on the way they process the HDR image. These categories are the global and the local tone mapping operators.

© Springer Nature Singapore Pte Ltd. 2018
R. Rameshan et al. (Eds.): NCVPRIPG 2017, CCIS 841, pp. 220–231, 2018.
https://doi.org/10.1007/978-981-13-0020-2_20

In all the global tone mapping operators, a tone mapping function is chosen once per processed scene based on its characteristics such as luminance. It is applied for all the pixels in the output image, independent of the values in the surrounding pixels [1]. Drago *et al.* discussed seven tone-mapping techniques in [2]. These techniques include, uniform rational quantization, visual adaption model, histogram adjustment, retinex, and photographic tone reproduction. They are explained in the context of global operators.

In local tone mapping operators, to compress the scope of luminance into a displayable range, it is mapped by a global tone mapping function first. After that, to improve the quality, a local adaption is performed. This adaption allows distinct exposures for each part of the input image. Early algorithms of such operators sometime caused undesirable halo-like objects.

Without an appropriate quality measure, we can not evaluate different Tone Mapping Operators. Subjective rating can be useful, but it can be time-consuming. Tone mapping quality index (TMQI) offers an objective criterion to evaluate Tone-mapped images. We use the TMQI index as described in [3]. It uses a modified structural similarity index (SSIM) alongside a naturalness measure.

Unlike machine learning, deep learning based methods work very well even without careful feature engineering. Deep learning works exceptionally well on natural data in its raw form. It represents the input in some other dimension to solve the problem. Nowadays, with the help of Graphics Processing Units (GPUs), the computational barrier in optimizing millions of parameters in deep learning is relieved. In this work, we explore deep learning [4] architectures such as convolutional neural networks (CNNs) [5], generative adversarial networks (GANs) [6] and GANs with residual functions [7] to address the problem of tone mapping HDR images. A CNN exploits spatial importance of an image and works well on Euclidean structured image data. A GAN can perform many tasks such as generating images, approximating a probability distribution, and generating text. Residual functions help optimize the neural network where there is some correspondence between input and output. Our method for generating images is different from the one used by Goodfellow *et al.* We do not use any latent code to generate images, instead we use a modified version of GANs. Such a method was proposed by Isola et al. for image-to-image translation [8]. Their generator consists of convolution layers followed by transposed convolution popularly called deconvolution layers [9].

The rest of the paper is organized as follows. We discuss the related works in Sect. 2. We describe the proposed method for tone mapping in Sect. 3. We present the results with detailed analysis in Sect. 4. We conclude the paper in Sect. 5 with some observations.

2   Related Work

The easiest way to tone map an HDR image to an LDR image is by compressing it to the range of 0–255. To improve results, many tone mapping operators have been proposed in the literature. They are categorized into local and global as stated above. Drago *et al.* [10] proposed a tone mapping model based on logarithmic compression of luminance values. They vary the base of logarithm to adjust the contrast of images. Reinhard and Devlin [11] proposed a fast and intuitive tone mapping operator modeled from photoreceptors to mimic the physiological response. In [12], Kuang *et al.* proposed a model which incorporated spatial processing models and photoreceptor light adaption functions.

Chiu *et al.* [13] introduced the concept of local adaption for tone-mapping of HDR images. Schlick focused on preserving the ratio of color primaries [14]. The local adaption method proposed by him was the first to take color into account in the tone-mapping of HDR images. Tumblin and Turk [15] proposed the concept of diffusion imaging. It included gradient mapping using a partial differential equation solver. Their work was extended and improved in efficiency by Fattal *et al.* [16].

In [17], Kim *et al.* proposed a global tone mapping operator that works well without any per-image user intervention. They leverage the assumptions that human vision sensitivity follows a Gaussian distribution and human vision sensitivity is concentrated in the averaged log luminance. A review of common TMOs is presented in [18]. In [19], Kshiteej et al. explored CNNs in the field of HDR imaging.

3   Method

We assembled the data-set from various vision groups across the world. References to all the data-sets we've used have been provided in Sect. 6. These images consist of natural scenes, buildings and other such structures. Because of varying sizes of the HDR images in the data-set, small patches of size 256×256 were generated from each of the images. The reason for this was to bring homogeneity in the input images to the deep learning architectures used in the study.

Supervised deep learning networks generally need lots of labeled data to train from. We did not have any such true labels to train the network. The objective of the work should be to maximize the tone mapping quality index (TMQI) of each generated tone mapped image [3]. However, the mathematical model of TMQI is not differentiable. Hence, it cannot be incorporated into any back propagation (chain rule of differentiation) based deep learning architecture.

The main contribution of this study is the exploration of the supervised deep learning techniques in the realm of HDR imaging. Because of the problems explained in the above paragraph, the authors pose this problem as a mapping problem where domain and co-domains are a set of images. Hence, any suitable image to image mapping methods of deep learning should work. We employ a different procedure to obtain the true label. The obtained HDR images were passed to various tone mapping operators available in the HDR toolbox [20] and the tone mapped images were generated. The list of Tone-mapping operators

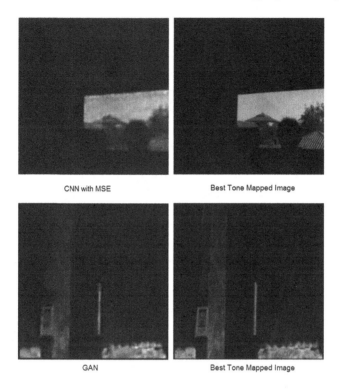

Fig. 1. Results of method 1 and method 2.

includes Banterle, Drago, Exponential, Fattal, Ferwerda, Gamma, Kim Kautz, Kuang, Reinhard Devlin, Schlick, Tumblin, Ward TMO. However, we need only one LDR image as the true label. This is why, for each HDR image, the tone mapped image with the best TMQI score was stored and the other tone mapped images were discarded. The deep network may learn some combinations of these TMOs which are used to obtain the true label. These combinations may lead to a better approach which indeed can generate better tone mapped images than the existing input TMOs. Let's say for Image-1, TMO-1 is giving good results and for Image-2, it is not. For Image-2, TMO-2 is giving good results, but for Image-1 it is not. However, our network may produce good results for both images because it learned the combinations of both the TMOs.

One of the obvious choice to obtain this is convolutional neural networks while keeping same spatial size of the input and output images. However, at best it can only approximate local tone mapping operators. This is because at a time the architecture can only see a filter sized image and not the full sized 256×256 images. This is why, we use different architectures in which a bottleneck enables the architecture to see the input and process it. First method was to use stacked convolutional layers while keeping the size of the input and output same using zero padding of size $(f-1)/2$ for each filter of size f. Mean squared error between the true tone mapped image and the output of the CNN was used as a loss function. Because of the mean squared error function, the output images were blurry. Since the data-set consisted of local and global TMOs, a CNN with a small receptive field would not be able to give a plausible result.

We have explored three different deep learning architectures which are essentially an image to image map.

1. Convolutional neural networks [21] with downsampling and upsampling with Mean Square Error between input and output images, This is the most basic and most naive method of all.
2. Generative adversarial networks in which the generator in the architecture explained in the first method. This method uses L1 loss as a reconstruction loss between true and generated images. This method also used binary cross entropy as the loss function of generator and discriminator. This generator network works better than the simple CNN architecture explained above because in this method we learn the distribution of the labeled tone mapped images and it helps the generator to generate real like images. Though this method is better than the first one, it does not have a crisp quality output.
3. Generative adversarial networks with skip connections between logically same sized upsample and downsample layers. The method is same as the one proposed by Isola et al. in [8] with modification is normalization to incorporate HDR images with better accuracy.

In the method 2, we keep the discriminator same as the one discussed in method 2, which is a CNN trying to predict 1 (true label) or 0 (fake label) for the true tone mapped image (obtained from the best of the existing TMOs) and tone mapped image generated from the generator, respectively.

In Fig. 1, results of the method 1 and method 2 are shown. The first image is generated by the CNN architecture of the method 1 and the image to its right is the corresponding true label obtained from Reinhard Devlin TMO [11]. We can see that the CNN alone cannot produce high quality images. The image below the first image is generated by a generator without residual skip blocks and in the right is its corresponding true label. Subjectively, we can see that the second method performs better than the first one, but it is a blurred image and does not look like a photo-realistic image.

In method 3, the reason why we use skip connections between same sized intermediate layers and between the input and the output is that the architecture loses the information at the pixel level because of the down-sampling layers. The max pooling or the double stride loses information of spatial position of pixel values. The skip connections make the signal strong again and it helps in generating sharp and clear images. We can use skip connection in our problem because there is a structural correspondence between the input HDR image and the output LDR image (tone mapped HDR image). The skip connections leverage this fact and export positional details directly to the output layers,

Table 1. Network details of the generator.

Layer type	Input channel	Number of filters	Filter size	Stride size	Dropout
Conv	3	64	4×4	2	0
Conv	64	128	4×4	2	0
Conv	128	256	4×4	2	0
Conv	256	512	4×4	2	0
Conv	512	512	4×4	2	0.5
Conv	512	512	4×4	2	0.5
Conv	512	512	4×4	2	0
DeConv	512	512	4×4	2	0
DeConv	512	512	4×4	2	0.5
DeConv	512	512	4×4	2	0.5
DeConv	512	256	4×4	2	0
DeConv	256	128	4×4	2	0
DeConv	128	64	4×4	2	0
DeConv	64	3	4×4	2	0

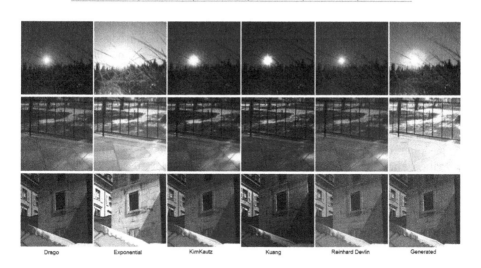

Drago   Exponential   KimKautz   Kuang   Reinhard Devlin   Generated

Fig. 2. Subjective and objective comparison with other tone mapping operators.

which helps the generator to generator sharp images. This is why the last method ought to give better results than the first two. We have compared only the third method with the existing tone mapping work in the Experimental results section.

Table 2. Network details of the discriminator.

Layer type	Input channel	Number of filters	Filter size	Padding applied	Stride size
Conv	3	64	4×4	1	2
Conv	64	128	4×4	1	2
Conv	128	256	4×4	1	2
Conv	256	512	4×4	1	2
Conv	512	512	4×4	1	2
Conv	512	1	4×4	1	1

In Table 1, the architecture details of the Generator used here are given. Here Conv represents a convolutional layer and DeConv represents a transposed convolutional layer. The difference between the method used by Isola *et al.* and ours is that their algorithm does not work on HDR images, we changed the normalization function to incorporate it with the architecture given below. The HDR pixel values were real values with different values for same intensity value. The images were scaled by subtracting from minimum pixel value and divided by difference of maximum and minimum pixel value. The resulting pixel values are in the range 0 to 1, same as dividing an LDR image with 255.0.

In Table 2, the proposed architecture for the discriminator architecture is shown. The discriminator network is a conventional CNN. The discriminator is forced to output a 30×30 matrix with sigmoid activated neurons. Despite having a single objective of outputting 1 for real label and 0 for the generated image, the discriminator is not down-sampled further after six convolutional layers. The logic behind this is to give more freedom to the discriminator to describe the difference between the real and the fake images.

Keeping configuration of the generator and the discriminator same as described above the training was carried out. In order to train the generator and the discriminator one by one, the batch size was kept to 1. Dropout of 0.3 was used to prevent overfitting. Random resize and crop were used to augment the training data. The HDR images were interpolated using bi-linear interpolation to resize the images. The GAN was trained for 30 epochs.

In Algorithm 1, the steps for the learning of the network are shown. Here, λ is the weight given to the L1 loss between labelled tone mapped images and generated LDR images. We have trained our network on a Titan X GPU for 30 epochs, which took 5 hours of training time. Once trained the generator is able to produce 29 images per second. The generator can also be used for real time tone mapping of videos, since it can generate tone mapped images at this rate.

Algorithm 1. Adversarial training process

1: From the training set of HDR images pick an image at random (Let us call it $real\_A$) and a corresponding labelled tone mapped image (Let us call it $real\_B$).
2: $real\_out =$ discriminator $(real\_B)$
3: $fake\_B =$ generator $(real\_A)$
4: $fake\_out =$ discriminator $(real\_B)$
5: $Loss\_discriminator = GAN\_Loss\_function(real\_out,1) + GAN\_Loss\_function\ (fake\_out,0)$
6: $Loss\_discriminator = GAN\_Loss\_function(fake\_out,1) + \lambda \times L1\_Loss\_function(fake\_B, real\_B)$

---

4   Results and Analysis

Using the configuration shown in Tables 1 and 2, the network was trained on 3000 cropped images of size 256×256. The learning rate was kept to 0.001. The cost function consists of a loss from discriminator and a loss from L_1 loss function between the generated image and the real label. The training was done on batches of size 10, which shows that a generator parameters are updated before updating the discriminator. In Fig. 2, subjective and objective comparison of the natural scene, balcony and the house image is shown. The tone mapping operators used are indicated below the images (Table 3).

Table 3. TMQI score of the images in the Fig. 2

	Natural scene	Balcony	House
Drago TMO	0.817	**0.9768**	0.914
Exponential TMO	0.823	0.857	0.829
KimKautz TMO	0.799	0.892	0.918
Kuang TMO	0.779	0.838	0.815
Reinhard Devlin TMO	0.8043	0.966	**0.986**
Generated image	**0.941**	0.7791	0.981

We can see that apart from the good objective score, the generated images look visually natural and real. Consider Fig. 3. Here left images are the images generated by the network and the right images are the corresponding tone mapped images with highest TMQI score from the five tone mapping operators we have used in the study. In (a), the right image has low TMQI because of the unusual brightness. It makes the image look a bit unnatural compared to the left image. In (b), the reason behind left image having the lower TMQI score is that it contains artifacts (connection between the bottom three beams). In (c), we can see that the architecture also works for natural scenery. From 500 testing samples the KimKautz [17], ReinhardDevlin [11], Drago [10], Exponential, Kuang [12] and the proposed method give the best result 112, 77, 73, 79, 57, and 102 times respectively. From the statistics, it can be seen that the method by KimKautz is better. But our method is closely second best and tries to give the best result for diverse images.

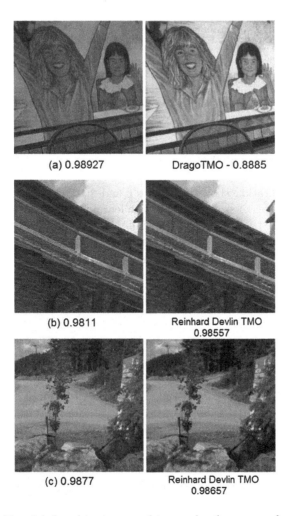

(a) 0.98927   DragoTMO - 0.8885

(b) 0.9811   Reinhard Devlin TMO
                               0.98557

(c) 0.9877   Reinhard Devlin TMO
                               0.98657

Fig. 3. True label and tone mapped images by the proposed method.

In Fig. 4, the comparison of TMQI score for different TMOs used in the study and the proposed methods is shown. The histogram of the TMQI for various TMOs is given in the image. We can see that the proposed method has more number of images in the range 0.85 to 0.97. In addition to this, the proposed method has very few number of images in the range 0.6 to 0.85. The reason for not performing well in 0.97 to 1 range is that essentially the generator approximates the true LDR label. Even though we are using skip connections, the generator has a very small bottleneck and that hinders it from very high pixel level accuracy. That is why it can not preserve very high structural similarity. From the histogram pattern, we can say that the proposed method is comparable and in many cases better than the other tone mapping operators.

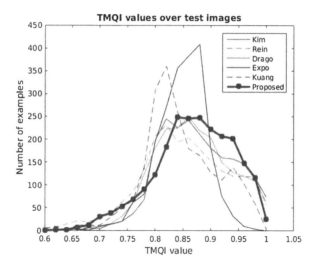

Fig. 4. Comparison of TMQI for different TMOs on test data-set.

5   Conclusion

We have explored deep learning methods to tone map high dynamic range images. CNN and simple GAN are not good enough for pixel level accuracy because of mean squared error and the bottle neck, respectively. Residual skip network helps the GAN to gain the pixel level accuracy lost while down-sampling. Even though the true label of any HDR image during the training is the competitor of the GAN while testing, the results are promising. Different types of tone mapping operators are used to create the training data-set, which is the primary reason behind the generator learning a complex combination of these TMOs resulting in higher TMQI in many images.

As a future work, we would like to improve the model to achieve better TMQI score on the present data-set. We would also like to build a larger data-set and determine the performance of the developed GAN for tone mapping. More elaborate subjective analysis will be carried out on the resulting tone mapped images to evaluate the quality.

6   HDR Image Sources

- Debevec Malik (5 images)
- EMPA (33 images)
- GL ICT USC (6 images)
- HDR EYE (44 images)
- HDRI HAVEN (5 images)
- HDRI HUB Freebies (8 images)
- HDRI SKIES (150 images)

- HDRLabs (116 images)
- HDRMAPS Freebies (75 images)
- HDR Stanford (88 images)
- HDRV Resources (12 images)
- IIT HDR (44 images)
- JVH (29 images)
- MPI (7 images)
- RIT MCSL 1 (104 images)
- RIT MCSL 2 (73 images)
- SFU (118 images)
- VizPeople (10 images)
- XTRAS (12 images)
- Z Vid Frames (19 frames from various videos)

Acknowledgment. The authors would like to thank Maharshi Vyas for helping with python scripts and NVIDIA for TitanX GPU card grant.

References

1. Yoshida, A., et al.: Perceptual evaluation of tone mapping operators with realworld scenes. Proc. SPIE **5666**, 192–203 (2005)
2. Drago, F., et al.: Perceptual evaluation of tone mapping operators with regard to similarity and preference. Max-Planck-Institut für Informatik (2002)
3. Yeganeh, H., Wang, Z.: Objective quality assessment of tonemapped images. IEEE Trans. Image Process **22**(2), 657–667 (2013)
4. LeCun, Y., Bengio, Y., Hinton, G.: Deep learning. Nature **521**(7553), 436–444 (2015)
5. LeCun, Y., et al.: Gradient-based learning applied to document recognition. Proc. IEEE **86**(11), 2278–2324 (1998)
6. Goodfellow, I., et al.: Generative adversarial nets. In: Advances in Neural Information Processing Systems, pp. 2672–2680 (2014)
7. He, K., et al.: Deep residual learning for image recognition. In: Proceedings of the IEEE Conference on Computer Vision and Pattern Recognition, pp. 770–778 (2016)
8. Isola, P., et al.: Image-to-image translation with conditional adversarial networks. arXiv preprint arXiv:1611.07004 (2016)
9. Zeiler, M.D., et al.: Deconvolutional networks. In: 2010 IEEE Conference on Computer Vision and Pattern Recognition (CVPR), pp. 2528–2535. IEEE (2010)
10. Drago, F., et al.: Adaptive logarithmic mapping for displaying high contrast scenes. In: Computer Graphics Forum, vol. 22, no. 3, pp. 419–426. Wiley Online Library (2003)
11. Reinhard, E., Devlin, K.: Dynamic range reduction inspired by photoreceptor physiology. IEEE Trans. Vis. Comput. Graph **11**(1), 13–24 (2005)
12. Kuang, J., Johnson, G.M., Fairchild, M.D.: iCAM06: a refined image appearance model for HDR image rendering. J. Visual Commun. Image Represent. **18**(5), 406–414 (2007)
13. Chiu, K., et al.: Spatially nonuniform scaling functions for high contrast images. In: Graphics Interface, pp. 245–245. Canadian Information Processing Society (1993)

14. Schlick, C.: Quantization techniques for visualization of high dynamic range pictures. In: Sakas, G., Müller, S., Shirley, P. (eds.) Photorealistic Rendering Techniques, pp. 7–20. Springer, Heidelberg (1995). https://doi.org/10.1007/978-3-642-87825-1_2
15. Tumblin, J., Turk, G.: LCIS: a boundary hierarchy for detail-preserving contrast reduction. In: Proceedings of the 26th Annual Conference on Computer Graphics and Interactive Techniques, pp. 83–90. ACM Press/Addison-Wesley Publishing Co. (1999)
16. Fattal, R., Lischinski, D., Werman, M.: Gradient domain high dynamic range compression. In: ACM Transactions on Graphics (TOG), vol. 21, no. 3, pp. 249–256. ACM (2002)
17. Kautz, M.H.K.J.: Consistent tone reproduction (2008)
18. Banterle, F., et al.: Multidimensional image retargeting. In: SIGGRAPH Asia 2011 Courses, p. 15. ACM (2011)
19. Sheth, K.: Deep neural networks for HDR imaging. arXiv preprint arXiv:1611.00591 (2016)
20. Banterle, F., et al.: Advanced High Dynamic Range Imaging: Theory and Practice. CRC Press, Boca Raton (2011)
21. Krizhevsky, A., Sutskever, I., Hinton, G.E.: ImageNet classification with deep convolutional neural networks. In: Advances in Neural Information Processing Systems, pp. 1097–1105 (2012)

Efficient Clustering-Based Noise Covariance Estimation for Maximum Noise Fraction

Soumyajit Gupta⑩ and Chandrajit Bajaj⁽⊠⁾⑩

University of Texas at Austin, Austin, TX 78705, USA
smjtgupta@utexas.edu, bajaj@cs.utexas.edu

Abstract. Most hyperspectral images (HSI) have important spectral features in specific combination of wave numbers or channels. Noise in these specific channels or bands can easily overwhelm these relevant spectral features. Maximum Noise Fraction (MNF) by Green *et al.* [1] has been extensively studied for noise removal in HSI data. The MNF transform maximizes the Signal to Noise Ratio (SNR) in feature space, thereby explicitly requiring an estimation of the HSI noise. We present two simple and efficient Noise Covariance Matrix (NCM) estimation methods as required for the MNF transform. Our NCM estimations improve the performance of HSI classification, even when ground objects are mixed. Both techniques rely on a superpixel based clustering of HSI data in the spatial domain. The novelty of our NCM's comes from their reduced sensitivity to HSI noise distributions and interference patterns. Experiments with both simulated and real HSI data show that our methods significantly outperforms the NCM estimation in the classical MNF transform, as well as against more recent state of the art NCM estimation methods. We quantify this improvement in terms of HSI classification accuracy and superior recovery of spectral features.

Keywords: Hyperspectral image · Maximum Noise Fraction
Noise Covariance estimation · Superpixel · Classification

1 Introduction

The emergence and development of hyperspectral (HS) remote sensing technology has made it possible to acquire data with large amounts of spatial and spectral information for image analysis applications such as classification, unmixing, subpixel mapping, and target detection [2]. HS imaging is applicable to a wide variety of fields, including agriculture, environment, mineral mapping, surveillance, and chemical imaging of biological tissue [3,4]. The acquired hyper spectral images (HSI) are often disturbed by radiometric noise such as sensor noise, photon (or shot) noise, calibration error, atmospheric scattering and absorption, which not only degrades the visual quality but also the final HSI analysis or interpretation via image classification techiques. The various aforementioned HSI

© Springer Nature Singapore Pte Ltd. 2018
R. Rameshan et al. (Eds.): NCVPRIPG 2017, CCIS 841, pp. 232–244, 2018.
https://doi.org/10.1007/978-981-13-0020-2_21

noise is generally represented as an additive normally distributed (Gaussian), zero-mean random process [5].

It was shown by Green *et al.* [1] that the variance of hyperspectral images did not necessarily reflect the real SNR, due to unequal noise variances in different channels or bands, with noise variance dominating the signal variance in some bands. As a result, a band with small variance does not necessarily mean poor image quality. It may have a high SNR compared to other bands with large variances but low SNR's. In order to deal with this problem, Green *et al.* [1] developed the Maximum Noise Fraction (MNF) transform based on maximization of SNR, so that the transformed principal components are ranked by SNR rather than variance as used in PCA.

One of the major disadvantages of this approach is that the Noise Covariance Matrix (NCM) must be estimated completely and accurately from the data apriori. This is generally difficult to do so, due to the stochastic nature of noise, and as pointed out in [1,6]. Several papers have been done to address this issue by considering the neighboring spatial information [7,8], as well as jointly considering neighborhood spatial and spectral information [9,10], leading to high complexity algorithms just for the NCM estimation.

Our main contributions are two-fold. First, we present a simple method to generate a panchromatic image from the HSI. Second, we propose two variants of NCM estimation approaches (neighborhood and cluster) based on the fast superpixel [11] SLIC algorithm. They depend only on the spatial information of the generated image, and can effectively recover a good estimate of the NCM, achieving good classification scores after MNF denoising. Being spatial based, they have lower computation cost (proportional to the number of pixels in the HSI), compared to spectral based methods. Our results, as demonstrated below, significantly outperforms both the spatial and spectral based approaches in terms of classification accuracy and recovery of spectral features. Both our algorithms remain unaffected with the scaling of the data in terms of size, hence provides a better NCM estimation for large datasets.

2   Theory

2.1   Notation

We are given a HSI $Y_{orig} \in \mathbb{R}^{W \times H \times S}$, where W, H are the spatial dimensions (width, height) and S is the number of spectral channels. It can be restructured/vectorized into a 2D matrix $Y \in \mathbb{R}^{N \times S}$, where $N = (W \times H)$ is the number of pixels. Each column $y_i, \forall i = [1 : S]$ represents the reshaped image for the i-th spectral channel and each row $y_j, \forall j = [1 : N]$ represents the spectral signature for the j-th pixel.

2.2   Related Work

The main difference between conventional PCA and MNF is that: MNF has a prior step of noise whitening, which needs a good estimate of the NCM. The original MNF method mainly adopts the spatial feature of image to estimate Σ_δ, such as minimum/maximum autocorrelation factor (MAF) by Switzer and Green [7], causal simultaneous autoregressive and quadratic surface by Nielsen [8].

As shown in studies by Roger [12], Greco *et al.* [13] and Liu *et al.* [9], spatial-based noise estimation method is data-selective and unstable. When HSI has low spatial resolution, the difference between pixels may mainly contain signal. Sometimes, noise with regular (interference) pattern may be considered as signal when spatial features are used in NCM estimation. When the structure/distribution of the noise is unknown, such methods always fall short in estimating Σ_δ.

In HSI there exists correlation between channels. Therefore, high correlations between channels can also be used for noise estimation, as in Liu *et al.* [9] by using uses both spatial and spectral domain information. The signal value of current pixel at a channel is estimated from the value of adjacent channels of the same pixel and adjacent pixels in the same channel, through multiple linear regression. Then difference between the estimated signal value and the raw value of the current pixel, is considered as noise.

The work of Optimized MNF by Gao *et al.* [10] extends the idea of Liu *et al.* [9] by computing noise over small non-overlapping sub-blocks locally, thereby further reducing the influence of spatial features. They solve multiple linear analysis over each sub-block to compute the residual noise, followed by computing the local standard deviation (LSD) for each of those sub-blocks, and binning those values over the range of computed LSD.

2.3 Superpixel

A superpixel is defined as a group of pixels having similar characteristics. We consider the Simple Linear Iterative Clustering (SLIC) superpixel of Achanta *et al.* [11]. It generates superpixels by clustering pixels based on their color similarity and proximity in the image plane. This is done in the five-dimensional [*labxy*] space, where [*lab*] is the pixel color vector in CIELAB color space, which is widely considered as perceptually uniform for small color distances, and [*xy*] is the spatial pixel position.

We use the SLICO[1] (the zero parameter optimized version of the SLIC algorithm) version, which adaptively chooses the compactness parameter for each superpixel differently, generating regular shaped groups in both textured and non textured regions alike, and can be used on grayscale and color images. The cost is $O(N)$, hence computationally efficient and real time.

3   Effect of Mixing of Pixels on NCM

Green *et al.* [1] uses the Maximum Autocorrelation Factor (MAF) [7] transform to obtain Σ_δ:

$$\Sigma_\delta = \frac{1}{2} Cov(Y_{j,i} - Y_{j+\Delta,i}) \tag{1}$$

---

[1] Code available at: http://ivrl.epfl.ch/research/superpixels.

where Δ denotes spatial shift in pixel. In Eq. 1, the subtractions between neighboring pixels is performed to estimate Σ_δ. If the spatial distribution of ground objects keeps getting complex as shown in Fig. 2, NCM estimates are very bad, hence classification results after MNF transform will be seriously affected as shown in Fig. 3, due to bad estimation of noise from pixels from different classes. In such scenarios, neighbors of each pixel would vary depending on the vectorization format (row or column wise), leading to poor noise estimation (Fig. 1).

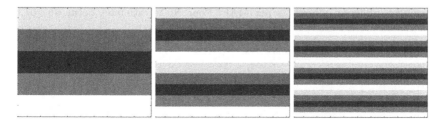

Fig. 1. Raw noisy spectrum of five classes of the Moffett HSI [14]. Light and dense vegetation contains spectral signature similarity. Same goes for the dry and wet soil. The parameters of the noise model are unknown.

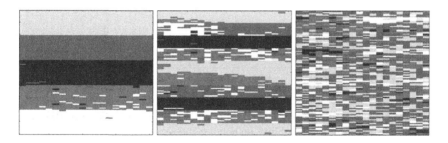

Fig. 2. Ground truth image of five materials of synthetic HSI over three levels of spatial rearrangement of pixels to demonstrate the effect of class mixing.

4 Spectral Based Approaches

Spectral approaches are state of the art in terms of effective noise estimation but time consuming. We ran the same experiment using Optimized MNF of Gao *et al.* [10], which considers noise estimation in the HSI cube, hence unaffected by vectorization of the data during MNF. Firstly, solving the system of regression for each pixel of each channel takes huge memory and time. Secondly, depending on the spectrum, this method at times becomes numerically unstable, which results in degraded noise estimation. This effect is clearly illustrated in Fig. 4, where at the first level the classification is fair. However, at subsequent levels, due to mixing of objects the regression solver suffers from being badly scaled and close to singular. This happens due to pixels from multiple materials participating in determining the noise level of a pixel from different class.

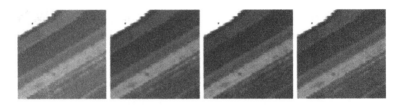

Fig. 3. Result of classification of the sample HSI after MNF denoising. K-Means is used for assigning labels. As classes keep on mixing, noise is computed between pixels belonging to different classes as per MAF. Poor NCM estimates occur due to bad estimation of noise, hence performance of MNF degrades.

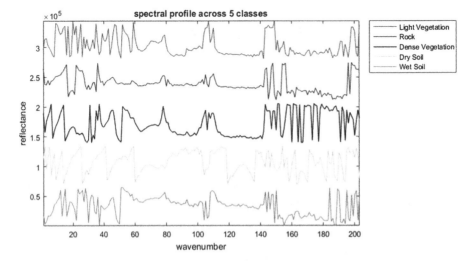

Fig. 4. Result of classification of the HSI after OMNF denoising. With further mixing the results degrade due to instability on solving the regressions.

5   Generating Panchromatic Image for SLIC

A HSI contains large number of continuous spectral bands with narrow bandwidth. To extract spatial features in a fast and simple way, we use a synthesized panchromatic image inspired by the work in Zhang *et al.* [15]. This generated panchromatic image $I \in \mathbb{R}^{W \times H}$ is used as input to the SLIC algorithm.

$$I = w_r I_r + w_g I_g + w_b I_b \tag{2}$$

where I_r, I_g, I_b are the spectral channels of the HSI with band centers corresponding to the red, green, and blue channels. In our experiments, the weights w_r, w_g, w_b are set to $0.06, 0.63, 0.27$ as per values suggested in [15], which are perceptually optimized on human visual data. A panchromatic image captures the variation in the spatial content of the HSI which is not always visible from the image of a single channel. This formulation of I tries to model the RGB version of the HSI.

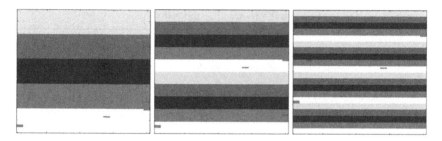

Fig. 5. Left to Right: original images corresponding to red (665.59 nm), green (589.31 nm), and blue (491.90 nm) wavelengths and simulated panchromatic image for the Salinas-A dataset. (Color figure online)

6   Methods: Two NCM Estimators

Spatial based noise estimators are fast but inaccurate when the data gets mixed. This issue is circumvented by considering spectral based noise estimators at the expense of increased computation cost. Another issue hampering the performance of spatial estimators like in Eq. 1, is the spatial dimensions of the data. For large vectorized images, there is absolutely no correlation between pixels at row/column skips even if they belong to the same material. Our spatial-based estimators handles both cases of accurately estimating noise at low computation cost, as well as being unaffected by spatial dimension. It computes the noise estimates from the 3D cube Y_{orig}, and then vectorizes it to Y, thereby maintaining proper correlations between neighboring pixels in the spatial domain.

6.1   Neighborhood Based (NCM-A)

This noise estimator of Algorithm 1 is inspired by earlier spatial based methods, where instead of just looking to the right neighbor, all surrounding eight neighbors of a pixel are accounted for computing the noise level for that pixel. To avoid estimating noise from neighbors of different material, only the ones that share the same superpixel label are considered. The noise is then computed as the difference between the current pixel's value and the weighted sum of values of its neighbors with same superpixel label. Hence the weighting factor is varies according to the layout of the data with ct being total of same label neighbors.

6.2   Cluster Based (NCM-B)

This noise estimator of Algorithm 2 is inspired by the classical K-means, where cluster centers are the true representation of the class spectrum, and all data within that class are some deviations away from the center due to noise and other effects. Once the superpixel labels are assigned, the mean spectrum of each label k is calculated as $\mu(k)$. The noise for each pixel is then computed as the difference between the current pixel's value and the mean spectrum of the same label.

Algorithm 1. NCM-A($I \in \mathbb{R}^{W \times H}, Y_{orig} \in \mathbb{R}^{W \times H \times S}$)

1: $\bar{I} = SLIC(I)$
2: **for** each pixel $(i, j) \in \bar{I}$ **do**
3:    **for** each neighbor (i', j') of pixel (i, j) **do**
4:        $ct = 0; elem = \Phi$
5:        **if** $label(\bar{I}(i, j)) == label(\bar{I}(i', j'))$ **then**
6:            $ct = ct + 1$
7:            $elem[ct] = Y_{orig}(i', j', :)$
8:        $\delta_{orig}(i, j, :) = Y_{orig}(i, j, :) - \frac{1}{ct}(\sum_{k=1}^{ct} elem[k])$
9: **Output**: $\delta_{orig} \in \mathbb{R}^{W \times H \times S}$ reshaped into $\delta \in \mathbb{R}^{N \times S}$

Algorithm 2. NCM-B($I \in \mathbb{R}^{W \times H}, Y_{orig} \in \mathbb{R}^{W \times H \times S}$)

1: $\bar{I} = SLIC(I)$
2: **for** each label $k \in K$ **do**
3:    $\mu(k) =$ mean of pixels with label k
4: **for** each pixel $(i, j) \in \bar{I}$ **do**
5:    $k = label(i, j)$
6:    $\delta_{orig}(i, j, :) = Y_{orig}(i, j, :) - \mu(k)$
7: **Output**: $\delta_{orig} \in \mathbb{R}^{W \times H \times S}$ reshaped into $\delta \in \mathbb{R}^{N \times S}$

7   Experiments

In this section, we provide simulations to showcase the effectiveness of our twin algorithms and their comparisons. We analyze results on both synthetic images created from real world spectrum as well as on public dataset, to show the robustness in presence of noise from any unknown distribution.

7.1   Data Description

For the synthetic image shown in Fig. 2, the spectrum contains reflectance values collected from the AVIRIS scene over Moffett Field[2], CA in 1997 [14]. We chose regions from five classes: Light vegetation, Rock, Dense vegetation, Dry soil and Wet soil. We chose this dataset because it is real-world and noise is included in the spectrum, hence no bias due to prior knowledge of the noise distribution. The data is arranged in stratified layers from each class in chunks of 20×20 pixels, with each spectrum containing 203 channels and 5 classes, resulting in an HSI of size $100 \times 20 \times 203$ of reflectance values.

7.2   Classification Metrics

We chose PCA for dimension reduction followed by K-means clustering to be the classification algorithm. Of course, other complex algorithms for pure pixel classification or end-member extraction can be employed, but those are out of scope

---

[2] Data available at http://aviris.jpl.nasa.gov/html/aviris.freedata.html.

for this work. The number of components for PCA was chosen as the number of channels that accounted for 97.5% of the total SNR after MNF transform. Loss is measured as the number of misclassified pixels after MNF denoising.

7.3 Different Variations of Spatial Mixing

We see that the number of misclassified samples in Figs. 6 and 7 is drastically less compared to the MNF with naive noise approximation in Fig. 3. Even though the number of intermixing of layers increased, both our algorithms were able to accurately approximate the noise, hence leading to better HSI denoising.

In order to further study the effect of mixing of objects, we shuffled the data blocks around to introduce more class skips along both horizontal and vertical directions, with patterns which occur in real-world datasets like Indian Pines or Salinas. We see that in these cases too, our approach is able to handle the spatial mixing of boundaries accurately. The two class boundary results are shown in Figs. 8 and 9 with the stride pattern corresponding to the Salinas dataset. However going by MAF [7] formulation, this is a very bad situation as all class boundary pixels have their noise estimated from their neighbor that belongs to a different class. Similarly, the multiple (four in cases of corner pixels of each class) class boundary results are shown in Figs. 10 and 11 respectively, where along each direction, a pixel encounters multiple classes, with the blocky checkerboard pattern corresponding to the Indian Pines dataset. Here also, due to computation of noise in the HSI cube Y_{orig}, results of MNF remain unaffected after vectorization.

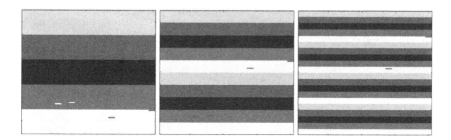

Fig. 6. Result of classification of the sample HSI after MNF denoising with NCM-A Algorithm 1. Across levels of mixing, the classification accuracy of a pixel does not degrade much due to proper estimation of noise from neighbors of same class.

7.4 Comparison Between the Two Approaches NCM-A, NCM-B

We compare our two approaches NCM-A (Algorithm 1) and NCM-B (Algorithm 2) in terms of quantitative and timing analysis. Over several experimentations, we found that the NCM-B variant performs better than NCM-A. Because of superpixel averaging, more the number of superpixel averaged, better is the cancellation of noise, under Gaussian noise models, hence better

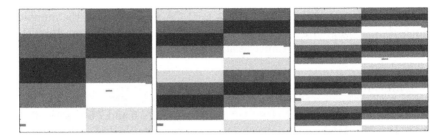

Fig. 7. Result of classification of the sample HSI after MNF denoising with NCM-B Algorithm 2. Across levels, the classification accuracy of a pixel does not degrade much due to proper estimation of noise from the mean spectrum of its superpixel.

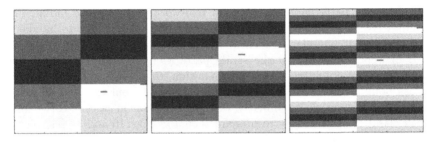

Fig. 8. Classification of the sample HSI after MNF denoising with NCM-A. Note that even when there are large class skips from inter- boundary pixels, NCM-A obtains proper noise estimates

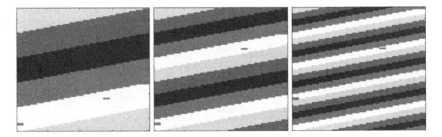

Fig. 9. Classification of the sample HSI after MNF denoising with NCM-B. Here too, NCM-B yields proper noise estimates.

performance of NCM-B (cluster-based method). This is also validated by the misclassified pixels rate of the two algorithms shown in Table 1, and better run-time efficiency.

7.5 Complexity

The cost for computing SLICO superpixel of the panchromatic image is $O(N)$. NCM-A computes the noise for each pixel by looking into its eight adjacent

Fig. 10. Classification of the sample HSI after MNF denoising with NCM-A. For this pattern, we get two neighboring classes for boundary pixels, with four for the corner ones. Weighting of neighbors with same labels gives better noise estimate.

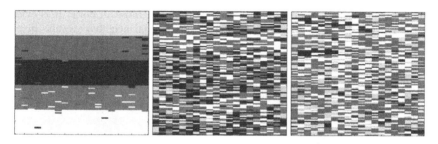

Fig. 11. Classification of the sample HSI after MNF denoising with NCM-B.

Table 1. Comparison of approaches: NCM-A (Algorithm 1) and NCM-B (Algorithm 2). Columns 3,4,5 shows the number of misclassified piexls in each case. We can see that given same patterns, NCM-B performs better than NCM in terms of errorenous pixels. NCM-B also has a speedup factor of 2 over NCM-A. Simulations carried out on a PC with Intel $i7 - 7700@3.6$ GHz CPU, 32 GB RAM.

Scenario	Execution time	# Pixels (left)	# Pixels (middle)	# Pixels (right)
Figure 6 NCM-A	∼0.024 s	7	8	8
Figure 7 NCM-B	∼0.011 s	4	4	4
Figure 8 NCM-A	∼0.024 s	6	5	5
Figure 9 NCM-B	∼0.011 s	5	5	5
Figure 10 NCM-A	∼0.024 s	7	8	8
Figure 11 NCM-B	∼0.011 s	4	4	4

neighbors, hence takes $O(NS)$. NCM-B computes the mean spectra of each superpixel in $O(P)$ time[3], the noise computation for all pixels is again $O(N)$, hence the total time is $O((N + P)S)$. For any HSI data $N \gg P$, hence P is relative constant depending on the dataset used. Hence, the time complexity of the both the algorithms is effectively $O(NS)$.

---

[3] P is the number of pixels grouped in a superpixel.

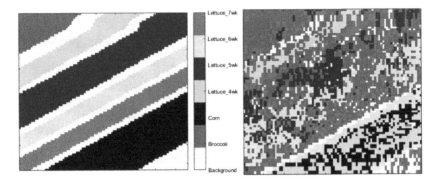

Fig. 12. Salinas-A HSI. Left: ground truth of 7 classes. Right: classification after MNF on the noisy cube, with added artificial band-correlated Gaussian noise. It is evident that the naive noise estimation by considering one spatial neighbor, results in poor denoising of the spectrum, hence bad classification accuracy.

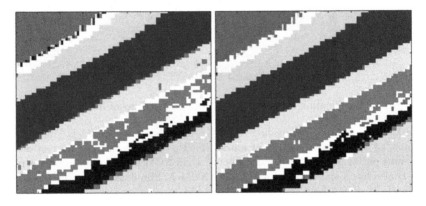

Fig. 13. Salinas-A HSI. Classification after noise estimation using Left: NCM-A (Algorithm 1), which takes 0.173 s. Right: NCM-B (Algorithm 2) which takes 0.099 s. The results are significantly improved compared to the naive approach. We also see that NCM-B performs better than NCM-A, specially near the pink, black and yellow patches at the bottom right, and in terms of computation time too. (Color figure online)

7.6 Experiments on Publicly Available Datasets

We chose the Salinas-A dataset for experimentation. It was collected by the 224-channel AVIRIS sensor over Salinas Valley, CA [14]. It has 86×83 pixels and six classes of radiance spectrum. The 20 water absorption channels were discarded. Figure 5 shows the generated image for SLIC. The spectrum are added with random Gaussian noise, which are correlated across channels, but independent of signal.

The naive algorithm badly estimates the noise, resulting in bad classification as shown in Fig. 12. The classification results from our twin methods are shown

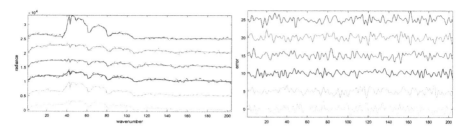

Fig. 14. Salinas-A HSI. Top: true spectra from six classes are shown with solid lines. Noise correlated across bands are shown in dashes. Bottom: difference between the true and estimated spectra. Low value of reflectance errors (<10) compared to the strength of signals (>1000) demonstrate that NCM-B accurately estimates the noise introduced in this HSI.

in Fig. 13. Both the algorithms can accurately recover the true spectral features of the data after MNF denoising, illustrated with low error between true and recovered spectrum in Fig. 14.

8   Conclusion

In this work we introduced two spatial based noise estimators for MNF, based on superpixel segmentation of a generated panchromatic image of a HSI. They perform with higher accuracy than the spectral based estimators while having the same computation cost as the spatial based estimators, and with no numerical instability issues. This is relevant in many research areas where the HSI datasets are large, hence a quick and accurate noise estimation method is required to maintain the integrity of MNF denoising.

Acknowledgment. This research was supported in part by National Institute of Health (NIH) grants R01 GM117594 and R41 GM116300.

References

1. Green, A.A., Berman, M., Switzer, P., Craig, M.D.: A transformation for ordering multispectral data in terms of image quality with implications for noise removal. IEEE Trans. Geosci. Remote Sens. **26**(1), 65–74 (1988)
2. Chang, C.-I.: Hyperspectral Imaging: Techniques for Spectral Detection and Classification, vol. 1. Springer, New York (2003). https://doi.org/10.1007/978-1-4419-9170-6
3. Shippert, P.: Why use hyperspectral imagery? Photogram. Eng. Remote Sens. **70**(4), 377–396 (2004)
4. Resonon: hyperspectral imaging applications, May 2017. https://www.resonon.com/applications_main.html
5. Corner, B., Narayanan, R., Reichenbach, S.: Noise estimation in remote sensing imagery using data masking. Int. J. Remote Sens. **24**(4), 689–702 (2003)

6. Lee, J.B., Woodyatt, A.S., Berman, M.: Enhancement of high spectral resolution remote-sensing data by a noise-adjusted principal components transform. IEEE Trans. Geosci. Remote Sens. **28**(3), 295–304 (1990)

7. Switzer, P., Green, A.A.: Min/max autocorrelation factors for multivariate spatial imagery. Comput. Sci. Stat. **16**, 13–16 (1984)

8. Nielsen, A.A.: Analysis of regularly and irregularly sampled spatial, multivariate, and multi-temporal data. Science **21**(4), 555–567 (1994)

9. Liu, X., Zhang, B., Gao, L., Chen, D.: A maximum noise fraction transform with improved noise estimation for hyperspectral images. Sci. Chin. Ser. F: Inf. Sci. **52**(9), 1578–1587 (2009)

10. Gao, L., Zhang, B., Sun, X., Li, S., Du, Q., Wu, C.: Optimized maximum noise fraction for dimensionality reduction of Chinese HJ-1A hyperspectral data. EURASIP J. Adv. Sig. Process. **2013**(1), 65 (2013)

11. Achanta, R., Shaji, A., Smith, K., Lucchi, A., Fua, P., Süsstrunk, S.: Slic superpixels compared to state-of-the-art superpixel methods. IEEE Trans. Pattern Anal. Mach. Intell. **34**(11), 2274–2282 (2012)

12. Roger, R.: Principal components transform with simple, automatic noise adjustment. Int. J. Remote Sens. **17**(14), 2719–2727 (1996)

13. Greco, M., Diani, M., Corsini, G.: Analysis of the classification accuracy of a new mnf based feature extraction algorithm. In: Remote Sensing, p. 63 650V. International Society for Optics and Photonics (2006)

14. Chartered Institute of Taxation. Jet Propulsion Lab: AVIRIS data - ordering free AVIRIS standard data products, July 2017. http://aviris.jpl.nasa.gov/html/aviris.freedata.html

15. Zhang, L., Zhang, L., Bovik, A.C.: A feature-enriched completely blind image quality evaluator. IEEE Trans. Image Process. **24**(8), 2579–2591 (2015)

GMM Based Single Depth Image Super-Resolution

Chandra Shaker Balure[1](✉)(iD), M. Ramesh Kini[1](iD), and Arnav Bhavsar[2]

[1] National Institute of Technology Karnataka, Surathkal, Mangalore, India
`balure1986a@gmail.com, rameshkinim@gmail.com`
[2] Indian Institute of Technology Mandi, Mandi, H.P., India
`arnav@iitmandi.ac.in`

Abstract. Super-resolution (SR) is a technique to improve the resolution of an image from a sequence of input images or from a single image. As SR is an ill-posed inverse problem, it leads to many suboptimal solutions. Since modern depth cameras suffer from low-spatial resolution and are noisy, we present a Gaussian mixture model (GMM) based method for depth image super-resolution (SR). We train GMM from a set of high-resolution and low-resolution (HR-LR) synthetic training depth images to learn the relation between the HR and the LR patches in the form of covariance matrices. We use expectation-maximization (EM) algorithm to converge to an optimal solution. We show the promising results qualitatively and quantitatively in comparison to other depth image SR methods.

1 Introduction

Super-resolution (SR) is a technique of increasing the resolution of a low spatial resolution image to a higher spatial resolution image. SR methods either works with sub-pixel shifted sequence of LR images of a same scene as input, or with a single input LR image. Most contemporary methods are based on the latter paradigm as it has been shown to be more effective. Such single-image SR methods typically also require a dictionary of local patches, which is used to learn the similarity between the local information from LR image and HR data (typically from training set of HR images, or multi-resolution pyramid by interpolation of the LR data).

While the notion of SR was traditionally motivated by resolution enhancement requirements for intensity images, in recent years the need for SR is also felt in case of depth images because of its use in varied applications like HD 3DTV, augmented reality, autonomous driving vehicle etc. wherein the current low-cost depth cameras or transmission/processing pipelines lack the resolution handling capabilities. Furthermore in many cases the depth data can also be noisy, which further makes the problem challenging.

© Springer Nature Singapore Pte Ltd. 2018
R. Rameshan et al. (Eds.): NCVPRIPG 2017, CCIS 841, pp. 245–256, 2018.
https://doi.org/10.1007/978-981-13-0020-2_22

In this paper, we are trying to address single depth image SR problem using Gaussian mixture model (GMM) learning. Similar to some earlier works on depth image SR, our framework is also based on a method which was originally proposed for intensity image SR [12]. We use external training depth images to learn the mapping between HR and LR images. A GMM model is used to learn the HR-LR mapping, and this learned mapping is then used in deriving the HR patch for the corresponding LR test patch. However, considering that the characteristics of the depth images are very different than those of intensity images (dominant edges and negligible texture), we believe it is important to demonstrate the effectiveness of such an approach especially for depth data.

Another important considering with depth image SR is that of considering high upsampling factors (e.g. 4, 8) which are typically not considered for intensity image SR. We adapt the GMM framework to be used in a hierarchical manner to achieve such high factor upsampling. Furthermore, we also demonstrate the performance of the GMM-based framework for super-resolution of noisy images, which is typically not considered in many depth SR works.

1.1 Related Work

We broadly classify the single depth image SR approaches into three different categories i.e. (1) SR from interpolation methods, (2) SR using guidance image, and (3) SR using training exemplars.

SR from interpolation methods include the classical interpolation methods like nearest neighbor, bilinear, bicubic, lenczos and more, which consider the smoothness constraints. It majorly results in edge blurring because of the implicit smoothing property. These methods have been improved further for better edge preservation. The work of Konno *et al.* [8] proposes residual interpolation (RI) method for depth image SR, which uses interpolation of the residuals to be added to the the tentative estimate obtained from the guidance image.

Single depth image SR using guidance image is yet another area which use RGB colour image as guidance image. The resolution of the guidance image is the target resolution for the input test depth image which needs to be super-resolved. As mentioned earlier, the work of Konno *et al.* [8] proposes residual interpolation (RI) method, which use guidance image to aid the SR operation. The use of guidance image for filtering, known as guidance image filtering (GIF) [6], has shown better smoothing results near edges without blurring it, which caught the attention of researchers to use HR colour guidance image as a cue for depth image SR problem. In [1–3,7], they have used HR colour guidance image, which gives an easy and convenient prior for SR problems under the assumption that the edges in the depth image coincide with the guidance image. The work in [2] use guidance image and use Markov random field (MRF) techniques to generate HR output. The use of BF filter [14] for upsampling the image, called joint bilateral upsampling (JBU) [9], suffer from texture copy, hence to address this issue, a noise aware filter for depth upsampling (NAFDU) method was proposed in [1], which used colour guidance image and proposed a technique which make SR objective function to work as standard JBU in less-noisy region, or work as BF filter in noisy region. In [7], authors use structure and gradient information from the guidance image to produce quality HR image. Authors in [3] use anisotropic diffusion tensor from guidance image to guide the upsampling.

The SR methods using external training examples have shown good performance for intensity image SR problems [4,5]. In [5], authors proposed intensity image SR, based on the observation that the patches redundantly recur within the same scale and across different scales, which can be used for creating patch database. The SR methods using the example database have been extensively used for depth images also [10,11]. In [11] the patching method is used to find the candidate HR patch from the database, and the SR problem is posed as MRF labeling problem. The work in [10] uses disassembling the input image based on the matching regions of HR training images and assembling of corresponding matched counterpart. A recent work on deep depth image super-resolution (DDSR) using deep convolutional neural network (CNN) has been proposed in [14], which uses deep network to learn the features, with added support from the HR guidance colour image and the use of depth field statistics to learn high-frequency components. However, typically such deep learning methods require a larger number of training examples and more training time, which are arguably lower in our approach.

Our proposed method falls into the third category of SR methods, wherein we employ an external training data, and learn the mapping between the HR and the LR training images using GMM model. Our key contributions are:

1. We adapt the GMM model of [12] for the depth image SR problem and train the GMM on synthetic depth images [11] which are sharp at edges to suit for our SR problem.
2. We propose stage-wise training of GMM for enabling the hierarchical SR framework, especially for higher up-sampling factors.
3. We demonstrate the effectiveness of the GMM-based approach for noisy depth images.

2   Proposed Method

Data preparation: Let us assume that we have HR and LR image set X and Y which comprise of T training examples each, which is represented as $[x_1, \cdots, x_T]$ and $[y_1, \cdots, y_T]$ respectively. We extract N number of patches each from sets X and Y, represented as patch sets PX and PY, which comprises of N patches $[px_1, \cdots, px_N]$ and $[py_1, \cdots, py_N]$ respectively. The patch sizes are $m \times m$ and $n \times n$ for HR and LR patches respectively, where $m = \alpha n$ and α is the upsampling factor. These HR and LR patches are then converted into vector form to create vector sets VX and VY respectively, where each set again comprises of N vectors each $[vx_1, \cdots, vx_N]$ and $[vy_1, \cdots, vy_N]$ respectively. The size of the HR and LR vectors will be $m^2 \times 1$ and $n^2 \times 1$ respectively. These HR and LR vectors are then concatenated to form an HR-LR pair as a single vector, the set of which is represented by V with N number of vector elements $[v_1, \cdots, v_N]$, each of size $(m^2 + n^2) \times 1 = n_D$. The vector set can be represented as shown in Eq. 1,

$$v_i = \begin{bmatrix} vx_i \\ vy_i \end{bmatrix} \tag{1}$$

where v_i is the concatenated vector with upper and lower part of the vector representing HR and LR vector respectively, and $i = 1 \cdots N$. The vector set V, whose size is n_D *rows* and N *columns*, is the training matrix given to GMM for training purpose.

GMM Training: GMM is a parametric model of probability distribution of the known measurement points. It can be used either to find the distribution of a new input point or to generate the multiple points from the estimate probability distribution. GMM is a weighted sum of K components of Gaussian densities, which can be written as Eq. 2:

$$p(x_i|\Theta) = \sum_{k=1}^{K} w_k \ g(x|\mu_k, S_k) \tag{2}$$

where x is n_D dimensional data vector, w_k, μ_k and S_k are weights, mean vectors and covariance matrices of kth Gaussian component which together constitute the GMM parameter Θ, and $g(\cdot)$ is the kth component of Gaussian density which can be written as Eq. 3,

$$g(x|\mu_k, S_k) = \frac{1}{\sqrt{(2\pi)^{n_D}|S_k|}} \exp\left\{-\frac{1}{2}(x - \mu_k)' S_k^{-1}(x - \mu_k)\right\} \tag{3}$$

The complete GMM model is parameterized by mixture weights, mean vectors and covariance matrices from all components of Gaussian densities, which is collectively represented as $\Theta = \{w_k, \mu_k, S_k\}$

The maximum likelihood (ML) parameter estimation method tries to find the Θ that best matches the distribution of the training vectors. It aims at maximizing the likelihood estimate. The ML estimate produces GMM likelihood, which is given by Eq. 4.

$$g(x|\Theta) = \sum_{i=1}^{N} p(x_i|\Theta) \tag{4}$$

where, x_i is the vector at calculation, and N is the total number of vectors in the training matrix. As Eq. 4 is a non-linear function of Θ, so the direct maximization is not possible. Hence, we use expectation maximization (EM) for parameter estimation, which iterates between E-step and M-step until convergence. **E-step:** It starts with an initial model Θ, and find the new model $\tilde{\Theta}$, such that $p(x_i|\tilde{\Theta}) \geq p(x_i|\Theta)$. **M-step:** It tries to increase the model likelihood value, as shown in Eq. 5. As the increase is monotonic, it guarantees the convergence.

$$w_k = \frac{1}{K} \sum_{i=1}^{N} Pr(k|x_i, \Theta)$$

$$\mu_k = \frac{\sum_{i=1}^{N} Pr(k|x_i, \Theta) \, x_i}{\sum_{i=1}^{N} Pr(k|x_i, \Theta)} \tag{5}$$

$$\boldsymbol{S}_k = \frac{\sum_{i=1}^{N} Pr(k|x_i, \Theta) \, x_i^2}{\sum_{i=1}^{N} Pr(k|x_i, \Theta)} - \mu_k^2$$

where, Pr is the posterior probability of kth component which is given by Eq. 6,

$$Pr(k|x_i, \Theta) = \frac{w_k \ g(x_i|\mu_k, \boldsymbol{S}_k)}{\sum_{k=1}^{K} w_k \ g(x_i|\mu_k, \boldsymbol{S}_k)} \tag{6}$$

The learned parameters μ_k (mean vectors) and $\boldsymbol{S}_k$ (covariance matrices) of kth Gaussian mixture is from the training vectors which were considered to be generated from the kth Gaussian component. Since the training vectors were composed of concatenated HR vectors and its corresponding LR vectors, the learned parameters μ_k and $\boldsymbol{S}_k$ can be effectively broken down into the means and covariances of HR vectors ($\mu_{H_k}, \boldsymbol{S}_{H_k}$) and the LR vectors ($\mu_{L_k}, \boldsymbol{S}_{L_k}$) respectively, as if the HR vector space and LR vector space existed separately. Similarly, $\boldsymbol{S}_{HL_k}$ and $\boldsymbol{S}_{LH_k}$ represents the covariance matrices between the HR vector space and LR vector space. The effective μ_k and $\boldsymbol{S}_k$ is represented as shown in Eqs. 7 and 8,

$$\mu_k = \begin{bmatrix} \mu_{H_k} \\ \mu_{L_k} \end{bmatrix} \tag{7}$$

$$\boldsymbol{S}_k = \begin{bmatrix} \boldsymbol{S}_{H_k} & \boldsymbol{S}_{HL_k} \\ \boldsymbol{S}_{LH_k} & \boldsymbol{S}_{L_k} \end{bmatrix} \tag{8}$$

Direct approach v/s Hierarchical approach: In direct approach, we train GMM model using appropriate HR-LR patch sizes, e.g. for upsampling factor ×8, we train using 32×32 and 4×4 patch sizes from HR and LR images of size 800×800 and 100×100. However, in Hierarchical approach, we train GMM model only for upsampling factor ×2, but with different HR and LR images sizes, e.g. we train the first GMM model (called TrainGMM1) for factor ×2 using patch sizes 8×8 and 4×4 from HR and LR images of size 800×800 and 400×400 respectively; similarly, we train second GMM model (TrainGMM2) which is also for upsampling factor ×2, but with smaller HR and LR image sizes of 400×400 and 200×200 respectively; and a third GMM model (TrainGMM3) for same upsampling factor and with same HR-LR patch sizes, but with different image sizes 200×200 and 100×100 for HR and LR training images.

Hence in hierarchical approach, we learn the small structure at the lowest resolution which will support to give accurate output at further stages for higher upsampling factors.

GMM Testing: For a given test input y, we extract the overlapping patches of size $n \times n$, where $m = \alpha n$. From the estimated GMM parameters $\Theta =$

$\{w_k, \mu_k, \boldsymbol{S}_k\}$ obtained from the training, we find the likelihood $q_i^{(k)}$ of the input patch being generated from k^{th} Gaussian component using Eq. 9, and choose the Gaussian component $\hat{k}_i$ which maximizes the likelihood $q_i^{(k)}$ using Eq. 10.

$$q_i^{(k)} = \omega_k \; p(y_i | \mu_{L_k}, \boldsymbol{S}_{L_k}) \tag{9}$$

$$\hat{k}_i = \underset{k \in 1 \cdots K}{\arg\max} \; q_i^{(k)} \tag{10}$$

From the selected k^{th} Gaussian component, we estimate the HR vector using the MMSE formula [12], which is given in Eq. 11,

$$\hat{x}_i = \mu_{H_{\hat{k}_i}} + \boldsymbol{S}_{HL_{\hat{k}_i}} \boldsymbol{S}_{L_{\hat{k}_i}}^{-1} \left(y_i - \mu_{L_{\hat{k}_i}} \right) \tag{11}$$

The estimated SR patches $\hat{x}_i$ from the learned parameters Θ is expected to be as close as the ground truth HR patch x_i. We estimate the SR patches for all the overlapping LR patches. The estimation at the overlapping region is obtained by averaging over all the SR patches sharing that region.

3   Results and Discussions

In this section we present the depth image SR results of our approach and its comparison with other SR methods. While we have trained GMM model with various numbers of Gaussian mixtures, here we only present the results obtained from 50 and 100 Gaussian mixtures, which were the best. Increasing the number of Gaussians further do not improve the results. We have chosen 8 test images from Middlebury dataset [13] and we compare our direct and hierarchical SRGMM results with bilinear and bicubic interpolation results and few other state-of-the-art depth image SR methods like ATGV [3], GIF [6] and RI [8] both qualitative and quantitative.

To simulate the LR data, we appropriately downsample the ground-truth HR images by following the LR modeling to generate an observed LR image. We have experimented with both the *noiseless* and *noisy* images. We use the LR modeling only to simulate our observed input LR image y, as shown in Eq. 12, and we do not use this model anywhere in our SR process.

$$y = DBx + \eta \tag{12}$$

where x the HR, D and B are the downsample matrix and blur matrix respectively, and η is the additive noise, and y is the observed LR image. For *noiseless* LR image creation, the HR image x is only downsampled and blurred, as in Eq. 12, but without having noise term ($\sigma = 0$). However, for *noisy* LR image creation the equation remains the same, but now with noise term in it with standard deviation $\sigma = 5$.

Noiseless scenario: The GMM training is performed with the set of HR-LR images. The HR image set is comprised of the synthetic depth images collected from [11], and LR image set is comprised of LR images generated from their HR image counterparts by following the downsampling procedure using Eq. 12, but without the noise term. The same model is used for generating the HR-LR image set for all the training types TrainGMM1, TrainGMM2 and TrainGMM3.

Figures 1 and 2 shows the comparative results for SR by factor ×4 and ×8 of depth image *Art* and *Baby* respectively. As we can see that our SRGMM method (either direct or hierarchical) does better job in retaining the edge discontinuities, and the overall shape of the image is retained without any artifacts. On contrary, we observe that ATGV method is not been able to preserve edges to larger extent and exhibit some jagged artifacts around edges, and similar is the case with GIF method. As shown in the inline zoomed region of the portion of the image in Fig. 1 (bottom row), the sticks in *Art* image produced by our methods has clear distinction from the background and has sharp edge discontinuities. Similarly, the arms in *Baby* images in Fig. 2 (bottom row) is sharper in our hierarchical approach than the interpolation methods and other state-of-the-art methods.

Table 1 shows the PSNR and SSIM [15] results on more images for *noiseless* scenario. We highlight the best score with *red* and second highest score with *blue* colour. We observe that our SRGMM method performs better than the classical interpolation methods for almost all the upsampling factors, and we also perform better than the state-of-the-art methods like ATGV, GIF and RI methods for most cases. For upsampling factor ×2, our SRGMM direct approach with 100 Gaussian mixtures performs better then all the other contemporary methods, and also our SRGMM direct approach with 50 Gaussian mixtures perform performs well then all other comparative methods, but stand second among the competitive methods. For upsampling factor ×4, the average results of our SRGMM direct approach with 50 Gaussian mixture is best and the SRGMM direct approach with 100 Gaussian mixture is second best among other methods.

Among the direct and hierarchical versions of our method, we note that at upsampling factor 4 the direct approach seems sufficient to learn the HR-LR mapping and yields somewhat better results than the hierarchical approach. However, for upsampling factor 8, clearly the hierarchical structure of learning GMM seems to help in producing better results, as the loss of information may be too high for a direct learning method.

Noisy scenario: The GMM training for noisy scenario is similar to the the training procedure followed for noiseless scenario, but with the included noise term for noisy case. The HR image set is as usual the high-resolution images, and now the LR image set is generated using Eq. 12 with noise term of standard deviation $\sigma = 5$.

Figures 3 and 4 shows the testing results and the comparisons of our direct and hierarchical approach with other SR method for upsampling factor ×4 and ×8 on *noisy* depth image *Art* and *Baby* respectively. Bottom row of Fig. 3 show results obtained from our SRGMM method using direct and indirect approaches for a given 100 Gaussian mixture. The zoomed portion of the image is shown inset to the image, and we can see that the sticks in *Art* image produced by our method (both direct and hierarchical approach) has better depth discontinuities

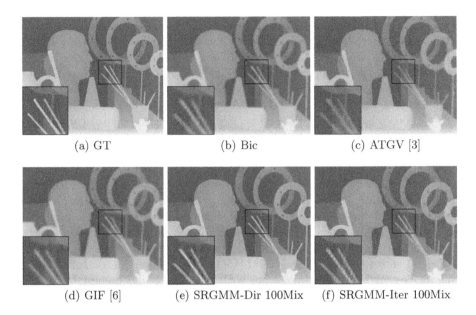

(a) GT   (b) Bic   (c) ATGV [3]

(d) GIF [6]   (e) SRGMM-Dir 100Mix   (f) SRGMM-Iter 100Mix

Fig. 1. Qualitative results comparison for SR by factor ×4_n0 (Image: *Art*)

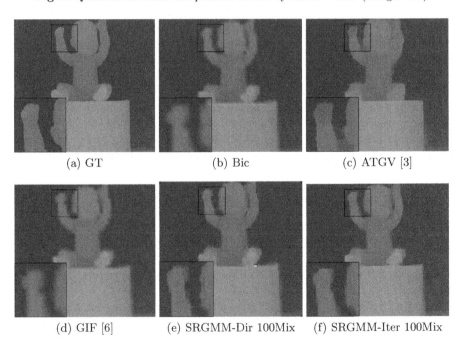

(a) GT   (b) Bic   (c) ATGV [3]

(d) GIF [6]   (e) SRGMM-Dir 100Mix   (f) SRGMM-Iter 100Mix

Fig. 2. Qualitative results comparison for SR by factor ×8_n0 (Image: *Baby*)

Table 1. PSNR/SSIM result comparison of SR for factor ×2, ×4 and ×8 on *noiseless* images (Red text indicate highest value and blue text indicate second highest value)

Images	Bil	Bic	ATGV [3]	GIF [6]	RI [8]	SRGMM-Dir 50Mix	SRGMM-Hier 50Mix	SRGMM-Dir 100Mix	SRGMM-Hier 100Mix
Aloe	33.36/0.95	33.67/0.95	34.41/0.96	33.83/0.96	35.42/0.97	37.58/0.98	-	37.96/0.98	-
Art	31.02/0.92	31.42/0.93	32.01/0.94	31.70/0.93	32.76/0.95	35.25/0.97	-	35.52/0.97	-
Baby	37.95/0.98	38.27/0.98	39.16/0.98	38.44/0.98	40.15/0.99	43.54/0.99	-	43.70/0.99	-
Cones	36.25/0.97	36.58/0.97	37.50/0.97	36.75/0.97	38.09/0.98	39.53/0.98	-	40.00/0.98	-
Plastic	39.28/0.99	39.57/0.99	41.64/0.99	40.14/0.99	41.72/0.99	44.92/0.99	-	45.76/0.99	-
Reindeer	34.17/0.96	34.51/0.97	35.10/0.97	34.87/0.97	35.99/0.98	38.40/0.98	-	38.64/0.98	-
Sawtooth	37.50/0.98	37.86/0.98	38.76/0.98	38.71/0.98	39.51/0.99	43.93/0.99	-	44.13/1.00	-
Venus	42.35/0.99	42.69/0.99	43.87/0.99	43.25/0.99	44.48/0.99	48.05/1.00	-	48.90/1.00	-
Avg. x2_n0	36.48/0.96	36.82/0.97	37.80/0.97	37.21/0.97	38.51/0.98	41.40/0.98	-	41.82/0.98	-
Aloe	30.10/0.92	30.11/0.92	31.90/0.94	30.47/0.93	34.82/0.97	34.82/0.96	33.42/0.96	34.72/0.96	35.66/0.97
Art	28.26/0.88	28.44/0.88	29.80/0.91	28.87/0.89	31.61/0.94	32.19/0.93	27.53/0.94	31.83/0.93	31.97/0.94
Baby	34.78/0.97	34.87/0.97	36.89/0.98	35.19/0.97	39.25/0.99	39.41/0.98	37.67/0.98	39.36/0.98	39.71/0.99
Cones	33.08/0.95	33.12/0.95	35.31/0.96	33.56/0.95	36.83/0.97	36.60/0.97	36.51/0.97	36.69/0.97	35.88/0.97
Plastic	36.27/0.98	36.33/0.98	41.55/0.99	36.76/0.98	38.47/0.99	41.45/0.99	37.32/0.98	38.65/0.98	41.87/0.99
Reindeer	31.16/0.94	31.25/0.94	34.01/0.97	31.73/0.95	35.12/0.97	35.04/0.96	34.12/0.97	35.09/0.96	34.65/0.97
Sawtooth	34.84/0.97	35.04/0.97	37.61/0.98	35.80/0.97	38.76/0.99	39.66/0.99	36.76/0.99	40.24/0.99	37.19/0.99
Venus	39.63/0.98	39.81/0.98	42.62/0.99	40.43/0.99	44.54/0.99	44.39/0.99	43.13/0.99	44.23/0.99	39.27/0.99
Avg. x4_n0	33.51/0.94	33.62/0.94	36.21/0.96	34.10/0.95	37.42/0.97	37.94/0.97	35.80/0.97	37.60/0.97	37.02/0.97
Aloe	26.46/0.88	26.17/0.87	26.12/0.90	26.36/0.88	30.27/0.92	29.32/0.89	30.11/0.92	29.54/0.90	30.45/0.93
Art	24.84/0.81	24.69/0.81	25.95/0.86	24.91/0.82	28.05/0.88	26.26/0.83	26.48/0.87	26.05/0.83	26.02/0.87
Baby	30.64/0.94	30.45/0.94	32.52/0.96	30.67/0.94	36.35/0.97	34.34/0.96	33.43/0.97	33.14/0.95	34.99/0.96
Cones	29.79/0.92	29.59/0.92	30.72/0.93	29.79/0.93	32.63/0.95	30.49/0.92	32.11/0.95	30.45/0.92	31.02/0.94
Plastic	31.11/0.96	30.93/0.96	33.46/0.97	31.08/0.96	36.39/0.98	34.23/0.97	29.35/0.97	33.31/0.97	36.36/0.97
Reindeer	27.91/0.92	27.73/0.91	29.64/0.94	28.02/0.92	31.39/0.95	28.60/0.92	29.94/0.93	28.94/0.92	29.43/0.94
Sawtooth	31.25/0.95	31.20/0.95	32.21/0.96	31.58/0.95	34.23/0.97	33.11/0.96	33.45/0.97	32.85/0.96	34.49/0.97
Venus	36.06/0.97	35.98/0.97	38.61/0.97	36.36/0.97	41.11/0.99	36.89/0.98	39.83/0.98	36.96/0.98	35.54/0.98
Avg. x8_n0	29.75/0.91	29.59/0.91	31.15/0.93	29.84/0.92	33.80/0.95	31.65/0.92	31.83/0.94	31.40/0.92	32.28/0.94

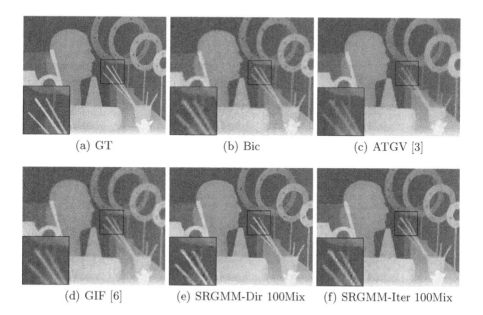

(a) GT   (b) Bic   (c) ATGV [3]

(d) GIF [6]   (e) SRGMM-Dir 100Mix   (f) SRGMM-Iter 100Mix

Fig. 3. Qualitative results comparison for SR by factor ×4_n5 (Image: *Art*)

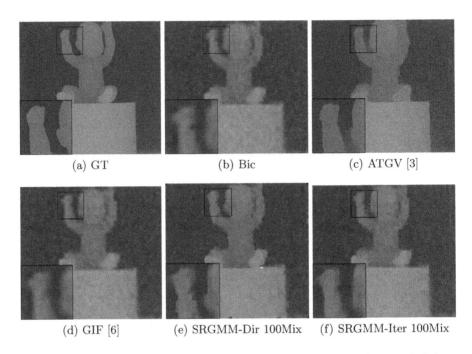

(a) GT   (b) Bic   (c) ATGV [3]

(d) GIF [6]   (e) SRGMM-Dir 100Mix   (f) SRGMM-Iter 100Mix

Fig. 4. Qualitative results comparison for SR by factor $\times 8\_n5$ (Image: *Baby*)

Table 2. PSNR/SSIM result comparison of SR for factor $\times 2$, $\times 4$ and $\times 8$ on *noisy* images (Red text indicate highest value and blue text indicate second highest value)

Images	Bil	Bic	ATGV [3]	GIF [6]	RI [8]	SRGMM-Dir 50Mix	SRGMM-Hier 50Mix	SRGMM-Dir 100Mix	SRGMM-Hier 100Mix
Aloe	32.15/0.87	31.70/0.81	32.56/0.85	33.12/0.92	32.51/0.82	35.48/0.96	-	35.60/0.96	-
Art	30.27/0.84	30.12/0.79	30.96/0.85	31.24/0.90	30.86/0.80	33.66/0.95	-	33.70/0.95	-
Baby	35.05/0.88	33.94/0.82	35.54/0.88	36.68/0.94	34.38/0.82	37.09/0.94	-	36.69/0.93	-
Cones	34.16/0.88	33.33/0.82	34.56/0.87	35.54/0.94	33.83/0.83	37.73/0.97	-	37.94/0.97	-
Plastic	35.75/0.89	34.44/0.82	37.01/0.89	38.00/0.95	34.85/0.82	41.61/0.98	-	41.77/0.98	-
Reindeer	32.76/0.87	32.21/0.81	33.77/0.88	34.10/0.94	32.86/0.82	36.56/0.97	-	36.59/0.97	-
Sawtooth	34.81/0.88	33.78/0.81	35.15/0.87	36.96/0.94	34.17/0.81	37.80/0.95	-	37.35/0.94	-
Venus	36.77/0.88	35.11/0.82	36.83/0.87	39.48/0.95	35.27/0.82	39.91/0.96	-	39.22/0.95	-
Avg. x2_n5	33.96/0.87	33.07/0.81	34.54/0.87	35.64/0.93	33.59/0.81	37.48/0.96	-	37.35/0.95	-
Aloe	29.39/0.87	29.08/0.84	31.24/0.91	29.76/0.88	32.25/0.88	33.27/0.93	33.12/0.94	33.06/0.93	33.45/0.94
Art	27.79/0.83	27.72/0.80	29.41/0.89	28.36/0.85	30.19/0.85	31.27/0.91	30.60/0.91	30.99/0.91	30.67/0.91
Baby	33.08/0.90	32.41/0.87	35.77/0.95	33.54/0.92	34.36/0.89	34.88/0.91	35.95/0.95	34.55/0.91	35.67/0.95
Cones	31.90/0.89	31.39/0.86	34.31/0.93	32.44/0.91	33.39/0.88	35.07/0.95	34.91/0.95	35.26/0.95	34.88/0.95
Plastic	34.01/0.91	33.18/0.87	39.20/0.97	34.63/0.93	34.55/0.89	39.10/0.98	38.17/0.97	37.95/0.97	37.85/0.97
Reindeer	30.31/0.88	30.00/0.85	33.22/0.94	30.91/0.91	32.44/0.88	33.81/0.95	33.39/0.95	33.83/0.95	33.67/0.95
Sawtooth	33.03/0.90	32.43/0.86	35.98/0.95	33.92/0.92	33.99/0.88	35.59/0.93	36.00/0.96	35.50/0.93	36.01/0.96
Venus	35.57/0.91	34.43/0.87	39.14/0.95	36.42/0.94	35.39/0.89	37.59/0.94	38.50/0.96	37.14/0.94	38.00/0.96
Avg. x4_n5	31.88/0.88	31.33/0.85	34.78/0.93	32.49/0.90	33.32/0.88	35.07/0.93	35.08/0.94	34.78/0.93	35.02/0.94
Aloe	26.16/0.86	25.75/0.84	25.87/0.89	25.98/0.85	29.40/0.89	29.12/0.88	29.61/0.90	28.98/0.88	29.83/0.90
Art	24.62/0.79	24.38/0.78	25.87/0.86	24.62/0.79	27.25/0.84	25.86/0.81	26.85/0.84	25.69/0.82	26.75/0.84
Baby	29.85/0.92	29.37/0.90	32.31/0.96	29.69/0.91	32.62/0.93	32.06/0.92	33.02/0.94	31.43/0.92	32.92/0.94
Cones	29.24/0.90	28.82/0.89	30.45/0.93	29.12/0.90	31.12/0.91	30.15/0.91	31.42/0.93	30.16/0.91	31.44/0.93
Plastic	30.28/0.94	29.77/0.92	33.81/0.97	30.07/0.93	32.97/0.94	33.10/0.95	34.89/0.96	32.27/0.95	31.43/0.95
Reindeer	27.51/0.89	27.17/0.88	29.56/0.94	27.52/0.89	30.00/0.91	28.31/0.90	30.10/0.92	28.43/0.90	30.01/0.92
Sawtooth	30.38/0.92	29.97/0.91	32.56/0.96	30.46/0.92	31.87/0.93	30.81/0.92	32.51/0.94	31.37/0.93	31.38/0.94
Venus	33.74/0.94	32.95/0.93	38.67/0.98	33.54/0.94	34.71/0.94	33.97/0.94	35.78/0.96	33.76/0.94	34.19/0.96
Avg. x8_n5	28.97/0.89	28.52/0.88	31.13/0.93	28.87/0.89	31.24/0.91	30.42/0.90	31.77/0.92	30.26/0.90	30.99/0.92

and the smoother regions are much smoother with lesser noise. Fig. 4 show results of SR by factor ×8, where our hierarchical approach performs better than the direct approach in terms of edge preservation and noise smoothing.

Table 2 shows the PSNR and SSIM values obtained from the SR methods on *noisy* depth images. Although the ATGV method performs well for the noisy images, but our proposed method, on an average, with 50 Gaussian mixture performs marginally better than ATGV method. In particular, on an average, we preform 2.80 dB and 3.25 dB better than bilinear and bicubic interpolation methods respectively, and perform about 0.64 dB, 2.90 dB and 0.53 dB better than ATGV, GIF and RI methods respectively in ×8_n5 case. Overall, our SRGMM hierarchical approach performs better then the contemporary methods for higher upsampling factors like ×4 and ×8 (best average value in red colour). Although our SRGMM direct approach does better, our SRGMM hierarchical approach does superior as it learns more finer mapping between the HR-LR patches in the iterative process of upsampling by factor 2 to reach the higher upsampling factors like 4 and 8.

4   Conclusion

We conclude by stating that the GMM models can also be used for depth image SR problem, and it can be performed with few training examples (31 in our case), and still produce better results by conserving edge discontinuities. The hierarchical approach learns finer structures better than the direct approach. The performance can vary with different number of Gaussian mixtures. We used EM algorithm to estimate GMM parameters, which makes it tractable and assures guaranteed convergence. As a future work, we are aiming at using some simpler methods of clustering the HR-LR patches, which needs to be faster and also able to give more accurate SR results.

References

1. Chan, D., Buisman, H., Theobalt, C., Thrun, S.: A noise-aware filter for real-time depth upsampling. In: 2008 Workshop on Multi-camera and Multi-modal Sensor Fusion Algorithms and Applications-M2SFA2 (2008)
2. Diebel, J., Thrun, S.: An application of markov random fields to range sensing. In: NIPS, vol. 5, pp. 291–298 (2005)
3. Ferstl, D., Reinbacher, C., Ranftl, R., Rüther, M., Bischof, H.: Image guided depth upsampling using anisotropic total generalized variation. In: Proceedings of the IEEE International Conference on Computer Vision, pp. 993–1000 (2013)
4. Freeman, W.T., Jones, T.R., Pasztor, E.C.: Example-based super-resolution. IEEE Comput. Graph. Appl. **22**(2), 56–65 (2002)
5. Glasner, D., Bagon, S., Irani, M.: Super-resolution from a single image. In: 2009 IEEE 12th International Conference on Computer Vision, pp. 349–356. IEEE (2009)
6. He, K., Sun, J., Tang, X.: Guided image filtering. In: Daniilidis, K., Maragos, P., Paragios, N. (eds.) ECCV 2010. LNCS, vol. 6311, pp. 1–14. Springer, Heidelberg (2010). https://doi.org/10.1007/978-3-642-15549-9_1

7. Hua, K.L., Lo, K.H., Wang, Y.C.F.F.: Extended guided filtering for depth map upsampling. IEEE Multimed. **23**(2), 72–83 (2016)
8. Konno, Y., Monno, Y., Kiku, D., Tanaka, M., Okutomi, M.: Intensity guided depth upsampling by residual interpolation. In: The Abstracts of the International Conference on Advanced Mechatronics, Toward Evolutionary Fusion of IT and Mechatronics (ICAM) Abstracts, vol. 2015, pp. 1–2 (2015)
9. Kopf, J., Cohen, M.F., Lischinski, D., Uyttendaele, M.: Joint bilateral upsampling. ACM Trans. Graph. (ToG) **26**, 96 (2007)
10. Li, J., Lu, Z., Zeng, G., Gan, R., Zha, H.: Similarity-aware patchwork assembly for depth image super-resolution. In: Proceedings of the IEEE Conference on Computer Vision and Pattern Recognition, pp. 3374–3381 (2014)
11. Mac Aodha, O., Campbell, N.D.F., Nair, A., Brostow, G.J.: Patch based synthesis for single depth image super-resolution. In: Fitzgibbon, A., Lazebnik, S., Perona, P., Sato, Y., Schmid, C. (eds.) ECCV 2012. LNCS, vol. 7574, pp. 71–84. Springer, Heidelberg (2012). https://doi.org/10.1007/978-3-642-33712-3_6
12. Sandeep, P., Jacob, T.: Single image super-resolution using a joint GMM method. IEEE Trans. Image Process. **25**(9), 4233–4244 (2016)
13. Scharstein, D., Szeliski, R.: A taxonomy and evaluation of dense two-frame stereo correspondence algorithms. Int. J. Comput. Vis. **47**(1–3), 7–42 (2002)
14. Tomasi, C., Manduchi, R.: Bilateral filtering for gray and color images. In: 1998 Sixth International Conference on Computer Vision, pp. 839–846. IEEE (1998)
15. Wang, Z., Bovik, A.C., Sheikh, H.R., Simoncelli, E.P.: Image quality assessment: from error visibility to structural similarity. IEEE Trans. Image Process. **13**(4), 600–612 (2004)

Patch Similarity in Transform Domain for Intensity/Range Image Denoising with Edge Preservation

Seema Kumari[1(✉)], Srimanta Mandal[2], and Arnav Bhavsar[1]

[1] MAS Lab, School of Computing and Electrical Engineering,
IIT Mandi, Mandi, India
seema_kumari@students.iitmandi.ac.in, arnav@iitmandi.ac.in
[2] IPCV Lab, Department of Electrical Engineering, IIT Madras, Madras, India
in.srimanta.mandal@ieee.org

Abstract. For the image denoising task, the prior information obtained from grouping similar non-local patches has been shown to serve as an effective regularizer. Nevertheless, noise may create ambiguity in grouping similar patches, hence it may degrade the results. However, most of the non-local similarity based approaches do not take care of the issue of noisy grouping. Hence, we propose to denoise an image by mitigating the issue of grouping non-local similar patches in presence of noise in transform domain using sparsity and edge preserving constraints. The effectiveness of the transform domain grouping of patches is utilized for learning dictionaries, and is further extended for achieving an initial approximation of sparse coefficient vector for the clean image patches. We have demonstrated the results of effective grouping of similar patches in denoising intensity as well as range images.

Keywords: Denoising · Sparsity · Non-local grouping · Dictionary
Edge preservation

1 Introduction

Image denoising aims to approximate the original noise-free scene from it's noisy observation. Typically, the noisy image $\mathbf{y}$ can be represented as

$$\mathbf{y} = \mathbf{x} + \mathbf{n}, \tag{1}$$

where $\mathbf{y}$ is the noisy image, which is obtained by adding additive white Gaussian noise (AWGN) $\mathbf{n}$ of standard deviation σ with the clean scene $\mathbf{x}$. Here, the objective is to estimate $\mathbf{x}$ from $\mathbf{y}$, which is an inverse problem, and can be addressed by regularizing the same with some prior knowledge. The main focus of the existing denoising approaches is to design a regularizer with appropriate prior knowledge, which evolves around the smoothness characteristics of the image.

© Springer Nature Singapore Pte Ltd. 2018
R. Rameshan et al. (Eds.): NCVPRIPG 2017, CCIS 841, pp. 257–268, 2018.
https://doi.org/10.1007/978-981-13-0020-2_23

Various approaches incorporate the prior information through total-variation (TV) [1], Gaussian mixture model (GMM) [2], sparsity inducing norms [3–5], non-local self similarity (NLSS) [5–9], and so on. TV modeling creates artifacts in uniform region because of its piecewise smooth structure. The performance of GMM based approaches depend on the number of mixtures and their corresponding weights. Whereas, sparsity inducing norm is dependent on goodness of dictionary for denoising an image. Further, non-local self similarity based approaches depends on the accurate grouping of similar patches. A few approaches have combined non-local similarity with sparsity to take the advantages of both the approaches by minimizing sparse coding noise in order to produce better results [5,10]. This combination becomes the cornerstone of our approach. Nevertheless, NLSS based approaches or combination of NLSS with sparsity, both require an appropriate grouping of similar patches. However, the very presence of noise may create ambiguity in grouping process by fabricating false similarity among the patches, thus result may degrade.

In this paper, we have addressed this issue by non-local grouping of patches using transform domain. Unlike most of the approaches that follow the non-local mean based methods, we group the patches using distant metric measured in a transform domain using few coefficients to avoid ambiguity that may arise due to noise. This transform domain similarity is used to learn dictionaries for sparse representation as well as in collecting similar patches to create an initial sparse representation. Further, we have used 2-step edge preserving strategy to preserve edges in an efficient way, as is done by the work [10]. Apart from denoising an intensity image we consider denoising of range images (or depth maps) also. The reason being that the inexpensive active depth sensors such as Kinect may capture a noisy inaccurate depth map due to surface reflections or sensor noise, which can also be approximated by AWGN, as [11,12]. Thus, the robustness of the proposed approach will be gauged by different image modalities under different noise strengths.

Hence, the contributions of this work can be summarized as: (i) Grouping of patches based on similarity in a transform domain, which is used in (a) learning dictionaries, and (b) achieving initial sparse representation. (ii) The edge preserving constraints are effectively used to preserve edges. (iii) The usefulness of the proposed denoising approach is demonstrated for intensity as well as range images.

2   Grouping Similar Patches: Noiseless vs Noisy

Here, we demonstrate the difference between grouping of similar patches in absence and presence of noise. We consider a natural image, as shown in left of Fig. 1(a). Then we extract patches of size 7×7 from the image, and cluster them into 3 groups depending on their mean intensity values[1]. After grouping,

---

[1] Note that the mean intensity values of patches are used on for this particular demonstration, for simplicity of interpretation. In our actual approach we use the vectorized patch values compute patch similarity using l2 norms.

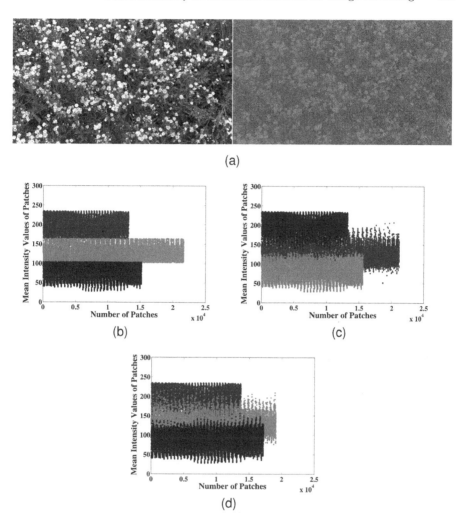

Fig. 1. (a) Left: ground-truth image, right: noisy version (AWGN, $\sigma = 100$) of the left image. Three groups of patches, achieved from K-means clustering of (b) the clean ground-truth image, (c) noisy image (AWGN, $\sigma = 100$), (d) noisy image based on transform domain (using DCT) similarity

the mean intensity values of the patches (y-axis) are plotted against the number of patches (x-axis) to generate the plot of Fig. 1(b). One can observe the distinct boundaries among the three groups of patches, which are represented by red, green and blue colors. The same experiment, we have repeated on the noisy image (right image of Fig. 1(a)), which is created by adding AWGN of $\sigma = 100$ to the left image of Fig. 1(a). Instead of directly plotting the resultant groups of noisy patches, we have used the indices of the noisy groups and plotted corresponding clean patches in order to reflect the effect of noise on grouping similar patches. The resultant plot of noisy image clustering can be observed in Fig. 1(c). One can note that due to noise, the group of red-colored patches are overlapped with the group of blue and green colored patches. In fact, all the three groups of noise-free patches have changed their positions due to noise with respect to their intensity values. This demonstrates the ambiguity in grouping similar patches under noise, which may degrade the results.

3 Proposed Approach

Our approach follows the denoising approach [5], which combines non-local similarity with sparsity by minimizing the sparse coding noise. In sparse representation framework, a target patch is represented by a sparse linear combination of dictionary patches i.e., $\mathbf{x} = \mathbf{Ac}$. Thus, using sparsity concept, we need to derive the coefficient vector $\mathbf{c}$ by solving

$$\hat{\mathbf{c}} = \arg\min_{\mathbf{c}} \left\{ ||\mathbf{y} - \mathbf{Ac}||_2^2 + \lambda\,||\mathbf{c}||_1 \right\}. \tag{2}$$

However, the $\mathbf{c}$ computed from the noisy image $\mathbf{y}$ may not be suitable for representing the clean image. Thus, a coefficient vector (ψ) for clean image is estimated by non-local similarity. Further the difference between $\mathbf{c}$ and ψ (known as sparse coding noise [5]), is minimized for every patch as

$$\hat{\mathbf{c}} = \arg\min_{\mathbf{c}} \left\{ ||\mathbf{y} - \mathbf{Ac}||_2^2 + \lambda\,||\mathbf{c} - \psi||_1 \right\}. \tag{3}$$

Once, we have the coefficient vector $\hat{\mathbf{c}}$, we can get an approximation of the clean image patch as $\hat{\mathbf{x}} = \mathbf{A}\hat{\mathbf{c}}$. Here, multiple dictionaries are created by grouping of similar patches across different scales of the noisy image.

However, the initial estimation of ψ as well as the dictionary $\mathbf{A}$ both require an robust grouping in presence of noise, which is challenging as demonstrated in previous section. Thus, we address to mitigate this issue by grouping in transform domain.

3.1 Patch Grouping Using Transform Domain Similarity

The underlying principle of our approach is that the l_2 distance between a pair of patches is identical in its original space as well as in its orthogonal transform space.

$$||\mathbf{Fx_1} - \mathbf{Fx_2}||_2^2 = ||\mathbf{x_1} - \mathbf{x_2}||_2^2, \tag{4}$$

where, the columns of $\mathbf{F}$ (e.g. DCT matrix) contains orthonormal vectors. Thus, $\mathbf{Fx_1}$ and $\mathbf{Fx_2}$ are the orthogonal transformations of vectors $\mathbf{x_1}$ and $\mathbf{x_2}$. This can be easily shown by considering $\mathbf{F}^T\mathbf{F} = I$, for an orthonormal basis.

The choice of transformation matrix $\mathbf{F}$ could be many such as DCT, Wavelet, DFT, etc. In our experiments, we choose DCT to demonstrate the denoising results and then provide comparisons of the performance using different transforms. In the transform space, the coefficients are thresholded using soft thresholding technique

$$\mathcal{S}(\mathbf{F}\mathbf{x}_i)_\lambda = \max\left(\mathbf{F}\mathbf{x}_i - \lambda, 0\right) \tag{5}$$

Here, $\mathcal{S}(\cdot)_\lambda$ is the soft thresholding operator that depends on $\lambda = c\sigma^2$ (c is small constant). Equation (5) shrinks the coefficients towards the origin. In the transform domain, shrinking coefficients, related to high frequencies can effectively reduce the effect of noise. Thus, these shrinked coefficients, can help in effective grouping of similar patches, as can be observed in plot of Fig. 1(d), which is generated by repeating the same experiment using the shrinked coefficients, as described in Sect. 2. For brevity, we have only shown this phenomena in Fig. 1(d) using DCT. One can notice that the overlapping of the groups are considerably reduced. Further, all the red, green and blue colored patches have regained their positions with respect to their intensity values as in case of clean image (Fig. 1(b)). This grouping strategy is used to learn dictionaries as well as creating an initial sparse coefficient vector for target patch.

Learning Dictionaries. We learn dictionaries from the noisy test image itself as in [5] by additional implementation of our transform domain grouping. Patches are extracted from the noisy image across different scales. These patches are grouped into K-clusters by initializing codebooks $(\mathbf{r}_1, \mathbf{r}_2 \cdots \mathbf{r}_K)$. If a patch $\mathbf{x}_i$ follows the condition

$$\mathbf{R}_k = \{i \mid \forall_{l \neq k}, \; ||\mathcal{S}(\mathbf{F}\mathbf{x}_i)_\lambda - \mathcal{S}(\mathbf{F}\mathbf{r}_k)_\lambda||_2 < ||\mathcal{S}(\mathbf{F}\mathbf{x}_i)_\lambda - \mathcal{S}(\mathbf{F}\mathbf{r}_l)_\lambda||_2\}, \tag{6}$$

then the patch will be kept in columnize mode into the cluster $\mathbf{R}_k$. Finally the codebook will be updated as

$$\mathbf{r}_k = \frac{1}{|\mathbf{R}_k|} \sum_{i \in \mathbf{R}_k} \mathbf{x}_i. \tag{7}$$

On each of the $\mathbf{R}_k$s, we apply principal component analysis (PCA) to represent the clusters more compactly as a dictionary through their significant eigenvectors. Finally, we have K dictionaries, made up of significant eigenvectors of the clusters and their representative $\mathbf{r}_k$s.

Estimation of Sparse Coefficient Vector. In order to solve Eq. (3), we need estimation of $\mathbf{c}_i$ and $\boldsymbol{\psi}_i$ along with a dictionary for target patch $\mathbf{x}_i$. A dictionary is selected based on minimum distance between the target patch $\mathbf{x}_i$ and $\mathbf{r}_k$. The selected dictionary $\mathbf{A}$ is used to represent the target patch as $\mathbf{x}_i = \mathbf{A}\mathbf{c}_i$. Since, the dictionary $\mathbf{A}$ is an orthogonal matrix, $\mathbf{c}_i$ can be estimated as $\mathbf{c}_i = \mathbf{A}^T\mathbf{x}_i$. Whereas, $\boldsymbol{\psi}_i$ is estimated from the sparse coefficient vectors of non-local similar patches as

$$\psi_i = \sum_{m \in \zeta} \frac{1}{W} \exp\left(-||\mathcal{S}(\mathbf{F}\mathbf{x}_i)_\lambda - \mathcal{S}(\mathbf{F}\mathbf{x}_{i,m})_\lambda||_2^2/h\right) \mathbf{c}_{i,m}. \qquad (8)$$

Equation (8), ψ_i can be interpreted as a weighted combination of sparse coefficient vectors $(\mathbf{c}_{i,m})$ of non-local similar patches $(\mathbf{x}_{i,m})$. Here, the weights are estimated from patch similarity via l_2 distance in the transform domain, and $\mathbf{c}_{i,m}$ are estimated as $\mathbf{c}_{i,m} = \mathbf{A}^T \mathbf{x}_{i,m}$. After achieving both the estimations along with the dictionary, we can solve Eq. (3) using iterative shrinkage algorithm [13] to estimate $\mathbf{c}$, which is further used to get denoised image estimate $\hat{\mathbf{x}}$. This is further enhanced by an edge-preserving strategy [10], as discussed next.

3.2 Edge Preservation

In order to preserve edges, we have incorporated two constraints, as is done in the approach [10]

$$\hat{\mathbf{x}} = \arg\min_{\hat{\mathbf{x}}} \left\{ ||\mathbf{y} - \hat{\mathbf{x}}||_2^2 + \beta\,||\mathbf{E}\mathbf{y}_l - \mathbf{EDH}\hat{\mathbf{x}}||_2^2 + \gamma\,||\mathbf{E}\hat{\mathbf{x}}^j - \mathbf{E}\hat{\mathbf{x}}^{j-1}||_2^2 \right\}, \quad (9)$$

where, $\mathbf{E}$, $\mathbf{D}$, $\mathbf{H}$ are the edge extraction, down-sampling, and blur matrices, respectively. $\mathbf{y}_l$ is the noisy image at low resolution. Here, the second term attempts to preserve the edges at the down-sampled version of the image as the level of noise drop drastically at down-sampled version [14]. The third term prevents transitional smoothing across iterations [10].

4   Experimental Results

In this section, the results of the proposed approach are compared with some state of the art existing approaches [3,5,7,15], including non-local similarity and sparsity based approaches. We have considered range images from Middlebury dataset [16,17] and standard intensity images for examining our strategy. The test images are synthesized from ground truth images by adding zero mean AWGN with $\sigma = 10, 20, 50, 100$, separately. We compare the results of the proposed approach with the existing approaches quantitatively, via the peak signal-to-noise ratio (PSNR) and structural similarity index (SSIM) [18]. In the proposed approach, we have used regularization parameters λ, α, β and γ, which are chosen similarly as is done in the approach [10]. Here, we provide the results using DCT for transformation, and provide comparison with DFT, wavelet transformations in the next subsection.

The quantitative results of the proposed approach are shown in Tables 1 and 2 for range and intensity images, respectively. The proposed approach yields comparable to the best results for intensity images, and outperforms the existing methods for range data for higher noise levels.

Range images are piecewise smooth in nature, hence they are more affected by noise as compared to the intensity images, which have more edges, textures etc. Moreover, range image has many more similar patches for a target patch at a

Table 1. Quantitative comparison of results for range images produced by denoising approaches via PSNR (top) and SSIM (bottom)

Approaches→ / Images, σ	EPLL [15] 10	20	50	100	K-SVD [3] 10	20	50	100	NCSR [5] 10	20	50	100	BM3D [7] 10	20	50	100	Proposed Approach 10	20	50	100
Cones	41.82	37.81	32.55	28.87	41.33	37.23	31.89	27.62	42.95	38.69	33.98	30.20	42.46	38.52	33.96	30.12	42.50	38.56	34.17	30.44
	0.9800	0.9564	0.8811	0.7687	0.9759	0.9513	0.8776	0.7501	0.9839	0.9700	0.9431	0.9078	0.9832	0.9645	0.9233	0.8560	0.9818	0.9676	0.9366	0.8900
Teddy	42.61	38.57	33.11	29.30	41.77	37.79	32.54	28.09	43.02	39.54	34.94	30.79	42.98	39.44	35.01	30.90	42.78	39.43	35.23	31.90
	0.9808	0.9577	0.8837	0.7716	0.9755	0.9533	0.8821	0.7560	0.9816	0.9707	0.9493	0.9185	0.9823	0.9653	0.9295	0.8617	0.9801	0.9681	0.9429	0.9020
Aloe	40.65	36.50	31.23	27.74	39.99	35.81	30.48	26.80	42.55	37.76	32.46	28.59	41.56	37.44	32.46	28.82	42.10	37.49	32.56	32.40
	0.9811	0.9550	0.8683	0.7490	0.9747	0.9480	0.8587	0.7302	0.9865	0.9704	0.9268	0.8775	0.9847	0.9652	0.9102	0.8303	0.9844	0.9667	0.9207	0.9076
Baby1	44.27	39.98	33.45	29.48	43.02	38.92	32.56	28.09	45.64	41.27	36.20	32.11	44.67	40.65	35.69	31.25	44.97	41.08	36.23	32.43
	0.9907	0.9732	0.9008	0.7841	0.9857	0.9696	0.8931	0.7614	0.9935	0.9872	0.9677	0.9362	0.9922	0.9813	0.9510	0.8845	0.9912	0.9844	0.9616	0.9189
Baby3	43.31	38.98	33.28	29.53	42.11	38.23	32.84	28.30	44.08	39.90	35.28	31.76	43.74	39.74	35.08	31.38	43.76	39.93	35.61	32.40
	0.9851	0.9635	0.8883	0.7762	0.9790	0.9578	0.8878	0.7627	0.9878	0.9755	0.9513	0.9238	0.9872	0.9715	0.9363	0.8775	0.9861	0.9738	0.9464	0.9075
Plastic	46.11	41.05	34.35	30.10	45.08	40.42	33.68	28.36	46.91	43.50	38.35	33.93	47.02	42.80	37.18	32.44	46.49	43.35	38.62	34.37
	0.9921	0.9762	0.9078	0.7941	0.9884	0.9733	0.9068	0.7739	0.9904	0.9783	0.9739	0.9535	0.9937	0.9851	0.9596	0.9015	0.9919	0.9881	0.9726	0.9366
Tsukuba	40.61	36.15	30.65	26.64	39.72	35.59	29.62	24.69	43.72	38.72	32.01	27.45	42.56	37.66	31.69	27.24	43.27	38.39	31.93	27.47
	0.9758	0.9436	0.8517	0.7192	0.9622	0.9213	0.8062	0.6373	0.9869	0.9684	0.9037	0.8029	0.9838	0.9591	0.8897	0.7780	0.9848	0.9620	0.8855	0.7683
Average	42.77	38.43	32.66	28.81	41.86	37.71	31.94	27.42	44.12	39.91	34.75	30.69	43.57	39.46	34.44	30.31	43.70	39.75	34.91	31.63
	0.9837	0.9608	0.8831	0.7662	0.9773	0.9535	0.8732	0.7388	0.9877	0.9761	0.9457	0.9029	0.9867	0.9703	0.9285	0.8556	0.9858	0.9730	0.9380	0.8901

Table 2. Quantitative comparison of results for intensity images produced by denoising approaches via PSNR (top) and SSIM (bottom)

Approaches→ / Images, σ	EPLL [15] 10	20	50	100	K-SVD [3] 10	20	50	100	NCSR [5] 10	20	50	100	BM3D [7] 10	20	50	100	Proposed Approach 10	20	50	100
Lena	35.56	32.60	28.42	25.30	32.28	31.23	27.78	24.49	35.81	32.92	28.89	25.66	35.92	33.05	29.04	25.91	35.81	32.97	29.03	25.72
	0.9126	0.8684	0.7713	0.6573	0.8608	0.8414	0.7603	0.6447	0.9149	0.8760	0.8026	0.7257	0.9167	0.8777	0.8004	0.7081	0.9158	0.8771	0.8031	0.7127
Barbara	33.59	29.75	24.83	22.10	30.59	29.42	25.43	21.87	34.98	31.72	27.10	23.30	34.92	31.70	27.16	23.70	34.92	31.67	26.95	22.93
	0.9319	0.8744	0.7031	0.5441	0.8757	0.8471	0.7128	0.5335	0.9411	0.9045	0.7962	0.6498	0.9419	0.9043	0.7914	0.6461	0.9414	0.9038	0.7881	0.6130
Couple	33.78	30.47	26.22	23.34	29.89	28.73	25.25	22.61	33.94	30.56	26.21	23.22	34.02	30.77	26.43	23.49	33.96	30.64	26.38	23.43
	0.9077	0.8364	0.6883	0.5380	0.8110	0.7739	0.6318	0.5012	0.9064	0.8363	0.6925	0.5554	0.9087	0.8467	0.7052	0.5652	0.9084	0.8432	0.7055	0.5719
Fingerprint	32.13	28.29	23.58	19.80	28.30	27.05	23.07	18.33	32.70	28.99	24.53	21.29	32.44	28.79	24.49	21.58	32.57	28.87	24.49	21.25
	0.9678	0.9262	0.8022	0.5877	0.9188	0.8920	0.7456	0.4406	0.9704	0.9327	0.8260	0.6816	0.9688	0.9297	0.8296	0.7101	0.9694	0.9304	0.8332	0.7069
Hill	33.49	30.47	26.91	24.37	30.04	29.08	26.25	24.01	33.69	30.61	26.86	24.13	33.59	30.71	27.13	24.57	33.66	30.66	27.02	24.43
	0.8859	0.7983	0.6597	0.5381	0.7715	0.7349	0.6193	0.5269	0.8864	0.8013	0.6586	0.5541	0.8830	0.8046	0.6708	0.5628	0.8866	0.8052	0.6661	0.5620
Man	33.90	30.53	26.63	23.96	29.97	28.93	26.03	23.40	33.96	30.52	26.60	23.97	33.95	30.55	26.76	24.21	33.97	30.55	26.66	23.89
	0.9093	0.8347	0.6943	0.5690	0.8083	0.7730	0.6628	0.5493	0.9069	0.8311	0.6976	0.6022	0.9077	0.8322	0.7013	0.5965	0.9082	0.8328	0.7000	0.5966
Peppers	34.51	31.18	26.60	22.93	30.57	29.43	26.08	21.69	34.66	31.26	26.53	22.64	34.65	31.22	26.69	23.23	34.56	31.13	26.62	22.71
	0.9273	0.8854	0.7847	0.6595	0.8700	0.8491	0.7662	0.6118	0.9262	0.8861	0.7969	0.6958	0.9269	0.8834	0.7849	0.6736	0.9248	0.8810	0.7803	0.6453
Average	33.85	30.47	26.17	23.11	30.23	29.12	25.70	22.34	34.25	30.94	26.67	23.45	34.21	30.97	26.81	23.81	34.21	30.93	26.74	23.48
	0.9204	0.8605	0.7291	0.5848	0.8452	0.8159	0.6998	0.5440	0.9217	0.8668	0.7529	0.6378	0.9220	0.8684	0.7548	0.6375	0.9221	0.8676	0.7538	0.6289

particular depth level. Hence, there is larger chance of error in grouping similar patches appropriately by the existing approaches, because of noise. Here, the proposed transform domain grouping strategy helps to better group the similar patches. This further helps in achieving better results as the performance of the grouping based techniques mostly depend on accuracy of measuring similarity of patches.

The results are further compared visually in Figs. 2, 3, 4, and 5 for $\sigma = 50$ & 100. One can observe that the visual results of the proposed approach is consistent with the quantitative improvements over existing approaches.

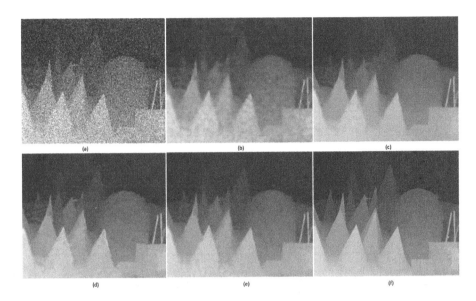

Fig. 2. Denoising results for noisy cones image ($\sigma = 50$): (a) the noisy image (PSNR = 14.12). Result of (b) K-SVD denoising [3] (PSNR = 31.89), (c) NCSR [5] (PSNR = 33.98), (d) BM3D [7] (PSNR = 33.96), (e) proposed approach (PSNR = 34.17), and (f) the ground truth image.

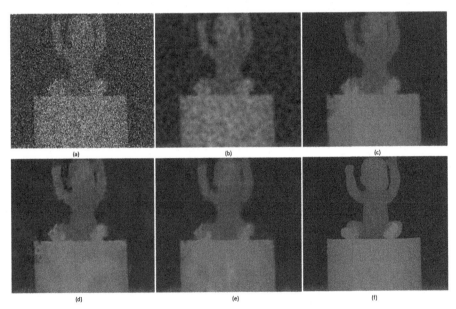

Fig. 3. Denoising results for noisy baby image ($\sigma = 100$): (a) the noisy image (PSNR = 8.11). Result of (b) K-SVD denoising [3] (PSNR = 28.09), (c) NCSR [5] (PSNR = 32.11), (d) BM3D [7] (PSNR = 31.25), (e) proposed approach (PSNR = 32.43), and (f) the ground truth image.

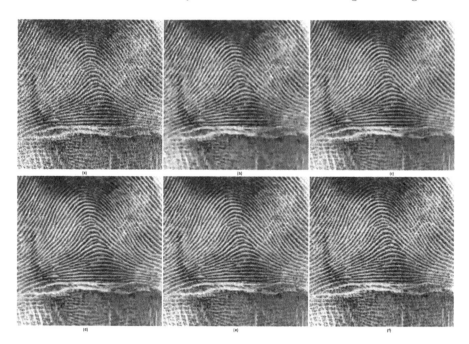

Fig. 4. Denoising results for noisy fingerprint image ($\sigma = 50$): (a) the noisy image (PSNR = 14.14). Result of (b) K-SVD denoising [3] (PSNR = 23.07), (c) NCSR [5] (PSNR = 24.53), (d) BM3D [7] (PSNR = 24.49), (e) proposed approach (PSNR = 24.49), and (f) the ground truth image.

4.1 Comparisons and Analysis Among Orthogonal Transformations and Filtering Technique

Here, we compare the results of different orthogonal transformations such as discrete cosine transform (DCT), Haar-wavelet and discrete Fourier transform (DFT). As contrast to these transformations, for comparison guided image filtering (GIF) technique [19] is also employed as pre-processing technique before the actual grouping of similar patches in order to observe the differences between filtering technique and orthogonal transformation techniques. The average PSNR and average SSIM of the 7 intensity and range images (mentioned in Tables) are shown in separate bar plots in Fig. 6 for different powers of noise (AWGN: $\sigma_n = 25, 50, 100$). The results of intensity image denoising are shown in Fig. 6(a) and (b). On the other hand, the results of range image denoising are shown in Fig. 6(c) and (d).

One can observe that the blue colored bars (DFT) are achieving almost similar heights as the yellow colored bars (DCT). This observation reminds us the similarity between DFT and DCT. Actually, computation of DCT of a sequence involves computation of DFT coefficients. However, the energy compaction property of DCT is better than that of DFT. Hence, the information after thresholding the coefficients of DCT is more than that of DFT. As a consequence, the results of DCT is slightly better than the DFT.

It has to be noted that the cyan colored bars (the results of Haar-wavelet transform) are bit shorter as compared to the other bars. The reason being that the energy compaction property of Haar-wavelet is poor as compared to DFT and DCT. Hence, thresholding operation leads to loss of much information, and the measured similarity between patches are not quite accurate as compared to the DCT and DFT. Thus, the produced results are lagging behind the other transformations.

In some cases, the results of GIF [19] (the red colored bar) is slightly trailing as compared to DCT. This is because, the GIF technique requires a guided image to process the target image. However, absence of guided image will compel the technique to use the target image as a guided image. Since, the target image is noisy, here the guidance may not be appropriate enough to produce a better result. However, using this technique as a pre-processing step will increase the computational load as it involves solving cost function with linear regression as compared to the proposed shrinkage operation, which does not involve any cost function minimization.

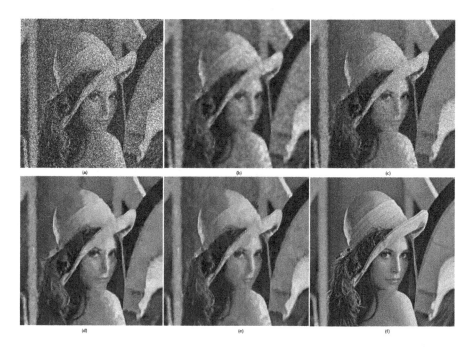

Fig. 5. Denoising results for noisy Lena image (σ = 100): (a) the noisy image (PSNR = 8.12). Result of (b) K-SVD denoising [3] (PSNR = 24.49), (c) NCSR [5] (PSNR = 25.66), (d) BM3D [7] (PSNR = 25.91), (e) the proposed approach (PSNR = 25.72), and (f) the ground truth image.

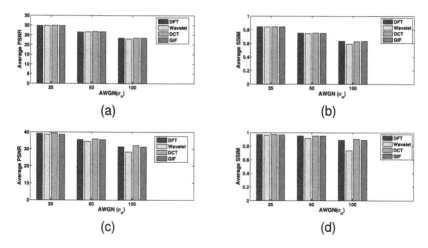

Fig. 6. Comparisons of results: DFT (Blue) vs. Wavelet (Cyan) vs. DCT (Yellow) vs. GIF (Red) [19] for different powers of noise (AWGN: $\sigma_n = 25, 50, 100$); (a) average PSNR for intensity images; (b) average SSIM for intensity images; (c) average PSNR for range images and (d) average SSIM for range images. (Color figure online)

Following the above observation and analysis, we can conclude that the DCT transformation produces better results in terms of average PSNR and SSIM for intensity as well as range images. Hence, in all our experiments, we have used DCT transformation for grouping of similar patches.

5 Summary

We have proposed a denoising strategy in the sparse representation framework based on non-local grouping of similar patches in transform domain. We demonstrate that the transform domain grouping is robust to noise. This transform domain similarity has been used to learn dictionaries as well as to estimate a sparse coefficient vector of clean image patches. The experimental results have demonstrated the effectiveness of the proposed transform domain patch similarity.

References

1. Rudin, L.I., Osher, S., Fatemi, E.: Nonlinear total variation based noise removal algorithms. Phys. D Nonlinear Phenom. **60**(1–4), 259–268 (1992)
2. Levin, A., Weiss, Y., Durand, F., Freeman, W.: Efficient marginal likelihood optimization in blind deconvolution. In: 2011 IEEE Conference on Computer Vision and Pattern Recognition (CVPR), pp. 2657–2664, June 2011
3. Elad, M., Aharon, M.: Image denoising via sparse and redundant representations over learned dictionaries. IEEE Trans. Image Process. **15**(12), 3736–3745 (2006)

4. Sulam, J., Elad, M.: Expected patch log likelihood with a sparse prior. In: Tai, X.-C., Bae, E., Chan, T.F., Lysaker, M. (eds.) EMMCVPR 2015. LNCS, vol. 8932, pp. 99–111. Springer, Cham (2015). https://doi.org/10.1007/978-3-319-14612-6_8

5. Dong, W., Zhang, L., Shi, G., Li, X.: Nonlocally centralized sparse representation for image restoration. IEEE Trans. Image Process. **22**(4), 1620–1630 (2013)

6. Buades, A., Coll, B., Morel, J.: A review of image denoising algorithms, with a new one. Multiscale Model. Simul. **4**(2), 490–530 (2005)

7. Katkovnik, V., Foi, A., Egiazarian, K., Astola, J.: From local kernel to nonlocal multiple-model image denoising. Int. J. Comput. Vis. **86**(1), 1–32 (2010)

8. Mairal, J., Bach, F., Ponce, J., Sapiro, G., Zisserman, A.: Non-local sparse models for image restoration. In: 2009 IEEE 12th International Conference on Computer Vision, pp. 2272–2279, September 2009

9. Zoran, D., Weiss, Y.: From learning models of natural image patches to whole image restoration. In: 2011 IEEE International Conference on Computer Vision (ICCV), pp. 479–486 (2011)

10. Mandal, S., Kumari, S., Bhavsar, A., Sao, A.K.: Multi-scale image denoising while preserving edges in sparse domain. In: 2016 6th European Workshop on Visual Information Processing (EUVIP), pp. 1–6, October 2016

11. Hu, W., Li, X., Cheung, G., Au, O.: Depth map denoising using graph-based transform and group sparsity. In: IEEE International Workshop on Multimedia Signal Processing (MMSP), pp. 001–006. IEEE (2013)

12. Jiao, J., Yang, Q., He, S., Gu, S., Zhang, L., Lau, R.W.: Joint image denoising and disparity estimation via stereo structure PCA and noise-tolerant cost. Int. J. Comput. Vis. **124**(2), 1–19 (2017). Please check and confirm if the inserted details for Ref. [12] is correct

13. Daubechies, I., Defrise, M., De Mol, C.: An iterative thresholding algorithm for linear inverse problems with a sparsity constraint. Commun. Pure Appl. Math. **57**(11), 1413–1457 (2004)

14. Zontak, M., Mosseri, I., Irani, M.: Separating signal from noise using patch recurrence across scales. In: 2013 IEEE Conference on Computer Vision and Pattern Recognition (CVPR), pp. 1195–1202 (2013)

15. Zoran, D., Weiss, Y.: From learning models of natural image patches to whole image restoration. In: IEEE International Conference on Computer Vision (ICCV), pp. 479–486, November 2011

16. Scharstein, D., Pal, C.: Learning conditional random fields for stereo. In: 2007 IEEE Conference on Computer Vision and Pattern Recognition, CVPR 2007, pp. 1–8, June 2007

17. Hirschmuller, H., Scharstein, D.: Evaluation of cost functions for stereo matching. In: 2007 IEEE Conference on Computer Vision and Pattern Recognition, CVPR 2007, pp. 1–8, June 2007

18. Wang, Z., Bovik, A., Sheikh, H., Simoncelli, E.: Image quality assessment: from error visibility to structural similarity. IEEE Trans. Image Process. **13**(4), 600–612 (2004)

19. He, K., Sun, J., Tang, X.: Guided image filtering. IEEE Trans. Pattern Anal. Mach. Intell. **35**(6), 1397–1409 (2013)

Multi-modal Image Analysis for Plant Stress Phenotyping

Swati Bhugra$^{(\boxtimes)}$, Anupama Anupama, Santanu Chaudhury, Brejesh Lall, and Archana Chugh

Indian Institute of Technology, Delhi, Delhi, India
{eez138301,santanuc,brejesh}@ee.iitd.ac.in,
{blz138031,achugh}@bioschool.iitd.ac.in

Abstract. Drought stress detection involves multi-modal image analysis with high spatio-temporal resolution. Identification of digital traits that characterizes drought stress response (DSR) is challenging due to high volume of image based features. Also, the labelled data that categorizes DSR are either unavailable or subjectively developed, which is a low-throughput and error-prone task. Therefore, we propose a novel framework that provides an automated scoring of DSR based on multi-trait fusion. k-means clustering was used to extract latent drought clusters and the relevant traits were identified using Support Vector Machine-Recursive Feature Extraction (SVM-RFE). Using these traits, SVM based DSR classification model was constructed. The framework has been validated on visible and thermal shoot images of rice plants, yielding 95% accuracy. Various imaging modalities can be integrated with the proposed framework, thus making it scalable as no prior information about the DSR was assumed.

Keywords: Support Vector Machines (SVM) · k-means clustering
Drought stress · Thermal images
Support Vector Machine-Recursive Feature Extraction (SVM-RFE)
Multi-modal analysis

1 Introduction

Drought is one of the major abiotic stress factor that limits crop productivity [1]. Therefore, there is a need to develop drought tolerant cultivars. In order to develop such cultivars, researchers rely on collection of specific traits related to plant structure and function such as temperature, water status, leaf area etc. (also termed as plant phenotyping) [2]. Different sensor technologies such as visible light imaging, thermal imaging, hyperspectral imaging etc. have been

Electronic supplementary material The online version of this chapter (https://doi.org/10.1007/978-981-13-0020-2_24) contains supplementary material, which is available to authorized users.

employed in a high throughput set-up to temporally monitor large plant populations non-destructively [3]. This results in huge amounts of data with high spatial and temporal resolution. Machine learning (ML) can be employed to discover the underlying governing principles of drought that are too complex to model mathematically using various image derived traits and sensor data [4]. For example, to detect leaf senescence in tomato due to drought stress, simplex volume maximisation (SiVM) was employed using hyperspectral images. This provided new insights by extracting hyperspectral signatures for different levels of senescence [5]. Another study in [6] used Dirichlet-aggregation regression (DAR) to detect leaf senescence in barley as a drought stress response using hyperspectral images. Smith et al. [7] employed Support Vector Machines (SVM) and Gaussian Processes Classifier (GPC) to classify between two categories i.e. well-watered and soil moisture deficit, using thermal and visible images of spinach canopy. However, this study did not capture the temporal evolution of drought stress response because the data was captured on a single day. A limitation of the aforementioned studies is that they are individually designed to study specific traits as a response to drought stress, whereas drought stress does not manifest itself in local symptoms [8]. Recently, Chen et al. [9] obtained image derived traits from various modalities. With no well-defined stress response classes, principle component analysis (PCA) was employed to obtain new set of features for qualitative visualisation the drought symptoms. However, this cannot be utilized to quantify drought stress response.

Under drought stress, the allocation of resources involves the whole plant and the stress response symptoms occur throughout the plant. This requires simultaneous analysis by multiple sensors [8,10]. Thus, in this work we suggest a more robust technique to obtain a discrete representation of progressive drought based on fusion of multiple digital traits for high-throughput analysis, by utilizing a time series of multi-modal images. We empirically demonstrate that automatically computed level of drought stress response based on multi-trait analysis allow for accurate quantification and interpretation of stress dispersion in rice. To the best of our knowledge, this is the first work based on simultaneous drought stress analysis by multiple sensors. The rest of the paper is organised as follows: In Sect. 2 the experiment protocol for data acquisition is elucidated, Sect. 3 explains the methodology of the proposed algorithm and in Sect. 4 the results are discussed.

2   Dataset

Two series of drought experiments were conducted on rice during kharif season of 2015 and 2016 (Table 1). In the first experiment (Dataset-2015), a visible camera (Canon 60D EOS) with eight mega-pixel resolution was employed to quantify leaf rolling and senescence. To quantify plant water status, a thermal camera (UNIQ Vision USS 301 CCIR) with an optical resolution of 752×582 was used. After the image data collection, leaf samples of the plants were collected for the estimation of relative water content (RWC) [11] and chlorophyll content [12]. The

Table 1. Experimental details

	Dataset-(2015)	Dataset-(2016)
Method	Non-destructive	Non-destructive
Genotype	Sahbhagi Dhan, CR262, MTU-1010, IR64	Pusa-44, Nerica L-44, CR262, MTU-1010
Imaging	Visible, thermal	Visible, thermal
Observation days	5	5
Modes	Top-view, 4 Side-view	Top-view, 4 Side-view
Number of visible images	200	100
Number of thermal images	200	100

second experiment (Dataset-2016) was conducted in a controlled environment, non-destructively to validate the proposed framework under different drought environments. The experimental set-up for the image data acquisition was similar to that used to acquire Dataset-2015. In the next section, the workflow of the proposed framework is discussed.

3 Methodology

The input to the framework (shown in supplementary Fig. 1) is a time series of plant images corresponding to different imaging modalities. In this study, we chose to record the images in the visible and thermal spectrum because of the relatively low cost and wide availability of these systems. The steps of the framework are explained below.

3.1 Feature Extraction Based on Visible Images

Leaf senescence and rolling are drought induced responses caused due to chlorophyll degradation and loss of turgidity in the plants respectively [13,14]. Plant canopy in visible images can be employed to characterize these aforementioned responses non-intrusively [15,16]. Since the visible images contain plant canopy and non-canopy elements such as soil, water and background, graph-cut segmentation is employed to extract the canopy [17]. Graph-cut is a binary (object/background) labelling algorithm based on global optimization of discrete cost function shown below:

$$E(A) = \lambda \sum_{p \in P} R_p(A_p) + \sum_{p,q \in N} B_{(p,q)} \delta_{A_p \neq A_q} \qquad (1)$$

where P is a set of pixels in the image, N is a set of all pairs $\{p, q\}$ of neighbouring elements in P. $A = \{A_1, A_2, \ldots A_p\}$ and A_p specify assignments (object/background) to pixels p in P. R describes the region property and B describes the boundary property of A. λ specifies the relative importance of region property versus boundary property.

Leaf color is a simple, but powerful pixel based feature which is robust to changes in scale, resolution and partial occlusion. Thus, to quantify leaf discolouration, segmented images are stored in three colour channels: RGB (red, green, blue), HSV (Hue, saturation, value) and $L^*a^*b^*$. This results in three histograms for each colour space. The skewness, kurtosis, mean, standard-deviation and mode are computed to characterize these distributions [18,19]. On the other hand, to quantify the degree of rolling, shape based descriptors namely compactness [15] is extracted from the segmented images (top-view). To achieve this, quick hull algorithm [20] is used to obtain a convex hull and then compactness (defined as the ratio between the top view leaf pixels and the convex hull) is computed.

3.2 Feature Extraction Based on Thermal Images

Thermal imaging can be employed for extracting the temperature profiles of plant canopy [21]. But, segmentation of the plant canopy in the grayscale thermal images is difficult due to the variable intensity between plant and background. Thus, using a fixed thermal threshold to separate plant canopy from background provided inaccurate segmentation. Therefore, the segmented canopy in the RGB images is used as a mask to obtain the corresponding thermal plant canopy. The thermal and colour images of rice genotypes, in the experiment were acquired simultaneously but with different sensors and from different viewpoints. Thus, the images must be aligned using a transformation such that the pixel location in both the images correspond to the same physical location. Leinonen [22] manually obtained corresponding points between the thermal and colour images to compute this transformation which is a low-throughput process. Hence for automatic registration, Mattes Mutual Information algorithm [23] is employed. In this algorithm, single set (S) of intensity samples is drawn from the images followed by computation of the marginal and joint probability density function (PDF) evaluated at discrete positions (uniformly spread bins) obtained from set (S). In this method, superposition kernel functions $K(.)$ are centred on the elements of S, given by:

$$P(x) = \frac{1}{N} \sum_{j \in S} K(x - s_j) \tag{2}$$

A zero order B-spline kernel is used to compute the PDF of the fixed image (thermal), while a third order B-spline kernel is used to compute the PDF of the moving image (visible). Mutual information (MI) is computed using the entropies as $I(X, Y) = H(X) + H(Y) - H(X, Y)$, where X and Y define the image intensities of the two images. The moving image is rotated and/or translated, until the MI between the two images is maximized. At maximum MI, the segmented visible image is used as a mask to overlay the thermal image to obtain the plant canopy. After the segmentation step, thermal map of the canopy is obtained as an intensity histogram feature vector. The skewness, kurtosis, mean, standard-deviation and mode are extracted from the thermal histogram to characterize the drought response of rice plants.

3.3   Quantification of Drought Stress

The digital traits extracted (previous subsections) are fused at the feature level after z-score normalisation to create a new feature vector ($\mathbf{f}_{new}$) that contains complementary information about different physiological and morphological information of rice plants under drought stress. However, well defined labels corresponding to these traits, are either not available or are subjectively created, which is a low-throughput and often error prone task. The lack of well-defined classes is due to (a) the differential response of plants after drought stress induction and, (b) its variance among the replicates of a cultivar (genotype). Since, drought is a latent variable that triggers the aforementioned physiological response, k-means [24] is employed to automatically compute different drought response levels using this feature ($\mathbf{f}_{new}$). k-means partitions data into k mutually exclusive clusters (hard assignment) and returns the index of the cluster to which it has assigned each data point. Silhouette coefficients [25] is estimated from each data point (for different values of k). The largest average silhouette width, over different k, indicates the best number of clusters and the resulting cluster indices are utilized as stress response labels for the training and testing of data points to be used in the subsequent steps.

Rice shows a large variation with respect to drought adaptation [26]. Hence, a large amount of features needs to be extracted from multiple modalities to obtain a comprehensive assessment of the drought response. However, the different drought responses (e.g. leaf senescence, leaf rolling etc.) are characterized by distinct digital traits [3]. Thus, to identify and select relevant features that accurately characterize different degrees of drought response, a wrapper approach SVM-RFE (Support Vector Machine-Recursive Feature Elimination) [27] is employed. In contrast to the filter and embedded based feature selection approach that have been developed in recent years, a wrapper based approach is used as the redundancies between the features do not affect its performance and it can easily adapt to the classification algorithm. The filter methods utilises single feature characteristics to obtain the feature ranking and its performance is affected by the presence of redundant features. On the other hand, embedded methods ranks features based on parameters obtained during the training phase of the machine learning algorithm. SVM-RFE [27] performs feature selection in a recursive backward manner, by discarding one feature at a time. Support Vector Machine (SVM) [28] is used as the learning algorithm in this wrapper approach. For binary problems, the decision function is given by, $f(\mathbf{x}) = \mathbf{w}^T \phi(\mathbf{x}) + b$, where the training data are mapped to higher dimensional space $\mathcal{H}$ by the function $\mathbf{x} \rightarrow \phi(\mathbf{x}) \in \mathcal{H}$ and b is a scalar. SVM minimizes the following optimisation problem:

$$\min_{\mathbf{w},b,\zeta} \quad \frac{1}{2}\|\mathbf{w}\|^2 + C\sum_{i=1}^{m}\zeta_i \tag{3}$$

$$subject\ to:\ \zeta_i \geq 0, \quad i = 1.......,m$$
$$y_i(\mathbf{w}^T.\phi(\mathbf{x}) + b) \geq 1 - \zeta_i, \quad i = 1...,m$$

where, C is a penalty parameter, ζ_i is the slack variable and y_i is the class label for the ith data point and m is the number of training data points. The optimal hyperplane is the one with the maximal distance (in $\mathcal{H}$) to the closest $\phi(\mathbf{x_i})$. The dual formulation with kernel function $K(\mathbf{x},\mathbf{y}) = \phi(\mathbf{x}).\phi(\mathbf{y})$ can be written as follows:

$$\max_{\alpha} \quad \sum_{i=1}^{m}\alpha_i - \frac{1}{2}\sum_{i,s=1}^{m}\alpha_i\alpha_s y_i y_s K(\mathbf{x_i},\mathbf{x_s}) \tag{4}$$

$$subject\ to:\ \sum_{i1}^{m}\alpha_i y_i = 0,\ 0 \leq \alpha_i \leq C, \quad i = 1,\ldots,m$$

After training SVM to obtain optimum hyperplane and α for each feature p, in the next step the feature with the smallest value of $|W^2(\alpha) - W^2_{-p}(\alpha)|$ is removed, where $W^2(\alpha)$ (given by Eq. (5)) measures the model predictive ability and is inversely proportional to the margin. $W^2_{-p}(\alpha)$ with feature p removed is given by Eq. (6).

$$W^2(\alpha) = \sum_{i,s=1}^{m}\alpha_i\alpha_s y_i y_s K(\mathbf{x_i},\mathbf{x_s}) \tag{5}$$

$$W^2_{-p}(\alpha) = \sum_{i,s=1}^{m}\alpha_i\alpha_s y_i y_s K(\mathbf{x_i^{-P}},\mathbf{x_s^{-P}}) \tag{6}$$

where, $\mathbf{x}_i^{-P}$ is the ith training data with feature p removed. This procedure is repeated until only one feature remains, which results in a list of features in the order of weights and can be used to obtain relevant features. In our case, this feature subset comprises of the relevant image-based phenotypic traits which are used to train the classification model for different levels of drought response.

4   Results and Discussions

In this section we demonstrate the effectiveness of our proposed framework by presenting the experimental results. The result of the Graph-cut segmentation is shown in Fig. 1(B). The segmented rice canopy in colour images was employed through the process of registration using maximisation of mutual information to extract the rice canopy in thermal images. After image registration between the colour and its corresponding thermal image, the segmented region in the colour image was used as a mask to extract the canopy in the thermal image (Fig. 2(B)).

(A)   (B)

Fig. 1. Segmentation of visible images using Graph-cut. (A) Corresponds to the visible image of plant canopy and (B) shows the corresponding segmented image of MTU-1010 under control.

(A)   (B)

Fig. 2. Segmentation of thermal images using multi-modal registration. (A) Corresponds to the colour image and right is the corresponding thermal image of MTU-1010 at 3rd day stress and (B) shows the overlay of segmented plant canopy (colour image) on thermal image after image registration. (Color figure online)

The image based phenotypic parameters obtained from visible and thermal images (as mentioned in previous subsections) were z-score normalised and fused at feature level to create a new feature set ($\mathbf{f}_{new}$) and k-means clustering was employed to extract latent drought clusters. Based on silhouette analysis, the average silhouette value was the largest for $k = 3$ (average silhouette value = .928, shown in supplementary Fig. 2(B)), suggesting it as the optimum k. The resultant indices were investigated and it was observed that the first cluster contained the control plant. Thus, we termed this cluster as "control". Similarly, second cluster contained the majority of the plants corresponding to first day of drought and second day of drought, thus we have assigned the label "mild-stress". Third cluster contained the plant belonging to fourth and the fifth days of drought stress, and thus it was labelled as "high-stress". Since three different drought responses were obtained using k-means, multiclass SVM approach [29, 30] was implemented by decomposing it into three binary problems with

One-vs.-One strategy. The reason to employ One-vs.-One in contrast to One-vs.-Rest was to build separate classification models that quantify the difference between individual drought response categories as they correspond to distinct phenotypic traits, whereas through one-versus-rest strategy the in-between drought response differences cannot be formulated. To obtain the multi-class model, following procedure was employed (shown in supplementary Fig. 3):

1. Given samples from every two classes i, j $(i, j \in 1, 2, 3$ and $i \neq j)$, feature ranking $F_{i,j}$ was obtained using SVM-RFE as explained in previous subsection.
2. For different binary SVMs the feature subset $(\hat{F}_{i,j} = f_1, f_2 \ldots, f_s)$ that corresponds to maximum prediction accuracy was obtained.
3. After feature selection, these binary SVMs were trained using their corresponding feature subsets.
4. In the evaluation step, each binary SVM extracts the corresponding $\hat{F}_{i,j}$ of the test data and the winning class is added a vote. The class with the maximum vote determines the final prediction.

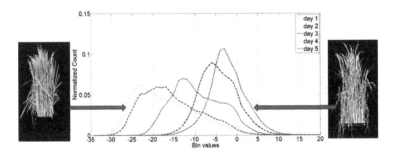

Fig. 3. Temporal evolution of a^* component distribution of MTU-1010 under drought. (Color figure online)

This procedure was employed to extract a different feature subset to discriminate between two different drought categories before building the final multiclass SVM model. Three relevant features were obtained: mean of a* component distribution, mode of thermal histogram and compactness. Since similar results were obtained from the four rice cultivars i.e. CR262, MTU-1010, IR64 and Sahbhagi Dhan, phenotypic features from the MTU-1010 dataset have been shown. Index a^* represents the visual perception of the green-red chroma $(+a^*$ reds, $-a^*$ greens) and from Fig. 3 the shift from the negative a^* values towards the positive a^* values can be observed as the magnitude of the increase in drought stress. The mean of a^* component has been denoted as leaf discolouration. Thus, chlorophyll content was correlated with the leaf discolouration to examine the relationship between them. Leaf discolouration showed a correlation of 0.85 $(p < 0.05)$ (figure not shown), which was the maximum in comparison to the other colour

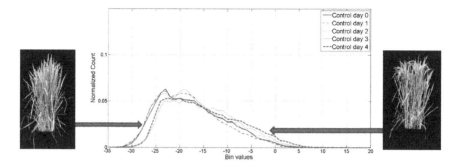

Fig. 4. Temporal evolution of a^* component distribution of MTU-1010 under control.

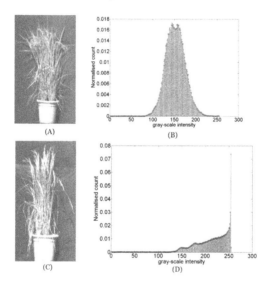

Fig. 5. Temporal evolution of gray-level histogram (A) and (B) shows the thermal image of MTU-1010 and gray-level histogram under control condition respectively. (C) and (D) shows the thermal image and gray-level histogram at 5th day of drought stress respectively.

histograms. The intensity histogram feature vector obtained from the thermal images is shown in Fig. 5. Since previous studies [31] have shown that canopy temperature was found to be negatively correlated with relative water content (RWC) across diverse wheat and rice genotypes, we have employed RWC as a proxy indicator of canopy temperature. Thermal-mode extracted from the distribution showed negative correlation of 0.88 ($p < 0.01$) (as shown in Fig. 6) with RWC. This implies that higher gray-scale intensity values corresponds to lower RWC (plant water status) and vice-versa. The high correlation between the image based phenotypic traits and the corresponding traditional traits (RWC & chlorophyll) further validates their importance.

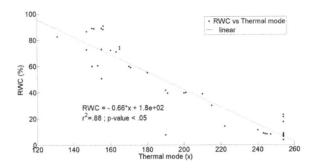

Fig. 6. Correlation between RWC and thermal mode of MTU-1010

Table 2. Confusion matrix for Dataset-2016

	Control	Mild-stress	High-stress
Control	38	2	0
Mild-stress	1	28	1
High-stress	0	1	29

Using these relevant features, final multi-class model was formulated to classify different levels of drought response and it was evaluated with Dataset-2016. The confusion matrix for Dataset-2016 (Table 2) shows that the misclassification was obtained only between the neighbouring classes with high separability between control and high-stress class. The classification model yielded an accuracy of 95%, thus showing the efficiency of the proposed framework for drought stress characterization.

5   Conclusion

In this study, we presented a novel framework based on integration of various image based phenotypic parameters that enables classification of drought stress response. The labelled data for different phenotypic responses under drought are either subjectively developed or are not available. This problem was resolved by combining supervised (SVM) and unsupervised (k-means) algorithms for drought stress response classification. The proposed framework yielded an accuracy of 95% on rice images, showing the efficiency for drought stress characterization in an accurate, reliable and high-throughput way. Drought tolerance is a complex process and various imaging modalities are needed to comprehensively study the overall drought responses. In this process, a large amount of data will be accumulated with redundant phenotypic features. Thus our framework, which is based on image processing and machine learning, will prove significant.

References

1. Furbank, R.T., Tester, M.: Phenomics–technologies to relieve the phenotyping bottleneck. Trends Plant Sci. **16**(12), 635–644 (2011)
2. Ghanem, M.E., Marrou, H., Sinclair, T.R.: Physiological phenotyping of plants for crop improvement. Trends Plant Sci. **20**(3), 139–144 (2015)
3. Li, L., Zhang, Q., Huang, D.: A review of imaging techniques for plant phenotyping. Sensors **14**(11), 20078–20111 (2014)
4. Singh, A., Ganapathysubramanian, B., Singh, A.K., Sarkar, S.: Machine learning for high-throughput stress phenotyping in plants. Trends Plant Sci. **21**(2), 110–124 (2016)
5. Romer, C., Wahabzada, M., Ballvora, A., Pinto, F., Rossini, M., Panigada, C., Behmann, J., Leon, J., Thurau, C., Bauckhage, C., et al.: Early drought stress detection in cereals: simplex volume maximisation for hyperspectral image analysis. Funct. Plant Biol. **39**(11), 878–890 (2012)
6. Kersting, K., Xu, Z., Wahabzada, M., Bauckhage, C., Thurau, C., Roemer, C., Ballvora, A., Rascher, U., Leon, J., Pluemer, L.: Pre-symptomatic prediction of plant drought stress using Dirichlet aggregation regression on hyperspectral images. In: AAAI (2012)
7. Smith, H.K., Clarkson, G.J., Taylor, G., Thompson, A.J., Clarkson, J., Rajpoot, N.M., et al.: Automatic detection of regions in spinach canopies responding to soil moisture deficit using combined visible and thermal imagery. PLoS ONE **9**(6), e97612 (2014)
8. Humplík, J.F., Lazar, D., Husickova, A., Spíchal, L.: Automated phenotyping of plant shoots using imaging methods for analysis of plant stress responses–a review. Plant Methods **11**(1), 1 (2015)
9. Chen, D., Neumann, K., Friedel, S., Kilian, B., Chen, M., Altmann, T., Klukas, C.: Dissecting the phenotypic components of crop plant growth and drought responses based on high-throughput image analysis. Plant Cell **26**(12), 4636–4655 (2014)
10. Minervini, M., Scharr, H., Tsaftaris, S.A.: Image analysis: the new bottleneck in plant phenotyping [applications corner]. IEEE Signal Process. Mag. **32**(4), 126–131 (2015)
11. Barrs, H., Weatherley, P.: A re-examination of the relative turgidity technique for estimating water deficits in leaves. Aust. J. Biol. Sci. **15**(3), 413–428 (1962)
12. Richardson, A.D., Duigan, S.P., Berlyn, G.P.: An evaluation of noninvasive methods to estimate foliar chlorophyll content. New Phytol. **153**(1), 185–194 (2002)
13. Munne-Bosch, S., Alegre, L.: Die and let live: leaf senescence contributes to plant survival under drought stress. Funct. Plant Biol. **31**(3), 203–216 (2004)
14. Pask, A., Pietragalla, J.: Leaf area, green crop area and senescence. In: Pask, A., Pietragalla, J., Mullan, D., Reynolds, M. (eds.) Physiological Breeding II: A Field Guide to Wheat Phenotyping, pp. 58–62 (2012)
15. Neilson, E.H., Edwards, A., Blomstedt, C., Berger, B., Moller, B.L., Gleadow, R.: Utilization of a high-throughput shoot imaging system to examine the dynamic phenotypic responses of a C4 cereal crop plant to nitrogen and water deficiency over time. J. Exp. Bot. (2015). https://doi.org/10.1093/jxb/eru526
16. Fahlgren, N., Feldman, M., Gehan, M.A., Wilson, M.S., Shyu, C., Bryant, D.W., Hill, S.T., McEntee, C.J., Warnasooriya, S.N., Kumar, I., et al.: A versatile phenotyping system and analytics platform reveals diverse temporal responses to water availability in Setaria. Mol. Plant **8**(10), 1520–1535 (2015)

17. Boykov, O.V.Y., Zabih, R.: Fast approximate energy minimization via graph cuts. IEEE Trans. Pattern Anal. Mach. Intell. **23**(11), 1 (2001)
18. Klukas, C., Chen, D., Pape, J.-M.: Integrated analysis platform: an open-source information system for high-throughput plant phenotyping. Plant Physiol. **165**(2), 506–518 (2014)
19. Breiman, L.: Statistics with a View Toward Applications, vol. 1. Houghton Mifflin Co., Boston (1973)
20. Barber, C.B., Dobkin, D.P., Huhdanpaa, H.: The quickhull algorithm for convex hulls. ACM Trans. Math. Softw. (TOMS) **22**(4), 469–483 (1996)
21. Jones, H.G., Serraj, R., Loveys, B.R., Xiong, L., Wheaton, A., Price, A.H.: Thermal infrared imaging of crop canopies for the remote diagnosis and quantification of plant responses to water stress in the field. Funct. Plant Biol. **36**(11), 978–989 (2009)
22. Leinonen, I., Jones, H.G.: Combining thermal and visible imagery for estimating canopy temperature and identifying plant stress. J. Exp. Bot. **55**(401), 1423–1431 (2004)
23. Raghunathan, S., Stredney, D., Schmalbrock, P., Clymer, B.D.: Image registration using rigid registration and maximization of mutual information. In: The 13th Annual Medicine Meets Virtual Reality Conference, Poster Presented at: MMVR13 (2005)
24. MacQueen, J., et al.: Some methods for classification and analysis of multivariate observations. In: Proceedings of the Fifth Berkeley Symposium on Mathematical Statistics and Probability, Oakland, CA, USA, vol. 1, no. 14, pp. 281–297 (1967)
25. Kaufman, L., Rousseeuw, P.J.: Finding Groups in Data: An Introduction to Cluster Analysis, vol. 344. Wiley, Hoboken (2009)
26. Hanson, A.D.: Drought resistance in rice. Nature **345**, 26–27 (1990)
27. Maldonado, S., Weber, R.: A wrapper method for feature selection using support vector machines. Inf. Sci. **179**(13), 2208–2217 (2009)
28. Cortes, C., Vapnik, V.: Support-vector networks. Mach. Learn. **20**(3), 273–297 (1995)
29. Liu, Y., You, Z., Cao, L.: A novel and quick SVM-based multi-class classifier. Pattern Recognit. **39**(11), 2258–2264 (2006)
30. Platt, J.C., Cristianini, N., Shawe-Taylor, J.: Large margin DAGs for multiclass classification. In: NIPS, vol. 12, pp. 547–553 (1999)
31. Blum, A.: Effective use of water (EUW) and not water-use efficiency (WUE) is the target of crop yield improvement under drought stress. Field Crop. Res. **112**(2), 119–123 (2009)

Source Classification Using Document Images from Smartphones and Flatbed Scanners

Sharad Joshi⬤, Gaurav Gupta, and Nitin Khanna(✉)

Multimedia Analysis and Security (MANAS) Lab, Electrical Engineering, Indian
Institute of Technology Gandhinagar (IITGN), Gandhinagar, Gujarat, India
{sharad.joshi,gaurav.gupta,nitinkhanna}@iitgn.ac.in

Abstract. With technological advancements, digital scans of printed
documents are increasingly used in many systems in place of the original hard copy documents. This convenience to use digital scans comes
at increased risk of potentially fraudulent and criminal activities due to
their easy manipulation. To curb such activities, identification of source
corresponding to a scanned document can provide important clues to
investigating agencies and also help build a secure communication system. This work utilizes local tetra patterns to capture unique device-
specific signatures from images of printed documents. In this first of its
kind work for scanner identification, the method uses all characters to
train a single classifier thereby, reducing the amount of training data
required. The proposed method depicts font size independence when
tested on an existing scanner dataset and a novel step towards font shape
independence when tested on a smart phone dataset of comparable size
(Supplementary material and code is available at https://sites.google.
com/view/manaslab).

Keywords: Scanner forensics · Source scanner identification
Smartphone identification · Printed documents · Local tetra patterns

1 Introduction

The fast-rising digital revolution being witnessed around the world comes against
a scare of security risks. Though digital documents are replacing paper in many
applications, use of printed documents cannot be completely replaced in the
foreseeable future owing to several reasons including issues with digital security,
ease of use, lack of expertise among members from specialized domains and
legal requirements. Also, relevant documents already printed in the past are
stored as digital archives to save on physical space and handling expenditures.
It also safeguards them against further wear and tears or natural calamities.
Such scanned archives provide an opportunity to access and use them from any
part of the world. As it provides a quick and environment-friendly solution,
so it is firmly establishing itself as a replacement for communicating printed

© Springer Nature Singapore Pte Ltd. 2018
R. Rameshan et al. (Eds.): NCVPRIPG 2017, CCIS 841, pp. 281–292, 2018.
https://doi.org/10.1007/978-981-13-0020-2_25

documents. Further, smart phones are becoming more prevalent instruments for generating digital scans of printed documents as compared to flatbed desktop scanners. However, any critical data archived in digital form is always prone to misuse. For example, a scenario where an unauthorized person makes a scanned archive of some important documents either from a flatbed scanner or a phone. Alternatively, a miscreant may interfere with sensitive legal or medical records of an adversary. To minimize damages caused by such acts, knowing the source scanner of a document image could provide valuable clues on its authenticity and potential perpetrators.

This paper addresses the problem of identifying source scanner/digital-camera/smart phone from a given image of a printed document. The proposed approach investigates input document image without the explicit knowledge of its content, based on the hypothesis that each scanner introduces some unique artifacts while scanning a page [3–7,10,14]. These artifacts/signatures depend upon the manufacturing defects in the scan head assembly (mirrors, lens, filter and CCD array), some other perturbations or on the drivers as sensors may blur and use some interpolation techniques [3]. In general, there can be more than one possible option for printers as well as scanners. In particular, for scenarios where a copy of document image is provided by a primary party to the secondary parties, the printer is already fixed and known beforehand. These documents may include medical records, insurance agreements, rental agreements, etc.

The problem of scanner source identification has recently started gaining attention of researchers [1,4–7,9,10,14]. It is worth noting that due to the presence of mostly saturated pixels (either completely black or white) and lack of continuous tones, the traditional camera source identification approaches are not applicable to this problem [9]. In [9], authors approach this problem by extracting gray level difference histogram (GLDH) based features from a group of 50 characters. However, its performance is not consistent across different font shapes and sizes. Another method based on dust and scratch detection [5] uses the absolute of a high-pass filtered image, and an image scanned with completely black or white background. It matches the two potential signatures based on their normalized cross-correlation values. An accuracy of 99.68% is reported with 150 images scanned at a resolution of 300 dpi from three scanners. In sharp contrast, the proposed method treats dust and scratches as unwanted noise since it will not be universal to the complete area of a scanned image and will strongly depend on time. In a recent work on detection of copy-move forgery in text documents [1], the authors use Zernike and Hu moments, PCA and KPCA. They report true positive rates up to 87% for varying font sizes on synthetically generated forgeries. The very nature of these features makes them shape dependent and unsuitable with a 'single' classifier (one classifier for all characters) approach or cross-font and cross-size experiments. In addition to these, there has been substantial research performed for identifying the source scanner of document images [4,6,7,10]. One recent method, which works on scanned hologram images [14], is based on correlation of color distributions. Such a method is specific to continuous toned color images. The methods discussed so far have not been analyzed with document images captured via smart phones and even the ones analyzed on scanners heavily depend on font shape and size. Though printed images captured from smart phones have been analyzed for copy-move forgery detection in [2]. Major contributions of this work are:

- A new single classifier based approach for source scanner identification which outperforms baseline method on the existing dataset.
- Font size independence by giving close to 100% page level accuracy with small differences in font sizes.
- Good performance on a new smartphone-based dataset for documents printed in three different fonts for both same font and cross font experiments.
- Substantial accuracy for decisions taken on every group of ten characters, thus paving the way for its use in sub-page level forgery detection.

2   Local Tetra Patterns

Local binary patterns (LBP) [12] based techniques have been very successful across multiple domains for texture classification. It provides a circular binary pattern in a small window based on the difference in pixel intensity values. It has also been used successfully in applications of forensics [8,16]. LBP, a 2-level pattern, was extended to local ternary patterns (LTP) [15] by accommodating for a transition interval thus achieving a 3-level pattern. Local derivative patterns (LDP) [17] extended LBP to higher orders by treating them as the first order. While, LTP and LDP work on the same fundamental principle as LBP, i.e., based on the difference of intensities of neighboring pixels, local tetra patterns (LTrP) [11] go a step further and encompass the relationship between intensity differences of neighboring pixels. In a comparison performed among the performance of various variants of LBP [13] for printer source identification [8], LTrP has shown the best performance. LTrP is a four directional code computed using two steps. First, the direction of each pixel in a given input image is computed from among four possibilities using the direction value at that pixel. The horizontal and vertical direction pairs at any pixel p is given as [11],

$$G_h(p) = I(q_h) - I(p) \text{ and } G_v(p) = I(q_v) - I(p).$$

Here, q_h and q_v are respectively the horizontal and vertical neighbors of central pixel p. They can be taken as either of the two possible neighbors. However, the order of neighbors must be kept fixed throughout an experiment. Based on this, the four direction are chosen as [11],

$$G_{dir}(p) = \begin{cases} 1, & G_h(p) \geq 0 \text{ and } G_v(p) \geq 0 \\ 2, & G_h(p) < 0 \text{ and } G_v(p) \geq 0 \\ 3, & G_h(p) < 0 \text{ and } G_v(p) < 0 \\ 4, & G_h(p) \geq 0 \text{ and } G_v(p) < 0 \end{cases} \tag{1}$$

Now, tetra patterns are estimated in a small window of size 3×3 by assigning a 'zero' corresponding to a neighboring pixel if its direction is same as the central pixel. Else, the direction of the neighboring pixel is assigned to that element as given by [11]

$$LTrP(p) = \{w_{LTrP}(G_{dir}(p), G_{dir}(q_0)),$$
$$w_{LTrP}(G_{dir}(p), G_{dir}(q_1)), \ldots, \tag{2}$$
$$w_{LTrP}(G_{dir}(p), G_{dir}(q_7))\},$$

where,

$$w_{LTrP}(G_{dir}(p), G_{dir}(q_n))$$
$$= \begin{cases} 0, & G_{dir}(p) = G_{dir}(q_n) \\ G_{dir}(q_n), & else \end{cases} \tag{3}$$

Each of these patterns have three non-zero distinct values. So, corresponding to each tetra pattern, three binary patterns could be formed. This gives a total of 12 binary patterns. Since magnitude and sign components when used together, work better than sign component alone, a magnitude based pattern is also introduced which is given by [11]

$$M(p) = \sum_{n=0}^{7} 2^n \times u[G_m(p) - G_m(q_n)] \tag{4}$$

where, $G_m(x) = \sqrt{(G_h(x))^2 + (G_v(x))^2}$.

3   Smartphone Attribution Method

The basic intuition behind this approach is that the desired signal remains the same irrespective of the content of the printed component. The same can be perceived from the zoomed characters of such documents as shown in Fig. 1. Further, the lowest unit of a potential forgery is a character. Forging could result in the insertion or replacement of the whole bounding box around a character or even only the printed area if an expert criminal is involved. Working on these ideas, the following steps are performed.

3.1   Segmentation

As discussed, the smallest unit of interest in a printed document is a text character. So, first, the input image is subjected to connected component analysis. This provides a bunch of segmented non-overlapping bounding boxes. Each page has approximately 3000 bounding boxes of interest. Boxes of very small or long length in either dimension or very small or very large area are filtered out to avoid spurious components. This is done separately for each input image by using adaptive thresholds based on the median of size and area of all the extracted boxes. This will in effect more or less segment out characters as long as the character set of the language comprises of connected components like English, Portugues, German, Hindi, etc. It is worth noting that in the proposed method, no preprocessing is applied before segmentation.

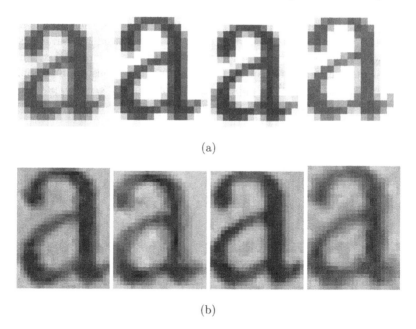

(a)

(b)

Fig. 1. Zoomed version of the letter 'a' captured from (a) four different scanners (top row) from the scanner dataset: S2, S3, S6, S7 (Table I in [9]) and (b) four different smartphones (bottom row) from the phone dataset: P2, P3, P6, P7 (Table 1).

3.2   Feature Extraction and Pooling

A feature vector is extracted from each of these bounding boxes. For this problem, LTrP [11] seemed to be an apt option which has been recently shown to work well on printer source identification [8]. The textures to be identified are situated inside both the printed and non-printed areas. This means that region of interest encompasses the whole bounding box of a connected component. For a particular bounding box, LTrP is extracted in the neighborhood of each pixel. Then a normalized 767 bin histogram is constructed from it. A total of 767 features (Sect. 2) are extracted from each bounding box. This is followed by post-extraction pooling (PoEP) [8] in which the feature vectors across a single document image are grouped into clusters of equal elements. Then an average feature vector is computed from each of those clusters. That is if there were 3000 feature vectors obtained from an image and they are divided into clusters of 10-elements each then only 300 feature vectors remain after application of PoEP. This step takes care of unwanted printer or scanner artifacts and averages them. In particular, the printer and scanner artifacts which are dependent on a character's shape are averaged by way of this technique [8], thereby, inducing font shape and size independence. As discussed, our feature vector is composed of counts of specific texture patterns captured from pixels inside the bounding box of a connected component. But some of these pattern counts will have a tendency to vary with a character's font shape and size. This can be inferred from zoomed versions of different characters shown in Fig. 2. In addition, there might be certain printer artifacts like tails and satellites [3] introduced in characters with varying frequency and at random locations inside the bounding box. Further, some non-recurring artifacts can occur due to instantaneous malfunctioning of printer mechanism. They may appear in the form of dark/light spots. Lastly, unwanted noise sources like dust and temporary scratches can be compensated for, by using this pooling technique.

Fig. 2. Zoomed version of the letters 'a', 'b', 'c' and 'd' printed from a specific printer and captured from a sample scanner.

3.3 Classification

The features are projected to a lower dimensional space using linear discriminant analysis (LDA). This results in a feature vector length of six. It not only improves performance but also reduces run time. Finally, the feature vectors with length six are fed into a support vector machine (SVM) which has proved to work successfully for many forensic applications.

4 Experimental Results

The proposed method is first tested on an existing dataset [9] which has eighty printed documents scanned each at 200 dpi resolution from seven different scanners. Forty of them comprise of different font sizes (14pt., 12pt., 10pt., 8pt.) printed in Times New Roman font while the remaining consist of four different fonts with equal distributions. All these documents were printed from a fixed reference printer. In the next experiment, our method is also tested on a new dataset comprising images of documents printed in three different fonts namely, Cambria, Arial, and Courier. There are five pages of each font captured using eight smartphones of seven different make and model (Table 1) and stored as .jpg files by the inbuilt mobile camera app at a resolution of 13 megapixels. All pages were printed from HP Laser Jet 1018. In all the experiments, the document images from different scanners/smart phones used to train and test, comprised of the same content.

Table 1. Details of smart phones used in experiments.

Id	Phone make and model	No. of docs	Image size (in pixels)
P1	Samsung Galaxy J5	15	4128 × 3096
P2	iPhone 5s	15	3264 × 2448
P3	Xiaomi Mi 3s	15	3120 × 4160
P4	Vivo 1601	15	3120 × 4160
P5	Moto G3	15	3120 × 4160
P6	Asus Zenfone 2	15	3072 × 4096
P7	Xiaomi Mi Note 4	15	3120 × 4160
P8	Xiaomi Mi Note 4	15	3120 × 4160

4.1 Experiments on Scanner Dataset

In the first set of experiments, feature vectors are extracted from each connected component. Then all the feature vectors are sequentially clustered into groups of ten and subjected to PoEP. LDA is applied so as reduce the dimensionality of feature vectors, thus reducing the feature vector length to six.

Table 2. Cross font size experiments on scanner data: average accuracy results for various possibilities of train and test fonts. (Accuracies for a group of 10 characters as well as a complete page (inside the square brackets [.]))

Train font size	Test font size			
	14pt.	12pt.	10pt.	8pt.
14pt.	**99.5 [100]**	97.6 [100]	**88.3 [93.6]**	62.5 [59.6]
12pt.	98.7 [100]	**99.83 [100]**	98.4 [100]	**76.5 [85.9]**
10pt.	**91.1 [94.4]**	99 [100]	**99.7 [100]**	90.5 [99.3]
8pt.	73.6 [79.4]	**81.6 [86]**	96.6 [97.1]	**96.6 [97.5]**

Same Font Type and Font Size Experiments. An SVM is trained using one page scanned from each scanner and is further used to test on 9 pages of the same font. It is repeated with all ten possibilities of training pages. This is done for pages printed from all three fonts. The average page level accuracy was 100% for all iterations except for four iterations of the Universal font. The average accuracy obtained on group of ten characters level is 100%, 99.9%, 99%, 95.9% respectively for URW, Arial, Calligra and Universal font. It is worth pointing out that even though Calligra and Universal look completely different from the other fonts, the proposed method achieves good performance with them. The second set of experiments is conducted on pages of different font sizes using the same settings as above. Here again, the page level accuracy was 100% for all iterations except for three iterations on the smallest font size (8pt.). This could be because of very small distances between certain consecutive characters at this font size. This converts multiple characters into a single connected component.

Cross Font Type and Font Size Experiments. The font shape independence of the proposed method is tested by training with a particular font type and testing on the other three font types. Similar to baseline method [9], the performance of proposed method severely deteriorates with cross font type experiments. In particular, most samples were misclassified into Canon scanner class. On the other hand, the effect of font size is also tested which suggests that the performance depends upon the difference in font sizes of the train and test documents. To be precise, accuracy decreases with increase in the difference between font sizes used for training and testing (Table 2). Nonetheless, the proposed method achieves close to 100% accuracy when the font sizes of train and test data differ by 2pt.

4.2   Comparison with Baseline

In comparison to [9], the proposed method achieves far higher accuracies on a group of 10 characters (connected components) as compared to 50 characters

Table 3. Cross font type experiments on smart phone data: average accuracy results for various possibilities of train and test fonts. Both the group of character level (10 characters) and page level accuracies (inside the square brackets [.]) have been listed.

Train font type	Test font type		
	Cambria	Arial	Courier
Cambria	89.7 [93.6]	82.2 [88.0]	85.3 [90.9]
Arial	88.8 [93.1]	92.5 [95.7]	82.9 [91.4]
Courier	75.5 [80.0]	65.8 [69.7]	95.3 [97.1]

Table 4. Average confusion matrix (over 5 iterations) for training on one document image and testing on four document images (Courier font, Smartphone dataset).

True	Predicted							
	S1	S2	S3	S4	S5	S6	S7	S8
S1	**95.5**	0.0	0.0	0.2	0.0	0.1	1.9	2.3
S2	0.0	**99.9**	0.0	0.0	0.0	0.0	0.0	0.0
S3	0.3	0.0	**99.1**	0.0	0.0	0.0	0.1	0.6
S4	8.9	0.0	0.5	**85.5**	0.0	0.4	3.6	1.1
S5	0.0	0.0	0.0	0.0	**100.0**	0.0	0.0	0.0
S6	0.0	0.0	0.0	0.0	0.0	**99.9**	0.1	0.0
S7	0.8	0.0	0.0	0.0	0.0	1.3	**64.3**	33.5
S8	0.7	0.0	0.0	0.0	0.0	0.2	31.5	**67.6**

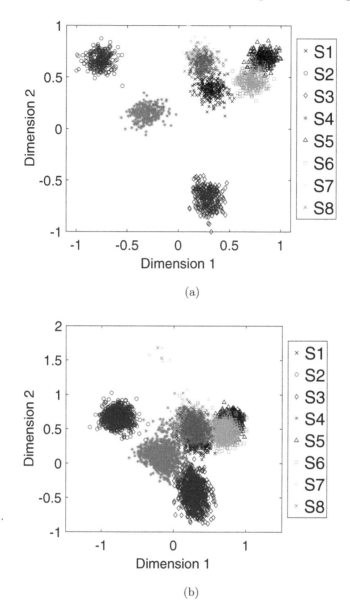

Fig. 3. Top two features of the proposed method applied on pages printed in courier font in smart phone dataset after projection using LDA with (a) train feature vectors (1 page, depicted in the top image) and (b) test feature vectors (4 pages, depicted in the bottom image).

required in the former. Secondly, the baseline method works well only with mixed font size data in training and testing while the proposed method works consistently with cross font size experiments having train and test of similar sizes.

4.3   Experiments on Smart Phone Dataset

With experiments on smart phone dataset, the features are extracted similarly to the previous pipeline. In all the experiments, except the last, only seven phones of different make and model are used.

Same Font Experiments. For images of documents printed in each of the three fonts, the number of training pages per smart phone is kept fixed at one while the other four pages are used in testing. The average page level accuracy obtained over five iterations for each possible option of training page is 93.6%, 95.7% and 97.1% respectively for documents printed with Cambria, Arial and Courier fonts. The corresponding character level accuracy obtained on a group of ten characters is 89.7%, 92.5% and 95.3% (Table 3). To analyze the effectiveness of the proposed method, the first two dimensions of train feature vectors and test feature vectors, are plotted in Fig. 3. Test feature vectors are projected using LDA weights of train feature vectors.

Cross Font Type Experiments. Here, one document image per smart phone of a particular font is used for training while all pages of some other font are used for testing. In contrast to scanner dataset, all of these three fonts are accepted in legal documents and other official works. The results in Table 3 suggest that training with either Cambria or Arial font performs better than Courier font (which covers lesser text area) for this small dataset. While the worst-case scenario is when SVM is trained with Courier font and tested on Arial font. It is worth noting that the accuracy for a group of characters, with training using Cambria or Arial, is significant enough to have a case for application in forgery detection. Experiments done with all the eight phones suggest that there is significant misclassification among phones of the same make and model as can be seen from the confusion matrix in Table 4.

5   Conclusion

This paper proposes a system for source classification using document images acquired by smartphones and flatbed scanners. Local tetra patterns based features are utilized to capture unique device-specific signatures. The proposed method uses all characters to train a single classifier, thereby, reducing the amount of training data required to a mere single document image. The available document images captured from a suspected source could comprise of specific font types and sizes while the document in question might consist of some other font shapes and types. The method proposed in this paper is a step in the direction of complete independence from the font shapes/sizes present in a document. Further, across all experiments, the accuracy has been reported on a group of ten characters which would roughly translate into less than the length of an average sentence. These results show promising improvements for their usage in potential forgery detection. Lastly, the results on smartphone dataset suggest that most wrongly classified characters occur in bunches as there is not much difference between character level and page level accuracy. This observation suggests that most of the characters which are wrongly classified may be located nearby on the same page. One possible reason could be blurring induced in certain areas of the image as a smart phone auto focuses on certain areas causing blurring at some other portions. This could be a useful direction to analyze further with different experiments. Future work will address such scenarios.

Acknowledgment. This material is based upon work supported by the Board of Research in Nuclear Sciences (BRNS), Department of Atomic Energy (DAE), Government of India under the project DAE-BRNS-ATC-34/14/45/2014-BRNS and Visvesvaraya Ph.D. Scheme, Ministry of the Electronics & Information Technology (MeitY), Government of India. Any opinions, findings, and conclusions or recommendations expressed in this material are those of the author(s) and do not necessarily reflect the views of the funding agencies.

References

1. Abramova, S., Bohme, R.: Detecting copy-move forgeries in scanned text documents. Electron. Imag. **8**, 1–9 (2016)
2. Amerini, I., Caldelli, R., Del Bimbo, A., Di Fuccia, A., Saravo, L., Rizzo, A.P.: Copy-move forgery detection from printed images. In: IS&T/SPIE Electronic Imaging, p. 90280Y (2014)
3. Chiang, P.J., Khanna, N., Mikkilineni, A.K., Segovia, M.V.O., Suh, S., Allebach, J.P., Chiu, G.T.C., Delp, E.J.: Printer and scanner forensics. IEEE Signal Process. Mag. **26**(2), 72–83 (2009)
4. Choi, C.H., Lee, M.J., Lee, H.K.: Scanner identification using spectral noise in the frequency domain. In: 17th IEEE International Conference on Image Processing, ICIP, pp. 2121–2124 (2010)
5. Elsharkawy, Z., Abdelwahab, S., Dessouky, M., Elaraby, S., El-Samie, F.: Identifying unique flatbed scanner characteristics for matching a scanned image to its source. In: 30th IEEE National Radio Science Conference, NRSC, pp. 298–305 (2013)
6. Gloe, T., Franz, E., Winkler, A.: Forensics for flatbed scanners. In: Proceedings of SPIE Security, Steganography, and Watermarking of Multimedia Contents IX, p. 65051I (2007)
7. Gou, H., Swaminathan, A., Wu, M.: Intrinsic sensor noise features for forensic analysis on scanners and scanned images. IEEE Trans. Inf. Forensics Secur. **4**(3), 476–491 (2009)
8. Joshi, S., Khanna, N.: Single classifier-based passive system for source printer classification using local texture features. arXiv preprint arXiv:1706.07422 (2017)
9. Khanna, N., Delp, E.J.: Intrinsic signatures for scanned documents forensics: effect of font shape and size. In: Proceedings of IEEE International Symposium on Circuits and Systems, ISCAS, pp. 3060–3063 (2010)
10. Khanna, N., Mikkilineni, A.K., Delp, E.J.: Scanner identification using feature-based processing and analysis. IEEE Trans. Inf. Forensics Secur. **4**(1), 123–139 (2009)

11. Murala, S., Maheshwari, R., Balasubramanian, R.: Local tetra patterns: a new feature descriptor for content-based image retrieval. IEEE Trans. Image Process. **21**(5), 2874–2886 (2012)

12. Ojala, T., Pietikäinen, M., Mäenpää, M.: Multiresolution gray-scale and rotation invariant texture classification with local binary patterns. IEEE Trans. Pattern Anal. Mach. Intell. **24**(7), 971–987 (2002)

13. Pietikäinen, M., Hadid, A., Zhao, G., Ahonen, T.: Computer Vision Using Local Binary Patterns. Springer, London (2011). https://doi.org/10.1007/978-0-85729-748-8

14. Sugawara, S.: Identification of scanner models by comparison of scanned hologram images. Forensic Sci. Int. **241**, 69–83 (2014)

15. Tan, X., Triggs, B.: Enhanced local texture feature sets for face recognition under difficult lighting conditions. IEEE Trans. Image Process. **19**(6), 1635–1650 (2010)

16. Xu, G., Shi, Y.Q.: Camera model identification using local binary patterns. In: IEEE International Conference on Multimedia and Expo, ICME, pp. 392–397 (2012)

17. Zhang, B., Gao, Y., Zhao, S., Liu, J.: Local derivative pattern versus local binary pattern: face recognition with high-order local pattern descriptor. IEEE Trans. Image Process. **19**(2), 533–544 (2010)

Homomorphic Incremental Directional Averaging for Noise Suppression in SAR Images

Shashaank M. Aswatha$^{(\boxtimes)}$, Jayanta Mukhopadhyay, Prabir K. Biswas, and Subhas Aikat

Indian Institute Technology Kharagpur, Kharagpur 721 302, West Bengal, India
mas@atdc.iitkgp.ernet.in, jay@cse.iitkgp.ernet.in, pkb@ece.iitkgp.ernet.in

Abstract. In recent days, it is found that Synthetic Aperture Radar (SAR) images can be a very useful mode for observing and understanding the surface of Earth. The images formed under SAR modality usually suffer from multiplicative noise, particularly in single-look-complex (SLC) mode. There are extensive works in the literature for denoising SAR data, which are usually applied on amplitude data, or on coherency/covariance data. In this paper, we propose a two-channel filtering technique for noise suppression in complex SAR data. The rectangular format of complex SAR data is represented in phasor form to execute noise filtering over amplitude and phase independently, and then converted back to the rectangular format for subsequent applications. In this approach, it is observed that, the surface texture information is visibly retained while suppressing the noise considerably well, in comparison to reference multi-look image. As an application, we show the advantage of proposed noise suppression technique in classification of SAR images.

Keywords: SAR image denoising · Homomorphic filtering
Incremental directional smoothing

1 Introduction

Among several modalities of remotely imaging the Earth's surface, Synthetic Aperture Radar (SAR) has been a very valuable resource for its ability to penetrate cloud-cover and being independent to solar illumination. Although SAR imaging module has given an advantage of choice of wide range of ground resolutions, the acquired data usually suffer from speckle noise due to coherent way of imaging. This imposes severe constraints on data interpretation and analysis, which calls for application of denoising techniques on SAR data. The speckle noise in SAR data can be modeled as a multiplicative noise process, which has been well explored and reported in the literature [23]. Some state-of-the-art SAR image denoising techniques include median filter, local statistics based filters, adaptive filters, information theory based filter, nonlinear filter based on

© Springer Nature Singapore Pte Ltd. 2018
R. Rameshan et al. (Eds.): NCVPRIPG 2017, CCIS 841, pp. 293–302, 2018.
https://doi.org/10.1007/978-981-13-0020-2_26

morphology, directional smoothing, wavelet based denoising approaches, [1,8–10,12,15,18,21,24,25], etc.

Since SAR acquisition is an active imaging method, the image is formed from scattered radiation from the surface. Scatters from different kinds of surfaces appear with different textures in the image. Since these textures contribute to the information of the surface characteristics, it is necessary to preserve them while suppressing the noise. Many of the denoising techniques in literature erode these texture information, while dealing with the noise. Also, the denoising is applied on the amplitude data, or on the basis of real elements of coherency/covariance data. This still retains some noise, which are particulary resulting from the imaginary components [13]. In our approach, we represent the rectangular form of single-look complex data in exponential form and then use denoising independently over amplitude and phase channels. In this paper, we discuss two main aspects: (i) Two Channel Processing; in particular, processing phase information separately, which has lead to significant improvement in retaining finer structure in the denoised image, while suppressing noise, and (ii) Incremental directional smoothing. The results of de-speckling are shown as Pauli RGB images, which show a satisfactory suppression of noise, in comparison with the reference multi-look image of the same scene.

2   Methodology

In general, a multiplicative noise in an image is represented as in Eq. 4. Here, $I_v(p,q)$ is an image corrupted by noise, $I_u(p,q)$ is noise free image, and $n(p,q)$ is the multiplicative noise, at pixel position, (p,q).

$$I_v(p,q) = I_u(p,q) \cdot n(p,q) \tag{1}$$

With reference to SAR image, $I_v(p,q)$ represents the values that is measured by the Radar instrument head, $I_u(p,q)$ represents the ideal radiometric values, and $n(p,q)$ represents the speckle noise.

The speckle noise is most prominent in single-look complex image, which is mainly used in polarimetric analysis of SAR data. In this case, we have complex data to consider, as shown below.

$$I_u(p,q) = |I_u(p,q)|e^{(j\phi(p,q))} \tag{2}$$

where, $I_u(p,q)$ is the complex SAR image in polar co-ordinates, and $|I_u(p,q)|$ and $\phi(p,q)$ are the amplitude and phase components of ideal radiometric signal. Similarly, the complex form of noise, $n(p,q)$, in phasor representation is given by Eq. 3.

$$n(p,q) = |n(p,q)|e^{(j\phi_n(p,q))} \tag{3}$$

where, $|n(p,q)|$ and $\phi_n(p,q)$ are the amplitude and phase components of the speckle noise, respectively. Therefore, the multiplicative noise process can be represented as,

$$I_v(p,q) = |I_u(p,q)||n(p,q)|e^{j(\phi(p,q)+\phi_n(p,q))} \tag{4}$$

where, $I_v(p, q)$ is the measured noisy complex signal at the Radar instrument head.

Usually, the complex SAR data is provided as individual real and imaginary channels in rectangular form. In polarimetric analysis, both the real and imaginary values are used for decomposition and classification applications. Generally, the amplitude image is obtained and the denoising is applied on it. When considering polarimetric applications like polarimetric decomposition, denoising is applied on coherency matrix (for full polarized data) or covariance data (for dual polarized data), which are computed from the noisy real and imaginary components of the signal. Given the real and imaginary components of radiometric signal, $I_{re}(p, q)$ and $I_{im}(p, q)$, respectively, the amplitude, $|I_A(p, q)|$, and phase, $I_\phi(p, q)$, are computed by Eq. 5.

$$|I_A(p, q)| = \sqrt{(I_{re}(p, q))^2 + (I_{im}(p, q))^2}$$
$$I_\phi(p, q) = \tan^{-1}\left(\frac{I_{im}(p, q)}{I_{re}(p, q)}\right) \tag{5}$$

Relating Eqs. 4 and 5, $|I_A(p, q)| = |I_u(p, q)||n(p, q)|$ and $I_\phi(p, q) = \phi(p, q) + \phi_n(p, q)$.

On the basis of their characteristics, the amplitude and phase channels are treated independently for denoising. After filtering them, they are converted back to complex numbers in rectangular representation, $I_{rect}(p, q)$ by the following equation.

$$I_{rect}(p, q) = |I_A(p, q)| \cdot e^{(jI_\phi(p, q))} \tag{6}$$

With the phasor representation in Eq. 4, we see that, the noise is multiplicative for amplitude values and additive for phase values. So, we filter the noise in two channels: (1) the amplitude channel is treated with homomorphic incremental directional averaging, and (2) the phase channel is simply Gaussian filtered to keep the phase variations smooth.

2.1   Directional Averaging

The amplitude image essentially captures the edge and texture information in the image. Edge-preserving denoising is preferred [3,11,17] to conventional filtering for retaining the edges while skimming off the noise. In directional averaging, the edges are preserved by smoothing along the direction of the edges in the images. This is achieved by spatially averaging the pixels within a fixed window size along a direction that has minimum distance with the center pixel.

Computationally, this method has an advantage of fast execution by using directional kernels when dealing with additive noise process, which is linear in nature. But, for multiplicative noise process, the filtering should be based on local statistics, which is usually nonlinear in nature [6,17]. Thus, the amplitude channel of SAR images is subjected to denoising in homomorphic domain, where the multiplicative noise becomes additive under log transformation [5].

2.2   Homomorphic Directional Averaging

Due to the use of fixed window size for filtering, there are chances of disturbing the underlying texture. If the chosen window size is too large, such texture may get eroded. If it is too small, the noise would leave some artifacts after filtering. Since the SAR image consists of various sizes of texture and edges, maintaining a balance to retain useful content and filtering the noise is necessary.

We perform this with a homomorphic incremental directional averaging on amplitude channel of SAR image. At first, the intensity image is transformed to logarithmic scale to make the noise additive. At each pixel location, the spatial average along different directions (0° to 360° with a 10° interval) within a fixed window is computed. The average value in a direction which is having a minimum distance with center pixel of the scaled image (scale factor of 2) is chosen in the filtered output. We compute the directional averaging for different window sizes, incrementing from a 3×3 window to 31×31, with an interval of 2 units. Mean of the filtered values from all the window sizes is computed and assigned to each pixel location. As a final step, the filtered image is subjected to inverse logarithmic transformation to obtain the denoised amplitude channel. The directional averaging is computed by directional kernels using the intensity profile, which speeds up the computation by nearly two times.

Accounting to the high dynamic range, the use of homomorphic filter is usually not suggested for SAR images while performing spatial averaging, which tends to suppress strong scatter responses [16]. However, we still use homomorphic filtering for denoising and show comparative results with some of the state-of-the-art techniques. Unlike mere averaging of neighborhood pixels, we perform oriented blurring along the edges, which does not suppress all strong scatters. While averaging, pixels with similar radiometric values (with less variation) are considered along a direction with reference to the center pixel value, and not a surrounding region as a whole. Therefore, only similar pixels in the neighborhood along minimally varying direction, whose scattering values are similar are averaged, which helps in preserving the strong scatters (strong scatters vary from the surrounding pixels with a very high margin). Since we perform incremental processing, the noise gets faded abruptly across scales, whereas, the edges show a gradual variation. By accumulating the filtered images with several scales, noise are suppressed while affecting the edges (which are more consistent) minimally.

2.3   Denoising Phases

The noise in phase channel is already additive in nature, which is shown in Eq. 4. Also, the edges and texture are essentially represented by amplitude, which is filtered by homomorphic incremental directional smoothing. Since the phase is expected to be smooth in its variation, we have used mere Gaussian filtering over the phase channel. The effect of phase filtering in suppression of noise can be observed in Fig. 1 We have experimented with both uniform kernels and Gaussian weighted kernels (with a range of σ = window size), and the results are shown in Sect. 3.

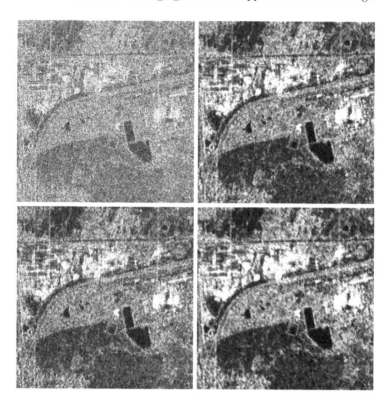

Fig. 1. Visualization of homomorphic incremental directional averaging performance. *Top left*: original unfiltered SAR image. *Top right*: homomorphic incremental directional averaging with uniform kernel and phase filtering. *Bottom left*: homomorphic incremental directional averaging with uniform kernel and without phase filtering. *Bottom right*: homomorphic incremental directional averaging with Gaussian weighted kernel and phase filtering.

Since surface scatters in SAR image appear as differently textured regions, outputs of varying window sizes retains different scales of edges. The output of the smallest window (finer scale) contains some artifacts due to filtering, which gradually decreases with increasing window size. Also, the output of largest window size (coarser scale) blurs the smaller edges, which are retained in smaller windows. The noisy artifacts usually vary abruptly across the scales, and actual edges vary smoothly across the scales attributing to the property of scale-space [22]. That is, the noisy artifacts are inconsistent across scales, whereas the actual edges remain prominent across the scales. Hence, averaging the outputs of varying window sizes (multi-scale edges) would essentially fade the inconsistent noise artifacts more, while affecting the prominent actual edges less.

2.4 Data Set

The proposed technique is tested on full-polarized (HH-HV-VH-VV) and dual-polarized (HH-HV) SAR images of Radar Imaging Satellite (RISAT) by Indian Space Research Organization (ISRO). They are imaged in C-band (frequency of 5.35 GHz) fine-resolution mode. Full-polarized and dual-polarized SAR data have a ground resolution of 9 meters and 3 meters, respectively. The data is in rectangular complex format with separate real and imaginary values at each pixel. The results shown in this paper correspond to the regions of Kolkata (urban), Kharagpur (semi-urban), and Nagpur (reservoir and vegetation) in India.

3 Results and Discussions

Figure 2 (top) shows an example of homomorphic incremental directional averaged data with Pauli RGB rendered image of Kharagpur region, India. This image is obtained by stacking the diagonal elements of coherency matrix as

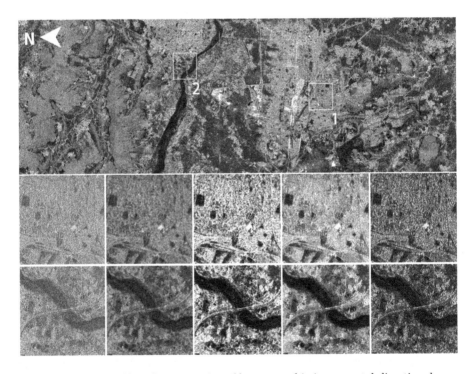

Fig. 2. *Top*: pauli RGB color composite of homomorphic incremental directional averaged SAR data of Kharagpur region, India. *Middle and bottom rows*: different filtering techniques applied on image patches numbered 1 and 2, respectively, as shown in the top image. Filtering techniques, from left to right: Original unfiltered SAR image, median filtering, Lee filtering [14], scaled-bilateral filtering [3], homomorphic incremental directional averaging with uniform kernel.

RGB channels to form a color composite image [16]. The depicted image is generated by a full-polarized complex SAR data. From the figure, it can be observed that, although median and Lee filtering perform denoising by preserving strong edges, they suffer from eroding the finer texture of some of the surface scatters, which can be used as features for certain applications. The filtering from scaled-bilateral filter shows a good amount of noise suppression, but it leaves residual noise and halo effect over the edges [3]. The output of homomorphic incremental directional average visually maintains a balance of noise suppression and texture retainment. Figure 1 shows the effect of phase filtering in noise suppression. Pecks of noise can be observed in Fig. 1 (*bottom left*), where the amplitude channel is filtered by averaging kernel, but the phase channel is left unfiltered. Figure 1 (*top right*) and (*bottom right*) show the denoised images using averaging and Gaussian weighted kernels, respectively, with phase filtering. It can be seen that, Gaussian weighted kernels are better in noise suppression, but the edges and texture appears to be little blurred.

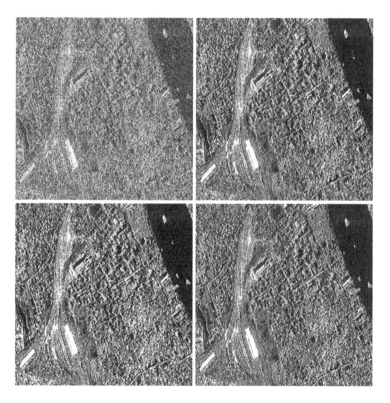

Fig. 3. Performance comparison of homomorphic incremental directional averaging with phase filtering. *Top left*: original unfiltered SLC SAR image. *Top right*: homomorphic incremental directional averaging with uniform kernel and phase filtering on SLC image. *Bottom left*: homomorphic incremental directional averaging with Gaussian weighted kernel and phase filtering SLC image. *Bottom right*: multi-look reference image (Gamma MAP filtered multi-look SAR image of the same scene).

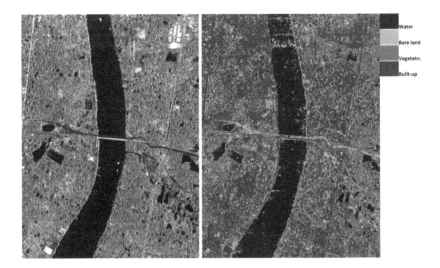

Fig. 4. Denoising application: classification of SAR images. *Left*: SLC SAR image of Kolkata region. *Right*: classified image.

Another example is shown in Fig. 3, where the proposed filtering technique of SLC SAR data is visually compared with gamma MAP filtered multi-look complex SAR data (obtained as a data product from ISRO) of the same scene [4, 7,20]. It can be observed that, in comparison to the reference image, the output of homomorphic incremental directional averaging with phase filtering performs satisfactorily well in suppressing the noise and preserving texture in SLC SAR data.

The average equivalent number of looks (ENL) [17] of original, proposed filtering output, and gamma MAP filtered multi-look images are found to be 1.674, 39.807, and 22.3902, respectively (lower ENL values represent higher impact of noise). As an example of application of the proposed noise suppression method, 4-class (water, vegetation, urban, and built-up) classification of a C-band dual polarized SAR image has been shown in Fig. 4. We have used k-nearest neighbor algorithm for classification ($k = 10$) with 2000 training samples per class and coherency/covariance matrices as features. Average classification accuracies of the proposed technique, refined Lee filter [26], Lee-Sigma filter [13], vector median filter [2,19], and without any filtering are 84%, 75%, 76%, 80%, and 51%, respectively.

4   Conclusion

In this paper, we have presented a two channel filtering techniques for suppressing noise in complex SAR images, particularly single-look-complex SAR images. The property of multiplicative speckle noise being additive in phase and log-transformed amplitude channels have been exploited. By combining the data filtered with a set of kernels at incremental scales, noise suppression and texture retainment have been balanced, which is necessary for certain polarimetric classification and recognition applications. Also, it is implemented in an efficient way by using kernels for computing the directional averages. As an application, we have shown its advantage in classification of polarimetric SAR images. An extensive objective performance analysis and the potential of this filtering approach in applications to SAR data decomposition and classification are yet to be explored.

Acknowledgments. This work has been carried out under a project entitled *Polarimetric Analysis of SAR Images for Segmentation, Classification, and Recognition of Objects*, sponsored by ISRO, Indian Space Research Organization (Grant no. IIT/KCSTC/Chair./NEW/P/17-18/01, dated 17-05-2017).

References

1. Aemand Lopes, R.T., Nezry, E.: Adaptive speckle filters and scene heterogeneity. IEEE Trans. Geosci. Remote Sens. **28**(6), 992–1000 (1990)
2. Astola, J., Haavisto, P., Neuvo, Y.: Vector median filters. Proc. IEEE **78**(4), 678–689 (1990)
3. Aswatha, S.M., Mukhopadhyay, J., Bhowmick, P.: Image denoising by scaled bilateral filtering. In: Third National Conference on Computer Vision, Pattern Recognition, Image Processing and Graphics, pp. 122–125 (2011)
4. Chen, G., Huang, Y.: To improve the GMAP for speckle filtering by consideration of the correlation of SAR images. In: 2007 International Symposium on Intelligent Signal Processing and Communication Systems, pp. 124–127 (2007)
5. Coltuc, D., Radescu, R.: On the homomorphic filtering by channels' summation. In: IEEE International Geoscience and Remote Sensing Symposium, vol. 4, pp. 2456–2458 (2002)
6. Cui, Y., Zhou, G., Yang, J., Yamaguchi, Y.: Unsupervised estimation of the equivalent number of looks in SAR images. IEEE Geosci. Remote Sens. Lett. **8**(4), 710–714 (2011)
7. Evans, A.N.: A gamma filter for multi-look synthetic aperture radar images. In: Fourth International Symposium on Signal Processing and Its Applications, vol. 2, pp. 829–832 (1996)
8. Frost, V.S., Stiles, J.A., Shanmugan, K.S., Holtzman, J.C.: A model for radar images and its application to adaptive digital filtering of multiplicative noise. IEEE Trans. Pattern Anal. Mach. Intell. **4**(2), 157–166 (1982)
9. Gagnon, L., Jouan, A.: Speckle filtering of SAR images: a comparative study between complex-wavelet-based and standard filters. In: Proceedings of Wavelet Applications in Signal and Image Processing V, pp. 28–29 (1997)
10. Jie, C., Jing, Z., Chunsheng, L., Yinqing, Z.: A novel speckle filter for SAR images based on information-theoretic heterogeneity measurements. Chin. J. Aeronaut. **22**(5), 528–534 (2009)
11. Lakshmanan, V.: A separable filter for directional smoothing. IEEE Geosci. Remote Sens. Lett. **1**(3), 192–195 (2004)
12. Lee, J.S.: Speckle suppression and analysis for synthetic aperture radar images. Opt. Eng. **25**(5), 636–643 (1986)

13. Lee, J.S., Ainsworth, T.L., Wang, Y., Chen, K.S.: Polarimetric SAR speckle filtering and the extended sigma filter. IEEE Trans. Geosci. Remote Sens. **53**(3), 1150–1160 (2015)
14. Lee, J.S., Grunes, M.R., de Grandi, G.: Polarimetric SAR speckle filtering and its implication for classification. IEEE Trans. Geosci. Remote Sens. **37**(5), 2363–2373 (1999)
15. Lee, J.S., Grunes, M.R., Schuler, D.L., Pottier, E., Ferro-Famil, L.: Scattering-model-based speckle filtering of polarimetric SAR data. IEEE Trans. Geosci. Remote Sens. **44**(1), 176–187 (2006)
16. Lee, J.S., Pottier, E.: Polarimetric Radar Imaging: From Basics to Applications (2009)
17. Mastriani, M., Giraldez, A.E.: Enhanced directional smoothing algorithm for edge-preserving smoothing of synthetic-aperture radar images. Measur. Sci. Rev. **4**(3), 1–11 (2004)
18. Melnik, V., Lukin, V., Egiazarian, K., Astola, J.: A method of speckle removal in one-look SAR images based on Lee filtering and wavelet denoising, pp. 243–246 (2000)
19. Novoselac, V., Zovko-Cihlar, B.: Image noise reduction by vector median filter. In: Proceedings of International Symposium on Electronics in Marine, pp. 57–62 (2012)
20. NRSC: Risat-1 data processing. https://nrsc.gov.in/RISAT-1. Accessed 05 Feb 2017
21. Parrilli, S., Poderico, M., Angelino, C.V., Verdoliva, L.: A nonlocal SAR image denoising algorithm based on llmmse wavelet shrinkage. IEEE Trans. Geosci. Remote Sens. **50**(2), 606–616 (2012)
22. Perona, P., Malik, J.: Scale-space and edge detection using anisotropic diffusion. IEEE Trans. Pattern Anal. Mach. Intell. **12**(7), 629–639 (1990)
23. Schulze, M.A., Wu, Q.X.: Nonlinear edge-preserving smoothing of synthetic aperture radar imagery. In: Proceedings of the New Zealand Image and Vision Computing 1995 Workshop, pp. 28–29 (1995)
24. Shi, Z., Fung, K.B.: A comparison of digital speckle filters. In: International Geoscience and Remote Sensing Symposium on Surface and Atmospheric Remote Sensing: Technologies, Data Analysis and Interpretation, IGARSS 1994, vol. 4, pp. 2129–2133 (1994)
25. Xu, L., Li, J., Shu, Y., Peng, J.: SAR image denoising via clustering-based principal component analysis. IEEE Trans. Geosci. Remote Sens. **52**(11), 6858–6869 (2014)
26. Yommy, A.S., Liu, R., Wu, S.: SAR image despeckling using refined Lee filter. In: 7th International Conference on Intelligent Human-Machine Systems and Cybernetics, pp. 260–265 (2015)

An EEG-Based Image Annotation System

Viral Parekh[1]([✉]), Ramanathan Subramanian[2], Dipanjan Roy[3]⬤,
and C. V. Jawahar[1]

[1] IIIT Hyderabad, Hyderabad, India
viral@live.in
[2] University of Glasgow, Singapore, Singapore
[3] National Brain Research Centre, Manesar, India

Abstract. The success of deep learning in computer vision has greatly
increased the need for annotated image datasets. We propose an EEG
(Electroencephalogram)-based image annotation system. While humans
can recognize objects in 20–200 ms, the need to manually label images
results in a low annotation throughput. Our system employs brain signals
captured via a consumer EEG device to achieve an annotation rate of
up to 10 images per second. We exploit the P300 event-related potential
(ERP) signature to identify target images during a rapid serial visual presentation (RSVP) task. We further perform unsupervised outlier removal
to achieve an F1-score of 0.88 on the test set. The proposed system does
not depend on category-specific EEG signatures enabling the annotation
of any new image category without any model pre-training.

Keywords: EEG · Image annotation · Active learning

1 Introduction

Image annotation is a critical task in computer vision, intended to bridge the
semantic gap between automated and human understanding via the use of tags
and labels. Image annotation is useful for building large-scale retrieval systems,
organizing and managing multimedia databases, and for training deep learning
models for scene understanding. A trivial way to annotate images is to tag them
manually with the relevant labels, but this approach is slow and tedious for huge
databases. Therefore, many efforts have been undertaken to address/circumvent
this problem. Some methods are completely automatic [1–5], while some others
are interactive [6–10]– these approaches have considerably reduced the human
effort required for annotation.

Human vision is a very powerful system for object recognition and scene
understanding. It is also robust to variations in illumination, scale or pose. We
are habitually used to recognizing objects even in cluttered scenes. Humans can
identify objects in tens of milliseconds [11,12], but the representation of the
perceived information via hand movements or verbal responses for annotation is
very slow compared to the processing speed of contemporary digital devices. In

© Springer Nature Singapore Pte Ltd. 2018
R. Rameshan et al. (Eds.): NCVPRIPG 2017, CCIS 841, pp. 303–313, 2018.
https://doi.org/10.1007/978-981-13-0020-2_27

this regard, the emerging field of brain-Computer Interfaces (BCI) offers us an innovative way to exploit the power of human brain for data annotation with minimal effort.

Brain-Computer Interfaces rely on various technologies for sensing brain activity such as Electroencephalography (EEG), MEG (Magnetoencephalography), PET (Positron Emission Tomography), SPECT (Single Photon Emission Computed Tomography), fMRI (functional Magnetic Resonance Imaging) and fNIRS (functional near infrared spectroscopy). Among these, EEG provides a high temporal resolution (sampling rate of up to 1 KHz) and adequate spatial resolution (1–2 cm). In this work, we specifically use the portable and easy-to-use consumer grade *Emotiv* EEG device, which enables a minimally intrusive user experience as users perform cognitive tasks, for sensing and recording brain activity. While having these advantages, consumer EEG devices nevertheless suffer from a high signal-to-noise ratio, which makes subsequent data analytics challenging.

In this work, we focus on the annotation of a *pre-selected* object category over the entire image dataset instead of labeling all categories at once. If the images are presented serially in a sequence for annotation, then the task is equivalent to that of *target detection*. Now whenever an image containing a target class instance is observed by the human annotator, an event-related potential (ERP) signature known as **P300** [13] is observed in the EEG data. By examining the EEG signals generated during image presentation, we can discover the images of interest and annotate them accordingly. In this paper, we provide the pipeline and architecture for image annotation via EEG signals.

2   Related Work

The use of EEG as an additional modality for computer vision and scene understanding tasks has been explored by a number of works. In [14], EEG signals are used to automate grab cut-based image segmentation. In [15], authors exploit ERP signatures such as P300 for image retrieval. In [16], authors use the N400 ERP to validate tags attached to video content. Emotions from movies and ads are inferred via EEG signals in [17,18].

Few studies directly use image category-based EEG signatures for recognizing aspects related to multimedia content as well as users. For example, the authors of [19] use EEG signals to classify images into three object categories– animals, faces and inanimate. In a recent work [20], the authors present how EEG features can be employed for multi-class image classification. Another recent work recognizes user gender from EEG responses to emotional faces [21]. Given the state-of-the-art, the key contributions of our work are we how how (i) the P300 ERP signature can be employed for image annotation; (ii) the model trained for one object category can be directly used for a novel category, and (iii) the image presentation time affects annotation system performance for complex images.

3   System Architecture

The proposed image annotation system consists of several components–RSVP generation, EEG data acquisition, EEG pre-processing, (binary) classification and outlier removal. Figure 1 presents an overview of the EEG-based annotation pipeline. The RSVP generation unit prepares the set of images for viewing, so that a few among those correspond to the target object category. The image sequence is created via random sampling from the whole dataset. A human annotator is then asked to identify the target category images as the sequence is presented rapidly, and the annotator's brain activity is recorded via an EEG headset during the visual recognition task. The compiled EEG data is first pre-processed for artifact removal. Then, the classification unit categorizes the EEG responses into *target* and *non-target* annotations based on P300 patterns. Images classified as *target* are annotated with the target label class. However, this labeling is noisy due to the presence of false positives and imbalance towards the negative (non-target) class. An outlier removal unit finally performs unsupervised dimensionality reduction and clustering to improve the labeling precision.

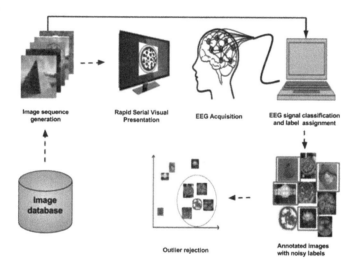

Fig. 1. EEG-based annotation pipeline: An exemplar illustration for the *pizza* object class is presented. Best viewed in color and under zoom.

3.1   Rapid Serial Visual Presentation and Oddball Paradigm

Rapid Serial Visual Presentation is popularly used in psychophysical studies, and involves a series of images or other stimuli types being presented to viewers with a speed of around 10 items per second. This paradigm is basically used to examine the characteristics pertaining to visual attention. In RSVP studies, the *oddball* phenomenon [22] is widely used. In the oddball paradigm, a deviant (target) stimulus is infrequently infused into a stream of audio/visual stimuli. For EEG-based annotation, we generated an RSVP sequence by combing a few *target* category images with many *non-target* images via random sampling from the original dataset. Each image in the sequence was then shown to the viewer for 100 ms, and a fixation cross was presented for 2 s at the beginning of the sequence to minimize memory effects and to record resting state brain activity (see Fig. 4).

3.2   EEG Data Preprocessing and Classification

We used the *Emotiv EPOC* headset to record EEG data. This is a 14 channels (plus CMS/DRL references, P3/P4 locations) Au-plated dry electrode system. For ERP analysis, the Emotiv provides signals comparable to superior lab-grade EEG devices with 32, 64 or 128 channels. The headset uses sequential sampling at 2048 Hz internally which is down-sampled to 128 Hz. The incoming signal is automatically notch filtered at 50 and 60 Hz using a 5th order sinc notch filter. The resolution of the electrical potential is $1.95\,\mu V$. The locations for the 14 channels are as per International 10–20 locations as shown in Fig. 2.

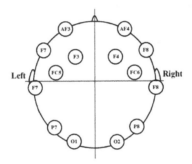

Fig. 2. Sensor configuration: Emotiv electrode locations as per International 10–20 system.

The recorded EEG data is contaminated by various noise undesirable signals that originate from outside the brain. For instance, while recording EEG, one often encounters 50/60 Hz power-line noise and artifacts caused by muscle or eye movements. We extracted one second long *epochs* corresponding to each 100 ms long *trial* denoting the presentation of an image, with 128 Hz sampling rate. Our EEG preprocessing includes (a) baseline power removal using the 0.5 s pre-stimulus samples, (b) band-pass filtering in 0.1–45 Hz frequency range, (c) independent component analysis (ICA) to remove artifacts relating to eye-blinks, and eye and muscle movements. Muscle movement artifacts in EEG are mainly concentrated between 40–100 Hz. While most artifacts are removed upon EEG band-limiting, the remaining are removed manually via inspection of ICA components.

The human brain's response to a stimulus can be measured as a voltage fluctuation resulting from the ionic current within the neurons. The event-related potential is one such measure that is directly related to some motor, cognitive or sensory activation. Out of various ERP components, the P300 signature is commonly elicited in the oddball paradigm where very few targets are mixed with a large number of non-targets. In our experimental setup, we employed a 1:12 ratio for target-to-non-target images. As shown in Fig. 3, the P300 ERP signature is observed between 250 to 500 ms post *target* stimulus presentation. Also, the ERP response is significantly different for target and non-target images, and therefore can be exploited for EEG-based image annotation.

We used the Convolutional Neural Network (CNN)-based EEGNet architecture [23] to classify our EEG data based on P300 detection in the RSVP task. The EEGnet architecture consists of only three convolutional layers. All layers use the Exponential Linear Unit (ELU) [24] as nonlinear activation function with parameter $\alpha = 1$. We trained the model using the minibatch gradient descent algorithm with categorical cross-entropy criterion and Adam optimizer [25]. The models were trained on a NVIDIA GEFORCE GTX 1080 Ti GPU, with CUDA 8 and cuDNN v6 using the Pytorch [26] based Braindecode [27] library.

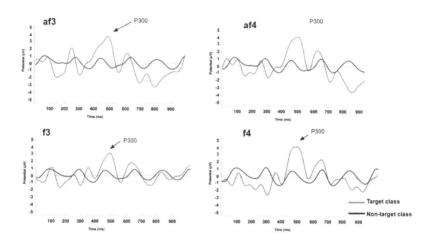

Fig. 3. ERP plots: ERP curves for the Emotiv af3, af4, f3 and f4 channels for *target* (red) and *not-target* (blue) images. P300 signatures are evident for targets but not for non-targets. (Color figure online)

3.3   Outlier Removal

We select one category at a time for the annotation task, which results in class imbalance for the RSVP task. The selected object category forms the *target* class, while all other categories collectively form the *non-target* class. Due to this heavy class imbalance and the characteristics of P300 as discussed in Sect. 5, the false positive rate of the predicted labels is high. Therefore we performed unsupervised outlier removal on the predicted *target* images. Deep learning features have proven advantages over hand-crafted features like SIFT and HoG [28]. We used a pre-trained VGG-19 model [29] to obtain the feature descriptors for the targets. These feature descriptors provide compact representation of raw images while preserving the information required to distinguish between image classes. Each target image was fed forwarded within the VGG-19 model to obtain the 4096 dimensional feature vectors. Target images need not belong to the image classes on which the model is pre-trained. Then, we perform dimensionality reduction with t-SNE [30] to generate low-dimensional features. The t-SNE algorithm retains the local structure of the data while also revealing some important global structure, and hence it performs better than principal component analysis (PCA) alone.

In our case, we assume that samples from the target class should be close in feature space as compared to non-target samples. By performing a grid search on hyper-parameters, we found that the algorithm works best with perplexity value 20, 50 PCA components and 3–5 output dimensions. Then, we performed k-means clustering for two classes assuming that target class samples will form a cluster distinct from the false positives. Also, since the false positive cluster would contain samples from many categories, the cluster would not be as dense as the target cluster.

4   Protocol Design and Experiments

4.1   Datasets

To evaluate the performance of our image annotation system, we used the Caltech101 (CT) [31] and Pascal VOC2012 (PV) [32] datasets. The CT dataset consists of 101 object categories with 40 to 800 images per category. The PV dataset contains a total of 11,530 images from 20 categories, and multiple object categories can be present in one image.

4.2   Experimental Setup

We utilized 2500 images for training, and 2500 images for testing. Both these image sets comprised 200 images of a particular target category that we wanted to annotate. All images were resized 512×512 pixels, and images were displayed at 10 Hz frequency in blocks of 100 in order to minimize viewer distraction and fatigue. During the RSVP task, participants were shown a fixation display for 2 s at the beginning of each 100 image sequence. Train and test EEG data were captured using an identical experimental setup with the temporal gap of 5 min. Target image categories were decided *a priori* before every experiment.

Our study was conducted with five graduate students (5 male, age 24.4 ± 2.1) with 10/20 corrected vision, seated at a distance of 60 cm from the display. A total of three sessions (each involving train and test set) were performed with

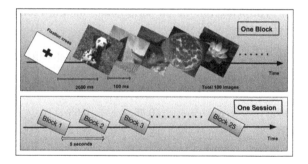

Fig. 4. Experimental protocol: Participants completed two identical sessions (one used for training and the other for test) which were 5 min apart. Each session comprised 25 blocks of 100 images, and lasted about six minutes.

each participant. To facilitate engagement, viewers were instructed to count the number of target images during the experiment. Target image classes were different for each session, and included categories like *bike, pizza, panda, sofa, etc.* Each participant performed two sessions on the CT dataset and one session on the PV dataset.

5   Results and Discussion

Due to a heavy class imbalance between *target* and *non-target* category images, we use the F1-score to evaluate our annotation results. The F1-score is a popular performance metric used in retrieval studies, and denotes the harmonic mean of the precision and recall scores. All reported results denote the mean F1 achieved with five-fold cross validation.

In Table 1, we report the averaged F1 and precision-recall values for the CT and PV datasets across all participants. Note that the precision and F1 scores improve significantly upon outlier removal due to a stark reduction in the number of false positives via feature-based clustering. Overall F1 scores for the PV dataset are lower than for the CT dataset. This can be attributed to the fact that the PV dataset is more complex, as it contains multiple object classes in many images, as compared to CT which contains only one object class per image.

As our annotation system is dependent on viewer ability, its performance is sensitive to human factors. One key factor is the image presentation rate. The image display latency (100 ms) is lower than the P300 response latency ($\approx$300 ms) [33]. The rapid image display protocol results in (i) viewers confusing between similar object classes, (ii) viewers unable to fully comprehend visual information from complex images, and (iii) EEG data for consecutive images having significant overlap leading to misclassification.

Therefore, we hypothesized that reducing the image display rate would (a) allow the viewer to better comprehend the visual content (especially for complex

Table 1. Results synopsis: Annotation performance obtained for the CT and PV datasets across total 15 sessions (5 viewers).

Dataset	Caltech101	Pascal VOC 2012
Before outliers removal		
F1 score	0.71	0.68
Precision	0.66	0.63
Recall	0.81	0.72
After outliers removal		
F1 score	**0.88**	**0.83**
Precision	0.99	0.97
Recall	0.81	0.72
Target image percentage	8%	8%
Image presentation speed	10 Hz	10 Hz
Number of images in test set	2500	2500

images), (b) better delineation of EEG responses, and (c) better manifestation of ERP signatures. These in turn, would improve our annotation performance while marginally reducing the annotation throughput. Figure 5 presents the observed results. Note that a 3% increase in F1-score is observed when the image presentation rate is reduced from 10 to 4 images/second, validating our hypothesis.

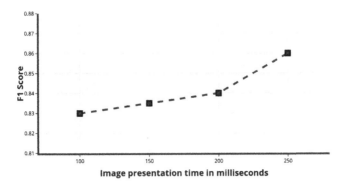

Fig. 5. Presentation rate vs annotation performance: Variation in F1-score with image display rate.

Conversely, since our annotation system is solely based on P300 signatures which are task specific but target class agnostic. Therefore, it is not mandatory to train the EEGNet with object class-specific EEG responses. To validate this aspect, we trained and tested the EEGNet with EEG responses corresponding to different object categories. Table 2 presents the F1 scores achieved for the five viewers with class-agnostic train and test EEG data. Note that only a marginal difference in annotation performance is noticeable with class-specific and class-agnostic EEG data across viewers. Since we are using the pre-trained VGG-19 model exclusively to extract feature descriptors, it can be used without further fine tuning for any new target class categories.

Table 2. Annotation performance with class-specific vs class-agnostic EEG data for five viewers.

F1 score	P1	P2	P3	P4	P5
Class-specific train and test	0.88	0.86	0.89	0.87	0.88
Class-agnostic train and test	0.85	0.85	0.84	0.86	0.86

6 Conclusion

In order to facilitate large-scale image annotation efforts for computer vision and scene understanding applications, we propose an EEG-based fast image annotation system. Our annotation system exclusively relies on the P300 ERP signature, which is elicited upon the viewer detecting a pre-specified object class in the displayed image. A further outlier removal procedure based on binary feature-based clustering significantly improves annotation performance.

Overall, our system achieves a peak F1-score of 0.88 with a 10 Hz annotation throughput. Another advantage of our method is that the P300 signature is specific to the target detection task, but not the underlying object class. Therefore, any novel image category can be annotated with existing models upon compiling the viewer EEG responses. Future work will focus on discovering and exploiting object-specific EEG signatures, and combining multiple human responses (*e.g.*, EEG plus eye movements) for fine-grained object annotation and classification.

References

1. Zhang, S., Huang, J., Huang, Y., Yu, Y., Li, H., Metaxas, D.N.: Automatic image annotation using group sparsity. In: CVPR (2010)
2. Verma, Y., Jawahar, C.V.: Image annotation using metric learning in semantic neighbourhoods. In: Fitzgibbon, A., Lazebnik, S., Perona, P., Sato, Y., Schmid, C. (eds.) ECCV 2012. LNCS, vol. 7574, pp. 836–849. Springer, Heidelberg (2012). https://doi.org/10.1007/978-3-642-33712-3_60
3. Yashaswi, V., Jawahar, C.: Exploring SVM for image annotation in presence of confusing labels. In: BMVC (2013)
4. Everingham, M., Van Gool, L., Williams, C.K.I., Winn, J., Zisserman, A.: The Pascal visual object classes (VOC) challenge. IJCV **88**(2), 303–338 (2010)
5. Fu, H., Zhang, Q., Qiu, G.: Random forest for image annotation. In: Fitzgibbon, A., Lazebnik, S., Perona, P., Sato, Y., Schmid, C. (eds.) ECCV 2012. LNCS, vol. 7577, pp. 86–99. Springer, Heidelberg (2012). https://doi.org/10.1007/978-3-642-33783-3_7

6. Wang, M., Hua, X.-S.: Active learning in multimedia annotation and retrieval: a survey. In: TIST 2011
7. Sychay, G., Chang, E., Goh, K.: Effective image annotation via active learning. In: IEEE International Conference on Multimedia and Expo Proceedings, vol. 1, pp. 209–212 (2002)
8. Bakliwal, P., Jawahar, C.: Active learning based image annotation. In: NCVPRIPG. IEEE (2015)
9. Katti, H., Subramanian, R., Kankanhalli, M., Sebe, N., Chua, T.-S., Ramakrishnan, K.R.: Making computers look the way we look: exploiting visual attention for image understanding. In: ACM International Conference on Multimedia, pp. 667–670 (2010)
10. Subramanian, R., Shankar, D., Sebe, N., Melcher, D.: Emotion modulates eye movement patterns and subsequent memory for the gist and details of movie scenes. J. Vis. **14**(3), 1–18 (2014)
11. Oliva, A.: Gist of the scene. Neurobiol. Attention **696**, 251–256 (2005)
12. Keysers, C., Xiao, D., Foldiak, P., Perrett, D.: The speed of sight. J. Cogn. Neurosci. **13**, 90–101 (2001)
13. Linden, D.E.: The P300: where in the brain is it produced and what does it tell us? Neuroscientist **11**(6), 563–576 (2005)
14. Mohedano, E., Healy, G., McGuinness, K., Giró-i Nieto, X., OConnor, N.E., Smeaton, A.F.: Improving object segmentation by using EEG signals and rapid serial visual presentation. Multimedia Tools Appl. **74**(22), 10137–10159 (2015)
15. Pohlmeyer, E.A., Wang, J., Jangraw, D.C., Lou, B., Chang, S.-F., Sajda, P.: Closing the loop in cortically-coupled computer vision: a brain-computer interface for searching image databases. J. Neural Eng. **8**(3), 036025 (2011)
16. Koelstra, S., Mühl, C., Patras, I.: EEG analysis for implicit tagging of video data. In: 3rd International Conference on Affective Computing and Intelligent Interaction and Workshops, ACII 2009, pp. 1–6. IEEE (2009)
17. Subramanian, R., Wache, J., Abadi, M., Vieriu, R., Winkler, S., Sebe, N.: ASCERTAIN: emotion and personality recognition using commercial sensors. IEEE Trans. Affect. Comput. **PP**, 1 (2016)
18. Shukla, A., Gullapuram, S.S., Katti, H., Yadati, K., Kankanhalli, M., Subramanian, R.: Affect recognition in ads with application to computational advertising. In: ACM International Conference on Multimedia (2017)
19. Kapoor, A., Shenoy, P., Tan, D.: Combining brain computer interfaces with vision for object categorization. In: CVPR (2008)
20. Spampinato, C., Palazzo, S., Kavasidis, I., Giordano, D., Shah, M., Souly, N.: Deep learning human mind for automated visual classification (2017)
21. Bilalpur, M., Kia, S.M., Chawla, M., Chua, T., Subramanian, R.: Gender and emotion recognition with implicit user signals. In: International Conference on Multimodal Interaction (2017)
22. Picton, T.W., et al.: The p300 wave of the human event-related potential. J. Clin. Neurophysiol. **9**, 456–456 (1992)
23. Lawhern, V.J., Solon, A.J., Waytowich, N.R., Gordon, S.M., Hung, C.P., Lance, B.J.: EEGnet: a compact convolutional network for EEG-based brain-computer interfaces. arXiv preprint arXiv:1611.08024 (2016)
24. Clevert, D.-A., Unterthiner, T., Hochreiter, S.: Fast and accurate deep network learning by exponential linear units (ELUS). arXiv preprint arXiv:1511.07289 (2015)
25. Kingma, D., Ba, J.: Adam: a method for stochastic optimization. arXiv preprint arXiv:1412.6980 (2014)

26. Paszke, A., Chintala, S., Collobert, R., Kavukcuoglu, K., Farabet, C., Bengio, S., Melvin, I., Weston, J., Mariethoz, J.: Pytorch: tensors and dynamic neural networks in python with strong GPU acceleration, May 2017. https://github.com/pytorch/pytorch

27. Schirrmeister, R.T., Springenberg, J.T., Fiederer, L.D.J., Glasstetter, M., Eggensperger, K., Tangermann, M., Hutter, F., Burgard, W., Ball, T.: Deep learning with convolutional neural networks for EEG decoding and visualization. In: Human Brain Mapping, August 2017. https://doi.org/10.1002/hbm.23730

28. Yosinski, J., Clune, J., Bengio, Y., Lipson, H.: How transferable are features in deep neural networks? In: Advances in Neural Information Processing Systems, pp. 3320–3328 (2014)

29. Simonyan, K., Zisserman, A.: Very deep convolutional networks for large-scale image recognition. CoRR, abs/1409.1556 (2014)

30. Maaten, L.V.D., Hinton, G.: Visualizing data using t-SNE. J. Mach. Learn. Res. 9(Nov), 2579–2605 (2008)

31. Fei-Fei, L., Fergus, R., Perona, P.: Learning generative visual models from few training examples: an incremental Bayesian approach tested on 101 object categories. Comput. Vis. Image Underst. 106(1), 59–70 (2007)

32. Everingham, M., Van Gool, L., Williams, C.K.I., Winn, J., Zisserman, A.: The PASCAL visual object classes challenge 2012 (VOC2012) Results

33. Polich, J.: Updating P300: an integrative theory of p3a and p3b. Clin. Neurophysiol. 118(10), 2128–2148 (2007)

Multimodal Registration of Retinal Images

Gamalapati S. Jahnavi$^{(\boxtimes)}$ and Jayanthi Sivaswamy

Center for Visual Information Technology, IIIT Hyderabad, Hyderabad, India
jahnavi.gamalapati@research.iiit.ac.in, jsivaswamy@iiit.ac.in

Abstract. Registration of multimodal retinal images such as fundus and Optical Coherence Tomography (OCT) images is important as the two structural imaging modalities provide complementary views of the retina. This enables a more accurate assessment of the health of the retina. However, registration is a challenging task because fundus image (2D) is obtained via optical projection whereas the OCT image (3D) is derived via optical coherence and is very noisy. Furthermore, the field of view of imaging possible in the two modalities is very different resulting in low overlap (5–20%) between the obtained images. Existing methods for this task rely on either key-point (junction/corner) detection or accurate segmentation of vessels which is difficult due to noise. We propose a *registration* algorithm for finding efficient landmarks under noisy conditions. The method requires neither accurate structure segmentation nor key-point detection. The Modality Independent Neighborhood Descriptor (MIND) features are used to represent landmarks to achieve insensitivity to noise, contrast. Similarity transformation is used to register images. Evaluation of the proposed method on 142 fundus-OCT pairs results in an RMSE of 2.61 pixels. The proposed method outperforms the existing algorithm in terms of robustness, accuracy, and computational efficiency.

1 Introduction

Fundus photography is based on projective imaging and has been widely used for several years to detect retinal abnormalities occurring in various diseases such as Diabetic Retinopathy (DR), Age related Macular Degeneration (AMD), etc. Optical Coherence Tomography (OCT) on the other hand is a newer modality which enables cross sectional imaging and is used to detect and localize pathologic changes within the retinal layers. A recent study [1] has shown that using fundus images to diagnose diabetic macular edema (DME), a serious condition requiring intervention, led to both false positive and negative results whereas OCT images provided the true condition. The study concluded that fundus images alone may not be a sufficient for retinal screening. OCT also provides unambiguous evidence for AMD which is marked by the appearance of Drusen in between the RPE and ISOS layers of OCT whereas they may or may not be visible in fundus image. Diagnosis of Glaucoma using the optic cup to disk ratio is also clearly detected from OCT than fundus image. In the proliferative

© Springer Nature Singapore Pte Ltd. 2018
R. Rameshan et al. (Eds.): NCVPRIPG 2017, CCIS 841, pp. 314–324, 2018.
https://doi.org/10.1007/978-981-13-0020-2_28

stages of DR and Retinopathy of Prematurity (ROP) where vessels are affected, fundus images provide clearer evidences as against the OCT. Thus, integrating information by registration of OCT-3D and fundus is of interest.

Multimodal retinal image registration is a challenging task [2,3] due to the many factors. 2D (color) Fundus images can be acquired with a wide field of view (FOV) with good clarity for vessels. 3D (greyscale) OCT in contrast can capture a much smaller FOV, is quite noisy due to the coherence phenomenon that underlies image capture and has poor clarity for vessels. Thus, extraction of reliable landmarks for registration from both modalities is difficult. Yet, existing methods rely on establishing correspondence between corners or junctions in the 2 images.

We propose an iterative solution for registering fundus images to an OCT volume. The key contributions of the proposed solution are:

- No requirement for accurate structure (vessel/OD/macula) segmentation or landmark such as corner detection.
- An adaptive and efficient landmark detection method which is capable of handling low FOV images.
- Feature-based registration which overcomes the noisy nature of OCT data and aids handling cross modal data.

2   Related Work

Two approaches are popular in registration literature: area based and feature based. Area based methods operate directly on image intensity values of a specific region or entire image without deriving structural information. This approach follows a typical pipeline of choosing a similarity measure and maximizing it with an optimization method to obtain the desired transformation model. Feature based methods rely on few salient points/features which are prominent in both the images and solving the correspondence between them.

Registration methods have been proposed for both OCT-fundus image pairs and Fluroscene fundus angiography-fundus (FFA) image pairs. FFA provide high contrast view of blood vessels due to the fluroscent dye used in imaging. Both blood vessel ridges [4] and vasculature network [5,6] have been used as features for registration of OCT-fundus image pairs. Similarity metrics based on pixel distance [4] or similarity between vessels [5] and local similarity [6] have been proposed. A coarse registration by brute force search [4,5] is followed by refinement using ICP algorithm [4] or higher order transform modelling [5,6].

Reported methods [2,3,7] for FFA and fundus registration are mostly feature based. Popular landmarks are Harris corners [3,7] or junctions [2]. Features include SIFT [7], orientation information [3] and a series of step patterns [2] around each obtained landmark. The extracted features are matched using bilateral matching [3,7] or nearest neighbour technique [2] and the final transformation is estimated using an affine model [2,3,7].

The limitation of methods in [4–6] comes from their dependence on vessel structure as a key feature. While this is relatively easy to extract in fundus images, it is not so in OCT due to the noisy nature of OCT. While Harris [3,7] and junction [2] detectors perform well on FFA and fundus images, they are unsuitable for the task at hand given the noisy OCT images. Our framework tries to solve these problems by finding landmarks without the need of accurate structure localization. MIND features are chosen so as to nullify the problem of noisy nature of OCT and complementary information provided by both modalities (Fig. 1).

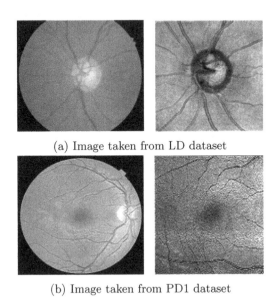

(a) Image taken from LD dataset

(b) Image taken from PD1 dataset

Fig. 1. Sample images of both macula and OD centric.

3   Methodology

The proposed method consists of the following modules: pre-processing and registration module. Pre-processing includes generating 2D OCT en-face images from 3D OCT volumes and illumination correction for OCT and fundus images. The registration module finds landmarks and registers images in an iterative manner. The MIND descriptor is extracted around each landmark and features are matched using Nearest neighbour technique. The obtained matches are finaly used to derive the transformation parameters.

3.1   Preprocessing of Images

OCT-Enface Creation
The 3D OCT volume is converted to a 2D OCT enface (see Fig. 2). The variance of the voxel values along columns (Y-axis) of all slices is computed for this

purpose. The variance measure is chosen for better visualization of vessels given that there is increased variability of vessels and background across the Y-axis. The final obtained 2D OCT enface is used for registration.

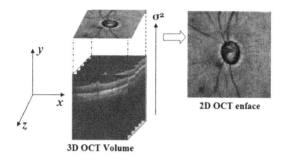

Fig. 2. 2D OCT en-face creation

Illumination Correction

Images suffer from non-uniform illumination and hence this is corrected using the luminosity and contrast normalization method proposed in [8]. Here, the image is modeled as:

$$I(x,y) = T(x,y) * L(x,y) + C(x,y) \qquad (1)$$

where $T(x,y)$ is the true image, $I(x,y)$ is the observed image, $L(x,y)$ and $C(x,y)$ are multiplicative and additive components. The recovery of the true image is based on estimation of the $L(x,y)$ and $C(x,y)$ components. Hence, the correction of observed image $I(x,y)$ can be obtained by:

$$T(x,y) = \frac{I(x,y) - L(x,y)}{C(x,y)} \qquad (2)$$

3.2 Registration Algorithm

The schematic of proposed registration method is shown in the Fig. 3. This is an iterative approach wherein the registration error is minimized with each iteration. Initial registration is performed with roughly initialized landmarks which are updated in each iteration. Unlike existing methods, the landmarks do not require any accurate structure localization/segmentation. The details of method is presented next. In our work, the enface OCT is used as floating image and registered to the reference fundus image.

Landmark Initialization

Rough initializations of both OD and macula are shown in Fig. 4. A circular Region of interest (cROI-*red*) is detected and a circle slightly larger than this cROI-*green* is initialized. The points of intersection of this circle with vessels

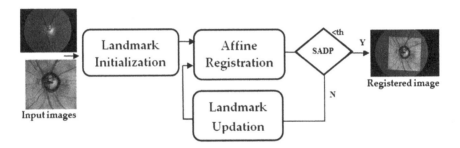

Fig. 3. Flow diagram for proposed registration framework

are considered as initial landmarks for registration. cROI can be the optic disc (OD) or macula depending on the imaging protocol. In order to find cROI from a fundus image, the OD (macula) boundary is detected by finding points of local maxima (minima) of intensity values whereas for an OCT en-face image, OD (macula) boundary is detected by finding points of local minima (minima) of the intensity values. These points are clustered and a best-fit circle is found for the boundary of largest central object. Let C_f (C_o) of radius R_f (R_o) be the circle of fundus(oct). A rough vessel map $I_{vf}(I_{vo})$, is obtained by thresholding the ROI images and thinning it to 1 pixel. The points of intersection of the $I_{vf}(I_{vo})$ with the circle $C_f(C_o)$ are identified as rough landmarks $P_f(P_o)$.

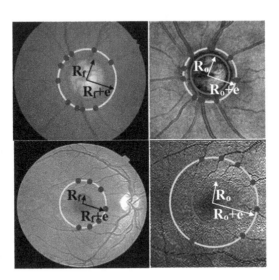

Fig. 4. Rough landmark initializations (marked in blue) (Color figure online)

Feature Based Affine Registration Feature Extraction

The MIND descriptor [9] is chosen to represent landmarks. MIND is based on the idea of image self-similarity. The assumption is that a local image can be approximated by considering the similarity between all small patches in the image. This approximation aims to extract the distinctive structure in a local neighborhood, which is preserved across modalities. MIND is computed as follows:

$$M(I, x, r) = \frac{1}{n} exp(-\frac{D_p(I, x, x + r)}{V(x, r)})$$ (3)

where D_p is the distance measure between two voxels x and $x + r$, r defines the spatial search region, V is variance estimate and n is normalization constant.

A patch of size $W \times W$ is extracted around each landmark from the enhanced image $I_f(I_o)$. Rotational invariance is achieved by rotating the patch to dominant direction found from Histogram of Orientation Gradients(HoG) prior to the descriptor computation. In our experiments, 12 bins were chosen for HoG computation and for the descriptor was computed over a patch of size $W = 12$. The resultant descriptor was vectorized (144 dimensional) to form a feature vector $M_f(M_o)$.

Feature Matching and Outliers Rejection
Given two sets of features M_f, M_o derived from the fundus and OCT images K-nearest neighbor search using normalized Euclidean distance metric was used to match them. Here K is chosen to be 3. So for each feature in set M_f, we obtain $K = 3$ neighbors in set M_o. The normalized Euclidean distance metric between i^{th} feature in set M_f and j^{th} feature in set M_o is given as

$$dist(M_{if}, M_{jo}) = \|M_{if} - M_{jo}\|_2^2$$ (4)

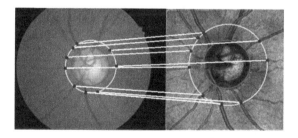

Fig. 5. Point correspondence after outliers rejection

The first set of outliers are rejected from the obtained neighbors by matching with dominant orientation of the landmark patch. Random sample consensus (RANSAC) [10] with similarity transformation is applied to all remaining matched pairs (see Fig. 5).

Transformation Estimation
The number of matched point pairs obtained from RANSAC is constrained by the number of detectable vessels and FOV of the floating image which is smaller than that of the fundus image. Given the anatomy of the retina, on average, 8–10

320   G. S. Jahnavi and J. Sivaswamy

matches are obtained for each image. In our problem the retina is a curved surface
that can be approximated with higher order model and OCT is a flat projection
with very less FOV. Thus, the transformation between two modalities can be
assumed to be locally rigid with possible deformations as scaling, translation,
rotation. Hence, a similarity model is used for the Transformation function.

Landmarks Updation
If the registration error from the initialized landmarks is greater than
threshold(th) then landmarks are to be updated. This is done in two steps.
One is at global level and other is at local level.

Global Level Update
At the global level, landmarks are updated by appropriate scaling of R_f and R_o.
Let their ratio be Q_R.

$$Q_R = R_f/R_o \tag{5}$$

Since the OCT image is taken to be the floating image, the aim is to update
R_o such that landmarks extracted from the circle with the updated radius R_{uo}
results in a registration error less than th. The registration error is taken to be
the sum of absolute distance between points (SADP). SADP is calculated from
two thinned vessel sets $I_{vf}(I_{vo})$ by finding matched point pairs in I_{vo} for every
point in I_{vf} using Nearest Neighbor search algorithm.

Local Level Update
For every global refinement step, the intersection points P_o are locally refined in
the angular direction. This local refinement is important because skeletonization
of vesse]ls can lead to perturbation of landmarks (see Fig. 6). The landmark
points are updated by making use of the principle that given two circles C_f
and C_o for a fixed angle, the ratio of their radii (Q_R) to the corresponding arc
lengths (Q_A) are equal where the arcs are defined to be between every pair of
successive points in P_f, P_o subtending angles θ_j, $j = 0, 1, 2 \ldots J$. The updation
rules for global and local refinement are shown below in Fig. 7. After updating
θ_j, the intersection points are also updated with appropriate angular shifts. This

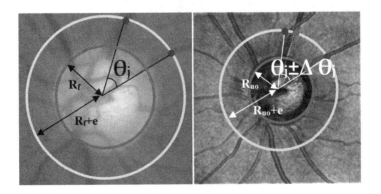

Fig. 6. Local refinement after updating radii

Global updating	Local updating
[1] **for:** $R_o \leftarrow R_o$ **to** $2R_o$	**for:** $\theta \leftarrow \theta_o$ **to** θ_j
[2] *Compute* $Q \leftarrow R_f/R_o$	$r_f \leftarrow R_f + e$
[3] **Local refinement of landmarks**	$r_o \leftarrow R_o + e$
[4] *Affine Registration*	*Compute* Q'
[5] *Error* $\leftarrow$ *SAD*	**if:** $Q > Q'$ **then:** $\theta \leftarrow \theta + 1$
[6] $R_o \leftarrow R_o + 1$ *and go to step 1*	**else:** $\theta \leftarrow \theta - 1$
[7] **if:** *Error is increasing* **then:** $R_o \leftarrow R_o - 1$	**Untill** $Q\text{-}Q'$ *equals* 0
[8] **end for**	**end for**

Fig. 7. Global and local updation rules

is done until the criterion of $Q_R - Q_A = 0$ is satisfied. The θ_j updated subject to it being in the range $min(\frac{\Delta\theta_j}{2}, \theta_{max})$ where θ_{max} is the upper bound for radial shift of landmarks. This is done to ensure that landmark update is bounded.

4 Datasets

Three datasets were considered for evaluation of proposed registration algorithm.

(1) **PD1** [5]: a public dataset, consisting of 22 pairs (Fundus-OCT) of which 17 pairs are of macular region and 5 pairs are of OD region with a variety of retinal diseases. Each OCT volume is of size $650 \times 512 \times 128$ voxels and the fundus image is of size 1200×1143 pixels.
(2) **PD2** [11]: a public dataset, consisting of 100 pairs (Fundus-OCT) of macular region, with no abnormalities. Each OCT volume is of size $650 \times 512 \times 128$ voxels and the fundus image is of size 1200×1143 pixels.
(3) **LD:** a locally sourced dataset, consisting of 42 pairs (Fundus and OCT) of OD region obtained. 20 pairs are of glaucoma cases and remaining are normal. Each OCT volume is of size $650 \times 304 \times 304$ and the fundus image is of size 4288×2848 pixels.

5 Experiments and Results

The MIND descriptor was computed with the following parameters $\{\sigma = 2, N = 6\}$ where σ is the variance estimate which controls the response of feature and N is the neighborhood of spatial search. For evaluating registration in every iteration the threshold th was chosen to be 5 pixels. The number of iterations depends on the error (SADP). If the SADP converges (<5 pixels) the least registration error (SADP) among next 5 iterations is considered.

Code was written in MATLAB 2016a and executed on a 2.5 GHz Intel Core i5 desktop with 8 GB memory. The average execution time for an image pair was 10.12 s, of which 5.8 s was for en-face creation and the remaining time was for registration (Fig. 8).

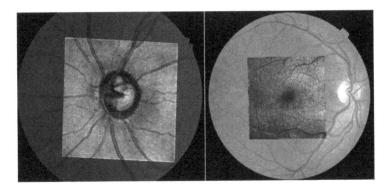

Fig. 8. Sample registration results

Accuracy of registration is evaluated by Root mean square error (RMSE), Mean median error (MME [3]), Mean maximum error (MAE [3]) and Sum of Absolute Distance between points (SADP [5]). Ground truth control points were manually marked mostly at reliable positions such as junctions of thin and thick vessels for measuring RMSE, MME, MAE. SADP was calculated from two sets of thinned vessel maps $I_{vf}(I_{vo})$ by finding the matched point pairs using Nearest Neighbour search Algorithm.

$$SADP = \sum_{i=1}^{n} |d(x_i, y_i)| / N \tag{6}$$

where x and y denote vessel pixels extracted from fundus image and OCT enface images, respectively; d is the distance between ith observation of x and y_i which is the corresponding closest point in y and N is the length of vector x. Table 1 shows the average SAD, RMSE, MME, MAE over all datasets. It is to be noted that for a total image set of 142 pairs 90.22% pairs are successfully registered with a average RMSE error of 2.61 pixels. The performance metrics of other methods are given below Table 2. Method [2] implementation is done and results are reported on LD dataset and method [5] results are mentioned in paper. In comparison with the our results it is observed that proposed algorithm performs exceptionally well considering the amount of data that is tested.

Table 1. Registration performance on datasets

Datasets	Success rate %	SDP	RMSE	MME	MAE
PD1	86.66	3.92	3.12	3.83	6.17
PD2	96	4.21	3.70	3.93	5.39
LD	90	1.51	1.01	2.22	2.46
Average	90.22	3.21	2.61	3.32	4.67

Table 2. Registration performance of existing methods

Method	Dataset	SDP	RMSE	MEE	MAE
[5]	PD1	6.01 ± 1.82 (stage-1)	-	-	-
[2]	LD	4.8	3.19	4.32	7.33

Next we report results of test of robustness of the proposed method for rotation invariance and scale sensitivity. This was tested by applying rotation and scaling to the floating images.

Scale Change Test

Floating images were up-sampled by a factor ranging from 1–10 and the results were registered to the fixed image. A registration error of ≤5 pixels is considered as perfect registration (or 100%). The success rate is proportionately reduced by 10% for an increase in error by 5 pixels. The plot in Fig. 9 indicates that the proposed registration is robust to a scale change of up to 1.6.

Rotation Invariance Test

Floating images were rotated by 0°–180° in steps of 30°. The registration was found to be robust for all angles in the tested range. This is to be expected as the patches used for feature computation are pre-rotated to dominant orientation. This makes the features invariant to rotation.

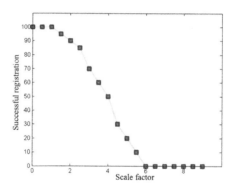

Fig. 9. Performance with scale change

6   Conclusion

Multimodal registration is a challenging task as the images are varied by FOV, noise, contrast etc. These differences affect the registration in terms of finding landmarks and extracting features. These problems are overcome in our proposed registration method by minimizing the registration error by simultaneously refining the landmark positions in an iterative framework. Unlike earlier methods, the proposed method does not require precise ROI/vessel segmentation which is usually challenging. The choice of MIND descriptor ensures robustness as the extracted features are insensitive to modality, noise and contrast across modalities. The proposed algorithm was found to achieve high registration accuracy and outperform existing algorithms when evaluated over three datasets i.e. 142 image pairs.

References

1. Wang, Y.T., Tadarati, M., Wolfson, Y., Bressler, S.B., Bressler, N.M.: Comparison of prevalence of diabetic macular edema based on monocular fundus photography vs optical coherence tomography. JAMA Ophthalmol. **134**(2), 222–228 (2016)
2. Lee, J.A., Cheng, J., Lee, B.H., Ong, E.P., Xu, G., Wong, D.W.K., Liu, J., Laude, A., Lim, T.H.: A low-dimensional step pattern analysis algorithm with application to multimodal retinal image registration. In: Proceedings of the IEEE Conference on Computer Vision and Pattern Recognition, pp. 1046–1053 (2015)
3. Chen, J., Tian, J., Lee, N., Zheng, J., Smith, R.T., Laine, A.F.: A partial intensity invariant feature descriptor for multimodal retinal image registration. IEEE Trans. Biomed. Eng. **57**(7), 1707–1718 (2010)
4. Li, Y., Gregori, G., Knighton, R.W., Lujan, B.J., Rosenfeld, P.J.: Registration of OCT fundus images with color fundus photographs based on blood vessel ridges. Opt. Express **19**(1), 7–16 (2011)
5. Golabbakhsh, M., Rabbani, H.: Vessel-based registration of fundus and optical coherence tomography projection images of retina using a quadratic registration model. IET Image Process. **7**(8), 768–776 (2013)
6. Niu, S., Chen, Q., Shen, H., de Sisternes, L., Rubin, D.L.: Registration of SD-OCT en-face images with color fundus photographs based on local patch matching (2014)
7. Ghassabi, Z., Shanbehzadeh, J., Sedaghat, A., Fatemizadeh, E.: An efficient approach for robust multimodal retinal image registration based on UR-SIFT features and PIIFD descriptors. EURASIP J. Image Video Process. **2013**(1), 1–16 (2013)
8. Joshi, G.D., Sivaswamy, J.: Colour retinal image enhancement based on domain knowledge. In: Sixth Indian Conference on Computer Vision, Graphics and Image Processing, ICVGIP 2008, pp. 591–598. IEEE (2008)
9. Heinrich, M.P., Jenkinson, M., Bhushan, M., Matin, T., Gleeson, F.V., Brady, M., Schnabel, J.A.: MIND: modality independent neighbourhood descriptor for multimodal deformable registration. Med. Image Anal. **16**(7), 1423–1435 (2012)
10. Fischler, M.A., Bolles, R.C.: Random sample consensus: a paradigm for model fitting with applications to image analysis and automated cartography. Commun. ACM **24**(6), 381–395 (1981)
11. Mahmudi, T., Kafieh, R., Rabbani, H., Akhlagi, M., et al.: Comparison of macular OCTs in right and left eyes of normal people. In: SPIE Medical Imaging, p. 90381W. International Society for Optics and Photonics (2014)

Segmentation, Retrieval, Captioning

Dynamic Class Learning Approach
for Smart CBIR

Girraj Pahariya[1,3](✉), Balaraman Ravindran[1,2], and Sukhendu Das[1,3]

[1] Department of Computer Science and Engineering, IIT Madras, Chennai, India
{giri,ravi}@cse.iitm.ac.in, sdas@iitm.ac.in
[2] Robert Bosch Centre for Data Science and AI, IIT Madras, Chennai, India
[3] Visualization and Perception Lab, IIT Madras, Chennai, India

Abstract. Smart Content Based Image Retrieval (CBIR) helps to simultaneously localize and recognize all object(s) present in a scene, for image retrieval task. The major drawbacks in such kind of system are: (a) overhead for addition of new class is high - addition of new class requires manual annotation of large number of samples and retraining of an entire object model; and (b) use of handcrafted features for recognition and localization task, which limits its performance. In this era of data proliferation where it is easy to discover new object categories and hard to label all of them i.e. less amount of labeled samples for training which raises the above mentioned drawbacks. In this work, we propose an approach which cuts down the overhead of labelling the data and retraining on an entire module to learn new classes. The major components in proposed framework are: (a) selection of an appropriate pre-trained deep model for learning a new class; and (b) learning new class by utilizing selected deep model with less supervision (i.e. with the least amount of labeled data) using a concept of triplet learning. To show the effectiveness of the proposed technique of new class learning, we have performed an evaluation on CIFAR-10, PASCAL VOC2007 and Imagenet datasets.

Keywords: CBIR · Triplet metric learning · CNN · Dynamic learning

1 Introduction

Content Based Image Retrieval (CBIR) systems retrieve images that are similar to a query image and rank order them on the basis of similarity to the query [15,16]. One of the chief drawbacks of traditional CBIR systems is the need to match the query against the entire gallery images in order to produce a rank order. Smart CBIR systems [6,9,19] address this issue by first identifying and localizing all the objects present in an image. These objects, and the corresponding images, are then categorized into multiple classes. While processing a query image, first the categories of the objects in the query are determined, and similar images are retrieved only from the corresponding categories in the image gallery. Clearly, locating and classifying objects in the images are important tasks in such systems. Doing this effectively gives rise to two challenges:

© Springer Nature Singapore Pte Ltd. 2018
R. Rameshan et al. (Eds.): NCVPRIPG 2017, CCIS 841, pp. 327–337, 2018.
https://doi.org/10.1007/978-981-13-0020-2_29

– Defining rich feature sets: The feature set chosen limits the performance of the system. Traditionally hand crafted features based on domain knowledge were chosen, but these were not always very discriminative. For example, use of shape features while useful for distinguishing classes such as apple and banana, would not be useful in telling apart a grapefruit and an orange.
– Addition of new categories: A dynamically changing gallery of images would require one to be able to add new categories of images/objects to the gallery. Typically this is a cumbersome process requiring large number of manually annotated samples, and expensive retraining of classification models.

In this work we propose a deep learning based new class learning framework for smart CBIR task that addresses the aforementioned issues. Inspired by the recent success of deep neural networks in image representation and pattern recognition, we build our framework on Convolutional Neural Networks (CNNs). It has been repeatedly shown that CNNs learn features at multiple granularities from low level features such as lines and edges; to high level features such as shape and texture [13]. With appropriate end-to-end training, features that are discriminative for the classes of interest are learned, and this addresses the first challenge discussed above.

While CNNs have shown tremendous success in object detection and categorization [13, 21, 25] there has not been much work on incremental addition of new object categories. Two conventional ways in which CNNs are trained to add new categories are:

1. Multi-class CNN model: freeze the model parameters and train only the last softmax layer to add new categories.
2. One vs All CNN models: train a separate model for new categories.

Both methods require huge amount of training samples and large number of iterations for effective training. The latter method is common in literature for the smart CBIR systems [6, 9].

In this work we have proposed a technique to efficiently learn or add new object category to the pre-trained CBIR system. We refer to this process of learning new class as *Dynamic Learning*. In the proposed dynamic learning system, one vs all model for the newly added categories are generated bootstrapping from the pre-trained system, with a few training samples. The bootstrap procedure first identifies from among the pre-trained categories, the category closest to the new category. While this provides a good starting point, we still require to fine-tune this classifier for the new category. In order to achieve this with minimal annotated data we use a modification of the triplet metric learning approach proposed in [27]. The proposed framework to learn new class is shown in Fig. 1.

The major contributions of this study are: (a) the method to select an appropriate model from the pre-trained system to add a new category; and (b) the triplet metric learning based approach to learn the new object categories by exploiting the existing deep learning techniques.

The main goal of paper is not to improve the performance of Smart CBIR technique, but to propose a framework which helps to learn new class using an existing models without effecting the overall performance of the system. Due to which, we have compared our work with state-of-the-art classification techniques only.

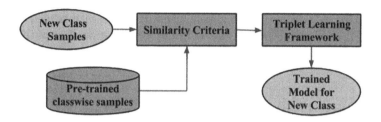

Fig. 1. Framework for proposed method

The paper is structured as follows, Sect. 2 provides a brief inspection of related work on CBIR, CNN and triplet metric learning. Section 3 discuss about the proposed framework. Section 4 provides details about the experiments and results to show the potency of our proposed method and Sect. 5 concludes the work.

2   Related Work

CBIR systems take a query image as input and retrieve similar images from a gallery of image samples. Existing CBIR algorithms [15,16] process one image into several steps of tasks. These steps include extracting the multidimensional features of an image query and compare it with images in the gallery. These features consist of color, shape, texture and other image characteristics [5]. Most of the CBIR systems in the earlier day's work by extracting global features from the entire image which captures a lot of background information, thus degrading the retrieval performance of the system.

To overcome the above problem, work published in [19] proposed a localized content based image retrieval as a CBIR task where a user is only interested inner portion of an image, and the background is irrelevant. The challenge in such advances is to localize the interested portion of an image. Graph-cut [2] is used for localization and SVM is used for recognition. Smart (object-centric) CBIR framework which extract the features from appropriate locations (region of interests), recognize each of them to one of the object categories and retrieves similar images from recognized categories only, which makes recognition an important task.

During the recent years deep learning approaches have been of particular interest for object classification task [26]. One major issue with deep learning approaches is it requires huge amount of data for better training, which is not available all the time. Data augmentation is one of the technique to increase training data size. General approaches for data augmentation are, scaling, rotary motion, translation, flips, color perturbation [13]. Work published in [8,17,23,24] uses data augmentation schemes to improve their performance.

However to avoid overfitting, it is desirable to use a variety of images, whereas data augmentation techniques mostly reproduce similar images. In [27], a deep metric learning framework has been proposed which use triplets for fine-grained image classification using CNN models. The advantage with triplets is that, a number of possible triplets increases cubically with the number of images and each triplet is unique in nature which generally solves the problem of huge data requirement and overfitting.

3   Proposed Dynamic Learning Framework

Dynamic Learning is the process of adding new object categories to a pre-trained CBIR system without affecting on its overall performance. It is challenging to build a CBIR system where new object classes can be added without retraining the whole system. In this study, we exploit the existing pre-trained models to learn the samples of new class efficiently.

The intuition is to make use of an existing class model to build the new class models with minimal number of samples. To achieve this, firstly we try to determine existing class that is most similar to new desired class by calculating similarity in feature space. Then fine-tune the parameters of selected model in previous step using triplet metric learning. The main intent is to exploit a shared feature space across desired and existing classes, pairwise.

The overall problem of dynamically adding new classes to CBIR system consists of two major tasks: (a) Selection of the most similar pre-trained model; and (b) Refining the parameters of the chosen model.

3.1   Selecting Most Similar Pre-trained Model

Pre-trained classes are trained using AlexNet [13] model, and a separate model is formed for each class. Each class model considers that class as positive and rest as negative.

The similarity between the pre-trained classes and the new class is assessed using the Eq. (1). In this work, similarity is defined as the inverse of the distance between mean of two classes in feature space.

$$sim(X,Y) \propto \frac{1}{dist\left(\frac{\sum_{i=1}^{n_x} \hat{f}(p_{ix})}{n_x}, \frac{\sum_{j=1}^{n_y} \hat{f}(p_{jy})}{n_y}\right)} \tag{1}$$

where, $sim(X,Y)$ is similarity between class X and class Y, X is one of the pre-trained classes and Y is a new class to be added, n_x and n_y are number of samples in class X, p_{ix} is the ith sample from class X, p_{jy} is the jth sample from class Y, $\hat{f}(p_{ix})$ and $\hat{f}(p_{jy})$ are the feature space representation for i^{th} and j^{th} sample from class X and Y respectively using pre-trained model of class X

and $dist(\frac{\sum_{i=1}^{n_x} \hat{f}(p_{ix})}{n_x}, \frac{\sum_{j=1}^{n_y} \hat{f}(p_{jy})}{n_y})$ evaluates the Euclidean distance between the means of feature space representation of samples from class X and Y.

Similarity of the new class is evaluated with each of pre-existing class in dataset. Similarity estimate outputs the class which is most similar to the new class. It is the class which gives maximum similarity with the objects of new class in feature space. The class which gives the maximum similarity is selected and pass to the next step for further processing.

3.2   Refining Selected Model

The second step for the proposed method is to exploit (retrain/refine) the parameters of the selected model in the previous subsection using Triplet Metric Learning using triplets designed from new class.

Triplets are set of three images $\{p_i, p_+, p_-\}$ where p_i (**Query Image**) is from training class, p_+ (**Positive Image**) is an image from the same class of query and p_- (**Negative Image**) is from a class other than the class of query sample. Overhead of collection and manual labelling of samples for new classes is high, which can be easily tackled using a proposed triplet learning based framework. For example, if we possess only 50 samples for training in a category "A" and we want to append that category to the pre-trained CBIR system having 10 different classes with 50 samples in each of them. The total number of possible triplets in this case are: $50(\#query\ samples) * 49(\#positive\ samples) * (10 * 50)(\#negative\ samples) = 1125\ K$ which is a huge number, providing adequate training data. Experiments performed in this paper also uses a minimal number of samples (only 50 to 100) which empirically shows that triplets are able to overcome the overhead of collection and manual labelling a lot of samples for training.

New class is considered as positive class and other classes are considered as negative classes. Generated triplets (from query, positive samples from new class and negative samples from rest of the classes) are fed to the triplet metric learning framework [27], as shown in Fig. 2, which incorporates 3 layers:

Triplet Sampling Layer. One way is to feed all the triplets to the network for training but number of triplets grows exponentially with data size so it is important to sample the relevant triplets. Sampling layer samples out the relevant triplets from the large set. In our approach we choose top 1 million triplets, half of which are from the most similar class as negative sample and rest of the triplets are from other classes as negative which are sampled uniformly over all other classes (except most similar one).

CNN Model Layer. It incorporates 3 identical CNN models (having similar weights) Q, P and N for each of query, positive and negative image of a Triplet. Each of the CNN model follows the AlexNet [13] architecture here except the last fully connected layer and initialized with the weights of the model of the most similar class to the new class. Selected relevant Triplets are fed to the respective CNN's for query, positive and negative image. Each CNN gives a feature space representation for each of query, positive and negative image represented by $\hat{f}(p_i)$, $\hat{f}(p_+)$ and $\hat{f}(p_-)$.

Ranking Loss Layer. It implements the Triplet loss or Hinge loss. Equation (2) depicts that the distance between query and positive image of a Triplet should always be less the distance between query and negative image in the feature space. This should always be true for a well trained model since query and positive image belongs to the same class, whereas the negative image is a sample from some other class.

$$dist(\hat{f}(p_i), \hat{f}(p_+)) < dist(\hat{f}(p_i), \hat{f}(p_-)) \tag{2}$$

Triplets which does not satisfy the constraint mentioned in Eq. (2) incorporates a Hinge loss which is given in Eq. (3). The hinge loss is a convex approximation to the 0–1 ranking-loss, which measures the model's violation of the ranking order specified in Eq. (2).

$$l(p_i, p_+, p_-) = max\{0, dist(\hat{f}(p_i), \hat{f}(p_+)) - dist(\hat{f}(p_i), \hat{f}(p_-)))\} \quad \forall p_i, p_+, p_- \tag{3}$$

where $l(p_i, p_+, p_-)$ is hinge/triplet loss for a Triplet. The objective function in order to minimize the loss is given as,

$$\min \sum_{i=1}^{n} l(p_i, p_+, p_-) + \lambda \|W\|_2^2 \tag{4}$$

where n is the number of query samples, λ is the regularization parameter and W are the model parameters. λ is set to 10^{-3} in this work which is measured empirically. Loss defined in Eq. (3) is back-propagated as gradients to the lower layers of the model, which adjusts the weight parameters of the model in order to minimize the objective function given in Eq. (4).

Figure 2 presents the Triplet Metric Learning. We feed a Triplet to the framework given in Fig. 2 which first samples the relevance of a Triplet and then passes it through the CNN models and give the feature space representation of query p_i, positive p_+ and negative p_- images, where ranking loss is incorporated to make positive sample closer and negative sample away from the query.

4   Results and Experiments

4.1   Datasets

1. **CIFAR-10** [12]: This dataset has 10 classes having 5000 samples in each class of size 32 * 32 pixels.
2. **Pascal VOC2007** [7]: This dataset includes 20 classes having a total of 9963 images of variable sizes. This is one of the most challenging dataset with variable no of samples in each class.

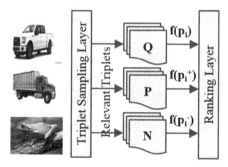

Fig. 2. Triplet learning framework

3. **Imagenet** [13]: Randomly chosen 50 out of 1000 classes are used for experimentation in this paper. Each of the 50 classes has 1000 samples in each of them having an average image size of $400 * 350$ pixels.

In each of the dataset, 70% of the data is used for training, 20% for testing and 10% for validation. 8, 15 and 40 classes are considered to be pre-trained in case of CIFAR, PASCAL and Imagenet categories and rest of the classes are added using our proposed approach.

4.2   Results

It is very important to recognize correct object category to retrieve only the correct samples as retrieval results. To indicate the effectiveness of the proposed approach of dynamic learning using triplets, we compared our approach with 5 different baseline methods and few other state-of-the-art techniques.

Baseline 1: In this approach, we train the CNN model with a multi-class classifier. To add a new class dynamically, an extra node is added to the last fully connected layer of CNN model and retrain with the samples of the new class by freezing weights of convolution layers.

Baseline 2: In this approach, one vs all classifiers are trained with initial classes and new classes are added incrementally by initializing model parameters from scratch.

Baseline 3: In this approach, one vs all classifiers are trained incrementally by initializing weights for new models from similar class as discussed in Sect. 3.1. This baseline is to show the effectiveness of starting point (choosing initial model parameters).

Baseline 4: In this approach, one vs all classifiers are trained for each class separately using triplets from the samples. New classes are added incrementally and model parameters are initialized from scratch. This baseline is to show the effectiveness of the triplet training over normal training.

Baseline 5: In this approach, one vs all classifiers are trained using Triplet learning by considering all classes available i.e. no incremental learning. This baseline is a benchmark as it assumes that all training data is available from the beginning.

For training purposes in baseline 1 to 4 and proposed method we are using 8, 15 and 40 classes as pre-trained classes initially. Rest of the classes in each of the dataset are added later with the help of incremental method and given approach in the baseline.

Proposed method is similar to baseline 4 except from the fact that initial model parameters are chosen as the parameters of one of the pre-trained similar model. Classification accuracy of 3 datasets are evaluated to show the comparison and effectiveness of the proposed methods as compared to the other baselines for dynamic learning.

Table 1. Classification accuracy (in %) on different datasets.

Dataset	B 1	B 2	B 3	B4	B 5	Proposed
CIFAR	89.4	94.6	93.7	96.8	97.9	97.6
PASCAL	74.8	79.95	79.3	82.1	83.3	82.7
Imagenet	92.6	91.4	90.6	92.4	93.6	93.4

Table 1 clearly shows that baseline 5 is a standard method, which is not easy to beat since it assumes that all classes are available for training at the beginning. Our proposed method is comparable to baseline 5 standards, which asserts the effectiveness of our proposed method. B 1–5 in Table 1 represents baseline 1–5 respectively.

Baseline 3 and proposed approach are able to converge almost 50% faster than other baselines 1, 2, 4 and 5 due to initialization of optimal parameters to perform incremental learning. Overall our approach is performing better than other baselines in terms of both speedup and accuracy which shows the superiority of our method.

The performance of the proposed method is comparable to a few state of the art approaches given in Tables 2 and 3 for CIFAR10 and PASCAL VOC2007 datasets respectively. Proposed method learns to classify all the classes by dynamically learning few classes whereas other methods mentioned in Tables 2 and 3 uses dataset as a whole (i.e. information about the full dataset is available).

Comparisons are not shown on Imagenet dataset as it is difficult to train all other models on selected 50 classes from Imagenet for baselines. Our aim in this paper is not to improve the classification accuracy, but the aim is to develop an approach which helps to dynamically learn or add a new class in an existing system. Classification results are compared to show the effectiveness of proposed method in learning a new categories.

For experimental purpose one other similarity criteria is used to find the most similar class i.e. by passing testing samples of new class with all other pre-trained models as positive class. The pre-trained class model which gives

Table 2. Comparison of classification accuracy on CIFAR-10 dataset.

Method	Accuracy (in %)
Graham [8]	96.53%
Springenberg et al. [23]	95.59%
Mishkin and Matas [17]	94.16%
Snoek et al. [22]	93.63%
Liang and Hu [14]	92.91%
Agostinelli et al. [1]	92.49%
Srivastava et al. [24]	92.40%
Proposed	**97.60%**

Table 3. Comparison of classification accuracy on PASCAL VOC2007 dataset.

Method	Accuracy (in %)
He et al. [10]	80.1%
Chatfield et al. [3]	**82.42%**
Sharif et al. [20]	77.2%
Oquab et al. [18]	77.7%
Chen et al. [4]	70.5%
Proposed	81.72%

the least classification error rate is considered to be the most similar class. New classes in CIFAR-10 and PASCAL datasets are added dynamically using this similarity criteria and for CIFAR-10 the selected similar classes are same as distance between their means in feature space. For PASCAL only one class, *cow* for which *horse* comes out to be the most similar class and it was *cat* when distance between mean is used as similarity criteria. Classification accuracy for CIFAR-10 dataset is similar for both similarity criterion, however for PASCAL dataset accuracy find out to be 80.5%.

5 Conclusion

In this work, we proposed a novel approach for training new object categories dynamically to a CBIR system. Our method is capable of training effectively (with the least number of samples) and also faster than training a model from scratch. One issue with the system is that we are using one vs all models which needs a model for each class which requires more memory for storage. But, now a days we have an abundance of storage space allowing us to lay in these models. Also, compression techniques like SqueezeNet [11] allows to minimize the model size. Similarity criteria between classes in feature space can also be improved. Using one vs all models for dynamic learning is overall time efficient and performing almost equivalent to other baselines.

References

1. Agostinelli, F., Hoffman, M., Sadowski, P., Baldi, P.: Learning activation functions to improve deep neural networks. arXiv preprint arXiv:1412.6830 (2014)
2. Boykov, Y., Funka-Lea, G.: Graph cuts and efficient nd image segmentation. Int. J. Comput. Vis. **70**(2), 109–131 (2006)
3. Chatfield, K., Simonyan, K., Vedaldi, A., Zisserman, A.: Return of the devil in the details: delving deep into convolutional nets. arXiv preprint arXiv:1405.3531 (2014)

4. Chen, Q., Song, Z., Dong, J., Huang, Z., Hua, Y., Yan, S.: Contextualizing object detection and classification. IEEE Trans. Pattern Anal. Mach. Intell. **37**(1), 13–27 (2015)
5. Deselaers, T., Keysers, D., Ney, H.: Features for image retrieval: an experimental comparison. Inf. Retrieval **11**(2), 77–107 (2008)
6. Dwivedi, G., Das, S., Rakshit, S., Vora, M., Samanta, S.: SLAR (simultaneous localization and recognition) framework for smart CBIR. In: Kundu, M.K., Mitra, S., Mazumdar, D., Pal, S.K. (eds.) PerMIn 2012. LNCS, vol. 7143, pp. 277–287. Springer, Heidelberg (2012). https://doi.org/10.1007/978-3-642-27387-2_35
7. Everingham, M., Van Gool, L., Williams, C.K., Winn, J., Zisserman, A.: The pascal visual object classes (VOC) challenge. Int. J. Comput. Vis. **88**(2), 303–338 (2010)
8. Graham, B.: Fractional max-pooling. arXiv preprint arXiv:1412.6071 (2014)
9. Gupta, N., Das, S., Chakraborti, S.: Revealing what to extract from where, for object-centric content based image retrieval (CBIR). In: Proceedings of the 2014 Indian Conference on Computer Vision Graphics and Image Processing, p. 57. ACM (2014)
10. He, K., Zhang, X., Ren, S., Sun, J.: Spatial pyramid pooling in deep convolutional networks for visual recognition. In: Fleet, D., Pajdla, T., Schiele, B., Tuytelaars, T. (eds.) ECCV 2014. LNCS, vol. 8691, pp. 346–361. Springer, Cham (2014). https://doi.org/10.1007/978-3-319-10578-9_23
11. Iandola, F.N., Han, S., Moskewicz, M.W., Ashraf, K., Dally, W.J., Keutzer, K.: Squeezenet: AlexNet-level accuracy with 50x fewer parameters and <0.5 MB model size. arXiv preprint arXiv:1602.07360 (2016)
12. Krizhevsky, A., Hinton, G.: Learning multiple layers of features from tiny images (2009)
13. Krizhevsky, A., Sutskever, I., Hinton, G.E.: Imagenet classification with deep convolutional neural networks. In: Advances in Neural Information Processing Systems, pp. 1097–1105 (2012)
14. Liang, M., Hu, X.: Recurrent convolutional neural network for object recognition. In: Proceedings of the IEEE Conference on Computer Vision and Pattern Recognition, pp. 3367–3375 (2015)
15. Lin, C.-H., Chen, R.-T., Chan, Y.-K.: A smart content-based image retrieval system based on color and texture feature. Image Vis. Comput. **27**(6), 658–665 (2009)
16. Liu, Y., Zhang, D., Lu, G., Ma, W.-Y.: A survey of content-based image retrieval with high-level semantics. Pattern Recogn. **40**(1), 262–282 (2007)
17. Mishkin, D., Matas, J.: All you need is a good init. arXiv preprint arXiv:1511.06422 (2015)
18. Oquab, M., Bottou, L., Laptev, I., Sivic, J.: Learning and transferring mid-level image representations using convolutional neural networks. In: Proceedings of the IEEE Conference on Computer Vision and Pattern Recognition, pp. 1717–1724 (2014)
19. Rahman, M.M., Antani, S.K., Thoma, G.R.: A query expansion framework in image retrieval domain based on local and global analysis. Inf. Process. Manage. **47**(5), 676–691 (2011)
20. Razavian, A.S., Azizpour, H., Sullivan, J., Carlsson, S.: CNN features off-the-shelf: an astounding baseline for recognition. In: Proceedings of the IEEE Conference on Computer Vision and Pattern Recognition workshops, pp. 806–813 (2014)
21. Simonyan, K., Zisserman, A.: Very deep convolutional networks for large-scale image recognition. arXiv preprint arXiv:1409.1556 (2014)

22. Snoek, J., Rippel, O., Swersky, K., Kiros, R., Satish, N., Sundaram, N., Patwary, M., Prabhat, M., Adams, R.: Scalable Bayesian optimization using deep neural networks. In: International Conference on Machine Learning, pp. 2171–2180 (2015)
23. Springenberg, J.T., Dosovitskiy, A., Brox, T., Riedmiller, M.: Striving for simplicity: the all convolutional net. arXiv preprint arXiv:1412.6806 (2014)
24. Srivastava, R.K., Greff, K., Schmidhuber, J.: Training very deep networks. In: Advances in Neural Information Processing Systems, pp. 2377–2385 (2015)
25. Szegedy, C., Liu, W., Jia, Y., Sermanet, P., Reed, S., Anguelov, D., Erhan, D., Vanhoucke, V., Rabinovich, A.: Going deeper with convolutions. In: Proceedings of the IEEE Conference on Computer Vision and Pattern Recognition, pp. 1–9 (2015)
26. Wan, J., Wang, D., Hoi, S.C.H., Wu, P., Zhu, J., Zhang, Y., Li, J.: Deep learning for content-based image retrieval: a comprehensive study. In: Proceedings of the 22nd ACM International Conference on Multimedia, pp. 157–166. ACM (2014)
27. Wang, J., Song, Y., Leung, T., Rosenberg, C., Wang, J., Philbin, J., Chen, B., Wu, Y.: Learning fine-grained image similarity with deep ranking. In: Proceedings of the IEEE Conference on Computer Vision and Pattern Recognition, pp. 1386–1393 (2014)

Exploring Memory and Time Efficient Neural Networks for Image Captioning

Sandeep Narayan Parameswaran$^{(\boxtimes)}$

Visualization and Perception Lab, Department of Computer Science and Engineering,
Indian Institute of Technology Madras, Chennai 600036, India
sandeepn@cse.iitm.ac.in

Abstract. Automatically describing the contents of an image is one of the fundamental problems in artificial intelligence. Recent research has primarily focussed on improving the quality of the generated descriptions. It is possible to construct multiple architectures that achieve equivalent performance for the same task. Among these, the smaller architecture is desirable as they require less communication across servers during distributed training and less bandwidth to export a new model from one place to another through a network. Generally, a deep learning architecture for image captioning consists of a Convolutional Neural Network (CNN) and a Recurrent Neural Network (RNN) clubbed together within an encoder-decoder framework. We propose to combine a significantly smaller CNN architecture termed *SqueezeNet* and a memory and computation efficient *LightRNN* within a visual attention framework. Experimental evaluation of the proposed architecture on Flickr8k, Flickr30k and MS-COCO datasets reveal superior result when compared to the state of the art.

1 Introduction

Generating a description for an image is at the heart of image understanding - a primary goal for computer vision. Many methods [1–4] have been devised to solve this problem. Much of these work focused on devising models that perform better on various metrics [5–7] for evaluating the quality of the generated descriptions. It is widely accepted that multiple architectural models can be constructed for achieving the same performance on a given metric. A model with fewer parameters and size has the following advantages:

- **Efficient distributed training:** A major limiting factor to the scalability of training a neural network using distributed systems is the communication overhead between the servers. This is a direct consequence of the number of parameters present in the network. Therefore, when performing a data-parallel training in a distributed environment, a small model will be able to train faster, since it requires lesser communication between the servers [8].
- **Reduced overhead during application update:** Many companies need to send new models from their servers to devices owned by their customers in

© Springer Nature Singapore Pte Ltd. 2018
R. Rameshan et al. (Eds.): NCVPRIPG 2017, CCIS 841, pp. 338–347, 2018.
https://doi.org/10.1007/978-981-13-0020-2_30

order to keep their applications updated. Today, majority of the architectures require models that require large data transfers for the model update. With smaller model sizes, such frequent updates become feasible.

In this work, we propose a smaller architecture with fewer parameters but equivalent performance in comparison to a popular model for the image captioning problem. We have identified a Convolutional Neural Network (CNN) architecture named SqueezeNet [9] and a modified Recurrent Neural Network (RNN) architecture called LightRNN [10] for the same. We introduce these components to the existing encoder-decoder architecture framework for performing image captioning introduced in [3]. The LightRNN, a variant of the familiar RNN introduces a 2-component shared embedding for the vocabulary. The overall architecture is as shown in Fig. 1. The model takes an image as input, performs a pass through the CNN and obtains a feature representation for the image. It then passes these features through the LightRNN, wherein the generation of each word involves the prediction of two components. We refer to these components as the row and column component of the word in accordance with the shared embedding table used for describing the words in the vocabulary. During the generation of each component of the word, the model focuses on different parts of the image similar to the visual attention mechanism for words [3].

We analyse and quantify the degradation in performance of our model in generating captions, where we trade off quality for lesser number of parameters, smaller size and computation with the help of three benchmark datasets: Flickr8k, Flickr30k and MS-COCO.

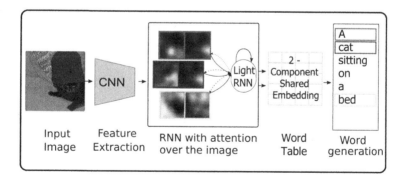

Fig. 1. The proposed architecture for generating sentences from images. The details about the component-wise attention can be found in Sect. 3.3.

2   Related Work

AlexNet [11] was the very first large deep convolutional neural network for classifying images performing exceptionally well on the ImageNet [12] data. The network achieved a top-5 error rate of 15.3% for the classification task with

60 M parameters. VGGNet [13] is a more recent deep network for classifying images with a top-5 error rate of 6.8% and 144 M parameters. ResNet [14] and GoogLeNet [15], two very deep networks perform even better with the incorporation of inception and residual layers. Recently, there has been substantial work directed towards reducing the model size without impacting accuracy. Deep Compression [16] uses pruning, trained quantization and Huffman coding to cut short the storage requirement of neural networks without affecting their accuracy. SqueezeNet [9] proposes a new architecture equivalent to AlexNet in terms of accuracy but with lesser number of parameters.

The Recurrent Neural Network (RNN) has been explored to be used for a wide variety of problems. It suffered a major drawback in the form of vanishing gradients when training the network, only to be solved by the introduction of gating in Long Short-Term Memory (LSTM) [17] and Gated Recurrent Unit (GRU) [18]. The softmax layer at the output embedding matrix is a compute intensive part of any model using RNN like framework. LightRNN [10] is one way to address this problem.

The models NIC [2], Show Attend and Tell [3] adapt the convolutional and recurrent architectures to solve the image captioning problem. The CNN acts as an encoder for the image while the RNN decodes, generating text. Both, NIC and Show Attend and Tell have used the VGGNet as the encoder for the image and LSTM as the decoder for generating captions. The NIC extracts features from a later layer while the Show attend Tell uses a earlier convolutional layer. Show Attend Tell also uses visual attention for describing images. LRCN (Long-Term Recurrent Convolutional Networks) [4] have used VGGNet and CaffeNet [19] for encoding the image. One notable difference between these architectures is the way they feed the encoded image. While the first two methods feed them as a initialization, the LRCN feed it to the LSTM at each time step.

3   Proposed Method

3.1   SqueezeNet

SqueezeNet is a CNN architecture that performs image classification. One among the core innovations of SqueezeNet is the fire module. A fire module consists of a squeeze convolutional layer which consists of only 1×1 filters followed by a mix of 3×3 and 1×1 filters named as the expand layer. It starts with a convolutional layer and is followed by 8 fire modules (fire 2–9) and a convolutional layer and ends by performing an average pooling into the classification layer. The result is a model which is 363 times smaller in size, 50 times lesser parameters [11] and also maintains the same level of accuracy on the ImageNet data in comparison to AlexNet [9].

3.2   LightRNN

The hyper-parameters of an RNN [20] that dictates the model size and computational resources needed are the word embedding size, the hidden layer size and the vocabulary size. LightRNN proposes to use a 2-component shared embedding for the vocabulary (V). With this a vocabulary of $|V|$ words can be represented with $2\sqrt{|V|}$ vectors, resulting in significant amount of reduction in computation when $|V|$ is large. Figure 2 shows a toy example of the shared word embedding table. A word is identified by two vectors: a row and a column component vector.

embedding	x_1^c	x_2^c	...	x_n^c
x_1^r	cat	dog	...	...
x_2^r	sit	stand	...	...
...	...	...	...	...
x_n^r	...	...	...	...

Fig. 2. An example of a 2-component shared embedding word table which indicates the row and column component for each word in the vocabulary.

The LightRNN model doubles the basic units of the vanilla RNN in order to incorporate this 2-component shared embedding. The modified architecture is depicted in Fig. 3. Let the dimensions of the row/column input vector and the hidden state vector be denoted by n and m respectively. The row and column vectors $x_t^r/x_t^c \in \mathbb{R}^n$ are formed from the embedding matrices $X^r/X^c \in \mathbb{R}^{n \times \sqrt{|V|}}$ at each time step t. The variables $h_t^r/h_t^c \in \mathbb{R}^m$ denote the hidden state vector for the row component and column component at time step t respectively. The update equations for the hidden state are

$$h_{t-1}^c = f(Wx_{t-1}^c + Uh_{t-1}^r + b), \tag{1}$$
$$h_t^r = f(Wx_t^r + Uh_{t-1}^c + b) \tag{2}$$

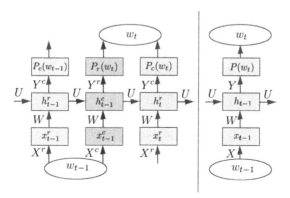

Fig. 3. LightRNN vs vanilla RNN [10].

Here, $W \in \mathbb{R}^{m \times n}$, $U \in \mathbb{R}^{m \times m}$ and $b \in \mathbb{R}^m$ and f is a non-linear activation function. The matrices $Y^r/Y^c \in \mathbb{R}^{m \times \sqrt{|V|}}$ is used to compute the row and column component probability respectively. The probability for the occurrence of word w_t at time step t, in terms of probability of its respective row and column components is as given below

$$P(w_t) = P_r(w_t).P_c(w_t) \tag{3}$$

Any recurrent unit like LSTM [17] or GRU [18] can be placed into the cell of the hidden state in this architecture [10].

3.3   Architecture

The base image captioning model we use is the Show, Attend and Tell [3] model. We replace the VGGNet [13] with the SqueezeNet architecture explained in Sect. 3.1 for encoding the image. The output from the fire9 module of the SqueezeNet, which preserves the spatial image information is used to generate the feature for the input image. The output of this module is a 13×13 feature map which can be used for enabling visual attention. We closely follow the deterministic soft attention mechanism described in Sect. 4.2 of [3]. Also, we have introduced the LightRNN detailed in Sect. 3.2 as a substitute to the LSTM unit. The attention framework has been expanded from the word level to the component level.

The convolutional network produces L vectors each of dimension D called as annotation vectors. Also, C is the length of the caption generated. Let a_i denote the annotation vector and α_i^r and α_i^c denote the attention weights for the row and column component respectively. $\hat{z}^r$ and $\hat{z}^c$ denote the context vectors for each of the two components. The weights α_i^r and α_i^c are associated with the annotation vector a_i for computing the context for the row and column component respectively. The attention model f_{att} uses a multilayer perceptron conditioned on the hidden state for the column component h^c of the previous time step for computing weight α_i^r while the same multilayer perceptron conditioned on the hidden state for the row component h^r of the current time step is used for computing weight α_i^c. The equations at a time step t are as given below:

$$e_{ti}^r = f_{att}(a_i, h_{t-1}^c) \tag{4}$$

$$e_{ti}^c = f_{att}(a_i, h_t^r) \tag{5}$$

$$\alpha_{ti}^r = \frac{exp(e_{ti}^r)}{\sum_{k=1}^{L} exp(e_{tk}^r)} \tag{6}$$

$$\alpha_{ti}^c = \frac{exp(e_{ti}^c)}{\sum_{k=1}^{L} exp(e_{tk}^c)} \tag{7}$$

$$\hat{z}_t^r = \Phi(\{a_i\}, \{\alpha_i^r\}) \tag{8}$$

$$\hat{z}_t^c = \Phi(\{a_i\}, \{\alpha_i^c\}) \tag{9}$$

Here, Φ denotes a function that returns a single vector given a set of annotation vectors and their weights.

The output probabilities for the row and column component of the word are computed as given below

$$P_r(w_t) \propto exp(L_0^r(X^r w_{t-1}^c + L_h^r h_t^r + L_z^r \hat{z}_t^r)) \tag{10}$$

$$P_c(w_t) \propto exp(L_0^c(X^c w_t^r + L_h^c h_t^c + L_z^c \hat{z}_t^c)) \tag{11}$$

where $L_0^r/L_0^c \in \mathbb{R}^{\sqrt{|V|} \times n}$, $L_h^r/L_h^c \in \mathbb{R}^{n \times m}$ and $L_z^r/L_z^c \in \mathbb{R}^{n \times D}$ are parameters that need to be learned. We minimize the following loss function

$$L_d = -\sum_t^C log(P(w_t)) + \lambda \sum_i^L \left(1 - \sum_t^C (\alpha_{ti}^c + \alpha_{ti}^r)\right)^2 \tag{12}$$

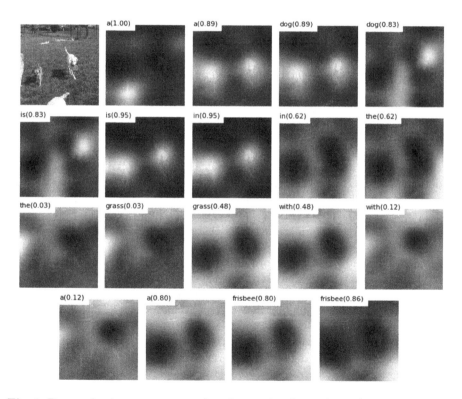

Fig. 4. Row and column component based attention for each word predicted by the model. The predicted sentence is "A dog is in the grass with a frisbee". The number enclosed in brackets is the probability with which each component was predicted.

A sample result for the component based attention is shown in Fig. 4, where we can see that for each predicted word, a pair of images are shown. The first image represents the attention weights for the row component of the word and the second image for the column component of the word.

The initialization of the hidden state and initial input for the column component at the first time step is performed the same way as mentioned in Sect. 3.1.2 of the base image captioning model [3]. Till now we have described the procedure assuming that a word allocation table exists. However, the way the words are allocated to each cell in the table can also become significant. We follow the bootstrap procedure as stated in [10] which uses the Minimum Cost Maximum Flow (MCMF) [21] algorithm to find a better state of the vocabulary which incorporates semantic meaning to the table. A random initialization is given in the beginning to the vocabulary and is periodically refined.

4   Experimental Results

We evaluate our model on the following datasets: Flickr8k [22], Flickr30k [23,24], MS-COCO [25]. The Flickr8k dataset and the Flickr30k dataset has about 8,000 images and 30,000 images respectively. The MS-COCO dataset has 82783 images. The Flickr8k dataset has clearly defined splits for training, validation and testing. We have used the splits defined in an earlier work [1] for the Flickr30k and MS-COCO datasets. We have applied only basic tokenization for all three datasets.

The performance of our model is tabulated in Table 1. We have used BLEU [6] and METEOR [5] metrics for evaluation which is consistent with the base model. We report here the performance of a model which uses the same architecture as proposed in [3] with the only difference of changing the encoder from the VGGNet architecture to the SqueezeNet architecture. We do this to better understand the nature of the trade-off between model size and model performance. The experiments were done without using any ensemble or augmentation methods. A single layer LSTM was used as the RNN unit.

We have also done a comparison of model size, parameter count and execution time and the results are tabulated in Table 2. We have maintained a consistent vocabulary size and a common word embedding and hidden state size throughout. The execution time was measured on a system with NVIDIA GeForce GTX 1080 GPU with 8 GB memory on a batch of 64 images.

From the tables it can be seen that we have achieved a model that is 6 times smaller in size, has 13 times lesser number of parameters and is 2 times faster compared to the Show Attend and Tell model using results obtained on the MS-COCO dataset. Also, the reduction in performance as measured by any metric is atmost a score difference of 3. On comparing the performance of our model on the MS-COCO dataset with the intermediate SqueezeNet with RNN model, we see that all metrics are close to each other suggesting that LightRNN is a good substitute.

The results on the smaller Flickr8k and Flickr30k datasets in comparison with MS-COCO, suggests that the smaller compute efficient models learn better on bigger datasets. On comparing the execution times, we see that to fully utilize the capability of LightRNN a bigger vocabulary is needed.

Table 1. Performance comparison on benchmark datasets.

Dataset	Method	BLEU-1	BLEU-2	BLEU-3	BLEU-4	METEOR
Flickr8k [22]	Show, Attend and Tell	67	44.8	29.9	19.5	18.93
	Show, Attend and Tell (SqueezeNet)	57.98	36.27	23.03	14.72	18.19
	Ours	56.72	35.03	21.91	14.20	18.32
Flickr30k [23, 24]	Show, Attend and Tell	66.7	43.4	28.8	19.1	18.49
	Show, Attend and Tell (SqueezeNet)	56.91	35.03	22.60	15.09	17.77
	Ours	55.87	34.45	22.05	14.67	17.67
MS-COCO [25]	Show, Attend and Tell	70.7	49.2	34.4	24.3	23.90
	Show, Attend and Tell (SqueezeNet)	67.74	47.10	32.57	22.91	22.41
	Ours	67.51	46.51	32.10	22.59	21.95

Table 2. Model size, parameter and execution time comparison.

Method	Model size (MB)	No of parameters (in millions)	Execution time (millisec/batch)
Show Attend Tell	956.4	178	534
Show Attend Tell (SqueezeNet)	421.4	36	194
Ours	150.3	13	219

5 Conclusion

In this work we have analysed the impact of substituting a small SqueezeNet and a compute efficient LightRNN in place of heavier CNN and RNN architectures respectively for performing image captioning. We were able to reduce the base model size 6 times with 13 times lesser parameters with minor impact on performance when trained on a large dataset. Our experimental results show that LightRNN is a good substitute for RNN for performing image captioning. We believe that by incorporating deep compression, we can further enhance our model's performance on the size related metrics.

References

1. Karpathy, A., Fei-Fei, L.: Deep visual-semantic alignments for generating image descriptions. In: Proceedings of the IEEE Conference on Computer Vision and Pattern Recognition, CVPR, pp. 3128–3137 (2015)
2. Vinyals, O., Toshev, A., Bengio, S., Erhan, D.: Show and tell: a neural image caption generator. In: Proceedings of the IEEE Conference on Computer Vision and Pattern Recognition, CVPR, pp. 3156–3164 (2015)
3. Xu, K., Ba, J., Kiros, R., Cho, K., Courville, A., Salakhudinov, R., Zemel, R., Bengio, Y.: Show, attend and tell: neural image caption generation with visual attention. In: Proceedings of the International Conference on Machine Learning, ICML, pp. 2048–2057 (2015)
4. Donahue, J., Anne Hendricks, L., Guadarrama, S., Rohrbach, M., Venugopalan, S., Saenko, K., Darrell, T.: Long-term recurrent convolutional networks for visual recognition and description. In: Proceedings of the IEEE Conference on Computer Vision and Pattern Recognition, CVPR, pp. 2625–2634 (2015)
5. Banerjee, S., Lavie, A.: METEOR: an automatic metric for MT evaluation with improved correlation with human judgments. In: Proceedings of the ACL Workshop on Intrinsic and Extrinsic Evaluation Measures for Machine Translation and/or Summarization, vol. 29, pp. 65–72 (2005)
6. Papineni, K., Roukos, S., Ward, T., Zhu, W.J.: BLEU: a method for automatic evaluation of machine translation. In: Proceedings of the 40th Annual Meeting on Association for Computational Linguistics, pp. 311–318. Association for Computational Linguistics (2002)
7. Lin, C.Y.: ROUGE: a package for automatic evaluation of summaries. In: Proceedings of the ACL Workshop, vol. 8 (2004)
8. Iandola, F.N., Moskewicz, M.W., Ashraf, K., Keutzer, K.: FireCaffe: near-linear acceleration of deep neural network training on compute clusters. In: Proceedings of the IEEE Conference on Computer Vision and Pattern Recognition, CVPR, pp. 2592–2600 (2016)
9. Iandola, F.N., Han, S., Moskewicz, M.W., Ashraf, K., Dally, W.J., Keutzer, K.: SqueezeNet: AlexNet-level accuracy with 50x fewer parameters and <0.5 MB model size. arXiv preprint arXiv:1602.07360 (2016)
10. Li, X., Qin, T., Yang, J., Hu, X., Liu, T.: LightRNN: memory and computation-efficient recurrent neural networks. In: Advances in Neural Information Processing Systems, NIPS, pp. 4385–4393 (2016)
11. Krizhevsky, A., Sutskever, I., Hinton, G.E.: ImageNet classification with deep convolutional neural networks. In: Advances in Neural Information Processing Systems, NIPS, pp. 1097–1105 (2012)
12. Deng, J., Dong, W., Socher, R., Li, L.J., Li, K., Fei-Fei, L.: ImageNet: a large-scale hierarchical image database. In: Proceedings of the IEEE Conference on Computer Vision and Pattern Recognition, CVPR, pp. 248–255 (2009)
13. Simonyan, K., Zisserman, A.: Very deep convolutional networks for large-scale image recognition. arXiv preprint arXiv:1409.1556 (2014)
14. He, K., Zhang, X., Ren, S., Sun, J.: Deep residual learning for image recognition. In: Proceedings of the IEEE Conference on Computer Vision and Pattern Recognition, CVPR, pp. 770–778 (2016)
15. Szegedy, C., Liu, W., Jia, Y., Sermanet, P., Reed, S., Anguelov, D., Erhan, D., Vanhoucke, V., Rabinovich, A.: Going deeper with convolutions. In: Proceedings of the IEEE Conference on Computer Vision and Pattern Recognition, CVPR, pp. 1–9 (2015)

16. Han, S., Mao, H., Dally, W.J.: Deep compression: compressing deep neural networks with pruning, trained quantization and Huffman coding. arXiv preprint arXiv:1510.00149 (2015)
17. Hochreiter, S., Schmidhuber, J.: Long short-term memory. Neural Comput. **9**(8), 1735–1780 (1997)
18. Chung, J., Gulcehre, C., Cho, K., Bengio, Y.: Empirical evaluation of gated recurrent neural networks on sequence modeling. arXiv preprint arXiv:1412.3555 (2014)
19. Jia, Y., Shelhamer, E., Donahue, J., Karayev, S., Long, J., Girshick, R., Guadarrama, S., Darrell, T.: Caffe: convolutional architecture for fast feature embedding. In: Proceedings of the 22nd ACM International Conference on Multimedia, pp. 675–678. ACM (2014)
20. Sutskever, I., Martens, J., Hinton, G.E.: Generating text with recurrent neural networks. In: Proceedings of the International Conference on Machine Learning, ICML, pp. 1017–1024 (2011)
21. Ahuja, R.K., Magnanti, T.L., Orlin, J.B.: Network Flows: Theory, Algorithms, and Applications. Prentice Hall, Upper Saddle River (1993)
22. Hodosh, M., Young, P., Hockenmaier, J.: Framing image description as a ranking task: data, models and evaluation metrics. J. Artif. Intell. Res. **47**, 853–899 (2013)
23. Young, P., Lai, A., Hodosh, M., Hockenmaier, J.: From image descriptions to visual denotations: new similarity metrics for semantic inference over event descriptions. Trans. Assoc. Comput. Linguist. **2**, 67–78 (2014)
24. Plummer, B.A., Wang, L., Cervantes, C.M., Caicedo, J.C., Hockenmaier, J., Lazebnik, S.: Flickr30k entities: collecting region-to-phrase correspondences for richer image-to-sentence models. In: Proceedings of the IEEE International Conference on Computer Vision, ICCV, pp. 2641–2649 (2015)
25. Lin, T.-Y., Maire, M., Belongie, S., Hays, J., Perona, P., Ramanan, D., Dollár, P., Zitnick, C.L.: Microsoft COCO: common objects in context. In: Fleet, D., Pajdla, T., Schiele, B., Tuytelaars, T. (eds.) ECCV 2014. LNCS, vol. 8693, pp. 740–755. Springer, Cham (2014). https://doi.org/10.1007/978-3-319-10602-1_48

Dataset Augmentation with Synthetic Images Improves Semantic Segmentation

Manik Goyal[1] , Param Rajpura[2], Hristo Bojinov[3], and Ravi Hegde[2(✉)]

[1] Indian Institute of Technology (BHU) Varanasi, Varanasi 221005, India
[2] Indian Institute of Technology Gandhinagar, Gandhinagar 382355, India
hegder@iitgn.ac.in
[3] Innit Inc., Redwood City 94063, USA

Abstract. Although Deep Convolutional Neural Networks trained with strong pixel-level annotations have significantly pushed the performance in semantic segmentation, annotation efforts required for the creation of training data remains a roadblock for further improvements. We show that augmentation of the weakly annotated training dataset with synthetic images minimizes both the annotation efforts and also the cost of capturing images with sufficient variety. Evaluation on the PASCAL 2012 validation dataset shows an increase in mean IOU from 52.80% to 55.47% by adding just 100 synthetic images per object class. Our approach is thus a promising solution to the problems of annotation and dataset collection.

1 Introduction

Deep Convolutional Neural Networks (CNNs) have achieved state-of-the-art performance on several image processing and computer vision tasks like image classification, object detection, and segmentation [1,2]. Numerous applications depend on the ability to infer knowledge about the environment through image acquisition and processing. Hence, scene understanding as a core computer vision problem has received a lot of attention. Semantic segmentation, the task of labelling pixels by their semantics (like 'person', 'dog', 'horse'), paves the road for complete scene understanding. Current state-of-the-art methods for semantic segmentation are dominated by deep convolutional neural networks (DCNNs) [3–5]. However, training end-to-end CNNs requires large scale annotated datasets. Even with a large enough dataset, training segmentation models with only image level annotations is quite challenging [6–8] as the architecture needs to learn from higher level image labels and then predict low-level pixel labels. The significant problem here is the need for pixel-wise annotated labels for training, which becomes a time-consuming and expensive annotation effort. The Pascal Visual Object Classes (VOC) [9] challenge considered to be a standard dataset for challenges like classification, detection, segmentation, action classification,

---

M. Goyal and P. Rajpura have contributed equally to this manuscript.

© Springer Nature Singapore Pte Ltd. 2018
R. Rameshan et al. (Eds.): NCVPRIPG 2017, CCIS 841, pp. 348–359, 2018.
https://doi.org/10.1007/978-981-13-0020-2_31

and person layout provides only 1464 (training) and 1449 (validation) pixel-wise labelled images for semantic segmentation challenge. Some researchers have extended training dataset [10] with 8.5k strong pixel-wise annotations (consisting of the same 21 classes as PASCAL VOC) to counter this problem. In practical applications, the challenge still stands since various classes of objects need to be detected, and annotated dataset for such training is always required.

To reduce the annotation efforts, recent reports use weakly-annotated datasets to train deep CNN models for semantic segmentation. Typically, such weak annotations take the form of bound-boxes, because forming bound-boxes around every instance of a class is around 15 times faster than doing pixel-level labelling [11]. These approaches rely on either defining some constraints [12] or on using multiple instance learning [13] techniques. [14] uses GraphCut for approximating bound-boxes to semantic labels. Although deep CNNs (such as the one proposed by [15] using DeepLab model [5]) significantly improved the segmentation performance using such weakly-annotated datasets, they failed to provide good visualization on test images.

There have been solutions proposed to reduce annotation efforts by employing transfer learning or simulating scenes. The research community has proposed multiple approaches for the problem of adapting vision-based models trained in one domain to a different domain [16–20]. Examples include: re-training a model in the target domain [21]; adapting the weights of a pre-trained model [22]; using pre-trained weights for feature extraction [23]; and, learning common features between domains [24]. Augmentation of datasets with synthetically rendered images or using datasets composed entirely of synthetic images is one of the techniques that is being explored to address the dearth of annotated data for training all kinds of CNNs. Significant research in transfer learning from synthetically rendered images to real images has been published [25,26]. Most researchers have used gaming or physics rendering engine to produce synthetic images [25] especially in the automotive domain. Peng et al. [27] have done progressive work in the Object Detection context, understanding various cues affecting transfer learning from synthetic images. But they train individual classifiers for each class after extracting features from pre-trained CNN. They show that adding different cues like background, object textures, shape to the synthetic image increases the performance [26,28] for object detection. There has not been an attempt yet to benchmark performances on the standard PASCAL VOC [9] semantic segmentation benchmark using synthetic images.

To the best of our knowledge, our report is the first attempt at combining weak annotations (generating semantic labels from bound box labels) and synthetically rendered images from freely available 3D models for semantic segmentation. We demonstrate a significant increase in segmentation performance (as measured by the mean of pixel-wise intersection-over-union (IoU)) by using semantic labels from weak annotations and synthetic images. We used a Fully Convolutional Network (FCN-8s) architecture [3] and evaluate it on the standard PASCAL VOC [9] semantic segmentation dataset. The rest of this paper is organized as follows: our methodology is described in Sect. 2, followed by the results we obtain reported in Sect. 3, finally concluding the paper in Sect. 4.

2   Method

Given an RGB image capturing one or many of the 20 objects included in PAS-
CAL VOC 2012 semantic segmentation challenge, our goal is to predict a label
image with pixel-wise segmentation for each object of interest. Our approach,
represented in Fig. 1, is to train a deep CNN with synthetic rendered images from
available 3D models. We divide the training of FCN into two stages: fine-tuning
FCN with the Weak(10k) dataset (real images with bound box labels) generated
from bound box labelled images, and fine-tuning with our own Syn(2k) dataset
(synthetic images rendered from 3D models). Our methodology can be divided
into two major parts: dataset generation and fine-tuning of the FCN. These are
explained in the following subsections.

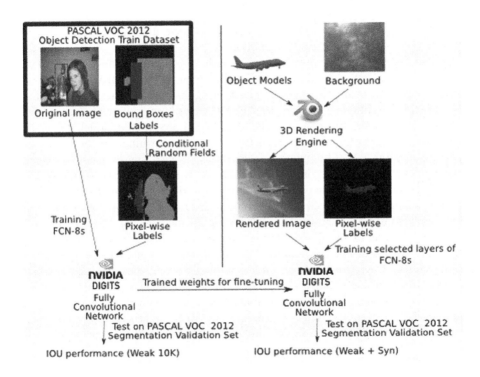

Fig. 1. Overview representing the approach for learning semantic segmentation from
weak bound-box labels and synthetic images rendered using 3D models.

2.1   Dataset Generation

Weakly Supervised Semantic Annotations: To train the CNN for semantic
segmentation, we use the available bound-box annotations in PASCAL-VOC
object detection challenge training set (10k images with 20 classes). Since the
bound-boxes fully surround the object including pixels from background, we filter

those pixels into foreground and background. Later the foreground pixels are given their corresponding object label in cases where multiple objects are present in an image. Two methods were chosen for converting bound-boxes to semantic segmentation namely Grab-Cut [14] and Conditional Random Fields (CRF) as deployed by [5,15]. Based upon the performance on a few selected images, we use the labels from CRF for training the CNN. Figure 2 shows the comparison of results from both methods. Grab-Cut tends to miss labelling smaller objects but is precise in labelling larger objects. CRF labels objects of interest accurately with a small amount of noise around the edges.

Synthetic Images Rendered from 3D Models: We use the open source 3D graphics software Blender for this purpose. Blender-Python APIs facilitates the loading of 3D models and automation of scene rendering. We use Cycles Render Engine available with Blender since it supports ray-tracing to render synthetic images. Since all the required information for annotation is available, we use the PASCAL Segmentation label format with labelled pixels for 20 classes.

Real world images have lot of information embedded about the environment, illumination, surface materials, shapes etc. Since the trained model, at test time must be able to generalize to the real world images, we take into consideration the following aspects during generation of each scenario:

1. Number of objects
2. Shape, Texture, and Materials of the objects
3. Background of the object
4. Position, Orientation of camera
5. Illumination via light sources

In order to simulate the scenario, we need 3D models, their texture information and metadata. Thousands of 3D CAD models are available online. We choose ShapeNet [29] database since it provides a large variety of models in the 20 categories for PASCAL segmentation challenge. Figure 3a shows few of the models used for rendering images. The variety helps randomize the aspect of shape, texture and materials of the objects. We use images from SUN database [30] as background images. From the large categories of images, we select few categories relevant as background to the classes of objects to be recognized.

For generating training set with rendered images, the 3D scenes need to be distinct. For every class of object, multiple models are randomly chosen from the model repository. Each object is scaled, rotated and placed at random location within the field of view of the camera which is placed at a pre-defined location. The scene is illuminated via directional light source. Later, a background image is chosen from the database and the image is rendered with Cycles Render Engine, finally generating RGB image and pixel-wise labelled image. Figure 3b shows few rendered images used as training set while Fig. 3c shows the subset of real images from PASCAL Object Detection dataset (Weak(10k)) used in training.

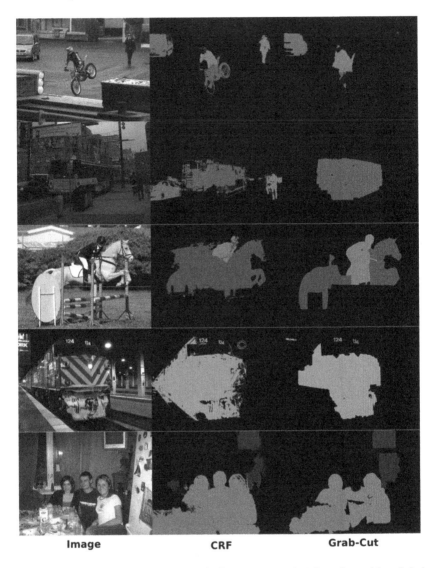

Image   **CRF**   **Grab-Cut**

Fig. 2. Comparision of CRF and Grab-Cut segmentation from bound box labels

2.2   Fine-Tuning the Deep CNN

We fine-tune FCN-8s [3] pretrained on ImageNet [31] initially with 10k real
images along with semantic labels generated from bound-boxes using CRF. All
layers in the network are fined-tuned with base learning rate of $1e^{-5}$. We further reference this model as baseline model. In next stage, we fine tune the
baseline model with synthetic images generated from Blender. Selected layers
(score_pool3, score_pool4, upscore2, upscore_pool4 and upscore8 shown in Fig. 4)
consisting of 2 convolutional and 3 deconvolutional layers are fine-tuned with

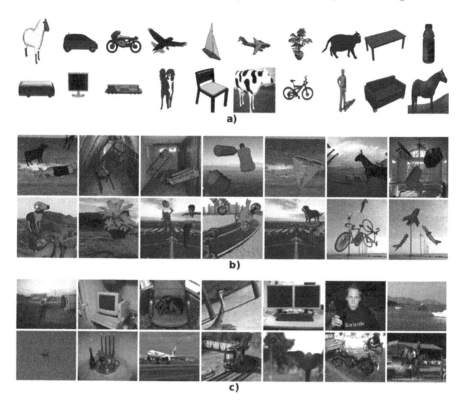

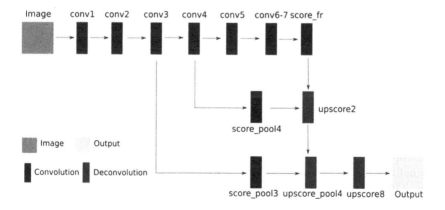

Fig. 3. (a) 3D models used for synthetic dataset (b) Synthetic images with multiple objects (c) Images from the training set of PASCAL VOC 2012 Object Detection Dataset

Fig. 4. FCN-8s architecture [3]

base learning rate of $1e^{-6}$. The network is trained with Adam optimizer for pixel-wise softmax loss function. Since the rendered images from 3D models are not rich in terms cues like textures, shadows and hence are not photo-realistic, we choose to fine-tune only few layers to capture majorly the higher hierarchical features like shape of the object.

3   Results and Discussion

The experiments were carried out using the workstation with Intel Core i7-5960X processor accelerated by NVIDIA GEFORCE GTX 1070. NVIDIA-DIGITS^{TM} (v5.0) [32] was used with Caffe library to train and manage the datasets. The proposed CNN was evaluated on the PASCAL-VOC 2012 segmentation dataset consisting of 21 classes (20 foreground and 1 background class). The PASCAL 2012 segmentation dataset consists of 1464 (train) and 1449 (val) images for training and validation respectively.

Table 1 shows the comparison of various CNN models trained on datasets listed in the first column. The performances reported are calculated according to the standard metric, mean of pixel-wise intersection-over-union (IoU). The first row lists the 21 classes and the mean IOU over all 21 classes.

The first row displays the performance when FCN is fine-tuned for real images with strong pixel-wise annotations from PASCAL VOC 2012 segmentation training dataset addressed as Real(1.5k). Using bound-box annotated images as weak annotations was an alternative proposed earlier by [15] which performed better than just using standard training dataset (with size of approximately 1.5k images). The second row showcases that the model trained with 10k weak bound-box annotated data (converted to pixel-wise labels using CRF) improved the mean-IoU performance from 47.68% to 52.80%. The predictions from CNN trained on Weak(10k) are represented in Fig. 5 third column. On comparing them with ground truth, it is observed that predictions miss the shape and sharp boundaries of the object.

Considering the CNN fine-tuned for Weak(10k) dataset as the baseline, we further fine-tuned it with rendered images of single class. Table 1 highlights the effect of using synthetic dataset on few classes namely car, bottle and aeroplane. Syn_Car(100) denotes the dataset of 100 synthetic images with car as the object of interest. We observed that by using few synthetic images from single class, the performance of segmenting car as well as 7 other classes improved. The improvement in other classes can be explained by common features learned from the car images. This trend can be observed for other classes like bottle (Syn_Bot(100)) and aeroplane (Syn_Aero(100)).

Finally, we fine-tuned the baseline model with complete set of synthetic images (100 images per class; 20 classes) addressed as Syn(2k). The mean IoU of this model increased from 52.80% to 55.47% as shown in Table 1 which clearly proves our hypothesis of supplementing synthetic images with weak annotated dataset. Some classes (car, bottle) showcased a significant improvement (10% for car, 8% for bottle) indicating the synthetic images in such cases to be more informative than others. While the classes like bicycle, dog, person and TV-monitor

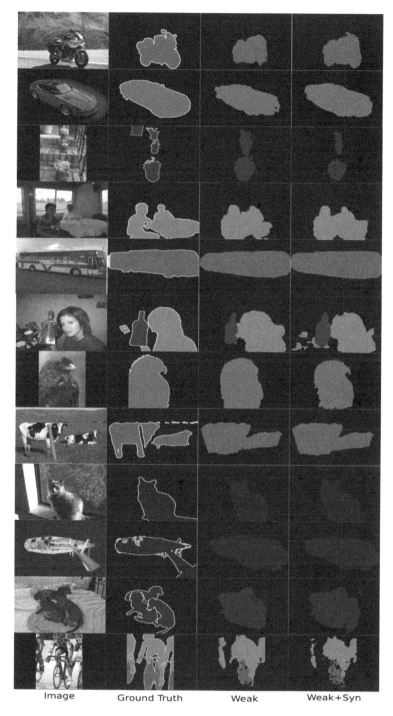

Image   Ground Truth   Weak   Weak+Syn

Fig. 5. Comparision of the segmented labels from ground truth, predictions from CNN trained with Weak(10k) and Weak(10k)+Syn(2k)

Table 1. IoU values for different classes evaluated on the PASCAL semantic segmentation validation set [9]. IoU values higher than baseline model have been highlighted

	Real(1.5k)	Weak(10k) (Baseline)	Weak(10k) +Syn_Car(100)	Weak(10k) +Syn_Bot(100)	Weak(10k) +Syn_Aero(100)	Weak(10k) +Syn(2k)
Background	**87.88**	87.12	**87.38**	86.78	85.39	**87.88**
Aeroplane	58.07	68.81	**69.75**	67.98	67.89	**69.39**
Bicycle	**46.47**	27.39	**27.48**	24.29	23.13	**27.65**
Bird	54.61	55.46	55.35	**57.65**	**63.90**	**57.23**
Boat	39.73	42.76	**46.25**	**45.62**	**48.89**	**47.76**
Bottle	41.56	47.25	44.38	**57.55**	27.83	**55.52**
Bus	61.67	73.96	**77.70**	73.15	68.51	**76.19**
Car	48.47	51.15	**69.31**	50.42	47.04	**61.83**
Cat	64.93	71.37	69.32	68.80	65.39	**72.58**
Chair	**16.92**	13.17	11.35	10.38	5.29	**14.91**
Cow	30.43	57.88	57.28	**58.98**	56.24	**59.23**
Dining table	39.47	42.95	42.93	**42.98**	27.21	**48.50**
Dog	53.43	**60.74**	59.65	58.71	54.36	60.56
Horse	44.40	54.92	54.34	54.70	51.41	**56.64**
Motor bike	59.03	54.99	**56.47**	50.58	44.46	**62.49**
Person	65.47	**66.01**	65.70	63.92	61.50	63.43
Potted plant	14.06	41.38	36.12	**41.46**	23.72	**49.54**
Sheep	56.05	65.71	**66.08**	**66.27**	61.90	**65.87**
Sofa	24.75	30.37	29.46	28.46	17.60	**36.95**
Train	54.05	67.48	66.47	64.04	56.34	**68.69**
Tv monitor	**38.62**	27.99	**28.26**	27.97	16.73	22.06
Mean IoU	47.62	52.80	**53.38**	52.41	46.42	**55.47**

had lower IoU values since we had fewer 3D models available for those object types. Since objects like cow, cat, person etc. have highly variable appearance compared to other object classes, we observe lesser improvement in performance.

To further explore the usefulness of synthetic and weak annotated dataset in conjunction with strong annotated real dataset, we fine-tune FCN with `Real(1.5k)+Weak(10k)+Syn(2k)`. The model achieves 58.27% (mean IoU) while `Real(1.5k)+Syn(2k)` achieves 5.08% (mean IoU) indicating the negative effect of non-photorealistic rendered images on strong annotation in real dataset.

Figure 5 shows the comparison of the semantic labels generated from network trained on `Weak(10k)` dataset and `Weak(10k)+Syn(2k)` dataset. The latter predictions are better since they produce sharper edges and shapes. The results prove that shape information from the synthetic models help eliminate the noise generated from CRF in labels. It is worth noting that even though synthetic images are non photo-realistic, and lack visual information from relevant backgrounds for objects, multiple object class in a single image or rich textures but they represent higher hierarchical feature like shape and thus can be used alongside weakly annotated images to achieve better performance on semantic segmentation tasks. The benchmark performance of FCN-8s on PASCAL test data when trained on augmented real image dataset released by [10] with strong annotations is 62.2% (mean IoU). While comparing with the benchmark performance, our model performs reasonably well with 55.47% (mean IoU) trained with the total of 12k images (`Weak(10k)+Syn(2k)`).

4   Conclusion

Our report demonstrates a promising approach to minimize the annotation and dataset collection efforts by using rendered images from freely available 3D models. The comparison shows that using 10k weakly annotated images (which approximately equals the annotation efforts for 1.5k strong labels) with just 2k synthetic rendered images gives a significant rise in segmentation performance.

This work can be extended by training CNN with larger synthetic dataset, with richer 3D models and relevant backgrounds. Adding other features like relative scaling and occlusions can further strengthen the synthetic dataset. The effect of using synthetic dataset with improved architectures for semantic segmentation are being explored further. Further investigation can be done on factors like domain adaptation, co-adaptation among deeper layers that affect the transfer learning from synthetic to real images.

Acknowledgment. We acknowledge funding support from Innit Inc. consultancy grant CNS/INNIT/EE/P0210/1617/0007.

References

1. Krizhevsky, A., Sutskever, I., Hinton, G.E.: ImageNet classification with deep convolutional neural networks. In: International Conference on Neural Information Processing Systems, pp. 1097–1105. Curran Associates Inc. (2012)
2. Szegedy, C., Liu, W., Jia, Y., Sermanet, P., Reed, S., Anguelov, D., Erhan, D., Vanhoucke, V., Rabinovich, A.: Going deeper with convolutions. In: Proceedings of the IEEE Computer Society Conference on Computer Vision and Pattern Recognition, 07–12 June 2015, pp. 1–9. IEEE, June 2015
3. Shelhamer, E., Long, J., Darrell, T.: Fully convolutional networks for semantic segmentation. arXiv Preprint arXiv:1605.06211, May 2016
4. Badrinarayanan, V., Handa, A., Cipolla, R.: SegNet: a deep convolutional encoder-decoder architecture for robust semantic pixel-wise labelling. arXiv Preprint arXiv:1505.07293, May 2015
5. Chen, L.C., Papandreou, G., Kokkinos, I., Murphy, K., Yuille, A.L.: DeepLab: semantic image segmentation with deep convolutional nets, atrous convolution, and fully connected CRFs. arXiv Preprint arXiv:1606.00915, June 2016
6. Vezhnevets, A., Ferrari, V., Buhmann, J.M.: Weakly supervised structured output learning for semantic segmentation. In: 2012 IEEE Conference on Computer Vision and Pattern Recognition, pp. 845–852. IEEE, June 2012
7. Verbeek, J., Triggs, B.: Region classification with Markov field aspect models. In: 2007 IEEE Conference on Computer Vision and Pattern Recognition, pp. 1–8. IEEE, June 2007

8. Xu, J., Schwing, A.G., Urtasun, R.: Tell me what you see and i will show you where it is. In: CVPR (2014)

9. Everingham, M., Eslami, S.M.A., Van Gool, L., Williams, C.K.I., Winn, J., Zisserman, A.: The pascal visual object classes challenge: a retrospective. Int. J. Comput. Vis. **111**(1), 98–136 (2015)

10. Hariharan, B., Arbelaez, P., Bourdev, L., Maji, S., Malik, J.: Semantic contours from inverse detectors. In: 2011 International Conference on Computer Vision, pp. 991–998. IEEE, November 2011

11. Lin, T.-Y., Maire, M., Belongie, S., Hays, J., Perona, P., Ramanan, D., Dollár, P., Zitnick, C.L.: Microsoft COCO: common objects in context. In: Fleet, D., Pajdla, T., Schiele, B., Tuytelaars, T. (eds.) ECCV 2014. LNCS, vol. 8693, pp. 740–755. Springer, Cham (2014). https://doi.org/10.1007/978-3-319-10602-1_48

12. Pathak, D., Krähenbühl, P., Darrell, T.: Constrained convolutional neural networks for weakly supervised segmentation. arXiv Preprint arXiv:1506.03648, June 2015

13. Pathak, D., Shelhamer, E., Long, J., Darrell, T.: Fully convolutional multi-class multiple instance learning. arXiv Preprint arXiv:1412.7144, December 2014

14. Rother, C., Kolmogorov, V., Blake, A., Rother, C., Kolmogorov, V., Blake, A.: GrabCut. In: ACM SIGGRAPH 2004 Papers on - SIGGRAPH 2004, vol. 23, p. 309. ACM Press, New York (2004)

15. Papandreou, G., Chen, L.C., Murphy, K.P., Yuille, A.L.: Weakly-and semi-supervised learning of a deep convolutional network for semantic image segmentation. In: 2015 IEEE International Conference on Computer Vision (ICCV), pp. 1742–1750. IEEE, December 2015

16. Li, W., Duan, L., Xu, D., Tsang, I.W.: Learning with augmented features for supervised and semi-supervised heterogeneous domain adaptation. IEEE Trans. Pattern Anal. Mach. Intell. **36**(6), 1134–1148 (2014)

17. Hoffman, J., Rodner, E., Donahue, J., Darrell, T., Saenko, K.: Efficient learning of domain-invariant image representations. arXiv Preprint arXiv:1301.3224, January 2013

18. Hoffman, J., Guadarrama, S., Tzeng, E., Hu, R., Donahue, J., Girshick, R., Darrell, T., Saenko, K.: LSDA: large scale detection through adaptation. In: Proceedings of the 27th International Conference on Neural Information Processing Systems, pp. 3536–3544. MIT Press (2014)

19. Kulis, B., Saenko, K., Darrell, T.: What you saw is not what you get: domain adaptation using asymmetric kernel transforms. In: CVPR 2011, pp. 1785–1792. IEEE, June 2011

20. Long, M., Cao, Y., Wang, J., Jordan, M.I.: Learning transferable features with deep adaptation networks. In: Proceedings of the 32nd International Conference on International Conference on Machine Learning, vol. 37, pp. 97–105. JMLR.org (2015)

21. Yosinski, J., Clune, J., Bengio, Y., Lipson, H.: How transferable are features in deep neural networks? In: Proceedings of the 27th International Conference on Neural Information Processing Systems, pp. 3320–3328. MIT Press (2014)

22. Li, Y., Wang, N., Shi, J., Liu, J., Hou, X.: Revisiting batch normalization for practical domain adaptation. In: International Conference on Learning Representations Workshop (2017)

23. Gupta, A., Vedaldi, A., Zisserman, A.: Synthetic data for text localisation in natural images. arXiv Preprint arXiv:1604.06646, April 2016

24. Tzeng, E., Hoffman, J., Zhang, N., Saenko, K., Darrell, T.: Deep domain confusion: maximizing for domain invariance. arXiv Preprint arXiv:1412.3474, December 2014

25. Ros, G., Sellart, L., Materzynska, J., Vazquez, D., Lopez, A.: The SYNTHIA dataset: a large collection of synthetic images for semantic segmentation of urban scenes. In: CVPR (2016)
26. Peng, X., Saenko, K.: Synthetic to real adaptation with generative correlation alignment networks. arXiv Preprint arXiv:1701.05524, January 2017
27. Peng, X., Sun, B., Ali, K., Saenko, K.: Learning deep object detectors from 3D models. In: 2015 IEEE International Conference on Computer Vision (ICCV), pp. 1278–1286. IEEE, December 2015
28. Peng, X., Saenko, K.: Combining texture and shape cues for object recognition with minimal supervision. arXiv Preprint arXiv:1609.04356, September 2016
29. Chang, A.X., Funkhouser, T., Guibas, L., Hanrahan, P., Huang, Q., Li, Z., Savarese, S., Savva, M., Song, S., Su, H., Xiao, J., Yi, L., Yu, F.: ShapeNet: an information-rich 3D model repository. arXiv Preprint arXiv:1512.03012, December 2015. https://doi.org/10.1145/3005274.3005291
30. Xiao, J., Hays, J., Ehinger, K.A., Oliva, A., Torralba, A.: SUN database: large-scale scene recognition from abbey to zoo. In: 2010 IEEE Computer Society Conference on Computer Vision and Pattern Recognition, pp. 3485–3492. IEEE, June 2010
31. Deng, J., Dong, W., Socher, R., Li, L.-J., Li, K., Fei-Fei, L.: ImageNet: a large-scale hierarchical image database. In: 2009 IEEE Conference on Computer Vision and Pattern Recognition, pp. 248–255. IEEE, June 2009
32. Heinrich, G.: Image Segmentation Using DIGITS 5 (2016). https://devblogs.nvidia.com/image-segmentation-using-digits-5/

Deep Neural Network for Foreground Object Segmentation: An Unsupervised Approach

Avishek Majumder[(✉)] and R. Venkatesh Babu[(✉)]

Indian Institute of Science, Bangalore 560012, Karnataka, India
{avishekm,venky}@iisc.ac.in

Abstract. Saliency plays a key role in various computer vision tasks. Extracting salient regions from images and videos have been a well established problem of computer vision. While segmenting salient objects from images depend only on static information, temporal information in a video can make non salient objects be salient due to movement. Besides the temporal information, there are other challenges involved with video segmentation, such as 3D parallax, camera shake, motion blur, etc. In this work, we propose a novel unsupervised end to end trainable, fully convolutional deep neural network for object segmentation. Our model is robust and scalable across scenes, as it is tested unsupervisedly and can easily infer which objects constitute the foreground of the image. We run various tests on two well established benchmarks of video object segmentation, DAVIS and FBMS-59 datasets. We report our results and compare them against the state of the art methods.

Keywords: CNN · Foreground segmentation · Object segmentation
Visual saliency · Image saliency

1 Introduction

Detecting foreground objects in a scene has a lot of applications in the field of computer vision. Tasks like, object recognition, scene summarization, classification etc. depend on the salient objects present in a scene. Recently Convolutional Neural Networks have gained popularity in the field of computer vision because of its success in various challenging tasks like, image classification [10,22], image segmentation [21], object localization [20], eye fixation prediction [11], summarization and captioning [3,14], which previously required a lot of effort to achieve high accuracy using hand crafted features. Not only images, but these Convolutional Neural Networks have been shown to work well with videos as well. In [5], 3D convolutional neural network has been shown to classify actions in videos very accurately.

Salient object segmentation in a scene is the task of segmenting out the object from a given image or video, on which a human is likely to fixate. Due to

© Springer Nature Singapore Pte Ltd. 2018
R. Rameshan et al. (Eds.): NCVPRIPG 2017, CCIS 841, pp. 360–371, 2018.
https://doi.org/10.1007/978-981-13-0020-2_32

the nature of the scene being static (images) or dynamic (videos), they possess very different criteria associated with them for being salient. In case of images, a salient object could be defined as an object which stands out in the scene, due to certain properties which could be, low level features like, color, illumination, texture, or it could be something conceptual like, a face, an animal or an object. On the other hand, saliency in videos could be due to the movement or action being performed. Unlike static images, certain frames in videos could suffer from motion blur, 3D parallax errors, camera shake, etc.

Fig. 1. A few frames from FBMS-59 dataset. Left: original RGB frames of the video. Right: segmentation map computed by our model.

In this paper, we design a novel deep neural network to segment out salient objects from an image sequence. Usually in a video the moving objects constitute the salient objects. In the datasets FBMS-59 and DAVIS, there are primarily a few main moving objects, which are considered salient. Thus the task of salient object segmentation is posed as moving foreground object segmentation. There have been many works, both using Deep neural networks [2,9] as well as traditional hand crafted features [1,18]. Some of these methods contains really interesting choice of features and model architectures. We train a deep neural network and test it in an unsupervised fashion to segment out foreground objects from a scene using just the static information of a frame. This makes our network transferrable to different scenes, without being finetuned to a specific scene before testing. Figure 1 illustrates a scene from FBMS dataset where our model is able to segment the moving objects even when motion blur and pose change occurs.

2   Related Work

For the task of video segmentation, the algorithm needs to be aware of the various challenges associated with any video sequence, such as, complex 3D parallax, non-rigid motion of both foreground and background, motion blur, camera shake, texture rich background etc.

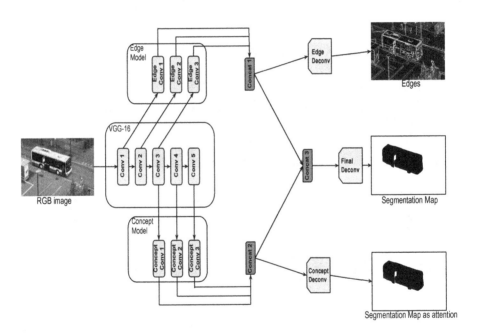

Fig. 2. Overview of the proposed approach: on top of the base network (VGG-16) we learn smaller filters to carry out specific auxiliary task to predict the final segmentation map.

To overcome these issues, researchers have focused on long range motion cues [4,6,23], grouping contours [1,18], point trajectories [8,15], etc.

Works [1,18] use pre-processing techniques to segment the moving objects in the video. In the paper [1], the contours are extracted from various scales of each frame, then grouped to segment out the salient objects in each scale. The work by Perazzi *et al.* [18] use the contrast of each frame separately to segment out the coarse foreground and background regions, then post process to get object segmentation from each frame. In other works like [25], we find that motion and appearance, both play a vital role. Works like [6,15,23] consider the temporal aspect separately and try to find clues from the long range relations among the objects in a scene. In another interesting approach by [23], occlusion relation between objects are considered for computing depth from the monocular frame information.

Other approaches in tackling this problems try to predict the salient regions from the static frames, then use the temporal information among the salient regions to link them, as seen in [4,12]. Work by Papazoglou and Ferrari [17] uses motion boundaries to derive object segmentation maps. Most of these approaches use highly specific hand crafted features, which are then used in a data agnostic way to segment the salient objects in these scenes. There are other methods [2,7,9] which use weak supervision, such as segmentation maps of a few frames from the video sequence to be tested for.

While our approach derives some motivation from these tasks, it is nevertheless different from the above mentioned unsupervised approaches as it is a fully convolutional neural network, trained end to end, and does not require any temporal information.

3 Methodology

We propose an end to end fully convolutional deep neural network, which takes in the raw RGB frame and outputs the moving object segmentation (Figs. 3, 4, 5 and 6). Since the scenes contain only a few moving objects, we consider the moving object to be the primary foreground object in a scene, and model our architecture to segment out the foreground objects. Figure 2 illustrates the proposed architecture. There are 3 key components in our network, we use a *base neural network* for extraction of robust features, then we employ some *Specialized filters* on top of the features of the base and finally we combine them to segment out the salient object. We also introduce *auxiliary tasks* to enhance the segmentation.

During training we use the segmentation maps provided by the datasets but during testing, the objects and scenes might be very different from what has been shown to the network. In these situations, it is quite common to use a weak supervision in the form of one or a few annotated frames from the sequence to be tested, be used for finetuning the network to locate the object of interest. But we bar our network to this finetuning, and hence our testing is purely unsupervised. The following sections describe our approach in detail.

3.1 Pre-trained Network

We start by using a neural network that has been trained on the 1.2M ImageNet dataset as base. This pre-trained network has the advantage of having filters

Fig. 3. A scene with the predicted segments by our method from FBMS-59 dataset. Lots of scale change and camera motion is present in the scene

Fig. 4. Predicted segments by our method on a scene from FBMS-59 dataset. Wide movement of primary object in the scene

Fig. 5. Predictions on a video sequence from DAVIS. Fluid motion present in the scene. Since the maps are not temporally linked, the segments generated are independent of the previous ones.

Fig. 6. A scene from DAVIS dataset, segmented by our method. The predicted mask tightly overlaps with the object of interest.

derived from a huge variety of images, across different scenes, involving different objects in them. The diversity in the ImageNet dataset makes the base network robust and scalable to wide variety of scenes. We take the VGG-16 image classi-fication network [22] as our base network. We remove the fully connected weights from the network, and keep only the convolutional part of it. We pose the prob-lem of segmentation as two class classification problem, where each pixel is to be classified as foreground or background.

3.2   Specialized Convolutions

Since the base network is able to generate robust convolutional features, we train a set of separate convolutional filters on top of these features, to transform the features to our need. Finetuning separate filters to perform different tasks has been shown to work by Maninis *et al.* [13], where they take the low level features to predict the contours of blood vessels in eyes and use the higher level features to predict the segmentation map of the retina.

We take a similar approach with our task as well, where we learn 6 small filter banks, on top of the existing VGG-16 filters. We call these specialized convolution layers, because these filter banks will be learnt to adapt to the scenes of the object segmentation task. As shown in the Fig. 2 we take the Conv 1, Conv 2 and Conv 3 features of the VGG-16 network, and feed it to 3 filter banks in the *edge model*, each containing 16 filters of size 3×3. We introduce an auxiliary task on the output of these filters.

We extract the Conv 3, Conv 4 and Conv 5 features as the input to the next set of filter banks, in the *concept model*. The higher level features of the VGG-16 network contain semantic information, like wheels, faces, text, etc. The activation of certain filters mark the existence of those concepts in a scene. We train these filter banks, containing 16 filters of size 3×3, to extract object information from the VGG-16 features.

We then upsample these features using nearest neighbour interpolation, L2 normalize them per channel and concatenate them to form a 96 channel feature map. Finally we use a 3×3 deconvolution filter on top of this map to predict our final segmentation map.

3.3   Auxiliary Task

To improve the segmentations, we use two auxiliary tasks to see if they might be able to help in improving the overall segmentation map. From the low level features, we predict the contour of the scenes, to make the network learn the precise boundaries of the objects. We use L2 loss between the predicted and ground truth edge map of each frame.

The other auxiliary task is to predict the object segmentation itself using just the final three filters, that is, the Concept conv 1, Concept conv 2 and Concept conv3. The idea is to arrive at the rough segmentation map from just these high level features itself, and then use the lower level information to fine tune the segments further.

We then further post-process the predicted segments with a dense CRF. The dense CRF takes into account the superpixels of the RGB image as well as objectness in the scene. Due to the post-processing most of the spurious false positive segments were removed, and the boundary of the original object was improved.

4   Experiments and Results

We trained our network using the Train set of DAVIS 2016 dataset. We then tested on the DAVIS 2016 validation and FBMS-59 dataset unsupervisedly, as mentioned before. We do not require any supervision from the scene to be tested for.

In the following sections we provide quantitative as well as qualitative results, along with our ablation study.

4.1   Datasets

DAVIS 2016 [19]. This dataset is the benchmark for video object segmentation. It contains approximately 50 videos. We use the 30 training videos in the dataset to train our model. It contains the various challenges associated with any wild video, such as camera shake, occlusion, varying backgrounds, etc. The validation set contains 20 videos, with animals, people, cars, etc. These scenes primarily have one moving object associated with them. Through our experiments, we show that across the various scenes, our network can predict which might be the moving object, from just one frame.

FBMS-59 [16]. This is another dataset, containing similar challenges to DAVIS, like occlusion, lighting changes, background change, confusing foreground and background textures, etc. Since we did not use any data from FBMS-59, we test our model on both the train and test set of FBMS-59. Due to non usage of temporal information and unsupervised testing, our model is able to separate foreground from background, even in wild scenes.

Table 1. Comparison of our method with the state of the art methods on DAVIS validation set. Please refer to the related works section for overview of each method. * Uses temporal information

Measure		Semi-supervised				Unsupervised							Pre-processing	
		[2]	[9]	[7]*	[24]*	Ours	[17]*	[8]*	[4]*	[15]*	[12]*	[23]*	[1]	[18]
J	Mean (↑)	79.8	79.7	70.2	68.0	56.1	55.8	55.2	55.1	53.3	49.8	48.2	70.7	16.8
	Recall (↑)	93.6	93.1	82.3	75.6	64.5	64.9	57.5	55.8	61.6	59.1	54.0	91.7	7.2
	Decay (↓)	14.9	8.9	12.4	26.4	8.4	0.0	2.2	12.6	2.4	14.1	10.5	1.3	−1.5
F	Mean (↑)	80.6	75.4	65.5	63.4	51.3	51.1	55.2	52.3	50.8	42.7	44.7	62.9	21.5
	Recall (↑)	92.6	87.1	69.0	70.4	56.2	51.6	61.0	51.9	60.0	37.5	52.6	76.7	2.7
	Decay (↓)	15.0	9.0	14.4	27.2	8.1	2.9	3.4	11.4	5.1	10.6	11.7	1.9	−1.6
T	GT(8.8) (↓)	37.8	21.8	32.4	22.2	50.5	36.6	27.7	42.5	30.1	26.9	25.0	70.4	81.1

Table 2. Comparison of our method with the state of the art methods on FBMS-59. *Precision* (P), *Recall* (R) and *F-measure* (F) are reported on binary masks of the ground truth. Higher score is better. * Uses temporal information

Method	Training set (29 sequences)			Test set (30 sequences)		
	P	R	F	P	R	F
[23]*	83.92	68.19	75.24	86.54	63.20	73.05
[12]*	64.86	52.70	58.15	62.32	55.97	58.97
[17]*	71.34	70.66	71.00	76.29	63.29	69.18
Ours	70.50	60.43	60.80	68.67	56.24	56.36

Table 3. Ablation study on the DAVIS validation set. We can see how certain parts of the model is responsible for increasing the performance.

Measure		Methods			
		No aux.	Concept aux.	Edge aux.	Both aux.
J	Mean (↑)	54.2	**55.9**	52.1	**56.1**
	Recall (↑)	**66.2**	63.5	61.6	**64.5**
	Decay (↓)	6.5	7.7	**4.6**	8.4
F	Mean (↑)	48.6	**51.4**	47.9	**51.3**
	Recall (↑)	51.3	**56.5**	50.6	**56.2**
	Decay (↓)	6.2	7.3	**4.7**	8.1
T	GT(8.8) (↓)	65.1	52.1	61.1	**50.5**

Fig. 7. Two most challenging sequence from DAVIS. In the first sequence due to texture rich background, our method includes some of the background into the foreground mask. In the second sequence, due to the object being very small and the scene being foggy, the car is not detected well until it comes closer to the camera in the scene.

4.2   Results

We report our quantitative results on the two datasets, DAVIS and FBMS-59, in Tables 1 and 2 respectively. We do not perform on par with the state of the art methods on FBMS-59, but that is partially due to the inclusion of the objects and the scenes, which are much more complex than DAVIS and non

Fig. 8. Some more qualitative results from FBMS-59 of our method. In the second sequence, our method predicts all the cars as foreground, which is correct but gets low score because only two of those cars are moving. The last sequence is from a television show Marple, where we see our method performs poorly, since it has not been shown such kind of low lit scenes. Even then it predicts the person as the foreground object.

inclusion of temporal information. Inclusion of scenes from a wide variety of lighting conditions, with wide variety of objects and inclusion of more than one moving objects, make this dataset a very challenging one. We report our numbers without finetuning and show we are able to achieve comparable performance on the dataset.

Fig. 9. More qualitative results generated by our method on DAVIS validation set. In crowded scenes, like the first and third sequence, our model tends to get slightly confused and predicts a bunch of people as foreground. In the second sequence, our model predicts the non-moving camel as foreground too. While sequence five shows even in non-rigid scene, our model predicts the foreground object perfectly.

We ran various experiments, with and without the auxiliary modules to justify the motivation for inclusion of each of the modules in our network architecture. Table 3 summarizes our ablation study. As we can see, by enforcing the network to learn the target auxiliary tasks, the final performance improves quite a bit. Specifically we see a huge boost by enforcing the network to learn semantic information from the features obtained by last three convolution layers of VGG-16. Even though the auxiliary task of predicting the edges do not improve the performance drastically, it is nevertheless required to make the segments more precise. We provide more qualitative results from the two datasets by our method in Figs. 8 and 9. We also provide results of some failure cases of our method in Fig. 7, where our method misses the object of interest or predicts part of the background as foreground.

5   Conclusion

The main contribution of this paper is to show that the task of foreground segmentation can be broken down into segmenting out salient object from each individual frame. Our method is a fully unsupervised method which can coarsely locate the foreground object in an image. We also conclude that in most situations, this foreground object is the moving salient object in videos. Thus our proposed approach can segment the foreground object in video frames without any temporal information. It can be transferred to other scenes without finetuning, due to the nature of our unsupervised training.

References

1. Arbeláez, P., Pont-Tuset, J., Barron, J.T., Marques, F., Malik, J.: Multiscale combinatorial grouping. In: Proceedings of the IEEE Conference on Computer Vision and Pattern Recognition, pp. 328–335 (2014)
2. Caelles, S., Maninis, K.K., Pont-Tuset, J., Leal-Taixé, L., Cremers, D., Van Gool, L.: One-shot video object segmentation. In: Proceedings of the IEEE Conference on Computer Vision and Pattern Recognition (2017)
3. Donahue, J., Anne Hendricks, L., Guadarrama, S., Rohrbach, M., Venugopalan, S., Saenko, K., Darrell, T.: Long-term recurrent convolutional networks for visual recognition and description. In: Proceedings of the IEEE Conference on Computer Vision and Pattern Recognition, pp. 2625–2634 (2015)
4. Faktor, A., Irani, M.: Video segmentation by non-local consensus voting. In: BMVC, vol. 2, p. 8 (2014)
5. Feichtenhofer, C., Pinz, A., Zisserman, A.: Convolutional two-stream network fusion for video action recognition. In: Proceedings of the IEEE Conference on Computer Vision and Pattern Recognition, pp. 1933–1941 (2016)
6. Fragkiadaki, K., Zhang, G., Shi, J.: Video segmentation by tracing discontinuities in a trajectory embedding. In: 2012 IEEE Conference on Computer Vision and Pattern Recognition (CVPR), pp. 1846–1853. IEEE (2012)
7. Jampani, V., Gadde, R., Gehler, P.V.: Video propagation networks. In: Proceedings of the IEEE Conference on Computer Vision and Pattern Recognition (2017)
8. Keuper, M., Andres, B., Brox, T.: Motion trajectory segmentation via minimum cost multicuts. In: Proceedings of the IEEE International Conference on Computer Vision, pp. 3271–3279 (2015)
9. Khoreva, A., Perazzi, F., Benenson, R., Schiele, B., Sorkine-Hornung, A.: Learning video object segmentation from static images. In: Proceedings of the IEEE Conference on Computer Vision and Pattern Recognition (2017)
10. Krizhevsky, A., Sutskever, I., Hinton, G.E.: Imagenet classification with deep convolutional neural networks. In: Advances in Neural Information Processing Systems, pp. 1097–1105 (2012)

11. Kruthiventi, S.S., Ayush, K., Babu, R.V.: DeepFix: a fully convolutional neural network for predicting human eye fixations. IEEE Trans. Image Process. **26**, 4446–4456 (2017)
12. Lee, Y.J., Kim, J., Grauman, K.: Key-segments for video object segmentation. In: 2011 IEEE International Conference on Computer Vision (ICCV), pp. 1995–2002. IEEE (2011)
13. Maninis, K.-K., Pont-Tuset, J., Arbeláez, P., Van Gool, L.: Deep retinal image understanding. In: Ourselin, S., Joskowicz, L., Sabuncu, M.R., Unal, G., Wells, W. (eds.) MICCAI 2016. LNCS, vol. 9901, pp. 140–148. Springer, Cham (2016). https://doi.org/10.1007/978-3-319-46723-8_17
14. Mopuri, K.R., Athreya, V.B., Babu, R.V.: Deep image representations using caption generators. arXiv preprint arXiv:1705.09142 (2017)
15. Ochs, P., Brox, T.: Object segmentation in video: a hierarchical variational approach for turning point trajectories into dense regions. In: 2011 IEEE International Conference on Computer Vision (ICCV), pp. 1583–1590. IEEE (2011)
16. Ochs, P., Malik, J., Brox, T.: Segmentation of moving objects by long term video analysis. IEEE Trans. Pattern Anal. Mach. Intell. **36**(6), 1187–1200 (2014)
17. Papazoglou, A., Ferrari, V.: Fast object segmentation in unconstrained video. In: Proceedings of the IEEE International Conference on Computer Vision, pp. 1777–1784 (2013)
18. Perazzi, F., Krähenbühl, P., Pritch, Y., Hornung, A.: Saliency filters: contrast based filtering for salient region detection. In: 2012 IEEE Conference on Computer Vision and Pattern Recognition (CVPR), pp. 733–740. IEEE (2012)
19. Perazzi, F., Pont-Tuset, J., McWilliams, B., Van Gool, L., Gross, M., Sorkine-Hornung, A.: A benchmark dataset and evaluation methodology for video object segmentation. In: Proceedings of the IEEE Conference on Computer Vision and Pattern Recognition, pp. 724–732 (2016)
20. Sermanet, P., Eigen, D., Zhang, X., Mathieu, M., Fergus, R., LeCun, Y.: OverFeat: integrated recognition, localization and detection using convolutional networks. arXiv preprint arXiv:1312.6229 (2013)
21. Shelhamer, E., Long, J., Darrell, T.: Fully convolutional networks for semantic segmentation. IEEE Trans. Pattern Anal. Mach. Intell. **39**(4), 640–651 (2017)
22. Simonyan, K., Zisserman, A.: Very deep convolutional networks for large-scale image recognition. arXiv preprint arXiv:1409.1556 (2014)
23. Taylor, B., Karasev, V., Soatto, S.: Causal video object segmentation from persistence of occlusions. In: Proceedings of the IEEE Conference on Computer Vision and Pattern Recognition, pp. 4268–4276 (2015)
24. Tsai, Y.H., Yang, M.H., Black, M.J.: Video segmentation via object flow. In: Proceedings of the IEEE Conference on Computer Vision and Pattern Recognition, pp. 3899–3908 (2016)
25. Wang, W., Shen, J., Porikli, F.: Saliency-aware geodesic video object segmentation. In: Proceedings of the IEEE Conference on Computer Vision and Pattern Recognition, pp. 3395–3402 (2015)

Document Image Segmentation Using Deep Features

K. V. Jobin$^{(\boxtimes)}$ and C. V. Jawahar

CVIT, IIIT-Hyderabad, Hyderabad, India
jobin.kv@research.iiit.ac.in, jawahar@iiit.ac.in

Abstract. This paper explores the effectiveness of deep features for document image segmentation. The document image segmentation problem is modelled as a pixel labeling task where each pixel in the document image is classified into one of the predefined labels such as text, comments, decorations and background. Our method first extracts deep features from superpixels of the document image. Then we learn an SVM classifier using these features, and segment the document image. Fisher vector encoded convolutional layer features (FV-CNN) and fully connected layer features (FC-CNN) are used in our study. Experiments validate that our method is effective and yields better results for segmenting document images in comparison to the popular approaches on benchmark handwritten datasets.

1 Introduction

Document image segmentation can be considered as the primary stage of document image analysis and understanding pipeline. The objective of this step is often to segment the image into semantically similar regions such as text, graphics, comments, decorations, backgrounds, etc. This problem is further challenging for historical documents. Analysis and understanding of historical document images is an active area of research. Challenges of historical handwritten document images such as unstructured layouts, degradation, various handwritten styles, etc. are exemplified in Fig. 1.

The early approaches for document segmentation (such as [1]) are based on binarization and connected component analysis. This approach fails with the images that have non-uniform background color (Fig. 1(b)). To get rid of this issue, instead of taking connected components, researchers started to classify image patches or superpixels to segment the image. Various features such as color and texture [2], SIFT, SURF, LBP, HOG, etc. are extracted for segmentation.

Various methods have been presented in the literature to perform the document image segmentation task. Most of these approaches focus on improving any of the stages of segmentation pipeline such as pre-processing, feature extraction, feature modeling, etc.

The recent paper on historical document images [3] utilizes the idea of autoencoder to learn the features automatically. Generally, an autoencoder is a neural

© Springer Nature Singapore Pte Ltd. 2018
R. Rameshan et al. (Eds.): NCVPRIPG 2017, CCIS 841, pp. 372–382, 2018.
https://doi.org/10.1007/978-981-13-0020-2_33

Fig. 1. Sample historical handwritten document images for layout segmentation from the following datasets: (a) St. Gall, (b) Parzival, (c) G. Washington, (d) CB55, (e) CSG18, (f) CSG863. The bottom part of each image is the zoomed view of red rectangular region. (Color figure online)

network trained to reconstruct its input. In this paper, the encoder output of the autoencoder is extracted as features and feed to an off-the-shelf classifier to segment an image. In the paper [5], incorporated the SLIC superpixel extraction stage inorder to speed up the process in [3]. Another paper [7] uses Conditional Random Field (CRF) [6] to model the local and contextual information jointly. This helps to refine the segmentation results of [5]. Another recent approach [8] segments document images with a simple CNN architecture. Inspired from [5], we consider the segmentation problem as a pixel labeling problem. In contrast to the above approaches, our work extracts deep features from each superpixel and classifies using SVM. Our results show that deep features are more robust than handcrafted features, the autoencoder based approach [3] and the CNN based approach [8]. In this paper, we explore the effectiveness of deep features in the document segmentation. Document images have many practical difficulties to use CNNs directly. The main difficulty is that the image should be resized to the size of input of the CNN architecture. It may poorly affect the performance of the method. Moreover, the time and data required to train deep neural networks are significantly large compared to standard statistical machine learning methods

Table 1. Details of the dataset used in our experiments. TR, TE, and VA denotes size of the training, test, and validation sets respectively.

Dataset	Image size (pixels)	TR	TE	VA
G. Washington [10]	2200 × 3400	10	5	4
St. Gall [11]	1664 × 2496	20	30	10
Parzival [12]	2000 × 3008	20	30	10
CB55 [13]	4872 × 6496	20	13	2
CSG18 [13]	3328 × 4992	20	10	10
CSG863 [13]	3328 × 4992	20	10	10

such as Support Vector Machines (SVM). We try to overcome this disadvantage. We pose the document image segmentation task as a semantic segmentation problem. Semantic segmentation is a popular problem in computer vision in which each pixel is assigned to its most appropriate label from a predefined label set. There are many approaches that use CNN for semantic segmentation [4]. In this work, we first extract deep features from document image pixels and train an SVM classifier to label the pixels. We compare the performance of the proposed approach with the following approaches: (i) local MLP [5], (ii) CRF [7] and (iii) CNN [8] on six different historical document image datasets. Our proposed method gives superior quantitative results consistently.

2   Proposed Method

We pose the document image segmentation problem as a pixel labeling problem. Consider an image I of size $w \times h \times d$, where w, h and d are the width, height and the number of color channel of the image respectively. Let $x_{i,j}$ is the pixel of image I at position (i, j), where $i \in \{1, \ldots, w\}$ and $j \in \{1, \ldots, h\}$. We train a statistical model which learns the label l from a set of labels L for each pixel $x_{i,j}$. The label set $\mathcal{L}$ for historical document images is set as $L = \{$body text, comments, decoration, background$\}$ similar to the past methods. We extract deep features proposed by Cimpoi et al. [9] from image patch surrounding each pixel x_{ij} in document image I. Finally, using an SVM classifier, on top of the extracted features, we assign a label l to each pixel x_{ij}.

2.1   Image Pre-processing

In our approach, we apply the superpixel segmentation algorithm SLIC. In document images, most of the pixels in a superpixel share the same label. The superiority of the superpixel based labeling approach over the pixel labeling approach for the page segmentation task has been demonstrated in [5].

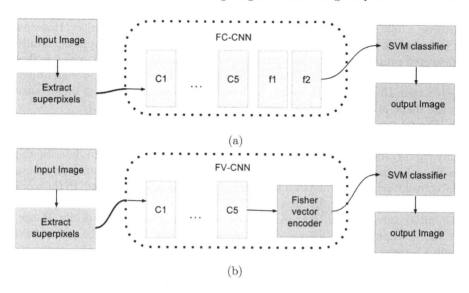

Fig. 2. The proposed approaches: (a) and (b) are separate pipelines for segmenting a document image using FC-CNN and FV-CNN features. The dotted box represents the feature extraction module, c1, ..., c5 represent convolutional layers of CNN and f1 and f2 represent the fully connected layers of CNN.

2.2   Texture of Document Images

In early works such as [14], texture is characterized with the arrangement of local patterns by the distribution of local filter bank responses. The filter banks are capable of capturing edges, spots, and bars at different scales and orientations. In the work [15] propose *textons* which are define by combining the filter responses. The idea of *textons* is improved by new pooling schemes such as soft-assignment [16] and Fisher Vectors (FVs) [18]. The work [17] uses FV encoding on the SIFT features, which achieved the state-of-the-art result in textures, objects and scene detection tasks.

One of the key observations made while visualizing the weights of a learned CNN [19] is that the initial layer learns to detect low level patterns such as dots, line edges, strokes, etc. While later layers in the network learn the higher level structures from images like face, the shape of an object, etc. Even if the CNN is trained with a different dataset or non-document images, the filters are capable of emphasizing various texture patterns in an image.

This paper proposes two types of deep features, namely FC-CNN and FV-CNN inspired from [9]. Both the descriptors are based on the same CNN features [20] obtained from an off-the-shelf CNN pre-trained on the ILSVRC 2012 dataset [21]. We evaluate the performance of segmentation using both features.

The FC-CNN descriptor is obtained by extracting the output of the penultimate fully connected layer of a CNN, including the nonlinear gating function, applied to an input image. This feature can be considered as an object descriptor because a fully connected layer captures the overall shape of an object. However it has some drawbacks in case of document images: (i) since it is using a fully connected neural network, the input image patch should be resized, which makes the feature faulty (ii) the FC-CNN feature represents the entire shape of an object rather than the texture. However, in document images, there is no importance in the shape of the object in a patch because it may very randomly.

The FV-CNN feature overcomes the above disadvantages because the feature is extracted by FV pooling of the convolutional filter response rather than the fully connected layer. Hence, the FV-CNN is a more efficient way to describe the texture of an image than the FC-CNN. Since the feature responses are taken from the convolutional layer, no rescaling of input patch/image is required. In the work [9], it is proved empirically that the efficiency of FV-CNN feature improve from the initial convolutional layer to final convolutional layer monotonically. Hence, in all our experiments, we use the final convolutional layer of the pre-trained neural network.

2.3 Document Image Segmentation

From the given training data, first, we generate superpixels by running the SLIC algorithm using an appropriate region size and regularization parameters. To get the contextual information about a superpixel, we crop each superpixel into patches of size $p \times p$ with the center aligned to the center of the superpixel. The optimum patch size p is calculated by minimizing the superpixel classification error (Fig. 4). Then we extract the deep features for each superpixel region from the corresponding patches.

In FV-CNN, from the densely pooled response of the input image in the convolutional layer, we learn a Fisher Vector (FV) encoder with 64 Gaussian components. This encoder is used for creating the FV-CNN features from the densely pooled response of the convolutional layer of pre-trained CNN architecture. In all our experiments, we use VGG-M [23] architecture trained on the ILSVRC 2012 dataset. The feature dimension in FV-CNN depends on the number of components of Fisher Vector encoder and the number of filters in the convolutional layer. However, the dimension of FC-CNN is the same as the dimension of the fully connected layer.

To model the extracted features, we train an SVM classifier with the predefined labels. In the testing stage, first we extract features from each superpixel. Then we classify the feature and label the superpixel region in the output image with the corresponding label of the superpixel. The proposed approaches using features FC-CNN and FV-CNN are described in the Fig. 2.

3   Experiments

In this section, we use various datasets to demonstrate the effectiveness of the proposed algorithm on different kinds of document images. We use the standard evaluation scheme to analyze the performance of the proposed method. Since

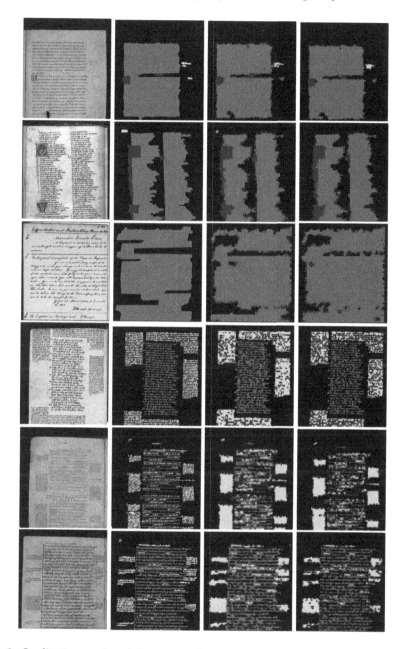

Fig. 3. Qualitative results of the proposed method. The first column shows the original test images from various datasets (1) St. Gall, (2) Parzival, (3) G. Washington, (4) CB55, (5) CSG18, (6) CSG863 from top to bottom respectively. The second column shows the ground-truth images. The third and fourth columns are the output of the proposed methods with FC-CNN and FV-CNN respectively. The black, red, green and blue color of ground truth and output images represent page/background, text, comments and decoration respectively. (Color figure online)

document image segmentation can be considered as a semantic segmentation task, for comparisons, we use pixel accuracy and region of intersection over union (IoU) [24] as the evaluation metrics. Let n_{ij} and n_{cl} are the number of pixels of class i predicted to belong to class j and the total number of classes respectively. Let $t_i = \sum_j n_{ij}$ is the total number of pixels of class i. The following are the metrics we use to evaluate the segmentation:

- pixel accuracy: $\sum_i n_{ii} / \sum_i t_i$
- mean accuracy: $(1/n_{cl}) \sum_i n_{ii} / \sum_i t_i$
- mean IoU: $(1/n_{cl}) \sum_i n_{ii} / (\sum_i t_i + \sum_j n_{ji} - n_{ii})$
- frequency weighted IoU:
  $(\sum_k t_k)^{-1} \sum_i t_i n_{ii} / (\sum_i t_i + \sum_j n_{ji} - n_{ii})$.

Table 2. Comparison on results of historical document image segmentation on the six different dataset with Local MLP, CRF, CNN and the proposed methods FC-CNN and FV-CNN.

Datasets	G. Washington				Parzival				St. Gall			
Evaluation	Pixel acc.	Mean acc.	Mean IoU	f.w. IoU	Pixel acc.	Mean acc.	Mean IoU	f.w. IoU	Pixel acc.	Mean acc.	Mean IoU	f.w. IoU
Local MLP [5]	87	89	75	83	91	64	58	86	95	89	84	92
CRF [7]	91	90	76	85	93	70	63	88	97	88	84	94
CNN [8]	91	91	77	86	94	75	68	89	98	90	87	96
FC-CNN (ours)	94	92	80	89	**97**	74	**71**	**94**	99	91	**88**	**98**
FV-CNN (ours)	**95**	**93**	**81**	**91**	**97**	**76**	**71**	**94**	99	91	**88**	**98**
Datasets	CB55				CSG18				CSG863			
Evaluation	Pixel acc.	Mean acc.	Mean IoU	f.w. IoU	Pixel acc.	Mean acc.	Mean IoU	f.w. IoU	Pixel acc.	Mean acc.	Mean IoU	f.w. IoU
Local MLP [5]	83	53	42	72	83	49	39	73	84	54	42	74
CRF [7]	84	53	42	75	86	47	37	77	86	51	42	78
CNN [8]	86	59	47	77	87	53	41	79	87	58	45	79
FC-CNN (ours)	91	64	52	86	89	64	52	85	91	66	55	87
FV-CNN (ours)	**95**	**73**	**64**	**91**	**92**	**72**	**60**	**89**	**94**	**71**	**61**	**91**

3.1 Evaluation on Historical Document Images

To evaluate the proposed method, we use six different historical handwritten document datasets whose details can be found in Table 1. G. Washington, Parzival, and St. Gall document images are from the IAM historical document database [25]. We use the annotations described in [26]. For the experiments, we choose the following four types of regions from annotation: page/background, text block, decoration, and comment. A new datasets with more complex layout introduced [13] are CB55, CSG18 and CSG863. The CB55 dataset consists of manuscripts from the 14th century which are written in Italian and Latin languages by one writer. The CSG18 and CSG863 datasets consist of manuscripts from the 11th century which are written in the Latin language. The number of writers of both these datasets is not specified. The details of the three datasets are presented in [13]. In SLIC superpixel extraction stage, we choose 10 pixels as the region size and the regularizing parameter as 0.01. The proposed method is compared with the current state-of-the-art method [8] and other two methods [5,7].

The quantitative results are shown in Table 2 and the qualitative results are shown in Fig. 3. From Table 2, we can see that the proposed method with FV-CNN feature achieves maximum of 9%, 19%, 19%, 14% improvements from the current state-of-the-art method [8] in pixel accuracy, mean accuracy, mean IoU and frequency weighted IoU respectively.

3.2 Deep Feature Analysis

To validate the utility of deep features in the document image, we visualize the deep features using t-SNE [22] method. The Fig. 5 represents the deep feature visualization of a sample image taken from the dataset CB55. From the figure, we can observe that even though the feature extraction technique is unsupervised, the feature representations of each class are clustered together.

The patch is a rectangular region we chose around the super pixels before feeding it to the CNN for feature extraction. Large patch size gives more contextual information about the superpixel it covers, it eventually reduces the importance of the superpixel because the local features are extracted uniformly from a patch. Hence the patch size needs to be optimum. The graph shown in Fig. 4 explains the effect on SVM classification accuracy while increasing the patch size for various document regions.

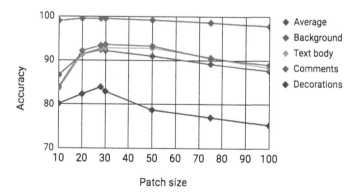

Fig. 4. The graph showing SVM classification accuracy of superpixels by extracting deep features with various patch sizes.

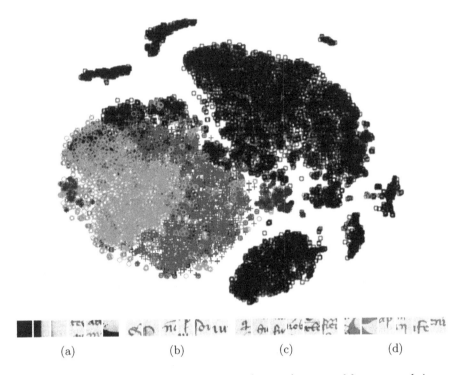

Fig. 5. T-SNE [22] visualization of deep feature (FC-CNN) extracted from a sample image from the CB55 dataset. The black squares, red pluses, green rounds and blue stars are representing background, text body, comments, and decorations features respectively. The subfigure a, b, c, d are the corresponding sampled image patches of these regions respectively (better viewed in colour).

4   Conclusion

We have proposed a deep feature based document image segmentation approach. This approach has the following advantages compared to other methods: (i) It provides better feature representation for document image regions compared to the previous methods. (ii) Since the proposed approach uses a pre-trained network, the training time is significantly reduced compared to an end-to-end CNN training approach [8] because the proposed method uses SVM to train the model. As a future work, we will try the FCN [24] architecture which will be more suites in document segmentation.

References

1. Zhong, Y., Karu, K., Jain, A.K.: Locating text in complex color images. In: ICDAR (1995)
2. Chen, K., Wei, H., Hennebert, J., Ingold, R., Liwicki, M.: Page segmentation for historical handwritten document images using color and texture features. In: ICFHR (2014)

3. Chen, K., Seuret, M., Liwicki, M., Hennebert, J., Ingold, R.: Page segmentation of historical document images with convolutional autoencoders. In: ICDAR (2015)
4. Ganin, Y., Lempitsky, V.: N4-fields: neural network nearest neighbor fields for image transforms. In: ACCV (2015)
5. Chen, K., Liu, C.L., Seuret, M., Liwicki, M., Hennebert, J., Ingold, R.: Page segmentation for historical document images based on superpixel classification with unsupervised feature learning. In: DAS (2016)
6. Lafferty, J., McCallum, A., Pereira, F.: Conditional random fields: probabilistic models for segmenting, labeling sequence data. In: ICML (2001)
7. Chen, K., Seuret, M., Liwicki, M., Hennebert, J., Liu, C.L., Ingold, R.: Page segmentation for historical handwritten document images using conditional random fields. In: ICFHR (2016)
8. Chen, K., Seuret, M.: Convolutional neural networks for page segmentation of historical document images. arXiv:1704.01474 (2016)
9. Cimpoi, M., Maji, S., Vedaldi, A.: Deep filter banks for texture recognition, segmentation. In: CVPR (2015)
10. Fischer, A., Keller, A., Frinken, V., Bunke, H.: Lexicon-free handwritten word spotting using character HMMs. P. R. Lett. **33**, 934–942 (2012)
11. Fischer, A., Frinken, V., Fornés, A., Bunke, H.: Transcription alignment of Latin manuscripts using hidden Markov models. In: Workshop on HDIP (2011)
12. Fischer, A., Wuthrich, M., Liwicki, M., Frinken, V., Bunke, H., Viehhauser, G., Stolz, M.: Automatic transcription of handwritten medieval documents. In: Virtual Systems, Multimedia (2009)
13. Simistira, F., Seuret, M., Eichenberger, N., Garz, A., Liwicki, M., Ingold, R.: DIVA-HisDB: a precisely annotated large dataset of challenging medieval manuscripts. In: ICFHR (2016)
14. Leung, T., Malik, J.: Recognizing surfaces using three-dimensional textons. In: CVPR (1999)
15. Julez, B., Bergen, J.R.: Human factors, behavioral science: textons, the fundamental elements in preattentive vision and perception of textures. In: Readings in Computer Vision (1987)
16. Liu, L., Wang, L., Liu, X.: In defense of soft-assignment coding. In: ICCV (2011)
17. Lowe, D.G.: Object recognition from local scale-invariant features. In: ICCV (1999)
18. Perronnin, F., Sánchez, J., Mensink, T.: Improving the fisher kernel for large-scale image classification. In: Daniilidis, K., Maragos, P., Paragios, N. (eds.) ECCV 2010. LNCS, vol. 6314, pp. 143–156. Springer, Heidelberg (2010). https://doi.org/10.1007/978-3-642-15561-1_11
19. Zeiler, M.D., Fergus, R.: Visualizing and understanding convolutional networks. In: Fleet, D., Pajdla, T., Schiele, B., Tuytelaars, T. (eds.) ECCV 2014. LNCS, vol. 8689, pp. 818–833. Springer, Cham (2014). https://doi.org/10.1007/978-3-319-10590-1_53
20. Krizhevsky, A., Sutskever, I., Hinton, G.E.: Imagenet classification with deep convolutional neural networks. In: PAMI (2012)
21. Russakovsky, O., et al.: ImageNet large scale visual recognition challenge. IJCV **115**, 211–252 (2015)
22. Imagenet classification with deep convolutional neural networks: visualizing data using t-SNE. In: JMLR (2008)
23. Chatfield, K., Simonyan, K., Vedaldi, A., Zisserman, A.: Return of the devil in the details: delving deep into convolutional nets. In: BMVC (2014)

24. Long, J., Shelhamer, E., Darrell, T.: Fully convolutional networks for semantic segmentation. In: CVPR (2015)
25. http://www.fki.inf.unibe.ch/databases/iam-historical-document-database
26. Chen, K., Seuret, M., Wei, H., Liwicki, M., Hennebert, J., Ingold, R.: Ground truth model, tool, and dataset for layout analysis of historical documents. In: DRR (2015)

Pattern Recognition Applications

MKL Based Local Label Diffusion for Automatic Image Annotation

Abhijeet Kumar$^{(\boxtimes)}$, Anjali Anil Shenoy, and Avinash Sharma

CVIT, KCIS, IIIT, Hyderabad, Hyderabad, India
abhijeet.kumar@research.iiit.ac.in, anjali.shenoy@students.iiit.ac.in,
asharma@iiit.ac.in

Abstract. The task of automatic image annotation attempts to predict a set of semantic labels for an image. Majority of the existing methods discover a common latent space that combines content and semantic image similarity using the metric learning kind of global learning framework. This limits their applicability to large datasets. On the other hand, there are few methods which entirely focus on learning a local latent space for every test image. However, they completely ignore the global structure of the data. In this work, we propose a novel image annotation method which attempts to combine best of both local and global learning methods. We introduce the notion of neighborhood-types based on the hypothesis that similar images in content/feature space should also have overlapping neighborhoods. We also use graph diffusion as a mechanism for label transfer. Experiments on publicly available datasets show promising performance.

1 Introduction

Automatic image annotation is a multi-label prediction problem that attempts to predict a set of semantic labels based on visual content of a given image [39]. It has potential application in image retrieval [18], caption generation [10], image description and classification [29].

The basic assumption in image annotation is that the visual content of an image captures a wide variety of semantics at different levels of granularity. Additionally, the label co-occurrence patterns also model the semantic similarity between images. Therefore, existing methods have tried to model label-to-label [18], image-to-image [9] and image-to-label [4] similarities or a combination of them [17,30].

In context of image-to-image and image-to-label similarities Nearest Neighbor (NN) based approaches have been largely successful and intuitive for image annotation. Recent methods either employ a global (metric) learning technique [9,28] or a local query specific model [14] for addressing the class-imbalance problem. However, while the former suffers from the problem of scalability due to global metric learning bottleneck, the latter fails to capture the global latent structure of the data as it is too focused on query specific neighborhood structure.

© Springer Nature Singapore Pte Ltd. 2018
R. Rameshan et al. (Eds.): NCVPRIPG 2017, CCIS 841, pp. 385–399, 2018.
https://doi.org/10.1007/978-981-13-0020-2_34

An alternate approach in [22] addresses the class-imbalance by performing scale-dependent label diffusion on global hypergraph in a transductive setup. However, their method also suffers from the scalability issue (due to SVD decomposition of large dense matrices). Many recent deep learning methods also propose to learn end-to-end network for solving image annotation task [21,32,37].

In this paper, we focus on bridging the gap between purely global and local modeling of the image annotation task. The key hypothesis is that similar images in feature space also have similar labels, hence two vicinal images in feature space should also have overlapping neighborhoods. Each of these neighborhoods (corresponding to an image) can be statistically characterized by constructing the label histogram of all their associated images. We refer to these label histogram features as Local Label Distribution (LLD) features. Thus, two similar images should have similar LLD feature representation which represent similarity in neighborhood. Hence we propose to learn a local label-transfer model for each such neighborhood-type (cluster) separately. This characterization of images by neighborhood-types also inherently captures the global latent structure of data.

Subsequently, each local model is formulated as Multiple Kernel Learning (MKL) task, using a family of multi-scale diffusion kernels. The MKL formulation minimizes the sum of squared error between the ground truth labels (known for each training image) and the labels predicted with multi-scale diffusion over the associated local graph. Such diffusion is performed by linearly combining a set of scale dependent diffusion kernels. A closed form solution exists for obtaining the optimal kernel combination coefficients (parameters of local model). Thus, MKL parameters per neighborhood-type are learnt over the training data. At test time, we construct and map the neighborhood structure of each query image to an existing neighborhood-type to retrieve the best parameter of local model. Finally, we construct the local graph for this query image and diffuse the label using these parameters for subsequent prediction.

1.1   Our Contributions

- We propose a new label histogram characterization (LLD features) of the image neighborhood enabling us to discover the neighborhood-types in the dataset.
- We propose a MKL formulation as local learning model and derived a closed form solution for obtaining the model parameters.
- We propose a diffusion scale normalization procedure for effectively combining diffusion over multiple graphs.

2   Literature Survey

2.1   Generative, Discriminative and Hybrid Models

Xinag et al. [34] proposed a Markov Random Field model, which captured many previously proposed generative models, but had an expensive training step as it learnt an MRF per label.

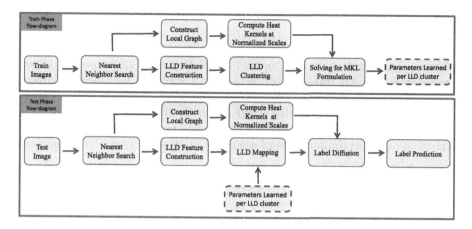

Fig. 1. Pipeline showing flow of testing & training phase

Discriminative models were proposed in [7,8,27,35]. These methods learn label-specific models to classify an image belonging to the particular label. However they fail to capture label-to-label correlations. A hybrid model was presented in [20] combining a generative [6] and discriminative (SVM) model aimed at improving the number of labels recalled.

2.2 Nearest Neighbor Approaches

Though simple and highly intuitive, NN methods are among the best performing ones. [9] introduced metric learning to fuse an array of low-level features. They used cross entropy loss in addition to weighted (based on distance or rank) label propagation. Recently, [28] defined a Bayesian approach with two pass kNN for addressing the class-imbalance challenge and subsequently used an extension of existing LMNN approach [33] as metric learning to fuse different feature sets. One major limitation of these approaches is that they are global methods and heavily rely on metric learning construct, which makes it difficult to scale them to large datasets.

Alternatively, a local variant of NN method proposed in [14] performs the Non-negative Matrix Factorization (NMF [15]) of features from images in a smaller neighborhood, which are made to follow a consensus constraint. Here, the class-imbalance is dealt by means of weighting different feature matrices. However, this is purely a local approach and hence fails to capture the global structure of the latent space.

Recently, [25,28] report performance improvement over the NN methods by using cross modal embedding such as Canonical Correlation Analysis (CCA) or Kernel Canonical Correlation Analysis (KCCA). This is again an attempt to learn global common latent space. However selection of an appropriate kernel function and scalability of KCCA poses a major challenge in these methods.

2.3 Graph Based Models

A graph based transductive method for explicitly capturing label-to-label and image-to-image similarities was proposed in [30]. Recently, [22] proposed a hyper-graph diffusion based transductive method and exploited multi-scale diffusion to address the class-imbalance problem. However, both these methods are semi-supervised in the sense that they need access to all test data for prediction. Additionally the hypergraph diffusion method is not scalable due to require-ment of storage and computation of eigen-decomposition of very large matrices.

2.4 Deep Learning Based Methods

Inspired by the recent success of deep neural net architectures in image classifi-cation [23,24], different approaches involving deep nets have been tried for multi-label classification [11,13,19,32]. [11] modeled these relationship on a hierarchi-cal model exploiting Long Short Term Memory (LSTM) by incorporating inter-level and intra-level label correlations which were parsed using WordNet. CNN-RNN [32] learns a joint image-to-label embedding and label co-occurrence model in an end-to-end way. Semantically Regularised CNN-RNN (S-CNN-RNN) [37] improves on the CNN-RNN model by using a semantically regularized embed-ding layer as an interface between the CNN and RNN which enables RNN to capture the relational model alone. [13] proposed exploiting image metadata to generate neighbors of an image and blend visual information using neural-nets. Recent works in Deep nets capture label-to-label relationships more explicitly than before. Another recent work in [21] converted labels to a word2vec vec-tor [19] and performed label transfer using nearest neighbor methods in embed-ding space computed using CCA or KCCA.

Recently deep-learning methods have been introduced in the context of graphs [31,38,40,42]. Gated Graph Neural Network (GGNN) [40] is a LSTM variant for graphs which learns a propagation model that transfers information between nodes depending on the edge types. [41] introduced Graph Search Neural Network (GSNN) which improves GGNN [40] by diminishing the computational issues. GSNN is able to reason about the concepts by capturing the information flow between nodes in the noisy knowledge-graphs. GSNN is different from our model in the propagation modeling in graphs. We explicit model the label propa-gation with diffusion framework on graphs constructed from neighboring images while GSNN learns the network propagation parameters in the knowledge-graph.

3 Proposed Approach

This section will provide a detailed description of each individual module in the proposed train and test phase flow pipeline depicted in Fig. 1. Let $\mathbf{X}^{tr} = \{\mathbf{x}_1, \cdots, \mathbf{x}_n\}$ be the feature-vector representation of training set of images with corresponding known ground truth labels $\mathbf{Z}^{tr} = \{\mathbf{z}_1, \cdots, \mathbf{z}_n\}$, where each $\mathbf{z}_i$ is a binary vector of size l denoting presence/absence of labels in the image $\mathbf{x}_i \in \mathbf{X}^{tr}$.

3.1   Nearest Neighbors Search

This module performs feature space NN search for a given image in order to discover a group of similar images. Instead of performing a global search, we opt for quantizing the feature space image representation by employing the parallelizable k-means clustering algorithm[1] on training data and finding a fixed g number of clusters in an offline manner. From all these clusters, we subsequently find the top η closest cluster centers in feature space, then we perform the local NN search in those clusters by retrieving a fixed δ number of similar images from each of them. All such retrieved images form the neighbourhood of a given image. We denote this set of nearest neighbor images obtained with this method for a given image $\mathbf{x}$ as $\mathcal{N}(\mathbf{x})$. Note that $|\mathcal{N}(\mathbf{x})| \leq \eta\delta$, as a cluster can have less than δ images. This naturally provides diversity and scalability over the exhaustive NN search.

3.2   Local Graph Construction

This module constructs an undirected weighted graph $\mathcal{G}(V, E, \mathcal{W})$ for an image $\mathbf{x}$ using the neighborhood $\mathcal{N}(\mathbf{x})$, where the input image and each of the selected images in $\mathcal{N}(\mathbf{x})$ images become nodes of the graph.

We construct a local graph by connecting each node to its k most similar nodes using an inverse euclidean distance similarity function over the corresponding image features. We use the standard Gaussian kernel over the feature space as the similarity function, i.e., $Sim(x_1, x_2) = \exp(-||x_1, x_2||_{l2}/\sigma^2)$ to assign weights to these edges.

Note that here $|V| = \zeta + 1 \leq \eta\delta + 1$ where $|\mathcal{N}(\mathbf{x})| = \zeta$.

3.3   LLD Feature Construction, Clustering and Mapping

This module first constructs an l-dimensional histogram feature $\mathcal{F}(\mathbf{x})$ for each image representing the LLD of a given image $\mathbf{x}$, by taking the sum of ground truth labels of all the samples in $\mathcal{N}(\mathbf{x})$:

$$\mathcal{F}(\mathbf{x}) = \sum_{\forall \mathbf{x_i} \in \mathcal{N}(\mathbf{x})} \mathbf{z}_i. \tag{1}$$

We employ parallelizable k-means clustering algorithm over the LLD features corresponding to all training images to get a fixed number of cluster-centers (c) which act as representatives of the neighborhood-types. To map an image to a neighborhood-type we just need to compute its closest neighborhood-type (cluster-centers) in this l-dimensional space. As discussed in Sect. 1, we discover the clusters in LLD space and learn a local model per cluster.

---

[1] https://github.com/serban/kmeans.

3.4 Diffusion Kernel

In this module we construct a family of diffusion kernels at different diffusion scales for a given local graph computed in the previous module. In each weighted graph $\mathcal{G}(V, E, \mathcal{W})$, training images with labels acts as heat sources that are diffused/propagated to all the other nodes in the graph where we aggregate the information and subsequently use for prediction.

Graph Laplacian. For (dyadic) undirected weighted graphs, diffusion kernels are derived from the spectra (constituted by both eigenvalues & eigenvectors) of the graph Laplacian matrix [1]. The unnormalized Laplacian L of a weighted undirected graph $\mathcal{G}$ with adjacency matrix A is defined as:

$$L = D - A = U \Lambda U^T \tag{2}$$

where D is the diagonal matrix with each diagonal entry $d_{ii} = \sum_{i=1}^{n} A_{ij}$, U is the matrix of eigenvectors and Λ is the diagonal matrix of corresponding real positive eigenvalues of the Laplacian matrix, i.e. $\Lambda = Diag(\lambda_1, \cdots, \lambda_{\zeta+1})$ and $0 = \lambda_1 \leq \lambda_2 \cdots \leq \lambda_{\zeta+1}$ for a connected graph.

Diffusion kernel is a positive semi-definite, non-linear family of kernels and can be used for defining distances over non-euclidean spaces and for multiscale-multilabel-diffusion in graphs. It has been used for multi-scale label diffusion over graphs [36], and a variety of other applications 3D Shape Matching [3] and Robotics graphSLAM [2]

Subsequently, the scale dependent diffusion kernel matrix is defined as:

$$H(t) = U e^{-\Lambda t} U^T \tag{3}$$

where $t > 0$ is the parameter of the diffusion. Every entry $H(i, j, t)$ of the diffusion kernel can be interpreted as the amount of heat diffused from node v_j to node v_i at scale t while considering v_j as a point heat source of unit magnitude. We use the diffusion kernel matrix at m different scales to diffuse each label.

This is different from [22] as we use multiple scales for all labels rather than using specific scales for different frequency type of labels.

Diffusion Scale Normalization. Instead of manually choosing diffusion scales for all local graphs, we propose to find a set of normalized scales per graph using the structure of the local graph. This structure is captured by the spectrum (eigenvalues) of the graph. Such a normalization is very important as the diffusion scale value is relative to the graph structure/topology. Interestingly, if we see the plot of exponential function

$$f(\lambda, t) = e^{-\lambda t} = \theta \tag{4}$$

in Fig. 2, we see that one can find the normalized values of the diffusion scale parameter t (varying from smaller to larger values) by fixing the values of θ and index of λ.

$$t = -log(\theta)/\lambda \tag{5}$$

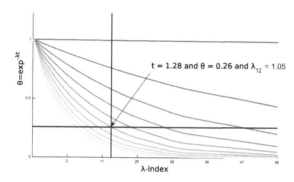

Fig. 2. Diffusion scale normalization on a sample graph of 56 nodes. In this case we use the 12th ($=0.2 * |56|$) eigenvalue and $\theta = 0.26$ for computing the scale normalized t value. In general a set of θ values will be chosen for defining bank of diffusion kernels

3.5 MKL Formulation for Label Diffusion

In this section, we outline our MKL formulation for learning the label diffusion parameters locally for each LLD cluster/neighborhood type.

Let $\mathbf{X}_c^{tr} \subset \mathbf{X}^{tr}$ be the subset of n_c training images and $\mathbf{Z}_c^{tr} \subset \mathbf{Z}^{tr}$ be the ground truth labels in c-th LLD cluster. We can write $\mathbf{X}_c^{tr} = [\mathbf{x}_1, \cdots, \mathbf{x}_{n_c}]$ and $\mathbf{Z}_c^{tr} = [\mathbf{z}_1, \cdots, \mathbf{z}_{n_c}]$.

For each image $\mathbf{x}_k \in X_{tr}^c$ there is a local graph $\mathcal{G}_k$ (Sect. 3.2) with $\zeta_k + 1$ nodes where the node with the last index is $\mathbf{x}_k$ itself. Let $\mathbf{z}_k$ be the ground truth label of $\mathbf{x}_k$ and $\mathbf{Y}_k = [\mathbf{y}_1 \cdots \mathbf{y}_l]$ be the transpose matrix of ground truth labels (i.e., $[\mathbf{z}_1 \cdots \mathbf{z}_k]^T$) for all the other ζ_k images (nodes) in the local graph appended with a $\mathbf{0}$ row vector representing labels for $\mathbf{x_k}$ itself. Note that $\mathbf{y}_i$ is a column vector of dimension $(\zeta_k + 1) \times 1$. The last row is appended for compatibility in matrix multiplication.

Let $\tau = [t_1, \cdots, t_m]^T$ be the set of m normalized diffusion scale parameters used for defining the diffusion kernels: $H_k(t_1), \cdots, H_k(t_m)$ (Sect. 3.4). Here each $H_k(t_i)$ is a $(\zeta_k + 1) \times (\zeta_k + 1)$ dimensional matrix. Let $\mathbf{e} = [0, \cdots, 0, 1]$ be a $(\zeta_k + 1) \times 1$ dimensional vector, then $h_k^i = e^T H_k(t_i)$ represents the last row of the (symmetric) diffusion kernel matrix.

It is important to note that since the training image $\mathbf{x}_k$ is kept at the last position in the index order in graph $\mathcal{G}_k$, only the last row of $H_k(t_i)$ (i.e., h_k^i) is sufficient to perform label diffusion (at scale t_i) from all other images (nodes) in the graph.

Since we know the ground truth labels for image $\mathbf{x}_k$, and if we take β_j^c to represent the diffusion contributions of the diffusion kernels $h_k^i \forall i \in \{1, \cdots, m\}$ for j^{th} label in the cth cluster, we can obtain an MKL formulation as a minimization criterion:

$$\min_{\beta_c} \sum_{k=1}^{n_c} ||\Gamma_k \beta_c - \mathbf{z}_k||^2, \tag{6}$$

where,

$$\beta_c^j = [\beta_c^{j1}, \beta_c^{j2}, ..\beta_c^{jm}]_{(1 \times m)} \tag{7}$$

$$\beta_c = [\beta_c^1, \beta_c^2, ..\beta_c^l]_{(lm \times 1)}^T \tag{8}$$

$$\Gamma_k = \begin{bmatrix} (\mathbf{M}_k \mathbf{y}_1)^T & & & \\ & \ddots & & \\ & & (\mathbf{M}_k \mathbf{y}_r)^T & \\ & & & \ddots & \\ & & & & (\mathbf{M}_k \mathbf{y}_l)^T \end{bmatrix}_{(l \times lm)} \tag{9}$$

and

$$\mathbf{M}_k = [h_k^{1T}, h_k^{2T}, \ldots, h_k^{mT}]_{(m \times (\zeta_k + 1))}^T. \tag{10}$$

By combining Eqs. 6, 8, 9 with simple algebraic manipulations, we can write the simplified MKL formulation as:

$$\min_{\beta_c} ||\hat{\Gamma}_c \beta_c - \mathcal{Z}_c||^2, \tag{11}$$

where,

$$\hat{\Gamma}_c = [\Gamma_1^T, \cdots, \Gamma_{n_c}^T]^T \tag{12}$$

is a $(n_c l \times lm)$ matrix and

$$\mathcal{Z}_c = [z_1^T, \cdots, z_{n_c}^T]^T \tag{13}$$

is a $(n_c l \times 1)$ vector.

The minimization of proposed MKL formulation Eq. 11 can be achieved by finding the optimal value of parameter β_c in a closed form manner as:

$$\beta_c = (\hat{\Gamma}_c^T \hat{\Gamma}_c + \epsilon I)^{-1} \hat{\Gamma}_c^T \mathcal{Z}_c, \tag{14}$$

It is important to note that the $\hat{\Gamma}_c$ is a very sparse and low rank matrix. This sparse structure can be useful in efficiently computing its singular value decomposition and hence the pseudoinverse of the $\hat{\Gamma}_c$ which is relatively inexpensive as KCCA or hypergraph Laplacian eigenvector-decomposition.

Since our method solves MKL at cluster level in a closed form manner, it is scalable to large data.

3.6   Label Diffusion and Prediction

For a test image $\mathbf{x_q}, \mathcal{F}(x_q)$ is used to find s nearest LLD neighborhood-types represented as $\mathbf{P} = [\mathbf{p}_1, \cdots, \mathbf{p}_s]$. The associated pre-learned MKL parameters $[\beta_1, \cdots, \beta_s]$ for the selected clusters are used for independent diffusion over the local graph $\mathcal{G}_q$ on $\mathbf{x}_q$. This is achieved by first computing the respective $\mathbf{\Gamma}_q$ matrix sized $(l \times lm)$ and then multiplying it with the pre-learned parameter vector β_c sized $(lm \times 1)$. Finally, we take an average of these diffused values. Label diffusion is performed as:

$$\mathbf{z}_q^{\text{diffused}} = \frac{1}{s} \sum_{c=1}^{s} \mathbf{\Gamma}_q \beta_c \tag{15}$$

where $\mathbf{z}_q^{\text{diffused}}$ is the $(l \times 1)$ vector of the diffused labels. Finally, a fixed set of r labels is predicted for $\mathbf{x}_q$ by choosing labels corresponding to top r values in $\mathbf{z}_q^{\text{diffused}}$.

4   Datasets

Table 1 provides details of datasets used in our experiments.

Table 1. Dataset details: rows 2–4 contain basic dataset information, rows 5–6 denote the statics in the order- median, mean and max.

Dataset information	PascalVOC-2007 [5]	MIRFlickr-25k [12]
Total number of images	9963	25000
Vocabulary size	20	38
Train/test split	5011/4092	12500/12500 [25]
Labels/images	1, 1.51, 6	5, 4.7, 17
Images/labels	257.5, 379.2, 2050	995.5, 1560, 5216

4.1   PascalVOC-2007

PASCAL Visual Object Classes (VOC) challenge [5] datasets are widely used as the benchmark for multi-label classification. The VOC 2007 dataset contains 9963 images. We follow a train/test split of 5011/4952 as in [32].

4.2   MIRFlickr-25k

This dataset contains images downloaded from Flickr and was introduced in [12] for evaluating keyword-based image retrieval. It consists of 25000 images and we follow an equal split of train and test (12500 images each) as used in [25]. 419 images in the dataset do not have any of the 38 semantic label annotations. Metadata, GPS and EXIF information are also provided in the dataset but we do not use any of these in our method.

5   Experiments and Results

5.1   Features and Evaluation Method

Deep-learning based features have proven to be effective in image representation [22,28] and hence we use outputs from *fc7-layer* of VGG16 network (pre-trained on ImageNet) [23] to represent an image. To analyze the annotation performance, we consider precision, recall, F1-score, average precision (AP) and mean average precision (mAP). We predict a fixed number of r labels per image which is set to be the mean number of labels per image in the dataset. Let a label w_i be present in $m1$ images as ground-truth and is predicted for $m2$ images where $m3$ of them are correct. The precision for w_i is $m3/m2$ and recall is $m3/m1$. Mean precision (P) and recall (R) is the precision and recall values averaged over all the labels. $F1$ measure is the harmonic mean of P and R. We also report AP and mAP by evaluating ranking of all the images.

5.2   Experiments

We set $s = 3$ for PascalVOC-2007 and $s = 5$ for MIRFlickr-25K. Additionally we set $k = 6$ in kNN graph construction in Sect. 3.2 and $m = 100$. θ is chosen as m equally spaced values between 0.001 to 1.0 (corresponding t will vary from large to small scales of diffusion) and the index of the eigenvalue is chosen as the closest integer value greater than $0.2 \times |V|$. Performance variation observed for varying m from 32 to 100 was less than 1%.

We find the values of the hyper-parameters via cross-validation by dividing the train dataset into two parts (5:1 ratio) while maximizing $F1$ and the best performing parameters on validation set were used to evaluate performance on the test data. For η and δ we explore from the following set $\{5, 12, 20, 28\}$ to find the best performing values. We also vary the number of cluster centers in LLD (c) and the number of clusters in image-feature space clustering (g). The best performing values for MIRFlickr-25k were found to be $\eta = 5, \delta = 12, c = 100$ and $g = 30$ and for PascalVOC-2007 were found to be $\eta = 5, \delta = 20, c = 45$ and $g = 20$.

5.3   Results

Tables 2 and 3 show the performance comparison of the proposed method with existing methods that uses VGG16 features. The obvious understanding one can make here is that there is non-agreement between F1 and mAP measures. The mAP considers the global ranking of all images corresponding to each label instead of just considering top r labels for computation of average precision.

We can see that our method performs very close to the state of the art 2PKNN method and also has similar mAP. This small disparity in performance can be attributed to the fact that our method does not consider KCCA and metric learning type of fully global operations.

Table 2. Comparison of popular methods on different evaluation metrics for MIRFlickr-25k Dataset for **r = 5**

Method	$P@r$	$R@r$	$F1@r$	mAP
TagRel [16]	41.5	72.1	52.7	68.9
TagProp [18]	45.5	70.1	55.2	70.8
2PKNN [28]	46.4	70.9	56.1	66.5
SVM [26]	38.8	72.4	50.5	72.7
HHD [22]	–	–	–	75.0
Our method	51.0	59.9	55.1	66.3

Table 3. Label specific (average precision in %) for all labels, mAP, P@r, R@r and F1@r with **r = 2** on PascalVOC-2007 dataset.

	CNN-RNN [32]	Our Method
plane	96.7	92.8
bike	83.1	84.7
bird	94.2	91.3
boat	92.8	81.7
bottle	61.2	41.3
bus	82.1	83.9
car	89.1	89.0
cat	94.2	86.3
chair	64.2	55.7
table	70.0	68.4

	CNN-RNN [32]	Our Method
cow	83.6	71.9
dog	92.4	86.7
horse	91.7	89.4
motor	84.2	82.7
person	93.7	91.8
plant	59.8	54.0
sheep	93.2	75.1
sofa	75.3	57.1
train	99.7	92.6
tv	78.6	66.9

	CNN-RNN [32]	Our Method
P@r	-	53.8
R@r	-	77.7
F1@r	-	63.6
mAP	84.0	77.2

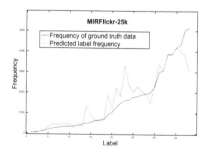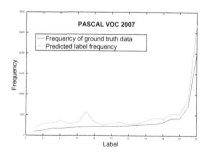

Fig. 3. Distribution of label frequency in MIRFlickr-25k and PascalVOC-2007 test images.

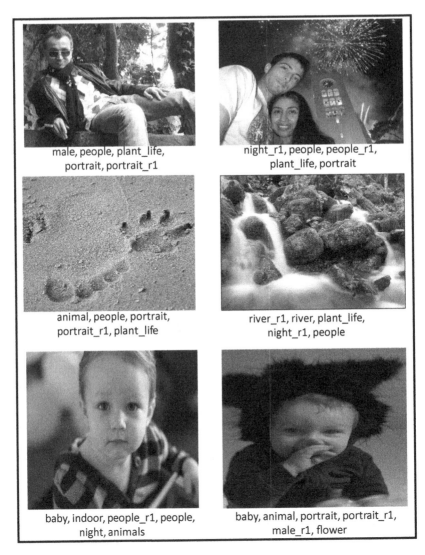

male, people, plant_life,
portrait, portrait_r1

night_r1, people, people_r1,
plant_life, portrait

animal, people, portrait,
portrait_r1, plant_life

river_r1, river, plant_life,
night_r1, people

baby, indoor, people_r1, people,
night, animals

baby, animal, portrait, portrait_r1,
male_r1, flower

Fig. 4. Qualitative results for label prediction on MIRFlickr-25k dataset. Row1: images with frequent labels (*male*, *people*); Row2: images with no ground truth label given; Row3: images with rare labels (*baby*, *potrait*). Green: labels present in ground truth and our model's predictions (true positives), Blue: Incorrect predictions by the model and Red: Labels are not present in ground truth but are semantically meaningful. Red and blue labels combined form False Positives (Color figure online)

Figure 3 shows the distribution of both ground-truth and predicted label frequency in test images on two datasets. For MIRFlickr-25k, a large section of predicted label frequency curve (including low and high frequency labels) closely overlaps with that of ground truth. However, the medium frequency labels (in the middle) are over-predicted at the cost of suppression of few frequent occurring labels (right tail). This is prevalent due to the nature of our approach, but we accept this as a trade-off in order to address the issue of class imbalance by accurately predicting lower frequency labels in images. In case of PascalVOC-2007, we observe our curve running parallel to the one of ground truth but with a shift of a few units. This shift is due to the difference that on an average only 1.5 labels are associated with image in the ground truth annotation but we predict 2 labels per image.

Figure 4 shows the qualitative results on a few examples from the MIRFlickr-25k dataset. Row1 depicts images which consists of frequent labels in the ground-truth (*male, people*) while Row2 consists of images with no ground-truth and Row3 contains images with rare labels (*baby, portrait*) in the ground-truth. From Row1 and Row3 we observe that our method performs well on the frequent and rare labels. We also observe that for images with no ground-truth (Row2) the predictions are semantically relevant to the image-content. Labels in red-color denote tags which are not present in the ground-truth of the image but are semantically meaningful. This indicates towards the incomplete-labeling in the dataset.

6 Conclusion

We have proposed a novel solution for automatic multi-label image annotation. Our method exploits the empirical observation that similar images have similar neighborhood-types in terms of their label distribution. We have introduced the notion of neighborhood-type and proposed to learn local MKL models per cluster/neighborhood-type with closed form learning solution. The MKL formulation exploits the multi-scale diffusion where we also proposed a novel diffusion scale normalization to be able to combine diffusion at different local graphs. The overall formulation is scalable as we have mainly proposed local models while clustering is employed twice (in original VGG16 feature space and as well as in histogram/LLD space). Finally, we have shown promising results on publicly available dataset.

As part of future work it will be interesting to explore the hypergraphs in the local space to model the higher order correlations between labels explicitly in conjunction with image correlations. Local metric learning construct in forming and/or manipulating LLD clusters can be used which may provide insights into the inherent nature of the problem.

Acknowledgments. We thank Yashashwi Verma for his helpful feedback.

References

1. Belkin, M., Niyogi, P.: Laplacian eigenmaps for dimensionality reduction and data representation. Neural Comput. **15**(6), 1373–1396 (2003)
2. Datta, S., Tourani, S., Sharma, A., Krishna, K.M.: SLAM pose-graph robustification via multi-scale Heat-Kernel analysis. In: CDC (2016)
3. Sharma, A., Horaud, R., Cech, J., Boyer, E.: Topologically-robust 3D shape matching based on diffusion geometry and seed growing. In: CVPR (2011)
4. Carneiro, G., Chan, A.B., Moreno, P.J., Vasconcelos, N.: Supervised learning of semantic classes for image annotation and retrieval. IEEE TPAMI **29**(3), 394–410 (2007)
5. Everingham, M., Van Gool, L., Williams, C.K.I., Winn, J.M., Zisserman, A.: The PASCAL visual object classes (VOC) challenge. IJCV **88**, 303–338 (2010)
6. Feng, S., Manmatha, R., Lavrenko, V.: Multiple Bernoulli relevance models for image and video annotation. In: CVPR (2004)
7. Fu, H., Zhang, Q., Qiu, G.: Random forest for image annotation. In: Fitzgibbon, A., Lazebnik, S., Perona, P., Sato, Y., Schmid, C. (eds.) ECCV 2012. LNCS, vol. 7577, pp. 86–99. Springer, Heidelberg (2012). https://doi.org/10.1007/978-3-642-33783-3_7
8. Grangier, D., Bengio, S.: A discriminative kernel-based approach to rank images from text queries. IEEE TPAMI **30**, 1371–1384 (2008)
9. Guillaumin, M., Mensink, T., Verbeek, J.J., Schmid, C.: TagProp: discriminative metric learning in nearest neighbor models for image auto-annotation. In: ICCV (2009)
10. Gupta, A., Verma, Y., Jawahar, C.V.: Choosing linguistics over vision to describe images. In: AAAI (2012)
11. Hu, H., Zhou, G.-T., Deng, Z., Liao, Z., Mori, G.: Learning structured inference neural networks with label relations. CoRR abs/1511.05616 (2015)
12. Huiskes, M.J., Lew, M.S.: The MIR flickr retrieval evaluation. In: Multimedia Information Retrieval (2008)
13. Johnson, J., Ballan, L., Li, F.-F.: Love thy neighbors: image annotation by exploiting image metadata. CoRR abs/1508.07647 (2015)
14. Kalayeh, M., Idrees, H., Shah, M.: NMF-KNN: image annotation using weighted multi-view non-negative matrix factorization. In: CVPR (2014)
15. Lee, D.D., Seung, H.S.: Algorithms for non-negative matrix factorization. In: NIPS (2000)
16. Li, X., Snoek, C.G.M., Worring, M.: Learning social tag relevance by neighbor voting. IEEE Trans. Multimed. **11**, 1310–1322 (2009)
17. Liu, J., Li, M., Liu, Q., Hanqing, L., Ma, S.: Image annotation via graph learning. Pattern Recogn. **42**, 218–228 (2009)
18. Makadia, A., Pavlovic, V., Kumar, S.: Baselines for image annotation. In: IJCV (2010)
19. Mikolov, T., Chen, K., Corrado, G.S., Dean, J.: Efficient estimation of word representations in vector space. CoRR abs/1301.3781 (2013)
20. Murthy, V.N., Can, E.F., Manmatha, R.: A hybrid model for automatic image annotation. In: ICMR (2014)
21. Murthy, V.N., Maji, S., Manmatha, R.: Automatic image annotation using deep learning representations. In: ICMR (2015)
22. Murthy, V.N., Sharma, A., Chari, V., Manmatha, R.: Image annotation using multi-scale hypergraph heat diffusion framework. In: ICMR (2016)

23. Simonyan, K., Zisserman, A.: Very deep convolutional networks for large-scale image recognition. CoRR abs/1409.1556 (2014)
24. Szegedy, C., Liu, W., Jia, Y., Sermanet, P., Reed, S.E., Anguelov, D., Erhan, D., Vanhoucke, V., Rabinovich, A.: Going deeper with convolutions. CoRR abs/1409.4842 (2015)
25. Uricchio, T., Ballan, L., Seidenari, L., Del Bimbo, A.: Automatic image annotation via label transfer in the semantic space. CoRR abs/1605.04770 (2016)
26. Verbeek, J., Guillaumin, M., Mensink, T., Schmid, C.: Image annotation with TagProp on the MIRFLICKR set. In: ACM MIR (2010)
27. Verma, Y., Jawahar, C.V.: Exploring SVM for image annotation in presence of confusing labels. In: BMVC (2013)
28. Verma, Y., Jawahar, C.V.: Image annotation by propagating labels from semantic neighbourhoods. IJCV **121**, 1–23 (2016)
29. Wang, H., Huang, H., Ding, C.H.Q.: Image annotation using multi-label correlated Green's function. In: ICCV (2009)
30. Wang, H., Huang, H., Ding, C.H.Q.: Image annotation using bi-relational graph of images and semantic labels. In: CVPR (2011)
31. Duvenaud, D.K., Maclaurin, D., Iparraguirre, J., Bombarell, R., Hirzel, T., Aspuru-Guzik, A., Adams, R.P.: Convolutional networks on graphs for learning molecular fingerprints. In: NIPS (2015)
32. Wang, J., Yang, Y., Mao, J., Huang, Z., Huang, C., Xu, W.: CNN-RNN: a unified framework for multi-label image classification. CoRR abs/1604.04573 (2016)
33. Weinberger, K.Q., Saul, L.K.: Distance metric learning for large margin nearest neighbor classification. JMLR **10**, 207–244 (2009)
34. Xiang, Y., Zhou, X., Chua, T.S., Ngo, C.W.: A revisit of generative model for automatic image annotation using markov random fields. In: CVPR (2009)
35. Zhang, H., Berg, A.C., Maire, M., Malik, J.: SVM-KNN: discriminative nearest neighbor classification for visual category recognition. In: CVPR (2006)
36. Szlam, A.D., Maggioni, M., Coifman, R.R.: Regularization on graphs with function-adapted diffusion processes. JMLR **9**, 1711–1739 (2008)
37. Liu, F., Xiang, T., Hospedales, T.M., Yang, W., Sun, C.: Semantic regularisation for recurrent image annotation. In: CVPR (2017)
38. Scarselli, F., Gori, M., Tsoi, A.C., Monfardini, G.: The graph neural network model. IEEE Trans. Neural Netw. **20**, 61–80 (2009)
39. Li, X., Uricchio, T., Ballan, L., Bertini, M., Snoek, C.G.M., Del Bimbo, A.: Socializing the semantic gap: a comparative survey on image tag assignment, refinement and retrieval. CSUR **49**(1) (2016)
40. Li, Y., Zemel, R.: Gated graph sequence neural networks. In: ICLR (2016)
41. Marino, K., Salakhutdinov, R., Gupta, A.: The more you know: using knowledge graphs for image classification. In: CVPR (2017)
42. Henaff, M., Bruna, J., LeCun, Y.: Deep convolutional networks on graph-structured data. arXiv preprint arXiv:1506.05163 (2015)

Semantic Multinomial Representation for Scene Images Using CNN-Based Pseudo-concepts and Concept Neural Network

Deepak Kumar Pradhan[1], Shikha Gupta[2], Veena Thenkanidiyoor[1(✉)], and Dileep Aroor Dinesh[2]

[1] Department of Computer Science and Engineering,
National Institute of Technology Goa, Ponda 401403, Goa, India
eb.deepakpradhan@gmail.com, veenat@nitgoa.ac.in
[2] School of Computing and Electrical Engineering,
Indian Institute of Technology Mandi, Mandi 175001, H.P., India
shikha_g@students.iitmandi.ac.in, addileep@iitmandi.ac.in

Abstract. For challenging visual recognition tasks such as scene classification and object detection there is a need to bridge the semantic gap between low-level features and the semantic concept descriptors. This requires mapping a scene image onto a semantic representation. Semantic multinomial (SMN) representation is a semantic representation of an image that corresponds to a vector of posterior probabilities of concepts. In this work we propose to build a concept neural network (CoNN) to obtain the SMN representation for a scene image. An important issue in building a CoNN is that it requires the availability of ground truth concept labels. In this work we propose to use pseudo-concepts obtained from feature maps of higher level layers of convolutional neural network. The effectiveness of the proposed approaches are studied using standard datasets.

1 Introduction

Scene image understanding is important for cognitive task such as scene classification. Early efforts in scene understanding shown that the rich semantic content comprising of multiple concepts can be effectively represented using set of local feature vectors comprising of SIFT [1] and HoG [2] that are low-level features. Our brain identifies a scene image from the composition of semantic content rather than colors or edges of the scene over small patches. For effective understanding of scene images, it is necessary to map them onto a suitable semantic representation. Some of the semantic scene representations are holistic scene representation [3], bag-of-visual-words representation [4], topic space representation [5], and concept occurrence vector representation [6] which represent the semantic content of an scene image. In this work, we explore semantic multinomial (SMN) representation for scene images.

R. Rameshan et al. (Eds.): NCVPRIPG 2017, CCIS 841, pp. 400–409, 2018.
https://doi.org/10.1007/978-981-13-0020-2_35

Semantic multinomial representation (SMN) is a semantic representation of a scene. SMN representation of a scene image is a vector of posterior probabilities corresponding to semantic concepts [7]. The value of a concept posterior probability can be computed by first building a suitable model for the concept. In [7], a GMM-based approach to obtain the SMN representation for a scene image is proposed. This method involves building a GMM for every semantic concept using the local feature vectors from all the images having that concept label in their ground truth. In [8], SVM based approaches to obtain SMN representation were explored. In this work, we propose to build a concept neural network (CoNN) to obtain the SMN representation for scene images. An important issue in building the concept models is that it requires the availability of ground truth concept labels for images. In [9], an approach to build concept models using pseudo-concepts in the absence of ground truth concept labels is proposed.

In this work we propose to use the pseudo-concepts obtained from feature maps of the higher level layers of convolutional neural network (CNN) [10]. We also propose to build a CoNN using the features extracted form CNN. Major contributions of this work are as follows: (1) Obtaining pseudo-concepts from CNN (2) Building CoNN to obtain SMN representation. The effectiveness of the approaches presented in this work are studied using standard datasets.

2   An Overview of Semantic Scene Representations

Semantic multinomial representation (SMN) is an intermediate scene representation. Several intermediate scene representations such as holistic scene representation [3], bag-of-visual-words representation [4], topic space representation [5], and concept occurrence vector representation [6] exist which represent the semantic content of an scene image. A holistic scene representation is be made up of structure or shape of a scene image using a set of spatial envelope properties such as degree of naturalness, degree of openness etc. [3]. The bag-of-visual-words [4] representation is a vector of frequencies of occurrence of visual words in the image. A visual word represents a specific local semantic pattern shared by a group of local feature vectors. The topic space (TS) representation of a scene image is a latent space representation that is a vector of posterior probabilities corresponding to the topics. Here, a topic corresponds to a 'theme' or a latent aspect that is related to a semantic concept as discussed in [5]. It is a generative process. The concept occurrence vector (COV) representation of a scene image corresponds to a vector of frequencies of occurrence of local semantic concepts in a scene image [6,11]. The COV representation of a scene image is obtained by assigning a concept label to every local feature vector of a scene image and the frequency of occurrence of every concept label is determined. In this method, it is necessary to build a suitable concept classifier to assign a local feature vector of an image to a semantic concept. For building a classifier to obtain a COV representation, we essentially need a data set where the concept label for each local feature vector of the image is available. It is difficult to have such a data set

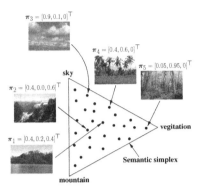

Fig. 1. Illustration of mapping of scene images onto points in a semantic simplex, where the number of concepts, $\mathcal{C} = 3$. Here, $\boldsymbol{\pi}$ for an image is the vector of posterior probabilities for the three concepts, 'sky', 'vegetation', and 'mountain' in that order.

because most of the datasets have the semantic information only at class level. Hence, it is better to have an intermediate scene representation such as SMN representation that can be obtained using the image level semantic information.

The semantic multinomial (SMN) representation of a scene image is a vector of posterior probabilities corresponding to semantic concepts [7]. An SMN representation $\boldsymbol{\pi}$ is given by $\boldsymbol{\pi} = [\pi_1, \pi_2, \ldots, \pi_k, \ldots, \pi_c]^\top$ where c corresponds to the number of semantic concepts and π_k is the posterior probability corresponding to kth concept. The SMN representation can be considered as a transformation that maps an image I onto a point in a C dimensional probability simplex as illustrated in Fig. 1. The SMN representation can be considered as a transformation that maps an image I onto a point in a C dimensional probability simplex, as illustrated in Fig. 1. To obtain the SMN representation of a scene image, it is necessary to build concept models. A concept model for kth concept can be built using all the images having that concept label. In [7], a GMM-based approach to obtain the SMN representation for a scene image is proposed. This method involves building a GMM for every semantic concept using the local feature vectors from all the images having that concept label in their ground truth. In [8], SVM based approaches to obtain SMN representation has been explored where dynamic kernels like intermediate matching kernel (IMK), GMM supervector kernel (GMMSVK) and GMM universal back-ground model mean interval kernel (GUMIK) for SVMs and used for obtaining SMN representation.

An important issue in obtaining SMN representation for an image by building concept models is that it requires ground truth concept labels for the images. All the datasets are not having the ground truth concept labels. In the absence of ground truth concept labels, alternative approaches to build the concept models may be explored. In [9], the usage of pseudo-concepts in the absence of ground truth concept labels was proposed. The paper proposed the usage of clusters of local feature vectors of all the images for getting pseudo-concept labels. The approach proposed in [9] cannot be used when the images are not represented as sets of local feature vectors. In this work, we propose an alternative way of obtaining pseudo-concepts using the convolutional neural networks. This work also proposes to build a neural network based concept model to obtain the SMN representation.

3   Concept Neural Network for Generating SMN Representation

In this work, we propose to build a concept neural network (CoNN) to generate SMN representation. The CoNN is a feed forward neural network (FFNN) that comprises of an input layer, an output layer and one or more hidden layers. Let $\mathcal{D} = \{I_1, I_2, \ldots, I_i, \ldots, I_N\}$ be the set of all scene images in a dataset. Let $\{\omega_1, \omega_2, \ldots, \omega_k, \ldots, \omega_c\}$ be a set of c concept labels. Let $\mathbf{X}_i \in \mathcal{R}^d$ be a d-dimensional feature vector representation for an image I_i. Let there be p concept labels associated with I_i. The CoNN comprises of d number of neurons in input layer and c number of neurons in the output layer. The number of neurons in the hidden layers need to be chosen carefully for a dataset. Weights in a CoNN are estimated using error back propagation method. However, the training of a CoNN differs from that of a FFNN in the way in which examples are presented. In a conventional FFNN, every input $\mathbf{X}$ is associated with a target vector $\mathbf{y}$ which need to be presented together during training process. Typically $\mathbf{y}$ is a c-dimensional vector encoded in one-hot-notation. As we know that a scene image comprises of multiple semantic concepts. Hence there are multiple concept labels associated with one image. Suppose that $\mathbf{Y}_i = \{\mathbf{y}_{i1}, \mathbf{y}_{i2}, \ldots, \mathbf{y}_{ip}\}$ is a set of one-hot target vectors corresponding to p concept labels of an image I_i. Here $\mathbf{y}_{ij}$ is a c-dimensional one-hot vector. During training, a scene image presented to CoNN multiple times with different target vectors unlike as in a conventional FFNN where a scene image is presented only once. The instance of training a CoNN using an image represented as 8-dimensional vector and comprising of 3 concepts is illustrated in Fig. 2a. The image is presented to the network thrice, every time with a different target vector.

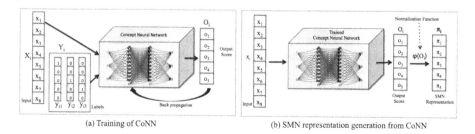

(a) Training of CoNN   (b) SMN representation generation from CoNN

Fig. 2. Illustration of the training (a) and testing (b) phase of CoNN. Here we assume that the input feature vector is 8-dimensional and there are total $c = 5$ concepts available in the dataset. The illustration also assumes that the particular scene image that is being fed to CoNN has $p = 3$ concepts in it.

The process of testing CoNN is shown in Fig. 2b. A feature vector $\mathbf{X}_i$ corresponding to a scene image I_i is fed to the CoNN and a c-dimensional score vector $\mathbf{O}_i = [o_1, o_2, \ldots, o_k, \ldots, o_c]^\top$ is obtained at the output layer. Score o_k for kth concept label, ω_k is mapped onto a pseudo probability using a logistic function as follows:

$$\tilde{P}(\omega_k \mid \mathbf{X}_i) = \frac{1}{1 + \exp(-\alpha o_k)} \tag{1}$$

where α is a parameter that controls the slope of the logistic function. The pseudo probability is then normalized to obtain the posterior probability value corresponding to a concept k as follows:

$$\pi_k = P(\omega_k \mid \mathbf{X}_i) = \frac{\tilde{P}(\omega_k \mid \mathbf{X}_i)}{\sum_{j=1}^c \tilde{P}(\omega_j \mid \mathbf{X}_i)} \tag{2}$$

The semantic multinomial representation of a scene image is obtained as a vector of posterior probabilities corresponding to the semantic concepts as $\boldsymbol{\pi}_i = [\pi_1, \pi_2, \ldots, \pi_k, \ldots, \pi_c]^\top$.

An important issue in building a CoNN is that it is necessary to have the ground truth (true) concept labels for the images. In the absence of ground truth concept labels, [9] proposed to obtain semantic scene representation using pseudo-concepts. In this work, we propose to obtain pseudo-concepts labels for images using convolutional neural networks.

4   Pseudo-concept Labels from Convolutional Neural Network

A convolutional neural network (CNN) is a deep neural network comprising of multiple convolutional layers and a fully connected layer [12]. The convolutional layers comprise of filters those when are convolved with the images extract certain specific features. It is important to note that in a CNN, filters are learnt from data. In the lower layers, the filters correspond to the primitive features like edge, texture etc. It is observed that the filters in higher level convolutional layers do contain semantic features [10]. We propose to consider these semantic features. The response of a filter to an image is known as feature map. All the images in a dataset are presented to a trained CNN. Feature maps in a layer for an image are considered. Every feature map is sum pooled and the filters corresponding to top c responses among all the images are considered as pseudo-concepts. Any image for which response of a particular filter chosen as pseudo-concept is above a threshold, that image is labelled with that pseudo-concept. While choosing c pseudo-concepts, it is necessary also to ensure that a particular pseudo-concept does not appear in a very few images in the dataset. This is because, with only a few example images, it becomes difficult to build concept models. It is also necessary to ensure that a particular pseudo-concept does not appear in almost all the images because then discriminating a pseudo-concept becomes difficult. We make sure that a particular pseudo-concept to be present in at least 'u' and at most 'v' number of scene images while considering total 'c' number of concepts.

5   Experimental Studies

The effectiveness of the proposed approaches is studied using MIT-8-scene [3] and Vogel-Schiele [13] scene image datasets. The MIT-8-scene dataset comprises of 2688 scene images belonging to 8 semantic classes. Every image in MIT-8-scene dataset is of 256×256 pixels in size. The results presented for this dataset correspond to 5-fold evaluation. In every fold, 100 scene images per class are used for training and the rest are used for testing. The Vogel-Schiele dataset comprises of 700 images belonging to 6 natural scene categories. The results presented for this dataset correspond to stratified 5-fold evaluation. Every image in Vogel-Schiele dataset is either 720×480 or 480×720 pixels in size. In this work, we propose to represent every scene image using features derived from a deep convolution neural network (CNN). We propose to use AlexNet [12] trained using Places 205 dataset [14]. We refer to this CNN as Places205-AlexNet. Though every layer in a CNN corresponds to a scene representation, we propose to consider convolutional layer 4 (Conv-4) and pooling layer 5 (Pool-5) features. The number of features in Conv-4 and Pool-5 layers correspond to 64896 and 9216 respectively.

First we study the proposed approach for obtaining the pseudo-concepts using the Places205-AlexNet. In this work we consider the feature maps of Conv-4 or Pool-5 layers and sum pool every feature map. The feature maps whose responses are above a threshold are chosen as pseudo-concepts. The suitable value for the threshold need to be chosen empirically. In this work, we considered 1600 as a threshold value for the Conv-4 layer and 220 as a threshold value for the Pool-5 layer. The above thresholds were used for both MIT-8-Scene and Vogel-Schiele datasets. In addition to this the redundant pseudo-concepts and the pseudo-concepts that may cause bias on the semantic scene modelling are removed. For this we consider only those pseudo-concepts that are present in at least 40 scene images and those do not occur in more than 80 scene images. The total number of pseudo-concepts for each fold of the two datasets are given in Table 1.

Table 1. Number of pseudo-concepts in each fold corresponding to MIT-8-Scene and Vogel-Schiele datasets corresponding to Conv-4 and Pool-5 layers of Places205-AlexNet.

	Fold1	Fold2	Fold3	Fold4	Fold5
Conv-4 (MIT-8-scene)	91	92	89	94	94
Pool-5 (MIT-8-scene)	101	100	95	100	101
Conv-4 (Vogel-Schiele)	74	75	70	74	77
Pool-5 (Vogel-Schiele)	167	165	167	167	166

Next we study the proposed approach to obtain the SMN representation using concept neural network (CoNN). The number of neurons in the input layer of CoNN correspond to the number of features and the number of neurons in output layer correspond to the number of pseudo-concepts. The number of neurons in

Table 2. Comparison of classification accuracy (in %) of SVM-based classifiers on MIT-8-scene and Vogel-Schiele datasets using CoNN-based SMN representation. Here, linear kernel (LK), histogram intersection kernel (HIK) and χ^2 kernel (χ^2) are explored for building SVM-based classifiers.

Method to obtain SMN representation	LK	HIK	χ^2
CoNN using Conv-4 features (MIT-8-scene)	85.88	87.00	87.87
CoNN using Pool-5 features (MIT-8-scene)	91.25	91.17	**91.39**
CoNN using Conv-4 features (Vogel-Schiele)	85.88	87.00	87.87
CoNN using Pool-5 features (Vogel-Schiele)	91.25	91.17	**91.39**

Table 3. Comparison of classification accuracy (in %) of SVM-based classifier that uses the SMN representation proposed in this work and CNN-based classifier on MIT-8-scene (MIT) and Vogel-Schiele (VS) datasets.

Representation	Classifier	MIT	VS
Places205-AlexNet Pool-5	CNN	90.75	74.45
CoNN-based SMN	SVM-χ^2 kernel	**91.60**	**77.30**

the hidden layer is chosen empirically by varying it from 2 to 2048. The slope of sigmoidal activation function is also chosen empirically. The effectiveness of the proposed approach to obtain SMN representation is studied by using SVM-based scene classification that uses the SMN representation. Since the SMN representation is a non-negative vector (like histogram vector), we consider SVM-based classifier using histogram intersection (HI) kernel and χ^2 kernel apart from linear kernel (LK). We have used LIBSVM [15] tool to build the SVM-based classifiers. Table 2 gives the accuracy of SVM-based scene classifiers using the SMN representation obtained using the proposed method for MIT-8-scene and Vogel-Schiele datasets. It is seen from Table 2 that the χ^2 kernel based SVM on SMN representation obtained using the CoNN performs better than the SVM-based classifier using HIK and LK. It is also seen that the performance of scene classification for SMN representation obtained from Pool-5 features is better than that obtained using Conv-4 features. One possible reason for this may be the huge dimensionality of the Conv-4 features. Building a CoNN using Conv-4 features as input requires a lot of data due to the large number of parameters to be estimated. For the rest of the studies, we consider SMN representation obtained using the Pool-5 features as input to CoNN.

Next we compare the performance of an SVM-based classifier that uses SMN representation obtained using the proposed approach with that of a CNN-based classifier. For this, the fully connected layer of Places205-AlexNet adapted to the given dataset. The number of nodes in the hidden layers are empirically chosen after exploring various options. The performance of the CNN-based classifier is compared with that of the SVM-based classifier that uses SMN representation in Table 3. It is seen from Table 3 that the performance of SVM-based classifier that

Table 4. Comparison of scene classification accuracy (ca) (in %) using the SMN representation obtained using clustering based and CNN-based pseudo-concepts and set of local feature vectors representation of scene images for Vogel-Schiele and MIT-8-scene dataset.

Image representation		Classification models	MIT-8-scene	Vogel-Schiele
Set of HOG vectors		GMM	66.92	64.13
		CIGMMIMK-based SVM	79.86	71.33
		GMMSPMK-based SVM	81.84	71.65
		IFK-based SVM	81.28	72.34
Pool-5 feature of Alexnet-Places-205		CNN	90.75	74.45
Clustering based pseudo-concepts	SMN from GMM-based approach	χ^2-kernel SVM	79.43	68.23
	SMN from GMMSPMK-based SVM		81.45	71.21
CNN-based pseudo-concepts	SMN from CoNN		91.60	77.30

uses SMN representation is significantly better than the CNN-based classifier. To adapt a CNN to a given dataset needs to tune hidden layers in the fully connected layers where the number of neurons need to be chosen. The results in Table 3 show the effectiveness of using the SMN representation for scene classification.

In Table 4, we compare the performance of SVM-based scene classification using SMN representation obtained using proposed approach with that obtained using clustering based approach proposed in [9]. We also compare the performance of scene classification using SMN representation with that using the set of local feature vectors representation for images. Due to the limitation of space, the details of the scene classification using set of local feature vectors representation can not be presented here. The details can be seen in [9]. It is seen from Table 4 that the classification accuracy obtained for the SMN representation of scene images is better than that obtained for the set of local feature vectors representation of scene images. It is also seen that performance of CNN-based classifier is better than that of the SVM-based classifier that uses SMN representation obtained using the clustering based pseudo-concepts. This shows the effectiveness of CNN in tasks involving scene understanding such as scene classification.

6   Conclusion

An approach to obtain SMN representation of scene images using concept neural network (CoNN) is proposed in this paper. An SMN representation is a semantic representation that is useful in cognitive tasks such as scene classification. Building a CoNN requires ground truth concept labels. In the absence of ground truth concept labels, the paper proposed to build CoNN using pseudo-concepts. An approach to obtain pseudo-concepts using the feature maps of higher level layers of convolutional neural network is proposed in this paper. The effectiveness of the proposed approach to obtain SMN representation is studied by building SVM-based scene classifiers that use the SMN representation. The SMN representation obtained using the proposed method is found to be very effective. The CoNN is found to be better in learning the semantic contents of an image. However the training time of CoNN is an issue to be addressed. In the future the proposed approaches need to be validated using larger datasets such as MIT-67-Indoor dataset and Scene Understanding (SUN) dataset.

References

1. Ke, Y., Sukthankar, R.: PCA-SIFT: a more distinctive representation for local image descriptors. In: Proceedings of the 2004 IEEE Computer Society Conference on Computer Vision and Pattern Recognition, CVPR 2004, vol. 2, p. II. IEEE (2004)
2. Dalal, N., Triggs, B.: Histograms of oriented gradients for human detection. In: 2005 IEEE Computer Society Conference on Computer Vision and Pattern Recognition, CVPR 2005, vol. 1, pp. 886–893. IEEE (2005)
3. Oliva, A., Torralba, A.: Modeling the shape of the scene: a holistic representation of the spatial envelope. Int. J. Comput. Vis. **42**(3), 145–175 (2001)
4. Chatfield, K., Lempitsky, V.S., Vedaldi, A., Zisserman, A.: The devil is in the details: an evaluation of recent feature encoding methods. In: BMVC, vol. 2, p. 8 (2011)
5. Rasiwasia, N., Vasconcelos, N.: Holistic context models for visual recognition. IEEE Trans. Pattern Anal. Mach. Intell. **34**(5), 902–917 (2012)
6. Perina, A., Cristani, M., Murino, V.: Learning natural scene categories by selective multi-scale feature extraction. Image Vis. Comput. **28**(6), 927–939 (2010)
7. Rasiwasia, N., Moreno, P.J., Vasconcelos, N.: Bridging the gap: query by semantic example. IEEE Trans. Multimed. **9**(5), 923–938 (2007)
8. Thenkanidiyoor, V., Chandra Sekhar, C.: Dynamic kernels based approaches to analysis of varying length patterns in speech and image processing tasks. In: Pattern Recognition and Big Data, p. 407 (2016)
9. Gupta, S., Dileep, A.D., Thenkanidiyoor, V.: The semantic multinomial representation of images obtained using dynamic kernel based pseudo-concept SVMs. In: National Conference on Communication (2017)
10. Zeiler, M.D., Krishnan, D., Taylor, G.W., Fergus, R.: Deconvolutional networks. In: 2010 IEEE Conference on Computer Vision and Pattern Recognition (CVPR), pp. 2528–2535. IEEE (2010)
11. Vogel, J., Schiele, B.: Semantic modeling of natural scenes for content-based image retrieval. Int. J. Comput. Vis. **72**(2), 133–157 (2007)
12. Krizhevsky, A., Sutskever, I., Hinton, G.E.: ImageNet classification with deep convolutional neural networks. In: Advances in neural information processing systems, pp. 1097–1105 (2012)

13. Vogel, J., Schiele, B.: Natural scene retrieval based on a semantic modeling step. In: Enser, P., Kompatsiaris, Y., O'Connor, N.E., Smeaton, A.F., Smeulders, A.W.M. (eds.) CIVR 2004. LNCS, vol. 3115, pp. 207–215. Springer, Heidelberg (2004). https://doi.org/10.1007/978-3-540-27814-6_27

14. Zhou, B., Lapedriza, A., Xiao, J., Torralba, A., Oliva, A.: Learning deep features for scene recognition using places database. In: Advances in Neural Information Processing Systems, pp. 487–495 (2014)

15. Chang, C.-C., Lin, C.-J.: LIBSVM: a library for support vector machines. ACM Tras. Intell. Syst. Technol. **2**(3), 27 (2011)

Automatic Synthesis of Boolean Expression and Error Detection from Logic Circuit Sketches

Sahil Dhiman, Pushpinder Garg, Divya Sharma,
and Chiranjoy Chattopadhyay[✉]

Indian Institute of Technology Jodhpur, Jodhpur, Rajasthan, India
{dhiman.1,pushpinder.1,sharma.12,chiranjoy}@iitj.ac.in

Abstract. Automatic techniques to recognize and evaluate digital logic circuits are more efficient and require less human intervention, as compared to, traditional pen and paper methods. In this paper, we propose LEONARDO (Logic Expression fOrmatioN And eRror Detection frame-wOrk), a hierarchical approach to recognize boolean expression from hand drawn digital logic gate diagram. The key contributions in the proposed approach are: (i) a novel hierarchical framework to synthesize boolean expression from a hand drawn logic circuit diagram; and (ii) identification of anomalies in drawing. Extensive experimentation was performed through qualitative and quantitative analysis. Results were also compared with existing techniques proposed on the similar problem. Upon experimentation and analysis, our system proved to be more robust to user variability in design and yielded an accuracy of 95.2%, which is a 4% gain over others.

Keywords: Sketch processing · Symbol spotting
Graphics recognition · Curvature Scale Space · Logic circuit
Boolean expression

1 Introduction

Sketching components using pen and paper is an essential part of various fields in engineering study. Sketch is more intuitive, easy to convey and represent ideas as compared to other modalities. With the popularity of digital hand-held devices users are keen on using them as compared to pen and paper to exchange ideas. Sketch interfacing comes with its own challenges of noisy input data, variability in pen movements from user-to-user, maintaining generality while recognition and grouping strokes into meaningful symbols.

Graphics recognition using sketch as modality can find application in recognition of UML class diagrams [8], circuit analysis [2] as well as CAD drawings [3]. Research on sketch recognition started with development of gesture based systems [11] that used hand markings entered with stylus or mouse and represented them using a single stroke. Such, a constraint-based system generally deviates

© Springer Nature Singapore Pte Ltd. 2018
R. Rameshan et al. (Eds.): NCVPRIPG 2017, CCIS 841, pp. 410–423, 2018.
https://doi.org/10.1007/978-981-13-0020-2_36

the user from a natural drawing environment. A statistical approach to identify the most important distinguishing features of ink for dividing text and shapes was proposed in [10]. In [9], the authors present a sketch recognition framework for chemical structure drawings combining various visual features using a jointly trained CRF. The work closely related to our approach is [6], where the authors proposed a system for recognizing the gates in a scanned image. However, in [6] the input mode was image and not sketch. A machine learning approach to recognize components taking user feedback was proposed in [4]. The major limitation of this technique was the low symbol recognition rate, resulting from usage of standard learning approach to identify and recognize the gate symbols.

In this paper, we mainly focus on interpretation and evaluation of logic circuit sketches. We propose, LEONARDO (Logic Expression fOrmatioN And eRror Detection framewOrk), a holistic sketch recognition environment for digital logic gate diagrams. Users can sketch the diagrams on a tablet in the same fashion as they would on paper. LEONARDO interprets these strokes, localizes and recognizes various logic gates, identifies connecting wires and synthesizes a boolean expression representing the digital circuit. Such an automated recognition system can help users to visualise the behavior of their designs and can help in automatically generating the final boolean expression from their circuit diagram. In order to recognize the objects created from multiple strokes by their geometrical properties, we have created a framework of recognition in which strokes are pre-processed, localized, recognized, and then identified. Further, we group all the semantic information together to result into a complete logical expression deduced from the hand-drawn gate diagram. Another aspect of LEONARDO is detection of errors in the sketch. If the user has wrongly drawn the circuit, then LEONARDO is able to identify and report the error.

Our work makes three significant contributions over the previous approaches: (i) we use improved features for recognizing various components in a logic gate diagram, instead of, relying on machine learning based methods, which in the past have proved to be less efficient, (ii) we have adopted a hierarchical approach towards sketch based recognition in the logic diagram. The resultant output is in the form of a complete boolean expression obtained after the evaluation of the diagram keeping in mind all the gates and their respective connections, (iii) our improved features make the system more robust towards user variability while drawing, as well as, identifying erroneously drawn circuits.

The rest of the paper is organized in the following manner. A brief description of LEONARDO is presented in Sect. 2. In Sect. 3 we describe the details of all the intermediate stags of LEONARDO. Results of the experiments with the rationale behind them are presented in Sect. 4. The concluding remarks and future scope of work is given in Sect. 5.

2   Brief Description of the Work

Figure 1 depicts the overall framework of LEONARDO. It can be observed that there are three main building blocks in the framework, indicated by three different colored arrows. Given a hand drawn sketch from the user, there are two

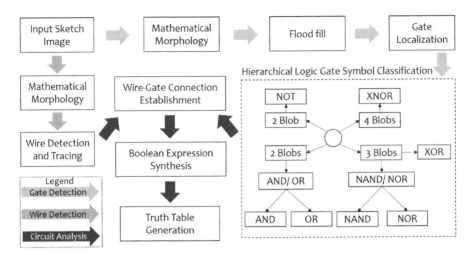

Fig. 1. A block diagram of LEONARDO's working principle. (Color figure online)

parallel operations, i.e. (i) gate recognition, (ii) wire detection and circuit analysis. We apply two different sets of mathematical morphology on the hand drawn sketches to isolate the pixels belonging to the gates and that to the wires. Once the potential locations of the logic gates are identified, we apply a set of rules (depending on the standardized structure of the logic gates) to split them into several components. We follow a hierarchical classification approach, where first connected component and blob analysis is performed on the candidate blobs for a coarse level of classification. Not only the blob structure but also the order of the blob position is also important property, which is taken into consideration by LEONARDO. For finer classification we adopt the Curvature Scale Space (CSS) feature. After the gates are recognized and connecting wires are identified, we synthesize the expression. To do so we perform a raster scan of the input sketch and detect the input, intermediate, and output connections. All the input wires and the output wires are given a unique identifier, which helps us to synthesize the correct expression for the hand drawn circuit.

2.1   Assumptions

To make the problem tractable, we make the following assumptions:

1. All the inputs are hand drawn and not scanned. Volunteers were asked to draw the circuit on a digital interface, from which the coordinates of the circuits were captured. Thus the noises that may get introduced due to scanning are not applicable in this work.
2. LEONARDO operates offline, i.e. we are not considering the time information and only capturing the visual information.
3. There is a single valid output of the circuit, i.e. not taking into consideration circuits with multiple outputs.

4. All the diagrams are to be parsed from left to right, i.e. the inputs are the left most components, where as the output is the right most component in the circuit.
5. There is no interconnected crossing wires.

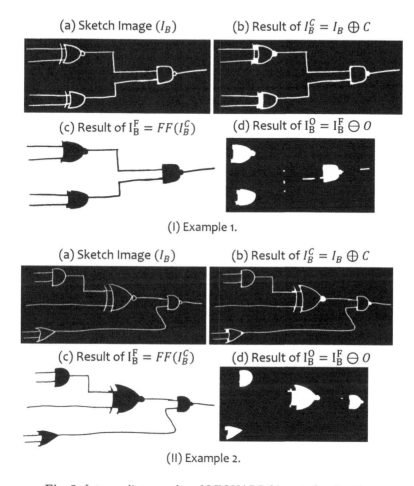

(a) Sketch Image (I_B)   (b) Result of $I_B^C = I_B \oplus C$

(c) Result of $I_B^F = FF(I_B^C)$ (d) Result of $I_B^O = I_B^F \ominus 0$

(I) Example 1.

(a) Sketch Image (I_B)   (b) Result of $I_B^C = I_B \oplus C$

(c) Result of $I_B^F = FF(I_B^C)$ (d) Result of $I_B^O = I_B^F \ominus 0$

(II) Example 2.

Fig. 2. Intermediate results of LEONARDO's gate localization.

3 Detailed Description of Intermediate Processing

In this section we give details of all the intermediate stages of processing involved in LEONARDO to correctly synthesize Boolean expression from sketches.

3.1 Gate Localization

Given a sketch of the digital logic circuit the first step is to localize "where are the logic gates?". To answer this question we propose a two step process. At first,

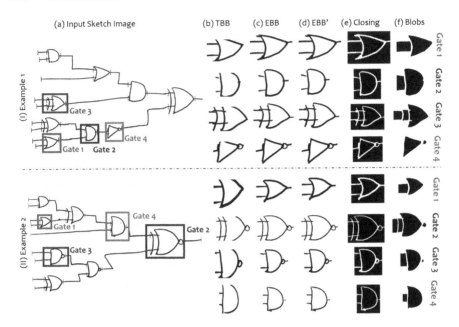

Fig. 3. Intermediate results of component extraction from blobs for logic gate recognition.

we binarize the gray level image (I_G) and invert it (I_B). We apply morphological closing operation on I_B, as $I_B^C = I_B \bullet C$. Here $\bullet$ is the closing operator and C is a square structuring element of dimension 10×10. The rationale behind closing is to close the small gaps in the drawing which may have creeped in to the image due to (i) fault in the drawing, (ii) the digitization process. After this we apply flood fill algorithm on the resultant image to identify the blobs. Inverting the flood filled image ends up with only the blobs having the potential gate regions. Figure 2 depicts stages of proposed gate localization technique for a particular circuit.

3.2 Gate Recognition

After blob localization in the given input sketch image, the next task is to recognize the gates. From the set of blobs obtained from I_B^O, there are two sets of blobs, gates and non-gates, respectively. We first use morphological operations to remove the insignificant blobs. From the resultant blobs we calculate the tight bounding box (TBB) around each of them. We also calculate an extended bounded box (EBB) by taking extra 10 pixels in every direction of the TBB and save the result for every blob. We apply flood-fill algorithm with EBB, and invert the same. As a result, for every gate we obtain a set of disjoint components. The intermediate results of extracting component blobs from two different logic circuit sketch are shown in Fig. 3. It can be observed that for the cases LEONARDO is successfully able to do the localization.

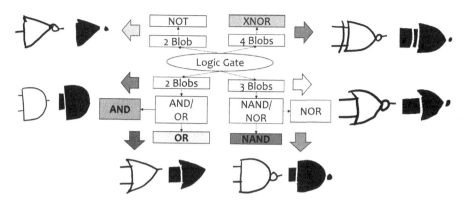

Fig. 4. Illustration of the hierarchical approach to classify blobs as logic gates.

Once the blobs, with EBB are extracted, we recognize the gates based upon that. We apply case based rule (hierarchical approach) for various gates. Figure 4 shows an illustration of how LEONARDO is able to differentiate between various logic gates. For a valid gate symbol the number of blobs present within an EBB is 2, 3 or 4. We also calculate the order of the blobs, from left to right. For each detected blob, we detect the size of the blob and there order in the horizontal direction. If the number of blobs within an EBB is 2 and the first blob is greater than the second, then that gate is recognized as NOT gate. Another, easy case is that of the XNOR gate. In this case the number of blobs are 4. The order of the blobs also helped in identifying XOR gate. Now, if we closely observe the other gates the basic building blocks (schematically) are that of the AND or OR gate. The largest size blob is the one that we need to check for. From the given set of blobs within an EBB, we detect the largest blob, and detect whether it resembles the shape of an AND or OR gate.

For matching, we adopt the idea of Curvature Scale Space (CSS) [1]. We define a canonical shape (Cn) for AND and OR gate referred from the text books. From the largest blob we first detect the edge, and then define the edge point coordinates as the shape of the gate. We calculate the CSS features from the curvature (θ) of the candidate blobs (Ca), i.e. the user-drawn blobs as well as the canonical blobs using:

$$\theta(u,\sigma) = \frac{X'(u,\sigma)Y''(u,\sigma) - X''(u,\sigma)Y'(u,\sigma)}{(X'(u,\sigma)^2 + Y'(u,\sigma)^2)^{3/2}} \tag{1}$$

Where, X and Y result from the convolution of the components of parameterized vector equation (parameter y) of the curve extracted from the contours of the blobs, with a Gaussian kernel of width σ. X', Y' are the 1st order derivatives, whereas X'' and Y'' are the 2nd order-derivatives of these convolved components. Thus, we obtain a feature for the curve for both the candidate and the canonical blobs. Maxima points are detected from the CSS contours as features. During matching, CSS features are extracted from the candidate shape, and matched

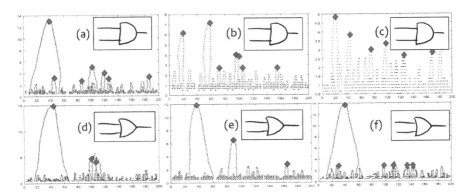

Fig. 5. CSS Feature of AND and OR gates. Inset: the hand drawn gate image. The star marks denote the CSS peaks.

with the canonical CSS features of both AND and OR gate and matching distance D is calculated for both the gates. Finally, the minimum distance (d) between the candidate and the canonical blobs is found using:

$$d = argmin_i(D(Cn_i, Ca)), \forall i \in (AND, OR) \qquad (2)$$

The candidate shape is categorized on the basis of its proximity, using distance d to canonical AND or OR gate. Figure 5 demonstrates the CSS features. Then, if there are 3 blobs within a EBB, it will be either AND or OR gate, where as for 4 blobs it will be NAND or NOR, based upon the results of CSS matching.

3.3   Path Tracing

Path tracing is critical in establishing the connection between a pair of gates, as well as for expression synthesis. We begin by subtracting the localized gate pixels from I_G, to obtain image I_W having only the wires. We then apply Canny edge detector on I_W and obtain a list of contours $W_1, W_2, \ldots, W_n$, where n is no of wires (path). The jth wire $W_j = p_1, \ldots, p_m$ is a set of points where each $p_k = <x, y>$ is a tuple. Next we sort the p_k's according to x coordinates to detect the input (p_I) and output (p_O) ends of W_j, respectively. Figure 6 depicts the start ("red" dots) and end ("green" dots) points of various path detected on three different circuit sketches.

After that we construct two data structures to store the gate and wire information to be used in expression evaluation. For a given logic gate $\mathscr{G}$, various fields of the gate data structure are: (i) The dimension of gate (x and y coordinate of the top left corner of bounding box, height, width), (ii) type, which denotes whether the gate is AND/OR/NOT/NAND/NOR/XOR/XNOR, (iii) IW, which is a set of input wires connected to $\mathscr{G}$, and (iv) IE, i.e. input expressions. IW is calculated by the intersection of p_O with EBB of $\mathscr{G}$. On

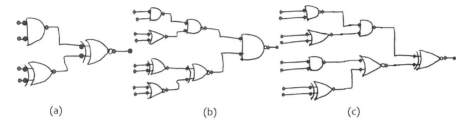

(a)   (b)   (c)

Fig. 6. Example of start and end point of a wire (path) detected from three different circuit sketches. (Color figure online)

the other hand, IE is implemented as a singular linked list of strings defined as $IE = \{string, *IE\}$, where $*$ denotes a pointer of type IE. In IE, number of nodes are equal to the number of input wires connected to it and there is a one to one correspondence between the 'string' field of a node and expression corresponding to one input wire. Similarly, for a given wire $\mathcal{W}$, various fields of the wire data structure are: (i) line id, obtained by sorting the p_I's along x and y direction, (ii) p_I, (iii) p_O, (iv) LG, i.e. gate attached to the left most end of $\mathcal{W}$ and (v) RG, i.e. gate attached to its right most end, and (iv) $\mathbb{E}$, to store the expression associated to $\mathcal{W}$. The fields LG or RG is set to -1 if there is no gate attached to left or right side of $\mathcal{W}$, i.e. for the input and output. Expression synthesis using these data structures is discussed next.

3.4 Expression Evaluation

All the wires with no left gate id are the input lines, and assigned with values $A, B, \ldots$, from top to bottom, in their respective expression fields. For all other wires, the expression field is assigned to an empty string. Algorithm 1 lists out the steps we proposed to synthesize the expression.

In line 2, the gate attached to the left side of the wire is identified. Line 4 indicates that we have reached the input line of a leftmost gate. If not then, all the input wires attached to $\mathcal{W}$ is stored in a set $\mathcal{I}$, which is a set of input wires attached to the gate $\mathcal{G}$. Now, for all the input wires, see whether it is processed already or not (line 9). If not then, recursively call the expression synthesis function for that wire, and store the synthesized expression in a singular linked list (line 11). After processing all the wires connected to gate $\mathcal{G}$, which is in turn connected to $\mathcal{W}$, next we synthesize the expression for $\mathcal{W}$. To do that, we traverse the list IE, and combine the expressions of the individual wires with the gate type (lines 14 to 25). The final expression is returned to the calling function. For any wire, if line 4 yields false then, the algorithm reaches a gate which is connected to the input line, and hence the expression for that path will be the input itself.

Figure 7 illustrates the expression synthesis process for one example sketch. For the logic sketch in Fig. 7(a) the recursive call of the proposed function is shown in Fig. 7(b). Here the called function is at the side pointed by the

Algorithm 1. Boolean expression synthesis algorithm

1: **function** SynExp($\mathcal{W}$)
2:     $\mathcal{G} \leftarrow \mathcal{W}.LG$ ▷ LG = Gate attached to the left of $\mathcal{W}$
3:
4:     **if** $\mathcal{G} \neq \phi$ **then**
5:         $\mathcal{I} \leftarrow \mathcal{G}.IW$ ▷ IW=Input Wires attached to gId
6:
7:         **for all** $I \in \mathcal{I}$ **do**
8:
9:             **if** I.visited $= 0$ **then**
10:                tempExp $=$ SynExpr(I);
11:                $\mathcal{G}$.IE.append(tempExp)   ▷ IE is a linked list
12:            **end if**
13:         **end for**
14:         $\mathcal{N} = \mathcal{G}$.IE.head   ▷ Head node of $\mathcal{G}$.IE
15:
16:         **while** $\mathcal{N} \neq \phi$ **do**
17:
18:             **if** $\mathcal{N} == \mathcal{G}$.IE.head **then**
19:                $\mathcal{W}.\mathbb{E} = \mathcal{N}$.value
20:
21:             **else**
22:                $\mathcal{W}.\mathbb{E} = \mathcal{W}.\mathbb{E} + \mathcal{G}$.type $+ \mathcal{N}$.val
23:             **end if**
24:             node $\leftarrow$ node.next   ▷ Next expression in $\mathcal{G}$.IE
25:         **end while**
26:     **end if**
27:     **return** $\mathcal{W}.\mathbb{E}$ ▷ Return the expression
28: **end function**

arrow head. The function call is initiated by calling SYNEXP() with w_0 as a parameter. The algorithm proceeds with calling all the wires and finally yields the expression $((A + B)) \oplus D$.

4   Experimental Study

There is a dearth of publicly available datasets for sketch based recognition of circuits. Dataset such as [7] is for natural objects and not suitable for document images. Hence, we have performed our experiments by asking volunteers to draw the circuit on a digital platform. To capture the drawing we have used Wacom Tablet, with a resolution of 1920×1080 pixels. Since we are working in the off-line mode, we stored the hand drawn circuit as an image and used the same for experimentation. All the images were saved in a gray scale format. Details of the results are discussed below.

4.1   Qualitative Results

Figure 8 depicts LEONARDO's performance on detecting logic gates, connecting wires, and expression synthesis on sixteen different sketches. The corresponding expressions synthesized by LEONARDO for a sketch is given as image captions. Each gate is highlighted by a colored bounding box based on what type of gate it is. The erroneously labeled gates are highlighted by thick 'red' bounding boxes. First four rows of Fig. 8(a)–(j), depicts LEONARDO's performance of circuit sketches where the circuits are not slanted. They also depict LEONARDO's robustness to other transformations.

Expression Synthesis from Correct Sketches. Figure 8(d), (e) shows that LEONARDO is invariant to the scale (size) of the logic gates. The XOR and the NAND gate in these two circuits, respectively are drawn larger as compared to others. LEONARDO could still identify them correctly. The area ratio feature is helping LEONARDO to achieve this scale invariance property. In Fig. 8(i), (j) it can be observed that even when the connections drawn are not straight, LEONARDO is able to trace the wires properly and capable to yield the correct expression. Figure 8(k)–(m) depicts a challenging situation of sketches drawn at a particular orientation. It is quite natural for human being to draw like that. Our proposed logic gate detection and wire tracing algorithm is able to correctly synthesize the correct expression in such scenarios. Once the logic gates are correctly localized in a rotated circuit the feature extraction technique further helps in performance. Usage of CSS features while recognition of the gates aids LEONARDO to capture rotation invariance. Figure 8(d) shows a sketch with many logic gates and complex connections successfully detected.

Identifying Errors in Circuit Sketch. LEONARDO detects errors in the circuit drawing. Error is defined in two ways, which are: (i) erroneously drawn logic gates, and (ii) dangling wires. We say a gate being drawn as erroneous one if (i) the shape is not properly drawn, (ii) number of input/output is not according to the classical definition of that gate. Figure 8(n) depicts various error cases such as: (i) invalid gate symbol, (ii) NOT gate with two inputs, (iii) gates are not drawn as a closed figure, and (iv) an OR gate with two outputs. In Fig. 8(o), there are two invalid gate symbols in a given circuit, and LEONARDO successfully detects them and reports.

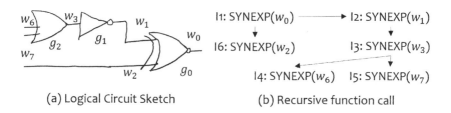

(a) Logical Circuit Sketch   (b) Recursive function call

Fig. 7. Illustration of the expression synthesis algorithm.

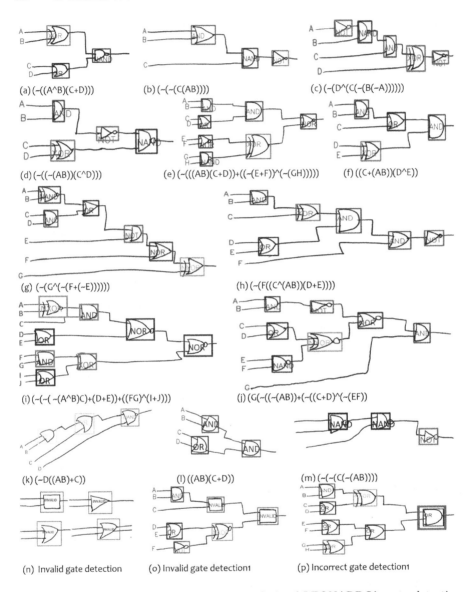

Fig. 8. Qualitative results and robustness analysis of LEONARDO's gate detection and expression synthesis on different examples. (Color figure online)

Failure Cases. LEONARDO fails to detect the correct type of gate in a few cases. Figure 8 depicts three such scenarios. For example, in Fig. 8(g), an XOR gate is labelled as XNOR gate. It can be observed that in Fig. 8(h), an OR gate is labelled as AND gate. In the last sub-figure, i.e. Fig. 8(p), there are two erroneous detection in one sketch. In that figure, XOR is labelled as XNOR and AND is labelled as OR. Possible reason could be that during morphological operation some of the blobs are merged due to crossover of lines during sketch. As a result the synthesized expression is also not correct.

4.2 Quantitative Results

Figure 9 quantifies LEONARDO's performance. There are two parts of the analysis, gate level and circuit level. The difference between these two analysis is that in the former we wanted to measure how LEONARDO performs when the gates are presented to it in isolation, i.e. not part of a circuit. The circuit level analysis captures LEONARDO's performance when an entire circuit is taken for analysis. Figure 9(a) depicts LEONARDO's performance while detecting individual gates. In this experiment, a volunteer is asked to draw a gate, and LEONARDO recognizes it in isolation. We have tested LEONARDO's performance on 100 samples/gate. It can be observed that the highest level of accuracy is obtained for the XNOR gate (99%), while the lowest accuracy is obtained for the OR gate (76%). In the next level of analysis, we measured LEONARDO's performance of gate recognition in a circuit. We captured 100 different sketches from a pool of 10 volunteers for this experiment.

Table 1 depicts LEONARDO's performance, i.e. accuracy of logic gate detection at circuit level. In the table the second and the third column denotes the number of samples correctly recognized by LEONARDO, and the total number of times a given symbol appears in the circuit sketches. This includes all the sketch samples taken for the experiments The right-most column denotes the % accuracy of different gates in circuit level analysis. It can be observed that apart from NOT gate, which is the easiest symbol to recognize, LEONARDO's performance for other gates is also very good in terms of percentage accuracy.

4.3 Comparison with Existing Techniques

We have also compared LEONARDO's performance with other existing techniques in the literature. We have compared with the technique proposed in [4,5]. Rationale behind choosing these two for comparison is that both the techniques used sketch as a modality for input. We have not compared with the technique

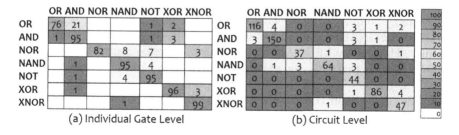

Fig. 9. Quantitative analysis of LEONARDO's performance.

Table 1. Percentage accuracy in circuit level recognition

Gate	No. of correct detection	No. of samples present	Accuracy
AND	116	126	92%
OR	150	157	95.50%
NOR	37	39	94.87%
NAND	64	71	90.14%
NOT	44	44	100%
XOR	86	91	94.5%
XNOR	47	48	97.91%

proposed in [6] as the modality is not sketch, but scanned images. Sketch based system has its own specific challenges, and hence it will be unfair to compare with a method proposed for different modality. Table 2 shows the result of comparison with the above mentioned two techniques. LEONARDO achieves an over all accuracy of 95.2%, as compared to 91.0% by, and 89% by for the input sketches, proving LEONARDO's superiority.

Table 2. Comparison of performance in terms of percentage accuracy between LEONARDO and others.

Technique	Accuracy
Cheng et al. [5]	89%
Alvarado et al. [4]	91%
LEONARDO	95.2%

5 Conclusion

LEONARDO accurately locates and recognizes the logic gates, and wires from the input sketch. After successful localization and recognition, LEONARDO synthesizes resulting expression, and the truth table as output. It can successfully handle complex circuits with any number of gates, having scale, layout variation. LEONARDO is also capable of handling circuits drawn in a slanted manner. That makes LEONARDO invariant to rotation also. The drawback of LEONARDO is that it is not able to handle circuit with interconnected crossing wires. The simplicity of the symbol detection algorithm makes LEONARDO time efficient, without compromising the accuracy. In the future, we would further explore and extend LEONARDO to handle more complex scenarios and real-time recognition.

References

1. Abbasi, S., Mokhtarian, F., Kittler, J.: Curvature scale space image in shape similarity retrieval. MS **7**(6), 467–476 (1999)
2. Alvarado, C., Davis, R.: SketchREAD: a multi-domain sketch recognition engine. In: UIST (2004)
3. Alvarado, C., Davis, R.: Resolving ambiguities to create a natural computer-based sketching environment. In: ACM SIGGRAPH 2006 Courses, p. 24. ACM (2006)
4. Alvarado, C., Kearney, A., Keizur, A., Loncaric, C., Parker, M., Peck, J., Sobel, K., Tay, F.: LogiSketch: a free-sketch digital circuit design and simulation SystemLogiSketch. In: Hammond, T., Valentine, S., Adler, A., Payton, M. (eds.) The Impact of Pen and Touch Technology on Education. HIS, pp. 83–90. Springer, Cham (2015). https://doi.org/10.1007/978-3-319-15594-4_8
5. Cheng, T., Khan, J., Liu, H., Yun, D.Y.Y.: A symbol recognition system. In: DAR, pp. 918–921 (1993)
6. Datta, R., Mandal, P.D.S., Chanda, B.: Detection and identification of logic gates from document images using mathematical morphology. In: NCVPRIPG (2015)
7. Eitz, M., Hays, J., Alexa, M.: How do humans sketch objects? ACM Trans. Graph. (Proc. SIGGRAPH) **31**(4), 44:1–44:10 (2012). (Proc. SIGGRAPH)
8. Hammond, T., Davis, R.: Tahuti: a geometrical sketch recognition system for UML class diagrams. In: ACM SIGGRAPH 2006 Courses, p. 25. ACM (2006)
9. Ouyang, T.Y., Davis, R.: ChemInk: a natural real-time recognition system for chemical drawings. In: IUIT, pp. 267–276. ACM (2011)
10. Patel, R., Plimmer, B., Grundy, J., Ihaka, R.: Ink features for diagram recognition. In: SBIM (2007)
11. Rubine, D.: Specifying gestures by example. SIGGRAPH Comput. Graph. **25**(4), 329–337 (1991)

Comparison of Edge Detection Algorithms in the Framework of Despeckling Carotid Ultrasound Images Based on Bayesian Estimation Approach

Y. Nagaraj$^{(\boxtimes)}$ and A. V. Narasimhadhan

National Institute of Technology Karnataka, Surathkal, India
nagraj.p.y@gmail.com

Abstract. Common carotid artery (CCA) ultrasound with estimation of Intima Media Thickness (IMT) is the safe and non-invasive technique for predicting the cardiovascular risks. The precise quantification of IMT is useful for evaluating the risk of cardiovascular disease. The presence of speckle noise in carotid ultrasound image reduces the quality of the image and automatic human interpretation. Carotid ultrasound images have multiplicative speckle noise and it is difficult remove compared to the additive noises. The speckle removal filters have a greater restriction in edges and characteristics preservation. In this paper, we propose an extension of our earlier work with a fully automated Region of Interest (ROI) extraction and speckle denoising using optimized bayesian least square estimation (BLSE) approach followed by edge detection. The objective of the paper is to reduce the speckle noise in the extracted ROI of carotid ultrasound images using state-of-art denoising techniques and then followed by edge detection techniques and compared them with the edges extracted by these edge operators of ground truth image. The proposed algorithm experiments with 50 B-mode carotid ultrasound images. Experimental analysis shows that proposed method achieves better results as compared to other edge detection methods in terms of structural similarity Index Map (SSIM), correlation of coefficient (CoC), peak signal to noise ratio (PSNR) and mean square error (MSE) measures. Based on results, proposed work more effective in terms of visual inspection and detail preservation in carotid ultrasound images.

Keywords: Common carotid artery · Intima media thickness
BLSE filter · Total Variation-L_1 norm · Edge detection

1 Introduction

In a recent survey of world health organization (WHO), it is found that 30% of the global death is due to cardiovascular diseases [1]. The main reason for having cardiovascular disease is atherosclerosis [2], which is the accumulation of plaque build-up on the arterial wall. The measurement of IMT in common

R. Rameshan et al. (Eds.): NCVPRIPG 2017, CCIS 841, pp. 424–435, 2018.
https://doi.org/10.1007/978-981-13-0020-2_37

carotid artery is the primary step for prediction of cardiovascular disease [3]. The IMT of the extracranial carotid arteries is a significant index of the presence of atherosclerosis [4]. Precise quantification of the IMT is useful for assessing the risk of stroke or its progress [5]. To accomplish the best possible diagnosis, the carotid ultrasound images required to be free of noise and artifacts. The measurement of IMT in the carotid wall is complex because of speckle noise in the carotid ultrasound images and leads to the reduction of contrast and resolution of the image [6]. To address this problem, several enhancement and speckle denoising methods have been proposed in carotid ultrasound images. Hassan and Akamatsu [7] used a sigmoid function in spatial domain for the process of image contrast enhancement. Zuo et al. [8] introduced a spatially weighted histogram equalization for enhancement of contrast in image. Coupe et al. [9] proposed an OBNLM denoising filter which is an adaptation of non-local mean filter and amount of image smoothing is determined directly by noise variance. Pandit et al. [10] uses Lee filter, which performs smoothing in lower variance regions and for higher variance region smoothing will not be performed. Li and Zhang [11] proposed SRAD filter to utilize the instantaneous coefficient of variation, which is the function of Laplacian operators and local gradient magnitude. In carotid ultrasound images edge detection is significant for identification of IMT in CCA [12]. The noise and edges contain high frequency component in an image so detection of the edge is very difficult in noisy images. The noisy images use operators in larger in scope to average enough data to localize noisy pixels. Generally, the edge is detected using algorithms such as Canny, Sobel, Prewitt, Robert and LoG operators [13]. Canny operator [14] smooths the data by means of Gaussian convolution and then performs the edge detection operation. Sobel operator [15] uses 2 Dimensional spatial gradient and high frequency regions are emphasized which are actually edges. Prewitt operator [16] is a desirable approach for estimating the magnitude and orientation of an edge in an image. Robert operator [17] performs the simple calculation of spatial gradients and used for grayscale images where input and output are grayscale values. LoG operator [18] used for an image to highlight the regions of abrupt change in the intensity value. The objective of the paper is to compare different edge detection techniques with different denoising filter in carotid ultrasound images for optimal reduction of speckle noise and detail preservation of edges. In the proposed algorithm framework presents speckle reduction using BLSE method based on conditional posterior distribution and canny operators are used to preserving the edges in carotid ultrasound images. The paper is structured as follows: Sect. 2 describes the proposed methodology. Section 3 shows comprehensive results of the proposed method. Section 4 presents the experimental analysis and followed by conclusion in Sect. 5.

2   Proposed Method

2.1   Ultrasound Image Data Acquisition

We have used two different datasets, dataset 1 and dataset 2. The dataset 1 consists 25 images collected from Cyprus Institute of Neurology of Nicosia [19,20].

The dataset 2 also consist of 25 images collected from the Father Muller medical hospital, Mangalore, India. Total 50 B-mode longitudinal images are used for performance evaluation of the proposed and existing methods. The textual marks are removed in order to facilitate the smooth processing, the original ultrasound images were automatically cropped into a size of 395×295 pixels.

2.2 Automatic ROI Extraction

Image pre-processing is one of the primary steps, which is highly required to ensure the high accuracy of the subsequent phase. In ultrasound images, because of speckle noise, the image resolution and contrast get reduced. The resolution of the carotid ultrasound image is enhanced by Total Variation L^1 (TV-L^1) norm [21] based on histogram equalization technique. The enhanced image is converted to binary form using Otsu thresholding technique [22]. Using morphological functions, area opening followed by dilation is applied to fill gaps and holes in the plaque contour and also cleans the edges. Here dilation is used because of the area opening, there was a possibility of breakage in the plaque contour. To overcome this problem, we used dilation with a structuring element of disk size 2 to seal the plaque contour. Canny edge detection is applied to extract the fine edges from resulted image. The Canny operator gives an accurate representation of the true edges of the artery while helping to eliminate the creation of false lines in the image. As ROI contains long thin lines, it is extracted automatically based on its longest length. Finally, the far wall cropped with the help of the longest line to find out the LI and MA boundaries [23]. The Fig. 1 depicts each step of automatic ROI extraction of the carotid ultrasound image.

2.3 Despeckling Filtering Using BLSE

The presence of speckle noise in carotid ultrasound images adversely effect the individual interpretation and diagnosis. Speckle noise is multiplicative noise present in carotid ultrasound images and reduces the ability of manual observer. The multiplicative speckle noise is expressed as [24]:

$$m(n) = g(n) * k(n) \tag{1}$$

where $m(n)$ represents measured data corresponding to the noiseless data $g(n)$ and speckle noise $k(n)$ of unknown distribution at location n respectively. Here n indicates the spatial locations that belong to the 2 Dimensional space of real numbers $n \in R^2$. To reduce the speckle noise in the ultrasound image we used the optimized BLSE filter for estimation of noiseless data in logarithmic component [25]. The logarithmic component affected due to the speckle noise such way that local mean tend to the local variance. As a result the speckle noise in the carotid ultrasound image turns in to Gaussian noise. Therefore, the measured data projected to the logarithmic component such way that distribution of noise becomes very close to the Gaussian. The expanded logarithmic component from the measures data is expressed as (from Eq. (1)):

$$m_L(n) = g_L(n) + k_L(n) \tag{2}$$

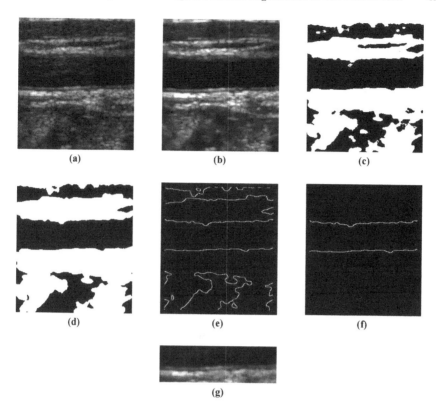

Fig. 1. (a) Original carotid longitudinal. (b) Enhancement using Total Variation L^1 (TV-L^1) norm. (c) Conversion of the binary image with automatic thresholding procedure. (d) Morphological operation on the binary image. (e) Canny edge detection. (f) Extraction of the near and far wall. (g) Automatic ROI extraction.

In the logarithmic component, the BLSE of $g_L(n)$ can be defined by the expression:

$$\widehat{g}_L(n) = \int p(g_L(n)|m_L(n))g_L(n)dg_L(n) \tag{3}$$

The Eq. (3) represents the optimized BLSE of the noiseless data $g_L(n)$ based on the measured data $m_L(n)$. The distributed probability of noiseless data $g_L(n)$ based on the measured data $m_L(n)$ is non linear and complicated due to the posterior distribution $p(g_L(n)|m_L(n))$ so $\widehat{g}_L(n)$ using Eq. (3) is difficult to solve. To overcome this problem we proposed to use posterior conditional approach to estimate $p(g_L(n)|m_L(n))$. The posterior distribution $p(g_L(n)|m_L(n))$ is calculated based on weighted histogram approach and it is described as [25]:

$$\widehat{p}(g_L(n)|m_L(n)) = \frac{\sum_{m=z} w(n'|n)\delta(g_L - m_L(s'_m))}{N} \tag{4}$$

where $\delta(.)$ represents the delta function and normalized factor N is defined as $\sum_{g_L} \widehat{p}(g_L(n)|m_L(n)) = 1$. Then, $g(n)$ can be calculated projecting back to Bayesian estimate $g_L(n)$ from the logarithmic component using $\widehat{g}(n) = exp(\widehat{g}_L(n))$. The BLSE denoising filter is implemented after the ROI is extracted. Finally, several edge detection operators are applied to the despeckled ROI and compared them with the other denoising filters.

3   Results

In this section, the experimental results obtained from the several edge detection techniques and compared them with existing denoising filters. The denoising techniques and edge detection algorithms are implemented in the MATLAB 2015a and tested on a 3 GHz machine of 2 GB RAM with Intel Core i7 processor. The mathematical expressions of performance metrics [18] are tabulated in Table 1. The performance of the proposed method is evaluated by addition of speckle noise with variance of 0.1 to the carotid ultrasound images. Denoising filters are applied to reduce the speckle noise in the image and improve the edge information. The purpose of edge detection is to retain the structural properties for further image processing. Figures 2 and 3 depict the carotid ultrasound images of Dataset 1 and Dataset 2, on which edges are detected by different edge detection techniques such as canny, sobel, prewitt, robert, LoG and compared them with the existing denoising methods such as SRAD, OBNLM, LEE filters by addition of speckle noise with variance of 0.1. From the Figs. 2 and

3 it is observed that Sobel, Prewitt, Robert operators are sensitivity to noise in detection of edges and their orientations. Canny and LoG operator preserve more edges compared to the other edge detection methods but we can notice that LoG operator have some discontinuity in the edges. Hence, LoG operator reduces the accuracy in finding out the orientation of the edges as compared to the canny operator. The structural similarity index (SSIM) is used to measure the similarity of the edges between denoised image and original image as shown in Figs. 4 and 5. From the visual inspection, the BLSE filter with canny edge detection in SSIM carotid images shows the difference between edges of ground truth image and denoised image is less as compared to the other denoising techniques. Therefore, canny edge detection is superior in terms of detail preservation in structural similarity images compared to the other edge detection techniques. From the

Table 1. The performance metrics for edge detection.

Performance metrics	Mathematical representation
Peak signal noise ratio	$PSNR = 10log_{10}(\frac{255}{\sqrt{MSE}})$
Mean square error	$MSE = \frac{1}{RC}\sum_{x=1}^{R}\sum_{y=1}^{C}(V_{x,y} - V'_{x,y})^2$
Coefficient of correlation	$CoC = \frac{\sum_{x=1}^{R}\sum_{y=1}^{C}(V'_{x,y} - \overline{V}'_{x,y})(V_{x,y} - \overline{V}_{x,y})}{\sum_{x=1}^{R}\sum_{y=1}^{C}(V'_{x,y} - \overline{V}'_{x,y})^2 \sum_{x=1}^{R}\sum_{y=1}^{C}(V_{x,y} - \overline{V}_{x,y})^2}$
Structural similarity	$SSIM(V,V') = \frac{(2\mu V \mu'_V + k_1)(2\sigma_{VV'} + k_2)}{(\mu_V^2 + \mu_{V'}^2, k_1)(\sigma_V^2 + \sigma_{V'}^2, k_2)}$

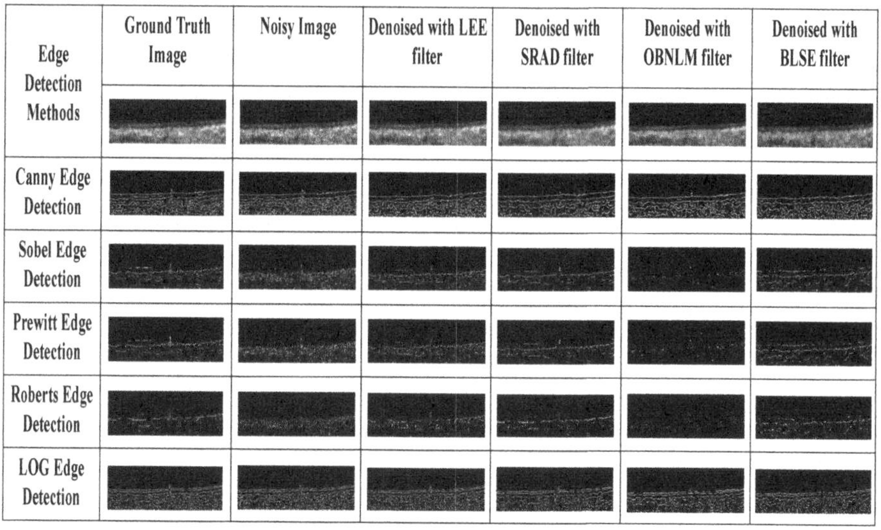

Edge Detection Methods	Ground Truth Image	Noisy Image	Denoised with LEE filter	Denoised with SRAD filter	Denoised with OBNLM filter	Denoised with BLSE filter
Canny Edge Detection						
Sobel Edge Detection						
Prewitt Edge Detection						
Roberts Edge Detection						
LOG Edge Detection						

Fig. 2. Edge detection techniques for carotid ultrasound images of Dataset 1 with noise variance of 0.1.

Edge Detection Methods	Ground Truth Image	Noisy Image	Denoised with LEE filter	Denoised with SRAD filter	Denoised with OBNLM filter	Denoised with BLSE filter
Canny Edge Detection						
Sobel Edge Detection						
Prewitt Edge Detection						
Roberts Edge Detection						
LOG Edge Detection						

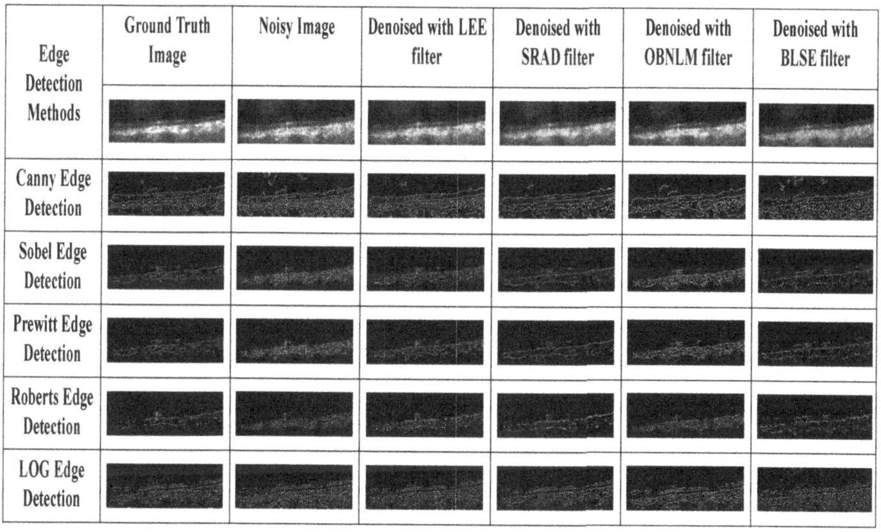

Fig. 3. Edge detection techniques for carotid ultrasound images of Dataset 2 with noise variance of 0.1.

qualitative analysis, the proposed work demonstrate a better edge preserving behaviour with the help of BLSE filter and also achieves better results in terms of the best visual inspection. Further, the various performance metrics such as PSNR, CoC, SSIM and MSE are evaluated for each denoising filter and from

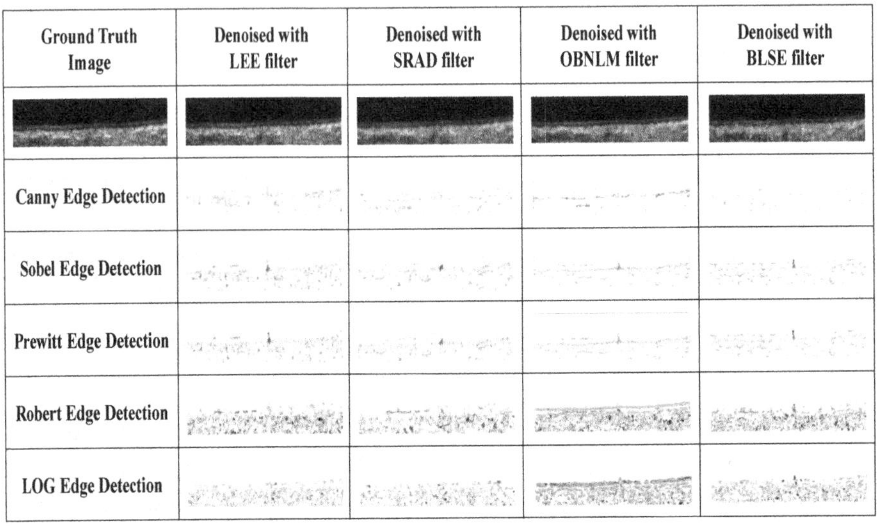

Ground Truth Image	Denoised with LEE filter	Denoised with SRAD filter	Denoised with OBNLM filter	Denoised with BLSE filter
Canny Edge Detection				
Sobel Edge Detection				
Prewitt Edge Detection				
Robert Edge Detection				
LOG Edge Detection				

Fig. 4. Structural similarity index carotid ultrasound images of Dataset 1 with variance of 0.1.

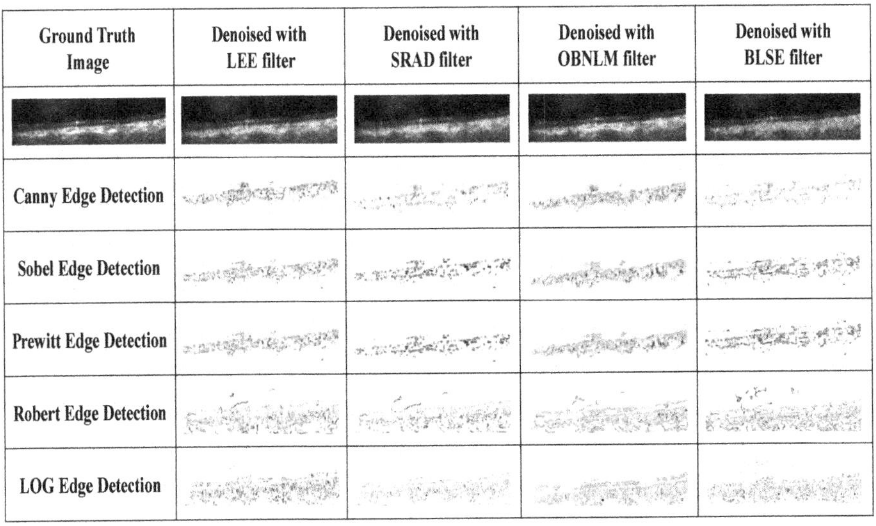

Ground Truth Image	Denoised with LEE filter	Denoised with SRAD filter	Denoised with OBNLM filter	Denoised with BLSE filter
Canny Edge Detection				
Sobel Edge Detection				
Prewitt Edge Detection				
Robert Edge Detection				
LOG Edge Detection				

Fig. 5. Structural similarity index of carotid ultrasound images of Dataset 2 with variance of 0.1.

the Tables 2, 3, 4, and 5, we can observe that canny edge detection with BLSE filter achieved the highest value of PSNR, CoC, SSIM and lowest value of MSE for the 50 carotid ultrasound images.

Table 2. Mean PSNR, Mean MSE, Mean CoC and Mean SSIM of LEE denoising filter with different edge detection techniques for 50 carotid ultrasound images.

Metric	Canny	Sobel	Prewitt	Robert	LoG
Dataset 1 with LEE filter					
PSNR ± Std	64.2808 ± 0.2462	63.6296 ± 0.2666	63.6850 ± 0.2538	62.5048 ± 0.5915	63.2677 ± 0.5608
MSE	0.0385 ± 0.0022	0.0355 ± 0.0021	0.0351 ± 0.0020	0.0583 ± 0.0079	0.0488 ± 0.0063
CoC	0.6562	0.4748	0.4757	0.2172	0.6558
SSIM	0.9993	0.9991	0.9992	0.9986	0.9990
Dataset 2 with LEE filter					
PSNR ± Std	65.8473 ± 0.8673	64.3143 ± 1.0513	64.9427 ± 1.0346	62.3705 ± 0.6478	63.4591 ± 0.6227
MSE	0.0272 ± 0.0047	0.0246 ± 0.0054	0.0244 ± 0.0053	0.0616 ± 0.0096	0.0457 ± 0.0063
CoC	0.5045	0.3970	0.4183	0.3378	0.5013
SSIM	0.9993	0.9992	0.9993	0.9985	0.9989

Table 3. Mean PSNR, Mean MSE, Mean CoC and Mean SSIM of SRAD denoising filter with different edge detection techniques for 50 carotid ultrasound images.

Metric	Canny	Sobel	Prewitt	Robert	LoG
Dataset 1 with SRAD filter					
PSNR ± Std	64.1425 ± 0.7999	63.6798 ± 0.6089	63.7140 ± 0.6074	60.4831 ± 0.4385	62.5281 ± 0.7766
MSE	0.0317 ± 0.0044	0.0353 ± 0.0049	0.0351 ± 0.0049	0.0735 ± 0.0074	0.0733 ± 0.0125
CoC	0.5407	0.4645	0.4748	0.4907	0.5860
SSIM	0.9988	0.9986	0.9982	0.9980	0.9964
Dataset 2 with SRAD filter					
PSNR ± Std	64.8027 ± 1.4865	64.0302 ± 0.9437	63.8864 ± 0.9721	61.8838 ± 0.3237	63.2194 ± 0.6539
MSE	0.0278 ± 0.0058	0.0274 ± 0.0057	0.0271 ± 0.0059	0.0669 ± 0.0049	0.0495 ± 0.0070
CoC	0.5130	0.3820	0.3902	0.4099	0.5150
SSIM	0.9994	0.9994	0.9991	0.9986	0.9988

4   Discussion

The aim of this paper is automatic edge detection using BLSE denoising filter for quantification of IMT in carotid ultrasound images. The edge detection in

Table 4. Mean PSNR, Mean MSE, Mean CoC and Mean SSIM of OBNLM denoising filter with different edge detection techniques for 50 carotid ultrasound images.

Metric	Canny	Sobel	Prewitt	Robert	LoG
Dataset 1 with OBNLM filter					
PSNR ± Std	64.8556 ± 0.7654	63.7264 ± 0.3482	62.7900 ± 0.4226	60.6984 ± 0.7315	63.3933 ± 0.7514
MSE	0.0340 ± 0.0055	0.0438 ± 0.0033	61.7900 ± 0.4226	59.6984 ± 0.7315	60.3938 ± 0.7514
CoC	0.6173	0.3898	0.3954	0.3596	0.6078
SSIM	0.9990	0.9989	0.9986	0.9984	0.9988
Dataset 2 with OBNLM filter					
PSNR ± Std	65.2727 ± 0.6500	64.7631 ± 0.7348	63.8424 ± 0.7720	61.3422 ± 1.1954	64.5376 ± 1.2255
MSE	0.0308 ± 0.0047	0.0348 ± 0.0065	0.0342 ± 0.0067	0.0780 ± 0.0222	0.0592 ± 0.0166
CoC	0.4966	0.3666	0.3707	0.2286	0.4963
SSIM	0.9992	0.9991	0.9990	0.9986	0.9988

Table 5. Mean PSNR, Mean MSE, Mean CoC and Mean SSIM of proposed denoising filter with different edge detection techniques for 50 carotid ultrasound images.

Metric	Canny	Sobel	Prewitt	Robert	LoG
Dataset 1 with BLSE filter					
PSNR ± Std	**65.1218 ± 0.4996**	63.3395 ± 0.4526	63.4135 ± 0.4670	61.2674 ± 0.5506	63.0588 ± 0.5644
MSE	**0.0255 ± 0.0037**	0.0381 ± 0.0040	0.0374 ± 0.0040	0.0615 ± 0.0078	0.0513 ± 0.0069
CoC	**0.6611**	0.4379	0.4695	0.4735	0.6362
SSIM	**0.9994**	0.9989	0.9991	0.9986	0.9990
Dataset 2 with BLSE filter					
PSNR ± Std	**65.7955 ± 1.2014**	64.4227 ± 1.0722	64.4337 ± 1.0216	63.1044 ± 0.5869	64.5946 ± 0.5137
MSE	**0.0209± 0.0065**	0.0302 ± 0.0069	0.0301 ± 0.0067	0.0639 ± 0.0090	0.0452 ± 0.0050
CoC	**0.5281**	0.3707	0.3603	0.3773	0.5244
SSIM	**0.9995**	0.9987	0.9992	0.9991	0.9989

carotid ultrasound images is important for recognition of IMT in common carotid artery (CCA) [26]. The experiment analysis in the previous section described that canny edge detection with BLSE filter is better than several commonly used edge detection techniques in terms of the reduction in speckle noise and preservation of edges in carotid ultrasound images. From the Tables 2, 3, 4, and 5, since the Lee filter [27] uses the local statistics of possible edge orientation for high variance areas of neighborhood pixels it cannot reduce noise in edges. SRAD filter [28] fails to give significance difference in speckle denoising in carotid ultrasound images. OBNLM filter [9] effective in preserving the edges but takes slightly more computational time. The BLSE filter with canny edge detection shows better for the preservation of intima media complex in the carotid ultrasound images and more efficient compared to the other techniques. The smoothing is achieved by the sobel operator along with the edge detection and merely adversely affects from the high frequency noises. In Prewitt operator, local edge orientation can be easily found but orientation estimates are not accurate. Robert operator is a simple method for edge detection and limitation of the method is very sensitive to noise. Finally, LoG operator is used for real time application and drawback of this method is image contrast may reduce. The performance evaluation of canny edge detection has some criteria such as it has a low error rate, a signal edge has only one response and the edge points should be well-localized [14]. The quantitative analysis from the Tables 2, 3, 4, and 5 show that the highest value of PSNR, CoC, SSIM and Lowest value of MSE are achieved from canny edge detection with BLSE denoising filter for 50 carotid ultrasound images. To estimate the non-parametric significance test between the edge detection techniques with denoising filter and ground truth image uses, P value test [29] is applied for 50 carotid ultrasound images. The result of PSNR show significance difference between canny edge detection with other edge detection conditions (P-value < 0.05). Similarly the results of MSE value, there is significant difference between canny edge detection status with respect to other edge detections statuses (P-value < 0.05). The CoC and SSIM are higher in the canny edge detection technique as compared to the other methods. Based on the results, by estimating PSNR, CoC, SSIM and MSE, this paper show that the canny edge detection with BLSE filter is better than the other edge detection techniques in terms of reduction of speckle noise and detail preservation in carotid ultrasound images.

5   Conclusion

In this paper, we proposed a new method for fully automatic ROI extraction and used contrast enhancement based on $TV - L^1$ norm for improving the robustness. The speckle present in ultrasound image has been reduced using the different denoising filters and compared them with the several edge detection techniques with respect to the preservation of edges. In all images, the proposed algorithm achieves better results in terms of image resolution and edge delineation. The measure parameters PSNR, MSE, CoC and SSIM of BLSE denoising filter with canny edge detection achieves better performance as compared to the other canny edge detection of denoising methods. Based on the obtained results and visual inspection, we conclude that the canny edge detection with BLSE denoising filter is superior to the other denoising methods and more effective in terms of detail preservation in carotid ultrasound images.

Acknowledgement. The authors would like to thank Department of Radiology, Father Muller Hospital, Mangalore for valuable contribution in collecting B-mode longitudinal ultrasound images of the patients.

References

1. WHO: World Health Organisation, cardiovascular disease (2013). http://www.who.int/cardiovasculardiseases/en/
2. Walker, M.D., Marler, J.R., Goldstein, M., Grady, P.A., Toole, J.F., Baker, W.H., Castaldo, J.E., Chambless, L.E., Moore, W.S., Robertson, J.T., et al.: Endarterectomy for asymptomatic carotid artery stenosis. JAMA **273**(18), 1421–1428 (1995)
3. Loizou, C.P.: A review of ultrasound common carotid artery image and video segmentation techniques. Med. Biol. Eng. Comput. **52**(12), 1073–1093 (2014)
4. Baldassarre, D., Amato, M., Bondioli, A., Sirtori, C.R., Tremoli, E.: Carotid artery intima-media thickness measured by ultrasonography in normal clinical practice correlates well with atherosclerosis risk factors. Stroke **31**(10), 2426–2430 (2000)
5. Molinari, F., Zeng, G., Suri, J.S.: A state of the art review on intima-media thickness (IMT) measurement and wall segmentation techniques for carotid ultrasound. Comput. Methods Programs Biomed. **100**(3), 201–221 (2010)
6. Kang, J., Lee, J.Y., Yoo, Y.: A new feature-enhanced speckle reduction method based on multiscale analysis for ultrasound B-mode imaging. IEEE Trans. Biomed. Eng. **63**(6), 1178–1191 (2016)
7. Hassan, N., Akamatsu, N.: A new approach for contrast enhancement using sigmoid function. Int. Arab J. Inf. Technol. **11**(1), 22–28 (2009)
8. Zuo, C., Chen, Q., Sui, X., Ren, J.: Brightness preserving image contrast enhancement using spatially weighted histogram equalization. Int. Arab J. Inf. Technol. **11**(1), 25–32 (2014)
9. Coupé, P., Hellier, P., Kervrann, C., Barillot, C.: Nonlocal means-based speckle filtering for ultrasound images. IEEE Trans. Image Process. **18**(10), 2221–2229 (2009)
10. Pandit, A., Sharma, M., Ramsankaran, R.: Comparison of the performance of the newly developed CDWM filter with Enhanced LEE and Enhanced Frost Filters over the SAR image. In: 2014 9th International Conference on Industrial and Information Systems (ICIIS), pp. 1–5. IEEE (2014)
11. Li, X., Zhang, Z.: Ultrasound speckle reducing anisotropic diffusion based on histogram curves matching. J. Med. Imaging Health Inform. **7**(1), 137–142 (2017)
12. Iwasaki, A., Takekawa, H., Okabe, R., Suzuki, K., Okamura, M., Nishihira, T., Suzuki, A., Tsukahara, Y., Hirata, K.: Increased maximum common carotid intima-media thickness is associated with smoking and hypertension in Tochigi Prefecture residents. J. Med. Ultrason. **44**, 315–321 (2017)
13. Maini, R., Aggarwal, H.: Study and comparison of various image edge detection techniques. Int. J. Image Process. (IJIP) **3**(1), 1–11 (2009)
14. Canny, J.: A computational approach to edge detection. IEEE Trans. Pattern Anal. Mach. Intell. **8**(6), 679–698 (1986)
15. Muthukrishnan, R., Radha, M.: Edge detection techniques for image segmentation. Int. J. Comput. Sci. Inf. Technol. **3**(6), 259 (2011)
16. Haider, W., Malik, M.S., Raza, M., Wahab, A., Khan, I.A., Zia, U., Tanveer, J., Bashir, H.: A hybrid method for edge continuity based on pixel neighbors pattern analysis (PNPA) for remote sensing satellite images. Int. J. Commun. Netw. Syst. Sci. **5**(09), 624 (2012)

17. Heath, M., Sarkar, S., Sanocki, T., Bowyer, K.: Comparison of edge detectors: a methodology and initial study. In: 1996 IEEE Computer Society Conference on Computer Vision and Pattern Recognition, Proceedings CVPR 1996, pp. 143–148. IEEE (1996)
18. Srivastava, R., Gupta, J., Parthasarthy, H.: Comparison of PDE based and other techniques for speckle reduction from digitally reconstructed holographic images. Opt. Lasers Eng. **48**(5), 626–635 (2010)
19. Cyprus: E-health laboratory *cs* department (2007). www.medinfo.cs.ucy.ac.cy/index.php/downloads/datasets
20. Loizou, C.P., Pattichis, C.S., Pantziaris, M., Tyllis, T., Nicolaides, A.: Snakes based segmentation of the common carotid artery intima media. Med. Biol. Eng. Comput. **45**(1), 35–49 (2007)
21. Ghita, O., Ilea, D.E., Whelan, P.F.: Texture enhanced histogram equalization using $TV - L1$ image decomposition. IEEE Trans. Image Process. **22**(8), 3133–3144 (2013)
22. Jun, O.: A threshold selection method from gray-scale histograms. IEEE Trans. Syst. Man Cybern. **9**(1), 62–66 (1988)
23. Nagaraj, Y., et al.: Segmentation of Intima Media Complex from Carotid Ultrasound Images using Wind Driven Optimization Technique, Biomedical Signal Processing and Control (2017). https://doi.org/10.1016/j.bspc.2017.08.009
24. Wong, A., Mishra, A., Bizheva, K., Clausi, D.A.: General Bayesian estimation for speckle noise reduction in optical coherence tomography retinal imagery. Opt. Express **18**(8), 8338–8352 (2010)
25. Nagaraj, Y., Asha, C., Narasimhadhan, A.: Assessment of speckle denoising in ultrasound carotid images using least square Bayesian estimation approach. In: 2016 IEEE Region 10 Conference (TENCON), pp. 1001–1004. IEEE (2016)
26. Taniguchi, N., Nagatsuka, K., Harada, R., Hirai, T., Fushimi, E., Yasaka, M.: Standard method for ultrasound evaluation of carotid artery lesions. J. Med. **36**, 219–226 (2009)
27. Lee, J.-S.: Speckle suppression and analysis for synthetic aperture radar images. Opt. Eng. **25**(5), 255636 (1986)
28. Yu, Y., Acton, S.T.: Speckle reducing anisotropic diffusion. IEEE Trans. Image Process. **11**(11), 1260–1270 (2002)
29. Wasserstein, R.L., Lazar, N.A.: The ASA's statement on p-values: context, process, and purpose. Am. Stat. **70**(2), 129–133 (2016)

A Two Stage Contour Evolution Approach for the Measurement of Choroid Thickness in EDI-OCT Images

George Neetha$^{(\boxtimes)}$ and C. V. Jiji

College of Engineering, Trivandrum, Thiruvananthapuram, Kerala, India
{neethageorge,jijicv}@cet.ac.in

Abstract. High resolution images of the choroid can be obtained using Enhanced Depth Imaging Optical Coherence Tomography (EDI-OCT). The thickness of the choroid can be measured from these images and is used widely in clinical application for diagnosing various eye related diseases. But analysis of the choroidal thickness is presently done manually which varies with the observer and is a time consuming task. In this paper we propose a two stage contour evolution approach using chan vese method for the segmentation of choroidal layers in EDI OCT images. First the EDI OCT image is prefiltered using Rotating Kernel Transformation (RKT) to reduce the effect of speckle noise. This is followed by first stage of contour evolution which effectively identifies the upper boundary, the Bruchs Membrane (BM). The second level of segmentation delineates the lower boundary of the choroid, the Choroid Sclera Interface (CSI). The choroid thickness measured as the distance between BM and CSI are compared with the manually segmented results by an ophthalmologist. Results show good consistency with the proposed method.

Keywords: EDI OCT · Chan vese · Choroid segmentation

1 Introduction

Optical Coherence Tomography (OCT) is a non invasive imaging technique used to obtain high resolution cross sectional images of microscopic structure of living tissues. This was introduced by Huang et al. in 1991 and is widely used for retinal analysis [5], and made the measurements like the different layer thickness, retinal vasculature, etc. easier. Choroid, the layer lying between Retina and Sclera, provides oxygen and nourishment to the outer layers of the retina. It is a vascular structure consisting of capillaries, nerves and blood vessels. Diseases affecting eye cause changes in these blood vessels and results in structural changes of the choroid. This causes changes in thickness of the layers which can be measured to analyse these diseases. But due to the presence of blood vessels which obstruct the passage of light, conventional OCT cannot be used to capture images of choroid.

© Springer Nature Singapore Pte Ltd. 2018
R. Rameshan et al. (Eds.): NCVPRIPG 2017, CCIS 841, pp. 436–445, 2018.
https://doi.org/10.1007/978-981-13-0020-2_38

In 2005, Margolis and Spaide introduced Enhanced Depth Imaging Optical Coherence Tomography (EDI-OCT) which made visualisation of choroid and analysis more easy [8]. EDI-OCT images of choroid can be segmented to obtain the thickness measure for easy diagnosis and prediction of eye related diseases. Presently quantification of the thickness of the choroid is done by the manual labeling of the two boundaries, the Bruch's Membrane (BM) and the Choroid - Sclera interface (CSI). This manual labeling is a time-consuming and tedious process and also varies with the observer. As the number of images increases, it becomes more complicated. This clearly suggests the need for developing an automatic segmentation algorithm that could detect the boundaries of choroid and extract thickness measure from this. There are large amount of works available in literature for retinal segmentation. But these algorithms fail to work when applied to choroid segmentation because the choroid layer has nonuniform reflectivity and appears to be of different brightness levels. In addition, the CSI is not at all visible in many cases and the texture is also nonuniform, making segmentation a difficult task.

2   Related Work

Automated segmentation of the retina provides various parameters, such as central macular thickness, retinal volume and sub field thickness [1], which have become crucial parts of patient management and research. But automated choroid segmentation is not yet available in clinical practice due to the lack of fast and accurate choroidal layer segmentation techniques. Here we review some of the automated segmentation techniques available in the literature particularly for choroid segmentation.

A statistical model based choroidal vessel segmentation with a multi scale 3D edge filtering technique was reported by Kajić et al. [6]. Statistical modelling provided robustness and demonstrated reliable performance to the changes in signal-to-noise ratio and shape properties. But this approach required extensive training for the statistical model. A fully automated algorithm for segmentation of choroidal images using texture based approach was proposed by Danesh et al. [4]. Dynamic programming was used to find the upper boundary and the lower boundary was segmented by constructing a gaussian mixture model using wavelet features. The algorithm was tested on larger data sets and border positioning errors were calculated. The error obtained was very less compared to existing methods. The disadvantage of this method was the need for manual segmentation to construct the model. A fully automated method to segment choroid from two different scanners was proposed by Zhang et al. [9]. The method used shape prior based soft-constraint graph-search and graph optimization and was capable of obtaining the thickness of the choroid. But there were significant differences between manual labelling and automated measurements for the outer choroid boundary. In this paper we propose a simple and efficient method to measure choroidal thickness using a two stage chan vese contour evolution approach. Our method does not require any training and shows good consistency with manual labellings obtained from ophthalmologists.

3   Proposed Method

In the proposed method the Retinal Pigment Epithelium (RPE) layer is detected first by searching pixels with maximum intensity. The EDI OCT image is then denoised to remove speckle noise. We use a rotating kernel transformation based algorithm for this purpose. The upper and lower boundaries of the choroid are then detected using active contour model. The first stage of contour evolution segments the BM. The second stage delineates the CSI as the lower boundary of the evolved closed contour. The block schematic of the proposed approach is shown in Fig. 1.

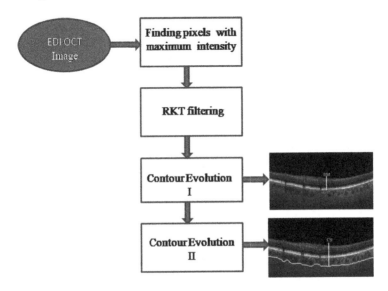

Fig. 1. Overview of the algorithm

3.1   Denoising Using Rotating Kernel Transformation

The OCT images are usually contaminated with speckle noise [1] and so it has to be de-noised before segmentation. The rotating kernel transformation we used is a modified version of the technique introduced by Lee and Rhodes [7]. In this method, directive masks are applied sequentially and the difference between maximum and minimum at each point is taken as the output. This suppresses noise and enhances the layer features emphasizing thin edges.

In RKT, the output image is obtained as the convolution of input image with a two-dimensional kernel that is rotated discretely in small steps through 360°. The convolved image is given by

$$I_\theta(x,y) = F(x,y) * S_\theta(x,y) \tag{1}$$

where F is the input signal I_θ the output signal and S_θ is the kernel oriented at angle θ.

For an image of size MXN, a set of KXK kernels ($K < M, K < N$) with $2K - 2$ different orientations are generated. The image is convolved with each of the kernels, generating a set of $2K - 2$ filtered outputs. As an example a set of templates for $K = 5$ is shown in Fig. 2. The template values are 0 and 1 and values of the template corresponding to 1 are enhanced.

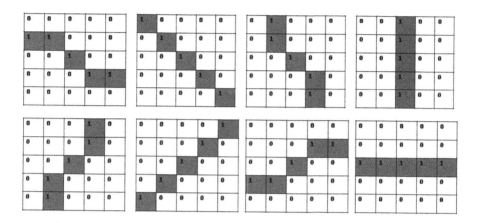

Fig. 2. Example of templates for $K = 5$

The convolution output $I_\theta(x, y)$ for each kernel rotation is monitored and the maximum and minimum values of $I_\theta(x, y)$ measured at each point (x, y) are stored. The difference is taken as the enhanced output.

3.2   Proposed Choroid Segmentation Approach

The anterior limit of the choroid is the BM and the lower boundary is the CSI. Figure 3 shows the cross sectional image of the choroid with manual labelling of the two interfaces and choroid is the region in between. We use a two stage contour evolution based on chan vese method for the segmentation of the above layers.

Chan vese contour evolution. Let I be the preprocessed image over the domain Ω and let C be the initial closed contour defined for segmentation. The initialised contour evolves minimising the energy function which is represented in Chan and Vese's model [3] as

$$E(C, c_1, c_2) = \mu.L(C) + \vartheta A(in\, C)$$
$$+ \lambda_1 \int_{in(C)} |I - c_1|^2 dxdy + \lambda_2 \int_{out(C)} |I - c_2|^2 dxdy \quad (2)$$

where $L(C)$ represents the length of C and $A(in\, C)$ represents the area inside C with c_1, c_2 are the averages of the image in the regions inside C and outside C

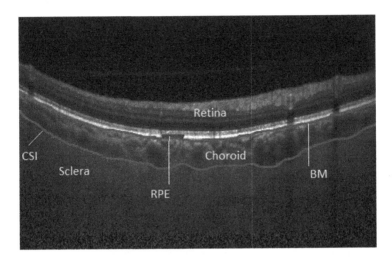

Fig. 3. EDI OCT image of the choroid with BM and CSI marked manually

respectively. The optimum values of the parameters $\mu, \vartheta, \lambda_1, \lambda_2$ are determined experimentally.

Level set method is widely used for curve evolution [3]. Here the curve C is represented by a Lipschitz function, ψ and the fitting energy to be minimised is

$$E(\Psi, c_1, c_2) = \mu. \int_{\Omega} \delta(\Psi)|\bigtriangledown \Psi| + \lambda_1 \int_{\Omega} |I - c_1|^2 H(\Psi) dx dy$$

$$+ \lambda_2 \int_{\Omega} |I - c_2|^2 (1 - H(\Psi)) dx dy \qquad (3)$$

H is the Heaviside function and δ is the one-dimensional Dirac measure concentrated at 0. c_1, c_2 are the averages of the image in the regions where $\Psi \geq 0$ and $\Psi < 0$ respectively. The area term is not included because this term is used when we force the curve to move only inside or only outside.

Using Heaviside function H, c_1, c_2 are expressed as

$$c_1(\Psi) = \frac{\int_{\Omega} I H(\Psi) dx dy}{\int_{\Omega} H(\Psi(x,y)) dx dy} \qquad (4)$$

$$c_2(\Psi) = \frac{\int_{\Omega} I(1 - H(\Psi)) dx dy}{\int_{\Omega} (1 - H(\Psi(x,y))) dx dy} \qquad (5)$$

Keeping c_1 and c_2 fixed and minimising the energy $E(\Psi, c_1, c_2)$ with respect to Ψ we obtain the Euler-Lagrange equation for Ψ. In the proposed approach we use the chan vese method twice for identifying the BM and CSI layers of the choroid as described below.

BM Detection. It is observed that RPE is the brightest layer in all EDI OCT images. This layer is detected by searching for pixels with highest intensities in the image. For the determination of BM, the initial closed contour is defined below RPE as shown in Fig. 4. Once the closed contour is evolved after sufficient iterations, the upper portion of the contour is identified as the BM layer.

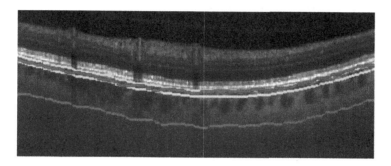

Fig. 4. Initial contour for BM is shown in green and for CSI in red. (Color figure online)

CSI detection. The lower boundary of the choroid is detected by second level of contour evolution. The initial contour for the second segmentation is selected from the segmented BM layer. When contour evolution stops, the lower portion of the contour is selected as CSI. The thickness of the choroid is then calculated by measuring the distance between the BM and CSI layers.

4   Experimental Results

The data set used in our experiments was the same available with [4]. This data set has both normal and abnormal OCT images. One hundred and fifty 2D EDI-OCT images from the dataset were tested with our algorithm. For denoising we used a 19×19 kernel which is rotated through $180°$ in steps of $5°$. For each image pixel, a maximum value and minimum value is calculated from the corresponding filtered images and the difference is taken as the output.

First contour evolution starts at points below RPE for BM segmentation, and second contour is defined below BM for CSI segmentation. Same segmentation is performed twice, since the CSI has different characteristics compared to BM.

In Eq. 3 we set the weight of first term, length term μ to 0.2. For the second and third term λ_1 and λ_2 are set to one. These terms represents the variance of the image level in the foreground region and the background region respectively and measures the uniformity in pixel intensity.

The upper boundary of the choroid is obtained from first curve evolution assigning the upper contour points as BM. For the second contour evolution, the lower boundary, CSI, is obtained as the lower contour points of the evolved curve. The results are shown in Fig. 5.

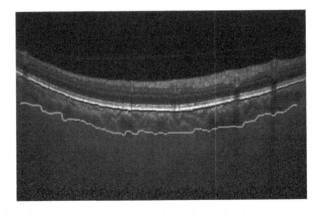

Fig. 5. Choroid upper and lower layer

For validation purpose we compared our results with the manual segmented images, the tracing by ophthalmologist. Results are shown in Fig. 6.

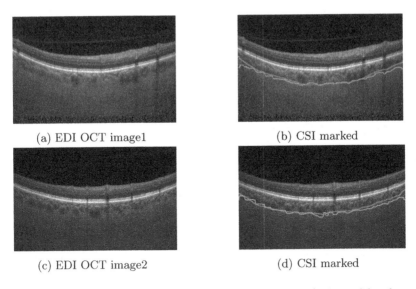

(a) EDI OCT image1

(b) CSI marked

(c) EDI OCT image2

(d) CSI marked

Fig. 6. Comparison of the results of the proposed algorithm (indicated by the green lines) and the ground truth, tracing by the expert (drawn in blue lines) (Color figure online)

The algorithm was tested on one hundred and fifty images from the data set. Bruchs membrane was correctly detected for all normal and diseased images. Choroid sclera interface was detected correctly for all normal images but some abnormalities could not be traced by the algorithm.

The mean signed and unsigned border positioning errors for each border were calculated using the tracing obtained by two ophthalmologists. The mean error is computed as the average distance between points along the length of the curve for automatic and manual segmentations. The calculations were done for both BM and CSI. The border positioning error between the curves of two observers were also calculated. Tables 1 and 2 summarises the result.

Table 1. Summary of mean signed border positioning error (mean ± std)

	Avg. obd versus our algorithm	Obs. 1 vs obs. 2
BM	1.1 ± 1.158	2.69 ± 1.79
Choroid	2.78 ± 1.238	3.27 ± 2.84

Table 2. Summary of mean un signed border positioning error (mean ± std)

	Avg. obd versus our algorithm	Obs. 1 vs obs. 2
BM	1.42 ± 0.975	2.8 ± 1.645
Choroid	5.48 ± 3.8	6.27 ± 4.93

The border positioning error obtained for BM and choroid is less compared to those obtained between two observers. For example, the mean signed error for choroid was 2.78 using our algorithm, the same was 3.27 using two observers. Since there is no gold standard for evaluating the accuracy of the algorithm, the ground truth is marked as the tracing made by the ophthalmologist [2]. We represent the border positioning error as the measure of accuracy. The pixel resolution for the data set was given as $3.9\,\mu m$/pixel. The border positioning error in μm is calculated as, for BM the signed error is $4.29\,\mu m$ and for choroid it is $10.8\,\mu m$ while between observers it is $10.49\,\mu m$ for BM and $12.7\,\mu m$ for choroid.

Precise measurement of the thickness of choroid is essential in the evaluation of choroid layer related diseases. The thickness of choroid in this work is obtained as the distance in pixels between the upper and lower layer of the choroid.

Figures 7 and 8 shows the thickness variations along the length of the choroid for the image in Fig. 6.

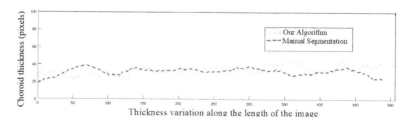

Fig. 7. Choroid thickness profile for image 1

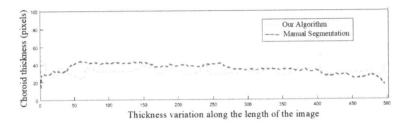

Fig. 8. Choroid thickness profile for image 2

Table 3. Summary of mean un signed and signed error in thickness (mean ± std)

	Avg. obd versus our algorithm	Obs. 1 vs obs. 2
Signed error	3.92 ± 6.22	4.24 ± 4.44
Unsigned error	6.52 ± 4.12	5.28 ± 4.24

Difference in thickness obtained using our algorithm over the length of the choroid and the thickness obtained using manual segmentation are calculated. The mean signed and unsigned differences obtained are compared with the values obtained in a similar method using the traces of two experts. Comparison between the two are shown in Table 3.

5 Conclusion

In this paper we proposed a two stage contour evolution method using chan vese approach for separately segmenting the BM and CSI in EDI OCT images after denoising the given image using rotating kernel transformation. Our method is simple and efficient and does not require any training examples. The results were compared with the ophthalmologist's labellings and showed good consistency. The fast and accurate thickness profile obtained using our method can be used for detecting various eye related diseases.

References

1. Anantrasirichai, N., et al.: SVM-based texture classification in optical coherence tomography. In: 2013 IEEE 10th International Symposium on Biomedical Imaging, pp. 1332–1335. IEEE (2013)
2. Beaton, L., Mazzaferri, J., Lalonde, F., Hidalgo-Aguirre, M., Descovich, D., Lesk, M., Costantino, S.: Non-invasive measurement of choroidal volume change and ocular rigidity through automated segmentation of high-speed OCT imaging. Biomed. Opt. Express **6**(5), 1694–1706 (2015)
3. Chan, T.F., Vese, L.A.: Active contours without edges. IEEE Trans. Image Process. **10**(2), 266–277 (2001)

4. Danesh, H., Kafieh, R., et al.: Segmentation of choroidal boundary in enhanced depth imaging OCTs using a multiresolution texture based modeling in graph cuts. Comput. Math. Methods Med. **2014** (2014)
5. Huang, D., Swanson, E.A., et al.: Optical coherence tomography. Science **254**(5035), 1178 (1991)
6. Kajić, V., et al.: Automated choroidal segmentation of 1060 nm OCT in healthy and pathologic eyes using a statistical model. Biomed. Opt. Express **3**(1), 86–103 (2012)
7. Lee, Y.K., Rhodes, W.T.: Nonlinear image processing by a rotating kernel transformation. Opt. Lett. **15**(23), 1383–1385 (1990)
8. Margolis, R., Spaide, R.F.: A pilot study of enhanced depth imaging optical coherence tomography of the choroid in normal eyes. Am. J. Ophthalmol. **147**(5), 811–815 (2009)
9. Zhang, L., Buitendijk, G.H., et al.: Validity of automated choroidal segmentation in SS-OCT and SD-OCT. Invest. Ophthalmol. Vis. Sci. **56**(5), 3202–3211 (2015)

Improved Low Resolution Heterogeneous Face Recognition Using Re-ranking

Sivaram Prasad Mudunuri, Shashanka Venkataramanan, and Soma Biswas[✉]

Department of Electrical Engineering, Indian Institute of Science, Bangalore, India
{sivaramm,shashankv,somabiswas}@iisc.ac.in

Abstract. Recently, near-infrared to visible light facial image matching is gaining popularity, especially for low-light and night-time surveillance scenarios. Unlike most of the work in literature, we assume that the near-infrared probe images have low-resolution in addition to uncontrolled pose and expression, which is due to the large distance of the person from the camera. To address this very challenging problem, we propose a re-ranking strategy which takes into account the relation of both the probe and gallery with a set of reference images. This can be used as an add-on to any existing algorithm. We apply it with one recent dictionary learning algorithm which uses alignment of orthogonal dictionaries. We also create a benchmark for this task by evaluating some of the recent algorithms for this experimental protocol. Extensive experiments are conducted on a modified version of the CASIA NIR VIS 2.0 database to show the effectiveness of the proposed re-ranking approach.

Keywords: Heterogeneous face recognition
Dictionary learning and re-ranking

1 Introduction

The task of recognizing low resolution facial images captured in uncontrolled settings has become a challenging area of research in the field of computer vision due to the increasing usage of surveillance cameras [1,2]. It has been observed that the performance of most of the current algorithms degrades if the images captured are of low resolution and also contain varying poses and poor illumination conditions which replicates real world scenarios [3–6].

To handle illumination variations at low-light or night-time conditions, researchers have started using near-infrared (NIR) facial images. But the gallery may consist of high resolution (HR), controlled visible images captured during enrolment. So our goal is to develop a heterogeneous face recognition algorithm which can match low resolution (LR) NIR face images captured under uncontrolled pose and expression with the HR visible face images captured with frontal pose and good illumination conditions (Fig. 1). This problem is more challenging since the probe and gallery faces differ in resolution, pose and illumination together with spectral variations. Addressing all these variations together has

© Springer Nature Singapore Pte Ltd. 2018
R. Rameshan et al. (Eds.): NCVPRIPG 2017, CCIS 841, pp. 446–456, 2018.
https://doi.org/10.1007/978-981-13-0020-2_39

not been well studied and needs to be addressed with special attention since these replicate the practical scenario [7]. The proposed re-ranking module can be used as an add-on for any other algorithm also.

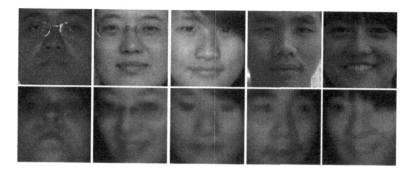

Fig. 1. Low resolution heterogeneous face recognition: matching HR VIS frontal faces (first row) with LR NIR non frontal faces (second row). Original images are taken from CASIA NIR VIS 2.0 database [8].

Recently, several approaches have been proposed for HR heterogeneous face recognition in the direction of dictionary learning framework. We build our re-ranking framework on the success of [9] to attempt this problem. Given a LR NIR probe and the HR visible gallery images, we select the k-nearest neighbors since even if the correct match is not at rank-1, it will likely be in the top few matches. We analyze the relative position of the probe and all the gallery in this set with respect to a set of reference images to re-rank these k-nearest neighbours. The assumption behind the re-ranking is that for the correct probe gallery pair, the nearest neighbors of both of them should match. The main contributions of our proposed work and differences with [9] are as follows:

– We provide a benchmark for the problem of LR heterogeneous face recognition and evaluate some of the recent approaches in literature for this task.
– We propose a re-ranking module that is evaluated as an add-on feature to an existing approach.
– The proposed re-ranking can potentially be used by other approaches to boost their performance.
– Extensive experiments conducted on a modified version of CASIA NIR VIS 2.0 database [8] show the effectiveness of the proposed approach.

2   Related Work

In this section, we provide some pointers regarding the recent approaches. A fusion based algorithm that uses restricted boltzman machine and stacked denoising auto encoders to address the problem of matching LR NIR and HR

VIS is proposed in [7]. A computationally efficient correlation analysis involving discriminant correlation analysis to compute the projection matrices which maximizes the correlation is described in [5]. A joint face hallucination and recognition approach based on sparse representation is described in [10]. Moutafis and Kakadiaris [11] propose a framework to match LR and HR faces by jointly learning two semi-coupled bases to exploit the optimal representations. Li et al. [12] uses local binary pattern for low resolution face recognition by combining multi-scale blocking center symmetric local binary pattern based on Gaussian pyramid. Mudunuri and Biswas [2] propose an approach that learns multi-dimensional scaling to construct a common transformation matrix to simultaneously transform both the probe and gallery faces into a common discriminative space. A template based face recognition which efficiently fuses discriminative information of deep features is proposed in [13]. An inter-session variability modelling approach using Gaussian mixture model to handle cross-modal faces is described in [14]. Peng et al. uses Markov models to represent heterogeneous image patches which considers the spatial compatibility between neighboring patches. Xing and Wang [15] describes a generalized bipartite graph to discretely approximate the manifold structure of face sets with different resolution.

A useful study on the effect of low resolution with deep learning techniques primarily involving pre-training by super resolution, domain adaptation and regression techniques is presented in [16]. A complex deep model to learn the relationship between cross-modal images is described in [17]. A single deep convolutional neural network architecture to map both NIR and VIS images to a compact Euclidian space is given in [18]. A neural network based architecture that captures the non-linear relationship between the two modalities of faces is proposed in [19]. A triplet loss based convolutional neural network framework is proposed in [20]. CNN based metric learning strategies to reduce discrepancies between the different modalities is proposed in [21].

3   Proposed Method

In this section, the details of the proposed approach is presented which addresses the problem of recognizing low resolution NIR faces captured under uncontrolled pose and expressions with HR visible (VIS) faces captured under frontal pose and good illuminations. The proposed re-ranking algorithm can be used as an add-on to any other algorithm to improve their matching accuracy for this problem. In this work, we use a recent work [9] as the baseline approach with certain modifications in which the authors addressed VIS-NIR face matching where NIR images are also of high resolution. For completion, first we will briefly describe the modified baseline approach [9] and then provide details of the re-ranking algorithm.

3.1   Baseline Approach

The baseline approach [9] has a training and a testing stage. During training, given images from both domains (NIR and VIS), we compute two orthogonal dictionaries for each of the domains respectively. Note that unlike [9], in this case, the NIR images are of low-resolution. Let $\mathbf{X} = \{\mathbf{x}_1, \mathbf{x}_2, \ldots, \mathbf{x}_{N_1}\} \in \mathcal{R}^{d \times N_1}$ and $\mathbf{Y} = \{\mathbf{y}_1, \mathbf{y}_2, \ldots, \mathbf{y}_{N_2}\} \in \mathcal{R}^{d \times N_2}$ be the data in the two domains, where d is the feature dimension of each sample and N_1, N_2 are the number of samples available for each of the respective domains. The main advantage of learning dictionaries separately for the two domains instead of in a coupled manner [22,23] is that we can avoid the requirement of paired training data. The other advantages of learning orthogonal dictionaries over the over-complete dictionaries are: (1) less computational complexity in computing the dictionaries and (2) redundancy of dictionary atoms is less.

The algorithm learns an orthogonal dictionary [24] $\bar{\mathbf{D}}_x = [\mathbf{J}_x \ \mathbf{D}_x]$ from the given data $\mathbf{X}$ such that $\bar{\mathbf{D}}_x^T \bar{\mathbf{D}}_x = \mathbf{I}_{d \times d}$. The optimization function is formulated as follows:

$$\min_{\mathbf{D}_x, \mathbf{\Lambda}} \| \mathbf{X} - [\mathbf{J}_x, \mathbf{D}_x] \mathbf{\Lambda} \|_2^2 + \alpha \| \mathbf{\Lambda} \|_0^2$$
$$\text{subject to } \mathbf{D}_x^T \mathbf{D}_x = \mathbf{I}_{m \times m}, \mathbf{J}_x^T \mathbf{D}_x = \mathbf{0}. \tag{1}$$

where d is the length of input feature vector and m is the number of atoms in the dictionary $\mathbf{D}_x$. The dictionary $\bar{\mathbf{D}}_x$ has two sub dictionaries: $\mathbf{D}_x$ is the orthogonal dictionary which has to be learnt from the given training data samples and $\mathbf{J}_x$ which can be used to control the required number of orthogonal dictionary atoms. The matrix $\mathbf{J}_x$ is set to a null matrix in our framework so that $\bar{\mathbf{D}}_x = \mathbf{D}_x$ and hence the dictionary atoms can span the entire space of d-dimensional vectors since they are orthogonal to each other (as per the constraint in Eq. (1)). The dictionary $\mathbf{D}_x$ is initialized to DCT matrix of size $d \times d$. During the ith iteration, we have $\mathbf{D}_x^i$ and the task is to find out $\mathbf{\Lambda}_x^i$ and is formulated as below:

$$\hat{\mathbf{\Lambda}}_x^i = \arg \min_{\mathbf{\Lambda}_x^i} \| \mathbf{X} - [\mathbf{J}_x, \mathbf{D}_x^i] \mathbf{\Lambda}_x^i \|_2^2 + \alpha \| \mathbf{\Lambda}_x^i \|_0^2$$
$$\text{subject to } \mathbf{D}_x^{i^T} \mathbf{D}_x^i = \mathbf{I}, \mathbf{J}_x^T \mathbf{D}_x^i = \mathbf{0}. \tag{2}$$

The optimization problem in (2) has a unique solution [24] and is given by:

$$\hat{\mathbf{\Lambda}}_x^i = T_\gamma(\bar{\mathbf{D}}_x^{i^T} \mathbf{X}) \tag{3}$$

Here $T_\gamma(\mathbf{v})$ represents a hard threshold operation on the vector $\mathbf{v}$ and we experimentally tuned the parameter γ. The objective function to update the dictionary at i^{th} iteration can be formulated as:

$$\hat{\mathbf{D}}_x^i = \arg \min_{\mathbf{D}_x^i} \| \mathbf{X} - [\mathbf{J}_x, \mathbf{D}_x^i] \mathbf{\Lambda}_x^{i-1} \|_2^2$$
$$\text{subject to } \mathbf{D}_x^{i^T} \mathbf{D}_x^i = \mathbf{I}, \mathbf{J}_x^T \mathbf{D}_x^i = \mathbf{0}. \tag{4}$$

Since the two dictionaries are orthogonal and span the same/similar space in the two domains, we can assume that their exists a one-to-one correspondence of the dictionary atoms. Consider $\mathbf{D}_x$ and $\mathbf{D}_y$ be the orthogonal dictionaries learnt from the two domains $\mathbf{X}$ and $\mathbf{Y}$. The one-to-one correspondence between the dictionary atoms is determined in a common space (here CCA space) and then the dictionaries are aligned similar to the subspace alignment approach [25]. A metric learning algorithm (here LSML [26]) is used to make the sparse coefficients discriminative. Please refer to [9] for more details of this baseline algorithm.

During the testing stage, given a low resolution NIR probe image, we need to identify the correct match from the database of gallery faces, which consists of HR visible images. In our work, the gallery and probe images differ in pose, illumination, resolution and spectral domain. We first compute the sparse coefficients from the respective aligned orthogonal dictionaries computed in the training stage for both the probe and gallery images. The sparse coefficients are transformed into the common space using the metric learnt using LSML approach.

3.2   Proposed Re-ranking Algorithm

Given a probe, the above procedure gives a list of gallery images, where the first image has the highest similarity with the probe, followed by the second one and so on. Now, we describe the proposed re-ranking algorithm which works with this retrieved set of images for improving the matching accuracy. It is based on two assumptions, (1) Even though the correct match may not appear in the first rank, it may appear in the top k-nearest neighbours; (2) An image can be very well described by taking into account its relation with some reference set of images [2].

Many of the existing algorithms including the considered baseline algorithm uses the subject labels for retrieving the correct match. In this work, we use the additional information of the relation with the reference set to improve the matching performance. The idea is that though the subject is captured in either VIS or NIR mode, his/her relation w.r.t the selected reference set should not change significantly in either of the domains. Let $\{\mathbf{r}_1, \mathbf{r}_2, \ldots, \mathbf{r}_{N_r}\} \in \mathcal{R}^d$ represent the features of N_r number of reference faces. If y_{te} is the probe face (sparse coefficient vector in the common space), then $\eta = [\eta_1, \eta_2, \ldots, \eta_{N_r}] \in \mathcal{R}^{N_r}$ is the vector which encodes the information (in our case distance) of how the probe face y_{te} is related to the set of reference faces. Each entry in the distance vector is computed as follows:

$$\eta_i = \parallel y_{te} - \mathbf{r}_i \parallel_2^2 \tag{5}$$

Similarly, we compute the vectors for the top k-nearest neighbors from the gallery faces for the given probe. Then the distances between the vectors of the probe and the k nearest galleries are computed. We take the weighted sum of previous distances (that are computed using transformed sparse coefficient vectors) and the new distances obtained with the computed vectors and then the first nearest neighbor is taken as the correct identity for the given probe. In our experiments, we used the training subjects itself as the reference subjects and we analyze the performance of our approach by varying the number of reference faces. In our experiments, we observe that 10 reference subjects give a reasonable boost in accuracy.

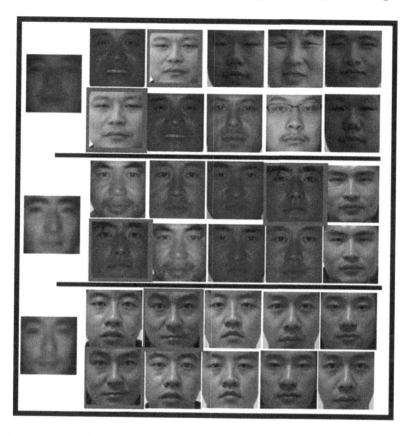

Fig. 2. Illustration of retrieval performance of our proposed re-ranking framework and comparison with the method [9]. For each probe (left column), the top row shows the 5 most similar images in the gallery for the approach [9] and the bottom row shows the results using the proposed framework. The red boxes indicate the correct identity for the given probe. (Color figure online)

The importance of these distance vectors is illustrated in Fig. 2. In the figure, for a given probe (shown in left column), the top row shows the 5 most similar images in the gallery for the approach [9] and the bottom row shows the results using the proposed framework. If we take the second example in the figure, the correct identity (marked with red box) as per [9] appears at the fourth position. By employing the proposed re-ranking approach, the distances are improved so that the correct match comes to the first position.

4   Experimental Results

Extensive experiments are conducted on CASIA NIR-VIS 2.0 database [8] as this is the largest publicly available database for matching NIR faces with VIS faces. The dataset consists of VIS-NIR images from 725 subjects. The dataset was collected over the years in 4 sessions. There are 1–22 visual and 5–50 NIR images per subject. There are 10 training-testing splits recommended by the authors. The subjects in the training and the corresponding testing set are non-overlapping, and the percentage of subjects in the training and testing set are both nearly 50%.

But in the database, both the VIS and NIR faces are high resolution images with size 128×128. So we converted the NIR faces into low resolution by down-sampling them to 20×20. They are then upsampled to the original size (128×128) so that the same features can be computed for all the images. We follow the same protocol as described in the database except that the NIR images used are of low resolution to mimic the real-world scenario. The rank-1 accuracy and the standard deviation of our approach over the 10 folds as per the protocol of the database is reported in Table 1. In all the cases, VGG face features (pool5, fc6 and fc7 features) [27] are used as image features. To reduce the dimensionality, we applied PCA and took the first 2500 coefficients as the feature vector.

First, we evaluated several algorithms on this modified CASIA NIR-VIS 2.0 database to create the benchmark results. Specifically, we evaluated several correlation-based approaches, metric learning and dictionary learning approaches. We have directly taken the codes from respective authors. The results of these approaches and also of the baseline algorithm [9] is given in Table 1 along with the results of the proposed re-ranking approach. We observe that the proposed re-ranking approach is able to improve upon the baseline approach and is superior to all the other compared approaches.

Table 1. Comparison of the performance (Rank-1 (%) ± Std) of the proposed approach on CASIA NIR-VIS 2.0 database [8] (NIR faces are of low resolution and the VIS faces are of high resolution) with state-of-the-art approaches.

Method	Rank-1 (%) ± **Std**
CBFD [28]	26.65 ± 0.35
GMA [29]	34.78 ± 0.89
CCA [30]	35.48 ± 1.46
Mean CCA [30]	35.93 ± 1.74
MvDA [31]	39.39 ± 1.86
Cluster CCA [30]	42.21 ± 1.55
Randomized kernel CCA [32]	45.59 ± 1.13
Dictionary alignment [9]	58.35 ± 1.37
Proposed Approach	$\mathbf{60.21} \pm 1.26$

Table 2. Effect of increasing number of reference images N_r. Fold 3 is chosen to conduct the experiment.

N_r	10	20	30	50	100	200
Rank-1 (%)	57.20	58.37	58.71	58.74	58.92	59.38

4.1   Analysis of the Proposed Approach

Now, we present some analysis done for the proposed approach.

Effect of Different Number of Reference Images: We evaluated with different number of reference images N_r which are used to compute the distance vectors and the variation of the Rank-1 recognition rate is given in Table 2. For this analysis, we took the third fold of the database protocol.

Effect of Applying Super-Resolution on LR NIR Images: One way of matching LR against HR faces is to first apply super resolution (SR) on LR images to improve their resolution and then perform the recognition. We experimented with three state-of-the-art super resolution approaches SR1 [33], SR2 [34] and SR3 [35] to make LR NIR images (of sizes 40×40 and 60×60) to HR and applied our approach to see the effectiveness. The resultant rank-1 recognition rates are shown in Fig. 3. We observe that the performance increases using SR techniques.

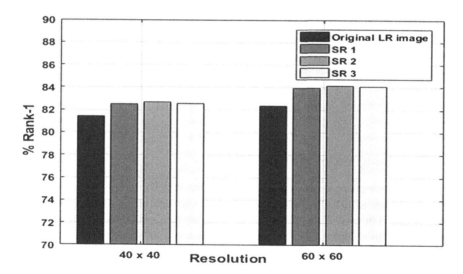

Fig. 3. Illustration of effect of applying super resolution techniques: SR1 [33], SR2 [34] and SR3 [35] on LR NIR faces before performing matching.

Effect of Different Probe Resolutions: To analyze the effectiveness of the proposed approach across different probe resolutions, we evaluated the approach with different resolutions of probe faces. We observe from Table 3 that the performance remains stable till probe resolution of around 40×40 and then suddenly decreases drastically, which also demonstrates the importance of handling this problem.

Table 3. Performance of the proposed approach for different NIR probe resolutions.

Resolution	Rank-1 (%)
10×10	24.38
20×20	59.45
40×40	82.35
60×60	83.80
80×80	84.28

Effect of LR Visible Images on the Performance: We also analyze the effect of resolution of the gallery VIS images. For this, we conducted experiments by varying the VIS face resolutions and the recognition accuracies are presented in Table 4. The NIR faces are fixed to the resolution 20×20. We observe that the accuracies are almost stable till gallery resolution of 20×20 and then suddenly drops.

Table 4. Performance of the proposed approach for different VIS gallery resolutions. Probe resolution is 20×20.

Resolution	Rank-1 (%)
10×10	24.59
20×20	51.36
40×40	58.51
60×60	58.16
80×80	59.03

5 Conclusion and Future Work

In this work, we proposed a re-ranking algorithm which can be used as an add-on to any existing algorithm for the problem of low resolution heterogeneous face recognition. The overall approach does not require one-to-one paired images for learning the dictionaries. Extensive experiments are conducted to show the usefulness of the proposed approach as well as the importance of the problem attempted in this work. Currently, there are no publicly available database which addresses this problem which has surveillance quality NIR images with large number of subjects. Collecting our own surveillance quality LR NIR database so as to advance research in this important field will be one of the future works.

Acknowledgment. This work is partly supported through a research grant from DeITY, India.

References

1. Zou, W.W., Yuen, P.C.: Very low resolution face recognition problem. IEEE Trans. Image Process. **21**(1), 327–340 (2012)
2. Mudunuri, S.P., Biswas, S.: Low resolution face recognition across variations in pose and illumination. IEEE Trans. Pattern Anal. Mach. Intell. **38**(5), 1034–1040 (2016)
3. Shekhar, S., Patel, V.M., Chellappa, R.: Synthesis-based robust low resolution face recognition. arXiv preprint arXiv:1707.02733 (2017)
4. Chu, Y., Ahmad, T., Bebis, G., Zhao, L.: Low-resolution face recognition with single sample per person. Sig. Process. **141**, 144–157 (2017)
5. Haghighat, M., Abdel-Mottaleb, M.: Low resolution face recognition in surveillance systems using discriminant correlation analysis. In: IEEE International Conference on Automatic Face and Gesture Recognition, pp. 912–917 (2017)
6. Jiang, J., Hu, R., Wang, Z., Cai, Z.: CDMMA: coupled discriminant multi-manifold analysis for matching low-resolution face images. Sig. Process. **124**, 162–172 (2016)
7. Ghosh, S., Keshari, R., Singh, R., Vatsa, M.: Face identification from low resolution near-infrared images. In: IEEE International Conference on Image Processing, pp. 938–942 (2016)
8. Li, S., Yi, D., Lei, Z., Liao, S.: The CASIA NIR-VIS 2.0 face database. In: IEEE Conference on Computer Vision and Pattern Recognition Workshops, pp. 348–353 (2013)
9. Mudunuri, S.P., Biswas, S.: Dictionary alignment for low-resolution and heterogeneous face recognition. In: IEEE Winter Conference on Applications of Computer Vision, pp. 1115–1123 (2017)
10. Yang, M.C., Wei, C.P., Yeh, Y.R., Wang, Y.C.F.: Recognition at a long distance: very low resolution face recognition and hallucination. In: International Conference on Biometrics, pp. 237–242 (2015)
11. Moutafis, P., Kakadiaris, I.A.: Semi-coupled basis and distance metric learning for cross-domain matching: application to low-resolution face recognition. In: International Joint Conference on Biometrics, pp. 1–8 (2014)
12. Li, J., Chen, Z., Liu, C.: Low-resolution face recognition of multi-scale blocking CS-LBP and weighted PCA. Int. J. Pattern Recogn. Artif. Intell. **30**(08), 1–13 (2016)
13. Bodla, N., Zheng, J., Xu, H., Chen, J.C., Castillo, C., Chellappa, R.: Deep heterogeneous feature fusion for template-based face recognition. In: IEEE Winter Conference on Applications of Computer Vision, pp. 586–595 (2017)
14. de Freitas Pereira, T., Marcel, S.: Heterogeneous face recognition using inter-session variability modelling. In: IEEE Conference on Computer Vision and Pattern Recognition Workshops, pp. 111–118 (2016)
15. Xing, X., Wang, K.: Couple manifold discriminant analysis with bipartite graph embedding for low-resolution face recognition. Sig. Process. **125**, 329–335 (2016)
16. Wang, Z., Chang, S., Yang, Y., Liu, D., Huang, T.S.: Studying very low resolution recognition using deep networks. In: IEEE Conference on Computer Vision and Pattern Recognition, pp. 4792–4800 (2016)
17. Reale, C., Nasrabadi, N.M., Kwon, H., Chellappa, R.: Seeing the forest from the trees: a holistic approach to near-infrared heterogeneous face recognition. In: IEEE Conference on Computer Vision and Pattern Recognition Workshops, pp. 54–62 (2016)

18. He, R., Wu, X., Sun, Z., Tan, T.: Learning invariant deep representation for NIR-VIS face recognition. In: Association for Advancements in Artificial Intelligence, pp. 2000–2006 (2017)

19. Sarfraz, M.S., Stiefelhagen, R.: Deep perceptual mapping for thermal to visible face recognition. arXiv preprint arXiv:1507.02879 (2015)

20. Liu, X., Song, L., Wu, X., Tan, T.: Transferring deep representation for NIR-VIS heterogeneous face recognition. In: International Conference on Biometrics, pp. 1–8 (2016)

21. Saxena, S., Verbeek, J.: Heterogeneous face recognition with CNNs. In: European Conference on Computer Vision Workshops, pp. 483–491 (2016)

22. Wang, S., Zhang, L., Liang, Y., Pan, Q.: Semi-coupled dictionary learning with applications to image super-resolution and photo-sketch synthesis. In: IEEE Conference on Computer Vision and Pattern Recognition, pp. 2216–2223 (2012)

23. Huang, D.A., Frank Wang, Y.C.: Coupled dictionary and feature space learning with applications to cross-domain image synthesis and recognition. In: IEEE International Conference on Computer Vision, pp. 2496–2503 (2013)

24. Bao, C., Cai, J.F., Ji, H.: Fast sparsity-based orthogonal dictionary learning for image restoration. In: IEEE International Conference on Computer Vision, pp. 3384–3391 (2013)

25. Fernando, B., Habrard, A., Sebban, M., Tuytelaars, T.: Unsupervised visual domain adaptation using subspace alignment. In: IEEE International Conference on Computer Vision, pp. 2960–2967 (2013)

26. Koestinger, M., Hirzer, M., Wohlhart, P., Roth, P.M., Bischof, H.: Large scale metric learning from equivalence constraints. In: IEEE Conference on Computer Vision and Pattern Recognition, pp 2288–2295 (2012)

27. Parkhi, O.M., Vedaldi, A., Zisserman, A.: Deep face recognition. In: British Machine Vision Conference (2015)

28. Lu, J., Liong, V.E., Zhou, X., Zhou, J.: Learning compact binary face descriptor for face recognition. IEEE Trans. Pattern Anal. Mach. Intell. $37(10)$, 2041–2056 (2015)

29. Sharma, A., Kumar, A., Daume, H., Jacobs, D.W.: Generalized multiview analysis: a discriminative latent space. In: IEEE Conference on Computer Vision and Pattern Recognition, pp. 2160–2167 (2012)

30. Rasiwasia, N., Mahajan, D., Mahadevan, V., Aggarwal, G.: Cluster canonical correlation analysis. In: Artificial Intelligence and Statistics, pp. 823–831 (2014)

31. Kan, M., Shan, S., Zhang, H., Lao, S., Chen, X.: Multi-view discriminant analysis. IEEE Trans. Pattern Anal. Mach. Intell. $38(1)$, 188–194 (2016)

32. Lopez-Paz, D., Sra, S., Smola, A., Ghahramani, Z., Schölkopf, B.: Randomized nonlinear component analysis. In: International Conference on Machine Learning, pp. 1359–1367 (2014)

33. Kim, K.I., Kwon, Y.: Single-image super-resolution using sparse regression and natural image prior. IEEE Trans. Pattern Anal. Mach. Intell. $32(6)$, 1127–1133 (2010)

34. Yang, J., Wright, J., Huang, T.S., Ma, Y.: Image super-resolution via sparse representation. IEEE Trans. Image Process. $19(11)$, 2861–2873 (2010)

35. Huang, J.B., Singh, A., Ahuja, N.: Single image super-resolution from transformed self-exemplars. In: IEEE Conference on Computer Vision and Pattern Recognition, pp. 5197–5206 (2015)

Description Based Person Identification:
Use of Clothes Color and Type

Priyansh Shah[1], Mehul S. Raval[1(✉)], Shvetal Pandya[1],
Sanjay Chaudhary[1], Anand Laddha[2], and Hiren Galiyawala[1]

[1] School of Engineering and Applied Science, Ahmedabad University,
Ahmedabad, India
{priyansh.s.btechi13,mehul.raval,sanjay.chaudhary,
hiren.galiyawala}@ahduni.edu.in, shvetalnp@gmail.com
[2] Bhabha Atomic Research Centre (BARC), Mumbai, India
anandl@barc.gov.in

Abstract. Surveillance videos can be searched for person identification using soft-biometrics. The proposed paper use clothes color and their type for person identification in a video. A height model and the ISCC-NBS color descriptors are used for human localization and color classification. Experimental results are demonstrated on the custom video database and compared with Gaussian mixture model based search model. It is shown that the proposed approach identifies a person correctly with high accuracy and outperforms Gaussian mixture based search model. The paper also develops a new vocabulary to describe the clothing type for a human.

Keywords: Color model · Classification · Person identification
Soft-biometrics

1 Introduction

Conventionally primary biometric based on physical traits are used for person identification [1], e.g. fingerprint, iris, voice, ears, palm print. Extraction of such trait requires; high quality equipments, controlled environment and cooperation from a person. Video surveillance systems have been used for monitoring wide area in real time [2,3]. Moreover, manual inefficiency has motivated work on automated video search for person identification. The task of person identification in video is very challenging due to occlusion, light condition, camera quality, pose, and zoom [4]. Person identification in video also require extraction of precise features which is possible only from near or mid field view sequences.

Recently researchers are pursuing person identification based on soft biometrics [5]. These traits are naturally described by humans e.g. gender, height, cloth color and type, hair color, ethnicity, and body accessory [6]. Soft biometrics are created in a way human naturally describes their peers. Moreover, such traits can be extracted from a poor quality video without subject's cooperation and they are simple to understand. Though soft biometrics provide information

© Springer Nature Singapore Pte Ltd. 2018
R. Rameshan et al. (Eds.): NCVPRIPG 2017, CCIS 841, pp. 457–469, 2018.
https://doi.org/10.1007/978-981-13-0020-2_40

about an individual but they lack distinctiveness. Also, search based on single trait is inefficient and unimodal systems under noisy conditions are inaccurate with high error rate [5]. Therefore, multiple traits are fused to decrease error rate and also forgery in many traits together is more likely to fail [7]. One of the challenge in using soft biometrics is to map human descriptions to computer understandable labels, which needs development of a special vocabulary.

Due to large number of soft biometrics it is important to find most discriminative ones. A study [8] identified 13 such traits including color. The use of color has following advantages; 1. color has better immunity against noise and affine transforms [9]; 2. color perception is also independent of dimension, direction and view angle [9]; 3. color also provide coarse information about a subject. The discussions between authors of the proposed work and local police officers also suggested that clothes color is amongst most distinctive trait received during investigation. Therefore, the proposed work uses clothes color and type as modalities to identify person(s).

Any color model which correctly maps eye perception increases classification accuracy. It has been shown in [10] that CIE-Lab color space is better than any other color model. It is designed to imitate non-linear eye responses and match human perception [11]. Therefore, the present work uses CIE-Lab color space. The identification through clothes color includes: (1) cloth segmentation; (2) cloth color classification. Mogelmose et al. [12] used part based histogram for cloth color identification. The upper and lower body part is divided into 20 bins per R-G-B channels to create 120 bins histogram. An undefined zone in middle body is not used for histogram computation. The subjects within 4 m of camera is only considered for re-identification. The system exhibits weakness for similarly dressed persons and assumes no occlusion. Moon and Pan [13] proposed an identification method using height and clothing color. Colors are extracted using octree-based color quantization technique and height is extracted using geometry. Euclidean distance is used for computing similarities.

Chien et al. [14] proposed a segmentation-and-descriptor based tracking algorithm with a Human Color Structure Descriptor (HCSD), where colors of body, legs, and shoes of each person are extracted. Hu et al. [15] modeled color distribution by creating color histograms for head, torso, and legs of each person and used condensation algorithm for person tracking. Nakajima et al. [16] extracted normalized color histograms and shaped features by representing each person by its color and shape based features and trained support vector machine (SVM) for person recognition. The method was made for indoor environment where lighting and background were invariant. Hahnel et al. [17] extended [16] by incorporating additional color, shape, and texture features. They used Radial Basis Function (RBF) classifier and a nearest-neighbor classifier for comparison. Ma et al. [18] developed a image representation for person re-identification named Gaussian descriptor based on Local Features (GaLF) which used single Gaussian model to represent color features.

Park et al. [19] designed a Visual Search Engine (ViSE) in multi-camera network. Clothing colors, height, and body build were extracted to represent the subject. Color matching is done by considering hue and the ten bin histogram.

The decision threshold is derived from the standard color charts. Jang et al. [20] proposed the method based on a color histogram and dominant color descriptor (DCD). Zhang et al. [9] proposed a person re-identification technique based on clothing features using spatial pyramid matching (SPM) and Gaussian Mixture model (GMM). The paper used R-G-B as dominant colors where dark or poor contrast images generated poor results. Kao et al. [21] proposed hierarchical structure to represent dominant colors and their probabilities by using GMM. A histogram is created only for torso color. The image is considered as a mixture of 5 Gaussian in R-G-B color space. The color model is learnt from pixels inside the bounding box.

Denman et al. [22] proposed an approach which used cloth color and height to build an *avatar* to search. A single dominant color is selected from 11 *culture colors* [10]. A GMM is trained in CIE-Lab space using patches from surveillance videos and no compensation technique was applied to deal with varying illumination. Video clips contained only *single* person in a frame and major error resulted due to ambiguity in color perception. Halstead et al. [23] extended [22] by incorporating many soft-biometrics like clothing type. The GMM is trained for each color in CIE-Lab space using patches from the videos of same camera set. Model heavily depends on range and number of patches used for training GMM. Summarzing, the GMM trained on color patches benefits due to *customized* learning. But it has some distinct disadvantages; 1. patches extraction is time consuming and noisy; 2. training GMMs over noisy patches may cause misclassification for *boundary* colors, e.g. light pink is treated as white; 3. trained model cannot be *generalized*; 4. it should retrained for newer set of conditions.

Another way of making color classification robust is to use a flexible color designation system; Inter-Society Color Council and National Bureau of Standards (ISCC-NBS) is one such system [24]. It uses 10 hues (pink, red, orange, yellow, brown, olive, yellow green, green, blue, purple) and 3 neutral categories(white, black, and gray) as Level-1 set. It is further divided into 29 Level-2 colors (e.g. reddish orange) while Level-3 has 267 colors compiled by using hue with modifiers (e.g. deep reddish orange). In this system colors are fairly well defined making color classification easy and accurate. An ideal color model would define tight color cluster such that intra and inter cluster distances are balanced. The ISCC-NBS defines such color clusters. This also motivates their use in the proposed approach. The 13 basic colors at Level-1 represents the coarsest clusters while 267 clusters at Level-3 are finest. The Level-1 representation sometimes can fall short to represent color exactness, while Level-3 seems to be an overkill. Level-2 set is a good balance between coarse and fine color clusters. It provides moderate color quantization and it is better equipped to match query given by a human. Therefore, the proposed work uses ISCC-NBS Level-2 centroids [25] for color classification.

Advantages of the proposed work as compared to GMM based approaches [9, 21–23, 26] are as follows;

1. It is generalized framework.
2. It does not need explicit patch collection which reduces noise.

3. It works on real world data.
4. It is a flexible framework which can scale from 13 basic colors in Level-1 to 267 in Level-3. This helps in specifying color at different levels; from coarse to fine.

The proposed work can identify criminal(s) using clothing information given by eye-witnesses at the crime scene. It should be noted that the proposed approach may produce multiple matches in a video with many subjects. The proposed approach takes clothes color and their type as input tuple for each individual. The algorithm is also capable of simultaneously handling such multiple tuples. The output will show a bounding box over matched individuals. The exactness in identification can be increased by using additional information like gender, age, hair color, and height.

The remainder of this paper is organized as follows: Sect. 2 presents the proposed approach; Sect. 3 has experimental results and discussions; Sect. 4 concludes the paper and outlines future work.

2   The Proposed Approach

Figure 1 shows block diagram of the proposed approach. A motion segmentation based on frame differencing is applied to detect a person. Morphological *closing* is then applied to reduce noise and a blob detection separates out region of interest (ROI) i.e. a person. Using the height model and clothing type, a search window is formed in which color classification is done using the ISCC-NBS model. A dominant color in window is determined using the color histogram and finally matching modules delivers the match.

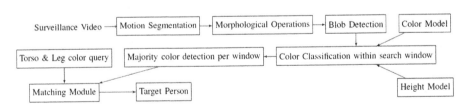

Fig. 1. Block diagram of the proposed approach

2.1   Height Model

A human body can be divided into three main parts: head, torso, and legs. An average human body is 7.5 *heads* high [27,28]. The face is about 1 *heads*, torso is 3 *heads*, and legs is 3.5 *heads* high [27,28]. The proposed height model is depicted in Fig. 2. The perfect bounding box is outlined in blue. The human body is divided into three-parts as follows: 0% to P_1 as head; P_1 to P_2 as torso; P_2 to 100% as legs. The values of P_1, P_2 are dependent on the clothing type.

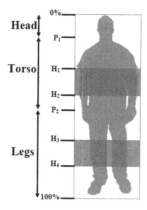

Fig. 2. Height model (Color figure online)

2.2   Color Model

The proposed work uses 11 culture color namely; pink, red, orange, brown, yellow, green, blue, purple, white, gray and black [23]. Further, culture color is mapped to finer Level-2 centroids. Table 1 captures this relationship. The centroid number for each Level-2 color is also specified in the Table 1. A pixel in the search window is compared with these 29 centroids and assigned a label for which distance is minimum.

2.3   Searching for the Clothes Type

During motion segmentation bounding box is formed only if its area measured by number of pixels is greater than threshold τ. This provides a non maximal separation and removes partial bounding box. In the proposed paper, new terminology has been developed to label clothing types: *average torso* is used for shirt, t-shirt, short kurta or any torso clothing of similar length; *long torso* is used for lengthy kurta or any clothing with length more than the *average torso*. *Average legs* is used for jeans, trousers, track pants, pajamas, leggings, or any clothing with similar length; *short legs* is used for shorts or any leg clothing with length shorter than *average legs*.

In this paper, torso is considered as the body region covered by *average* or *long* torso clothing while legs is considered as the clothing covered by *average legs* or *short legs*. Depending on combination of clothing type, the values of P_1, P_2 are shown in Table 2. The % values in Table 2 are with respect to top of the perfectly fitting bounding box. It can be seen that P_1 (head) in all the three cases is 20%, while P_2 varies depending on torso clothes.

2.4   Searching for Clothes Color

Figure 2 shows brown search windows for torso (H_1 to H_2) and legs (H_3 to H_4). Height of the search window is dependent on the clothing type. Table 2 shows

Table 1. Mapping between culture color and Level-2 colors

Culture	Level-2
Pink	1. Pink
	3. Yellowish Pink
	25. Purplish Pink
Red	2. Red
	4. Reddish Orange
	5. Reddish Brown
Orange	6. Orange
	8. Orange Yellow
Brown	7. Brown
	9. Yellowish Brown
	11. Olive Brown
Yellow	10. Yellow
	12. Greenish Yellow
	13. Olive
Green	14. Yellow Green
	15. Olive Green
	16. Yellowish Green
	17. Green
Blue	18. Bluish Green
	19. Greenish Blue
	20. Blue
	21. Purplish Blue
	22. Violet
Purple	23. Purple
	24. Reddish Purple
	26. Purplish Red
White	27. White
Gray	28. Gray
Black	29. Black

Table 2. Relationship between height model and clothing type

Clothing type	P_1	P_2	H_1	H_2	H_3	H_4
Avg. torso and avg. legs	20%	55%	33.33%	40%	66.66%	80%
Avg. torso and short legs	20%	55%	33.33%	40%	60%	65%
Long torso and avg. legs	20%	70%	33.33%	40%	75%	90%

H_1 to H_4 based on the clothing type which are empirically chosen to determine dominant color with high precision. For *average* (Avg.) or *long* torso the range 33% to 40% determine the dominant color with high confidence. The legs window varies depending on the clothing. The *short legs* is fixed at 60% to 65% from the top. The window occupies 75% to 90% for *long torso and average legs*.

The width of the search window is kept less than the bounding box to avoid background cluttering. The CIEDE2000 [29] metric is used to compute distance between a pixel in the search window and 29 Level-2 centroids. A pixel is assigned label of the nearest centroid as specified in Table 1. After all pixels are labeled, histogram is formed to find dominant color for torso and legs.

3   Experimental Results

The constrained video dataset is built to negate segmentation error. The assumptions while capturing videos are as follows: 1. frame has person(s) in upright position with visible head and torso; 2. background is fairly uncluttered; 3. clothes color are different for each subject; clothes color and clothing style of the person remains same throughout the sequence. The videos were captured using 4 Mega pixel (MP) bullet network color camera. The videos were recorded with help of 15 student volunteers. Such 18 sequences were recorded at 20 frames per second (fps) and 1080×720 pixels resolution. Each clip covers at most three subjects. The true positive (TP), i.e. the percentage of frames in which subjects are correctly identified is used as the performance measure.

3.1   Person Localization Evaluation

Threshold for frame difference is set to 30 and it has been empirically determined after testing several videos from the dataset. The τ for bounding box formation is set to 72; i.e. one-tenth of the frame height (720). Figure 3 shows results of person identification as described by the input tuple. The bounding box in Fig. 3 represents correct identification. The linguistic queries are: Fig. 3(a) green kurta and blue leggings (*long torso, avg. legs*), Fig. 3(b) red t-shirt and black leggings (*avg. torso, avg. legs*), Fig. 3(c) black shirt and brown pants (*avg. torso, avg. legs*), Fig. 3(d) blue shirt and blue jeans (*avg. torso, avg. legs*), Fig. 3(e) white t-shirt and blue jeans (*avg. torso, avg. legs*), Fig. 3(f) gray t-shirt and blue shorts (*avg. torso, short legs*), Fig. 3(g) red t-shirt and blue jeans (*avg. torso, avg. legs*), Fig. 3(h) red t-shirt and black trousers (*avg. torso, avg. legs*), Fig. 3(i) pink t-shirt and blue jeans (*avg. torso, avg. legs*), Fig. 3(j) white t-shirt and blue jeans (*avg. torso, avg. legs*) and blue t-shirt and gray shorts (*avg. torso, short legs*), Fig. 3(k) has two subjects with gray t-shirt and blue jeans (*avg. torso, avg. legs*) and one subject with black shirt and blue jeans (*avg. torso, avg. legs*), Fig. 3(l) black shirt and blue jeans (*avg. torso, avg. legs*) and yellow short kurta and blue jeans (*avg. torso, avg. legs*), Fig. 3(m) blue t-shirt and black leggings (*avg. torso, avg. legs*), Fig. 3(n) purple t-shirt and blue shorts (*avg. torso, short. legs*), and Fig. 3(o) yellow t-shirt and blue jeans (*avg. torso, avg. legs*).

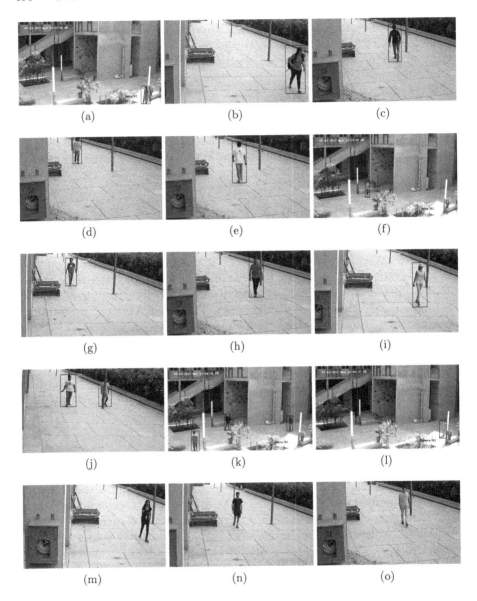

Fig. 3. Outputs by the proposed system (Color figure online)

The proposed approach is able to deal with different colors and type of clothing. The system correctly identifies person in near field (viz. Fig. 3(b)) or far field region (viz. Fig. 3(f) and (l)), frontal pose (cf. Fig. 3(g) and (i)) or back pose (cf. Fig. 3(c) and (e)). It also correctly identifies a person irrespective of minor occlusion (cf. Fig. 3(j)). Note that Fig. 3(j) has two subjects while Fig. 3(k) has three persons. In both the cases all subjects are correctly identified by the proposed system.

Table 3. Accuracy for torso and legs. A: No. of frames with correct identification in the proposed method; B: TP rate in % for the proposed method; C: No. of frames with correct identification for GMM; D: TP rate in % for GMM

Seq. No.	Total frames	A	B	C	D
1	550	477	86.72%	299	54.36%
2	380	269	70.78%	261	68.68%
3	470	252	53.61%	84	17.87%
4	600	377	62.83%	14	2.33%
5	280	156	55.71%	261	93.21%
6	440	354	80.45%	347	78.86%
7	430	347	80.69%	333	77.44%
8	800	602	75.25%	616	77%
9	300	94	31.33%	206	68.66%
10	300	53	17.66%	192	64%
11	450	297	66%	108	24%
12	400	320	80%	260	65%
13	220	103	46.81%	161	73.18%
14	220	129	58.63%	30	13.63%
15	220	99	45%	27	12.27%
16	360	324	90%	6	1.66%
17	360	303	84.16%	0	0%
18	360	297	82.5%	0	0%
Total	7140	4853	67.96%	3205	44.88%

The proposed approach is compared with 11 culture color [10] based GMM trained on patches of custom videos and SAIVT database [23]. The approach operates in CIE-Lab space without using normalization. The comparisons of color and type for both torso and legs are shown in Table 3. It can be observed that on average TP for the proposed method (67.96%) is better than GMM (44.88%) approach. In another variation, experiments are also performed to identify person based on the color and type of torso clothes. The results of experimentation are shown in Table 4. It turns out that average TP for the proposed method (83.99%) is better than GMM (55.44%). Interestingly the average TP rates in this case are higher than shown in Table 3.

An attempt to narrow down search space and also to reduce false positives is made by performing logical AND operation between separate results of torso and leg colors. However, it affects TP and reduces effectiveness. In this experiment TP for legs is found to be lower than torso. This results in lower accuracy when torso and legs colors are combined. TP for legs is lower due to different shades and variation in color of jeans. For instance, light blue jeans are labeled as white or sometimes gray because of high brightness (cf. Fig. 3(o)), whereas dark blue

Table 4. Accuracy for only torso. A: No. of frames with correct identification in the proposed method; B: TP rate in % for the proposed method; C: No. of frames with correct identification for GMM; D: TP rate in % for GMM

Seq. No.	Total frames	A	B	C	D
1	550	514	93.45%	389	70.72%
2	380	348	91.57%	376	80%
3	470	333	70.85%	93	19.78%
4	600	531	88.5%	20	3.33%
5	280	238	85%	264	94.28%
6	440	360	81.81%	371	84.31%
7	430	369	85.81%	361	83.95%
8	800	702	87.75%	647	80.87%
9	300	234	78%	238	79.33%
10	300	270	90%	292	97.33%
11	450	300	66.66%	109	24.22%
12	400	326	81.5%	261	65.25%
13	220	173	78.63%	189	85.9%
14	220	186	84.64%	186	84.64%
15	220	143	65%	156	70.9%
16	360	325	90.27%	7	1.94%
17	360	339	94.16%	0	0%
18	360	306	85%	0	0%
Total	7140	5997	83.99%	3959	55.44%

color for T-shirt (cf. Fig. 3(m)) or short (Fig. 3(n)) is labeled black because of low brightness.

In case multiple person wear same type of clothes e.g. Fig. 3(k), then color plays a dominant role in person identification. In another variation multiple subjects in frame wear clothes of same color e.g. Fig. 3(k), then clothing type is used to narrow down the search. However, if many persons put on clothes with same color and type then additional information like gender, age, height, is required to uniquely identify the subjects.

While training GMM, enormous overlap between color patches were observed in 2D scatter plot of 'a', 'b' components of CIE-Lab. This means GMM is likely to fail for boundary colors like cyan or greenish blue. Further validation for color classification using the proposed approach and GMM is done based on; 1. 528 images of e-bay database [30]; 2. 69 boundary colors from Level-3 of the ISCC-NBS. The result of these experiments are shown in Table 5. It can be observed from Tables 3, 4, and 5 that on average color classification accuracy of the proposed method is better than GMM. Boundary colors like cyan or greenish blue is poorly classified owing to significant color overlap between clusters resulting into

Table 5. Color classification accuracy

Database	GMM TP (%)	Proposed TP (%)
E-bay color dataset	79.35%	81.43%
ISCC-NBS	59.42%	72.46%

ambiguity. Whereas, in the proposed method color centroids are non-overlapping resulting into well defined boundaries from one color cluster to another resulting in non-dubious classification. The proposed method can do a *coarse* color classification using Level-1 colors only or very *fine grain* using all 267 hues at Level-3. The proposed method can also overcome the camera sensing issue by *forceful* mapping of perceived color to its *true* color.

The proposed system also mis-classifies, e.g. in Fig. 3(n), *short legs* is actually *dark blue* and classifier labels it as *black* color and similarly in Fig. 3(m), *avg. torso* is actually *dark blue* and classifier labels it as *black* color. This is due to low intensity and also color tone being very close to black. Whereas in Fig. 3(o), *avg. legs* is actually *light blue* and classifier labels it as *white* color. This is due to high intensity and also color tone being very close to white. The proposed approach can also fail when eye witness cannot correctly perceive and describe colors.

4   Conclusion

The paper presented person identification through clothes color and type. It is shown that the proposed approach works quite well under various constraints. It is dependent on motion segmentation and an error in it may reduce accuracy of the proposed method. The approach is flexible, universal and outperforms GMM. It works on every pixel making it computationally expensive. Currently, motion segmentation operates at 10 fps which reduces due to excessive computation during classification. A GPU based parallel computing can help to increase the speed. Incorporating tracking and robust motion segmentation can improve performance of the proposed method in future.

Acknowledgments. The authors would like to thank Board of Research in Nuclear Sciences (BRNS) for generous grant (36(3)/14/20/2016-BRNS/36020) to carry out this research work. We would also like to thank the SAIVT Research Labs at Queensland University of Technology (QUT) for freely supplying us with the SAIVT-SoftBioSearch database for our research. The authors are also thankful to volunteers for their participation in creation of the dataset.

References

1. Reid, D., Samangooei, S., Chen, C., Nixon, M., Ross, A.: Soft biometrics for surveillance: an overview. Mach. Learn. Theory Appl. **31**, 327–352 (2013)
2. Demirkus, M., Garg, K., Guler, S.: Automated person categorization for video surveillance using soft biometrics. In: SPIE Defense, Security, and Sensing, International Society for Optics and Photonics, p. 76670P (2010)

3. Thornton, J., Baran-Gale, J., Butler, D., Chan, M., Zwahlen, H.: Person attribute search for large-area video surveillance. In: 2011 IEEE International Conference on Technologies for Homeland Security (HST), pp. 55–61. IEEE (2011)

4. An, L., Chen, X., Kafai, M., Yang, S., Bhanu, B.: Improving person re-identification by soft biometrics based reranking. In: 2013 Seventh International Conference on Distributed Smart Cameras (ICDSC), pp. 1–6. IEEE (2013)

5. Raval, M.S.: Digital video forensics: description based person identification. CSI Commun. **39**, 9–11 (2016)

6. Dantcheva, A., Velardo, C., Dangelo, A., Dugelay, J.L.: Bag of soft biometrics for person identification. Multimedia Tools Appl. **51**(2), 739–777 (2011)

7. Kim, M.G., Moon, H.M., Chung, Y., Pan, S.B.: A survey and proposed framework on the soft biometrics technique for human identification in intelligent video surveillance system. BioMed Res. Int. **2012**, 1–7 (2012)

8. MacLeod, M.D., Frowley, J.N., Shepherd, J.W.: Whole body information: its relevance to eyewitnesses. Adult eyewitness testimony: current trends and developments, pp. 125–143 (1994)

9. Zhang, G., Jiang, P., Matsumoto, K., Yoshida, M., Kita, K.: Reidentification of persons using clothing features in real-life video. Appl. Comput. Intell. Soft Comput. **2017**, 9 (2017)

10. D'Angelo, A., Dugelay, J.L.: Color based soft biometry for hooligans detection. In: Proceedings of 2010 IEEE International Symposium on Circuits and Systems (ISCAS), pp. 1691–1694. IEEE (2010)

11. Kakumanu, P., Makrogiannis, S., Bourbakis, N.: A survey of skin-color modeling and detection methods. Pattern Recogn. **40**(3), 1106–1122 (2007)

12. Mogelmose, A., Moeslund, T.B., Nasrollahi, K.: Multimodal person re-identification using RGB-D sensors and a transient identification database. In: 2013 International Workshop on Biometrics and Forensics (IWBF), pp. 1–4. IEEE (2013)

13. Moon, H.M., Pan, S.B.: A new human identification method for intelligent video surveillance system. In: 2010 Proceedings of 19th International Conference on Computer Communications and Networks, pp. 1–6 (2010)

14. Chien, S.Y., Chan, W.K., Cherng, D.C., Chang, J.Y.: Human object tracking algorithm with human color structure descriptor for video surveillance systems. In: 2006 IEEE International Conference on Multimedia and Expo, pp. 2097–2100. IEEE (2006)

15. Hu, M., Hu, W., Tan, T.: Tracking people through occlusions. In: Proceedings of the 17th International Conference on Pattern Recognition, ICPR 2004, vol. 2, pp. 724–727. IEEE (2004)

16. Nakajima, C., Pontil, M., Heisele, B., Poggio, T.: Full-body person recognition system. Pattern Recogn. **36**(9), 1997–2006 (2003)

17. Hahnel, M., Klunder, D., Kraiss, K.F.: Color and texture features for person recognition. In: Proceedings of 2004 IEEE International Joint Conference on Neural Networks, vol. 1, pp. 647–652. IEEE (2004)

18. Ma, B., Li, Q., Chang, H.: Gaussian descriptor based on local features for person re-identification. In: Jawahar, C.V., Shan, S. (eds.) ACCV 2014. LNCS, vol. 9010, pp. 505–518. Springer, Cham (2015). https://doi.org/10.1007/978-3-319-16634-6_37

19. Park, U., Jain, A.K., Kitahara, I., Kogure, K., Hagita, N.: Vise: visual search engine using multiple networked cameras. In: 18th International Conference on Pattern Recognition, ICPR 2006, vol. 3, pp. 1204–1207. IEEE (2006)

20. Jang, K., Han, S., Kim, I.: Person re-identification based on color histogram and spatial configuration of dominant color regions. arXiv preprint arXiv:1411.3410 (2014)
21. Kao, J.-H., Lin, C.-Y., Wang, W.-H., Wu, Y.-T.: A unified hierarchical appearance model for people re-identification using multi-view vision sensors. In: Huang, Y.-M.R., Xu, C., Cheng, K.-S., Yang, J.-F.K., Swamy, M.N.S., Li, S., Ding, J.-W. (eds.) PCM 2008. LNCS, vol. 5353, pp. 553–562. Springer, Heidelberg (2008). https://doi.org/10.1007/978-3-540-89796-5_57
22. Denman, S., Halstead, M., Bialkowski, A., Fookes, C., Sridharan, S.: Can you describe him for me? A technique for semantic person search in video. In: 2012 International Conference on Digital Image Computing Techniques and Applications (DICTA), pp. 1–8. IEEE (2012)
23. Halstead, M., Denman, S., Sridharan, S., Fookes, C.: Locating people in video from semantic descriptions: a new database and approach. In: 2014 22nd International Conference on Pattern Recognition (ICPR), pp. 4501–4506. IEEE (2014)
24. Kelly, K.L., Judd, D.B.: Color: Universal Language and Dictionary of Names, vol. 440. US Department of Commerce, National Bureau of Standards, Washington, D.C. (1976)
25. Centore, P.: sRGB centroids for the ISCC-NBS colour system (2016)
26. Sivic, J., Zitnick, C.L., Szeliski, R.: Finding people in repeated shots of the same scene. BMVC **3**, 909–918 (2006)
27. Bjorndahl, K.: Learn to Draw. http://www.learn-to-draw.com/figure-drawing/02-draw-male-proportions.shtml
28. Bjorndahl, K.: Learn to Draw. http://www.learn-to-draw.com/figure-drawing/05-draw-female-proportions.shtml
29. Sharma, G., Wu, W., Dalal, E.N.: The ciede2000 color-difference formula: Implementation notes, supplementary test data, and mathematical observations. Color Res. Appl. **30**(1), 21–30 (2005)
30. Van De Weijer, J., Schmid, C., Verbeek, J.: Learning color names from real-world images. In: IEEE Conference on Computer Vision and Pattern Recognition, CVPR 2007, pp. 1–8. IEEE (2007)

Towards Accurate Handwritten Word Recognition for Hindi and Bangla

Kartik Dutta$^{(\boxtimes)}$, Praveen Krishnan, Minesh Mathew, and C. V. Jawahar

CVIT, IIIT Hyderabad, Hyderabad, India
{kartik.dutta,praveen.krishnan,minesh.mathew}@research.iiit.ac.in,
jawahar@iiit.ac.in

Abstract. Building accurate lexicon free handwritten text recognizers for Indic languages is a challenging task, mostly due to the inherent complexities in Indic scripts in addition to the cursive nature of handwriting. In this work, we demonstrate an end-to-end trainable CNN-RNN hybrid architecture which takes inspirations from recent advances of using residual blocks for training convolutional layers, along with the inclusion of spatial transformer layer to learn a model invariant to geometric distortions present in handwriting. In this work we focus building state of the art handwritten word recognizers for two popular Indic scripts – Devanagari and Bangla. To address the need of large scale training data for such low resources languages, we utilize synthetically rendered data for pre-training the network and later fine tune it on the real data. We outperform the previous lexicon based, state of the art methods on the test set of Devanagari and Bangla tracks of RoyDB by a significant margin.

Keywords: Handwriting recognition · Lexicon free · Indic scripts

1 Introduction

The creation and dissemination of handwritten documents remains pervasive for humans as a personal choice of communication other than speech. Handwritten text recognition is the process of automatic conversion of such handwritten documents into machine encoded text. It has been a popular research area for many years due to various applications such as digitizing handwritten manuscripts [1], postal automation [2], matching documents [3], digitizing handwritten medical forms [4], etc. Most of these works have focused on Latin scripts, with very few works in the space of Indic scripts. In this work, we address the challenges of building a handwritten word recognizer for two popular Indic scripts – Devanagari and Bangla. A lot of handwritten documents in these scripts have been made available by scanning historical documents, ancient manuscripts and literary resources with cultural significance. Extracts from such Bangla and Devanagari manuscripts is shown in Fig. 1.

© Springer Nature Singapore Pte Ltd. 2018
R. Rameshan et al. (Eds.): NCVPRIPG 2017, CCIS 841, pp. 470–480, 2018.
https://doi.org/10.1007/978-981-13-0020-2_41

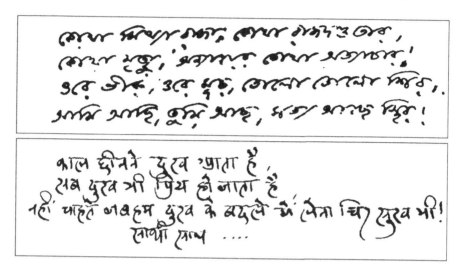

Fig. 1. The top box shows an excerpt from the Bangla poem "Namashkar" (1907) written by Rabindranath Tagore, while the bottom box shows an example of Devanagari writing from a Hindi poem written by Amitabh Bachchan.

Devanagari and Bangla are the two most popular Indian scripts, also being the fifth and sixth most popular language in the world [5]. Both these scripts are read left to right. Both scripts contain 11 vowels whereas the number of consonants is 38 for Devanagari and 39 for Bangla. Figure 2 shows the basic set of characters in both the scripts. As one can notice both the scripts contains a horizontal line running across the characters and words (for word images see Fig. 4) which is referred as *Shirorekha*. The shape of the consonant is modified in case it is followed by a vowel in either script, and such a character is referred to a *modified* character or modifier. In certain cases, when a consonant follows one or more consonant(s), a new character gets formed which has an orthographic shape and is called a *compound* character. For more details about the Bangla and Devanagari scripts, the reader can look at [6]. Due to the presence of modifiers and compound characters, the number of distinct characters possible in both Bangla and Devanagari is far higher than Latin scripts (roughly 400 distinct characters in Bangla compared to only 62 in English), making word recognition for these Indic scripts more challenging as compared to English.

In addition to the script level challenges, a handwritten word recognizer for Indic scripts has to deal with challenges associated with writers having different styles and the cursive nature of the handwriting. The cursive way of writing [7] results in merging of adjacent characters, variable skew and modified shapes which further increases the complexity in recognition. Another important challenge is the lack of publicly available handwritten data in Indian languages. This inhibits training of modern deep learning architectures, which contain millions of parameters and require substantial data for generalization of features.

Vowels: অ আ ই ঈ উ ঊ ঋ এ ঐ ও ঔ
Modifiers: কি কু কূ কৃ কে কা কী কে কৈ কো কৌ
Consonants: ক খ গ ঘ ঙ চ ছ জ ঝ ঞ ট ...
Conjuncts: ক্র কৃখ চ্ছ ঙ্ছ ঙ্জ ঘ্ঙ ঘ্চ ঙ্ম গ্ঘ খ্ক খ্খ ...

(a)

Vowels: अ आ इ ई उ ऊ ऋ ए ऐ ओ औ
Modifiers: पु पू पे पै पो पौ पृ पी पा पि
Consonants: क ख ग घ ङ च छ ज झ ञ ट ...
Conjuncts: क्र क्ल क्स ख्म ख्म न्स प्र फ्र र्त र्च श्र ...

(b)

Fig. 2. Few examples of vowels, modifiers, consonants and conjuncts in (a) Bangla and (b) Devanagari

Most of the previous works [8–10] on recognizing Devanagari and Bangla scripts were limited to printed documents. In this work we focus on handwritten word images which are more challenging than machine printed words. Initial works in offline Bangla and Devanagari handwritten word recognition used Hidden Markov Models (HMM). HMM based approaches can be categorized as – (i) trained on recognizing the whole word or finding the holistic representation (ii) segmenting the image into different zones and using the HMM to recognize individual characters. Works such as [11,12] for Bangla and [13,14] for Devanagari, extract features from the entire word and use lexicon dependent HMM decoding to recognize the whole word. In [15] for Bangla and Devanagari word recognition, the authors first segment the word image into three regions, namely the upper, middle and lower zone, using image processing techniques such as skeletal analysis and shape matching. The upper and lower zones are recognized by using support vector machines while the middle zone was recognized using a HMM decoded with a lexicon of middle zone characters. Finally, the results from the recognizers in all three zones are combined. Both these methods are limited to lexicon based decoding. More recently, with the proliferation of deep learning based methods, modern text recognizers are built using a combination of convolutional neural networks (CNN) and recurrent neural networks (RNN) such as BLSTMs [16]. In [17], Garain et al. uses BLSTM's with CTC loss, while in [7] CNN's are used for feature extraction along with RNN's for sequence classification. Both these methods show results for offline Bangla handwritten recognition. While our work is similar to that in [7] in terms of basic architecture, our network is much deeper, uses residual connections and contains spatial transformation layer to better handle geometric distortions present in handwriting. Also, in [7] each modifier and compound character is treated as a unique character, while we model it as a sequence of characters.

In this work, we address the challenges associated with recognizing the handwritten word images of Devanagari and Bangla scripts, in an unconstrained setting, by using a CNN-RNN hybrid network. The main contributions of this work are as follows- (i) To address the lack of data we pre-train our network on synthetic data created from fonts and fine tune the network of real world images, (ii) We use a network similar to the one used in [18], containing a spatial transformer layer, residual convolutional blocks and BLSTM layers along with the CTC loss function for sequence to sequence transcription and (iii) We present results in both lexicon-based and lexicon-free (unconstrained) setting. Our proposed method gives state of the results on both Bangla and Devanagari tracks of RoyDB [15].

The paper is structured as follows: In Sect. 2, we discuss about the CNN-RNN hybrid architecture and its notable components. In Sect. 3, we discuss how we train our deep model and the result of applying our pre-trained model to both the Bengali and Devanagari track of the RoyDB dataset. Sect. 4 concludes our work.

2   Methodology

Figure 3 illustrates the proposed deep architecture for lexicon free handwritten word recognition which consists of a spatial transformer layer (STN) [19], followed by a set of residual convolutional blocks, which is proceeded by a stacked bi-directional LSTM module and ends with a transcription layer for label prediction.

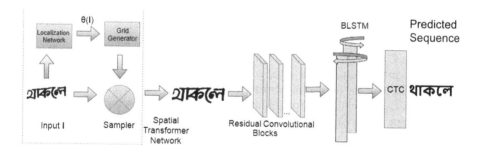

Fig. 3. Overview of the proposed CNN-RNN hybrid architecture. The various important components of the architecture are highlighted such as the spatial transformer network, residual convolutional blocks, BLSTM layers and the CTC loss function.

2.1   Synthetic Data

The availability of huge amount of data is crucial for successful training of deep architectures which typically contain millions of parameters. In [20, 21], a framework for rendering synthetic word images from standard fonts is proposed which practically enables building an nearly infinite vocabulary dataset. In this work, we follow a pipeline similar to [21] for rendering word images from Bangla and Devanagari fonts to pre-train our deep network. The word is rendered onto the image in one of the following three ways: with a horizontal bottom text line or following a random curve or following a straight line. We apply varying amounts of kerning while rendering along with gaussian noise.

2.2   CNN-RNN Hybrid Architecture

In this work, we use the convolutional recurrent neural network (CRNN) [22] architecture along with STN layer [18,23] proposed for scene text recognition. In our work we show that such a network can be adapted for robust recognition of handwritten word images for Indic scripts. A CRNN architecture consists of a set of convolutional layers, followed by a recurrent neural network units whose output is given to a transcription layer which is modeled using connectionist temporal classification [24]. In general, convolutional neural networks have been found to be excellent spatial feature extractors [25–27] with translation invariant properties while recurrent neural units can take a sequence of feature vectors of variable length and can perform sequence to sequence (seq-2-seq) transcription tasks. In our case, the input sequence of features is constructed from the feature maps of the last convolutional layer by concatenating column features across different channels. For example given the feature map of size $512 \times 5 \times 10$, it results in a sequence of 10 feature vectors with dimension $\mathbb{R}^{5 \times 512}$. Here we choose the column width to be single pixel. Given a sequence of feature vectors $f_1, f_2, \ldots, f_T$, we forward it to a stacked set of recurrent layers which is our case is a bi-directional LSTM [16] network. The BLSTM network considers both the forward and backward context (history) while making prediction from the label space at each time step. In our case, the label space consists of the basic (no modifiers and conjuncts) character set of the given language, plus a blank symbol. Finally, the CTC layer converts the predictions generated by the BLSTM output layer into a maximal probable label sequence for the target language. One of the key advantages of the above framework is that the input images can take varying input sizes, thus avoiding distortion in the aspect ratio, since both convolutional and recurrent layers can operate with variable size images and feature sequences respectively.

2.3   Spatial Transformer Network (STN)

The spatial transformer network [19] is an end-to-end trainable layer which can perform an explicit geometric transformation to the input. The transformation parameters are learnt through backpropagation. As seen in Fig. 3 it has three main components, the localization network, the grid generator and the sampler. The localization network takes as input a feature map and outputs θ, the transformation parameters that is to be applied to the input feature map. The size of θ depends on the kind of transformations being modeled-affine, thin plate spline, etc. The localization network in itself is modeled as a neural network having a $|\theta|$ dimensional FC layer at the end. The grid generator generates a grid of coordinates in the input feature map corresponding to each pixel from the output feature map. Finally, the sampler generates the output feature map using bilinear interpolation by sampling the pixels given by the grid generator after applying the learnt transformation. As [18,23] show, this layer transforms the input feature map such that the geometric transformation is removed from the input and only the relevant part of the input is forwarded to subsequent layers. In the case of handwritten images the role of STN layer is particularly important to handle the variations caused due to the variable hand movements.

2.4   HW Word Recognition Network

Recent studies in deep learning [27,28] on the Imagenet challenge have shown that deeper architectures lead to an improvement in classification accuracy. However, merely increasing the number of layers would bring challenges during training such as exploding/vanishing gradients, internal covariate shifts [29], and the degradation problem [30]. In our architecture, we take into account the best practices proposed in the recent literature to overcome these problems. We use smaller size 3×3 convolutional filters which enable us to obtain a bigger receptive field with lesser number of parameters. Batch Normalization [29] is applied before each convolutional layer to prevent internal covariate shifts. The convolutional filters are arranged into multiple residual blocks with skip connections as proposed in [31]. The residual layers enables to overcome the degradation problem which prevents the network to learn efficiently. Also, as [32] demonstrated that using dropout in the recurrent layers improved accuracy, we apply dropout with $p = 0.2$ at the BLSTM layers in our proposed model.

3   Recognition Experiments

In this work, we use the public benchmark **Indic Word Database/RoyDB** [15] to conduct experiments and validate our results. It has been compiled by 60 writers and consists of a Bengali and a Devanagari track. The Bengali track comprises of 17,091 binarized HW word images, while the Devanagari track comprises of 16,128 HW grayscale word images. On an average, an image in either track represents a word consisting of 4 characters. We use the word level annotations that is provided along with RoyDB and follow the training, validation and testing partition provided along with the dataset. We use the standard evaluation metrics of Character Error Rate (CER) and Word Error Rate (WER) to compare the various models. CER is defined as (where RT: recognized text and GT: ground truth text in the below equation)-

$$CER = \frac{\sum EditDistance(GT, RT)}{\#Characters}$$

Table 1. Summary of the network configuration. The width, height and number of channels of each convolution layer is shown in square brackets, with the number of layers that are stacked together. After all but the last block, max pooling is applied. The width and height of the max pooling kernel are shown below each block. The number of units in each BLSTM layer is shown in square brackets, with the number of layers that are stacked together.

Block1 (2 × 2)	Block2 (2 × 2)	Block3 (1 × 2)	Block4 (1 × 2)	Block5	BLSTM
[3 × 3, 64] × 5	[3 × 3, 128] × 4	[3 × 3, 256] × 4	[3 × 3, 512] × 4	[3 × 3, 512] × 1	[256] × 2

i.e. the sum of insertions, deletions and substitutions in terms of characters required to transform RT to GT, divided by the number of characters in the ground truth. WER is the defined as the mean number of words wrongly transcribed.

Architecture Details: Table 1 lists the architecture of our network, along with the details of the convolution and recurrent layers used. For the localization network in our STN, we used three plain convolutional blocks and two linear layers. All the convolutional blocks have filter size, stride and padding of 3×3, 1 and 1 respectively. The number of channels in these layers were 64,64,128. 2×2 max pooling is applied before the first convolutional block and after each convolutional block as well. The first linear layer has 30 units and the second one has 6 units for learning the parameters of the affine transformation.

Pre-Training: To address the lack of enough training data, we use 1M word images, generated for both Bangla and Devanagari as described in Sect. 2.1, comprising of 50 different fonts for both the scripts. We use the train and validation corpus of RoyDB, for either track, as the rendering vocabulary to avoid undue advantages while comparing with other methods. In practice, the generation of synthetic data can span to nearly infinite vocabulary.

Data Augmentation and Fine-Tuning: To make the network invariant to affine transformations, we augmented each train image in RoyDB by applying a random amount of rotation ($\pm 5°$), shearing ($\pm 0.5°$ along horizontal direction) and perform translation in terms of padding on all fours sides to simulate incorrect segmentation of words. After the model converges on the synthetic dataset, we fine tune the network using the augmented train data of RoyDB in individual tracks.

3.1 Results and Analysis

Table 2 shows the quantitative results of our model on both Bengali and Devanagari tracks of RoyDB, alongside the state of art methods in either track. We present our results in three different settings- (i) Lexicon based decoding, where the CTC layer selects a sequence from the test corpus lexicon with the highest likelihood during decoding. The methods proposed in [7,15] show results in

Table 2. Word recognition performance of the CNN-RNN hybrid model in comparison with state of the art methods on the test set of RoyDB.

Track	Method	WER	CER
Bangla	Roy et al. [15] – lexicon	16.61	-
	Adak et al. [7] – lexicon	14.58	-
	Ours – lexicon	**4.30**	**2.05**
	Ours – unconstrained	**10.71**	**3.49**
	Ours (without synth. data)– unconstrained	12.77	3.85
Devanagari	Roy et al. [15] – lexicon	15.76	-
	Ours – lexicon	**4.62**	**2.67**
	Ours – unconstrained	**11.89**	**4.9**
	Ours (without synth. data) – unconstrained	14.09	5.53

Fig. 4. Recognition results for the CNN-RNN hybrid model on RoyDB dataset. First 3 rows show results for Bangla and the rest for Devanagari. Other than binarization and segmentation issues in the images, most of the errors are caused by ambiguities in the original handwritten image.

this setting, (ii) Lexicon free or "unconstrained" setting in which decoding is not restricted to any target lexicon and finally (iii) we also present our results without using any synthetic data, in the lexicon free setting. In all these scenario we improve the state of the art results with significant margins. When compared to previous lexicon based methods [7,15], we report an WER 4.30 and 5.13 for Bangla and Devanagari respectively. In this work, we primarily focus on the unconstrained lexicon setting. In this setting, we report better results from lexicon based methods with a relative improvement in WER of about 26% in the Bangla and 22% in the Devanagari tracks. We also observe that our networks perform better even without using synthetic data when compared with previous methods. The use of synthetic data provides us an absolute additional reduction of WER by 2% in both scripts. Figure 4 shows the recognized outputs for few sample images from both tracks of RoyDB. Figure 5 visualizes the activations of a few channels from the 2nd convolution layer when an image is passed through the network.

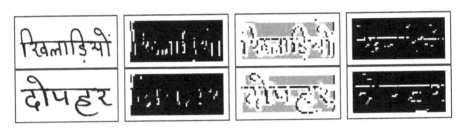

Fig. 5. Visualization of few channels from layer 2 activations. (From Left) first column shows the two input images. Second column shows the activation of a channel which detects vertical lines. The third column shows a channel which activates on the image background while the fourth column shows a channel which acts like a horizontal line detector.

3.2 Implementation Details

In all the experiments, the network is trained using stochastic gradient descent with the ADADELTA [33] optimizer. We initialize the parameters of the STN to represent the identity transformation. The input images are resized to 96×256. We used a batch size of 64 for training. Both Bangla and Devanagari models took around 15 h to train on a single NVIDIA GTX 1080 Ti GPU. The character set for each language was taken from the set of unique characters in the respective Bangla and Devanagari track of the RoyDB database.

4   Conclusion

We demonstrate state of the art lexicon free handwritten word recognizers for Devanagari and Bangla scripts using a CNN-RNN hybrid model using modern architectural components. The idea of pre-training the network on synthetic data can pave way for solving text recognition problems for languages where datasets of adequate sizes are not available. As a future work, we would like to work with historical manuscripts and also relax the assumption of having pre-segmented words by incorporating automatic text localization.

Acknowledgement. This work was partly supported by IMPRINT scheme, Govt. of India. The authors would also like to thank Oishika, Sounak and Sreya for their help in verifying the results for Bangla.

References

1. Rath, T.M., Manmatha, R.: Word spotting for historical documents. IJDAR **9**, 139–152 (2007)
2. Srihari, S.N., Kuebert, E.J.: Integration of hand-written address interpretation technology into the united states postal service remote computer reader system. In: DAS (1997)
3. Krishnan, P., Jawahar, C.V.: Matching handwritten document images. In: Leibe, B., Matas, J., Sebe, N., Welling, M. (eds.) ECCV 2016. LNCS, vol. 9905, pp. 766–782. Springer, Cham (2016). https://doi.org/10.1007/978-3-319-46448-0_46
4. Milewski, R.J., Govindaraju, V., Bhardwaj, A.: Automatic recognition of hand-written medical forms for search engines. IJDAR **11**, 203–218 (2009)
5. Simons, G.F., Fennig, C.D.: Ethnologue: languages of the world. In: SIL International (2017)
6. Pal, U., Chaudhuri, B.: Indian script character recognition: a survey. PR **37**, 1887–1899 (2004)
7. Adak, C., Chaudhuri, B.B., Blumenstein, M.: Offline cursive Bengali word recognition using CNNs with a recurrent model. In: ICFHR (2016)
8. Chaudhuri, B., Pal, U.: A complete printed bangla OCR system. PR **31**, 531–549 (1998)
9. Bansal, V., Sinha, R.: A complete OCR for printed hindi text in Devanagari script. In: DAS (2001)
10. Mathew, M., Singh, A.K., Jawahar, C.: Multilingual OCR for Indic scripts. In: DAS (2016)
11. Bhowmik, T.K., Parui, S.K., Roy, U.: Discriminative HMM training with GA for handwritten word recognition. In: ICPR (2008)
12. Bhowmik, T.K., Roy, U., Parui, S.K.: Lexicon reduction technique for bangla handwritten word recognition. In: DAS (2012)
13. Shaw, B., Bhattacharya, U., Parui, S.K.: Combination of features for efficient recognition of offline handwritten Devanagari words. In: ICFHR (2014)
14. Shaw, B., Parui, S.K., Shridhar, M.: Offline handwritten Devanagari word recognition: a holistic approach based on directional chain code feature and HMM. In: ICIT (2008)
15. Roy, P.P., Bhunia, A.K., Das, A., Dey, P., Pal, U.: HMM-based Indic handwritten word recognition using zone segmentation. PR **60**, 1057–1075 (2016)
16. Graves, A., Liwicki, M., Fernández, S., Bertolami, R., Bunke, H., Schmidhuber, J.: A novel connectionist system for unconstrained handwriting recognition. PAMI **3**, 855–868 (2009)
17. Garain, U., Mioulet, L., Chaudhuri, B.B., Chatelain, C., Paquet, T.: Unconstrained Bengali handwriting recognition with recurrent models. In: ICDAR (2015)
18. Liu, W., Chen, C., Wong, K.Y.K., Su, Z., Han, J.: STAR-Net: a spatial attention residue network for scene text recognition. In: BMVC (2016)
19. Jaderberg, M., Simonyan, K., Zisserman, A., et al.: Spatial transformer networks. In: NIPS (2015)
20. Jaderberg, M., Simonyan, K., Vedaldi, A., Zisserman, A.: Synthetic data and artificial neural networks for natural scene text recognition (2014)

21. Krishnan, P., Jawahar, C.: Generating synthetic data for text recognition. arXiv preprint arXiv:1608.04224 (2016)
22. Shi, B., Bai, X., Yao, C.: An end-to-end trainable neural network for image-based sequence recognition and its application to scene text recognition. PAMI **39**, 2298–2304 (2016)
23. Shi, B., Wang, X., Lyu, P., Yao, C., Bai, X.: Robust scene text recognition with automatic rectification. In: CVPR (2016)
24. Graves, A., Fernández, S., Gomez, F., Schmidhuber, J.: Connectionist temporal classification: labelling unsegmented sequence data with recurrent neural networks. In: ICML (2006)
25. Krizhevsky, A., Sutskever, I., Hinton, G.E.: Imagenet classification with deep convolutional neural networks. In: NIPS (2012)
26. Jaderberg, M., Simonyan, K., Vedaldi, A., Zisserman, A.: Reading text in the wild with convolutional neural networks. IJCV **116**, 1–20 (2016)
27. Simonyan, K., Zisserman, A.: Very deep convolutional networks for large-scale image recognition. arXiv preprint arXiv:1409.1556 (2014)
28. Szegedy, C., Liu, W., Jia, Y., Sermanet, P., Reed, S., Anguelov, D., Erhan, D., Vanhoucke, V., Rabinovich, A.: Going deeper with convolutions. In: CVPR (2015)
29. Ioffe, S., Szegedy, C.: Batch normalization: accelerating deep network training by reducing internal covariate shift. In: ICML (2015)
30. He, K., Zhang, X., Ren, S., Sun, J.: Deep residual learning for image recognition. In: CVPR (2016)
31. He, K., Zhang, X., Ren, S., Sun, J.: Identity mappings in deep residual networks. In: Leibe, B., Matas, J., Sebe, N., Welling, M. (eds.) ECCV 2016. LNCS, vol. 9908, pp. 630–645. Springer, Cham (2016). https://doi.org/10.1007/978-3-319-46493-0_38
32. Pham, V., Bluche, T., Kermorvant, C., Louradour, J.: Dropout improves recurrent neural networks for handwriting recognition. In: ICFHR (2014)
33. Zeiler, M.D.: ADADELTA: an adaptive learning rate method. arXiv preprint arXiv:1212.5701 (2012)

NrityaGuru: A Dance Tutoring System for Bharatanatyam Using Kinect

Achyuta Aich, Tanwi Mallick, Himadri B. G. S. Bhuyan,
Partha Pratim Das[(⊠)] [iD], and Arun Kumar Majumdar [iD]

Indian Institute of Technology Kharagpur, Kharagpur 721302, India
send2aich@gmail.com, tanwimallick@gmail.com, himadribhuyan@gmail.com,
{ppd,akmj}@cse.iitkgp.ernet.in

Abstract. Indian Classical Dance (ICD) is a living heritage of India. Traditionally *Gurus* (teachers) are the custodians of this heritage. They practice and pass on the legacy through their *Shishyas* (disciples), often in undocumented forms. The preservation of the heritage, thus, remains limited in time and scope. Emergence of digital multimedia technology has created the opportunity to preserve heritage by ensuring that it can be accessible over a long period of time. However, there have been only limited attempts to use effective technologies either in the pedagogy of learning dance or in the preservation of heritage of ICD. In this context, the paper presents *NrityaGuru* – a tutoring system for *Bharatanatyam* – a form of ICD. Using Kinect Xbox to capture dance videos in multimodal form, we design a system that can help a learner dancer identify deviations in her dance postures and movements against the prerecorded benchmark performances of the tutor (*Guru*).

1 Introduction

Till date ICD has been passed on to the students by the teacher, from one generation to the next, through the traditional method of *Guru-Shishya Parampara*. We focus on *Bharatanatyam* - a specific form of Indian Classical Dance. To learn *Bharatanatyam* one has to go to a guru, watch her/him perform the steps and then mimic. During the reproduction, the guru provides feedback on the performance of the learner to help her correct the steps. However, while the learner needs to practice these steps at home she neither has the benchmark performance to mimic nor the feedback to correct. Recording the performance of the guru can help getting the benchmark to follow, but instructional feedback remains an open issue.

In this paper we build *NrityaGuru* – an autonomous tutoring system to provide real-time instructional feedback about the correctness of *Bharatanatyam* as performed by a learner. To keep the complexity of the problem manageable, we work only with *Adavus* of *Bharatanatyam*. An *Adavu* is a basic unit of *Bharatanatyam* performance comprising well-defined sets of postures, gestures, movements and their transitions, and is typically used to train the dancers.

© Springer Nature Singapore Pte Ltd. 2018
R. Rameshan et al. (Eds.): NCVPRIPG 2017, CCIS 841, pp. 481–493, 2018.
https://doi.org/10.1007/978-981-13-0020-2_42

The system builds on the skeleton tracking of Kinect as a computational model for *Adavus*. Using Kinect recording (skeletal as well as RGB videos) of benchmark performances of *Adavus* by an expert; we employ different approaches to align the time-scales of the learner and the expert to first determine the best match of steps, and then to detect when and how the steps of the learner deviates from the expert. Also, we provide specific feedback on the steps and rate the performance overall.

In Sect. 2 we discuss related work in tutoring and identify the requirements in Sect. 3. The system architecture is outlined in Sect. 5. After discussing the results in Sect. 6, we conclude in Sect. 7.

2   Related Work

Over nearly a decade, there have been several attempts, mostly in non-Indian dance forms, to develop autonomous tutoring systems with variety of approaches, sensors, and features. We classify these below.

Virtual/Conceptual Models: In [12,13] Nakamura et al. proposed a dance movement training systems in 2005 where a user learns to dance by imitating the model (benchmark) dance demonstrated by a virtual teacher. This just supports demonstration. There is no feedback as the user's dance is not captured. Ramadoss et al. [14] made a proposal for a tutoring system to store and retrieve dance data from *Labanotation*.

Force Sensors: Drobny et al. [5], in 2009, developed a system which acquires data from force sensors mounted under the dancers' feet, detects steps, and compares their timing to the timing of beats in the music and help the dancer stay in sync with the music. Force sensors are intrusive and cannot be used for bare-foot dance forms as in ICD.

RGB Videos: In [4,7], some work was done on storing and synthesizing choreography from RGB video though no full-scale tutoring system was built.

Kinect: Since the introduction of Kinect in 2010, tutoring systems have become more viable and effective. Kinect is the first sensor of its kind that is low-cost, non-intrusive, and multi-modal in audio, RGB-D video and skeleton streams. Understandably there has been proliferation of activities. Efforts include the usage of Kinect based skeleton tracker by Alexiadis et al. [1], Essid et al. [6], and Anderson et al. [2] to develop systems that automatically/semi-automatically evaluate performances of a dancer against a benchmark and provide visual feedback to the performer. Further, Marquardt et al. [11] proposed the Super Mirror that combines the functionality of studio mirrors and prescriptive images to provide the user with instructional feedback in real-time.

All the work reported above focus on western dance forms like Ballet, Samba, or Salsa. There has been no attempt to tutor for any Indian Classical Dance (ICD) form.

3   Requirements Analysis

At the initial stages of development of *NrityaGuru*, we identified a few challenges that defined the requirements.

- *Recorded Data Set:* There is no data set for *Bharatanatyam*. We need to create one (Sect. 4).
- *Aligning Dance Sequences:* Typically two distinct dance sequences may have different number of frames as they may not be performed for the same duration. Further, the start of skeletal tracking differs across sequences depending on the time taken by the tracking module to detect the dancer and start the tracking process. So we need to align the dance sequences.
- *Identifying Similarity Measure:* Even when two dancers would be performing identical postures, their recorded frames would differ. So we need to define proper similarity measures between two dance frames (learner against expert) based on various parameters.
- *Feedback:* We need way (interface) to provide feedback to the learner in terms of deviations in dance poses. Ideally, this should be real-time. Practically, it could be based on an offline playback. The interface should make it easy to have repeated views and highlight specific areas of deviation.
- *Score Computation:* The correctness of a performance need to be quantified at a frame as well as overall levels in terms of normalized scores.

NrityaGuru system attempts to address the above requirements as explained in Sect. 5.

4   Data Set Creation and Annotation

No data set for *Bharatanatyam Adavus* is available for research. Hence, we start by recording 8 different *Adavus* performed by *Bharatanatyam* dancers – experts as well as learners. A part of the data set is available at [10]. We also get the learners' videos annotated by the experts for deviations.

We use Kinect to capture RGB, depth and skeleton videos at a rate of 30 fps. The skeleton information is used to align videos and compute similarity scores, and RGB and skeleton information are used to provide the visual feedback to the learner. A Kinect skeleton is represented by 20 joint points (Fig. 1) with the root of the Cartesian 3D coordinate system positioned at the hip joint and oriented in alignment with the sensor. Each point is marked as *tracked* or *inferred* – the latter typically denoting the estimate of an occluded body part.

Though the Kinect was found to be mostly adequate for our purpose, yet the following limitations need to be emphasized:

1. Inferred joints of the occluded body parts commonly have substantial noise, which has been taken care of by defining a suitable threshold of error
2. Due to the Limited Field of View dancers needed to perform within a defined space

3. The IR camera is susceptible to noise from various light sources that may contain emissions in the IR band. Hence, special light sources have been used.

Keeping the above in view the following studio setup was created for data recording.

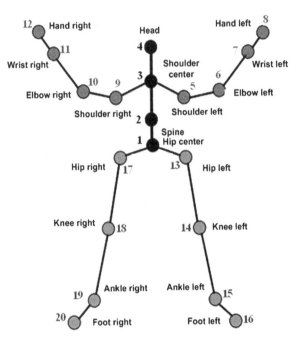

Fig. 1. Different skeletal joints tracked by Kinect

4.1   Studio Setup, Sensors and Tools

The selection of our sensor devices and studio items are listed in Table 1 and our studio setup is illustrated in Fig. 2.

The setup is done based on the following considerations:

- In spite of the limitations of FoV and DoF, we have decided to use a single Kinect as both the use of multiple Kinects or mirrors inject various kinds of noise and/or artifacts that can be seriously detrimental to the quality required for dance postures and movements.
- The dancer is provided a 3 m by 3 m area at a distance of roughly 4 m from Kinect to perform. This was found to be adequate[1] for performing the *Adavus*. Also, the dancers rehearse in the space before the recording.

---

[1] Such a setup, however, may not work effectively for a performances with a lot of movement.

– Unnecessary space in the background is constrained by three backdrop screens at about 45° angle with the imaging plane (Fig. 2(a)). This ensures that the maximum depth values do not vary widely, remains within Kinect's DoF, and thus limits the depth noise.
– All shiny/specular surfaces, mirror etc. are avoided in the studio. The backdrop is made with special material suitable for high quality imaging both in RGB and in depth.
– The lighting is done with uniformity to minimize shadows. This ensures good quality for RGB images.
– The audio (a *Sollukattu*) is first recorded with an Audio Recorder. The audio is played back while the dancer performs and Kinect records the audio. This helps orthogonalize the video against the audio and ensures that all *Adavus* having the same *Sollukattu* use the same audio file (identical beat structure etc.)
– The Studio is acoustically designed to minimize various audio noise including echoes.

Table 1. Studio and sensors as used in recording

Item	Details
Acoustic studio	The sound isolation requirement is met by acoustic treatment of the room to keep the reverberation time between 1–1.2 sec. A layer of glass wool having a density of 48 Kg/cubic meter and thickness of 50 mm along with 12 mm thick gypsum acoustic panels with NRC 0.85 are used on the walls to achieve the desired isolation criteria. For ceiling, 18 mm thick similar gypsum acoustic boards are used
Ambient noise	Studio ambient noise level is maintained within 25 dBA using centralized air-conditioning system
Lights	Philips 4 ft 36 Watt cool white (6500k) Fluorescent lights
Curtains	Grey/blue/chocolate colored heavy duty wrinkle free 100% polyester material is used for uniform background and to minimize reflection
RGBD sensor	Kinect XBox 360 (Kinect 1.0)
Audio recorder	Zoom H2N portable handy recorder Recording media: SD/SDHC cards Built-in memory: Up to 1 min in 96 kbps MP3 format Mic arrangements: 90° X/Y stereo, MS stereo Microphone types: directional & Bidirectional (MS side mic) Maximum sound pressure input: 120 dB spl Stereo/4ch uncompressed PCM, Compressed MP3 Input gain: 0 to +39 dB Rated output level: −10 dBm Headphones: 20 mW + 20 mW Built-in speaker: 400mW, 8O, mono

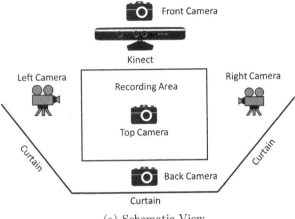

(a) Schematic View

(b) Front View

(c) Rear View

Fig. 2. Set-up for recording of *Adavus*

5   System Architecture

The architecture of *NrityaGuru* is shown in Fig. 3. At a time it takes two videos – one pre-recorded by an expert (E) and the other recorded by a learner (L) who is trying to follow the performance of the expert. We attempts to align the videos frame-by-frame so that the learner's performance in a frame can be compared against the corresponding (matching) frame of the expert's performance. If the postures in these matching frames significantly differ, we declare wrong performance by the learner and highlight on the interface (User interface, Sect. 5.4). Treating the videos as sequences of frames, we first align the start frames of the sequences by detecting the movement in the first beat. Next we match and align frames pairwise between the two sequences using Dynamic Time Warping (DTW). For matching we define suitable measures. If the measure exceeds a threshold we declare wrong performance. We explain the steps below.

5.1   Alignment of First Frames

To align the first frames between two videos, we note that both the expert and the learner perform to the same musical beats and start the performance with a specific starting movement of stamping a foot. So one option is to analyze the audio of the music, detect the first beat and then align based on the audio. However, in the present work we do not use the audio clue. Rather, we note that at the time of the first beat, the dancer raises her foot (usually right) and puts it down to stamp on the floor. We estimate the velocity of the corresponding joint (ankle right) and detect a zero crossing in its vertical component (Fig. 4) with joint moving up treated as positive. To eliminate errors due to small movements, we use a threshold. Hence in the figure we ignore the crossing around frame 10 and detect the one around frame 100 as the starting. Starting frames so detected in each video ($e_s \in E$ and $l_s \in L$) are used as the first alignment pair.

5.2   Dissimilarity Measure

To match the frames (in DTW and in scoring) we define two similarity measures between every pair of frames from the two videos. The first measure is based on angular dispersion at five major joints while the second is based on the difference in directions of movement of each of the 20 joints. Final measure is computed as a weighted sum of these two measures.

Angles at Joints. For any skeletal frame we consider angles formed by bones at 5 joints[2]: HKA_L & HKA_R, SEW_L & SEW_R, and LH_HC_RH. These are

---

[2] HKA: hip–knee–ankle, SEW: shoulder–elbow–wrist, LH_HC_RH: left hip–hip center–right hip.

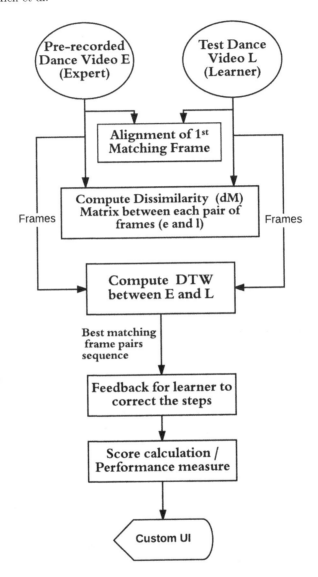

Fig. 3. Architecture of *NrityaGuru*

marked α_0 through α_4. The dissimilarity dM_1 between two frames $e \in E$ and $l \in L$ of the two dancers is then defined as:

$$dM_1(e,l) = \sum_{i=0}^{4} |\alpha_i(e) - \alpha_i(l)| \tag{1}$$

Velocity of Joints. For a frame, we compute the unit velocity vector $\|\hat{u}_j\|$ of every joint $j = 1, 2, \cdots, 20$ by considering 5 preceding and 5 following frames.

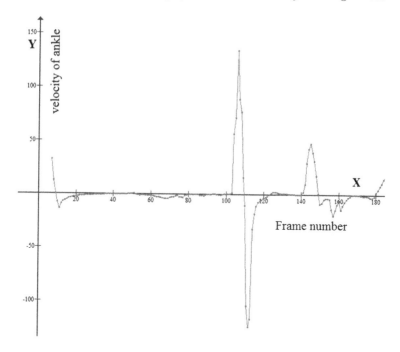

Fig. 4. Vertical component of the velocity of the right ankle joint

The dissimilarity dM_2 between two frames e and l of the two dancers is then computed as inverse of the cosine similarity as:

$$dM_2(e,l) = \left(\sum_j \frac{\hat{u}_j(e) \cdot \hat{u}_j(l)}{\|\hat{u}_j(e)\|_2 \|\hat{u}_j(l)\|_2} + \delta \right)^{-1} \tag{2}$$

A small positive constant δ is added in the denominator to avoid division by zero. Finally, the dissimilarity dM is computed as a weighted sum of dM_1 and dM_2 as:

$$dM(e,l) = w * dM_1(e,l) + (1 - w) * dM_2(e,l) \tag{3}$$

where $0 \leq w \leq 1$. This gives the frame–to–frame score.

Defining the Threshold. Since two dancers (frame wise) are not exactly same in the temporal/spatial domain, a set of $Thresholds$[3] are required while comparing the similarity between them. Consider a same joint J of two frame e and l, denoted by $J(e)$ and $J(l)$. We calculate the distance, say ds, between these two

---

[3] Threshold of sudden change = 0.08, Threshold of fast motion = 1.5, Threshold of slow motion = 0.5.

similar joints. If the following condition (similarity measure) satisfies for each of the joints of e and l then the two frames e and l are considered similar.

$$ds <= (FrameIndex(e) - LastViewedFrameIndex(l)) * Threshold \qquad (4)$$

5.3 Frame Correspondence by Dynamic Time Warping

Next we need to correspond every frame of video L with the best matching frame of video L. To arrive at a best matching frame we use *Dynamic Time Warping* (DTW) [3] algorithm to obtain the matching frame pair sequence. For this we first compute the dissimilarity matrix between pair of frames from both videos and then find the path in the matrix that minimizes the sum of dissimilarity measure dM along that path. In other words we need to find the shortest possible path in the matrix from the first matching frame pair to the last matching frame pair. This path will give us the best matching frame pairs.

Note that a frame of one video may match multiple frames of another video, or vice versa. Figure 5 shows a plot of the matching frames between dancer-1 (expert E) and dancer-2 (learner L). For example, the frame 1200 of dancer-1 matches (marked by a pair of green lines) multiple frames of dancer-2. In that case we select the frame which is at the shortest distance from the one in expert's video.

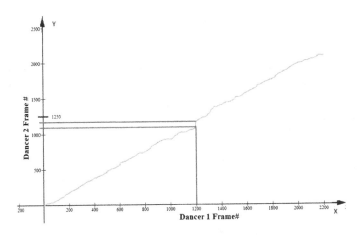

Fig. 5. 2205 frames of Dancer-1 (expert) matched against 2400 frames of Dancer-2 (learner) by DTW (Color figure online)

5.4 User Interface

NrityaGuru supports a custom user interface (Fig. 6) to visualize the dance of the learner (in sync with the dance of the expert). The learner may freeze (pause) at a frame, go forward/backward in steps, or play back continuously to accurately analyze her dance moves. We provide evaluation on the movements in terms of angular difference. We have 5 windows – HKA_L, HKA_R, SEW_L, SEW_R, and

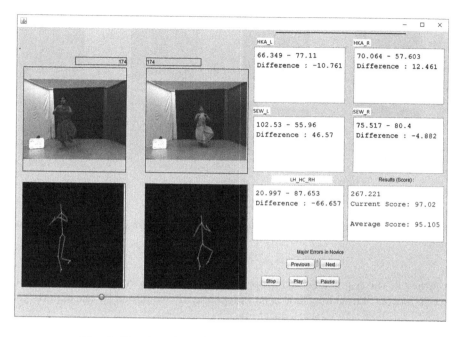

Fig. 6. User interface of *NrityaGuru* (Color figure online)

LH_HC_RH (between legs) – for this feedback and one window for score display for the learner to know the percentage of accuracy of her/his performance. A set of minimum (-25^0) and maximum ($+25^0$) angular thresholds determines the extent of possible variations between the real–time angles (of learner) and prerecorded angles (of expert) that can still result in a match. When a miss occurs the corresponding window is displayed in red.

5.5 Score Computation

The system provides two scores – *Current Frame Score* and *Average Frame Score*[4] to help the learner. For the last matched frame, average frame score is the final score of the performance.

$$Score = Constant/(Constant + dM(e,l))$$ (5)

6 Results

A sample matching for *Pakka Adavu* is shown in Fig. 7.

While it is difficult to provide quantitative accuracy measures for a tutoring system, using the annotated data set (Sect. 4) we could check the correctness of the flagged (scored red) frames. On the 8 learners' videos, we could achieve 83%

---

[4] Score of match from starting to current frame.

Fig. 7. Sequence of matching frames between two dancers for a *Pakka Adadu* performance

accuracy at the frame level. Appropriateness of the performance scores are subjective matter. These have not been independently evaluated by the experts yet.

7   Conclusions

We present *NrityaGuru* – a dance tutoring system for *Bharatanatyam Adavus*. A learner can use this system to record performances and compare against the correct ones as performed by the experts (prerecorded). The system is low cost, non-intrusive, easy to use, and the first of its kind for Indian Classical Dance.

The implementation of the system has been a non-trivial task. First, the multi-modal data of Kinect has a lot of noise [8] due to various factors. Particularly, the skeletons are often ill-formed (especially when one body part overlaps on another). Hence, we needed to use various filters (at image as well as skeleton levels) and tune a couple of threshold to stabilize the computations. Second, the Kinect views the dance from one side and all postures (critical for defining correctness) are not completely discernible from the view. Use of multiple Kinect for more complete 3D view has its own issues [9]. Finally, the dancing rules of *Bharatanatyam* are not standardized, allowing for substantial permissible variation at the frame level. In the present system most of these have been craftily handled by tuning the parameters and threshold. However, for scaling up and to generalize to a larger number of *Adavus*, more in-depth analysis (and partial automated interpretation of the dance form) may be required.

The different types of dance forms have their own set of rules and may require additional features (for example facial features) to be considered. Thus *NrityaGuru* has to be extended to deal with such dance forms. However the angular features of the joints may still be applicable.

The system works in offline mode. We are working to make it real-time. Also, the feedback visualization needs to be improved. We intend to use specific highlight for the errant limbs on the skeleton as well as RGB views.

References

1. Alexiadis, D., Kelly, P., Boubekeur, T., Moussa, M.B.: Evaluating a dancers performance using Kinect-based skeleton tracking. In: Proceedings of the 19th ACM International Conference on Multimedia, pp. 659–662 (2011)
2. Anderson, F., Grossman, T., Matejka, J., Fitzmaurice, G.: YouMove: enhancing movement training with an augmented reality mirror. In: Proceedings of the 26th Annual ACM Symposium on User Interface Software and Technology, pp. 311–320. ACM, October 2013
3. Bellman, R., Kalaba, R.: On adaptive control processes. IRE Trans. Autom. Control **4**(2), 1–9 (1959)
4. Chan, J.C., Leung, H., Tang, J.K., Komura, T.: A virtual reality dance training system using motion capture technology. IEEE Trans. Learn. Technol. **4**(2), 187–195 (2011)
5. Drobny, D., Weiss, M., Borchers, J.: Saltate!: a sensor-based system to support dance beginners. In: CHI 2009 Extended Abstracts on Human Factors in Computing Systems, pp. 3943–3948. ACM, April 2009
6. Essid, S., Alexiadis, D., Tournemenne, R., Gowing, M., Kelly, P., Monaghan, D., Daras, P., Drémeau, A., O'Connor, N.E.: An advanced virtual dance performance evaluator. In: 2012 IEEE International Conference on Acoustics, Speech and Signal Processing (ICASSP), pp. 2269–2272. IEEE, March 2012
7. James, S., Fonseca, M.J., Collomosse, J.: ReEnact: sketch based choreographic design from archival dance footage. In: Proceedings of International Conference on Multimedia Retrieval, p. 313. ACM, April 2014
8. Mallick, T., Das, P.P., Majumdar, A.K.: Characterizations of noise in Kinect depth images. IEEE Sens. J. **14**, 1731–1740 (2014)
9. Mallick, T., Das, P.P., Majumdar, A.K.: Study of interference noise in multi-Kinect set-up. In: Proceedings of 9th National Conference on International Conference on Computer Vision Theory and Applications VISAPP 2014, pp. 173–178 (2014)
10. Mallick, T., Bhuyan, H., Das, P.P., Majumdar, A.K.: Annotated Bharatanatyam Data Set (2017). http://hci.cse.iitkgp.ac.in
11. Marquardt, Z., Beira, J., Em, N., Paiva, I., Kox, S.: Super mirror: a Kinect interface for ballet dancers. In: CHI 2012 Extended Abstracts on Human Factors in Computing Systems, pp. 1619–1624. ACM, May 2012
12. Nakamura, A., Tabata, S., Ueda, T., Kiyofuji, S., Kuno, Y.: Dance training system with active vibro-devices and a mobile image display. In: 2005 IEEE/RSJ International Conference on Intelligent Robots and Systems, (IROS 2005), pp. 3075–3080. IEEE, August 2005
13. Nakamura, A., Tabata, S., Ueda, T., Kiyofuji, S., Kuno, Y.: Multimodal presentation method for a dance training system. In: CHI 2005 Extended Abstracts on Human Factors in Computing Systems, pp. 1685–1688. ACM, April 2005
14. Ramadoss, B., Kannan, R., Andres, F.: Intelligent tutoring systems for dance media environments. In: International Advance Computing Conference (IACC 2009) (2009)

Automated Translation of Human Postures from Kinect Data to Labanotation

Anindhya Sankhla, Vinanti Kalangutkar, Himadri B. G. S. Bhuyan,
Tanwi Mallick, Vivek Nautiyal, Partha Pratim Das(✉),
and Arun Kumar Majumdar

Indian Institute of Technology Kharagpur, Kharagpur 721302, India
anindhya.sankhla@gmail.com, vinantivishesh@gmail.com,
himadribhuyan@gmail.com, tanwimallick@gmail.com,
vivek.engi01@gmail.com, {ppd,akmj}@cse.iitkgp.ernet.in

Abstract. We present a non-intrusive automated system to translate human postures into *Labanotation*, a graphical notation for human postures and movements. The system uses Kinect to capture the human postures, identifies the positions and formations of the four major limbs: two hands and two legs, converts to the vocabulary of *Labanotation* and finally translates to a parseable *LabanXML* representation. We use the skeleton stream to classify the formations of the limbs using multi-class support vector machines. Encoding to XML is performed based on *Labanotation* specification. A data set of postures is created and annotated for training the classifier and to test its performance. We achieve 80% to 90% accuracy for the 4 limbs. The system can be used as an effective front-end for posture analysis applications in various areas like dance and sports where predefined postures form the basis for analysis and interpretation. The parseability of XML makes it easy for integration in a platform independent manner.

1 Introduction

Most physical human activities like standing, walking, running, dancing, playing, acting etc. involve varied set of postures, gestures, and movements. While a posture is a quasi-static state of the human body, gestures and movements naturally are composed of temporal sequences of postures at varying granularity of time and body details. Hence, postures form the fundamental descriptor for an activity[1]. Usually, a posture is created from certain formations of the limbs, torso, and the head and a system to recognize and represent postures can be very effective to analyze wide range of human activities. Here we build a system to recognize postures from Kinect [2] recordings and then symbolize them into a standard notation (*Labanotation* [1]), encoded in a parseable XML format.

---

[1] This, of course, overlooks the semantics dimension of gestures where rate and nature of change defines varied languages for an activity.

© Springer Nature Singapore Pte Ltd. 2018
R. Rameshan et al. (Eds.): NCVPRIPG 2017, CCIS 841, pp. 494–505, 2018.
https://doi.org/10.1007/978-981-13-0020-2_43

The system can be used as an effective front-end for posture analysis applications in various areas like dance, sports, dramatics, and others where predefined postures form the basis for analysis and interpretation. The parseability of the output representation (XML) makes it easy for integration in a platform independent manner.

The paper is organized as follows. We introduce *Labanotation* briefly in Sect. 2. We survey related work in Sect. 3. The system is discussed in Sect. 4 with data sets. Section 5 presents the results and we conclude in Sect. 6.

2   *Labanotation*

Labanotation [1,4], designed by Rudolf von Laban, is a system for analyzing and recording human postures and movements. *Labanotation* uses a *staff* (Fig. 1) consisting of 9 columns (standard one) and runs vertically. The score is read from the bottom to top. Anything that happens on the left (right) side of the body is shown on the left (right) side of the staff. *Labanotation* uses 9 directions and 3 levels (Fig. 2) and 6 degrees of folding (Fig. 3).

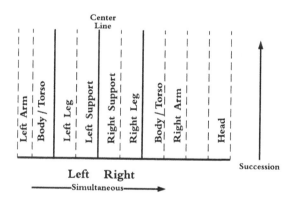

Fig. 1. Laban staff [1]

2.1   LabanXML

LabanXML[2], designed by Nakamura and Hachimura [11], is an XML representation for the graphical Labanotation. ⟨*laban*⟩ is the root element corresponding to the stuff. Columns are represented as ⟨*left*⟩, ⟨*support*⟩, and ⟨*right*⟩. ⟨*direction*⟩ specifies one of the 9 directions and ⟨*degree*⟩ specifies one of the 3 levels.

---

[2] *LabanXML* is designed after *MusicXML* [3] for use in encoding dance with music. It uses several tags specific to music and keeps a time line. As we intend to use *LabanXML* only for encoding posture, we ignore these details.

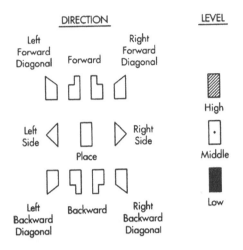

Fig. 2. *Labanotation*: directions and levels [1]

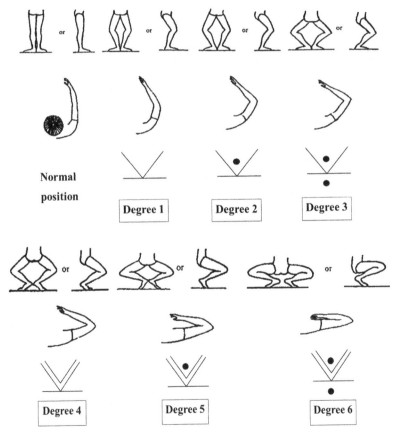

Fig. 3. Folding postures in legs and arms with the symbol [1]

3   Related Work

There have been attempts to encode human activities:

Loke et al. [6] present a design tool for movement-based interaction. Movements of the human body are input using motion detection by Eyetoy [7]. They are transcribed in *Labanotation* for players of two different Eyetoy[TM] games. Eyetoy needs a well-lit room and usually can recognize hand gestures alone. Transcription, however, is manual.

Wolofsky [5] takes *Labanotation* commands consisting of directional, level and timing information as input and outputs an animated character (avatar) performing the body movement as mentioned in the commands. Input is manually driven and works only for basic Laban commands. There is no automation of Laban symbol generation. The final output is a graphic representation or animation of posture not the Laban symbols.

Brown et al. [8] work on a graphics editor for *Labanotation*. They present the design of a machine-independent data structure for the creation and alteration of *Labanotation* diagram in *LABA*, an interactive graphic editor. However, most of the work is done manually and in the whole process, real body postures are not considered. Kojima et al. [15] present *LabanEditor* – an interactive graphical editor for writing and editing *Labanotation* scores. Later, Choensawat et al. [9] added a unique feature to *LabanEditor* for handling highly stylized classical Japanese performances, *Noh*. *Noh* is a characteristic Japanese classical performing art that takes the form of a musical drama. *Noh* body movement is peculiarly stylized and is not like ordinary human movement.

Guo et al. [10] generates *Labanotation* automatically from human motion capture data stored in BVH (Bio-vision Hierarchy) files. To capture the motion data, they use special bodysuits with markers and image with monocular camera. They produce the *Labanotation Data* (LND) to draw Labanotation diagrams. The paper, however, does not discuss the accuracy of the results or reveal what types of motions the system can handle. Naturally, the body-attached markers for capturing the motion data is intrusive and prone to errors.

We develop a novel non-intrusive approach using Kinect generated data set for automatic translation of different human postures to *Labanotation*.

4   System Overview

Recognizing a human posture as a whole is difficult. Hence, we attempt to individually categorize the four important limbs – left hand, right hand, left leg and right leg. We generate the notation for the posture based on these four limbs.

4.1   Data Set Generation

The data set for this paper was recorded indoors[3] with Kinect 1.0 in normal room conditions with ambient lighting. The subjects used casual

---

[3] This means that the approach cannot be directly used for outdoor games where the open field has a lot of potential IR interference.

clothing[4]. The Kinect was placed at a distance of about $2\,\mathrm{m}^5$ for its depth of field with proper directional alignment with the subjects (subject facing the Kinect and mostly parallel to Kinect's imaging plane).

Each Kinect video file contains the depth, skeletal and RGB data of various human postures. The postures are performed by male and female volunteers having various body types, but in similar age groups. The postures are limb specific. The video files are then annotated based on a particular limb postures in the form of file name. For example:

$$066\_Aman\_right\_leg\_right\_side\_low\_d02.dcl$$

represents the 2nd recording of a posture by *Aman* where right leg was on the right side with level low and degree 0. Recordings are done for 4 limbs, each limb having 9 directions, each direction having 3 levels, and each level having 3 degrees of bending[6] for different persons. So there are total of 9*3*3 = 81 possible classes for each limb. However, most volunteers cannot perform all theses classes[7]. Also, some classes are infeasible – a class with two legs up is not valid. So, we identify 39 classes for hands and 30 for legs. Every posture class is recorded by 3 different volunteers 10 times each. The Process of creation of data set is shown in the Fig. 4.

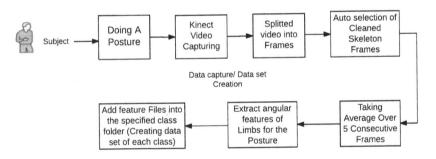

Fig. 4. Data set creation

4.2   Encoding Posture Classes

We represent every limb class with an 11-bit id that encodes its posture. First 3 bits[8] indicate the 4 limbs (left hand = 0, right hand = 1, left leg = 2, right leg = 3).

---

[4] Since target applications include dance and sports, the effect of dress on the quality of the skeletons as captured by Kinect was specifically studied. It was observed that Kinect can produce fairly good and stable skeleton for both genders wearing wide range of dresses (even Sarees).

[5] This is a limitation for typical auditorium format where deeper depth of field and wider field of view are needed.

[6] Out of 6 degrees we consider only 3 here, namely, 1 = No bending, 3 = Bending 90° and 6 = Bending 180°.

[7] There are folding of limbs, for example, that only trained people can do.

[8] An extra bit is considered for future extension to head and torso.

Next 4 bits indicate the 9 directions (starting with Place = 1, Forward = 2, and so on clockwise), the next 2 bit indicates the 3 levels, and the last 2 bits indicates the 3 degrees. For example, a right hand (= 1 ≡ 001) extended in Forward direction (= 2 ≡ 0010) at High level (= 3 ≡ 11) and folded perpendicular (degree = 2 ≡ 10) will be encoded as 001-0010-11-10 or 302.

Encoding and decoding for first 10 classes for right hand (one of the limb) is shown in the Table 1. The parameters are given in Table 2.

Table 1. Decoding for first 10 classes for right hand

Class	Binary	Limb	Direction	Level	Degree
277	001 - 0001 - 01 - 01	1	1	1	1
281	001 - 0001 - 10 - 01	1	1	2	1
293	001 - 0010 - 01 - 01	1	2	1	1
294	001 - 0010 - 01 - 10	1	2	1	2
295	001 - 0010 - 01 - 11	1	2	1	3
297	001 - 0010 - 10 - 01	1	2	2	1
298	001 - 0010 - 10 - 10	1	2	2	2
301	001 - 0010 - 11 - 01	1	2	3	1
302	001 - 0010 - 11 - 10	1	2	3	2
309	001 - 0011 - 01 - 01	1	3	1	1

Table 2. Details of parameters used in Table 1

Directions details		Limb details	
1	Place	0	Left hand
2	Forward	1	Right hand
3	Left side	2	Left leg
4	Left diagonal front	3	Right leg
5	Backward	Levels details	
6	Left diagonal back	1	Low
7	Forward	2	High
8	Right side	3	Mid
9	Right diagonal front	Degrees details	
10	Backward	1	No bending
11	Right diagonal back	2	Partial bending
		3	Complete bending

4.3 Feature Selection

In *Labanotation* major limb information is encoded in terms of direction and level. Hence, we use the skeleton stream of Kinect video that can help identify – (1) the human figure (as a *player*), (2) the limbs in terms of joints (and bones connecting them), and (3) the coordinates of the joints that can estimate the orientation of bones. We, therefore, use angular features as descriptors of the postures.

In a Kinect skeleton the joints are organized in a hierarchy (Fig. 5(a)). At a joint point, Y–axis is along the parent bone, X–axis is 90° right to Y–axis and Z–axis is coming out of the plane of X and Y–axes (Fig. 5(b)). To calculate the angle between two adjacent bones (B_1 and B_2) formed by 3 joint co-ordinates J_1, J_2 and J_3 (where B_1: $J_1 \rightarrow J_2$ and B_2: $J_2 \rightarrow J_3$), we convert them into vectors $V_1 = J_1 - J_2$ and $V_2 = J_3 - J_2$ by treating J_1 as the parent joint (Fig. 5(a)).

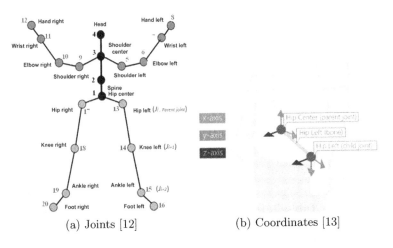

(a) Joints [12]   (b) Coordinates [13]

Fig. 5. Hierarchy of Kinect skeleton joints

Kinect provides the 3D (camera) coordinates and a hierarchical orientation information[9] at every joint. So to convert the camera co-ordinate space to local co-ordinate system we multiply camera coordinate vectors (V_1 and V_2) with the orientation matrix. The resultant vectors are V_1' and V_2'. Next we normalize and compute the arc cosine of each component in X, Y and Z directions to get the angle between B_1 and B_2.

To understand the features better, let us take an example. Suppose a man has spread both his hands wide in sideways in a given posture. So we can describe the posture as right hand making an angle in the range of +90° to +100° from spine and left hand making –90° to –100° angle from spine. These angles succinctly describe the upper body posture (of hands). In Laban diagram, direction and level are best described by angular information. Hence we choose such angular information as feature for classification. These angles are created by *bones* connecting 20 skeletal joint points.

---

[9] In the form of quaternions and rotation matrices [13].

Often skeleton frames have errors where skeletons may be distorted or ill-formed. So we use filters to select a set of clean skeleton frames. We then take average over 5 consecutive frames to compute candidate frames for training and test.

4.4   LabanViewer Tool

We build *LabanViewer* (Fig. 6), to annotate the features in the data sets. It can play, pause, and extract features of 4 limbs for any frame. A limb is selected by *Generate Features* button and a total of 6 sets of angles are extracted for each limb and annotated based on the name of the video. The *Bad Skeleton* check box is used for removing bad data from files. Finally, the laban diagram is generated with *Generate Laban* button.

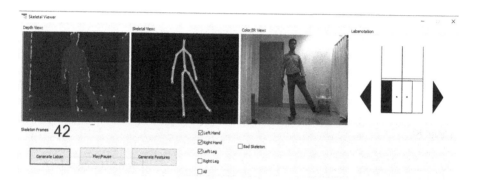

Fig. 6. *LabanViewer* tool for annotation and laban generation

4.5   Training of Classifiers

We use multi-class *Support Vector Machine* (SVM) [14] for classification. The classifier is trained and tested with the created data set as shown in the Fig. 7. Four separate classifiers (left leg, right leg, left hand, and right hand) for predicting the class of each limb are built. Multi-class SVM uses the multi-class formulation, but optimizes it with an algorithm that is very fast in the linear case. For a training set $(x_1, y_1) \cdots (x_l, y_l)$ where $x_i \in R^d$ (d is the dimension of the vector R) with labels $y_i \in [1..k]$, it finds the solution of the following optimization problem during training.

$$\min_{\substack{W_m \in H, \\ b \in R^K, \\ \xi \in R^{l \times k}}} \frac{1}{2} \sum_{m=1}^{k} W_m^T W_m + C \sum_{i=1}^{l} \sum_{t \neq y_i} \xi_{i,t}$$

subject to $W_{yi}^T \varphi(x_i) + b_{yi} \geq W_t^T \varphi(x_i) + b_t + 2 - \xi_{i,t}$. The resulting decision function is

$$argmax_m (W_m^T \varphi(x) + b_m)$$

where $\xi_{i,t} \geq 0$ ($\xi_{i,t}$ denotes the pairwise margin violation between the true class y_i and some other class t), $i = 1...l, t \in \{1....k\}$, W is the weight vector, C is the regularization constant, and the mapping function φ projects the training data into a suitable feature space H so as to allow for nonlinear decision surfaces.

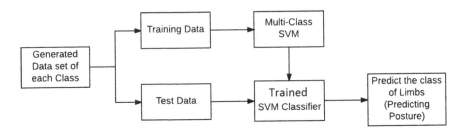

Fig. 7. The classifier

4.6   Decoding of Class to Laban XML and Labanotation

After training the classifier for 4 limbs, the system predicts the class of new posture and decodes the class predicted by the classifier to generate *LabanXML*. This is used as input to generate *Labanotation* diagrams. The process is shown in Fig. 8.

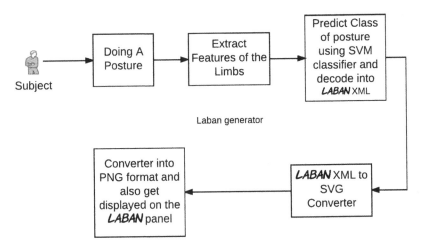

Fig. 8. Decoding of class to laban XML and labanotation

5   Experimental Results

We illustrate the results with Right Hand limb. For this we recorded 1170 samples – 39 right hand limb classes performed by 3 volunteers (10 repeats for every class).

Table 3. Confusion matrix for right hand

Class ID	Self	Error	Total	Class ID	Self	Error	Total
277	3		3	389	2		2
281	3	2,409	5	390	2	1,342	5
293	3		3			2,438	
294	1	1,295	2	391	3		3
295	3	1,294	4	393	4		4
297	3	1,329	4	394	4		4
298	4		4	397	4		4
301	5		5	398	4		4
302	2		2	399	1		1
309	1		1	405	2		2
325	1		1	406	7		7
326	4	1,297	5	407	6		6
327	0	1,334	1	409	3		3
329	3	1,409	4	410	0	2,301	2
333	4		4	413	1		1
334	1		1	414	4		4
341	2		2	415	5		5
342	2		2	437	2		2
349	0	1,445	1	438	3		3
350	1		1	445	2	1,397	3
Total	46	9	55	Total	59	6	65

There 39 classes are coded as in Sect. 4.2. For test data, the diagonal entries (cases of correct recognition) of the confusion matrix are shown as 'Self'. Entries for wrong recognition are shown under 'Error' with the id of the mis-classified class. For example, for class id = 281, the diagonal entry is 3 (correct cases) and it is mis-classified as class 409 in 2 cases. 'Total' shows the number of samples in the class.

100 of these samples, however, had to be discarded due to various noise and recording errors. Hence the experiments are performed with 1070 samples.

We train an C-SVM classifier (Sect. 4.5) with polynomial kernel function of degree 6 using 950 samples. First the model is tested on the training data itself. It is found to be 100% accurate. This proves that the features are 100% separable under polynomial kernel with degree 6. We then test it on remaining 120 samples. The confusion matrix for this is shown in Table 3. 105 out of 120 samples are correctly recognized. Hence **we achieve 87.5% accuracy**.

Many of the mis-classifications are due to wrong estimation of degree of bending which often are border line. Like class 294 (90° bending) as 295

(180° bending) and vice versa. In some cases, however, the direction of the limb is grossly mis-classified – like class 390 (direction 8 or left side) as class 342 (direction 5 or right backward diagonal). This is due to wrong skeleton formation.

We repeated similar procedure for the other limbs too. Finally, **we could get 86.0%, 89.5%, and 80.5% accuracy for left hand, right leg, and left leg respectively**.

6   Conclusions

We present a non-intrusive automated system to translate human postures into *Labanotation* using Kinect video of human postures and movements. We use Kinect skeletons and represent every posture in terms of angles between bones of 4 major limbs – hands and legs. We build a multi-class SVM to classify the formation of every limb into Laban primitives and represent in *LabanXML*. We also prepare a data set of postures and develop a *LabanViewer* tool annotate them. The system can be used as an effective front-end for posture analysis applications in various areas like dance and sports where predefined postures form the basis for analysis and interpretation. The parseability of the output representation (XML) makes it easy for integration in a platform independent manner.

The implementation of the system has been a non-trivial task. First, the multi-modal data of Kinect has a lot of noise [16] due to various factors. Particularly, the skeletons are often ill-formed (especially when one body part overlaps on another). Hence, we needed to use various filtering (at image as well as skeleton levels) and tune a couple of threshold to stabilize the computations. Second, the Kinect views the postures from one side and all postures (critical for defining correctness) are not completely discernible from the view. Use of multiple Kinect for more complete 3D view has its own issues [17].

Going forward we plan to train the separate classifiers for head and torso too. But we need to be careful while deciding feature vector for these, since these two form a rigid structure in Kinect skeleton frames that moves a little. With this we hope to move on the human body movements as movement is just a sequence of postures with time.

References

1. Guest, A.H.: Labanotation: The System of Analyzing and Recording Movement, 4th edn. Routledge, Abingdon (2005)
2. Kinect. https://en.wikipedia.org/wiki/Kinect. Accessed 24 Apr 2016
3. Michael Good, MusicXML. http://www.musicxml.com/. Accessed 17 Aug 2017
4. Griesbeck, C.: Introduction to Labanotation, Frankfurt University (1996). http://user.uni-frankfurt.de/~griesbec/LABANE.HTML. Accessed 24 Apr 2016
5. Wolofsky, Z.: Computer Interpretation of Selected Labanotation Commands, Vancouver, B.C., Canada (1974). summit.sfu.ca

6. Loke, L., Larssen, A.T., Robertson, T.: Labanotation for design of movement-based interaction. In: IE 2005 Proceedings of the Second Australasian Conference on Interactive Entertainment, Sydney, Australia (2005)
7. EyeToy-Wikipedia. https://en.wikipedia.org/wiki/EyeToy. Accessed 26 Apr 2016
8. Brown, M.D., Smoliar, S.W.: A graphics editor for labanotation. In: SIGGRAPH 1976 Proceedings of the 3rd Annual Conference on Computer Graphics and Interactive Techniques, New York, NY, USA (1976)
9. Choensawat, W., Takahashi, S., Nakamura, M., Hachimura, K.: LabaNOHtation: Laban meets Noh. In: SIGGRAPH 2012 ACM SIGGRAPH 2012 Posters, New York, NY, USA (2012)
10. Guo, H., Miao, Z., Zhu, F., Zhang, G., Li, S.: Automatic labanotation generation based on human motion capture data. In: Li, S., Liu, C., Wang, Y. (eds.) CCPR 2014. CCIS, vol. 483, pp. 426–435. Springer, Heidelberg (2014). https://doi.org/10.1007/978-3-662-45646-0_44
11. Nakamura, M., Hachimura, K.: An XML representation of Labanotation, LabanXML, and its implementation on the notation editor LabanEditor2. Rev. Natl. Cent. Digitization 9, 47–51 (2006)
12. Tracking Users with Kinect Skeletal Tracking, 24 April 2016. https://msdn.microsoft.com/en-us/library/jj131025.aspx
13. Joint Orientation, 24 April 2016. https://msdn.microsoft.com/en-us/library/hh973073.aspx
14. Boser, B.E., Guyon, I.M., Vapnik, V.N.: A training algorithm for optimal margin classifiers. In: COLT 1992 Proceedings of the Fifth Annual Workshop on Computational Learning Theory, New York, USA (1992)
15. Kojima, K., Hachimura, K., Nakamura, M.: Labaneditor: Graphical editor for dance notation. In: Proceedings of 11th IEEE International Workshop on Robot and Human Interactive Communication, pp. 59–64. IEEE (2002)
16. Mallick, T., Das, P.P., Majumdar, A.K.: Characterizations of noise in Kinect depth images. IEEE Sens. J. 14, 1731–1740 (2014)
17. Mallick, T., Das, P.P., Majumdar, A.K.: Study of interference noise in multi-Kinect set-up. In: Proceedings of 9th International Conference on Computer Vision Theory and Applications VISAPP 2014, pp. 173–178 (2014)

Emotion Based Categorization of Music Using Low Level Features and Agglomerative Clustering

Rajib Sarkar[1]([⊠])(iD), Saikat Dutta[2], Aneek Roy[2], and Sanjoy Kumar Saha[2]

[1] Computer Science Department, Derozio Memorial College,
Kolkata 700136, West Bengal, India
rjbskar@gmail.com
[2] Computer Science and Engineering Department,
Jadavpur University, Kolkata 700032, West Bengal, India
saikat.dutta779@gmail.com, aneek.roy5@gmail.com, sks_ju@yahoo.co.in

Abstract. Music emotion recognition (MER) has become an eminent field of interest in music information retrieval (MIR) group with the objective to provide more flexibility in content based music retrieval. It is quite important to categorize the music according to the emotional characteristics as it enables the users to retrieve the music according to their cognitive state. In this work, we have considered low level time-domain and spectral features extracted from the music signal. Instead of considering a wide range of features, they are judiciously considered based on our perception about the particular emotion. For classification, unsupervised approach based on *K-means* and *Agglomerative* clustering are considered. Experiment is carried out on a benchmark dataset. Performance comparison with existing work reflects the superiority of our proposed work.

Keywords: Music emotion recognition · Time-domain features
Spectral features · Clustering

1 Introduction

Music is an universal form of communication that conveys emotional information transcending language boundaries. It also influences cognitive state of the listener. To perceive the emotions in music, Russell's emotion model [1] has been accepted by researchers. According to this model, emotion is represented in a two dimensional space where *valence* and *arousal* are the two dimensions. Perceived energy level of a musical excerpt is the measure of *arousal*. The energy level extends from low energy indicating calmness to high energy indicating excitement [2]. *Valence* indicates the attractiveness (goodness or positivity) or ugliness (badness or negativity) of a music clip [3].

Music emotion recognition has gained tremendous importance in recent times. Emotional characterization of music is an important task especially when

© Springer Nature Singapore Pte Ltd. 2018
R. Rameshan et al. (Eds.): NCVPRIPG 2017, CCIS 841, pp. 506–516, 2018.
https://doi.org/10.1007/978-981-13-0020-2_44

we want to divide large collections of music into emotional clusters. This can be useful for the users to download music from the websites according to their emotional/mental state. This idea can also be integrated into music players on mobile-phones or computers which eases the task for user to pick music according to their mood. The main challenge in this work comes in the form of subjectivity of emotion. Unfortunately, the state-of-the-art techniques are yet to achieve desired level of success.

The paper is organized as follows. A brief survey of past work is presented in Sect. 2. Proposed methodology is discussed in Sect. 3. Sections 4 and 5 provide experimental results and concluding remarks.

2 Past Work

The ethos of human life is captured in the essence of music [4]. A extensive database of music files has been created and a huge collection of music files are accessed daily. The conventional meta data based cataloging approaches are inadequate to manage such vast collection of music. An effective system is required to organize and retrieve music information to meet the demands of drastically growing music industry. In this context, music emotion recognition has become very popular and challenging topic among acoustic domain researchers [5–7].

It is not always effective to label a music excerpt by exactly one emotional tag and it may have multiple emotional aspects. One way of representing the emotional aspect of music clips is to place them in a two dimensional plane, as proposed by Thayer [8] and Russell [1]. The two dimensions in the plot are pleasure/valence and arousal. Russell's work is considered as the pioneer in MER field to describe human emotions. Thayer adopted Russell's emotion model. This two-dimensional emotion plane can be divided into quadrants or octant denoting four or eight emotional state. According to Thayer's emotion plane, emotion of a music can be depicted by a two dimensional model where the X and Y axes are valence and arousal respectively. So, regression model for both valence and arousal can be trained to find the position of the song in the plane which gives us an impression about the emotional aspect of the music.

Gómez and Cáceres [9] proposed feature based multi-label music emotion detection system. A set of features are used as descriptor. The descriptor includes mean and standard deviation of spectral centroid, spectral roll-off and mel-frequency cepstral coefficients (MFCCs). The classification algorithm k-Nearest Neighbors (kNN) is used to classify song clips according to their emotional labels. Chen et al. [10] proposed a regression based method. They have extracted MFCC coefficients, tonal intensity value, linear predictor coefficients of the spectral envelope, spectral flux and spectral shape descriptors like spectral centroid, spectral spread, spectral skewness, and spectral kurtosis. The valence and arousal values of each music clip is regressed with ground truth using Gaussian mixture model (GMM). Koch et al. [11] proposed a method for recommendation of online videos. The low level audio features are extracted to determine the emotion.

MIRtoolbox [12] is used to extract the low level audio features and for classification support vector machines (SVM) is used. Zhang et al. [13] proposed a feature based emotion detection approach where features like root mean square (RMS) energy, MFCC's, zero crossing rate (ZCR), fundamental frequency (f_0) are considered along-with voicing probability and statistical features. They have used Random Forest for classification. Media-Eval competition [14] considers emotion in music as a task. Participants deal with the prediction of static and dynamic emotion [15].

The work of Saari et al. [16] focused on feature selection criteria. They have used a wide range of features to represent various aspects like dynamism, rhythm, structure, timbre, harmony and pitch. They have worked with different combination of feature selection methods and classifiers. For feature selection: wrapper selection method, forward selection and backward elimination are tried. Classifiers like Naive Bayes, k-NN and SVM are utilized.

From the past work, the general observation is that it is quite difficult to capture and map the emotion in terms of low level features. But indeed the emotion will have some sort of bearings in the low level features. Researchers have used wide range of features and relied on the supervised classifier for the outcome. One major issue with supervised approach lies in the availability of proper training data. Very often, it is not possible to categorize a music clip to a single emotional class. It is likely to affect the learning process. In our approach, we are motivated to select the features in a judicious manner based on the perception of emotion and subsequently follow the unsupervised classification to avoid the issues of proper learning.

3   Proposed Methodology

Music is very complex structure of sounds whose different parameters affect the perception of different emotion. The way musical accents are patterned through time leads listeners to anticipate the emotional essence spread over the musical clip. In this work, feature set is designed considering the relation between emotional response and musical structure. The feature set combines both time and frequency domain low level features. The features are standardized using z-score normalization. The music excerpts are then clustered into a number of clusters same as the number of classes in ground truth using the standardized features. Finally, quality of clusters are evaluated. In the following sections, details of the extraction of features, classification method along with evaluation process are discussed.

3.1   Feature Extraction

Different features considered in our work are as follows.

RMS Energy: Energy varies depending on the emotional content. For an excitement, energy is indeed high with respect to sad state. Hence, it can play role in identifying the emotion. It is calculated as root mean square of amplitude of the samples in the audio signals [17]. Let x is the time domain normalized signal with n samples, then its RMS energy is given by

$$E = \sqrt{\frac{\sum_1^n (x(i))^2}{n}}$$

Time domain signal is divided into number of frames, each consisting of 512 samples. Average and standard deviation of the frame level RMS energy are taken as the features. Figure 1(a) shows the average frame level energy for five samples of different emotional categories. Its discriminating capability is also visible in the plot.

Zero Crossing Rate (ZCR): ZCR is a gross approximation of the signal frequency. Strong emotion is expected to have relative higher frequency content (so higher ZCR) in comparison to a sad or tender mood. The time domain signal x is divided into number of frames consisting of N samples (it is 512 for our case). For each frame ZCR is computed as follows.

$$ZCR = \sum_{m=1}^{N-1} sign(x(m) \times x(m-1))$$

where *sign* function is

$$sign(a) = \begin{cases} 1, & if & a > 0 \\ 0, & if & a = 0 \\ -1, & otherwise \end{cases}$$

Finally, average and standard deviation of the frame level ZCR are used as features. Figure 1(b) reflects the variation of average ZCR for different categories of emotions.

Linear Prediction Cepstral Coefficients (LPCC): Variation in the time domain signal depends on the emotion. A flat or neutral emotion is likely to have less variation in the signal and variation increases otherwise. Low variation allows better predictability. With this intuition, we have considered features based on linear predictive coding [18]. LPC uses a linear model to represent the spectrum of an audio signal in compressed form. It basically uses a linear model to predict n_{th} value using previous p samples of the signal as follows.

$$Predicted\ Sample, \hat{x}(n) = \sum_{i=1}^{p} (a_i \times x(n-i))$$

a_is are the linear predictive coefficients and $x(t)$ is the t-th sample value of the signal. a_is are computed based on first $(p+1)$ autocorrelation co-efficients of the estimated samples. LPCC, C_is are extracted from LPC's using the following recursive equation.

$$C_i = a_i + \sum_{k=1}^{i-1} \frac{k}{i} C_k \times a_{i-k} \qquad for\ 1 \le i \le p \quad and$$

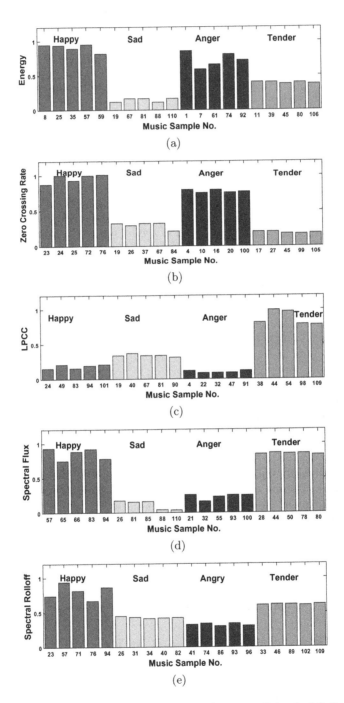

Fig. 1. Plot for (a) Energy, (b) ZCR (c) LPCC (first co-efficient), (d) Spectral flux, and (e) Spectral rolloff respectively for different category of emotion.

$$C_i = \sum_{k=i-p}^{i-1} \frac{k}{i} C_k \times a_{i-k} \qquad for\ i > p$$

In our case, p is taken as 12 and twelve C_is are considered. Signal is divided into equal sized frames and for each frame the co-efficients are computed. Finally, average and standard deviation of each co-efficient over the frames are used as features. Figure 1(c) shows the plot for average value of the first co-efficient for different samples belonging to different emotions.

We have considered a set of spectral features. In order to compute these features, first of all the time domain signal is divided into number of frames consisting of N samples. Discrete Fourier transform [19] is applied on the frame to obtain the frequency spectrum. Let $X_i(k)$ denotes the k-th co-efficient of the i-th frame. For each frame N such coefficients form the corresponding spectral frame.

Spectral Flux (SF): It measures the changing rate of power spectrum of an audio signal by computing the sum of differences of consecutive normalized spectral frames as follows.

$$F_r = \frac{1}{N} \sum_{k=1}^{N} (|\ X_r(k)\ | - |\ X_{r-1}(k)\ |)^2$$

Variation in the power of spectral components over successive frames is captured by SF. Average and standard deviation of the variations over the frames are taken as features. Figure 1(d) shows the plot for different category of emotion.

Spectral Rolloff (SR): It is defined as the qth percentile of the power spectral distribution [20]. It characterizes the inclination of the frequency spectrum. In our case q is taken as 85. Average and standard deviation of the SR point over the frames are taken as features. The plot of average value for different emotion classes is shown in Fig. 1(e).

Spectral Flatness Measure (SFM): It is the ratio of the geometric mean to the arithmetic mean of a power spectrum [17,21], as shown below,

$$SFM = \frac{\sqrt[N]{\prod_{k=0}^{N-1} X(k)}}{\frac{1}{N} \sum_{k=0}^{N-1} X(k)}$$

Average and standard deviation of SFMs over the frames are considered as the features. For uniform (flat) distribution of power spectral component it provides higher value.

Spectral Crest Factor (SCF): It is the measurement of the quality of a acoustic signal [17]and defined as peak to root mean square ratio. It is inversely proportional to the flatness. SCF is computed as the ratio of maximum spectrum power and mean spectrum power of a sub-band. In our case, 24 for sub-bands are considered in each frame. Finally, for each sub-band mean and standard deviation of frame level values are considered.

3.2   Classification

We have followed unsupervised approach based on clustering. Two clustering methodology namely, *k-means* and *Agglomerative Clustering* have been considered.

K-Means clustering is a method to divide data into a pre-specified number of clusters(K) [22]. Value of K is taken as the number of emotional groups. In the initialization phase, K data-points are assigned as cluster-centroids. For the rest of the data-points, they are assigned to the cluster with closest cluster-centroid. Now, position of cluster-centroids are updated by averaging over the points present in respective clusters. Again, data-points are assigned to cluster having closest cluster-centroid followed by cluster-centroid updation. This cluster-assignment and updation loop is continued until sum of squared distances of nodes in a cluster from their nearest cluster center is below a specified tolerance level. Major problem arises from the fact that selection of initial cluster centers is non trivial and it influences the final clusters. As an alternative scheme, we have considered Agglomerative Clustering.

Agglomerative clustering [23] is a *bottom-up* approach to hierarchical clustering. Initially it is assumed that each data points belong to a separate cluster. Then the distance between the clusters is measured. Smallest distance among all possible pairs of elements of two groups (single-link clustering) or the maximum distance between the pairs (complete link clustering) may be taken as the distance between two clusters. In each iteration two closest clusters are identified and merged. The process continues till a criteria is met. In our case when number of clusters reaches the number of emotional category the process stops. The result of the agglomerative clustering can be represented using a hierarchical structure known as dendogram, which tend to be generally compact in case of complete-link clustering. We have used agglomerative clustering along with complete-linking and *Manhattan distance* is taken as the distance metric.

Once the clusters are formed, based on the ground-truth category of the music clips the clusters are labeled. The category which becomes the majority is considered as the cluster label. This assignment problem is solved by applying the concept of Hungarian method [24]. The emotional category is a subjective matter. Normally, in a benchmark dataset corresponding to each music clip ratings are provided for all emotions with certain confidence value that ranges in $[0, 1]$. In deciding the cluster label, we have considered the primary category which is the category with highest confidence. To evaluate the accuracy of clustering, along with primary, another secondary category is also considered. It is the category with second highest rating. It is taken in to account provided the confidence value is with in a threshold of the primary confidence. In our experiment, it is taken as 0.1. Inclusion of secondary category in evaluating the clusters addresses the subjectivity issue of the emotion. On the other hand, closeness of confidence values of primary and secondary tag ensures that both are applicable.

Table 1. Performance comparison

Method	Features used	Accuracy
K-means	Set A – Energy, Spectral Rolloff, ZCR	59.09%
Agglomerative clustering	Set B – Spectral Crest Factor, Spectral Flatness, Spectral Rolloff, Spectral Flux, LPCC	**63.63%**
SVM	Set A	51.43%
SVM	Set B	58.08%
k-NN BE [16]	Mode Majorness and Key clarity, combined with dynamical, rhythmical and structural features	56.5%
SVM BE [16]	Dynamical, rhythmical, structural, timbral harmony & pitch features *Wrapper selection* method used for feature selection	54.3%

4   Experimental Results

Most of the researchers have worked with their own dataset. Saari et al. [16] have worked with a benchmark dataset namely, *SoundTracks dataset* [25]. To carry out the experiment we have also worked with the same dataset. It consists of audio-clips collected from background tracks of movies with duration ranging from 10 seconds to 30 seconds. The songs are well distributed over different emotional categories like anger, fear, sadness, happiness and tenderness. A panel of twelve musicology experts rated a set of 360 music-clips (*Set-1*). Set-1 is then refined such that participants' ratings are consistent, thereby providing a set of 110 excerpts (*Set-2*). For *Set-2*, ratings are consistent and have achieved Cronbach's alpha [26] over 0.99. Fear and Anger emotions have high correlation (0.69) making these emotions difficult to distinguish. For this reason, we consider anger and fear belonging to the same class giving rise to a total number of four classes as ground truth - Anger/Fear, Happy, Sad and Tender as considered in [16].

The common practice is to design the descriptors for the items to be classified at first level. At the next level, based on the descriptors items are categorized. For classification supervised or unsupervised approach may be followed. In supervised approach training data is required for learning the inherent pattern for different categories. So, availability of suitable training data of sufficient volume is very important. Emotion being a subjective attribute, different listeners may not fully agree on the emotional category of a music. Ground truth also reflects the same as the clips bear multiple tags. It has motivated us to focus on unsupervised classification. However, we have carried out our experiment using both unsupervised (K-means and Agglomerative clustering) and supervised classifier (SVM).

In our work, features are extracted using MARSYAS [27], an open-source software. Features are standardized using z-score normalization. Clustering is implemented using Scikit-learn [28], a Machine Learning library in Python. It is difficult to adjudge the contribution of the features and classification techniques. In our effort, different feature combination has been tried for both the clustering techniques. Best feature combination for each of the clustering techniques and their corresponding performances are presented in Table 1. For K-means clustering, best performance is achieved with feature Set A comprising of energy, spectral rolloff and ZCR. But, *Agglomerative* clustering with feature Set B comprising of spectral Crest factor, spectral flatness, spectral roll-off, spectral flux and LPCC provides better result. For comparison, we have also worked with SVM classifier with RBF kernel. It is implemented using Scikit-learn [28]. Both the feature sets A and B have been used as the descriptors. As shown in Table 1, its performance is inferior. While working with feature set A, K-means clustering performs better than SVM and for feature set B, *Agglomerative* clustering performs better. As discussed earlier, a music clip may not be mapped to a single emotional class. Thus, ensuring proper training for SVM classifier is difficult. Lack of optimal training data (both, in terms of the purity of its category and size) is a possible reason behind its low performance.

The proposed system is further compared with the work of Saari et al. [16] and the comparative result is shown in Table 1. Their best result is based on k-NN with backward elimination (BE) on mode majorness, key clarity, combined with dynamical, rhythmical, and structural features. It is observed that performance of proposed *Agglomerative* clustering based methodology is superior.

5 Conclusion

In this work we have presented a simple methodology for low level feature based music emotion recognition. Both time and frequency domain features are considered to match our perception about emotion. For classification, unsupervised approach is followed. Two clustering algorithms namely, *K-means* and *Agglomerative* clustering are considered. Experiment is carried out for different combinations of the features and clustering algorithms on a benchmark dataset. Performance is compared with the existing works on the same dataset and proposed methodology outperforms those. In future, a deep learning architecture may be deployed to learn the features to capture the subtlety of the cognitive and emotional aspect.

References

1. Russell, J.: A circumspect model of affect, 1980. J. Pers. Soc. Psychol. **39**(6), 1161–1178 (1980)
2. Sammler, D., Grigutsch, M., Fritz, T., Koelsch, S.: Music and emotion: electrophysiological correlates of the processing of pleasant and unpleasant music. Psychophysiology **44**(2), 293–304 (2007)

3. Krumhansl, C.L.: An exploratory study of musical emotions and psychophysiology. Can. J. Exp. Psychol./Rev. canadienne de psychologie expérimentale **51**(4), 336 (1997)
4. Miyashita, H., Nishimoto, K.: What is the essence of music? A case study on a Japanese audience. In: Proceedings of the Sound and Music Computing (2005)
5. Kim, Y.E., Schmidt, E.M., Migneco, R., Morton, B.G., Richardson, P., Scott, J., Speck, J.A., Turnbull, D.: Music emotion recognition: a state of the art review. In: Proceedings of the ISMIR, pp. 255–266 (2010)
6. Yang, Y.H., Chen, H.H.: Machine recognition of music emotion: a review. ACM Trans. Intell. Syst. Technol. **3**(3), 40:1–40:30 (2012)
7. Han, B., Rho, S., Jun, S., Hwang, E.: Music emotion classification and context-based music recommendation. Multimedia Tools Appl. **47**(3), 433–460 (2010)
8. Thayer, R.E.: The Biopsychology of Mood and Arousal. Oxford University Press, Oxford (1990)
9. Gómez, L.M., Cáceres, M.N.: Applying data mining for sentiment analysis in music. In: Proceedings of the PAAMS, pp. 198–205 (2017)
10. Chen, Y.A., Wang, J.C., Yang, Y.H., Chen, H.: Component tying for mixture model adaptation in personalization of music emotion recognition. IEEE/ACM Trans. Audio. Speech Lang. Process. **25**(7), 1409–1420 (2017)
11. Koch, C., Krupii, G., Hausheer, D.: Proactive caching of music videos based on audio features, mood, and genre. In: Proceedings of the MMSys, pp. 100–111 (2017)
12. Lartillot, O., Toiviainen, P.: A matlab toolbox for musical feature extraction from audio. In: Proceedings of the DAFx, pp. 237–244 (2007)
13. Zhang, F., Meng, H., Li, M.: Emotion extraction and recognition from music. In: Proceedings of the ICNC-FSKD, pp. 1728–1733 (2016)
14. Soleymani, M., Aljanaki, A., Yang, Y.H., Caro, M.N., Eyben, F., Markov, K., Schuller, B.W., Veltkamp, R., Weninger, F., Wiering, F.: Emotional analysis of music: a comparison of methods. In: Proceedings of the 22nd ACM International Conference on Multimedia, pp. 1161–1164. ACM (2014)
15. Weninger, F., Eyben, F., Schuller, B.W.: The TUM approach to the mediaeval music emotion task using generic affective audio features. In: MediaEval (2013)
16. Saari, P., Eerola, T., Lartillot, O.: Generalizability and simplicity as criteria in feature selection: application to mood classification in music. IEEE Trans. Audio Speech Lang. Process. **19**(6), 1802–1812 (2011)
17. Lerch, A.: An Introduction to Audio Content Analysis: Applications in Signal Processing and Music Informatics. Wiley, Hoboken (2012)
18. Huang, X., Acero, A., Hon, H.W., Foreword By-Reddy, R.: Spoken Language Processing: A Guide to Theory, Algorithm, and System Development. Prentice Hall PTR, Upper Saddle River (2001)
19. Welch, P.: The use of fast fourier transform for the estimation of power spectra: a method based on time averaging over short, modified periodograms. IEEE Trans. Audio Electroacoust. **15**(2), 70–73 (1967)
20. Zhang, T., Kuo, C.C.J.: Audio content analysis for online audiovisual data segmentation and classification. IEEE Trans. Speech Audio Process. **9**(4), 441–457 (2001)
21. Gray, A., Markel, J.: A spectral-flatness measure for studying the autocorrelation method of linear prediction of speech analysis. IEEE Trans. Acoust. Speech Sig. Process. **22**(3), 207–217 (1974)
22. Hartigan, J.A., Wong, M.A.: Algorithm as 136: a k-means clustering algorithm. J. Roy. Stat. Soc.: Ser. C (Appl. Stat.) **28**(1), 100–108 (1979)

23. Beeferman, D., Berger, A.: Agglomerative clustering of a search engine query log. In: Proceeding of the SIGKDD, pp. 407–416 (2000)
24. Kuhn, H.W.: The Hungarian method for the assignment problem. Nav. Res. Logist. (NRL) **2**(1–2), 83–97 (1955)
25. Eerola, T., Vuoskoski, J.K.: A comparison of the discrete and dimensional models of emotion in music. Psychol. Music **39**(1), 18–49 (2011)
26. Cronbach, L.J.: Coefficient alpha and the internal structure of tests. Psychometrika **16**(3), 297–334 (1951)
27. Tzanetakis, G., Cook, P.: MARSYAS: a framework for audio analysis. Organ. Sound **4**(3), 169–175 (2000)
28. Pedregosa, F., Varoquaux, G., Gramfort, A., Michel, V., Thirion, B., Grisel, O., Blondel, M., Prettenhofer, P., Weiss, R., Dubourg, V., et al.: Scikit-learn: machine learning in python. J. Mach. Learn. Res. **12**(Oct), 2825–2830 (2011)

Transfer Learning by Finetuning Pretrained CNNs Entirely with Synthetic Images

Param Rajpura[1], Alakh Aggarwal[2], Manik Goyal[2]📷, Sanchit Gupta[3]📷,
Jonti Talukdar[4], Hristo Bojinov[5], and Ravi Hegde[1](✉)📷

[1] Indian Institute of Technology Gandhinagar, Gandhinagar 382355, India
Hegder@iitgn.ac.in
[2] Indian Institute of Technology (BHU) Varanasi, Varanasi 221005, India
[3] BITS Hyderabad, Hyderabad 500078, India
[4] Nirma Institute of Technology, Ahmedabad 382481, India
[5] Innit Inc., Redwood City 94063, USA

Abstract. We show that finetuning pretrained CNNs entirely on synthetic images is an effective strategy to achieve transfer learning. We apply this strategy for detecting packaged food products clustered in refrigerator scenes. A CNN pretrained on the COCO dataset and finetuned with our 4000 synthetic images achieves mean average precision (mAP @ 0.5-IOU) of 52.59 on a test set of real images (150 distinct products as objects of interest and 25 distractor objects) in comparison to a value of 24.15 achieved without such finetuning. The synthetic images were rendered with freely available 3D models with variations in parameters like color, texture and viewpoint without a high emphasis on photorealism. We analyze factors like training data set size, cue variances, 3D model dictionary size and network architecture for their influence on the transfer learning performance. Additionally, training strategies like fine-tuning with selected layers and early stopping which affect transfer learning from synthetic scenes to real scenes were explored. This approach is promising in scenarios where limited training data is available.

1 Introduction

Deep Convolutional Neural Networks (CNNs) have fulfilled the demand for a robust feature extractor and have achieved state-of-the-art performance on image classification, object detection, and segmentation [1,2] tasks. The availability of large sets of training images has been a prerequisite for successfully training CNNs [1]. Manual annotation of images for object detection is a time-consuming and mechanical task; what is more, in some applications the cost of capturing images with sufficient variety is prohibitive. In fact the largest image datasets are built upon only a few categories for which images can be feasibly curated (20 categories in PASCAL VOC [3], 80 in COCO [4], and 200 in ImageNet [5]).

There have been solutions proposed to reduce annotation efforts by employing transfer learning or simulating scenes to generate large image sets. The research

© Springer Nature Singapore Pte Ltd. 2018
R. Rameshan et al. (Eds.): NCVPRIPG 2017, CCIS 841, pp. 517–528, 2018.
https://doi.org/10.1007/978-981-13-0020-2_45

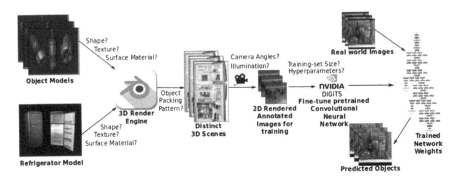

Fig. 1. Overview of our approach to train object detectors for real images based on rendered images.

community has proposed multiple approaches for the problem of adapting vision-based models trained in one domain to a different domain [6–10]. Examples include: re-training a model in the target domain [11]; adapting the weights of a pre-trained model with adaptive batch normalization [12]; overlaying synthetic text on real background images [13]; and, learning common features by maximizing domain confusion between source and target domains [14]. Donahue et al. [15] introduced the concept of learning linear classifiers for target dataset over DeCAF (features) extracted from CNN trained on large public datasets. Though Tommasi et al. [16] report that DeCAF not only does not solve the dataset bias problem in general, but in some cases (both class- and dataset-dependent) they capture specific information that induce worse performance than what can be obtained with less powerful features. Oquab et al. [17] used mid-level representation and finetuned them for target datasets which has been considered standard practice given annotated dataset is available for target domain.

Attempts to use synthetic data for training CNNs to adapt in real scenarios have been made in the past. Peng et. al. used available 3D CAD models to render images (after varying the projections and orientations of the objects) for evaluation on 20 categories in the PASCAL VOC 2007 data set [18]. They aimed to study the effects of texture and background by training the classifier. Su and coworkers [19] used the rendered 2D images from 3D on varying backgrounds for pose estimation. Their work also uses an object proposal stage and limits the objects of interest to a few specific categories from the PASCAL VOC data set. Georgakis and coworkers [20] propose to learn object detection with synthetic data generated by object instances being superimposed into real scenes at different positions, scales, and illumination. They propose the use of existing object recognition data sets such as BigBird [21] rather than using 3D CAD models. They limit their synthesized scenes to low-occlusion scenarios with 11 products in GMU-Kitchens data set. Gupta et. al. generate a synthetic training set by taking advantage of scene segmentation to create synthetic training examples, however the goal is text localization instead of object detection [13]. Tobin et. al. perform domain randomization with low-fidelity rendered images from 3D meshes, however their objective is to locate simpler polygon-shaped objects restricted to a table top in world coordinates [22]. In [23,24], the Unity game engine is used to generate RGB-D rendered images and semantic labels for outdoor and indoor scenes. They show that by using photo-realistic rendered images the effort for annotation can be significantly reduced. They combine synthetic and real data to train models for semantic segmentation, however the network requires depth map for semantic segmentation.

In this paper, we report performance of transfer learning by finetuning a pretrained network (with standard public datasets) to identify objects in refrigerator with reasonably small sized dataset of synthetic images rendered from available 3D models. We automate the process of rendering 3D models with variations in viewpoints, cues etc. and annotating the 2D images to use it for object detection in real scenes. We report the study of cues or hyper-parameters involved to efficiently achieve transfer learning from synthetic to real images. Our experiments explore the effects of data set size, 3D model repository sizes. While lesser attention has been given to understanding selective layer fine-tuning for transfer learning, we explore it and report significant improvements. Furthermore, training strategy like early stopping [25] is also used for transfer learning from simulation to reality. Hence, this approach is particularly relevant in the detection of object candidates in scenes with large intra-class variance as opposed to one with only a few specific categories using synthetic datasets which do not require extensive effort towards achieving photorealism. The rest of this paper is organized as follows: our methodology is described in Sect. 2, followed by the results we obtain reported in Sect. 3, finally concluding the paper in Sect. 4.

2   Method

To study transfer learning from synthetic to real images we choose the object detection task where given an RGB image captured inside a refrigerator, our goal is to predict a bound-box for each object of interest. In addition, there are few objects in the scene that need to be neglected. Our approach is to train a deep CNN with synthetic rendered images from available 3D models. Overview of the approach is shown in Fig. 1. Our work can be divided into two major parts namely synthetic image rendering from 3D models and transfer learning by fine-tuning the deep neural network with synthetic images.

2.1   Synthetic Generation of Images from 3D Models

We use Blender and its Python APIs to load 3D models and automate the scene rendering. We use Cycles Render Engine with Blender since it supports ray-tracing to render synthetic images. Since all the required annotation data is available, we use the KITTI [26] format with bound-box co-ordinates, truncation state and occlusion state for each object in the image.

Considering the information embedded about the environment, illumination, surface materials, shapes etc. in real world scenes, we include following aspects like (a) Number of objects, (b) Shape, Texture, and Materials of the objects, (c) Texture and Materials of the refrigerator, (d) Packing pattern of the objects, (e) Position, Orientation of camera and (f) Illumination via light sources while rendering each scene.

To simulate the real world scenario, we need 3D models, their texture information and metadata. Thousands of 3D CAD models are available online. We choose ShapeNet [27] database and Archive3D [28]. Among various categories from ShapeNet like bottles, tins, cans and food items, we selectively add 616 various object models including objects of interest and distractor objects to the repository (R_0) for generating scenes. The variety helps randomize the aspect of shape, texture and materials of the objects. For the refrigerator, we choose a model from Archive3D [28] suitable for the application. The design of refrigerator remains same for all the scenarios though the textures and material properties are dynamically chosen.

For generating training set, the refrigerator model with 5–25 randomly selected objects from R_0 are imported in each scene. To simulate object packing in refrigerator, we use three patterns namely grid, random and bin packing for 3D models. The grid places the objects at predefined distances on the refrigerator tray. Random placements drop the objects at random locations while bin packing tries to optimize the usage of tray top area placing objects very close and clustered in the scene to replicate real world scenarios in refrigerator. To replicate the packing in 3D, we also stack few objects vertically. The light sources are placed such that illumination is varied in every scene and the images are not biased to a well lit environment since refrigerators generally tend to have dim lighting. Multiple cameras are placed at random location and orientation to render images from each scene. The refrigerator texture and material properties are dynamically chosen for every rendered image.

2.2 Transfer Learning by Fine-Tuning CNN and Evaluation

For neural network training we use NVIDIA-DIGITS^{TM}-DetectNet [29] along with GoogleNet weights pretrained on ImageNet using Caffe [30] library in backend. For a comparison among various architectures we also use Faster-RCNN [31] (with ResNet-101 [32] as feature mapping network) and SSD [33] using Tensorflow and weights pretrained on COCO [4] dataset. During training, the labelled RGB images with resolution (in pixels) 512×512 are used. We neglect objects truncated or highly occluded in the images in the ground truth label.

We evaluate our object detector using manually annotated crowd-sourced refrigerator images. Figure 3 illustrates the variety in object textures, shapes, scene illumination and environment cues present in the test set. The real scenarios also include other objects like vegetables, fruits, etc. which need to be neglected by the detector. We address them as distractor objects. For performance evaluation, we compute Intersection over Union (IoU) score. With a threshold parameter, predicted bound boxes are classified as True Positives (TP), False Positives (FP) and False Negatives (FN). Precision (PR) and Recall (RE) are calculated using these metrics and a simplified mAP score is defined by the product of PR and RE [34].

All the experiments were carried on workstation with $Intel^R$ $Core^{TM}$ i7-5960X processor accelerated by $NVIDIA^R$ $GEFORCE^{TM}$ GTX 1070. Hyper-parameters search on learning rate, learning rate policy, training epochs, batch-size were performed for training all neural network models.

3   Results and Discussion

The purpose of our experiments was to evaluate the efficacy of transfer learning from rendered 3D models on real refrigerator scenarios. Hence we divide this section into two parts:

– Factors affecting Transfer Learning: We study following factors using the DetectNet architecture:
  (a) Training Dataset Size
  (b) Selected Layer Fine-tuning: Features learned at each layer in CNNs have been distinct and found to be general across domains and modalities. Fine-tuning of the final fully-connected linear classification layers has been used in practice for transfer learning across applications. Hence, we fine-tune selected layers of the network and report the performance.
  (c) Object Dictionary Size: Variance in objects used for rendering has been observed to increase detection performance significantly [19]. Hence, we report performance for various object repository size used while finetuning.
– Detection Accuracy: Here, we represent the analysis of the performance on real dataset achieved with three different architectures and three training datasets with varying cues and complexity[1].

3.1   Factors Affecting Transfer Learning

Considering other parameters like object dictionary size and fine-tuned network layers, we vary the training data size from 500–6000. We observe an increase in mAP up to 4000 images followed by a slight decline in performance as shown in Fig. 2(a). Note that the smaller dataset is a subset of the larger dataset size. After an extent, we observe decline in accuracy as we increase the dataset size.

We use GoogleNet FCN architecture with 13 hierarchical levels including inception modules as single level. mAP vs. number of epochs chart is presented in Fig. 2(b) for models with different layers selected for fine-tuning. Starting from training just the final coverage and bounding-box regressor layers we sequentially open deeper layers for fine-tuning. We observe that fine-tuning all the inception modules helps transfer learning from synthetic images to real images in our

---

[1] Trained network weights and synthetic dataset are available at https://github.com/paramrajpura/Syn2Real.

a) Effect of training data-set size on detection performance

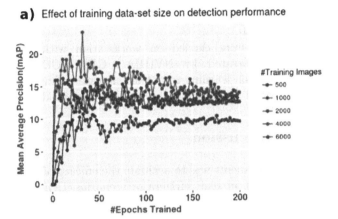

b) Effect of fine-tuning selected layers on detection performance

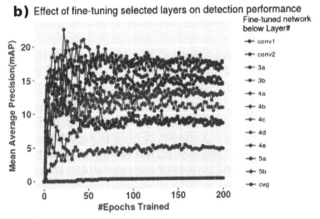

c) Effect of 3D object dictionary size on detection performance

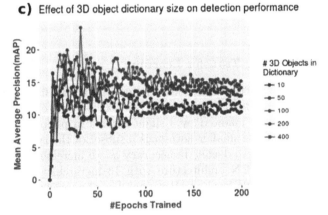

Fig. 2. (a) Detection results on the validation image-set varying train dataset size. (b) Neurons in layers of CNN learn distinct features. Network weights were fine-tuned by freezing layers sequentially. The figure represents the performance with weights fine-tuned till mentioned layers. (c) Variety in training data affects the capability of generalizing object detection in real scenarios.

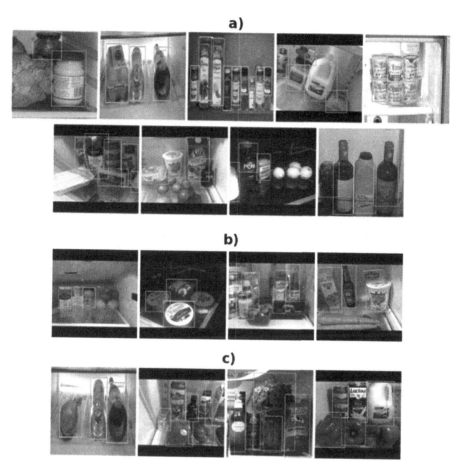

Fig. 3. Scenes representing variance in scale, background, textures, illumination, packing patterns and material properties wherein (a) Object detector correctly predicts the bound boxes for all objects of interest. (b) Object detector misses objects of interest. (c) Object detector falsely predicts the presence of an object. (Color figure online)

application. The results show that selection of the layers to fine-tune proves to be important for detection performance.

To study the relationship of variance in 3D models with performance, we incrementally add distinct 3D models to the dictionary starting from 10 to 400. We observe an increase in mAP up to 200 models and slight decline later on as represented in Fig. 2(c).

We report in Fig. 2 mAP vs. epochs trained plots over mAP vs. variance in factor to also represent the relevance of early stopping [25]. The networks trained by varying factors, show their peak performances for 25–50 epochs of training while the performance declines contrary to saturating which suggests over-fitting to synthetic images.

Fig. 4. Figure illustrates the improvement in object detection by finetuning CNN with synthetic rendered dataset. First row highlights the prediction from baseline model trained on COCO dataset with white bound-boxes. Second row marks predictions (with green bound-boxes) from fine-tuned CNN with synthetic dataset.

3.2 Detection Accuracy

We build 3 training datasets with increasing variance and cues. Dataset A consists only the objects of interest (positives) packed inside the refrigerator with grid, random and bin packing. The refrigerator wall is assigned a random solid color for every scene. Dataset B consists of a subset of Dataset A and images with distractor objects and refrigerator wall with glossy or glass material properties. While, Dataset C with few images from Dataset A and B also contains scenes where objects were vertically stacked on each other bringing the scenario more closer to the real world in terms of object arrangement. We evaluate three architectures namely DetectNet, Faster-RCNN and SSD on a set of 170 crowd-sourced refrigerator scenes with variation in cues, scale, illumination and blur, covering 150 distinct objects of interest considered as positives and 25 distractor objects as negatives. Figure 3 shows the variety in test set. The best model achieves mAP @ 0.5 IOU of 52.59 on this dataset which is a promising result considering that no real images were used while fine-tuning. In order to compare our performance with benchmark results, we consider Faster-RCNN (with ResNet-101 as feature mapping network) pretrained on COCO dataset as baseline model. Considering objects classes like bottle, cup and bowl from COCO object detection dataset as objects of interest, 24.15% mAP @ 0.5 IoU and 20.27% mAP @ 0.7 IoU is achieved on our test set. Figure 4 shows few images where our model outperforms the predictions from baseline model. It is observed that objects missed by baseline model were detected by model trained with synthetic images.

We observe that detector handles scale, shape and texture variance. Though packing patterns like vertical stacking or highly oblique camera angles lead to false predictions. Few vegetables among the distractor objects are falsely predicted as objects of interest suggesting the influence of pre-training on real dataset and lack of variety in distractor objects models available in object repository (Table 1).

Table 1. Performance on datasets with various architectures.

Dataset A	Size: 3576	
Architecture	mAP@0.5IOU	mAP@0.7IOU
FRCNN	49.24	39.61
SSD	23.97	10.92
DetectNet	32.53	11.83
Dataset B	Size: 2750	
Architecture	mAP@0.5IOU	mAP@0.7IOU
FRCNN	49.35	24.13
SSD	17.83	5.17
DetectNet	35.31	9.38
Dataset C	Size: 3696	
Architecture	mAP@0.5IOU	mAP@0.7IOU
FRCNN	52.59	37.28
SSD	30.86	17.79
DetectNet	30.32	7.83

4   Conclusion

The study with selected layer fine-tuning and freezing gives an insight of the important cues for efficient transfer learning from synthetic to real while comparison in architectures shows the significance of region proposal networks in detecting class-agnostic objects of interest.

We further observe scope in understanding the factors affecting transfer learning from synthetic to real images. The reported experiments hinted that few deeper layers were required to be fine-tuned with domain specific dataset (images rendered from 3D models) to achieve better performance compared to using pretrained CNN as feature extractor. Study related to the visualization of features transferred from synthetic dataset by controlling the visual cues like texture, background, color, shape, illumination shall be useful. Further improvement in the performance can be achieved by training CNNs for semantic segmentation using synthetic images and adding depth information to the training sets to help in cases with high degree of occlusion. The results also inspire to use similar approach to build object detector using rendered images for larger set of object classes within varying environments.

Acknowledgment. We acknowledge funding support from Innit Inc. consultancy grant CNS/INNIT/EE/P0210/1617/0007.

References

1. Krizhevsky, A., Sutskever, I., Hinton, G.E.: ImageNet classification with deep convolutional neural networks. In: International Conference on Neural Information Processing Systems, pp. 1097–1105. Curran Associates Inc. (2012)
2. Szegedy, C., Liu, W., Jia, Y., Sermanet, P., Reed, S., Anguelov, D., Erhan, D., Vanhoucke, V., Rabinovich, A.: Going deeper with convolutions. In: Proceedings of the IEEE Computer Society Conference on Computer Vision and Pattern Recognition, 12 June, vol. 07, pp. 1–9. IEEE, June 2015
3. Everingham, M., Eslami, S.M.A., Van Gool, L., Williams, C.K.I., Winn, J., Zisserman, A.: The pascal visual object classes challenge: a retrospective. Int. J. Comput. Vis. **111**(1), 98–136 (2014)
4. Lin, T.-Y., Maire, M., Belongie, S., Hays, J., Perona, P., Ramanan, D., Dollár, P., Zitnick, C.L.: Microsoft COCO: common objects in context. In: Fleet, D., Pajdla, T., Schiele, B., Tuytelaars, T. (eds.) ECCV 2014. LNCS, vol. 8693, pp. 740–755. Springer, Cham (2014). https://doi.org/10.1007/978-3-319-10602-1_48
5. Deng, J., Dong, W., Socher, R., Li, L.-J., Li, K., Fei-Fei, L.: ImageNet: a large-scale hierarchical image database. In: 2009 IEEE Conference on Computer Vision and Pattern Recognition, pp. 248–255. IEEE, June 2009
6. Li, W., Duan, L., Xu, D., Tsang, I.W.: Learning with augmented features for supervised and semi-supervised heterogeneous domain adaptation. IEEE Trans. Pattern Anal. Mach. Intell. **36**, 1134–1148 (2014)
7. Hoffman, J., Rodner, E., Donahue, J., Darrell, T., Saenko, K.: Efficient learning of domain-invariant image representations. In: ICLR, pp. 1–9, January 2013
8. Hoffman, J., Guadarrama, S., Tzeng, E., Hu, R., Donahue, J., Girshick, R., Darrell, T., Saenko, K.: LSDA: large scale detection through adaptation. In: Proceedings of the 27th International Conference on Neural Information Processing Systems, pp. 3536–3544. MIT Press (2014)
9. Kulis, B., Saenko, K., Darrell, T.: What you saw is not what you get: domain adaptation using asymmetric kernel transforms. In: Proceedings of the IEEE Computer Society Conference on Computer Vision and Pattern Recognition, pp. 1785–1792. IEEE, June 2011
10. Long, M., Cao, Y., Wang, J., Jordan, M.I.: Learning transferable features with deep adaptation networks. In: Proceedings of the 32nd International Conference on International Conference on Machine Learning, vol. 37, pp. 97–105 (2015)
11. Yosinski, J., Clune, J., Bengio, Y., Lipson, H.: How transferable are features in deep neural networks? In: Proceedings of the 27th International Conference on Neural Information Processing Systems, pp. 3320–3328. MIT Press (2014)
12. Li, Y., Wang, N., Shi, J., Liu, J., Hou, X.: Revisiting batch normalization for practical domain adaptation. arXiv Preprint arXiv:1603.04779, March 2016. https://doi.org/10.1016/B0-7216-0423-4/50051-2
13. Gupta, A., Vedaldi, A., Zisserman, A.: Synthetic data for text localisation in natural images. arXiv Preprint arxiv:1604.06646, April 2016. https://doi.org/10.1109/CVPR.2016.254
14. Tzeng, E., Hoffman, J., Zhang, N., Saenko, K., Darrell, T.: Deep domain confusion: maximizing for domain invariance. arXiv Preprint arXiv:1412.3474, December 2014

15. Donahue, J., Jia, Y., Vinyals, O., Hoffman, J., Zhang, N., Tzeng, E., Darrell, T.: DeCAF: a deep convolutional activation feature for generic visual recognition. In: Proceedings of the 31st International Conference on International Conference on Machine Learning - Volume 32, ICML 2014, pp. I-647–I-655. JMLR.org (2014)

16. Tommasi, T., Patricia, N., Caputo, B., Tuytelaars, T.: A deeper look at dataset bias. In: Gall, J., Gehler, P., Leibe, B. (eds.) GCPR 2015. LNCS, vol. 9358, pp. 504–516. Springer, Cham (2015). https://doi.org/10.1007/978-3-319-24947-6_42

17. Oquab, M., Bottou, L., Laptev, I., Sivic, J.: Learning and transferring mid-level image representations using convolutional neural networks. In: Proceedings of the 2014 IEEE Conference on Computer Vision and Pattern Recognition, CVPR 2014, pp. 1717–1724. IEEE Computer Society, Washington, DC (2014)

18. Peng, X., Sun, B., Ali, K., Saenko, K.: Learning deep object detectors from 3D models. In: Proceedings of the IEEE International Conference on Computer Vision 2015 Inter, pp. 1278–1286, December 2015

19. Su, H., Qi, C.R., Li, Y., Guibas, L.J.: Render for CNN: viewpoint estimation in images using CNNs trained with rendered 3D model views. In: Proceedings of the IEEE International Conference on Computer Vision 2015 Inter, pp. 2686–2694, May 2015

20. Georgakis, G., Mousavian, A., Berg, A.C., Kosecka, J.: Synthesizing training data for object detection in indoor scenes. arXiv Preprint arXiv:1702.07836, February 2017

21. Singh, A., Sha, J., Narayan, K.S., Achim, T., Abbeel, P.: BigBIRD: a large-scale 3D database of object instances. In: Proceedings - IEEE International Conference on Robotics and Automation, pp. 509–516. IEEE, May 2014

22. Tobin, J., Fong, R., Ray, A., Schneider, J., Zaremba, W., Abbeel, P.: Domain randomization for transferring deep neural networks from simulation to the real world. arXiv Preprint arXiv:1703.06907, March 2017

23. Ros, G., Sellart, L., Materzynska, J., Vazquez, D., Lopez, A.M.: The SYNTHIA dataset: a large collection of synthetic images for semantic segmentation of urban scenes. In: 2016 IEEE Conference on Computer Vision and Pattern Recognition (CVPR), pp. 3234–3243. IEEE, Jun 2016

24. Handa, A., Patraucean, V., Badrinarayanan, V., Stent, S., Cipolla, R.: SceneNet: Understanding Real World Indoor Scenes With Synthetic Data. arXiv Preprint arXiv:1511.07041, November 2015. https://doi.org/10.1109/CVPR.2016.442

25. Yao, Y., Rosasco, L., Caponnetto, A.: On early stopping in gradient descent learning. Constr. Approximation **26**(2), 289–315 (2007)

26. Sharp, T.: 2012 IEEE Conference on Computer Vision and Pattern Recognition (CVPR), 16–21 June 2012. IEEE (2012)

27. Chang, A.X., Funkhouser, T., Guibas, L., Hanrahan, P., Huang, Q., Li, Z., Savarese, S., Savva, M., Song, S., Su, H., Xiao, J., Yi, L., Yu, F.: ShapeNet: an information-rich 3D model repository. arXiv Preprint arXiv:1512.03012, December 2015. https://doi.org/10.1145/3005274.3005291

28. Archive 3D (2015)

29. Barker, J., Sarathy, S., July, A.T.: DetectNet: deep neural network for object detection in DIGITS (2016)

30. Vlastelica, M.P., Hayrapetyan, S., Tapaswi, M., Stiefelhagen, R.: Kit at MediaEval 2015 - evaluating visual cues for affective impact of movies task. In: CEUR Workshop Proceedings, vol. 1436, pp. 675–678. ACM Press, New York (2015)

31. Ren, S., He, K., Girshick, R., Sun, J.: Faster R-CNN: towards real-time object detection with region proposal networks. IEEE Trans. Pattern Anal. Mach. Intell. **39**(6), 1137–1149 (2017)

32. He, K., Zhang, X., Ren, S., Sun, J.: Deep residual learning for image recognition. In: Proceedings of the IEEE Conference on Computer Vision and Pattern Recognition, pp. 770–778 (2016)
33. Liu, W., Anguelov, D., Erhan, D., Szegedy, C., Reed, S., Fu, C.-Y., Berg, A.C.: SSD: single shot MultiBox detector. In: Leibe, B., Matas, J., Sebe, N., Welling, M. (eds.) ECCV 2016. LNCS, vol. 9905, pp. 21–37. Springer, Cham (2016). https://doi.org/10.1007/978-3-319-46448-0_2
34. Hoiem, D., Chodpathumwan, Y., Dai, Q.: Diagnosing error in object detectors. In: Fitzgibbon, A., Lazebnik, S., Perona, P., Sato, Y., Schmid, C. (eds.) ECCV 2012. LNCS, vol. 7574, pp. 340–353. Springer, Heidelberg (2012). https://doi.org/10.1007/978-3-642-33712-3_25

Detection of Coal Seam Fires in Summer Seasons from Landsat 8 OLI/TIRS in Dhanbad

Jit Mukherjee[1]([✉]), Jayanta Mukherjee[2], and Debashish Chakravarty[3]

[1] Advance Technology Development Centre,
Indian Institute of Technology Kharagpur, Kharagpur, West Bengal, India
jit.mukherjee@iitkgp.ac.in
[2] Department of Computer Science and Engineering,
Indian Institute of Technology Kharagpur, Kharagpur, West Bengal, India
jay@cse.iitkgp.ac.in
[3] Department of Mining Engineering, Indian Institute of Technology Kharagpur,
Kharagpur, West Bengal, India
dc@mining.iitkgp.ernet.in

Abstract. Surface and sub-surface coal seam fires are detected by estimating Land Surface Temperature (LST). The LST of an area depends on several factors such as, seasonal variation, nature of soil, urban settlements, etc. Temperatures of several areas of Dhanbad region of Eastern India are affected by the presence of surface and sub-surface coal seam fires. Coal seam fire detection has several challenges. Specially in summer season, thermal anomalies provide false classifications of such fires. It has been observed that during summer season, water bodies have high temperatures, and thus affecting the performance of detection of fires. This paper proposes a novel method to detect surface and subsurface fires in summer from satellite data by removing the high temperature water bodies.

Keywords: LST · LSE · NDVI · Water body removal · Landsat
Coal seam fires

1 Introduction

The catastrophic coal seam fires are threats to social, economical, environmental welfares of India. Coal seam fires are non-stop smouldering of coals. Depending upon the location of fires, there are two kinds of coal seam fires such as, surface, and sub-surface. Underground coal seam fires are denoted as sub-surface fire whereas fires which are visible from the ground are marked as surface coal seam fires. These fires are generated by several factors such as mine-related activities, surface fires caused by lightning, external burning, auto-oxidation, etc. [1]. Coal seam fires can be detected by a physical procedure like borehole technique [2], but this kind of procedure is tedious and risky. There is an alternative way to

© Springer Nature Singapore Pte Ltd. 2018
R. Rameshan et al. (Eds.): NCVPRIPG 2017, CCIS 841, pp. 529–539, 2018.
https://doi.org/10.1007/978-981-13-0020-2_46

detect these fires. Using the concept of land surface temperature (LST) [3], these fires can be detected and located in satellite images. Computation of LST has various challenges. From satellite images brightness temperature can be computed. Surface temperature can be produced from brightness temperature using the knowledge of Land Surface Emissivity (LSE). Apart from LSE, atmospheric correction, radiometric calibration, and cloud screening are also needed to compute the LST. This separates the computation of LST into three different type of approaches [3], such as (i) retrieval with known emissivity [4,5], (ii) retrieval with unknown emissivity, and (iii) retrieval with unknown emissivity and unknown atmospheric quantities [6]. The LSE computation can be performed by several methods such as, by using *Normalized Difference Vegetation Index (NDVI)* [7], classifiers [8], two-temperature method [9], day/night operation methods [10], etc. Temperature emissivity separation (*TES*) method over Advanced Spaceborne Thermal Emission and Reflection Radiometer (*ASTER*) data has achieved significant accuracy for detecting LST and LSE [11]. But this technique needs multiple thermal infrared bands and information of sky irradiance, and *ASTER* data, which provides such information, is not acquired in regular time interval over the same location. In this paper, the *NDVI* based LSE computation is used to determine the surface temperature as atmospheric correction is not required for such computation [3]. Further, *TES* algorithm over *ASTER* data has been used for validation of surface temperature. Temperatures of Dhanbad region in summer seasons are higher than that in other seasons, and land surface temperature has distinct characteristics in this period. In this work, we present this observation by performing statistical hypothesis testing from satellite. High temperature water bodies, observed in this period, may lead to erroneous detection of surface and sub-surface fires. Hence, this paper presents a novel technique, where water is removed from the LST image to separately determine the fire regions. Water body detection in satellite images has also several aspects. In [12], an index named as Normalized Difference Water Index (*NDWI*) is proposed to detect water bodies. It proposed to use spectral ratio between near infra-red and short wave infra-red. There have been several works on detection of water regions such as, locating the areas of water bodies [13], wetland estimation [14], flood area detection [15], etc. In [16], water bodies are detected by a spectral slope method, which is used here because of its high accuracy. In summer season, several areas of water bodies are dried out, but these areas still have high temperatures. Detection of such regions are also considered by taking account of the presence of water bodies in non-dry seasons. In the past, a few techniques for detection of surface and sub-surface fires had been advanced such as, use of empirical hard, or adaptive threshold values by analyzing the temperature histograms [17–19], etc. However, these works did not specifically consider the challenges of finding fire regions in summer seasons.

In this paper, we propose a novel method to find surface and sub-surface fire regions in summer from Landsat 8 images, where water bodies are detected and removed beforehand using multi-spectral analysis of Landsat data.

2 Methodology

The detection of coal seam fire regions is carried out in three stages. First, brightness temperature and surface temperature are computed using values of *LSE*. Next, water bodies are detected and corrected by change detection technique. Finally, these water bodies are removed from the temperature image to analyse it further to detect fire regions. An overview of the computation is shown in Fig. 1. In Fig. 1, input images, intermediate results and final result, are shown in grey, white and red boxes respectively. Bounding boxes with other colours in Fig. 1, represent outputs of different stages of the proposed algorithms.

Computation of *LST* using *LSE* from the *NDVI* of Landsat images goes through several steps. First, the pixel values are corrected by band-specific multiplicative and additive rescaling factor [20], and brightness temperature is computed as given by the following equations.

$$L_\lambda = M_L \times Q_{CAL} + A_L$$
$$T_B = \frac{K_2}{\ln\left(\frac{K_1}{L_\lambda} + 1\right)} \tag{1}$$

Here, T_B is the brightness temperature (in Kelvin), K_1 is the first calibration constant (watts/m^2.sr.μm), K_2 is the second calibration constant (Kelvin). Values of K_1 and K_2 are obtained from meta-data file of the Landsat image [20]. M_L and A_L are band-specific multiplicative and additive rescaling factors [20]. Q_{CAL} is quantized and calibrated pixel values retrieved from an image. L_λ is the corrected spatial value of the image. The computation of surface temperature requires the knowledge of land surface emissivity (*LSE*).

2.1 Computation of LSE

In this paper, the *LSE* is computed using the NDVI which assumes that emissivity is linearly dependent on vegetation. The NDVI is computed by the reflectance values of red and near-infra-red bands of Landsat images as follows [21].

$$NDVI = \frac{\lambda_{NIR} - \lambda_{RED}}{\lambda_{NIR} + \lambda_{RED}} \tag{2}$$

Here λ_{NIR} and λ_{RED} are the values of reflectance obtained from visible red and near-infra-red bands. It is considered as soil emissivity, if $NDVI < 0.2$. Emissivity of vegetation is taken into consideration, if $NDVI > 0.6$ [7]. Emissivities where the values of NDVI are between 0.2 and 0.6, are computed as follows [22].

$$P_v = \left(\frac{NDVI - NDVI_{min}}{NDVI_{max} - NDVI_{min}}\right)^2$$
$$d\varepsilon = (1 - \varepsilon_s) \times (1 - P_v) \times \varepsilon_v \times F$$
$$\varepsilon = \varepsilon_v \times P_v + \varepsilon_s \times (1 - P_v) + d\varepsilon \tag{3}$$

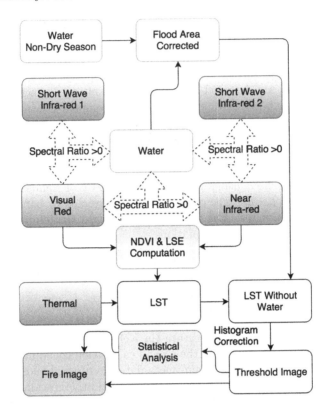

Fig. 1. Flow diagram of the proposed method (Color figure online)

where ε_v and ε_s are emissivities of vegetation and soil, respectively. P_v is the vegetation proportion. The value of F is taken as 0.55 as reported in [23]. This procedure occurs in the green box of Fig. 1. Finally, the surface temperature (in kelvin) is computed as.

$$LST = \frac{T_B}{1 + (\frac{\lambda.T_B}{\rho}) \times \ln(\varepsilon)} \tag{4}$$

Here λ is the band wavelength, and ρ is defined as $(h \times c)/\kappa$ where κ is Boltzmann's constant, h is Planck's constant, and c is the velocity of light. These surface temperatures are validated by temperature emissivity separation (*TES*) method over Advanced Spaceborne Thermal Emission and Reflection Radiometer (*ASTER*) data [11]. The *TES* method uses an iterative approach to remove sky irradiance from land surface temperature. It detects surface temperatures and emissivities within the ±1.5 K and ±0.015, respectively [11]. Because of such high accuracy, the *TES* method is used to validate surface temperatures. First, while computing normalized emissivity, the *TES* method computes initial temperature and emissivity by iteratively subtracting sky irradiance with all the thermal bands of *ASTER* data [11]. In ratio module [24], the β spectrum for each band is computed with average emissivity values over all the bands. Finally in min-max difference (MMD) module, using this β spectrum, final emissivities and temperatures are computed [11,25,26].

2.2   Water Body Removal

Using the above procedure, it has been found that in Landsat 8 summer data, water bodies show high temperatures which create anomalies for detecting coal seam fires. Hence in this paper, water bodies are separately detected and removed from the LST image. As described in [16], water bodies are detected using the spectral slope method. Spectral slope of reflectance of two spectrums ρ_1 and ρ_2 is defined as follows.

$$\theta_{(\rho_1,\rho_2)} = \rho_1 - \rho_2 \tag{5}$$

ρ_1, and ρ_2 are reflectance values obtained from different wavelengths after radiometric corrections. Spectral slopes of red and near infra-red ($\theta_{(RED,NIR)}$), red and short wave near infra-red one ($\theta_{(RED,SWIR1)}$), and near infra-red and short wave infra-red two ($\theta_{(NIR,SWIR2)}$) are computed. Water pixel is detected, if $\theta_{(RED,NIR)}$, $\theta_{(RED,SWIR1)}$, and $\theta_{(NIR,SWIR2)}$ are found to be positive for that pixel as shown in the orange box of Fig. 1. But, in summer season many regions do not contain water due to heat but contain high moistures which may provide high temperatures. In this paper, these high moisture regions are assumed to have visible water bodies in other seasons of the year. Hence, change of locations of water bodies in consecutive summer and non-dry seasons are used to locate these areas. Water region in rainy season is excluded in such a case because non water areas could have been marked as water regions. The LST image without water bodies are statistically analyzed to get the fire regions.

2.3   Fire Region Detection

The process first goes through a histogram based modification. First, for an image with N bins, the algorithm finds the bin position M (where $M < N$) where histogram of that image has the highest value. Next, depending upon the position of M, it finds an increasing slop position S in the histogram. If $M < \frac{N}{2}$, S is computed within $\frac{N}{2}^{th}$ bin to N^{th} bin. Otherwise, it finds S starting from $(M + 1)^{th}$ bin to N^{th} bin. After getting S, the image is thresholded to preserve only high temperatures for further statistical analysis. The blue block in Fig. 1 refers to this statistical analysis. Spatial values of that histogram corrected image which have higher values than μ_1 are considered as, fire regions where μ_1 is the mean of spatial values of that image. Standard deviation, σ_1, of that image has also been computed. Mean μ_2 and standard deviation σ_2 of these fire regions are further computed. Here, values greater than μ_2 are considered as surface fire regions, and others as sub-surface fire region. Let spatial value of a pixel location be considered as v. If $v \geqslant \mu_2$, that spatial location is considered as a surface fire location. It is considered as sub-surface fire location if $\mu_1 < v < \mu_2$, and others are considered as non fire locations.

3   Data and Study Area

In this work Landsat 8 (Path 140, Row 43 as per Landsat Reference System) and Aster data (Earthdata [27], marking Dhanbad as a point centre) are used over the Jharia region in Dhanbad district of the state of Jharkhand in India. Operational land imager (OLI) and thermal infra-red sensors ($TIRS$) are two instruments of Landsat 8 which provide nine bands with different wavelengths and two thermal bands, respectively. Resolution of thermal bands are 100 m which are rescaled to 30 m in the end product of Landsat 8. Aster provides several data on demand such as thermal radiance, sky irradiance, emissivity map, temperature map, etc. Thermal images of Aster are of 90 m resolution. For the high accuracy of the TES algorithm, surface temperatures of soils are validated by this. Jharia coal field is located between latitudes 23°38′ N and 23°50′ N and longitudes 86°07′ E and 86°30′ E with vast geographical features of reserve forests, dry crop-lands, fresh water bodies, mining areas, river banks, grassland and urban areas, etc. Observed data consisting of latitude, longitude and type of fires from [17,28] are used here for validation. In [17], fire region information of ten locations are provided.

4   Results

For experimentation, a sample Landsat 8 thermal image is taken from 9th April 2016 of Path 140, Row 43 as per Landsat Reference System as shown in Fig. 2(A). In this work, detection of fire regions is divided into three parts. First, surface temperature of every pixel values are computed. In this segment, the spatial values of a thermal image are converted to top of atmosphere radiance [20]. Then, the corrected spatial values are used to compute brightness temperature in kelvin for every pixels. From the multi-spectral Landsat bands, the $NDVI$ is computed using visual red and near infra-red images. Values of $NDVI$ lie in the range of -1 to 1. As it is assumed that the LSE is linearly dependent with the $NDVI$, it is computed as described in Sect. 2. This computed LSE is used to produce surface temperature as shown in Fig. 2(B). This image is the negative image of actual LST image for better representation. It is evident from the image, the areas covered with water bodies show higher temperature than other places by this procedure. This high temperature water bodies classified several region as fire regions. It has been found that in $NDVI$ based LSE and LST computation, estimated temperatures in water bodies are higher than the mean temperature found in other areas in summer seasons. Whereas, in winter, temperatures found in water bodies are lower than the mean temperature found in other areas.

Samples taken from water body and non-water body regions of a summer time LST image, are analyzed over the null hypothesis of $\mu_{water} = \mu_{nonWater}$. 100 random samples are taken from both water body and non-water body region from a summer LST image, and mean, and standard deviation of both samples are computed. A two tail t-test is applied here with mentioned null hypothesis. Here, we have considered $S_1 \neq S_2$ where S_1 and S_2 are variances of water and

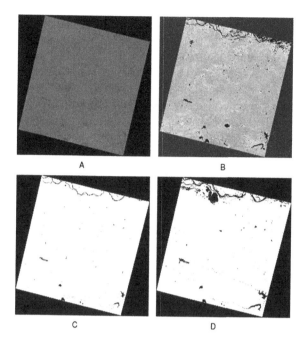

Fig. 2. A. A sample thermal image of summer season, B. LST of such image, C. Water detected in summer, D. Water in non-dry season

non water samples. Student t-test produces values of t_0 and degree of freedom as 164.428 and 179, respectively. The null hypothesis is rejected against the alternative hypothesis $\mu_{water} > \mu_{nonWater}$ as P-value is <0.00001 where $S_1 \neq S_2$. One sample data from December is also analyzed. A double tail t-test is performed over 100 randomly selected data from both the population of water body and non water body. It provides t-statistic and degree of freedom as -3.91 and 180, respectively. Thus, the null hypothesis is rejected against the alternative hypothesis $\mu_{water} < \mu_{nonWater}$ as the obtained P-value is 0.000131 where $S_1 \neq S_2$.

Hence, for summer season, water bodies are detected beforehand, and removed from the LST image in the third stage. In this stage, three spectral slopes are computed for every pixel as discussed in Sect. 2. Pixels where all the spectral slopes are positive, are detected as water pixels as shown in Fig. 2(C). Figure 2(C) shows the detected water in April season. During this time, Dhanbad region provides high temperatures, and there are dams in this region which can control the water flow. Therefore, water bodies detected in such season can be associated with smaller regions. Figure 2(D) shows an image of water body from a non-dry season. The shown image is from 18th October 2016 of the same location. In both images of Fig. 2(C) and (D), the black pixels are represented as water bodies, and white pixels are represented as non-water regions. It can be observed that water regions detected in October have more areas which are not detected in summer season. LST images after removing water bodies, which are detected only in summer, are also shown in Fig. 3(A). This image shows a portion of the whole image where Dhanbad, and Panchet dam regions are visible. The black pixels in the image are shown as high temperatures after applying a threshold value (as discussed in Sect. 2.2) and white pixels are treated as low temperature pixels. If the image, where water is detected in October as shown in Fig. 2(D), is considered, it can be observed that several regions which are detected as high temperature in Fig. 3(A), are actually water segments in non-dry seasons. Therefore, water bodies in non-dry season are selected, and changes in water body locations are marked. For change detection, image ratio method [29] is used here. Using these changes, a modified water map is created to discard the temperature anomalies in summer data as shown in Fig. 3(B). This modified water map is further used in the LST image to find the high temperature regions. The LST image discarding these water bodies provides high temperature regions, where coal seam fires may occur. As mining areas may have water bodies, sub-surface fire locations under any water body remain undetected by this algorithm, and it needs to be carefully looked into in future. In the final stage, of the algorithm, this modified LST image is further analyzed. First, most frequently occurring bin M is detected. Depending upon the positions of M, threshold operation is performed over the LST image as described in Sect. 2. This is used to remove the highest bin from histogram of the image such that it does not create a bias in further analysis. The final output image is shown in Fig. 3(C). The red, orange, and white portions of the image represent detected surface, sub-surface, and no fire regions. The green and blue dots in the image show sample locations, where information of fires are known and validated. Green and blue dots are surface and sub-surface fire, respectively. In Chasnala, a surface fire locations at 23.6606° N and 86.44224° E has been observed. The output image shows the surface fire position at Chasnala as represented by a green dot in Fig. 3(C). Otherwise, the images are validated by the observation provided in [17,28]. Latitude and longitude of ground truth data are checked with the processed image to find a match within a 5 pixel radius of that position. As, the size of ground truth is relatively small with respect to the selected region, recall[1] is considered here. In [17], a manual thresholding technique is considered where seasonal variations are not taken into account. Therefore, water bodies with high temperature are erroneously detected by this method. Method in [19] considered $\mu + 2\sigma$ as a threshold to detect fire regions where μ and σ are mean and standard deviation of the spatial values. This method does not provide significant results in summer season as $\mu + 2\sigma$ may go beyond the range of spatial values. The proposed approach provides a recall value of 60% (for both with and without water body removal) with observations in [17]. In this paper two threshold values are experimentally chosen. First, the fire regions are selected by the threshold value μ_1. Second, μ_2 is selected to differentiate between surface and sub surface fire regions. In this paper, experimentation with different threshold values have been performed. The proposed method has been checked with $\mu_1 + \sigma_1$, and $\mu_1 - \sigma_1$ as first threshold values. Second threshold value has been

---

[1] Recall is defined as $t_p/(t_p + f_n)$ where t_p, and f_n are true positives, and false negatives, respectively.

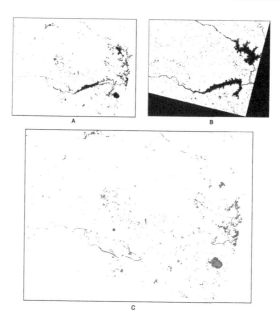

Fig. 3. A. High temperature regions after removing water bodies detected from summer, B. Detected water bodies using changes over seasons, C. Final output. Red, orange denote surface and sub-surface fires. Green and blue dot represents validate surface and sub-surface fire location (Color figure online)

varied between $\mu_2 + \sigma_2$, and $\mu_2 - \sigma_2$ for experimentation. In the given image, there are no significant differences, if the threshold value has been changed to $\mu_1 + \sigma_1$ from μ_1. But, if the threshold value is selected as $\mu_1 - \sigma_1$, number of potential fire regions are increased drastically which increase false positive for both surface and sub surface fire regions. If the second threshold value is changed to $\mu_2 - \sigma_2$, false positive in case of surface fire increases. No significant change has been detected for the given image, if the second threshold value is changed to $\mu_2 + \sigma_2$ from μ_2. The range and dependency can only be further analysed if a detailed fire map of the region can be used as ground truth. Water bodies of this region are marked by Google Earth[TM] very high resolution images. The major water bodies such as, Panchet dam, are marked as surface fire regions by the proposed method without removal of water bodies. On the other hand, mine areas have small water bodies, which are detected and removed, but may have sub-surface fires. This may degrade the performance of the algorithm in some cases, but if water bodies are not removed, several regions are classified falsely as surface fire regions.

5 Conclusion

This paper provides a novel method by which surface and sub-surface fire regions are detected using Landsat data in summer seasons. It has been found that the technique of estimation of temperature by the *NDVI* based *LSE* and *LST* computation in summer season provides high temperatures in water bodies. The proposed method detects and discards the regions containing water bodies, and the resultant image is further analyzed to detect fire regions. But, as mine areas have shallow water bodies, where sub-surface fires may occur, the performance degrades for some cases. The procedure to retain those shallow water bodies, and detection of possible sub-surface fire locations are future agendas of this work. Aerosol band of Landsat can be used to detect shallow water bodies which is also considered as future work.

References

1. Stracher, G.B., Taylor, T.P.: Coal fire burning out of control around the world: thermodynamic recipe for environmental catastrophe. Int. J. Coal Geol. **59**, 7–17 (2004)
2. Sinha, A., Singh, V.K.: Spontaneous coal seam fires: a global phenomenon. In: International Conference on Spontaneous Coal Seam Fires: Mitigating a Global Disaster, pp. 42–65 (2005)
3. Li, Z.-L., Tang, B.-H., Wu, H., Ren, H., Yan, G., Wan, Z., Trigo, I.F., Sobrino, J.A.: Satellite-derived land surface temperature: current status and perspectives. Remote Sens. Environ. **131**, 14–37 (2013)
4. Jimenez-Munoz, J.C., Cristobal, J., Sobrino, J.A., Soria, G., Ninyerola, M., Pons, X.: Revision of the single-channel algorithm for land surface temperature retrieval from landsat thermal-infrared data. IEEE Trans. Geosci. Remote Sens. **47**(1), 339–349 (2009)
5. Sória, G., Sobrino, J.A.: ENVISAT/AATSR derived land surface temperature over a heterogeneous region. Remote Sens. Environ. **111**(4), 409–422 (2007)
6. Wang, N., Li, Z.-L., Tang, B.-H., Zeng, F., Li, C.: Retrieval of atmospheric and land surface parameters from satellite-based thermal infrared hyperspectral data using a neural network technique. Int. J. Remote Sens. **34**(9–10), 3485–3502 (2013)
7. Sobrino, J.A., Jimenez-Munoz, J.C., Paolini, L.: Land surface temperature retrieval from LANDSAT TM 5. Remote Sens. Environ. **90**(4), 434–440 (2004)
8. Peres, L.F., DaCamara, C.C.: Emissivity maps to retrieve land-surface temperature from MSG/SEVIRI. IEEE Trans. Geosci. Remote Sens. **43**(8), 1834–1844 (2005)
9. Watson, K.: Two-temperature method for measuring emissivity. Remote Sens. Environ. **42**(2), 117–121 (1992)
10. Jiang, G.-M., Li, Z.-L., Nerry, F.: Land surface emissivity retrieval from combined mid-infrared and thermal infrared data of MSG-SEVIRI. Remote Sens. Environ. **105**(4), 326–340 (2006)
11. Gillespie, A., Rokugawa, S., Matsunaga, T., Cothern, J.S., Hook, S., Kahle, A.B.: A temperature and emissivity separation algorithm for advanced spaceborne thermal emission and reflection radiometer (ASTER) images. IEEE Trans. Geosci. Remote Sens. **36**(4), 1113–1126 (1998)
12. Gao, B.-C.: NDWI–a normalized difference water index for remote sensing of vegetation liquid water from space. Remote Sens. Environ. **58**(3), 257–266 (1996)
13. Alsdorf, D.E., Rodriguez, E., Lettenmaier, D.P.: Measuring surface water from space. Rev. Geophys. **45**(2) (2007)

14. Rebelo, L.-M., Finlayson, C.M., Nagabhatla, N.: Remote sensing and GIS for wetland inventory, mapping and change analysis. J. Environ. Manag. **90**(7), 2144–2153 (2009)
15. Chignell, S.M., Anderson, R.S., Evangelista, P.H., Laituri, M.J., Merritt, D.M.: Multi-temporal independent component analysis and landsat 8 for delineating maximum extent of the 2013 colorado front range flood. Remote Sens. **7**(8), 9822–9843 (2015)
16. Aswatha, S.M., Mukherjee, J., Biswas, P.K., Aikat, S.: Toward automated land cover classification in landsat images using spectral slopes at different bands. IEEE J. Sel. Top. Appl. Earth Obs. Remote Sens. **PP**(99), 1–9 (2016)
17. Mishra, R., Bahuguna, P., Singh, V.: Detection of coal mine fire in Jharia coal field using landsat-7 ETM+ data. Int. J. Coal Geol. **86**(1), 73–78 (2011)
18. Huo, H., Jiang, X., Song, X., Li, Z.-L., Ni, Z., Gao, C.: Detection of coal fire dynamics and propagation direction from multi-temporal nighttime landsat SWIR and TIR data: a case study on the Rujigou coal field, Northwest (NW) China. Remote Sens. **6**, 1234–1259 (2014)
19. Huo, H., Ni, Z., Gao, C., Zhao, E., Zhang, Y., Lian, Y., Zhang, H., Zhang, S., Jiang, X., Song, X., Zhou, P., Cui, T.: A study of coal fire propagation with remotely sensed thermal infrared data. Remote Sens. **7**(3), 3088–3113 (2015)
20. Using the USGS landsat8 product. https://landsat.usgs.gov/using-usgs-landsat-8-product. Accessed 29 Mar 2017
21. Silleos, N.G., Alexandridis, T.K., Gitas, I.Z., Perakis, K.: Vegetation indices: advances made in biomass estimation and vegetation monitoring in the last 30 years. Geocarto Int. **21**(4), 21–28 (2006)
22. Giannini, M.B., Belfiore, O.R., Parente, C., Santamaria, R.: Land surface temperature from landsat 5 TM images: comparison of different methods using airborne thermal data. J. Eng. Sci. Technol. Rev. **8**, 83–90 (2015)
23. Sobrino, J.A., Caselles, V., Becker, F.: Significance of the remotely sensed thermal infrared measurements obtained over a citrus orchard. ISPRS J. Photogramm. Remote Sens. **44**, 343–354 (1990)
24. Watson, K.: Spectral ratio method for measuring emissivity. Remote Sens. Environ. **42**(2), 113–116 (1992)
25. Payan, V., Royer, A.: Analysis of temperature emissivity separation (TES) algorithm applicability and sensitivity. Int. J. Remote Sens. **25**(1), 15–37 (2004)
26. Pivovarník, M., Khalsa, S.J.S., Jiménez-Muñoz, J.C., Zemek, F.: Improved temperature and emissivity separation algorithm for multispectral and hyperspectral sensors. IEEE Trans. Geosci. Remote Sens. **55**(4), 1944–1953 (2017)
27. Earthdata Login. https://search.earthdata.nasa.gov/. Accessed 28 July 2017
28. Singh, A., Raju, A., Pati, P., Kumar, N.: Mapping of coal fire in Jharia coalfield, India: a remote sensing based approach. J. Indian Soc. Remote Sens. **45**, 369–376 (2016)
29. Singh, A.: Review article digital change detection techniques using remotely-sensed data. Int. J. Remote Sens. **10**(6), 989–1003 (1989)

Classification of Indian Monuments into Architectural Styles

Saurabh Sharma[1]([⊠]), Priyal Aggarwal[1], Akanksha N. Bhattacharyya[2],
and S. Indu[2]

[1] Department of Computer Science and Engineering, Delhi Technological University,
Delhi, India
saurabhsharma.1295@gmail.com, aggarwalpriyal27@gmail.com
[2] Department of Electronics and Communication Engineering,
Delhi Technological University, Delhi, India
akanksha.nb@gmail.com, s.indu@dce.ac.in

Abstract. We propose two novel approaches to classify Indian monuments according to their distinct architectural styles. While the historical
significance of most Indian monuments is well documented, the details of
their architectural styles are not as well recorded. Different Indian architectural styles often show certain similar features which makes classification a difficult task. Previous work has focused on European architecture
and standard datasets are available for the same, but no standard dataset
exists for Indian architecture. Therefore, we have curated a dataset of
Indian monuments. In this paper, we propose two approaches to classify
monuments according to their styles: Radon Barcodes and Convolutional
Neural Networks. The first approach is fast and consumes less memory,
but the second approach gives an accuracy of 82%, which is better than
the 76% accuracy of the first method.

Keywords: Convolutional Neural Networks · Radon transform
Barcodes · Classification · Monuments · Architectural styles
Image processing

1 Introduction

Each architectural style has certain features that make it distinguishable from
other forms of architecture. These characteristic features play a key role in
the identification of such monuments. For instance, bulbous domes and slender
minarets are often found in monuments of the Mughal architectural style. India
has been a hotbed of architectural innovation over the ages. Monuments have
traditionally been major tourist attractions, Taj Mahal being the best example.

In this paper, we propose methods of classification of these monuments
according to their architectural styles which are closely associated with different dynasties in our history. These historical factors often led to styles which
were influenced from other monuments. This makes classification of Indian monuments a tedious task. Moreover, these historic buildings are useful references

© Springer Nature Singapore Pte Ltd. 2018
R. Rameshan et al. (Eds.): NCVPRIPG 2017, CCIS 841, pp. 540–549, 2018.
https://doi.org/10.1007/978-981-13-0020-2_47

for architects designing contemporary architecture, thus information about the architectural styles of these monuments seems necessary. The naked eye can find some distinguishing features for each category, but the challenge was to find methods to automatically learn those features for better classification (Fig. 1).

Fig. 1. Images from our dataset. Two images from each style are shown. Line 1: Mughal and Buddhist architecture. Line 2: Kalinga and Dravidian architecture.

2   Related Work

Previous work on image classification tasks has utilized several different models. The Bag of Visual Words [1] introduced by Sivic et al. was a landmark approach, quantizing image features as visual words and building a vocabulary of these words. A histogram is maintained for each image which measures the frequency of occurrence of these words. SIFT [2] and Histogram of Oriented Gradient (HOG) [3] features have previously been used with the BoW model. Fei-Fei et al. [4] proposed the Dense SIFT approach of finding descriptors at all points within the image. Bay et al. [5] developed a faster alternative to SIFT, called SURF feature descriptors.

Millions of features may be extracted and added to the Bag of Words which leads us to the need of using clustering algorithms to cluster similar features together. Siagian et al. [6] have used a gist feature extraction approach which includes spatial information by dividing the image into a grid and computing on these parts of the grid. Nowozin et al. [7] used a multiple-graph mining algorithm to capture frequent structures of visual words across images. Wei-Ta Chu et al. [8] proposed their visual pattern discovery approach for classification of Architectural styles. Philbin et al. [9] proposed the use of spatial verification during retrieval. Hauagge et al. [10] proposed a novel approach of finding local symmetric features in images. They used a window based approach to find local rather than global symmetry.

LeCun et al. [12] in 1998 used Convolutional Neural Networks on the MNIST dataset and set forth a new state of the art metric with an accuracy of 99.2%. Ever since, Convolutional Neural Networks have been extensively used in Image

Analysis, object recognition and more recently in building agents playing complex games, such as Go. The ImageNet challenge has seen the development of many different architectures like AlexNet [13], VGGNet [14].

We propose novel approaches for classification of Indian monuments. We curated our own dataset, consisting of 3559 images, since none other existed for the particular domain. We first propose the use of Convolutional Neural Networks for this task, a technique which has hitherto been unexplored for classifying Indian monuments. CNNs are effective in classification tasks, as they can model different kinds of features, such as texture and shapes. Our second approach using Radon transform to generate binary barcodes is one of a kind for classifying monuments according to their architectural styles. Similar techniques have previously been limited to medical image databases. Since the overall architecture of different monuments belonging to the same class is similar, multiple projections are able to model these styles considerably well.

2.1 Problem Definition

Classifying Indian monuments presents several problems that were not encountered with similar tasks of classifying European Monuments. The cause of these problems is rooted in history because one period often tended to influence later periods with its culture. Indian history is highly intertwined and different periods and dynasties had some cultural influence on contemporary or later dynasties. This influence also trickled into architecture. This led to some medieval architects deriving some features from other periods. Thus, these common features present problems to the classifier/predictor system.

We first used the previously established state of the art methods for classification of European monuments on the dataset provided by [8]. This dataset consists of 423 images belonging to 4 distinct styles - Korean, Islamic, Gothic and Georgian. We then compared the results by running the same experiments on our dataset of Indian Monuments. The details of the methods used are mentioned in the Experiments section. The results are listed in Table 1.

To investigate why our dataset gets unfavorable results when compared with state of the art methods for European datasets, we introduce a metric to quantify how "different" the various classes really are from each other i.e. how easy it is to classify them. In the proposed metric, we first calculated the feature vector corresponding to the Bag of Words model for each image. We took the mean of such feature vectors for all images of each class to result into one vector representing the class. Then, the Euclidean distances between different classes belonging to the same dataset were calculated.

If $a = (x_1, x_2, \ldots, x_n)$ and $b = (y_1, y_2, \ldots, y_n)$ then Euclidean distance from a to b in $\mathbb{R}^n$ space can be defined as

$$d(a,b) = \sqrt{(x_1 - y_1)^2 + (x_2 - y_2)^2 + \ldots, + (x_n - y_n)^2} \qquad (1)$$

The results showed that distances between the classes of European dataset were $150\% - 300\%$ more than those between classes of the Indian dataset.

Resolution as defined by optics means the minimum distance of separation to clearly identify two objects. Using this analogy, since distances between classes of Indian dataset are less, it is, therefore, more difficult to resolve them to their correct classes.

In this work, we propose two approaches to overcome this problem. First, we use a Convolutional Neural Network for the classification task. Second, we propose generating Radon barcodes [11] and using SVM for classification. These approaches are further detailed in the remainder of the paper.

3   Proposed Approach

In this work, we propose two approaches to classify Indian monuments. We first propose using a Convolutional Neural Network for the task. Our second approach involves generating a binary radon barcode for each image of the dataset and training an SVM using these barcodes as features.

3.1   Convolutional Neural Network

Convolutional Neural Networks [12–14] have previously been used for various image classification tasks. The ability of a multilayer network to learn complex relationships using gradient based learning [15] makes it suitable for the presented task.

We show the architecture of the network that we used in Fig. 2. The architecture has been inspired by previous work on the ImageNet dataset but is limited by the size of our dataset. We thus used only three convolutional layers followed by two fully connected layers. We used scaled down versions of AlexNet and VGGNet to build our own network and we proceeded to further modify them to minimize the number of parameters while maintaining accuracy.

The mainstay of the Convolutional Neural Network is the Convolution layer which has multiple filters which are convolved with the training image. Figure 3 shows how these filters are able to model relevant features better than SIFT feature detectors. Convolution is a mathematical operation given by:

$$f(x) * g(x) = \int_{-\infty}^{\infty} f(\tau).g(x - \tau)d\tau \tag{2}$$

These feature maps can then be passed through several kinds of activation functions. We have used the ReLu (Rectified Linear Unit) [16] activations for all of our layers. A major concern when dealing with CNNs is the problem of overfitting. CNNs are susceptible to overfitting due to an imbalance between the size of the dataset and the number of parameters to be learned. First, when the amount of data is less, the network will tend to fit the limited data perfectly and this can lead to skewed cross validation results. Additionally, a smaller dataset would lead the network to capture noise instead of the important features. Second, a deeper network will lead to a greater number of parameters to be learned.

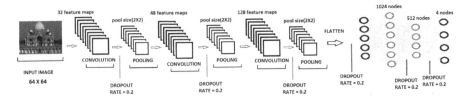

Fig. 2. Architecture of CNN: each images, re-sized to 64 × 64, is first convoluted with 3 × 3 feature detectors to give 32 feature maps. The first convolutional layer is followed by a dropout layer to prevent over-fitting where 20% of the units are removed. The feature maps undergo max pooling (with pool size 2 × 2), where the pooling operator maps the sub-region to its maximum value to achieve spatial invariance. This is followed by another convolution layer outputting 48 feature maps whose output is given as input to the next dropout and pooling layers. Another Convolution layer - Dropout layer - Pooling layer triplet follows. A single vector of pixel values as input nodes to the neural network is obtained from the pooled layer using flattening technique. This vector is an input to the Artificial Neural Network. Two fully-connected layers: one with 1024 nodes and other with 512 nodes are used, with dropout rate of 20% after each layer. The four output nodes correspond to each Architecture- Mughal, Dravidian, Kalinga, Buddhist.

Fig. 3. Comparing the interest points as detected by the CNN filters and those of conventional SIFT detectors using the Bag of Visual Words approach, we note the significant number of peripheral keypoints being detected by SIFT, whereas CNN focuses more on the important architectural patterns. For instance, in the middle image of line 1, the regions highlighted by violet show features such as minarets and the tomb being identified by the CNN.

Consequently, the network shows a proclivity towards fitting the large number of parameters according to the training data.

To prevent it, we have used dropout layers [17] after each convolutional layer to ensure that some neurons are not considered during a learning step in each batch. We also used the max pooling layer which performs the function of down-sampling an image. The image reduces in size and such loss of information is essential in order to lessen computational overhead for the upcoming layers of the network and prevent overfitting. Mathematically, max pooling is given as:

$$a_j = max_{N \times N}(a_i^{N \times N} u(n, n))$$

where u(x, y) is the window function to the input patch size of $N \times N$ and computes the maximum in the neighbourhood.

We also used data augmentation to reduce overfitting by extending our dataset by applying label preserving transformations [13] to images of our dataset. For this purpose, we configured random transformations and normalization operations, such as width shift, height shift, zooming, horizontal flip, and shear, on our image data during training. Open source library Keras for used for the same.

3.2   Radon Barcodes

As proposed in [11], we try to classify images using Barcodes to Radon Transform of normalized images.

In [18], the use of Radon transform to identify global features by local peak detection is discussed. Such an approach seemed a promising direction for classification and retrieval tasks and therefore this method was investigated further.

Radon transform [19] on an image $f(x, y)$ for a given set of angles computes a projection of the image at different angles. The resulting projection is the sum of intensities of the pixels in each direction. The new image R(ρ, θ), or the Radon transform, can be defined as the line integral along a line inclined at θ and at a distance ρ from the origin.

$$R(\rho, \theta) = \int_{-\infty}^{\infty} \int_{-\infty}^{\infty} f(x, y)\delta(x cos\theta + y sin\theta - \rho)dxdy \qquad (3)$$

where $\delta(\cdot)$ is the Dirac Delta function which is non-zero only on s axis and its integral, and $-\infty < \rho < \infty$, $0 \leq \theta < \pi$.

Before calculating Radon Transform, we processed the images. Preprocessing steps include converting images to grayscale and resizing them to (128, 128). This is because we want same length features for all images. Radon Transform of each preprocessed image is then computed on 128 evenly spaced projection angles in the range 0 to π. Further, we normalize each resulting projection ray. This is done by dividing by the maximum value in the array. We then binarize the result using thresholding, wherein the threshold value is calculated as the median of the non-zero values in the normalized projection. We, thereby, assemble the barcode [20] of a single image by concatenating all binary outcomes for every projection angle.

For each image, the barcode is used as feature vector. Barcodes are passed as input to a multiclass SVM classifier, whose hyperparameters are optimized using Grid Search method. 10-fold cross validation is performed to limit overfitting.

Table 1. Results of the baseline and proposed approaches on european and Indian datasets. (Values given are average for all classes.)

Method	European dataset				Indian dataset			
	Accuracy	Precision	Recall	F1-score	Accuracy	Precision	Recall	F1-score
$SIFT + BoVW$	91.04%	0.92	0.91	0.91	51.05%	0.50	0.51	0.51
$SURF + BOVW$	90.1%	0.90	0.90	0.90	54.10%	0.52	0.55	0.54
$DenseSIFT$	95.44%	0.94	0.95	0.95	70.05%	0.70	0.71	0.71
CNN	**85.85%**	**0.87**	**0.86**	**0.86**	**82.31%**	**0.81**	**0.82**	**0.81**
Radon Barcodes	**78.30%**	**0.79**	**0.78**	**0.78**	**75.53%**	**0.76**	**0.75**	**0.75**

This is done for both European and Indian Monuments datasets for comparison. The results are listed in Table 1.

Fig. 4. Example of radon barcode on a query image

This algorithm runs very fast in comparison to other approaches and also takes significantly less memory. The exact time taken for creation of barcode features for 3559 images for our dataset is 857 s, which is about 4.15 s per image. In addition to this, each barcode takes less than 10 Kbs to be stored. This approach can be used in areas where time and memory are constrained, such as an application in Mobile phones (Fig. 4).

4   Experiments

4.1   Dataset

India, with its incredibly rich cultural history, has been an archaeological treasure chest. To truly capture the diversity, we found the four most frequently occurring styles of architecture, namely, Buddhist, Dravidian, Kalinga, and Mughal. The four classes have been chosen after careful deliberation in order to capture the most of India, both historically and geographically.

We have created a database of 3559 carefully curated images from Google Search and Flickr. The number of images belonging to each class has been kept fairly equal so as to avoid bias; Buddhist category has 819 images, Dravidian has 835, Kalinga has 1117 and Mughal has 788 images. We used specific monument names and their styles as the search terms. The membership of each monument in its respective category was verified using Wikipedia. The dataset was then manually pruned to remove duplicates and incorrectly retrieved images. We have included images of the interior and exterior of these monuments from varying angles and illumination to ensure that extracted features pertain only to the architecture of the monument. Furthermore, using both interior and exterior parts of monuments, the classifier can identify texture and wall art patterns that are distinctive features. Also, both high and low-resolution images have been included to make the dataset robust. The smallest and largest sizes of images in the dataset are $(100, 100)$ and $(3924, 8867)$ respectively.

This dataset is available online here: https://goo.gl/ijKXY1

4.2 Evaluation

We performed our classification experiments using varied approaches on the European dataset and the Indian dataset. The results are mentioned in Table 1. We have set the Bag of Visual Words approach with SIFT feature detector as the baseline [21]. We split the data set in 75:25 ratio to get the training and test sets. None of the images in the cross-validation set have been used for training the models. We employed the Bag of Visual Words Approach [1] after feature extraction using various feature descriptors with different properties: scale invariance, color contours, histograms of gradients. We used K Means Clustering to cluster the feature points to vocabulary sizes of 1000/4000. We have also used Dense SIFT [4] approach and SURF [5] feature detectors to compare our proposed approaches. Dense SIFT gave better results and motivated us to find alternative solutions to further improve accuracy.

The CNN was built and compiled using Keras Framework for Python on top of Google's open source TensorFlow library. The momentum was set at 0.9, the learning rate was kept at 0.005. Learning was done in batch sizes of 128 images and decay rate of 0.0001. Categorical cross-entropy was used as loss function, a fairly standard choice when working with datasets with more than two class labels. We used a softmax classifier at the output layer.

For our second approach, an SVM with a polynomial kernel was used for experiments using Radon barcodes and hyper-parameter tuning was done using Grid-Search. We produced different length barcodes by changing the number of projection angles and we present the best results with a barcode of length 128.

Implementation and experimentation was performed on a 2.2 GHz Intel 7th Generation core i5 machine with 8GB RAM and NVIDIA 940M GeForce GPU with a clock speed of 1.1 GHz.

5   Conclusion and Future Work

We have succeeded in our aim of classifying Indian monuments to their respective architectural styles. We also introduced a metric to quantify 'resolution' of an image into a particular class, to attribute a quantity to the difficulty of the problem at hand. We proposed two approaches for the task and also compared the same with the established baseline measures. While Convolutional Neural Networks prove to be the most accurate, the approach of Radon Barcodes is also an effective technique which can be used to build time and memory efficient applications. Future work includes a similar method that can be employed in tourist centric applications which provide accurate annotations using the phones camera as an image source.

References

1. Sivic, J., Zisserman, A.: Video google: a text retrieval approach to object matching in videos. In: ICCV (2003)
2. Lowe, D.G.: Distinctive image features from scale-invariant keypoints. IJCV **60**, 91–110 (2004)
3. Dalal, N., Triggs, B.: Histograms of oriented gradients for human detection. In: CVPR (2005)
4. Fei-Fei, L., Perona, P.: A bayesian hierarchical model for learning natural scene categories. In: IEEE Computer Society Conference on Computer Vision and Pattern Recognition, CVPR 2005, vol. 2, pp. 524–531. IEEE, June 2005
5. Bay, H., Tuytelaars, T., Van Gool, L.: SURF: speeded up robust features. In: Leonardis, A., Bischof, H., Pinz, A. (eds.) ECCV 2006. LNCS, vol. 3951, pp. 404–417. Springer, Heidelberg (2006). https://doi.org/10.1007/11744023_32
6. Siagian, C., Itti, L.: Rapid biologically-inspired scene classification using features shared with visual attention. IEEE Trans. Pattern Anal. Mach. Intell. **29**(2), 300–312 (2007)
7. Nowozin, S., Tsuda, K., Uno, T., Kudo, T., BakIr, G.: Weighted substructure mining for image analysis. In: Proceedings of CVPR (2007)
8. Chu, W.-T., Tsai, M.-H.: Visual pattern discovery for architecture image classication and product image search. In: ACM ICMR (2012)
9. Philbin, J., Chum, O., Isard, M., Sivic, J., Zisserman, A.: Object retrieval with large vocabularies and fast spatial matching. In: CVPR (2007)
10. Hauagge, D., Snavely, N.: Image matching using local symmetry features. In: CVPR (2012)
11. Zhu, S., Tizhoosh, H.R.: Radon features and barcodes for medical image retrieval via SVM arXiv:1604.04675v1 [cs.CV] (2016)
12. LeCun, Y., Bottou, L., Bengio, Y., Haffner, P.: Gradient-based learning applied to document recognition. Proc. IEEE **86**(11), 2278–2324 (1998)
13. Krizhevsky, A., Sutskever I., Hinton G.: ImageNet classification with deep convolutional networks. In: Advances in Neural Information Processing Systems, pp. 1097–1105 (2012)
14. Simonyan, K., Zisserman, A: Very deep convolutional networks for large-scale image recognition. In: ICLR (2015)
15. Bottou, L.: Large-scale machine learning with stochastic gradient descent. In: Lechevallier, Y., Saporta, G. (eds.) Proceedings of COMPSTAT, pp. 177–186. Springer, Heidelberg (2010). https://doi.org/10.1007/978-3-7908-2604-3_16
16. Nair, V., Hinton, G.E.: Rectified linear units improve restricted Boltzmann machines. In: ICML, pp. 807–814 (2010)

17. Srivastava, N., Hinton, G.E., Krizhevsky, A., Sutskever, I., Salakhutdinov, R.: Dropout: a simple way to prevent neural networks from overfitting. JMLR **15**(1), 1929–1958 (2014)
18. Toft, P.A., Srensen, J.A.: The radon transform - theory and implementation. Technical University of Denmark, Kgs. Lyngby, Denmark (1996)
19. Radon, J.: On the determination of functions from their integral values along certain manifolds. IEEE Trans. Med. Imaging **5**(4), 170176 (1986)
20. Tizhoosh, H.R.: Barcode annotations for medical image retrieval: a preliminary investigation. In: IEEE International Conference on Image Processing ICIP, pp. 818–822 (2015)
21. Goel, A., Juneja, M., Jawahar, C.V.: Are buildings only instances? Exploration in architectural style categories. In: Proceedings of the Eighth Indian Conference on Computer Vision, Graphics and Image Processing, 16 December 2012

Predicting Word from Brain Activity Using Joint Sparse Embedding with Domain Adaptation

Akansha Mishra[✉]

Department of Computer Science and Engineering,
IIT Guwahati, Guwahati, India
ak.kkb@iitg.ernet.in

Abstract. In the proposed work machine learning algorithm is applied on Functional Magnetic Resonance Imaging (fMRI) data to analyze the human brain activity and then predicting the word that the subject was thinking. The algorithm that can learn to identify and track the cognitive processes and gives rise to predict the word from observed fMRI data is developed. The major problem here is that we have limited data in very high dimensional feature space. Thereby, making the model susceptible to overfit the data. Also, the data is highly noisy through most of the dimensions, leaving only a few features that are discriminative. Due to high noise domain shift problem is very likely to occur. Most of the previous approach focused only on feature selection and learning the embedding space. Here our main objective is to learn the robust embedding space and handling the domain shift problem [11] in an efficient way. Unlike the previous approach instead of learning the dictionary that projects the visual space to the word embedding space, we are using the joint dictionary learning approach based on the matrix factorization. Our experiment shows that the proposed approach based on the joint dictionary learning and domain adaptation method has the significant advantage over the previous approaches.

1 Introduction

One of the motivation to study brain imaging is to make it possible to answer what someone is currently thinking based only on measurements of their brain activity. In this paper, we deal with a very simplified version to do the same. Advances in the field of cognitive science and technology for imaging human brain activity, such as Functional Magnetic Resonance Imaging (fMRI), Magnetoencephalography(MEG) offers a wonderful opportunity to analyze the activity of the brain. fMRI is a neuroimaging procedure which measures the activity of the brain (while speaking, reading, writing and listening as shown in Fig. 1 [1]) by detecting changes in the flow of blood using Magnetic Resonance Imaging Technology (MRI). This technique relies on the fact that cerebral blood flow and neuronal activation are coupled. When an area of the brain is in use, blood flow to that region also increases.

© Springer Nature Singapore Pte Ltd. 2018
R. Rameshan et al. (Eds.): NCVPRIPG 2017, CCIS 841, pp. 550–559, 2018.
https://doi.org/10.1007/978-981-13-0020-2_48

Whenever a person reads or writes, the semantic content corresponding to every word will activate in the brain, as a result, some pattern is generated for the activity of neurons. Thus, the prediction of the word from brain imaging techniques becomes a new area of research. It is thus concluded that if the brain activity data could encode the semantics, then the model generated using brain activity data along with ground truth semantic data could be more consistent. In 2008 [2] Mitchell et al, has introduced a new task to decode the semantic features of a noun from neural activity in the brain. It was done using a semantic model to learn the mapping between the concepts and activity of neurons in the brain, captured during brain activity imaging experiments.

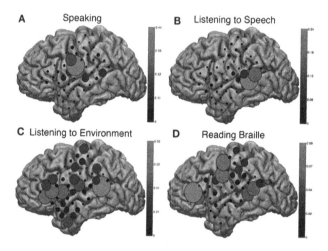

Fig. 1. fMRI image (A) Speaking, (B) Listening to speech, (C) Listening to environmental sounds, (D) Reading Braille [1]

In the proposed work we have fMRI scan data corresponding to 60 noun class and for each noun, we have human annotated attribute vector of 218 *dimension*. Here, each dimension of the attribute vector is the existence of some clue corresponding to that word. In our approach for predicting the word from brain activity, a joint embedding of activity of brain and word attribute is learn and our mapping is such that fMRI image in the embedding space is close to the corresponding real word. fMRI data is very high dimensional and for learning the embedding space we need a function that transforms the visual space (fMRI data) to word-attribute space. There are many approaches [6,9] proposed based on the matrix factorization that transforms the visual attribute to the word-attribute. While proposed approach significantly differs from the previous approach. Here each fMRI and word attribute data is factorized individually such that they have a common sparse dictionary. Here more parameters are to learn but learning is in such a way that it generalizes well for the individual fMRI and attribute data. Also if a common parameter minimizes the reconstruction error of many problems it has less chance of over-fitting [12]. Sparsity in the dictionary helps in the feature selection without using any external feature selection technique. fMRI image has very high sensitivity towards the noise. A small noise has the significant disturbance in the activation of the neuron. To overcome this problem the domain adaptation method [11] is applied that helps to adapt the significant domain shift at the test time.

Section 2 of the paper describes the work related to the prediction of words. In Sect. 3 proposed methodology is presented in detail. Results and Experiments are shown in Sect. 4. The whole work is concluded in Sect. 5.

2   Related Work

A lot of work can be found in the literature for predicting the word from human brain activity images. In [3] Palatucci et al., presented the use of zero-short learning that uses semantic knowledge to extrapolate to novel classes. By using a rich semantic encoding of the classes, the classifier may be able to extrapolate and recognize novel classes. Linear regression with l2 regulariser was used for predicting the attribute vector of a word from the fMRI data. Comparative information from different models with behavioural data integrated is presented in [5], Models that represent word meanings based on linguistics as well as perpetual data.Distributional models of lexical semantics have seen incredible success with including wide range of behavioural data in tasks involving semantic cognition. Models with visual content [4,8] have been integrated with semantic models giving multimodal distributional semantic space. Results demonstrate that visual attributes improve the performance of distributional models across the board showing that image-based and text-based features are complementary. Also adding visual data to distributed semantic models showed more human like word meaning interpretation. [7] Murphy et al., for mapping of concepts and neural activity in the brain have introduced an automatically derived representation of corpus on basis of co-occurrence of text. It is also based on neuro-semantic decoding using a linear model with regularised linear combinations of semantic features. The trained linear model could generate vector for activations of specific features of different concepts. [6,9] have correlated Vector Space Models built with text or images with brain activation data. In 2012 [6] linear regression model was used to learn the mapping from semantic features to brain activity levels and it was observed that Non-Negative Sparse Embedding uses a larger number of dimensions per word, but even then, the resulting embeddings are significantly sparser, effective and highly interpretable. In [10] uses hybrid Vector Space Model (VSMs) learned using Joint Non-Negative Sparse Embedding (JNNSE), to predict words from brain activation images and text data. In this paper, multiple output linear regression is used to predict semantic features. [11] learns dictionaries in the training and in the testing explores domain adaptation which shows the better result on most of the standard datasets.

3   Proposed Methodology

3.1   Sparse Embedding Description

Non Negative Sparse Embedding produces the latent representation using matrix factorization, the matrix factorized consists of positive entries or zero values, this method is one of the popular state-of-the-art methods for the predicting the word from the brain activity [6,10].

In propose work, a Joint Sparse Embedding (JSE) algorithm that produces a latent representation (embedding) using matrix factorization is used. The model is called Joint JSE because it learns a joint sparse dictionary for the visual space and attribute space that is used to reconstruct the original matrix. Using the JSE we can predict the attribute of the visual space.

Let for training, the fMRI data is $X_s = [x_1, x_2, \dots x_{N_s}]$ and each $x_i \in \mathbb{R}^d$ here each x_i represents the voxel feature corresponding to the each nouns neurons activation value. The word-attribute vector $Y_s = [y_1, y_2, \dots, y_{N_s}]$ each $y_i \in \mathbb{R}^{\shortmid\shortmid}$ is the human annotated word attribute description. Here each x_i and y_i are arranged in the column manner.

3.2   Objective Function for Training

The objective function for training of model is given as:

$$
\min_{D_s, W_s, \alpha_s} \|X_s - D_s \alpha_s\|_2^2 + \|Y_s - W_s \alpha_s\|_2^2
$$
$$
+ \lambda_1 \|D_s\|_2^2 + \lambda_2 \|W_s\|_2^2 + \lambda_3 \|\alpha_s\|_1 \tag{1}
$$

where $X_s \in \mathbb{R}^{d \times N_s}$, N_s is the number of train data, $D_s \in \mathbb{R}^{d \times K}$, $\alpha_s \in \mathbb{R}^{K \times N_s}$, $Y_s \in \mathbb{R}^{q \times N_s}$, $W_s \in \mathbb{R}^{q \times K}$ X_s, Y_s are known, while D_s, W_s and α_s are to be estimated. The proposed objective function is defined as we want to factorize the fMRI data into D_s and α_s. Also, we want to factorize the word attribute data into W_s and α_s. This factorization is done based on the common dictionary that has the sparse representation. This common representation helps in the better generalization. Here Eq. (1) also use the l_2 regularizer that helps to reduce overfitting because it forces parameter to have a small value. The proposed objective function has the analytical solution for D_s and W_s that can be found directly by differentiating Eq. (1) with respect to D_s and W_s and equate to zero.

For minimization differentiate the equation w.r.t W_S, D_s, α_s and equate to zero,

$$
\frac{\partial(Eq:1)}{\partial D_s} = 0
$$
$$
\Rightarrow \quad -2(X_s - D_s \alpha_s)\alpha_s^t + 2\lambda_1 D_s = 0
$$
$$
\Rightarrow \quad X_s \alpha_s^t - D_s \alpha_s \alpha_s^t + \lambda_1 D_s = 0
$$
$$
\Rightarrow \quad D_s(\alpha_s \alpha_s^t + \lambda_1) = X_s \alpha_s^t
$$
$$
\Rightarrow \quad D_s = (X_s \alpha_s^t)(\alpha_s \alpha_s^t + \lambda_1)^{-1}
$$

we get closed form solution of D_s and W_s as

$$D_s = (X_s \alpha_s^t)(\alpha_s \alpha_s^t + \lambda_1 I)^{-1} \tag{2}$$

$$W_s = (Y_s \alpha_s^t)(\alpha_s \alpha_s^t + \lambda_2 I)^{-1} \tag{3}$$

We can not obtain the direct solution for α_s since the $l1$ regularizer is not differentiable. So iterative optimization is needed to solve this. SPAMS [13] toolbox is used to solve the lasso problem.

$$\alpha_s = lasso([X_s; Y_s], [D_s; W_s]) \tag{4}$$

For solving Eqs. (2) and (3) we initialize the α_s randomly using Gaussian sampling i.e. $\alpha_s \sim \mathcal{N}(0, I)$. Once we have solved for α_s, Eqs. (2), (3) and (4) are iterated till convergence or fix the number of iteration using the validation data. If iterated more it starts over-fitting. So the number of iterations is tuned with the help of validation data.

3.3   Objective Function for Testing with Domain Adaptation

In case of testing the same class data suffers from the domain shift problem. If we are not handling the domain shift problem carefully its accuracy decreases significantly. So the domain adaptation is the key challenge in case of the sensitive data, or the data that is coming from a different domain. Here a very simple domain adaptation method [11] is used that is easy to implement and fast to learn. The objective function proposed with the help of domain adaptation for the test data is given as:

$$\min_{D_t, W_t, \alpha_t} ||X_t - D_t \alpha_t||_2^2 + ||Y_t - W_t \alpha_t||_2^2 + \lambda_1 ||D_t - D_s||_2^2$$
$$+ \lambda_2 ||W_t - W_s||_2^2 + \lambda_3 ||\alpha_t||_1 \tag{5}$$

where $X_t \in \mathbb{R}^{d \times N_t}$, N_t is the number of test data. $D_t \in \mathbb{R}^{d \times K}$, $\alpha_s \in \mathbb{R}^{K \times N_t}$, $Y_t \in \mathbb{R}^{q \times N_t}$, $W_t \in \mathbb{R}^{q \times K}$ Here X_t is known D_s and W_s are learned from the Eqs. (2) and (3), while D_t, α_t, W_t, and Y_t are to be estimated. Again for estimating these parameters we have to initialize α_t and Y_t randomly but here we can use a better initialization based on previously learned parameter during the training.

$$\frac{\partial(Eq:9)}{\partial D_t} = 0$$

$$\Rightarrow \quad -2(X_t - D_t \alpha_t)\alpha_t^t + 2\lambda_1(D_t - D_s) = 0$$

$$\Rightarrow \quad -X_t \alpha_t^t + D_t \alpha_t \alpha_t^t + \lambda_1 D_t - \lambda_1 D_s = 0$$

$$\Rightarrow \quad D_t(\alpha_t \alpha_t^t + \lambda_1 I) = X_t \alpha_t^t + \lambda_1 D_s = 0$$

$$\Rightarrow \quad D_t = (X_t \alpha_t^t + \lambda_1 D_s)(\alpha_t \alpha_t^t + \lambda_1 I)^{-1}$$

Similarly,

$$\frac{\partial(Eq:9)}{\partial W_t} = 0 \tag{6}$$

Here in Eq. (5) we have a similar objective function as in Eq. (1) the main difference is that we know only X_t. Y_t is unknown and our objective is to predict that. The learned dictionary D_s and W_s are not used. A new dictionary D_t and W_t are to be learned but the constraint is that the new dictionary should be close to the old one. function as D_t, W_t are forced to be close to D_s, W_s respectively. So instead of using the same dictionary, we are using the similar dictionary. This formulation helps in the domain adaptation. Now with minimizing the loss we are learning the dictionary for the new domain.

Initialize D_t, Y_t and α_t

$$D_t = (X_t \alpha_t^t + \lambda_1 D_s)(\alpha_t \alpha_t^t + \lambda_1 I)^{-1} \tag{7}$$

$$\alpha_t = Lasso(X_t, D_t) \tag{8}$$

$$Y_t = (W_s \alpha_t) \tag{9}$$

Now we can see the advantage of initialization based on previously learned parameters. Here we have to initialize only one parameter α_t randomly instead of the both α_t and Y_t. This gives the faster convergence and less prone to over-fitting. Therefore, it results in better performance. If we are using equation Eq. (9) only for the prediction of the test data, it gives the prediction accuracy without domain adaptation. We will see the improvement using the domain adaptation in the result section.

Once we have initialized Y_t and α_t we can use it for the alternating optimization.

$$D_t = (X_t \alpha_t^t + \lambda_1 D_s)(\alpha_t \alpha_t^t + \lambda_1 I)^{-1} \tag{10}$$

$$W_t = (Y_t \alpha_t^t + \lambda_2 W_s)(\alpha_t \alpha_t^t + \lambda_2 I)^{-1} \tag{11}$$

$$\alpha_t = Lasso([X_t; Y_t], [D_t; W_t]) \tag{12}$$

$$Y_t = (W_t \alpha_t) \tag{13}$$

Equations 10, 11, 12 and 13 are iterated till convergence. For the test data prediction, we have only two outputs i.e., correct and incorrect. Here we have Y_t, the predicted attribute value that is obtained based on the projection of the visual feature obtained using fMRI into the embedding space. After finding the attribute value we can measure the l_2 distance in the embedding space. The predicted attribute belongs to the class that has the minimum distance from the predicted attribute to the given two classes (correct/incorrect).

4 Experimentation and Results

4.1 Brain Activation of Data

The fMRI data [14] was originally collected by Marcel Just and his colleagues in Carnegie Mellon University's CCBI. Nine right-handed adults (5 female, age between 18 and 32) from the Carnegie Mellon community participated and gave

---

Algorithm 1. Algo Description

   Input : $X_s, Y_s, \lambda_1, \lambda_2, \lambda_3$
   Output: Predicted Attribute value Y_t
1 Initialize $\alpha_s = N(0,I)$ and α_t = random;
2 $i \leftarrow 1$
3 **while** $i <=$ *fixed no.of iterations* **do**
4   update D_s by Eq. (2)
5   update W_s by Eq. (3)
6   update α_s by Eq. (4)
7       $i \leftarrow i + 1$
8 **end**
9 D_t = compute from Eq. (7)
10 α_t = compute from Eq. (8)
11 Y_t = compute from Eq. (9)
12 **while** *not converge* **do**
13   update D_t by Eq. (10)
14   update W_t by Eq. (11)
15   update α_t by Eq. (12)
16   update Y_t by Eq. (13)
17 **end**

---

informed consent approved by the University of Pittsburgh and Carnegie Mellon Institutional Review Boards. Two additional participants were excluded from the analysis due to head motion greater than 2.5 mm. To ensure that each participant had a consistent set of properties to think about, they were asked to generate and write a set of properties for each exemplar in a separate session prior to the scanning session (such as "cold, knights, stone" for castle). However, nothing was done to elicit consistency across participants. MEG measures the magnetic field caused by many thousands of neurons firing together and has good time resolution (1000 Hz) but poor spatial resolution. fMRI measures the change in blood oxygenation that results from differential neural activity and has a good spatial resolution but poor time resolution (0.5–1 Hz). We have fMRI data and MEG data for 18 subjects (9 in each imaging modality) viewing 60 concrete nouns ([2,6]). The 60 words span 12-word categories (animals, buildings, tools, insects, body parts, furniture, building parts, utensils, vehicles, objects, clothing, food). Each of the 60 words was presented with a line drawing, so word ambiguity is not an issue. For both recording modalities, all trials for a particular word are averaged together to create one training instance per word, with 60 training instances in all for each subject and imaging modality.

The entire set of 60 stimuli was presented 6 times during the scanning session, in a different random order each time. Participants silently viewed the stimuli and were asked to think of the same item properties consistently across the 6 presentations. Each stimulus was presented for 3s, followed by a 7s rest period, during which the participants were instructed to fixate on an X displayed in the center of the screen. There were two additional presentations of the fixation,

31s each, at the beginning and at the end of each session, to provide a baseline measure of activity.

In the dataset, we have 360 data from the 60 noun class. Each data point is 21764-*dim* feature vector of the voxel intensities corresponding to fMRI image. Each noun class is defined by the 218-*dimension* word-attribute annotated by the human. From the whole set of 360 data, 300 data is used for training and remaining 60 are used for testing. In the testing we are given the fMRI feature and corresponding two words from this we have to predict, one is correct while other is incorrect.

4.2 Results

The proposed method is compared with existing algorithm presented in [10] and without domain adaptation. The results are shown in Table 1. Accuracy of predicting the word with domain adaptation is 91.67% which is higher than the prediction without domain adaptation i.e., 78.34%. This shows that to handle the domain adaptation shift problem is a key task in the case of fMRI data. As the fMRI data is very high dimensional, we also experimented our algorithm by reducing the dimension of data using Principal Component Analysis (PCA) [15]. Using PCA, 21764 dimensional data is projected into a space of 300 dimension that is very much lower than the dimension of original data. Here dimension of data is highly reduced but from Table 1 it is clear that while we have reduced 21764 to 300 dimension we are still getting quite good results i.e, 86.67%. If data could be reduced to dimension higher than 300 it is expected that it will give better results. Graphical comparison of the performance of proposed method and other existing ones is shown in Fig. 2. This experiment shows that out of all the neuron activity only few neurons are important. This motivates us to learn a sparse dictionary that helps in selecting feature. For fMRI data, feature selection and domain adaptation are very important but difficult to handle. The proposed algorithm handles all these scenarios efficiently. The efficacy of proposed method can be seen in Table 1.

Table 1. Comparison of proposed method with other

Method	Accuracy
fMRI data + text data [10]	81%
fMRI data + text data	78.34%
fMRI data + text data + PCA	76.34%
fMRI data + text data + PCA + Domain Adaptation	86.67%
fMRI data + text data + Domain Adaptation	**91.67%**

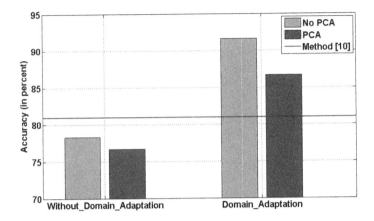

Fig. 2. Performance graph of different methods of word prediction

5   Conclusion and Future Work

fMRI dataset is of huge dimension but very limited in size. This leads to high computational cost. Defining a robust classifier is always a challenging task because of the higher dimensionality of the data and limited availability. Out of all these dimensions only few are important, which is clear by the PCA experiment. We have seen that reducing the feature space from 21764 to 300 does not degrade the performance much. Thus one can conclude that there is a huge similarity in the way brain interprets meanings of words and semantic features of words obtained from the large text corpus. Also, it is clear that different individuals visualize different words in the same manner in terms of pure physiology in the brain. The result of the second experiment of sparse dictionary learning shows that for the fMRI data feature selection is a key task. The whole performance of the classifier depends on the how good the selected feature is and how well it generalizes. In the proposed work these two problems are handled efficiently and achieving the state of art performance. The result shown in Table 1 justified all the claims we made. The proposed approach is simple, robust and an efficient for predicting the word from fMRI data. Though the fMRI data available for corresponding words is small, the proposed methodology has shown a significant improvement over the existing ones.

The proposed experimental setting is very simple but accurately can read the subject's mind in the binary case. In future, we would like to extend this work in the complex setting like when the subject is thinking about a lot of objects and using the better feature selection technique we can further improve the accuracy.

References

1. Roland, J.L., Hacker, C.D., Breshears, J.D., Gaona, C.M., Hogan, R.E., Burton, H., Corbetta, M., Leuthardt, E.C.: Brain mapping in a patient with congenital blindness-a case for multimodal approaches. Front. Hum. Neurosci. **7**, 431 (2013)
2. Mitchell, T.M., Shinkareva, S.V., Carlson, A., Chang, K.-M., Malave, V.L., Mason, R.A., Just, M.A.: Predicting human brain activity associated with the meanings of nouns. Am. Assoc. Adv. Sci. **320**(5880), 1191–1195 (2008)
3. Palatucci, M., Pomerleau, D., Hinton, G.E., Mitchell, T.M.: Zero-shot learning with semantic output codes. In: Advances in Neural Information Processing Systems, pp. 1410–1418 (2009)
4. Bruni, E., Tran, G.B., Baroni, M.: Distributional semantics from text and images. In: Proceedings of the GEMS 2011 Workshop on Geometrical Models of Natural Language Semantics, pp. 22–32 (2011)
5. Silberer, C., Lapata, M.: Grounded models of semantic representation. In: Proceedings of the 2012 Joint Conference on Empirical Methods in Natural Language Processing and Computational Natural Language Learning, pp. 2452–2460 (2012)
6. Murphy, B., Talukdar, P.P., Mitchell, T.: Learning effective and interpretable semantic models using non-negative sparse embedding. In: Association for Computational Linguistics (2012)
7. Murphy, B., Talukdar, P., Mitchell, T.: Selecting corpus-semantic models for neuro-linguistic decoding. In: Proceedings of the First Joint Conference on Lexical and Computational Semantics-Volume 1: Proceedings of the main conference and the shared task, and Volume 2: Proceedings of the Sixth International Workshop on Semantic Evaluation, pp. 114–123 (2012)
8. Silberer, C., Ferrari, V., Lapata, M.: Models of semantic representation with visual attributes. In: PACL, vol. 1, pp. 572–582 (2013)
9. Anderson, A.J., Bruni, E., Bordignon, U., Poesio, M., Baroni, M.: Of words, eyes and brains: correlating image-based distributional semantic models with neural representations of concepts. In: EMNLP, pp. 1960–1970 (2013)
10. Fyshe, A., Talukdar, P.P., Murphy, B., Mitchell, T.M.: Interpretable semantic vectors from a joint model of brain-and text-based meaning. In: Proceedings of the Conference on Association for Computational Linguistics, Meeting, p. 489 (2014)
11. Kodirov, E., Xiang, T., Fu, Z., Gong, S.: Unsupervised domain adaptation for zero-shot learning. In: Proceedings of the IEEE International Conference on Computer Vision, pp. 1423–1433 (2015)
12. Zhang, Y., Yang, Q.: A survey on multi-task learning. arXiv preprint arXiv:1707.08114 (2017)
13. Mairal, J.: SPAMS: A SPArse Modeling Software, v2. 3 (2012)
14. http://www.cs.cmu.edu/afs/cs/project/theo-73/www/science2008/data.html
15. Wold, S., Esbensen, K., Geladi, P.: Principal component analysis. In: Chemometrics and Intelligent Laboratory Systems, pp. 37–52 (1987)

Author Index

Printed in the United States
By Bookmasters